Crime and Public Policy

Crime and Public Policy

EDITED BY

James Q. Wilson & Joan Petersilia

OXFORD
UNIVERSITY PRESS

OXFORD
UNIVERSITY PRESS

Oxford University Press, Inc., publishes works that further
Oxford University's objective of excellence
in research, scholarship, and education.

Oxford   New York
Auckland   Cape Town   Dar es Salaam   Hong Kong   Karachi
Kuala Lumpur   Madrid   Melbourne   Mexico City   Nairobi
New Delhi   Shanghai   Taipei   Toronto

With offices in
Argentina   Austria   Brazil   Chile   Czech Republic   France   Greece
Guatemala   Hungary   Italy   Japan   Poland   Portugal   Singapore
South Korea   Switzerland   Thailand   Turkey   Ukraine   Vietnam

Copyright (c) 2011 by Oxford University Press

Published by Oxford University Press, Inc.
198 Madison Avenue, New York, New York 10016
www.oup.com

Oxford is a registered trademark of Oxford University Press

Library of Congress Cataloging-in-Publication Data

Crime and public policy / edited by James Q. Wilson, Joan Petersilia.
p. cm.
Includes bibliographical references and index.
ISBN 978-0-19-539935-6 (pbk.: alk. paper)—ISBN 978-0-19-539936-3 (cloth: alk. paper)
1. Crime prevention—United States.   2. Crime—United States.   3. Crime.
4. Criminology.   I. Wilson, James Q.   II. Petersilia, Joan.
HV9950.C743155 2010
364.973—dc22
2010007432

10

Printed in Canada
on acid-free paper

Dedicated to serious students of criminal justice who, despite their disagreements, have profoundly deepened our knowledge of what works and what does not.

Contents

Contributors

Robert Apel is an Associate Professor in the School of Criminal Justice at the University at Albany, State University of New York.

Eric Beauregard is an Assistant Professor at the School of Criminology, Simon Fraser University (Canada) and co-director of the Centre for Research on Sexual Violence.

David A. Boyum is Director of Research at Aquiline Advisors.

Anthony A. Braga is a Professor in the School of Criminal Justice at Rutgers University and a Senior Research Fellow in the Program in Criminal Justice Policy and Management at Harvard University.

Shawn D. Bushway is an Associate Professor of Criminal Justice and an Associate Professor of Public Administration and Policy at the University at Albany, State University of New York.

Jonathan P. Caulkins is H. Guyford Stever Professor of Operations Research at Carnegie Mellon University's Heinz College and Qatar campus.

Philip J. Cook is ITT/Sanford Professor of Public Policy and Professor of Economics and Sociology at Duke University.

Francis T. Cullen is Distinguished Research Professor of Criminal Justice and Sociology at the University of Cincinnati.

David P. Farrington is Professor of Psychological Criminology at the Institute of Criminology, Cambridge University.

Brian Forst is Professor of Justice, Law and Societyat the School of Public Affairs, American University.

Peter Greenwood is the President and CEO of Greenwood & Associates and Executive Director of the Association for Advancement of Evidence Based Practice.

Randall Kennedy is the Michael R. Klein Professor at Harvard Law School.

Mark A. R. Kleiman is Professor of Public Policy at University of California, Los Angeles.

Cheryl Lero Jonson is an Assistant Professor of Criminal Justice at Northern Kentucky University.

Roxanne Lieb is the Associate Director of the Washington State Institute for Public Policy, a nonpartisan organization that conducts research for the state legislature.

James P. Lynch is the current director of the Bureau of Justice Statistics, U.S. Department of Justice and formerly a Distinguished Professor at John Jay College of Criminal Justice in New York.

Cheryl Maxson is an Associate Professor in the Department of Criminology, Law and Society at the University of California, Irvine.

Terrie E. Moffitt is Knut Schmidt Nielsen Professor in the Department of Psychology and Neuroscience at Duke University, and Professor of Social Behaviour and Development, King's College London.

Anne Morrison Piehl is Associate Professor of Economics and Director of the Program in Criminal Justice at Rutgers University.

Mark H. Moore was formerly the Guggenheim Professor of Criminal Justice Policy and Management at Harvard's Kennedy School of Government. He is now the Hauser Professor of Nonprofit Management at Harvard's Kennedy School, and the Herbert Simon Professor of Management, Organization, and Education at Harvard's Graduate School of Education.

Daniel S. Nagin is Teresa and H. John Heinz III University Professor of Public Policy and Statistics in the Heinz College at Carnegie Mellon University.

Joan Petersilia is the Adelbert H. Sweet Professor of Law at Stanford Law School and co-director of the Stanford Criminal Justice Center (SCJC).

William Alex Pridemore is Professor and Director of Graduate Studies in the Department of Criminal Justice at Indiana University.

Adrian Raine is University Professor and the Richard Perry Professor of Criminology, Psychiatry, and Psychology at the University of Pennsylvania.

Kevin R. Reitz is the James Annenberg La Vea Professor of Criminal Procedure at the University of Minnesota.

Richard Rosenfeld is Curators Professor of Criminology and Criminal Justice at the University of Missouri-St. Louis.

Stephen Ross currently works with Terrie E. Moffitt at Duke University.

Robert J. Sampson is Chairman of the Department of Sociology and the Henry Ford II Professor of the Social Sciences at Harvard University.

Lawrence W. Sherman is the Wolfson Professor of Criminology and Director of the Jerry Lee Centre for Experimental Criminology in the Institute of Criminology at Cambridge University, and Distinguished University Professor in the Department of Criminology and Criminal Justice at the University of Maryland.

Susan Turner is a Professor in the Department of Criminology, Law and Society and Director of the Center for Evidence-Based Corrections at the University of California, Irvine.

Bert Useem is Professor of Sociology and Department Head at Purdue University.

James Q. Wilson, an emeritus professor at UCLA, and is now the Ronald Reagan Professor of Public Policy at Pepperdine University and a Distinguished Fellow at the Clough Center at Boston College.

Crime and Public Policy

Chapter 1

Introduction

James Q. Wilson, Joan Petersilia

Trying to keep up with the growing research on crime and criminal justice has become a full-time job. When the crime rates rose dramatically in the 1960s, criminologists knew a few interesting facts but not nearly enough to either explain the rise in crime or tell policymakers what to do about it.

But the growth in crime rates, while it created a serious problem for the country, had at least one small benefit: it brought to the study of crime a sizable new group of scholars, some of them trained in criminology but others with backgrounds in economics, operations research, anthropology, and political science.

In an effort to keep up with the sharp rise in knowledge about the likely causes and possible remedies for crime, the two editors of this book have spent much of the last 25 years trying to present—for the lay reader as well as for fellow scholars—an interesting account of what we have learned. In 1983 one of us (Wilson) published a volume that brought together the best thinkers on this subject in an edited book called *Crime and Public Policy*. He quickly learned that one person could not keep up with what was being discovered, and he eagerly joined with Joan Petersilia to produce in 1995 a new volume entitled *Crime*. This was followed in 2002 with a revised and expanded book called *Crime: Public Policies for Crime Control*. Now we bring forth a brand new edition, much longer, called *Crime and Public Policy*.

The books have become longer because there have been so many new discoveries in the field. Here are some of the issues about which few people could have written authoritatively in earlier years. In 1983, nobody had much reliable evidence about:

- Whether imposing criminal sanctions deterred crime
- Whether there were many programs that actually prevented children from becoming delinquent
- Whether programs that claimed to rehabilitate offenders really worked
- What kinds of gun control, if any, might affect the murder rate
- Whether there was any way to get offenders to stop using drugs.

Today we know a lot about these matters. But that does not mean there are no disagreements. The more we learn about the causes of crime, the more opportunities there are for drawing different conclusions about criminal justice policies. The average person usually has strong views about criminal justice policy, and this will guide what he or she wants done. Many scholars, though expert in some aspect of criminology, also have strong views.

In this book the editors have not tried to impose any policy perspective; we have instead sought out (and, we think, largely found) the best thinkers on these topics. If you think crime can be sharply reduced by eliminating its root causes, read chapter 3 by Terrie Moffitt, Stephen Ross, and Adrian Raine on biological factors in criminality and chapter 6 by Cheryl Maxson on the puzzle of managing criminal gangs. If you think it is easy to deter crime by imposing prison sentences on offenders, read chapter 14 by Robert Apel and Daniel Nagin on the complex effects of deterrence. If you think that legalizing cocaine and heroin would reduce crime, read chapter 13 by David Boyum, Jonathan Caulkins, and Mark Kleiman.

None of the chapters in this book was written by authors who think there is some silver bullet that will easily cut crime rates. But at the same time, *something* has driven down crime rates in America, as is shown in chapter 19 by Richard Rosenfeld—so much so that, as James Lynch and William Pridemore point out, American property crime rates are lower than they are in many parts of Europe.

This edition of our book treats subjects that were ignored in earlier versions. There are new chapters on race and crime (by Randall Kennedy), the impact of gangs on crime (by Cheryl Maxson), sex offenders (by Eric Beauregard and Roxanne Lieb), life in and around prisons (by Anne Piehl and Bert Useem), sentencing policies (by Kevin Reitz), and changing crime rates (by Richard Rosenfeld).

This book is not offered to readers because its message will "solve" the crime problem but rather because it will demonstrate how to think about this problem. Read these chapters not only to learn what the authors conclude but also to learn how talented people address a major national issue.

Chapter 2

Crime in International Perspective

James P. Lynch, William Alex Pridemore

Cross-national comparisons of crime and criminal justice policy have a unique place in criminology and policy research. Simple comparisons of crime rates or imprisonment rates across nations have tremendous power to sway popular opinion and the public debate. No one wants to be the nation first in the ranking of bad national indicators or last in the ranking of good ones. For all of their influence, however, cross-national comparisons are difficult to do well and may be therefore often misleading rather than enlightening. Nations that make extensive use of mental institutions for serious violent offenders, for example, will have lower imprisonment rates than those that do not, but when secure mental health facilities are included, the imprisonment rates may be the same. Moreover, simple rate comparisons should be the first step in understanding cross-national comparisons of crime and punishment, not the last. This chapter examines the common wisdom about the place of the United States relative to other nations in terms of crime and punishment. It revisits the common wisdom, taking account of more recently available information, to see if these beliefs hold up. We also explore how recent changes in the array of nations and the varieties of data available may reduce our reliance on simple rate comparisons and increase our understanding of cross-national differences in crime and justice policy.

The first of the following sections addresses common beliefs about the place of the United States with respect to crime and punishment and how that has changed over time. It also addresses the proper role of cross-national comparisons in producing research to guide policy. The second section describes changes in the number of nations on which we have cross-national data, the quality of those data, and the ways in which this information has been used. The third section examines differences in crime across nations over time and addresses some of the methodological complexities involved in making accurate comparisons. The fourth section does the same for punishment policy. The concluding section reassesses the common wisdom regarding the relative position of the United States on crime and punishment in light of the new data. It also suggests how recently available data can help us understand cross-national differences in crime and punishment.

As a result of these inquiries we reached the following conclusions:

1) The common wisdom that the United States is the most punitive and crime-ridden nation in the world is both accurate and too simple.

a. The United States has higher levels of serious violence than other developed nations, but similar levels of minor violence and property crime.

b. Punitive responses to serious violence are similar across nations, but the higher level of serious violence in the United States contributes substantially to higher incarceration rates.

c. The United States is unique in its aggressive response to drug offenses, and this too is a major determinant of prison populations.

2) Simple comparisons of aggregate rates of crime and punishment can be misleading, even when they are technically correct.

a. These comparisons often fail to control adequately for differences in the nature of national populations of persons and crime events.

b. The effects of national culture or social structure on levels of crime and punishment may be small when differences in population and the crime problem are taken into account.

c. Newly available data on persons and crime incidents across nations will tell us a great deal about the role of the nation-state in producing cross-national differences

COMMON WISDOM AND THE ROLE OF CROSS-NATIONAL COMPARISONS

For most of the last 50 years, the common wisdom has been that the United States was the most crime-ridden of industrialized democracies and that this was particularly the case for violence. At the same time, punishment policies in the United States were perceived to be the most punitive in that group of nations. The point was often made that only the former Soviet Union and South Africa made greater use of prisons than the United States (Doleschal 1977). Gradually this view became more nuanced as scholars began to admit that the high imprisonment rate may have something to do with the high crime rate (Lynch 1988, 1995). The common wisdom evolved to the point at which the United States was viewed as having high rates of violence and reacting to this violence in roughly the same manner as other industrialized democracies, but the United States was substantially more punitive than these other nations when it came to less severe offenses like property crimes and drug offenses

(Blumstein, Tonry, and Van Ness 2005; Lynch 1995, 2002). More recently, with the massive increases in the prison population and the large reductions in crime, the United States is seen as the most punitive nation in the world with moderate crime rates (except for lethal violence, and especially lethal violence with firearms, which are comparatively high in the United States) (Liptak, 2008). This is the current common wisdom.

Making cross-national comparisons of crime and crime control policy and getting them right is important for a number of reasons. First, cross-national comparisons get peoples' attention and are a popular means of bringing a policy issue to the fore. Second, cross-national comparisons demand explanations that go beyond individual-level factors or single program solutions that so much criminological research addresses. Cross-national differences can be the product of many things—some of which result in positive differences and others negative ones. They make us ask: What are other nations doing that we are not, and can the explanation offered produce differences at the national level? Can what we know about crime and its causes at the individual or neighborhood level be aggregated to explain the large cross-national differences we observe? Germany, for example, may use fines more extensively as a criminal sanction than the United States, but does that difference in sentencing policy affect enough cases to produce the differences in incarceration rates across nations? Cross-national comparisons provide a useful reality check in a policy area where statistical significance is often given more weight than substantive significance. These comparisons force us to think about crime control policy in a more holistic way where factors such as inequality, the housing market, or the length of the school day—which are not policies created with crime control in mind—can have unintended consequences for crime control.

At the same time, simple cross-national comparisons of rates of crime or punishment are often not very useful for helping us understand why nations differ in terms of crime and punishment. Nations are large and heterogeneous, and aggregate rates of behavior like national crime or imprisonment rates will mask that heterogeneity and provide a misleading picture of crime nationally (Ouimet 1999). Differences in the population composition of nations, their social organization, and their crime control policy may account for the differences in crime rates, but this cannot be determined by comparisons of nation-level rates. More recently available cross-national data collected at the crime, victim, or offender level suggest these characteristics may hold much greater promise for correctly estimating cross-national differences and understanding why these differences occur.

So the role of cross-national comparison of crime and crime control policy is to bring attention to issues using aggregate rate comparisons and to suggest the plausibility of various explanations for differences by disaggregating these rates. These analyses must be supplemented with multilevel, multivariate analyses in order to test the speculations that emerge for cross-national comparisons of aggregate national rates.

STUDYING CRIME CROSS-NATIONALLY

Common Types of International Criminological Studies

There are three main genres of international criminological studies that appear most often in criminology and sociology journals: studies of a single nation (or carried out within a single nation) other than the United States; comparative studies of two (or some other very small number of) nations; and studies that compare crime in a larger number of nations.

Since most readers of this chapter will be in the United States, we would consider studies from any other single country to be "international" in scope. In general, these studies can be separated into two types. The first includes studies in which there is a conscious intent to examine a particular country either because there might be something unique or different about crime in the nation (e.g., particularly high or low rates, a unique type of criminal behavior, etc.) or to see' if relationships found elsewhere are generalizable to that nation. Although there are often general comparisons of findings from these analyses with other nations, these types of studies usually do not contain systematic or formal comparisons. Recent examples include studies of reporting crime to police in China (Zhang, Messner, and Liu 2007), neighborhood characteristics and individual homicide risk in the Netherlands (Nieuwbeerta et al. 2008), a criminological analysis of genocide in Darfur (Hagan and Rymond-Richmond 2008), a study of incarcerated drug offenders in Iran (Aliverdinia and Pridemore 2007), an analysis of homicide rates in Finland for the last 250 years (Savolainen, Lehti, and Kivivuori 2008), the impact of an international ban on ivory sales on elephant poaching in Africa (Lemieux and Clarke 2009), the social ecology of rural violence in Mexico (Villarreal 2004), and the effects of social structure on the variation of regional homicide rates in Russia (Pridemore 2005a). The second subtype of this genre includes studies carried out in another nation but where there are no expectations that local or national culture plays an overriding role in any associations found. Examples include the Dunedin Multidisciplinary Health and Development Study (e.g., Moffitt, Lynam, and Silva 1994; Odgers et al. 2008) or the Cambridge Study in Delinquent Development (e.g., Lussier, Farrington, and Moffitt, 2009; Piquero, Farrington, and Blumstein 2007).

A second main genre is comparative studies of two nations, or a small set of nations. In these studies, unlike those in the third genre described below, explicit comparisons are made between the nations in terms of offending, victimization, or aspects of their criminal justice systems. This allows for a more in-depth analysis of each of the nations under study and for more careful and meaningful comparisons. Recent examples of this type of work include a comparison of homicide clearance rates in the United States and Japan (Roberts 2008), a test of the generalizability of general strain theory using individual-level data from Russia, Ukraine,

and Greece (Botchkovar, Tittle, and Antonaccio 2009), the impact of
economic conditions and imprisonment on property crime rates in the
United Kingdom and the United States (Rosenfeld and Messner 2009),
trajectories of delinquency among Puerto Rican youth in New York City
and San Juan, Puerto Rico (Maldonado-Molina et al. 2009), and an
analysis of legal services operated by indigenous groups in Australia and
Canada (Nielsen 2006).

A third main genre in international criminology is cross-national studies
that use a large sample of nations, using the nation as the unit of analysis
and employing multivariate models. These studies examine the variation
in national crime rates, usually focusing on social structural theories of
crime and normally including at least a few dozen countries. Due to
measurement issues discussed below, these studies most often employ
homicide rates as their dependent variable. There have been about 50
such studies published in the last few decades. These include studies of
the effects on the variation in cross-national national homicide rates of
institutional anomie (Messner and Rosenfeld 1997; Savolainen 2000),
inequality (Fajnzylber, Lederman, and Loayza 2002), population diversity
(Avison and Loring 1986), routine activities (Bennett 1991), and poverty
(Pridemore 2008), as well as studies of the structural correlates of homicide rates in Latin America (Neapolitan 1994) and post-communist East-
Central Europe (Stamatel 2009). A variation on this theme is international
studies that stem from a single data source, the International Crime Victims Survey (ICVS, discussed below). These include studies that examine
cross-national attitudes toward punishment (Mayhew and van Kesteren
2002), fear of street crime in Europe (Aromaa and Heiskanen 2002),
gender differences in violent victimization in industrialized nations (Verweij and Nieuwbeerta 2002), repeat victimization (Farrell, Tseloni, and
Pease 2005), victimization in post-socialist nations (Gruszczynska 2002),
crime in 13 African nations (Naudé, Prinsloo, and Ladikos 2006), and a
comparative study of support for the police (Kutnjak Ivković 2008).

Most Common Data Sources

There are four main sources of data employed by scholars carrying out
cross-national research using nations as the unit of analysis. These include
the United Nations surveys, Interpol, homicide victimization data from
the World Health Organization, and the International Crime Victims
Survey (ICVS). There are also a few regional efforts to collect comparable
administrative data on crime and criminal justice, most notably the *European Sourcebook* (Killias et al. 2003), and a growing number of special
multinational studies in which nation is not treated as the unit of analysis
but as the social context for crime or punishment (Johnson, Ollus, and
Nevala 2007; Junger-Tas, Terlouw, and Klein 1994).

The main source of crime data at the national level is the United Nations
Surveys on Crime Trends and the Operations of Criminal Justice Systems

(United Nations 2009). The UN has completed 10 waves of data collection thus far, with the 11th wave of the survey sent to member states in August 2009. The first wave was fielded in the late 1970s and covered 1970–1975. Since then, the waves have covered varying numbers of years, though since 2000 the survey has been administered once every two years. The survey not only requests data on crimes and offenders as reported by the police, but also detailed information about various aspects of the criminal justice system, including sections on police, prosecution, courts, and prisons. Of the 191 nations to which the instrument was distributed during the 10th wave (2005–2006), 86 responded. It is not uncommon for nations to provide information on some criminal justice categories (e.g., police, prisons) but not for others, or for nations to provide data on some crimes (e.g., completed homicides, total recorded thefts, automobile thefts) but not for others (e.g., major thefts, burglaries, bribery crimes). A major limitation of comparing levels of crime among countries is that definitions of crime (e.g., what is included in the theft category? assault?) vary from nation to nation. While the UN survey provides instructions to nations on how to categorize crimes in an attempt to obtain uniform data for country comparisons, the likelihood that nations follow this charge is probably small; nor are there systematic procedures for validating the wide-ranging data provided by each nation before its release by the United Nations.

A second source of crime data at the national level traditionally has been the Interpol crime survey. Like the UN survey, the Interpol survey is based on police data. One advantage of the Interpol data is that the survey has been fielded for much longer than the UN survey. Another is that Interpol has dedicated contacts for the survey with national law enforcement agencies in each nation, as the survey is completed as part of ongoing relations between Interpol and member nations. On the other hand, like the UN survey, these crime data come from police records and so are subject to the same limitations. The Interpol survey is also smaller in scope than the UN survey, focusing mainly on issues related to crime and the police. Unlike the UN survey, the Interpol survey does not have uniform definitions of crime; responding nations simply report crime data using their own definitions. All this information about the Interpol survey is largely moot, however, as the 2005 survey was the last to be undertaken. After more than 50 years of data collection, Interpol decided in 2006 to discontinue its data collection efforts with this survey (Rubin et al. 2008). In short, Interpol stated flatly that "the compilation and publication of statistics is of limited interest for international police co-operation" due to the many limitations associated with these types of data. This is because "the number of Members . . . which provide statistics, as well as the quality of statistics provided, are insufficient to ensure the compilation and publication of statistics which fulfill in a satisfactory manner the requirements of accuracy and reliability" and "the publication of statistics is likely to create difficulties in the way they are used" (The International Criminal Police Organization 2006).

Some region-specific compilations of official data have emerged, such as the *European Sourcebook on Crime and Criminal Justice Statistics* (Killias et al. 1999, 2003, 2006), which collects data on 40 nations that are mostly in the European Union. It includes information on offenses reported to the police, offenders, convictions, sentences, admissions to prison, and persons in prison and under supervision.[1] All of this information is broken out by offense categories and there is extensive documentation that explains sources of non-comparability in the data. Three editions of the Sourcebook are available.

The third main source of cross-national data contains information only on homicide. The World Health Organization (WHO 2001) began collecting annual data on deaths by cause from nations in the early 1950s. Approximately 100 nations currently provide this information to WHO, though the number of reporting nations varies from year to year and the number of nations reporting homicide data in recent years has been somewhat lower. The WHO data come from member nations' vital statistics registration systems and are based on cause of death—as reported on death certificates—using the International Classification of Diseases (ICD) codes. The ICD-10 codes for "Homicide and injury purposely inflicted by other persons" include the categories X85-Y09 and Y87.1. The various subcategories provide information about the method of homicide (e.g., firearms, strangulation, blunt objects, etc.). Of course, many less-developed nations may lack complete coverage in their vital statistics registration systems and either may not provide data or provide unreliable data. The WHO Mortality Database contains data for nations that are believed to report quality data. For scholars studying homicide cross-nationally, these WHO data are now the most commonly used source, as they are considered more reliable than police data, they do not include attempts (as police data on murder from several nations sometimes do), and they are available for a large number of nations.

The final main data source for scholars undertaking cross-national criminological studies is the International Crime Victims Survey (ICVS). The ICVS was created out of recognition of the limitations of official data for making cross-national comparisons of crime. Unlike the instruments discussed thus far, data from the ICVS are not based on police records but instead on interviews of crime victims. The first survey was carried out in 1989 and included 17 nations (van Dijk, Mayhew, and Killias 1990). Four more surveys have been carried out since, with the last fielded in 2004 and 2005. In developed nations, nationally representative samples are usually drawn and interviews are done using computer-assisted telephone interviewing (CATI) techniques. In developing nations, alternative sampling techniques are employed, and usually data are collected only from one large city (often the capital). Sample sizes are small, averaging around 2,000. Respondents are asked screener questions about any victimization experiences with 10 crime types during the five years prior to the interview. For each victimization, respondents are then asked to provide information about the circumstances of the event. Victims also are asked if the victimization was reported to the police and, if so, the satisfaction of the victim with police response. Finally, the survey also gathers information from all respondents on fear of crime, attitudes toward law enforcement, and attitudes about the appropriate punishment for a specific type of crime.

Limitations of These Data

Although the data described above are the most commonly used sources by researchers studying crime cross-nationally, they have several important limitations. First, all of these data sources focus on a narrow range of criminal behavior like violence, rape, robbery, burglary, automotive theft, and larceny. White collar crimes and so-called victimless crimes are largely absent from these systems, which limits the scope of cross-national analyses. Second, the UN and Interpol surveys are based on police data, which of course only include crimes that come to the attention of the police, and as we know only a relatively small proportion of even serious non-lethal assaults of various types are reported to the police. More importantly, the rate at which crimes are reported to police varies substantially from nation to nation, making cross-national comparisons difficult for all but a few types of crimes like homicide, motor vehicle theft, and burglary with forcible entry (all of which are reported to police at similarly high rates in most nations). On the other hand, comparing nations on crimes like theft, robbery, vandalism, and assault is suspect, given that there is much greater variability among nations in how often these crimes are reported to police and, in turn, what proportion of the crimes reported are actually recorded by the police.

Another problem with official police data is that definitions of crime vary from nation to nation. For example, the range of behaviors that might be classified under assault varies widely. When most people think of assault, they think of violence, perhaps even serious violence. In actuality, however, a large and heterogeneous group of behaviors can fall into this crime category. For example, an assault might include anything from serious acts of interpersonal violence, including sexual assault, to unwanted sexual advances to less serious offenses such as threats and verbal abuse. How this category is handled by police and prosecutors, de jure and de facto, can vary tremendously both within and between nations. Even if the definitions are similar across nations, there can be other questions about similarities of events. The annual proportion of robberies involving firearms in the United States is a little over one-third, for example, but this proportion is much smaller in other Western nations. Thus, while robbery may be defined similarly in these nations, robbery events in the United States involve the use or threat of much greater force. This type of limitation is alleviated somewhat when using victimization surveys like the ICVS, since standardized behavioral definitions are employed instead of legal definitions. Another type of limitation is that national-level data are rather inflexible in how they can be used. For example, within a given nation, criminal offending and victimization rates will vary widely by age, sex, ethnicity, and place (e.g., urban relative to suburban or rural areas). Yet it is usually impossible to disaggregate on these variables the summary statistics provided by the UN and Interpol surveys. Again, however, victimization data like that from the ICVS is incident-based, allowing for disaggregation on various characteristics.

Finally, while the ICVS provides the potential for scholars to be more nimble in some respects, this victimization survey also has limitations. Sample sizes within nations are relatively small, meaning that estimates of rare events like serious violence and even some serious property crimes will be unreliable. Another potential limitation is that samples have not always been representative of entire nations but instead carried out in a single city within a particular nation. This will not only misrepresent the distribution of crime within a single country, but can make cross-national comparisons suspect if samples from different nations represent different populations (e.g., a large city in one nation relative to a small city or even the entire country in a different nation). Nevertheless, Lynch (2006) concludes that ICVS victimization data yield more comparable cross-national comparisons of property crime than comparisons of nation-specific victimization surveys.

Given these limitations, as well as the construction and goals of the different instruments themselves, it makes little sense to argue that one of these data sources is better than the other. As should be the case with any study, the question being asked should dictate the type and source of data to be used. Even then, however, scholars must be careful. Questions related to the cross-national differences in crime and its causes are compelling, and the easy availability of these data sources can entice scholars to use them. Simply because data exist and are readily available, however, does not mean they are valid, that they are useful for making cross-national comparisons, or that they are capable of supporting statistical analyses.

Summary

These changes in the amount of information available and in the range of nations for which these data are available stand to substantially increase our ability to understand cross-national differences in crime and punishment. Including a larger range of nations not only increases the variability in crime and punishment but also the range of variables that can be used to understand that variability. Large samples of nations over longer periods of time permit multivariate analyses of crime and punishment that, in turn, facilitate holding population composition and other potential explanations constant when examining cross-national differences at the national level. More exciting still is the availability of individual- and incident-level data on crime and punishment in data collections like the

ICVS or International Self Report Delinquency (ISRD) study. This allows for the use of multi-level models that can hold constant attributes of individuals and places while looking at the effect of national-level characteristics. The few multilevel studies that have been done suggest that the nation-state explains very little of the variation in crime or other behavior like calling the police (Goudriaan, Lynch and Nieuwbeerta 2003). If this finding holds up with more investigation, it would mean that many of the national-level studies done to date are not explaining much of the variation in crime risk or other behavior. Indeed, much of what passes for cross-nation differences in these studies may be due to their inability to adequately control for person or incident level characteristics in their analysis. This would fundamentally change our view of the importance of the nation-state in producing difference in the risk of crime and punishment. This awaits more multi-level data and analysis. While we wait this data and analysis, we can see what simple rate comparison tell us about the current state of crime and punishment around the world.

What Do These Data Tell Us about Crime Rates Around the World?

Table 2.1 provides official data on crime and victimization. The first column (following the list of country names) provides homicide victimization rates as reported by the World Health Organization. Rates for most of these nations are for 2000, though for a few nations the rate comes from the late 1990s or early 2000s. Data in the second column are also completed homicides, but are based on official police data as reported to the United Nations. Columns three and four provide data on automobile theft and burglaries, respectively. All rates are per 100,000 residents.

While the homicide rates in columns one and two are not directly comparable, due to differing years and differing case definitions, they give the reader an idea of the difficulties faced by cross-national researchers even when examining what most people think of as the most reliably measured crime from country to country. Rates are available for some years and not others, or from one instrument and not another, and when data are available from both instruments there is often not a close correspondence between them. With that caveat, of the 88 nations listed in table 2.1, 77 have homicide victimization rates available via the World Health Organization. Some nations with the highest rates include El Salvador (38 per 100,000 residents), Zimbabwe (33), Sri Lanka (30), Russia (28), Brazil (26), Venezuela (26), Uganda (25), Philippines (21), Swaziland (21), Guatemala (18), and Ecuador (17). Five of these top 11 nations are in Central and South America, and three are in Africa. The U.S. rate of 5.90 is lower than many nations on this list, but much higher than most other developed nations, especially those in western Europe.

Table 2.1. Homicide, Automobile Theft, and Burglary Rates per 100,000 Residents, by Nation[a]

	Homicide (WHO)[b]	Homicide (UN)[c]	Automobile theft[c]	Burglaries[c]
Algeria	9.6	1.43	3.49	7.85
Armenia	3.3	2.46	4.16	---
Argentina	5.80	---	---	---
Australia	1.58	1.31	450.57	1580.40
Austria	0.92	---	---	---
Azerbaijan	2.8	2.44	1.15	10.15
Bahrain	1.1	1.01	90.38	---
Belarus	10.2	8.22	17.85	0.33
Belgium	1.74	2.07	180.52	586.93
Bermuda	---	1.58	1,352.82	1,292.91
Brazil	26.37	---	---	---
Brunei	1.1	1.43	40.64	142.51
Bulgaria	3.55	3.04	97.72	324.10
Canada	1.50	1.99	541.48	877.46
Chile	5.21	1.75	59.21	137.01
China	2.2	---	---	---
Costa Rica	6.13	6.47	116.26	4.10
Croatia	---	1.84	54.64	575.34
Cyprus	0.2	1.74	412.29	---
Czech Republic	1.50	2.22	236.48	631.40
Denmark	1.09	0.80	386.48	1,690.67
Dominican Republic	7.66	---	---	---
Ecuador	16.80	18.87	48.68	82.36
El Salvador	37.68	---	---	---
England and Wales	---	1.63	460.05	1,293.46
Estonia	8.9	6.75	46.58	40.50
Finland	2.63	2.77	371.27	1,141.70

(continued)

Table 2.1. Continued

	Homicide (WHO)[b]	Homicide (UN)[c]	Automobile theft[c]	Burglaries[c]
France	0.85	1.66	328.17	631.53
Georgia	3.7	6.09	31.58	79.75
Germany	0.73	0.98	71.43	1,203.53
Greece	1.15	—	—	—
Guatemala	17.79	—	—	—
Hong Kong	—	0.65	25.58	102.92
Hungary	2.53	2.08	73.30	439.06
Iceland	1.0	1.05	152.78	965.88
India	5.5	—	—	—
Iran	—	2.98	139.69	622.24
Ireland	1.00	0.94	340.50	1,910.25
Israel	2.07	2.73	486.10	191.58
Italy	1.04	1.23	323.60	—
Japan	0.61	—	—	—
Kyrgyzstan	8.6	8.20	4.68	423.15
Latvia	12.52	8.49	126.35	264.64
Lithuania	9.86	9.32	169.18	8.51
Maldives	—	1.28[d]	103.40	197.44
Malta	0.7	1.77	201.48	163.52
Mauritius	2.7	2.56	6.45	—
Mexico	10.84	—	—	—
Moldova	8.2	6.67	3.65	354.70
Monaco	—	2.93	35.18	96.92
Mongolia	3.2	13.13	1.96	5.85
Morocco	1.1	0.48	3.56	—
The Netherlands	1.13	1.27	—	—

New Zealand	1.43	—	—	—
Nicaragua	6.82	—	—	—
Norway	1.19	0.79	392.48	86.51
Panama	9.76	—	—	—
Paraguay	12.28	—	—	—
Peru	1.73	5.70	39.73	—
Philippines	21.0	4.47		—
Poland	2.07	1.64	132.47	690.43
Portugal	0.95	1.81	283.01	449.26
Qatar	—	0.87	9.18	58.72
Romania	—	2.35	5.10	45.58
Russia	28.43			
Scotland	—	2.57	322.83	712.46
Singapore	1.3	0.50	26.83	29.71
Slovakia	2.0	2.26	111.06	493.94
Slovenia	2.1	1.47	46.92	1,144.35
South Korea	2.2	2.20		4.42
Spain	1.02		—	
Sri Lanka	29.76	6.81	4.07	84.75
Surinam	—	10.44	9.08	495.38
Swaziland	21.1	13.64	29.71	808.13
Sweden	1.01	2.41	682.64	1,335.35
Switzerland	0.79	2.95	862.31	976.01
Syria	2.6	1.20	3.23	0.12
Thailand	5.65			
Turkey	2.9	3.94	36.52	97.81
Turkmenistan	8.8	8.06	0.17	26.87
Uganda	25.2	7.89	2.24	—
Ukraine	12.0	7.26	12.19	—

(continued)

Table 2.1. Continued

	Homicide (WHO)[b]	Homicide (UN)[c]	Automobile theft[c]	Burglaries[c]
United Arab Emirates	0.5	0.72	13.82	57.32
United Kingdom	0.89	---	---	---
United States	5.90	5.7[e]	421.4[e]	729.4[e]
Uruguay	5.54	5.72	137.92	246.89
Venezuela	26.23	---	---	---
Zimbabwe	32.9	8.54	8.57	528.40

Note: Data are from World Health Organization (2006), United Nations Office on Drugs and Crime (2009a), and United Nations Office on Drugs and Crime (2009b).
[a] The WHO and UN homicide data are not directly comparable, as they do not come from the same years, nor do they have the exact same case definitions.
[b] World Health Organization victimization data. Data are for various years. Most are for 2000, with others from the late 1990s or early 2000s.
[c] Data from United Nations from 2004.
[d] Based on 2003 data.
[e] These rates are taken from *Crime in the United States, 2004* (FBI, 2005).

Rates of automobile theft are highest in Bermuda (1,353 per 100,000 residents), Switzerland (862), Sweden (683), Canada (541), and England and Wales (460). The U.S. rate as reported by the Federal Bureau of Investigation (FBI) was substantially lower at 429 per 100,000.[2] One must be wary of the meaning of these auto theft figures. First, the rates reported by some nations seem unlikely. Second, the rates are expressed per 100,000 residents, and thus do not represent the number of cars available to steal (or the attractiveness of some automobiles), which varies considerably by nation. Still further, this figure does not take into account other preferred forms of transportation in many nations, such as bicycles or motorcycles. The final column of table 2.1 shows the burglary rate by nation as reported to the police. The highest rates are found in Israel (1,910 per 100,000 residents), Denmark (1,691), Australia (1,580), Sweden (1,335), Bermuda (1,293), and England and Wales (1,293). While burglaries are probably high in some non-reporting nations or in nations that report lower rates, the high burglary rate in the nations listed here is likely associated with the attractiveness of the targets in these nations. Again the burglary rates for the United States are substantially lower at 729 per 100,000.

Table 2.2 shows data from the 2004–2005 wave of the International Crime Victims Survey and the corresponding 2005 European Survey of Crime and Safety (van Dijk et al. 2008). Data are provided for 30 nations (means are shown in bold near the bottom of the table), as well nine cities in which the survey was carried out between 2001 and 2005. One-year prevalence estimates for car theft, burglary, robbery, and assaults (including verbal threats) are shown in columns one through four, respectively. Among the 30 nations in the survey, the prevalence of automobile theft was highest in England and Wales (1.8 percent), New Zealand (1.8 percent), Portugal (1.5 percent), and Northern Ireland (1.4 percent), and lowest in Austria (0.1 percent), Japan (0.1 percent), Germany (0.2 percent), Hungary (0.2 percent), and Switzerland (0.2 percent). Recall that Switzerland had the second highest rate of automobile theft according to the UN data above.

The prevalence of burglary was highest in England and Wales (3.5 percent), New Zealand (3.2 percent), and Mexico (3.0 percent), and lowest in Sweden (0.7 percent), Finland (0.8 percent), and Spain (0.8 percent). Notice that Sweden was among the countries with the highest rates of burglary according to the UN data. Mexico (3.0 percent), Ireland (2.2 percent), and Estonia (1.6 percent) had the highest prevalence of robbery according to these victimization data, with Japan (0.2 percent), Finland (0.3 percent), Italy (0.3 percent) showing the lowest prevalence of robbery victimization. Finally, the prevalence of assaults and threats was highest in Northern Ireland (6.8 percent), Iceland (5.9 percent), England and Wales (5.8 percent), Ireland (4.9 percent), and New Zealand (4.9 percent), and lowest in Japan (0.6 percent), Italy (0.8 percent), and Portugal (0.9 percent).

Table 2.2. One-Year Prevalence Estimates of Car Theft, Burglary with Entry, Robbery, and Assaults and Threats, and Percent of Crimes Reported to the Police and Percent of Respondents Fearful of Going Outside at Night (Numbers are Percentages)[a]

	Car theft	Burglary	Robbery	Assault	Reporting[b]	Fear[c]
Australia	1.1	2.5	0.9	3.8	52	27
Austria	0.1	0.9	0.4	1.8	70	19
Belgium	0.5	1.8	1.2	3.6	68	26
Bulgaria	1.2	2.5	0.9	1.7	35	53
Canada	0.8	2.0	0.8	3.0	48	17
Denmark	1.3	2.7	0.9	3.3	60	17
England and Wales	1.8	3.5	1.4	5.8	61	32
Estonia	0.5	2.5	1.6	2.7	43	34
Finland	0.4	0.8	0.3	2.2	48	14
France	0.6	1.6	0.8	2.1	54	21
Germany	0.2	0.9	0.4	2.7	61	30
Greece	0.3	1.8	1.4	2.4	49	42
Hungary	0.2	1.7	0.9	1.2	58	26
Iceland	1.0	1.6	0.8	5.9	40	6
Ireland	1.2	2.3	2.2	4.9	51	27
Italy	1.0	2.1	0.3	0.8	50	35
Japan	0.1	0.9	0.2	0.6	54	36
Luxembourg	0.6	1.7	0.7	2.3	48	35
Mexico	0.9	3.0	3.0	2.2	16	34
Netherlands	1.0	1.3	0.5	4.3	58	18
New Zealand	1.8	3.2	1.1	4.9	57	30
N. Ireland	1.4	1.4	1.1	6.8	59	26
Norway	0.7	1.2	0.7	2.9	53	14
Poland	0.7	1.4	1.3	3.0	46	33
Portugal	1.5	1.4	1.0	0.9	51	34
Scotland	0.3	1.5	0.9	3.8	61	30

Spain	1.0	0.8	1.3	1.6	47	33
Sweden	0.5	0.7	1.1	3.5	64	19
Switzerland	0.2	1.6	0.8	2.5	63	22
United States	1.1	2.5	0.6	4.3	49	19
Mean for nations Cities	**0.8**	**1.8**	**1.0**	**3.1**	**48**	**27**
Buenos Aires	2.1	2.0	10.0	3.2	21	66
Johannesburg	2.6	5.4	5.5	11.2	35	57
Hong Kong	0.0	0.6	0.4	1.2	24	5
Istanbul	0.9	4.6	0.9	0.6	38	51
Lima	0.3	6.8	7.4	11.0	16	—
Maputo	1.9	12.6	7.6	6.2	17	65
Phnom Penh	0.2	15.8	1.8	6.8	14	48
Rio de Janeiro	1.7	1.0	5.1	1.5	18	57
Sao Paulo	4.2	1.5	5.4	2.6	12	72

Note: Data are from van Dijk, van Kesteren, and Smit (2008), Tables 4, 8, 11, 13, 19, and 27.

[a] National data are from the 2004-2005 wave of the International Crime Victims Survey or from the 2005 European Survey of Crime and Safety. City data at the bottom of the table are from ICVS in various years 2001–2005.

[b] Reporting rates are based on five crimes: theft from a car, bicycle theft, burglary, attempted burglary, and theft of personal property.

[c] Percentage of the population feeling "unsafe" or "very unsafe" on the street after dark.

Table 2.2 also reports information on the proportion of crime reported to the police. These reporting rates are based on an aggregate of five crimes: theft from a car, bicycle theft, burglary, attempted burglary, and theft of personal property. Reporting rates are highest in Austria (70 percent), Belgium (68 percent), Sweden (64 percent), and Switzerland (63 percent). Denmark, England and Wales, Germany, and Scotland also were all above 60 percent. Nations with the lowest levels of reporting of these five crimes included Mexico (16 percent), which was by far the lowest, Bulgaria (35 percent), Estonia (43 percent), and Iceland (40 percent). The final column of table 2.2 shows the percentage of all respondents who feel "unsafe" or "very unsafe" on the street after dark. The citizens of the northern European nations of Iceland (6 percent), Finland (14 percent), and Norway (14 percent) felt the safest. Bulgarians (53 percent) were by far the most fearful, followed by Greece (42 percent), Japan (36 percent), Italy (35 percent), and Luxembourg (35 percent).

Finally, for similar information from the ICVS about other nations and cities—including those in Africa, East-Central Europe, the Baltics, and Latin America—readers are encouraged to consult *Crime Victimization in Comparative Perspective* (Nieuwbeerta 2002), especially the article by Lynch (2002) on the effects of design differences on rate comparisons in the International Crime Victims Survey.

Emerging Topics in the International Literature on Crime

In recent years, several studies have appeared that, while not necessarily cross-national or comparative in nature, are of interest to those examining crime and justice throughout the world. One group of these studies examines the impact of specific policies and/or the functioning of the criminal justice system. Examples include studies of the variation in crime clearance rates and the causes of this variation (Roberts 2008; Smit, Meijer, and Groen 2004); studies from Russia, the United Kingdom, and the United States that suggest that needle exchange centers and methadone treatment are not associated with increases in crime and that examine the difficulties of implementing such harm-reduction policies when police and lawmakers are not supportive (Butler 2005; Healey et al. 2003; Marx et al. 2000); an analysis of Portugal's successful decriminalization of marijuana (Greenwald 2009); and studies from the United Kingdom, Slovenia, and elsewhere that hint at the potential reduction in violence associated with various alcohol policies (Livingston, Chikritzhs, and Room 2007; Nowill and Lavin 1988; Pridemore and Snowden 2009). Although policies and criminal justice practices from one culture do not always translate well to another, success (and failure) stories often can provide an evidence-based road map to other nations facing similar challenges.

Another recent area of interest for scholars has been the impact of democratization and marketization on crime. Since the first volume of this book was published there have been major fundamental changes in

Russia, Eastern Europe more generally, and China. It is not only interesting to examine the impact of social, economic, political, and cultural change on crime and justice in these nations, but more generally we now have access to information on these issues in these nations (which comprise a considerable proportion of the world's landmass and population) that previously was unavailable. As such, we have seen the recent publication of general and historical discussions of crime and justice in Russia (Pridemore 2005b) and China (Liu, Zhang, and Messner 2001; Mühlhahn 2009), as well as studies that examine various aspects of crime in these nations (without special attention given to democratization), including analyses from Russia of social capital and victimization (Stickley and Pridemore 2010), domestic violence (Cubbins and Vannoy 2005; Lysova and Hines 2008), human trafficking (Glonti 2001; Shelley and Orttung 2005), and the development of illicit drug markets (Paoli 2005); and studies of China on gang crime (Zhang et al. 1997), bicycle theft (Zhang, Messner, Liu 2007b), and official punishments for delinquency (Zhang and Messner 1994). Other studies have focused more specifically on the effects of change and democratization (or at least movement away from political economies of the past), including the effects of socioeconomic change (Pridemore and Kim 2007) and democratization and political change (Pridemore and Kim 2006) on homicide rates in Russia, and the effects of varying paths toward democratization and marketization on homicide rates in post-communist Eastern-Central Europe (Stamatel 2009). Finally, focusing on democratization more generally and using nations as units of analysis, several recent studies have examined how criminal justice in democratizing nations tends to move from a crime control perspective to a due process model (Sung 2006), the relationship between democratization and intellectual property theft (Piquero and Piquero 2006), and the effect of democratization and transition on national homicide rates (LaFree and Tseloni 2006) and more general crime rates (Lin 2007). In general, these studies tend to show that although there is commendable movement toward democratic principles and institutions, the transition toward democratization in a nation creates tremendous tensions for both citizens and criminal justice systems.

In spite of the increasing amount and improving quality of international criminological research, there are still fundamental areas that deserve more attention. One of these is geographic coverage. Many parts of the world are underrepresented in the English-language criminological literature. The most notable, unfortunately, is Africa. Africa as a continent—as well as many individual nations within it—faces considerable challenges related to crime, justice, and policy. While there is no dearth of information on these difficulties (we see them every day in the headlines), there is a clear and present need for more systematic research on crime in the region. The different cultures and wide range of topics—from high rates of interpersonal and sexual violence (Jewkes Abrahams 2002) in some areas to environmental degradation (Bojö 1996) and poaching (Lemieux and Clarke 2009) in other areas to terrorist activity in yet other areas (Lyman and Morrison 2004)—demand careful and sensitive analysis that will inform not only science but national and international policymaking and harm reduction strategies. Other underrepresented geographic regions in the English-language criminological literature include Asia and Central and South America. As mentioned earlier, the former has recently received greater attention as China becomes more important on the world stage and faces tremendous social, economic, and political change. The Asian continent holds a diverse array of cultures, nations, and crime and justice issues, however, that deserve greater systematic criminological attention. The same is true of Central America and South America, which not only contain some nations with very high rates of violence but also others that suffer from the illicit narcotics trade and issues of environmental injustice.

Another fundamental issue that demands more attention—from both research and practical perspectives—is creating and improving surveillance systems. A major conclusion of the World Health Organization's recent *World Report on Violence and Health* (Krug et al. 2002) was to "enhance the capacity for collecting data on violence." Simply put, neither utilitarian nor scientific goals can be met without valid measurement. This is necessary within and across nations. That is, individual nations must enhance their abilities to discover and record incidents of violence and to collect the type of information about these events required to analyze them for public health and scientific purposes. This would best be implemented, however, using an overarching framework based on best practices. Data collection happens at the local level, and so must be designed to be simple and inexpensive. Of course, the process must result in valid data, and so must also conform to national and international standards. There must also be transparency, and thus a mechanism that allows public health agencies, scientists, law enforcement agencies, and policymakers to share information. As noted by WHO's *Report*, the current lack of accepted standards for collecting data on violence could look to examples such as the *International Classification of External Causes of Injury* (World Health Organization 2001) and the *Injury Surveillance Guidelines* (Holder et al. 2001) created by WHO and the U.S. Centers for Disease Control (CDC). Unfortunately, with a few notable exceptions, criminologists have been largely absent from hands-on discussion about and creation of such surveillance systems, with public health experts and epidemiologists largely taking the lead.

Some Final Thoughts about the International Criminological Literature

There are a few final thoughts about the international criminological literature worth considering. First, while there has been a substantial increase in the size of this literature in recent years, many familiar problems remain. One is that much of this work is descriptive, even journalistic, in nature, providing little new information and therefore failing to add to the systematic accumulated knowledge on a subject. Another continuing problem is the lack of reliable data from many parts of the world on many of the subjects that criminologists are used to studying. Few systematic and methodologically rigorous studies have been carried out in many individual nations, and for those interested in cross-national comparisons, reliable data even on violent crime are difficult to find. Further, just because data are available (e.g., on various crimes like theft or robbery or assault) does not mean they are reliable enough to subject them to statistical analysis. Gibson and Kim (2007), for example, have analyzed the factors influencing the rate at which crime victims report crime to the police in different nations, and have shown that this reporting rate affects the parameter estimates of associations between economic factors and crime cross-nationally.

Another item that traditional criminologists must consider is the growing empirical literature appearing in the disciplines of epidemiology and public health. Nearly every issue of the leading journals in these disciplines contains studies of violence, often from international or cross-national studies. Unfortunately, this body of research is almost never cited (and thus, we assume, almost never read) by criminologists publishing in more traditional criminological journals. Criminology remains an insular discipline generally, and this is especially true of the international research published by traditional criminologists. This level of insularity is unhealthy both scientifically in terms of accumulating knowledge about crime and violence, and more generally in terms of growth and development as a viable discipline that is to be taken seriously.

Finally, we must consider the commonly held belief that the United States is the most violent industrialized nation in the world. In terms of lethal violence, there is little doubt that the United States stands out when compared to other Western nations (Zimring and Hawkins 1997), even given the low U.S. rates during the last several years. But this rate is still lower than in nations like Brazil, South Africa, and several nations in eastern Europe, including Russia. The claim becomes even more suspect when we compare non-lethal violence in the United States to other developed nations. Aside from the countries just mentioned, the robbery and assault rates in table 2.2 reveal several Western nations that rival the United States. So, while the level of lethal violence in the United States is probably the highest in the Western world, it is hard to make the case for U.S. exceptionalism when it comes to non-lethal violence.

STUDYING PUNISHMENT CROSS-NATIONALLY

Differences in Punishment across Nations

Our understanding of crime control and especially prevention has become more sophisticated over the past few decades. We understand that things other than punishing offenders can affect the level of crime in a specific area (Clarke and Cornish 1986). There is an increasing appreciation that not only negative but positive incentives can affect the motivation to commit crime and that changes in the opportunity to commit crime can be as effective as changes in the motivation to offend (Clarke 1995; Clarke and Newman 2006). Nonetheless, punishment is viewed as an important instrument in social control, and there is great interest in the amount of punishment used in a society. Consequently, most cross-national comparisons of punishment focus on the administration of state coercion such as arrest, fines, imprisonment and non-custodial supervision (Kutataladze 2007; Frost, 2008).

By far the most often used indicators of the severity of punishment in a society is the incarceration rate—the number of persons in prison on a given day over the population of the nation (Walmsley 2008, 2009). This is the case because imprisonment is a severe form of punishment, prison populations are relatively easy to count, and imprisonment counts are broadly available compared to other data on state coercion. Imprisonment is to cross-national comparisons of punishment what homicide is to cross-national comparisons of crime.

While incarceration rates are an important indicator of punishment policy, they have their limitations. The concept of severity of punishment implies a certain level of punishment or coercion for a given level of provocation. A nation that inflicts a higher level of pain for the same unit of provocation is more punitive. Population-based incarceration rates do not take account of variation in provocation, such as the volume of crime in a society or differences in the types of crimes committed. They also do not tell us much about the source of punishment differences across nations. Imprisonment is the result of a long linked chain of choices from the offender's decision to commit a crime, to the victim's decision to report it to the police, to decisions of criminal justice system actors to arrest, prosecute, convict, and imprison. Nations can achieve the same incarceration rates in very different ways, and it is useful to break down the process into its component parts. Finally, cross-national comparisons of imprisonment rates are subject to all of the comparability issues identified in the crime rate discussion. Differences in the definition of incarceration or the counting rules used to enumerate prisoners can distort these comparisons. In this section, we compare the use of imprisonment across nations beginning with population-based incarceration rates and then refine these rates to take account of some of the limitations mentioned above. We will see how these refinements affect the rates, our understanding of why they differ, and their implications for the common wisdom about the relative punitiveness of the United States.

In doing this analysis, we rely on some of the newly available data referred to in the previous section, specifically the *European Sourcebook on Crime and Criminal Justice Statistics* (Killias et al. 1999) and a study conducted by a consortium led by David Farrington, Patrick Langan, and Michael Tonry (2004). The latter study is particularly useful because the authors took great pains to define comparable crime classes across nations, and they provided detailed information on each stage of processing, from the offense to the time served in prison for that offense.

Population-based Stock Incarceration Rates

In terms of population-based incarceration rates, the United States is clearly the most punitive nation in the world. According to data from the International Center for the Study of Prisons (ICSP), the United States in 2008 incarcerated 760 persons per 100,000 population (Walmsley 2009).[3] The closest competitors are St. Kitts with 660 prisoners for each 100,000 population and the Russian Federation with 626 per 100,000 population. When comparisons are restricted to other industrialized democracies, the gap between the United States and other nations grows much wider. In the same period, for example, France had an incarceration rate of 96 per 100,000 and Germany 90. Our common-law kin—the United Kingdom, Canada, and Australia—had rates of 153, 116, and 129 per 100,000, respectively. With the exception of the Russian Federation, these differences in incarceration rates have been relatively stable for the past decade or more. In 1999, the United States had an incarceration rate of 678 per 100,000 and was edged out by the Russian Federation with a rate of 688. The rates in other industrialized democracies were considerably lower, with the differences among nations of about the same magnitude as those found in 2008. In 1999, the United Kingdom was incarcerating 124 per 100,000, France 90, and Germany 84. So for at least the last decade, the United States has incarcerated its residents at a rate that is 5 to 12 times that of other industrialized democracies.

The incarceration rate in the United States increased about 12 percent between 1999 and 2008, but this is not unique among industrialized democracies. Virtually all of the nations to which the United States is commonly compared have experienced increases in incarceration rates over this period. Only Canada and Switzerland have had declines in their incarceration rates during this time. Some of the increases in incarceration have been substantially greater in nations other than the United States. For example, the incarceration rate has increased 20 percent in Sweden, 23 percent in the United Kingdom, and 48 percent in Japan over the same time period. There appears to have been a general increase in the use of imprisonment among industrialized democracies in the last decade (Farrington, Langan, and Tonry 2004).

Taking Account of Differences in Crime

It is conceivable that these differences in incarceration rates are due to differences in the level of provocation and specifically in the scope and nature of criminal activity in these nations. If other nations define criminal

Table 2.3. Population-based Stock Incarceration Rates by Nation[a]

Nation	Years		Percent Change
	1999	2008	
United States	678.4	760	12.0
England and Wales	124.2	153	23.2
Australia	113.8	129	13.4
Canada	116.6	116	−0.5
Netherlands	75.3	100	32.8
Austria	86.2	99	14.9
Italy	92.9	97	4.4
France	89.7	96	7.1
Germany	84.4	90	6.7
Switzerland	81.7	76	−6.9
Sweden	61.9	74	19.5
Japan	42.6	63	47.9

[a] *Source*: Walmsley (2007, 2009).

acts much more narrowly than the United States, for example, these differences in scope could account for the observed differences in incarceration rates. So if drug use and sale are not treated as crimes in some nations but are in others, this narrowing in the scope of the criminal law can bring fewer persons to sentencing and fewer persons to prison. In a sense the relative broadness of the criminal law can be seen as a form of punitiveness, but it is not punitiveness in terms of sentencing policy, and this is a distinction worth making. On the other hand, the scope of the criminal law can be the same across nations, but the volume of crimes within the shared crime classes can be different, which can drive incarceration rates even when the punitiveness of sentencing policies is the same. Finally, the mix of crimes committed can vary across nations such that nations with a greater proportion of violent crime or more serious property crime can have higher incarceration rates than other nations with a greater representation of less severe crimes. Previous comparative studies have taken into account the differences in the volume of crime but not in the scope and mix of crimes in a given nation (Farrington and Langan 1992; Tonry and Farrington 2005).

Assessing differences in the scope of crime and its effect on incarceration rates has generally been avoided in comparisons of punishment because it makes the provocation non-comparable across nations. Researchers usually want to determine if incarceration is used as prevalently across nations in response to the same provocation (Farrington and Langan 1992; Feeney 1998; Frase 2001; Lynch 1988; Tonry and Farrington 2005), so they restrict comparisons to a common set of crimes. Doing so, however, obscures the effect of the scope of the criminal law across societies. One approach to this issue is to simply take that group of crimes that a nation believes should be reported on as an indicator of the crime problem and treat it as a reflection of a society's definition of crime.[4] This, of course, assumes that other factors such as the nature of federalism in a nation or technological deficiencies or bureaucratic intransigence does not prevent these crime indicators from reflecting popular definitions of crime.[5] Another way to assess differences in scope is to compare nations on a group of crimes that includes not only those crimes for which there is broad agreements across nations, such as homicide and robbery, but also some crimes that reflect differences in the criminalization of behavior. The prime examples of the latter would be traffic offenses and possession and sale of illicit drugs. This will not completely reflect differences in the criminalization of behavior, but it will provide some idea of a nation's tendency to regulate behavior through the criminal law.

As noted in the previous section, the International Crime Victims Survey (ICVS) indicates that the overall prevalence of crimes measured by the survey in the United States is similar to that in a number of other industrialized democracies.[6] The crime prevalence rate in the United States is 17.5 per hundred population, which is lower than the rate of 21.8 in England and Wales, 19.7 in the Netherlands, and 18.1 in Switzerland. It is also similar to the prevalence in Australia (16.3), Canada (17.2), and Sweden (16.1). Crime is somewhat less prevalent in Austria, Germany, and France and considerably lower in Japan. Overall crime rates are driven mostly by theft. When we start to examine subclasses of crime, burglary seems to be more prevalent in the United States (6.1) and England (6.2) compared to these other nations. What is somewhat more surprising is the fact that the prevalence of violent crime in the United States is not greater than many of the other industrialized nations. The prevalence rate for robbery in the United States (0.6) is lower than the rates in 6 of the 11 nations compared. In the case of assault, the United States has higher prevalence than most nations except England and Sweden, although Australia too is reasonably similar. These findings on violence are somewhat less reliable than the property crime estimates because of the small sample sizes and the fact that violence is so rare. The estimates of robbery victimization are in many cases not appreciably different from 0 once sampling error is taken into account. Assaults are less rare, but this category includes a wide range of events, from threats to attacks with a weapon. Nations can have very different rates of relatively rare but serious forms of violence, such as assault with grievous injury, that can contribute substantially to differences in the incarceration rate but they would not be distinguishable in the ICVS data. Further, victimization surveys omit crimes like homicide (for obvious reasons) and vice crimes like drug possession or sale that can be very consequential for prison populations. For these reasons, it is also useful to make comparisons of the crime problems using police data when our focus is incarceration.

Table 2.4. Victimization Prevalence by Crime and Nation 2004–2005

Nation	Crime			
	Overall	Burglary	Robbery	Assaults
Australia	16.3	4.9	0.9	3.4
Austria	11.6	2.3	0.4	1.8
Canada	17.2	3.7	0.8	3
England and Wales	21.8	6.2	1.4	5.8
France	12	2.8	0.8	2.1
Germany	13.1	2.2	0.4	2.7
Italy	12.6	4.6	0.3	0.8
Japan	9.9	1.6	0.2	0.6
Netherlands	19.7	2.7	0.5	4.3
Sweden	16.1	0.8	1.1	3.5
Switzerland	18.1	2.8	0.8	2.5
United States	17.5	6.1	0.6	4.3

Source: Van Dijk, Van Kesteren and Smit (2008) Appendix Table 1.

When police data are used to characterize crime, the crime problem in the United States becomes more distinctive. The incidence of serious property crime like burglary is higher in many European countries than it is in the United States, which is generally consistent with findings from the ICVS. The rates of serious violent crime, like homicide and rape, however, are substantially higher in the United States than in other nations. Rates of robbery are also much higher in the United States than most other industrialized democracies, but there are a few nations like the United Kingdom and France that have rates similar to the United States. The other distinctive feature of the crime mix in the United States is that the rate of police recorded drug offending is considerably higher than that in most other nations except Switzerland.

This distinctive mix of higher rates of serious violence and aggressive criminalization of victimless crime contribute to the higher incarceration rates in the United States. The higher rates of serious violence contribute to incarceration rates because serious violence results in longer sentences in virtually every nation (Lynch 1988, 1993). As a result, even a small number of violent crimes can contribute disproportionately to the incarceration rate because violent offenders accumulate in prisons over time. At the same time, drug crimes are identified at high volume[7] relative to serious violence and thereby contribute to the prison population by increasing admissions rates. In the United States, drug crimes are identified at a rate more than 100 times that of homicide and 4 times that of robbery. In contrast, in the Netherlands the robbery rate is about 2.5 times the drug offense rate. The Dutch have clearly chosen not to criminalize drug sale and possession, while the United States has chosen the opposite strategy. Although sentences for most drug crimes are relatively

Table 2.5. Crime Rates per 100,000 Population by Nation and Type of Crime, 1999

Nations	Murder	Rape	Robbery	Assault[c]	Burglary	MVT	Larceny	Drugs[d]
				Type of Crime				
United States[a]	5.70	32.68	150.23	820.89	769.99	420.73	2551.39	571.01
United Kingdom[b]	1.58	15.89	154.74	889.52	1666.72	707.92	3480.09	265.37
Netherlands	1.47	11.26	111.04	268.40	3045.64	194.20	2114.14	48.22
Austria	0.76	12.38	28.60	405.41	957.01	87.59	1648.70	204.50
Italy	1.51	3.35	69.23	57.00	411.62	517.89	1672.49	79.14
France	1.85	13.23	157.83	161.63	615.17	658.17	2254.75	169.29
Germany	1.58	9.22	74.87	453.66	626.51	171.43	3021.58	276.17
Switzerland	1.25	6.27	59.98	76.35	1071.41	297.44	2537.71	622.49
Sweden	1.22	23.76	97.44	676.71	1454.46	883.37	5635.08	412.49

[a] All crime information for the United States is taken from *Crime in the U.S. 1999* (FBI 2000).
[b] All crime information for nations other than the U.S. is taken from the *European Sourcebook on Crime and Criminal Justice Statistics, 1995–2000* (Killias et al. 2003).
[c] Assault data from *Crime in the U.S., 1999* combined aggravated assault and arrests for simple assault to make the category more comparable to the *European Sourcebook*.
[d] Drug offenses recorded by the police in the U.S. is estimated by drug arrests in *Crime in the U.S. 1999*.

short, the volume of drug offenses makes them a major contributor to the U.S. prison population.

To get some sense of how much the uniqueness of the crime mix and the volume of crime in the United States contribute to the observed differences in population-based incarceration rates, we can compare offender-based incarceration rates to population-based rates. The number of offenders identified is a function of the scope and volume of crime, which is exactly what we want to know. It is also affected by the effectiveness and efficiency of the police, which introduces some distortion. When population-based incarceration rates are used to compare the United States to other industrialized democracies, the average ratio of the U.S. rate to rates of other nations is 7.25. When nations are compared using offender-based incarceration rates, the average ratio of U.S. rates to those of other nations is 2.3. While this is a sizable reduction in the difference in incarceration rates, the United States still incarcerates at a much higher rate per offense than other industrialized democracies. We will return to this issue of parsing out the effect of the crime problem on incarceration rates below.

Taking Account of Differences in Sentencing

In an effort to determine how much differences in sentencing policies contribute to differences in the incarceration rates, we focus on a number of similarly defined offenses across nations to see how nations differ with respect to the probability of conviction, the likelihood of incarceration, and the length of sentence imposed. In making these comparisons, we draw heavily on the work of Farrington, Langan, and Tonry (2004) and Blumstein, Tonry, and Van Ness (2005) referred to previously. Their comparisons were restricted to homicide, rape, robbery, assault, burglary, and motor vehicle theft. Data from the European Sourcebook were used to make comparisons on drug offenses (Killias et al. 2003).

The probability of conviction per offense varies considerably across nations with many, in fact most, industrialized nations having much higher conviction rates than the United States.[8] In the case of homicide, England, Switzerland, and the Netherlands have higher rates of conviction than the United States, and Sweden's rate is essentially the same. Australia and Scotland have lower conviction rates. The United States has higher conviction rates for rape than any of the other nations in the study except for the Netherlands. With respect to robbery, the United States convicts at a rate substantially lower than Switzerland, Australia, and the Netherlands, but higher than England, Sweden, and Scotland. The conviction rate for assault is the lowest in the United States, and the conviction rate for burglary is the highest, with the conviction rate for motor vehicle theft in the middle of the distribution of nations. In terms of the propensity to convict a person given the occurrence of a crime, the United States is not consistently more likely to convict across all crime classes.

Table 2.6. Probability of Conviction Given Offense by Nation and Crime[a]

| Nation | Crime | | | | | |
	Homicide	Rape	Robbery	Assault	Burglary	MVT
England and Wales	69.2	7.8	7.1	15.5	3.6	4.0
United States	63.8	18.5	11.8	10.3	6.5	4.7
Sweden	62.5	7.6	8.1	15.0	4.0	3.0
Australia	42.1	22.4	25.6	43.0	5.7	7.4
Scotland	55.9	7.6	5.4	19.6	5.6	5.5
Switzerland	107.9	12.2	16.9	11.6	3.0	2.9
Netherlands	78.4	19.0	21.0	29.9	3.9	17.2

[a] Data taken from Farrington, Langan and Tonry (2004).

One reason that the offense-based conviction rates in the United States are low could have to do with the relatively high rates of plea bargaining and charge reduction that go on in the pre-trial stage in the United States. Someone can be charged with burglary and robbery in the same instance, but pleads guilty in return for being charged only with the burglary. In police-recorded offense statistics, this crime is coded as a robbery, but the conviction is recorded as a burglary. This would be treated as non-conviction for the robbery offense. With the data currently available on the pre-trial process in the United States, it is impossible to determine the magnitude of this bargaining and its effect on these rates (Lynch 1988). We do know that plea bargaining is not nearly as prevalent in the other nations examined here (Langbein 1979).

The probability of being sentenced to incarceration given conviction varies across nation by type of crime. It is highest for homicide and lowest for assault and motor vehicle theft. In the case of homicide, most nations incarcerate in the neighborhood of 90 percent of those convicted, with Sweden being the highest at 95 percent and Switzerland by far the lowest at 76 percent. The United States incarcerates 94 percent of persons convicted of homicide. The variation in the use of incarceration becomes

Table 2.7. Probability of Incarceration Given Conviction by Nation and Crime[a]

Nation	Homicide	Rape	Robbery	Assault	Burglary	MVT
England and Wales	91.86	96.8	72.61	29.5	61.8	28.8
United States	94.48	75.6	75.01	59.3	54.9	54.7
Sweden	95.24	89.8	62.67	33.5	48.3	26.1
Australia	85.82	55.9	57.01	8.2	32.9	27.6
Scotland	89.39	88.9	69.60	15.0	50.5	31.0
Switzerland	75.61	53.1	21.60	16.5	40.5	22.6
Netherlands	93.92	65.0	62.53	14.9	66.0	44.0

[a] Data taken from Farrington, Langan and Tonry (2004).

greater in the case of rape, with England having the highest rate at 97 percent and Switzerland having the lowest at 53 percent. The United States incarcerates 75 percent of persons convicted of rape. The probability of incarceration decreases for robbery compared to homicide and rape, but the variability across nations is less. For most nations, the probability of incarceration for robbery given conviction is between 60 and 75 percent, except for Switzerland, which incarcerates only 22 percent of those convicted of robbery. The United States is at the high end of the range of incarcerating for robbery with a rate of 75 percent. The average probability of incarceration for assault is less than that for homicide, rape, and robbery, and the variability in the incarceration rate given conviction is greater. The United States is highest with an incarceration rate of 59 percent of those convicted of assault, and Australia is lowest with an incarceration rate of 8 percent of convictions. There seems to be a grouping of nations with regard to use of incarceration for assault with the United States, England, and the Netherlands having relatively higher rates and Sweden, Switzerland, Scotland, and Australia having lower rates of incarceration. The probability of incarceration given conviction ranges between 66 and 32 percent, with the Netherlands having the highest and Australia the lowest rates. The United States is right around the average for these nations at 54 percent. Finally, the United States has by far the highest probability of incarcerating persons convicted of motor vehicle theft at 55 percent, followed by the Netherlands at 44 percent. The Swiss have the lowest incarceration for motor vehicle theft at 23 percent of those convicted.

The United States then is not distinctively and uniformly more likely to incarcerate persons convicted of crimes than other industrialized nations. In the case of serious violence such as homicide and rape, the U. S. uses incarceration in ways similar to other industrialized nations, even somewhat lower than some. In the case of lesser violence, such as assault and robbery, the United States is somewhat more likely to use incarceration than other nations, but it does have close company in some instances. Comparisons on these classes of crimes may be particularly imprecise due to the widespread use of firearms in these offenses in the United States relative to other nations (FBI 2007, Lynch 1988). The United States is not distinctive in using incarceration for burglary, with several other nations sentencing greater proportions of convicted burglars to prison than the United States. The United States does use incarceration substantially more than other nations for motor vehicle theft. Earlier studies have also identified this pattern in the likelihood of incarceration across nations and offenses (Blumstein, Tonry, and Van Ness 2005; Lynch 1988).

Finally, the United States generally imposes longer sentences on persons sentenced to incarceration than other industrialized nations. This difference between the United States and other nations is more uniform across types of crime than was the probability of conviction, but there are other industrialized nations with relatively similar time served. In the case

Table 2.8. Time Served Given Incarceration by Nation and Crime[a] (Months)

Nation	Homicide	Rape	Robbery	Assault	Burglary	MVT
England and Wales	104.70	48.8	23.00	7.3	10.20	4.2
United States	126.20	59.2	37.40	21.6	15.20	10.1
Sweden	49.42	11.68	14.33	3.54	6.36	2.97
Australia	132.60	57.3	40.90	24.4	21.40	8.4
Scotland	106.83	46.23	10.91	8.89	4.08	2.72
Switzerland	63.80	33.86	24.50	12.49	15.60	10.5
Netherlands	66.90	19.2	12.50	4.7	11.40	3.53

[a] Data taken from Farrington, Langan and Tonry (2004).

of homicide, for example, Australia (133 months) has a longer average time served than the United States (126 months), with England (105 months) and Scotland (107 months) not far behind. Sentences for homicide are much shorter in Sweden, Switzerland, and the Netherlands. The pattern is essentially the same for rape with the United States imposing the longest sentences (59 months), followed very closely by Australia (57 months) and somewhat more distantly by England (48 months) and Scotland (46 months). Sweden, Switzerland, and the Netherlands have much shorter terms of imprisonment for rape. This pattern gets a little more complicated with burglary. Australia has the longest prison terms (21.4 months) followed by the United States (15.2 months) and Switzerland (15.6 months) and more distantly by the Netherlands (11.4 months) and England (10.2 months). Sweden and Scotland have the shortest sentences. The distinctiveness of the United States is greatest for assault and motor vehicle theft, where only Australia comes close to having prison terms as long as those of the United States.

Thus far we have attributed the massively higher population-based incarceration rate in the United States to the nature of the crime problem and the punitiveness of our sentencing policy. The United States has higher levels of serious violence than other nations, and this contributes disproportionately to the prison population because of both the propensity to incarcerate perpetrators of these crimes and the longer time served. The foregoing tables complicate this story somewhat. The United States is not distinctively the most likely to incarcerate given conviction across all offenses, nor does it always impose the longest sentences.

In order to sort out the contribution of the crime problem and sentencing policy more clearly, we estimated the stock prison population using the number of offenses, the probability of conviction given an offense, the probability of being sentenced to incarceration, and the time served if sentenced.[9] We then changed the components of this calculation for each nation to reflect the crime problem and sentencing policy in the United States to see how much of the difference between the incarceration rate of the United States and other nations is due to the crime problem or sentencing policy.[10] If, for example, the crime problem accounts for most of the difference in the incarceration rate, then when other nations are assumed to have the same crime problem as the United States, the incarceration rates of those nations and the United States will become more similar. We assessed the similarity of incarceration rates as the ratio of the U.S. incarceration rate to the incarceration rate for another nation, and we used the changes in these ratios to indicate the importance of each factor.

When we estimate the incarceration rate in each nation with the original data on crime, conviction, incarceration sentence, and time served in prison, the average ratio of incarceration rates in the United States to the incarceration rate in other nations is 5.66. England is the most similar to the United States with a ratio of 3.02 and Sweden the most different with a ratio of 9.04. When these other nations are assumed to have the same mix and rate of crime as the United States, the average ratio falls to 2.97, or 47.6 percent relative to the original average rate. England and the Netherlands are the most similar to the United States with ratios of 2.16 and 2.12, respectively, when assuming the same mix and rate of crime as the United States Sweden still has the smallest imprisonment rate relative to the United States with a ratio of 4.57. When other nations are assumed to have the same crime problem and the same propensity to incarcerate given conviction, the average ratio decreases to 2.22 or an additional 13 percent. With this adjustment the Netherlands and Switzerland become the nations most similar to the United States and the ratio for England changes relatively little. This indicates that much of the difference between the United States and the Netherlands and Switzerland is driven by the propensity to incarcerate, while the difference between the United States and England is not. When other nations are assumed to have the same crime problem, propensity to incarcerate, and time served in prison as the United States, the average incarceration rate ratio falls to .96 or an additional 22.25 percent. The incarceration rates for all nations become considerably more similar to that of the United States as a result of this adjustment, with Sweden experiencing the most change.

In sum, the very high incarceration rates in the United States are a product of both its distinct crime problem and its sentencing policy. Of these two forces, the nature of the crime problem is somewhat more consequential. Of the two components of sentencing policy, the longer prison sentences served by offenders are a more important factor than differences in the propensity to incarcerate.

The Special Case of Drug Crimes

Drug crimes were left out of the foregoing discussion of the effects of the crime mix in a nation on the use of incarceration. This was done in part because drug crimes were not included in the comparative study done by Farrington, Langan, and Tonry (2004), so we must go to other, perhaps less refined sources of data to address this issue. Also, the crimes

Table 2.9. Ratios of Incarceration Rates in U.S. to Other Nations by Nation and Adjustments

Nation	Original Estimates[a]	With crime standardized	With crime and comits standardized	With crime, comits and time standardized
England and Wales	3.02	2.16	1.94	1.13
United States	1.00	1.00	1.00	1.00
Sweden	9.04	4.57	3.87	1.16
Scotland	3.82	3.18	2.23	1.07
Switzerland	7.98	2.82	1.40	0.86
Netherlands	4.46	2.12	1.66	0.57
Average	5.66	2.97	2.22	0.96
Pct Reduction		47.58	13.24	22.25

[a] Data in this table taken from Farrington, Langan and Tonry (2004).

addressed in that study are broadly considered morally objectionable and are viewed as something that nations must address. The consensus regarding the morality of using and selling drugs, however, is less uniform across nations, and the creation and enforcement of drug laws are seen more as policy decisions rather than as imperatives. Nonetheless, drug offenses comprise a substantial proportion of the prison population in the United States and other nations, and differential treatment of drug use and sale can go a long way in explaining differences in prison populations.

The *European Sourcebook on Crime and Criminal Justice Statistics* (Killias et al. 2003) provides well-documented data on drug offenses for a number of European nations and when these data are combined with information on the United States from the Uniform Crime Reports (UCR) we can obtain some idea of the relative magnitude of drug offenses known to the police. The *Sourcebook* also includes data on the number of persons convicted of drug crimes, the number sentenced to incarceration, and the number of persons in prison for drug offenses. Data on convictions and incarceration sentences for drug crimes in the United States were obtained from the *Felony Sentences in State Courts: 2000* (Durose and Langan 2003).

Based on these data, the United States is not unique in the extent of drug offending or the degree to which drug offenses are recorded by the police. While the United States has high rates of drug offending per 100,000 (587), so do other nations like Scotland (623) and Switzerland (622). At the other end of the spectrum is the Netherlands with a rate of 48 per 100,000. Given that drug enforcement is highly discretionary, these big differences in drug offense rates are most likely driven by differences in policy (Lynch 2002). The Dutch, for example, have low drug offense rates because they have essentially decriminalized use of illicit drugs while allowing some prosecution of those who sell these drugs inappropriately.

The nations do not differ much in the probability of conviction given an offense, with most nations convicting in about 20 percent of the offenses. England and Wales and the Netherlands are the outliers here with a rate of conviction given offense of 40 and 91 percent respectively.

Much greater differences appear in the use of incarceration and the length of custodial sentences for drug offenses. The United States imposes prison and jail sentences in 67 percent of drug cases, followed distantly by the Netherlands at 46 percent and then Switzerland (38 percent) and France (35 percent). England and Wales, Scotland, and Sweden are much less likely to incarcerate drug offenders.[11] In terms of time served, the United States imposes much longer sentences than any of the other nations studied. The average expected time to be served for drug crimes is 23 months in the United States The average time served in England and Wales is the next longest at 12 months, followed by Scotland at 10 months. Switzerland has the shortest time served for drug offenses at

Table 2.10. Drug Offenses and the Processing of Drug Offenders by Nation

Nation	Drug Offense Rate	P(conviction/offense)	P(prison/conviction)	Time Served[c]
England andWales[a]	231.2	0.4	0.179	11.89
United States[b]	586.9	0.205	0.67	23
France	169.2	0.237	0.346	7.2
Sweden	412.6	0.198	0.202	8.17
Scotland	622.5	0.201	0.148	10.13
Switzerland	621.7	0.181	0.384	5.34
Netherlands	48.22	0.91	0.459	8.31

[a] Data for all nations except the U.S. are taken from the *European Sourcebook on Crime and Criminal Justice Statistics* (Killias, et al. 2003).

[b] Drug offenses for the U.S. are estimated from arrest data in Crime in the U.S. 1999 (FBI 2000).
Probability of conviction, incarceration and time to be served were taken from *Felony Sentencing in State Courts, 2000* (Durose and Langan 2003).

[c] Time served for all nations but the U.S. is estimated by the ratio of the stock populations to admissions in a given year.

5.3 months, followed by France (7.2 months), Sweden (8.2 months) and the Netherlands (8.3 months).

These data suggest that nations take very different approaches to drug control. Some nations, like the United States, Scotland, and Switzerland, tend to cast a broad net and aggressively arrest drug offenders, while others like the Netherlands are much more selective in whom they target for police attention. Once drug offenders are in the criminal justice system, some nations are more likely to incarcerate than others and for longer periods. The Netherlands, for example, is more likely to incarcerate drug offenders than any other nation in the study with the exception of the United States, and the length of the sentences they serve are not particularly short. Switzerland, in contrast, seems to cast a much broader net than the Netherlands and incarcerate at nearly the same rate, but the time served is substantially lower than that in the Netherlands. Nations tend be punitive toward drug offenders in some ways and less so in others. The United States is distinct in that it casts a broad net for drug offenders, makes more extensive use of incarceration and has longer custodial sentences. The United States is punitive toward drug offenders on every dimension.

In an effort to determine how differences in criminal justice policies toward drug offenders might be contributing to differences in incarceration across nations, we added the data on drug offenses to the data on other offenses presented in previous sections. We made the same adjustments as in table 2.7, sequentially setting the crime rate, the probability of incarceration and the time served in custody equal to the U.S. rate to see how it would affect the difference in incarceration between the United States and other nations. The crime mix in a nation still has the largest

Table 2.11. Average Ratio of U.S. Incarceration to Incarceration in Other Nations by Adjustment with and without Drug Crimes

		Original Estimates	With crime standardized	With crime and comits comits standardized	With crime, comits and time standardized
Without Drug Crimes					
	Average	5.66	2.97	2.22	0.96
	Pct Change		47.58	13.24	22.25
With Drug Crimes					
	Average	6.80	3.66	2.01	0.84
	Pct Change		55.27	29.30	20.55

effect on the differences in incarceration rates. The average ratio of U.S. incarceration rates to those of other nations decreases by 47.58 percent when the crime mix in other nations is set to that of the United States. The average ratio decreases by 13.02 percent when the propensity to incarcerate is also set to the U.S. level in these other nations and by an additional 22.25 percent when time served is set to U.S. level. Adding drug offenses increases the effect of crime mix from a 47.58 percent to a 55.27 percent decrease in the ratio and caused the importance of propensity to incarcerate to increase from 13.02 to 29.30 percent. The effect of time served on the average ratios decreased slightly from 22.25 percent to 20.55 percent. The effect of differences in the propensity to incarcerate has a larger effect when drugs were added to the crime mix. It is clear that the aggressive policy that the United States has taken toward the use and sale of illicit drugs is a major contributor to its high incarceration rate. This aggressiveness includes the greater propensity to criminalize drug-related activity, to sentence to prison those convicted of drug crimes, and to make those imprisoned serve longer sentences.

The Role of Supervision in Generating Incarceration Rates xxx

Virtually all cross-national comparisons of punishment have ignored the role that post-conviction supervision plays in generating prison populations (Lynch 1988, 1993; Farrington and Langan 1992; Tonry and Farrington 2005). Supervision refers to that period after serving a custodial sentence in which the former inmate is under the supervision of a parole or probation officer who monitors his behavior and sees that the conditions imposed by the court for the inmate's release are complied with. It also refers to supervision in the community that occurs as an alternative to prison. Former inmates under supervision can be re-incarcerated if they commit a new offense or violate the terms of their release. The same is the case for persons sentenced directly to supervision. Typically, persons under supervision can have their supervision revoked in an administrative hearing that may never appear in court conviction statistics and certainly not in offense-specific statistics. This is the back door into prison and a potentially important determinant of the prison population. Moreover, the specific nature of the interrelationship of supervision and incarceration in a nation can change the very meaning of supervision with respect to what is punitive. If supervision is more therapeutic than regulatory, then it can be seen as a less punitive alternative to incarceration, but if supervision is strictly regulatory, it constitutes a substantial broadening of the control net and intrusiveness approaching incarceration. Comparing supervision practices across nations adds a whole new dimension to punishment and new complexities to cross-national comparisons.

Data on supervision populations and supervision policies are not as readily available as data on prison use. Nonetheless, we were able to assemble data on the supervision populations in the United States and

Table 2.12. Size of the Supervision Populations in U.S. and England and Wales

		United States 2007[a]	England and Wales 2008[b]	Ratio of U.S. to EW
Stock	Total	5,117,528	176,220	29.04
	Parole	824365	30874	26.70
Supervision Pop to Prison Pop		2.23	2.20	1.01
Supervision Pop to Population per 100k		1683.07	323.70	5.20
Parole Pop to Prison Pop		0.359	0.386	0.93
Parole Pop to Population per 100k		271.12	56.71229	4.78

[a] These data are taken from *Probation and Parole in the United States, 2007: Statistical Tables* (Gaze and Bonczar 2009).
[b] These data are taken from *Offender Management Caseload Statistics, 2008* (Wickens 2009).

England and Wales to provide a limited comparison. The rate of supervision in the United States is 5.2 times that of England and Wales. The stock supervision population—including probation and parole—is 5,117,528 in the United States compared to 176,220 in England and Wales. Expressed as a rate per 100,000 population, the United States has a rate of 1,683 and England and Wales a rate of 324. When comparisons are restricted to post-release supervision, the rate for the United States is 271 per 100,000 and the rate for England and Wales is 57 per 100,000. The parole rate in the United States is 4.8 times that of England and Wales. With more people under supervision there is a greater chance that those being monitored will be detected either violating the technical conditions of their supervision or committing a new offense. So having larger per capita populations under supervision will mean that more persons should be entering prisons through the "back door" in the United States than in England and Wales, even if the rate at which persons under supervision is the same in both nations (Blumstein and Beck 1999).

The rate at which persons on parole are returned to prison for violating the conditions of supervision in the United States is 4.7 times the rate in England and Wales. The ratio of technical revocations to the stock population of persons on parole is .16 in the United States compared to .03 in England and Wales. Being returned to prison for a new offense is also substantially more likely for parole populations in the United States than in England and Wales. The ratio of revocations for new offenses to the stock population of persons on parole is .06 in the United States compared to .02 in England and Wales.[12] It is difficult to say with certainty whether these differences are due to stricter supervision policies in the United States or higher levels of non-cooperation among supervision populations in the United States. It is clear that the "back door" is substantially more ajar in the United States than it is in England and Wales. Given the similarity of the United States and England and Wales on other aspects of their sentencing policies, it seems likely that supervision may be even less of a contributor to the prison population in the other industrialized nations examined here. More generally, these observations make it clear that greater attention should be given to the role of supervision policies in generating differences in prison populations cross-nationally.

Table 2.13. Ratio of Re-admissions to Stock Parole Population by Nation and Reason

Reason	United States	England and Wales	Ratio of U.S. to EW
Revocation	15.72	3.34	4.71
New Offense	5.74	1.54	3.74

CONCLUSION

This chapter set out to reassess the common wisdom that the United States is both the most punitive and the most crime-ridden of industrialized democracies. It also set out to review cross-national comparisons of crime and criminal justice policy more broadly to assess how they might help us more accurately describe and understand cross-national differences. We find that the common wisdom about crime and punishment in the United States relative to other nations is accurate, though simplistic and misleading. The United States has levels of serious violence (and especially lethal violence) that are higher than any other industrialized democracy, but its levels of lesser violence and property crime are similar to or lower than many other nations to which it is commonly compared. Incarceration rates are much higher in the United States than other comparable nations, but this is due in large part to the higher levels of serious violence in the United States, since sentences for serious violence are long everywhere. The aggressive stance that the United States has taken toward drug crime is also a major contributor to the prison population. The United States is more likely to treat drug activity as a crime than most other nations, more likely to sentence convicted persons to prison, and more likely to require offenders to serve more time. Other nations may be similar to the United States in one of these aspects, but none is as punitive in all of these respects. The other major contributor to the high incarceration rates in the United States is the general tendency to require more time served for offenses other than serious violence. So the United States is the most crime-ridden of developed nations with respect to very serious violence and the criminalization of illicit drug activity, but not with regard to other common-law crimes. It is punitive in that it imposes longer sentences than other nations for most crimes and it aggressively pursues drug crimes at every stage. If other nations had the same levels of serious violence as the United States, their incarceration rates would look substantially more similar to that of the United States, but the U.S. rates would still be considerably higher.

The changes that have occurred over the last decade in our ability and eagerness to conduct cross-national comparisons hold promise for improving the accuracy of those comparisons and for understanding why nations differ. The inclusion of nations from the former Soviet Union and China in the world community and in commonly used data bases provides variation on major institutional arrangements that will allow us to assess the effect of these institutions on crime and criminal justice policy, including punishment. The unique problems of these emerging democracies also have pushed other crimes such as human trafficking and corruption to the fore. These topics will give new energy to cross-national studies, since they are almost of necessity comparative. While the demise of the INTERPOL database on crime is a blow to cross-national comparisons, some regional data collections have risen to provide data on police-recorded crime that are arguably of higher quality, albeit for fewer nations. Most importantly, the prevalence of comparable individual- and incident-level data on crime (though not yet on punishment) in a number of nations holds the promise of more accurately determining cross-national differences and understanding the sources of this variation. With these data, sub-national information on the characteristics of victims, offenders, and incidents that influence the risk of crime and punishment can be distinguished from country characteristics. In conclusion, the nature of international research on crime and punishment is evolving, as is its potential to contribute meaningfully to the scientific record on these subjects. In order to meet this potential, however, there must be a greater focus on international research and greater care on the part of scholars carrying out this research.

References

Aliverdinia. A., and W. A. Pridemore. 2007. "A First Glimpse at Narcotics Offenders in an Islamic Republic: A Test of an Integrated Model of Drug Involvement among a Sample of Men Incarcerated for Drug Offenses in Iran." *International Criminal Justice Review* 17: 27–44.

Aromaa, K., and M. Heiskanen. 2002. "Fear of Street Violence in Europe." In *International Comparison of Crime and Victimization: The ICVS*, ed. H. Kury Willowdale. Ontario: de Sitter Publications.

Avison, W. R., and P. L. Loring. 1986. "Population Diversity and Cross-national Homicide: The Effects of Inequality and Heterogeneity." *Criminology* 24: 733–749.

Bennett, R. R. 1991. "Routine Activities: A Cross-national Assessment of a Criminological Perspective." *Social Forces* 70: 147–163.

Blumstein, Alfred, and Allen Beck. 1999. "The Growth in the American Prison Population, 1980–1996." In *Prisons*, eds. Michael Tonry and Joan Petersilia. Chicago: University of Chicago Press.

Blumstein, Alfred, Michael Tonry, and Asheley Van Ness. 2005. "Cross-national Measures of Punitiveness." In *Crime and Punishment in Western Countries, 1980–1999*, eds. Michael Tonry and David P. Farrington, 347–376. Chicago: University of Chicago Press.

Bojö, J. 1996. "The Costs of Land Degradation in Sub-Saharan Africa." *Ecological Economics* 16: 161–173.

Botchkovar, E. V., C. R. Tittle, O. Antonaccio. 2009. "General Strain Theory: Additional Evidence using Cross-cultural Data." *Criminology* 47: 131–176.

Butler, W. E. 2005. "Injecting Drug Use and HIV: Harm-reduction Programs and the Russian Legal System." In *Ruling Russia: Law, Crime, and Justice in a Changing Society*, ed. A. Pridemore, 205–224. Lanham, MD: Rowman and Littlefield.

Clarke, Ronald V. 1995. "Situational Crime Prevention." In *Building a Safer Society: Strategic Approaches to Crime Prevention*, eds. Michael Tonry and David Farrington, 91–150. Chicago: University of Chicago Press.

Clarke, Ronald V., and Derek Cornish. 1986. *The Reasoning Criminal: Rational Choice Perspective on Offending*. New York: Springer Verlag.

Clarke, Ronald V., and Graham Newman. 2006. *Outsmarting the Terrorists*. Portsmouth, NH: Greenwood Publishing.

Cubbins, L. A., and D. Vannoy. 2005. "Socioeconomic Resources, Gender Traditionalism, and Wife Abuse in Urban Russian Couples." *Journal of Marriage and Family* 67: 37–52.

Doleschal, Eugene. 1977. "Rate and Length of Imprisonment: How Does the U.S. Compare with the Netherlands, Sweden and Denmark?" *Crime and Delinquency* 23: 51.

Durose, Matthew, and Patrick A. Langan. 2003. *Felony Sentences in State Courts: 2000.* Washington, DC: Bureau of Justice Statistics.

Fajnzylber, P., D. Lederman, and N. Loayza. 2002. "Inequality and Violent Crime." *The Journal of Law and Economics* 45: 1–39.

Farrell, G., A. Tseloni, and K. Pease. 2005. "Repeat Victimization in the ICVS and the NCVS." *Crime Prevention and Community Safety: An International Journal* 7 (3): 7–18.

Farrington, David P., and Patrick Langan. 1992. "Changes in Crime and Punishment in England and Wales and America in the 1980s." *Justice Quarterly* 9 (1): 6–46.

Farrington, David, Patrick Langan, and Michael Tonry, eds. 2004. *Cross-national Studies in Crime and Justice.* Washington, D.C.: Bureau of Justice Statistics.

Federal Bureau of Investigation. 2008. *Crime in the United States, 2007.* Washington, DC: Federal Bureau of Investigation.

Federal Bureau of Investigation. 2007. *Crime in the United States, 2006.* Washington, DC: Federal Bureau of Investigation.

Federal Bureau of Investigation. 2005. *Crime in the United States, 2004.* Washington, DC: Federal Bureau of Investigation.

Federal Bureau of Investigation. 2000. *Crime in the United States, 1999.* Washington, DC: Federal Bureau of Investigation.

Feeney, Floyd. 1998. *German and American Prosecutions: An Approach to Statistical Comparison.* Washington, DC: Bureau of Justice Statistics.

Frase, Richard. 2001. *Sentencing in Germany and the United States: Comparing Äpfel with Apples.* Freiburg: Max Planck Institute.

Frost, Natasha. 2008. "The Mis-measurement of Punishment." *Punishment and Society* 10 (3): 277–300.

Gibson, J., and B. Kim. 2007. "The Effect of Reporting Errors on the Cross-country Relationship between Inequality and Crime." *Journal of Development Economics* 87: 247–254.

Glase, Lauren, and Thomas Bonzcars. 2009. *Probation and Parole in the United States, 2007 Statistical Tables.* Washington, DC: Bureau of Justice Statistics.

Glonti, G. 2001. "Trafficking Human Beings in Georgia and the CIS." *Demokratizatsiya* 9: 382–398.

Goundriaan, Heike, James P. Lynch, and Paul Niewbeerta. 2004. "Reporting to the Police in Western Nations: The Effects of Country Characteristics." *Justice Quarterly* (December)21: 933–969.

Greenwald, G. 2009. *Drug Decriminalization in Portugal: Lessons for Creating Fair and Successful Drug Policies.* Washington, DC: Cato Institute.

Gruszczynska, B. 2002. "Victimization, Crime, and Social factors in Post-socialist Countries." *International Journal of Comparative Criminology* 2: 77–89.

Hagan, J., and W. Rymond-Richmond. 2008. *Darfur and the Crime of Genocide.* Cambridge: Cambridge University Press.

Healey, A., M. Knapp, J. Marsden, M. Gossop, and D. Stewart. 2003. "Criminal Outcomes and Costs of Treatment Services for Injecting and Non-injecting

Heroin Users: Evidence from a National Prospective Cohort Survey."*Journal of Health Services Research and Policy* 8:134–141.

Holder, Y., M. Peden, E. Krug, J. Lund, G. Gururaj, and O. Kobusingye. 2001. *Injury Surveillance Guidelines*. Geneva: World Health Organization.

International Criminal Police Organization. *Resolution AG-2006-RES-19*. 2006. Available online at http://www.interpol.int/Public/ICPO/GeneralAssembly/AGN75/resolutions/AGN75RES19.pdf. Accessed September 24, 2009.

Jewkes, R., and N. Abrahams. 2002. "The Epidemiology of Rape and Sexual Coercion in South Africa: An Overview." *Social Science and Medicine* 55: 1231–1244.

Johnson, Holly, Natalia Ollus, and Sami Nevala. 2007. *Violence against Women: An International Perspective*. New York: Springer.

Junger-Tas, J., Gert-Jan Terlouw, and Malcolm Klein, eds. 1994. *Delinquent Behavior among Young People in the Western World*. New York: Kugler.

Killias, Martin, Gordon Barclay, Paul Smit, Marcelo Fernando Aebi, Cynthia Tavares, Bruno Aubusson de Cavarlay, Jörg-Martin Jehle, Hanns von Hofer, Beata Gruszczyñska,Vasilika Hysi, and Kauko Aromaa. 2006. *European Sourcebook on Crime and Criminal Justice Statistics*. Den Haag: Boom Jurische.

Killias, Martin, Gordon Barclay, Paul Smit, Marcelo Fernando Aebi, Cynthia Tavares,Bruno Aubusson de Cavarlay, Jörg-Martin Jehle, Hanns von Hofer, Beata Gruszczyñska,Vasilika Hysi, and Kauko Aromaa. 2003. *European Sourcebook on Crime and Criminal Justice Statistics*. Den Haag: Boom Jurische.

Killias, Martin, Gordon Barclay, Paul Smit, Marcelo Fernando Aebi, Cynthia Tavares,Bruno Aubusson de Cavarlay, Jörg-Martin Jehle, Hanns von Hofer, Beata Gruszczyñska,Vasilika Hysi, and Kauko Aromaa. 1999. *European Sourcebook on Crime and Criminal Justice Statistics*. Den Haag: Boom Jurische.

Krug, E. G., L. L. Dahlberg, J. A. Mercy, A. B. Zwi, and R. Lozano. 2002. *World Report on Violence and Health*. Geneva: World Health Organization.

Kutnjak Ivković, S. 2008. "A Comparative Study of Public Support for the Police." *International Criminal Justice Review* 18: 406–434.

Kutateladze, B. 2007. "Raising and Addressing Some Methodological Problems of an International Comparison of Punishment and Sentencing Law." Paper presented at the annual meeting of the American Society of Criminology, Atlanta Marriott Marquis, Atlanta, Georgia, November 13, 2007.

LaFree, G., and A. Tseloni. 2006. "Democracy and Crime: A Multilevel Analysis of Homicide Trends in Forty-four Countries, 1950–2000." *The Annals of the American Academy of Political and Social Science* 605: 25–49.

Langbien, John. 1979. "Land Without Plea Bargaining: How the Germans Do It." *Michigan Law Review* 78: 204–210.

Lemieux, A. M., and R. V. Clarke. 2009. "The International Ban on Ivory Sales and Its Effects on Elephant Poaching in Africa." *British Journal of Criminology* 49: 451–471.

Lin, M. J. 2007. "Does Democracy Increase Crime? The Evidence from International Data." *Journal of Comparative Economics* 35: 467–483.

Liu, J., J. Zhang, and S. F. Messner. 2001. *Crime and Social Control in Changing China*. Westport, CT: Greenwood Press.

Liptak, Adam. 2008. "U.S. Prison Populations Dwarf That of Other Nations." *New York Times*, April 23, 2008.

Livingston, M., T. Chikritzhs, and R. Room. 2007. "Changing the Density of Alcohol Outlets to Reduce Alcohol-related Problems." *Drug and Alcohol Review* 26: 557–566.

Lussier, P., D. P. Farrington, and T. E. Moffitt. 2009. "Is the Antisocial Child Father of the Abusive Man? A 40-Yyear Prospective Longitudinal Study on the Developmental Antecedents of Intimate Partner Violence." *Criminology* 47: 741–780.

Lyman, P. N., and J. S. Morrison. 2004. "The Terrorist Threat in Africa." *Foreign Affairs* 83: 75–86.

Lynch, J. P. 2006. "Problems and Promise of Victimization Surveys for Cross-national Research." *Crime and Justice* 34: 229–287.

Lynch, J. P. 2002. "Effects of Design Differences on Rate Comparisons in the ICVS." In *Crime Victimization in Comparative Perspective: Results from the International Crime Victims Survey, 1989–2000*, ed. P. Nieuwbeerta, 431–457. The Hague: Boom Legal Publishers.

Lynch, James P. 2002. "Crime in International Perspective." In *Crime: Public Policies for Crime Control*, eds. James Q. Wilson and Joan Petersilia. Oakland, CA: Institute for Contemporary Studies Press.

Lynch, James P. 1995. "Crime in International Perspective." In *Crime: Public Policies for Crime Control*, eds. James Q. Wilson and Joan Petersilia. Oakland, CA: Institute for Contemporary Studies Press, 1995.

Lynch, James P. 1993. "A Cross-national Comparison of the Length of Custodial Sentences for Serious Crimes." *Justice Quarterly* 10: 639-660.

Lynch, James P. 1988. "A Comparison of Imprisonment in the United States, Canada, England, and West Germany:A Limited Test of the Punitiveness Hypothesis." *Journal of Criminal Law and Criminology* 79: 180–217.

Lysova, A. V., and D. A. Hines. 2008. "Binge Drinking and Violence against Intimate Partners in Russia." *Aggressive Behavior* 34: 416–427.

Maldonado-Molina, M. M., A. R. Piquero, W. G. Jennings, H. Bird, and G. Canino. 2009. "Trajectories of Delinquency among Puerto Rican Children and Adolescents at Two Sites." *Journal of Research in Crime and Delinquency* 46: 144–181.

Marshall, I. H., and C. R. Block. 2004. "Maximizing the Availability of Cross-national Data on Homicide." *Homicide Studies* 8: 267–310.

Marx, M. A., B. Crape, R. S. Brookmeyer, B. Junge, C. Latkin, D. Vlahov, and S. A. Strathdee. 2000. "Trends in Crime and the Introduction of a Needle Exchange Program." *American Journal of Public Health* 90: 1933–1936.

Mayhew, P., and J. van Kesteren, J. 2002. "Cross-national Attitudes to Punishment." In *Changing Attitudes to Punishment, Public Opinion, Crime and Justice*, ed. J. V. Roberts and M. Hough, 63–02. Portland, OR: Willan Publishing.

Messner, S. F., and R. Rosenfeld. 1997. "Political Restraint of the Market and Levels of Criminal Homicide: A Cross-national Application of Institutional-Anomie Theory." *Social Forces* 75: 1393–416.

Moffitt, T. E., D. R. Lynam, and P. A. Silva. 1994. "Neuropsychological Tests Predicting Persistent Male Delinquency." *Criminology* 32: 277–300.

Mühlhahn, K. 2009. *Criminal Justice in China: A History*. Cambridge: Harvard University Press.

Mumola, Christopher, and Allen Beck. 1997. *Prisoners in 1996*. Washington, DC: Bureau of Justice Statistics.

Naudé, C. M. B, J. H. Prinsloo, and A. Ladikos. 2006. *Experiences of Crime in Thirteen African Countries: Results from the International Crime Victims Survey*. Available online at http://rechten.uvt.nl/icvs/pdffiles/ICVS13Africancountries.pdf.

Neapolitan, J. 1994. "Cross-national Variation in Homicides: The Case of Latin America." *International Criminal Justice Review* 4: 4–22.

Nielsen, M. O. 2006. "Indigenous-run Legal Services in Australia and Canada: Comparative Developmental Issues." *International Criminal Justice Review* 16: 157–178.

Nieuwbeerta, P. 2002. *Crime Victimization in Comparative Perspective: Results from the International Crime Victims Survey 1989–2000*. The Hague: Boom Legal Publishers.

Nieuwbeerta, P., P. L. McCall, H. Elffers, and K. Wittebrood. 2008. "Neighborhood Characteristics and Individual Homicide Risks: Effects of Social Cohesion, Confidence in the Police, and Socioeconomic Disadvantage." *Homicide Studies* 12: 90–116.

Nowill, R., and S. Lavin. 1988. *Pub Watch*. South Yorkshire Police, Sheffield.

Odgers, C. L., T. E. Moffitt, J. M. Broadbent, N. Dickson, R. J. Hancox, H. Harrington, R. Poulton, M. R. Sears, W. M. Thomson, and A. Caspi. 2008. "Female and Male Antisocial Trajectories: From Childhood Origins to Adult Outcomes." *Development and Psychopathology* 20: 673–716.

Ouimet, M. 1999. "Crime in Canada and in the United States: A Comparative Analysis." *The Canadian Review of Sociology and Anthropology* 36: 389–410.

Paoli, L. 2005. "The Ugly Side of Capitalism and Democracy: The Development of the Illegial Drug Market in Post-Soviet Russia." In *Ruling Russia: Law, Crime, and Justice in a Changing Society*, ed. W. A. Pridemore, 183–202. Lanham, MD: Rowman and Littlefield.

Piquero, A. R., D. P. Farrington, and A. Blumstein. 2007. *Key Issues in Criminal Career Research: New Analyses of the Cambridge Study in Delinquent Development*. Cambridge: Cambridge University Press.

Piquero, N. L., and A. R. Piquero. 2006. "Democracy and Intellectual Property: Examining Trajectories of Software Piracy." *The Annals of the American Academy of Political and Social Science* 605: 104–127.

Planty, Michael. 2007. "Series Victimizations and Divergence." In *Understanding Crime Statistics: Revisiting the Divergence of the NCVS and the UCR*, eds. James P. Lynch and Lynn Addington, 156–182. New York: Cambridge University Press.

Pridemore, W. A. 2005a. "Social Structure and Homicide in Post-Soviet Russia." *Social Science Research* 34: 732–756.

Pridemore, W. A. 2005b. *Ruling Russia: Law, Crime, and Justice in a Changing Society*. Lanham, MD: Rowman and Littlefield.

Pridemore, W. A. 2008. "A Methodological Addition to the Cross-National Empirical Literature on Social Structure and Homicide: A First Test of the Poverty-Homicide Thesis." *Criminology* 46: 133–154.

Pridemore, W. A., and S. W. Kim. 2007. "Negative Socioeconomic Change and Crime in a Transitional Society." *The Sociological Quarterly* 48 (2007): 229–251.

Pridemore, W. A., and S. W. Kim. 2006. "Democratization and Political Change as Threats to Collective Sentiments: Testing Durkheim in Russia." *The Annals of the American Academy of Political and Social Science* 605: 82–103.

Pridemore, W. A., and A. Snowden. 2009. "Reduction in Suicide Mortality Following a New National Alcohol Policy: An Interrupted Time Series Analysis of Slovenia." *American Journal of Public Health* 99: 915–920.

Roberts, A. 2008. "Explaining Differences in Homicide Clearance Rates Between Japan and the United States." *Homicide Studies* 12: 136–145.

Rosenfeld, R., and S. F. Messner. 2009. "The Crime Drop in Comparative Perspective: The Impact of the Economy and Imprisonment on American and European Burglary Rates." *British Journal of Sociology* 60: 445–471.

Rubin, M. M., R. Culp, P. Mameli, and M. Walker.2008. "Using Cross-national Studies to Illuminate the Crime Problem: One Less Data Source Left Standing." *Journal of Contemporary Criminal Justice* 24: 50–68.

Savolainen, J. 2000. "Inequality, Welfare State, and Homicide: Further Support for the Institutional Anomie Theory." *Criminology* 38: 1021–1042.

Savolainen, J., M. Lehti, and J. Kivivuori. 2008. "Historical Origins of a Cross-national Puzzle: Homicide in Finland, 1750 to 2000." *Homicide Studies* 12: 67–89.

Shelley, L. I., and R. W. Orttung. 2005. "Russia's Efforts to Combat Human Trafficking: Efficient Crime Groups versus Irresolute Societies and Uncoordinated States." *Ruling Russia: Law, Crime, and Justice in a Changing Society*, ed. William A. Pridemore, 167–182. Lanham, MD: Rowman and Littlefield.

Smit, P. R., R. F. Meijer, and P.-P. J. Groen. 2004. "Detection Rates, an International Comparison." *European Journal on Criminal Policy and Research* 10: 225–253.

Stamatel, J. P. 2009. "Correlates of National-level Homicide Variation in Post-Community East-Central Europe." *Social Forces* 87: 1423–1448.

Stickley, A., and W. A. Pridemore. 2010. "The Effects of Binge Drinking and Social Capital on Violent Victimization: Findings from Moscow." Forthcoming in *Journal of Epidemiology and Community Health*.

Sung, H. E. 2006. "Democracy and Criminal Justice in Cross-national Perspective: From Crime Control to Due Process." *The Annals of the American Academy of Political and Social Science* 605: 311–337.

Tonry, Michael, and David P. Farrington, eds. 2005. *Crime and Punishment in Western Countries 1980–1999*. Chicago: University of Chicago Press.

United Nations. 2009. *United Nations Surveys on Crime Trends and the Operations of Criminal Justice Systems*. Available online at http://www.unodc.org/unodc/en/data-and-analysis/United-Nations-Surveys-on-Crime-Trends-and-the-Operations-of-Criminal-Justice-Systems.html. Accessed October 30, 2009.

United Nations Office on Drugs and Crime. 2009[SNL15].*International Homicide Statistics*. Available online at http://www.unodc.org/documents/data-and-analysis/IHS-rates-05012009.pdf. Accessed September 28, 2009.

United Nations Office on Drugs and Crime. 2009 *Responses by Indicator to Questionnaire for the Ninth United Nations Survey on Crime Trends and Operations of Criminal Justice Systems, covering the period 2003–2004*. Available online at http://www.unodc.org/documents/data-and-analysis/CTS9_by_indicator.pdf. Accessed September 28, 2009.

United States Census Bureau. 2009 *Annual Estimates of the Resident Population for the United States, Regions, States, and Puerto Rico: April1, 2000 to July 1, 2008 (NST-EST2008-01)*. Available on line at http://www.census.gov/popest/states/NST-ann-est.html. Accessed September 20, 2009.

van Dijk, J. J. M., P. Mayhew, and M. Killias. 1990. *Experiences of Crime across the World: Key Findings of the 1989 International Crime Survey*. Deventer, the Netherlands: Kluwer Academic Publishers.

van Dijk, J. J. M., J. N. van Kesteren, and P. Smit. 2008. *Criminal Victimisation in International Perspective: Key Findings from the 2004–2005 ICVS and EU ICS*. The Hague, Boom Legal Publishers.

Verweij, A., and P. Nieuwbeerta. 2002. "Gender Differences in Violent Victimization in Eighteen Industrialized Countries: The Role of Emancipation." In *International Comparison of Crime and Victimization: The ICVS*, ed. H. Kury. Willowdale, Ontario: de Sitter Publications.

Villarreal, A. 2004. "The Social Ecology of Rural Violence: Land Scarcity, the Organization of Agricultural Production, and the Presence of the State." *American Journal of Sociology* 110: 313–348.

Walmsley, R. 2008. *The World Prison Population List*. London: International Centre for Prison Studies.

Walmsley, R. 2009. *World Prison Brief*, rev. September 7, 2009. Available online at http://www.kcl.ac.uk/depsta/law/research/icps/worldbrief/. Accessed September 15, 2009.

Wickins, Justin. 2009. *Offender Management Caseload Statistics, 2008*. London: Ministry of Justice.

World Health Organization. 2007. *World Health Organization Statistical Information System* (WHOSIS). Available online at http://www.who.int/healthinfo/morttables/en/index.html. Accessed December 2007.

World Health Organization. 2001. *International Classification of External Causes of Injuries*. Amsterdam: Consumer Safety Institute.

Zhang, L., and S. F. Messner. 1994. "The Severity of Official Punishment for Delinquency and Change in Interpersonal Relations in Chinese Society." *Journal of Research in Crime and Delinquency* 31: 416–433.

Zhang, L., S. F. Messner, and J. Liu. 2007. "Bicycle-theft Victimization in Contemporary Urban China: A Multilevel Assessment of Risk and Protective Factors." *Journal of Research in Crime and Delinquency* 44: 406–426.

Zhang, L., S. F. Messner, Z. Lu, and X. Deng. 1997. "Gang Crime and Its Punishment in China." *Journal of Criminal Justice* 25: 289–302.

Zimring, F. E., and Hawkins, G. 1997. *Crime Is Not the Problem: Lethal Violence in America*. New York: Oxford University Press.

Notes

1. Information on case processing is only available in the 1999 and 2003 versions of the *Sourcebook*.

2. The United States did not report burglary and motor vehicle theft data in the UN Survey that year, but traditionally the FBI data has been the source of responses to questions about police-recorded crime in the survey.

3. The rates presented here include both pre-trial and sentenced prisoners as well as juveniles and adults. If nations differ in the level of juvenile crime, in the nature of the response to that crime, or in terms of the keeping of statistics on these populations, the comparison of rates can be affected. The ICPS data do distinguish these populations for some contributing nations. Analysis of these data indicates that the relative position of nations does not change much when the pre-trial prisoners are excluded. Rates decrease approximately 20 percent across nations, with some deviations like France and the Netherlands, which have larger pre-trial populations and consequently larger decreases in rates when they are removed. These data also suggest that juveniles are a small proportion of the incarcerated population in most developed nations—between .1 and 7 percent—and will not affect comparisons much.

4. Traffic laws are a good example of a class of crimes that can be subject to wide variation in the way in which they are treated across nations. Some nations take drunk driving very seriously, for example, and others do not. In the past, the claim has been made that, on any given day, one-third of the Swedish prison population were drunk drivers.

5. In the United States, for example, law enforcement is largely a local function, and federal authorities must gain the cooperation of more than 18,000 police departments without many inducements. Moreover, each of the 50 states has a different criminal code. Hence the FBI restricts its crime statistics to seven broad classes that are serious, prevalent, and well reported to the police. Nations without these constraints might report on a broader array of crimes.

6. We use prevalence rather than incident because the method the ICVS uses to count multiple victimizations is not that precise. See Lynch (2006) and Planty (2007).

7. Drug crimes are usually not reported by victims but are uncovered through police initiative.

8. Because the conviction rate is based on offenses and not arrests or charged persons, it includes many more decisions than simply determining if a charged person is indeed guilty.

9. In an equilibrium state, where admissions are equal to releases and time served is constant over time, the product of admissions times average time served will be the stock population. The equation described here is essentially that. This methodology will not provide an exact estimate of the prison population because these systems are not in equilibrium, and this illustration does not include many of the offenses that result in incarceration, such as drug offenses, larceny, fraud, and public order offenses, among others. In 1995, these offenses accounted for about 40 percent of the stock prison population in the United States (Mumola and Beck, 1997).

10. In this illustration the probability of conviction given an offense was not set to levels observed in the United States because it was unclear whether conviction is part of sentencing policy or a function of efficiency or the availability of due process protections. As a result ratios of incarceration rates in the United States to rates in other nations need not equal 1.0 when all adjustments for crime and sentencing are made.

11. The estimate of the probability of incarceration given conviction and the time expected to be served may be somewhat high because the National Judicial Reporting Program data that is used in the publication *Felony Sentencing in State Courts* are restricted to felonies and exclude misdemeanors. The latter would result in lower rates of incarceration and shorter sentences.

12. These ratios are not the same as the probabilities of a parolee returning to prison that one would obtain from monitoring a release cohort for a year. These are simply the ratio of the number of persons revoked for violating conditions of parole or committing a new offense over the number of persons who entered parole status that year.

Chapter 3

Crime and Biology

Terrie E. Moffitt, Stephen Ross & Adrian Raine

The first edition of this book contained a chapter entitled "The Biological Basis of Crime," which focused on investigations of heritability, psycho-physiology, neuroimaging, neurotransmitters, birth complications, and hormones as potential causes of crime (Raine, 2002a). This new chapter updates these topics, and also takes a somewhat broader approach, in order to introduce readers to the current explosion in ways of thinking about connections between crime and human biology. We invite readers to think beyond biological research into the etiology of antisocial behavior, and to consider the wonderful array of connections between crime and biology. Some illustrative examples follow.

Forensic science is inherently biological—studying, for example, effects of law-enforcement tasers on the heart muscle, the uses of injury patterns to detect child abuse, the application of physical anthropology to crime-scene evidence, and the uses of DNA in offender identification (Rapley and Whitehouse 2007).

Psychobiologists are uncovering biological underpinnings of many individual differences that predict criminal involvement, for example, intelligence, neuro-cognitive deficits, physical size and strength, hyperactivity, and personality traits, including low self-control (Zuckerman 2005). Some of these biologically based individual differences are likely to be important for crime theory because they help to explain one of the most fundamental mysteries of antisocial behavior: the sex difference (Moffitt et al. 2001).

Mental-health researchers are looking for biological explanations for the dis-inhibiting effects of alcohol on violent behavior, and for the precipitating effects of paranoid delusions and command hallucinations on violence by individuals who suffer from psychotic illnesses (Hoptman et al. 2009; Naudts and Hodgins 2006).

Ethologists have observed that in almost all mammalian species, including ours, males begin to seek novelty, search for stimulation, roam afar from family, and engage in risk-taking around the age of reproductive maturity (Handley and Perrin 2007; Spear 2007). This phenomenon, called "dispersal," has origins in a biological imperative to avoid inbreeding and promote genetic variation, thereby enhancing group fitness and survival. Evolutionary psychologists think that dispersal has intriguing implications for our understanding of the adolescent peak of the age-crime curve (Steinberg and Belsky 1996).

Cognitive neuroscience researchers are finding biological explanations for why cognitive processes such as risk-appraisal and decision-making differ between adolescents and adults (Spear 2007). This research is having real consequences for the handling of juvenile offenders by the criminal courts (Scott and Steinberg 2008).

Health researchers are investigating the effects of crime on biology. There are studies of the effects of domestic violence on the health of women victims (Campbell 2002; Coker et al. 2002), the effects of child abuse on victims' immune systems and physical health as adults (Danese et al. 2007; Danese et al. 2010), and the damaging effects of life-course persistent offenders' antisocial lifestyle on their health when they reach midlife (Odgers et al. 2007a).

Developmental psychologists are studying the effects of biological puberty on delinquent offending. In particular, girls who reach physical maturity before their age peers are highly likely to become offenders and victims of crime. Uncovering why this is so makes great science (reviewed by Celio et al. 2006;[1] Haynie and Piquero 2006).

Toxicologists and nutritionists are uncovering consequences for crime of childhood exposure to toxins such as lead (Needleman et al. 2002) and to deprivation of basic nutrition (Liu et al. 2004). A follow-up study of babies born to Dutch women who were starved while pregnant during the German food blockade of Holland in World War II revealed that when these children reached adulthood, their prevalence of antisocial personality disorder more than doubled as compared to the general Dutch population of that generation (Neugebauer et al. 1999).

Even economists are venturing into population biology to explain crime by studying abortion. Abortion is most often utilized by teenage mothers, single mothers, mothers who are economically disadvantaged, and mothers who do not want the baby—all circumstances known to increase a child's likelihood of becoming a criminal offender. In 1991 the first post–*Roe v. Wade* cohort was 17 years old and entering the peak age-range for criminal activity. One controversial study argued that the U.S. crime rate fell in the 1990s because the increase in abortion of unwanted pregnancies in the 1970s selectively reduced the population of young people with criminal propensity in the 1990s (Donohue and Leavitt 2001).

Of course one chapter cannot review all of these topics. This chapter reviews four areas of research into biological influences on criminal propensity: biomarkers, genetics, psychophysiology, and neuroimaging. In addition, the chapter briefly describes how developmental neuroscience is informing juvenile justice, and reviews the effects of a criminal lifestyle on offenders' health. The main aim of the chapter is to acquaint young criminologists with the existence of these areas of research, and to attract readers to incorporate biological information into their thinking about crime: its causes, consequences, control, and prevention.

Our results suggest the following conclusions

- There is marked variation between people in their response to all social causes of crime, which prompts research into biological vulnerability to the social causes of crime.
- A rule of thumb is biosocial interaction: biological vulnerabilities to crime operate most strongly on people living in criminogenic environments, and environmental causes of crime affect most strongly the subgroup of biologically vulnerable individuals.
- Many offenders do not have marked biological vulnerabilities. Biological vulnerabilities are concentrated among individuals whose antisocial behavior onsets in childhood, persists for years thereafter, and involves frequent and violent victimization of others.
- Because it is not ethical to experimentally alter biological risk to test whether antisocial behavior results, causation remains unclear. However, biological characteristics assessed during childhood in prospective longitudinal studies predict antisocial behavior in adolescence and adulthood.
- Crime is concentrated in families. More than 100 twin and adoption studies converge to show that approximately half of the variation in antisocial behavior among people is under genetic influence.
- Genetic studies show association between genetic polymorphisms and antisocial behavior. The most replicated and validated genetic finding is that the *MAOA* gene is associated with moderation of the cycle of violence from childhood maltreatment to risk for violent crime.
- The most replicated and validated psychophysiological findings show that antisocial individuals are chronically under-aroused, as shown through slow heart rate, weak skin conductance activity, and excessive slow-wave electroencephalogram readings.
- The most replicated and validated findings from brain-imaging research show that impaired communication between self-control areas in the brain's frontal lobes and emotional areas in the brain's temporal lobes results in deficient learning from punishment, lack of empathy and remorse, exaggerated reactions to perceived threats, and weak control over impulses, fear, and anger.
- Legal scholars argue that a defendant's biological characteristics are like any other information that can be considered in court. The question of whether a defendant's biological vulnerability to crime precludes free will and mitigates criminal culpability remains much more controversial.

- Offenders who have lived an antisocial lifestyle for years show early declines in physical health as compared to their age-mates, suggesting that the cost of crime to society involves not only criminal-justice costs, but also health-care costs.
- Technical and ideological barriers to biological research in criminology are crumbling fast. Biological research into antisocial behaviors will be hugely improved as more criminologists take part.

A word about terminology: this book is about crime, but researchers whose work contributes to this chapter publish in fields of psychology and medicine as well as criminology, and they study children as well as adolescents and adults. As such, biological research uses a variety of different measures: Official records of criminal conviction, self-reports of delinquent behaviors from research participants, reports from other informants such as parents and teachers, and even observational measures. Biological studies assess participants' antisocial behaviors on a frequency continuum, as well as diagnostic categories of conduct disorder and antisocial personality disorder. This wide variety of measurements offers advantages for inference, because each outcome measurement's weaknesses are offset by the strengths of other measurement methods. Importantly, the pattern of biological findings turns out to be remarkably consistent across different measures of antisocial behavior. Thus, to simplify, this chapter uses generic terms such as antisocial behavior or criminal propensity.

BIOLOGICAL VULNERABILITY TO CRIMINAL PROPENSITY

The non-biological, social causes of crime are well-known and are presented in the other chapters of this book. Yet, there is marked variation in people's responses to all of the social causes of crime. Most people who are socially disadvantaged do not become involved in an antisocial, criminal lifestyle, and many wealthy people do commit crimes. Most people who live in a neighborhood with low collective efficacy, who encounter opportunities for crime, or who venture into a crime hot-spot location do not actually commit crimes. This simple observation provides the rationale for research into individual variation in vulnerability to the social causes of crime. Such research often addresses individual differences in crime-related constructs such as social learning, delinquent peer affiliation, intelligence, self-control, and social bonds in relationships. Because it has now been confirmed that these and virtually all other human behaviors are partially under biological influence (Beaver et al 2009a; Plomin et al. 2008; Rutter 2006), much of vulnerability to the social causes of crime is inherently biological vulnerability. This section reviews research on biological causes of vulnerability to criminal propensity.

Biomarkers in Vulnerability to Crime: Hormones, Neurotransmitters, and Perinatal Complications

Increasing evidence supports the general rule that biomarkers such as hormones, neurotransmitters, and birth complications operate in interaction with the social environment to predict antisocial behavior (Raine 2002b; Beaver 2009a). For example, studies have indicated that such things as minor physical anomalies, prenatal exposure to nicotine, obstetric delivery complications, and low birth weight predict antisocial conduct problems most strongly in children and adolescents who were rejected by their mothers, who grew up in unstable families, or who were raised in deprived environments (Arseneault et al. 2002; Piquero and Tibbetts 1999; Raine et al. 1994a, 1997a). These perinatal complications are assumed to engender or signal fetal brain damage, which in turn may cause neuropsychological deficits that are known risk factors for persistent and serious antisocial behavior (Brennan et al. 2003; Moffitt, 2006).

The activity of the body's stress hormone system (called the hypothalamic-pituitary-adrenal axis) has also been associated with antisocial conduct. Studies have shown that children, adolescents, and adults with antisocial behaviors have low resting levels of the stress hormone cortisol, and that when antisocial research participants are subjected to stressful challenges in the laboratory they show underreactive cortisol responses (Susman 2006; van Goozen et al. 2008). The theory is that the normal stress response has been blunted by chronic exposure to neglect, abuse, and emotional distress. The differences between antisocial groups and control groups are moderate, for both resting cortisol (effect size .40 standard deviations) and reactive cortisol following a stressful challenge (effect size .42 standard deviations) (van Goozen et al. 2007).

Other hormones such as testosterone have been linked to aggression and violent behavior. Elevated testosterone has been observed in antisocial samples, and testosterone administered experimentally can exacerbate aggressive responses in humans (Glenn and Raine 2008; Nelson 2006). Abnormalities in the brain's chemical messengers (called neurotransmitters), particularly serotonin, have also been linked to antisocial behavior (van Goozen et al. 2007). A meta-analysis of 20 studies of adults and 5 studies of children reported a moderate association between reduced serotonin metabolite levels and measures of antisocial conduct (Moore et al. 2002).

Most studies on biomarkers are cross-sectional and correlational. It is not ethical to experimentally alter biomarker levels to test whether antisocial behavior follows. Therefore, as is true of many social risk factors, it remains unclear whether these biomarkers cause vulnerability to antisocial conduct, or whether they are the consequence of an adverse, antisocial lifestyle. Both may be true. However, some biomarkers (e.g. perinatal complications, slow heart rate) have been studied during childhood in the context of prospective longitudinal studies and shown to predict later-emerging antisocial behavior.

FAMILY HISTORY VULNERABILITY

Crime is known to be concentrated in families; studies in London and Pittsburgh have shown that over 60 percent of crimes are committed by members of fewer than 10 percent of families (Farrington et al. 1996, 2001). This observation was followed up in the Dunedin longitudinal cohort study, which has followed a cohort of 1,037 New Zealanders (52 percent male) from birth to age 32 years. A family history of so called "externalizing problems" (conduct disorder, antisocial personality disorder, alcohol abuse, drug abuse) assessed in cohort members' parents and grandparents especially characterized the cohort's life-course persistent subgroup of offenders (Odgers et al. 2007b). This subgroup had childhood-onset of antisocial behavior and subsequent persistent offending adulthood, termed "life course persistent" (Moffitt 1993a). However, family history did not characterize the subgroups with childhood-limited or adolescence-limited antisocial behaviors. A similar finding was reported from a Minnesota sample; early-starter delinquents had more biological relatives who were offenders, as compared to late-starter delinquents (Taylor et al. 2000). Family history predicts serious offending careers very powerfully because it comprises both a family's genetic and social contributions to crime. The next section describes research that disentangles genetic risk from social risk.

Quantitative Twin and Adoptee Estimates of Heritable Vulnerability

Genetic influence on antisocial behavior has been studied in twins reared together, adoptees, and twins reared apart (Moffitt 2005a, 2005b; Rhee and Waldman 2002). The basic logic used to make inferences about genetic influences is straightforward. In adoption studies, the correlation between adoptee and biological parent represents genetic transmission, whereas the correlation between adoptee and adoptive parent represents social (i.e., environmental) transmission. In twin studies, genetic influence is inferred if dizygotic (DZ, or fraternal) twins' behavior is less similar than that of monozygotic (MZ, or identical) twins. DZ twins share their upbringing and also share on average only half of the genes that vary among humans; they are no more similar than are ordinary siblings. But MZ twins share their upbringing and also all their genes. In other words, if there were no genetic influence on a person, it should not matter whether the twins are fraternal or identical. However, for a wide variety of human behaviors, including crime, whether twins are fraternal or identical makes a big difference. (For a good explanation of genetics written for social scientists, see Carey 2003).

A number of potential flaws apply to adoption studies. First, adoption agencies may attempt to maximize similarity between the adoptee's biological and adoptive families to increase the child's chance of fitting in with the new family (this is called "selective placement"). Relatedly, biological mothers who intend to give their baby away may neglect prenatal care and continue to abuse substances during pregnancy, and many unwanted babies experience institutionalization before they are adopted (Mednick et al. 1986). If adoptive homes, prenatal care, and institutional care are selectively worse for the babies given up by antisocial biological mothers, this could bias estimates of heritability upward by adding the criminogenic influences of these three unmeasured non-genetic factors to any criminogenic influence of genes. Second, both adoptees and twins reared apart are likely to be reared in home environments that are unusually good for children because adoptive parents are carefully screened. The resulting restricted range of rearing environments could lead to an overestimation of heritability (Stoolmiller 1999). However, this flaw of adoption studies is offset by studies of national twin registers (e.g., Cloninger and Gottesman 1987; Viding et al. 2008) or stratified high-risk twin samples (Arseneault et al. 2003) because such sampling frames accurately represent the complete population range of environmental and genetic backgrounds.

Studies of twins avoid the potential flaws of adoption studies, but they suffer several potential flaws of their own. First, the logic of the twin design assumes that all of the greater similarity between MZ than DZ twins can safely be ascribed to MZ twins' greater genetic similarity. This "equal environments assumption" requires that MZ twins are not treated more alike than DZ twins on the causes of antisocial behavior (Kendler et al. 1994). Because MZ twins look identical, in theory they might be treated more similarly than DZ twins in some way that promotes antisocial behavior, and as a result, estimates of heritability from studies of twins reared together could be biased upward. However, studies of adoptees do not suffer this flaw. Neither do studies of twins reared apart, because MZ twins reared apart do not share environments. Grove and colleagues (1990) studied 32 sets of monozygotic twins who were separated and reared apart shortly after birth and found statistically significant heritabilities for antisocial behavior in both childhood (0.41) and adulthood (0.28). Furthermore, one must consider that twin studies have methodological problems which can *decrease* estimates of heritability as opposed to artificially increasing them. For example, there is evidence that some twins make attempts to "de-identify" or to be different from one another, and this is expected to be greater in MZ pairs, with the result of artificially *reducing* heritability estimates. Also, identical twinning can result in biological differences that can accentuate human differences. For example, there is a greater discrepancy between MZ twins in a pair relative to DZ twins on factors such as in-utero nutrition and birth weights, and such birth complications can create sibling differences in behavior. This non-genetic, biological factor will exaggerate behavioral differences in MZ twins and thus reduce heritability estimates. The methodological problems of twin studies are just as likely to *decrease* heritability estimates as opposed to *inflate* them. In all probability, these effects tend to cancel each other out.

The greatest confidence can be attained in science when studies represent different people, times, and places, and use measurements and research designs that have complementary strengths and weaknesses and yet converge on similar findings (Robins 1978). Studies of antisocial behaviors range in participants' age from 19 months to 70 years, cover the period from the Great Depression to the present, represent numerous Western nations, use a wide variety of measures of antisocial behavior, and comprise twin, adoption, and sibling designs. When taken together, all of these studies converge on similar findings. The resulting pool of more than 100 heritability estimates ranges from 0 percent heritability to 80 percent heritability, with a modal average of 50 percent. This means that approximately half of the variation in antisocial behavior among people is under genetic influence (Moffitt 2005a). The most reliable estimates come from the past 15 years of research in Australia, the Netherlands, Norway, Sweden, the United Kingdom, and the United States, which examined large, population-representative samples using advanced quantitative modeling techniques. These studies' estimates tend to converge quite tightly around 50 percent. In addition, large twin studies have recently shown that genetic influences are strongest in the particular type of criminal career that begins at an early age and is persistent, severe, and involves callous unemotional symptoms, such as lack of remorse (Arseneault et al. 2003; Moffitt 2005a; Viding et al. 2008).

What Does a Heritable Liability toward Antisocial Behaviors Mean?

To answer this question, it is useful to revisit what heritability does not imply. First, evidence of genetic influence for antisocial behavior does not imply resistance to intervention. The mean height of the population increased notably this century due to better nutrition, while the amount of variation between individuals' heights attributable to genes remained constant across the century. Second, evidence of genetic influence does imply that biological processes are involved in the etiology of antisocial behaviors, but biological etiology does not imply that change can only be brought about through biological intervention. Indeed, adoption studies have repeatedly illustrated that adoption into a good home can be an effective treatment, counteracting a genetic liability to antisocial behavior (Cadoret et al. 1995; Mednick et al. 1984). Third, the omnibus 50 percent estimate of genetic influence does not imply that the causal role of non-genetic social factors is trivial. To the contrary, it is now recognized that estimates of heritability from twin studies include not only the direct effects of genes, but also the effects of interactions between genes and environments (Moffitt 2005a, 2005b).

Undeniable evidence that the genetic and environmental causes of crime do interact was provided years ago by adoption studies. A good example is the now-famous study conducted by Mednick and colleagues (1984). These researchers studied 14,427 adoptions that took place in Denmark between 1927 and 1947. Court conviction records were obtained on 65,516 biological parents, adoptive parents, and adoptees. When neither the adoptive or biological parents had been convicted of a crime, 14 percent of the adoptees had a crime record. This increased to 15 percent when only the adoptive parents were convicted, and to 20 percent when only the biological parents were convicted. However, when both adoptive and biological parents were convicted (i.e., both genetic and environmental predispositions were present), the adoptees' conviction rate increased further, to 25 percent. Such gene-environment interactions mean that the effect of an environmental risk factor may be even stronger than previously reported, among a subgroup of individuals carrying a vulnerable genotype. This truism is likely to be the case for antisocial behaviors, and it is addressed in the next section.

Molecular Genetic Studies of Inherited Vulnerability

Studies of gene-to-crime associations consist of several types. The first type is genome-wide association studies (GWAS) that compare cases with a condition (e.g., antisocial personality disorder) against controls who do not have that trait. These studies scan hundreds of thousands of genetic variants at once to search for any locations on the genome that show variation that is statistically associated with the disease beyond chance. The second type is candidate-gene studies. They investigate direct associations between antisocial behavior and a genetic variant, which is called a "candidate" because there is enough information known about the gene's biological function to state advance hypotheses that explain its probable connection to behavior. For example, a gene known to increase muscle strength, or to lead to impaired judgement under the influence of alcohol, might become a candidate for hypotheses about violence. The third type is studies of genotype-by-environment interaction (GxE). These studies test whether a candidate genetic variant is associated with increased or diminished vulnerability to an environmental cause of antisocial behavior. Evidence for all three of these types of associations has emerged.

This research is in its infancy, and discovery is very fast-paced, making any review almost obsolete soon after it is written, but this chapter covers key findings to date.

As soon as technology allowed genome-wide scans, GWAS of antisocial cases were undertaken (Dick et al. 2004; Kendler et al. 2006; Stallings
et al. 2005). Each tentatively suggested regions on chromosomes that
might harbor antisocial-related genes (specific genes must now be identified in these regions). However, the three studies have not converged on
the same chromosomal regions, except possibly regions 1q and 2p. These
genome-wide scans were carried out in samples originally recruited to
study people at high risk for substance dependence. As noted in this
chapter's section on family history, a familial liability to substance abuse
is characteristic of persistent antisocial personalities, and thus the combined antisocial+substance-abuse phenotype is considered ideal for gene-
hunting.

Several candidate-gene studies have reported an association between
polymorphisms in the serotonin transporter gene *5HTTLPR* and antisocial behavior (Beitchman et al. 2006; Haberstick et al. 2006; Sakai et al.
2007). (Each gene has sections within it that can take different forms for
different people; these sections are called polymorphisms, meaning "bodies that come in different forms.") Candidate genes in the dopamine
neurotransmitter system that have also been implicated in antisocial
conduct include the dopamine receptor *DRD4* (Holmes et al. 2002),
the dopamine transporter *DAT1* and the catechol O-methyltransferase
gene *COMT* (Caspi et al. 2008; Thapar et al. 2005).

New findings of gene-environment interaction are emerging in relation
to crime, and we expect this area of research to grow rapidly (Beaver et al.
2009b; DeLisi et al. 2009). A now well-known GxE study showed that a
polymorphism in the *MAOA* gene is associated with moderation of the
cycle of violence from childhood maltreatment to risk for adolescent
conduct disorder, aggressive personality, and violent crime in adulthood
(Caspi et al. 2002). The gene encodes the *MAOA* enzyme, which selectively metabolizes serotonin, norepinephrine, and dopamine (neurotransmitters linked by previous research to maltreatment victimization and to
aggressive behavior). Drugs inhibiting the action of the *MAO* enzyme
have been shown to prevent animals from recovering from the stress that
results from maltreatment, and to make them overly reactive to signals
of threat. Among the boys in the Dunedin study cohort who had the
combination of the low-*MAOA*-activity allele and severe maltreatment,
85 percent developed some form of antisocial outcome. Males having
the combination of the low-activity allele and maltreatment were only
12 percent of the male birth cohort, but they accounted for 44 percent of
the cohort's violent convictions, because they offended at a higher rate on
average than other violent offenders in the cohort.

Since 2002 at least seven studies have attempted to replicate the
original *MAOA* GxE finding, with varying success. A meta-analysis of
studies showed that the interaction between *MAOA* genotype and childhood maltreatment predicting antisocial outcomes averaged across all of

the studies is modest but statistically significant (Taylor and Kim-Cohen 2007). Pooling the different samples, the correlation between childhood maltreatment and antisocial outcome was .30 in individuals with the low-activity genotype, but only .13 in individuals with the high-activity *MAOA* genotype.

Studies published after the meta-analysis replicate and extend the original finding. In 1,100 males from the National Longitudinal Study of Adolescent Health, three genetic polymorphisms, in *MAOA*, *DAT1*, and *DRD2*, were significant predictors of serious and violent juvenile delinquency when added to a social-control model of delinquency. In this sample, the genetic effects of *DRD2* and *MAOA* were conditional and interacted with family processes, school processes, and friendship networks (Guo et al. 2008). Also in this Adolescent Health sample, *MAOA* genotype was found to be associated with gang membership and weapon use (Beaver et al. 2010).

One American study has been able to look at race differences and reported that the *MAOA* GxE applied to Caucasian Americans but not to African Americans (Widom and Brzustowicz 2006). The researchers followed up adjudicated cases of child abuse in an American Midwestern state. Whites who had the combination of the low-*MAOA*-activity allele and child abuse had elevated rates of crime, but this pattern did not apply to African Americans in the sample. That race or ethnicity should make a difference is not surprising, because the way that polymorphisms are located near or far from each other within the *MAOA* gene is known to be somewhat different for individuals of European versus African descent. One speculative theory is that because the origin of Europeans is more recent than that of Africans, areas of the genomic DNA sequence (called a haplotype) that are inherited together as a block in Europeans may have been broken up by the many more generations of recombination in African populations. If the biological function of a genetic polymorphism depends on contributions from other polymorphisms located nearby it, which is very likely, then a gene's function in relation to environmental stress could potentially differ by the region of the world where one's ancestors lived.

In addition to replication of genetic findings, validation of these findings in experimental research is essential (Caspi and Moffitt 2006). Additional validation of this gene-environment interaction comes from McDermott et al.'s (2009) study in the laboratory. The authors genotyped 78 college-age males for either high or low *MAOA* activity. Participants were told that they could earn up to $10 based on their performance on a vocabulary quiz. They were then led to believe that they were linked via computer with a partner participant in a different testing room. The partner could choose to take 0 percent, 20 percent, or 80 percent of the participant's earnings. Subsequently, the participants were given the choice of either (a) punishing their partner by making them eat hot sauce or (b) trading in the hot sauce for more money. The participants were allotted 10 one-eighth teaspoons of hot sauce from which they could choose the amount of punishment. In reality, there was no partner and a computer randomly took either 20 percent or 80 percent of participants' earnings. When 80 percent was taken, participants with the *MAOA* low-activity genotype punished significantly more than participants with the *MAOA* high-activity genotype. The *MAOA* low-activity participants also chose to give the harshest punishment (all 10 spoonfuls) significantly more frequently. These results suggest that *MAOA* genotype and social provocation of aggression interact to predict aggressive behavior in the laboratory.

Psychophysiological Vulnerability to Antisocial behavior

Since the 1940s an extensive body of research has accrued on the psychophysiological basis of antisocial behavior. The most influential psychophysiological theory of antisocial behavior posits that antisocial individuals are chronically under-aroused. Under-arousal is the strongest psychophysiological finding in the field of antisocial and criminal behavior. Under-arousal is measured through slow heart rate, weak skin conductance activity (less sweating in response to stress), and excessive slow-wave EEG (electroencephalogram) readings. Why should low physiological arousal predispose to antisocial behavior? One theory is that low arousal equates to low capacity to feel fear (Raine 1997). A second theory is that low arousal represents an unpleasant physiological state that drives under-aroused people to seek stimulation through risky antisocial activities to bring their arousal levels up to an optimal level (Raine 1997; Van Goozen et al. 2007).

EEG is recorded from scalp electrodes that measure the electrical activity of the brain. A significant number of studies implicate EEG abnormalities in groups who show violent recidivistic offending, with the most common abnormalities being excessive slow-wave EEG. The bulk of this research implicates the more frontal regions of the brain, areas that regulate self-control (Raine 1993). These abnormalities are present and associated with antisocial behavior early in life. Studies of young children with conduct disorder show that they have reduced P300 EEG amplitude (a brain response that measures attention) at the frontal region of the brain during tasks requiring decision-making and sustained attention (Bauer and Hesselbrock 2003; Kim et al. 2001; Costa et al. 2000). A recent meta-analysis of 38 studies confirms small but significant effect sizes for both reduced P300 amplitudes ($d = 0.25$) and longer P300 latencies ($d = .13$) in antisocial groups. EEG latencies are especially slower at frontal brain sites (Gao and Raine). (Latency is the time between a stimulus, such as a sound, and the EEG response to it.) Overall, results suggest impaired attention in antisocial individuals. One caveat is that such impairments are less evident for psychopathic offenders (Gao and Raine, 2009s).

Slow resting heart rate (or pulse rate) is another of the most replicated of all biological markers associated with antisocial behavior. A meta-analysis of 40 studies concluded that slow heart rate, when people are either resting or when they are undergoing stress, is a robust correlate of antisocial behaviour (Ortiz and Raine 2004; Lorber 2004). Effect sizes were moderate for resting heart rate (-.44) and large for heart rate during a stress challenge (-.76). Low heart rate characterizes life-course persistent antisocial individuals in particular (Moffitt et al. 2001); the highest probability of violence is among individuals who show a combination of slow resting heart rate and other social risk factors (e.g., large family size, poor relationship with parents) (Farrington 1997). A twin study has shown that the relation between slow heart rate and delinquent behavior arises from shared genetic vulnerability (Baker et al. 2009). Intriguingly, slow heart rate has a specific relation to antisocial behavior, while alcoholism, depression, schizophrenia, and anxiety disorders have, if anything, been linked to faster resting heart rate.

Prospective longitudinal studies have confirmed that slow childhood heart rate predicts antisocial behavior ascertained years later in adulthood (Farrington 1997; Ortiz and Raine 2004) as do skin conductance and EEG (Mednick et al. 1981; Petersen et al. 1982). A key prospective study has shown that slow resting heart rate, low resting skin conductance activity, and more slow-wave EEG measured in 15-year-old British schoolboys predicted variation in their criminal offending when they were followed up at age 24 (Raine et al. 1990). The boys who later became offenders were also characterized by abnormal electrical brain responses to the warning signal in a test that required them to be ready to react to an impending stimulus. In this same British sample, followed to age 29, men who had desisted from offending had faster heart rates and greater arousal on all psychophysiological measures as 15-year-olds, as compared to men who persisted in offending to age 29 (Raine et al. 1995; 1996). This protective effect of high arousal against persistent offending has been replicated (Brennan et al. 1997). A clinical study has shown that resting heart rate predicts outcomes when children are treated for disruptive behavior disorders; children with pretreatment faster heart rate were more responsive to behavior therapy (Stadler et al. 2008). Overall, the psychophysiological profile of young offenders who desist from crime includes heightened information processing (better orienting), being more responsive to environmental stimuli (fast skin conductance recovery), greater sensitivity to cues predicting punishment in particular (better classical conditioning), and higher fearfulness (faster heart rate).

Autonomic conditioning theory is familiar from the classic case of Pavlov's dog, who was conditioned to associate a bell cue with saliva-inducing food, and afterward salivated at the sound of the bell, in anticipation of food. Poor autonomic fear conditioning is another well-replicated correlate of crime and psychopathy in adults (Lorber 2004; Patrick 2006). Children ordinarily avoid committing antisocial acts because they learn to associate mental cues that accompany their transgressions with fear of getting caught and punished. Once conditioned, children feel fear when they consider transgressing, and this fearful anticipation of potential punishment deters antisocial acts. Studies testing this theory have focused almost exclusively on adults. One recent study, however, assessed autonomic fear conditioning in 1,795 three-year-old children and showed that poor conditioning at the age of three predicted risk of criminal offending at age 23 (Gao et al., 2010). Psychopathic adolescents also show a deficit in autonomic fear conditioning (Fung et al. 2005). Fear emotions are experienced by a brain structure called the amygdala, and therefore weak fear conditioning suggests amygdala dysfunction. This suggests that neurological vulnerability may be involved in propensity to crime, our next topic.

Neurological Vulnerability Studied Through Neuroimaging

In the past, the idea of peering into the mind of a murderer to gain insights into his acts was the province of science fiction. But advances in brain imaging techniques in the past 20 years have provided the opportunity to gain dramatic new insights into the brain mechanisms involved in antisocial behavior. Today we can literally look into the living brain using imaging techniques that are currently revolutionizing our understanding of the biology of behavior. The imaging techniques include: structural magnetic resonance imaging (MRI), which identifies abnormalities in the anatomy of the brain; functional magnetic resonance imaging (fMRI), which reveals the activity of brain structures while the subject performs a task inside the scanner; and positron emission tomography (PET), which measures the metabolic activity of different regions of the brain to show which regions are using energy while subjects perform a mental task. As fMRI measures blood flow within brain tissue, it thus allows assessment of the functional properties of the brain. In this sense, fMRI is like PET, but unlike PET, participants are not exposed to radioactivity. Furthermore, fMRI detects activity in brain regions as small as 1 millimeter with fine resolution. Diffusion tensor imaging (DTI) is the newest technology. This technique makes it possible to directly examine the microscopic fibers that carry communications between brain structures. A caveat for all of these technologies is that they are costly and cumbersome to perform, and therefore most studies have examined only a small number of very serious offenders, such as individuals convicted for homicide, or individuals diagnosed with psychopathic personality or antisocial personality disorder.

Brain-imaging studies of antisocial samples (Crowe and Blair 2008; Yang et al. 2008) consistently support the theory that poor functioning of the brain's frontal and temporal regions predisposes to offending. These regions are important for criminological theory because, with only a bit of oversimplification, we can say that self-control and conscientiousness are the responsibility of the brain's frontal lobes (the part of the brain lying above the eyes and behind the forehead that is specifically called the prefrontal cortex), whereas processing strong negative emotions such as anger and fear is the responsibility of the mesial (or middle) temporal lobes (the part of the brain near the ears that contains the limbic system emotion circuitry structures called the amygdala, cingulate gyrus, and hippocampus). These new findings of structural, functional, and metabolic abnormalities in frontal and temporal brain regions revealed by imaging are consistent with the large preexisting neuropsychological testing literature that predated neuroimaging technology and showed that children and adults with antisocial behavior have deficits in executive functions of self-control and also with processing information that has emotional content (Moffitt 1990, 1993b; Nigg and Huang-Pollock 2003; Blair et al. 2006). The new imaging findings are also consistent with clinical studies of patients who suffer injury to the frontal and temporal lobes of their brain as a result of an accident. For example, injury to the orbitofrontal cortex (situated above the eye orbits) leaves many patients with personality and emotional problems that resemble criminal psychopathic behavior, a brain-injury syndrome termed "acquired sociopathy" (Damasio 1994). Finally, the new human brain-imaging findings are also consistent with earlier contentions from animal studies that showed that frontal and temporal brain regions regulate non-human aggression. Here we will review a few studies, the very earliest landmark imaging studies, and the most recent innovative studies (as of 2009).

Neuroimaging Findings in Homicide Offenders

The first published brain imaging study of murderers (Raine et al. 1994b) PET-scanned the brains of 22 murderers pleading not guilty by reason of insanity (or otherwise found incompetent to stand trial), and compared them to the brains of 22 normal controls matched with the murderers on sex and age. Subjects performed a task that required them to maintain focused attention and be vigilant for a continuous period of time. The prefrontal cortex in part serves this vigilance function. The key finding was that the murderers showed significantly poorer functioning of the prefrontal cortex—the very front part of the brain. A further study showed that it was in particular the impulsive, emotionally under-controlled murderers who were especially likely to show prefrontal deficits (Raine et al. 1998).

What other brain deficits, apart from prefrontal dysfunction, characterized these murderers? The imaging study was taken a step further by expanding the sample from 22 to 41 murderers, and also by increasing the size of the control group to 41 (Raine et al. 1997b). This increase in sample size gave more statistical power to detect group differences. The results were interesting for many reasons. First, the report confirmed that there was a significant reduction in the activity of the prefrontal region in murderers. Second, this larger sample revealed that the left angular gyrus was functioning more poorly in the murderers. The angular gyrus lies at the junction of the temporal (side of head), parietal (top and back of head), and occipital (very back of head) regions of the brain and plays a key role in integrating information from these three lobes. Reductions in activity of the left angular gyrus have been correlated with reduced verbal ability, while damage to this region has been linked to deficits in reading and arithmetic. Such cognitive deficits could predispose to educational and occupational failure, which in turn predisposes to crime and violence. The fact that learning deficits have been found to be common in violent offenders supports this interpretation. The angular gyrus also plays a role in moral decision-making (Raine and Yang, 2006). Poor functioning of this brain region may help partly explain the immoral, rule-breaking behavior of violent offenders. Third, the murderers showed reductions in the functioning of the corpus callosum, the band of white nerve fibers that carry communication between the brain's left and right hemispheres. It is possible that a poor connection between the hemispheres may mean that the right hemisphere, which is involved in the generation of negative emotion (Davidson and Fox 1989), may experience less regulation and control by the inhibitory processes of the more dominant left hemisphere, a factor that may contribute to the expression of violence. Furthermore, split-brain patients, who have had their corpus callosum surgically severed, show inappropriate emotional expression and have difficulty grasping the future implications of situations. This implies that the inappropriate emotional expression of violent offenders and their long-term planning difficulties may be partly accounted for by poor functioning of the corpus callosum. Nevertheless, callosal dysfunction by itself is unlikely to cause aggression. Instead, it may only contribute to violence in those who also have other brain abnormalities and criminogenic early life experiences.

Neuroimaging Findings in Antisocial Personality Disorder and Psychopathy

Neurological patients who have suffered demonstrable damage to both gray and white matter in the prefrontal region of the brain often acquire the above-mentioned antisocial personality syndrome, "acquired sociopathy" (Damasio 1994; Damasio et al. 1990; Stuss and Benson 1986). Gray matter comprises neurons in the brain's outer layers; white matter comprises connective tissues and the brain's inner structures. When patients with prefrontal brain injuries are tested, they also show deficient autonomic arousal and deficient attention in response to socially-meaningful information and experiences (Damasio 1994; Damasio et al. 1990). For example, they fail to show a skin conductance (sweat rate) response to threatening pictures that would normally evoke an emotional reaction in most people. These findings are consistent with the prefrontal cortex's role of modulating the expression of emotion, arousal, and attention by the brain's temporal-limbic system (Stuss and Benson 1986; Davidson 1993; Raine et al. 1991).

The volume of prefrontal gray and white matter was assessed in a structural magnetic resonance imaging (MRI) study of volunteers from the community who had antisocial personality disorder (Raine et al. 2000; Yang et al. 2009b). Psychophysiological measures of skin conductance and heart rate activity during a social stressor were also assessed, as were social and demographic risk factors for violence. Volunteers were recruited from temporary employment agencies in Los Angeles and consisted of 21 males with antisocial personality disorder, a normal control group of 34 males, and a psychiatric control group of 27 males who had substance dependence. Antisocial participants had significantly lower prefrontal gray volumes than both controls and substance-dependent participants. In contrast, groups did not differ in white matter prefrontal volume, indicating a specific deficit in gray matter. Furthermore, antisocial participants also showed reduced autonomic reactivity during the social stressor, compared to both controls and substance-dependent participants. When each particiants' prefrontal gray matter was calculated as a function of volume of his whole brain, the groups again differed significantly, so the results were not due to general difference in brain size, but reflected a specific difference in prefrontal cortex size. After the demographic and social risk factors for antisocial personality were statistically controlled, the prefrontal and autonomic deficits still significantly discriminated the antisocial group from the control group. As such, the brain deficits could not be wholly accounted for by the antisocial participants' worse social-risk history, and instead appeared to reflect a partly independent risk process. When both brain measures and social measures were used together, they correctly classified 88 percent of participants into the antisocial versus control groups, indicating the importance of a biosocial perspective that integrates biological and social factors in one study.

Structural impairments have also been observed in the amygdala—an inner part of the brain critically involved in emotion. Psychopaths have a reduction in the size of the left amygdala (17 percent volume reduction) and the right amygdala (19 percent) compared to controls (Yang et al 2009a). Nevertheless, the amygdala is a very complex structure, made up of 13 different nuclei. Reductions in volume were localized to the basolateral, lateral, cortical, and central nuclei of the amygdala. Lesioning (damaging) of these sub-regions of the amygdala in non-human animals has shown that they play an important role in fear conditioning and good parenting. Reduced amygdala volume may consequently account for deficient fear conditioning, emotions, and social bonds observed in some serious criminal offenders (Raine et al. 2008).

Moral decision-making was associated with brain function in a study of 17 community participants diagnosed with psychopathic personality (Glenn et al. 2009). The participants were asked to make judgments on ten moral dilemmas in the scanner, while fMRI images of the amygdala and prefrontal cortex were recorded. The moral dilemmas were designed to evoke a range of emotional salience. Participants that scored higher on psychopathy showed reduced amygdala activity while considering the most emotionally salient dilemmas. Those who scored highest on conning, manipulation, and deceitfulness displayed reduced activity in all the regions of the neural circuit from limbic to frontal regions. These brain areas are known to be involved in complex social processing that is essential to empathetic reasoning. Empathetic reasoning is the basis for moral decision-making; without it, there is no gauge of the appropriate-ness of using people as a means to an end. Reduced activity in these brain areas suggest limited capacity for empathy and therefore deficits in moral decision-making among psychopaths.

In an innovative study, Craig and colleagues (2009) investigated the fibers connecting the orbitofrontal and prefrontal cortexes (involved in social cognition) as well as the amygdala (involved in moral and emotional cogni-tion). This study provided unique data because a newer technology (diffu-sion tensor magnetic resonance imaging—DTI)) was used, which creates three-dimensional images of the branching fibers that connect different parts of the brain. This technique was used to measure volume and micro-structural integrity of connective fibers called the uncinate fasciculus in 18 participants: 9 highly psychopathic individuals and 9 controls. There were no significant group differences in the volume of the fibers, but significantly reduced structural integrity of the fibers was found in the psychopathic participants compared to controls. This study suggested that abnormalities in the network that connects the orbitofrontal/prefrontal cortex to the amygdala contribute to the emotional detachment of psychopaths.

Neuroimaging Findings in Young Children

Initially, imaging was reserved for adults, but recently, the technology became suitable for use with children. The existing, small neuroimaging literature with young children shows that the same frontal and temporal abnormalities observed in adults are present early in life and are associated with conduct disorder (persistent antisocial behavior problems such as lying, stealing, fighting, and truancy). Data from fMRI studies show that antisocial children have reduced functioning of the anterior cingulate (a part of the frontal lobe) to emotional stimuli, which is taken to reflect poor emotional regulation (Sterzer et al. 2005; Stadler et al. 2006). In addition, antisocial children show amygdala under-reactivity to emotional stimuli (Sterzer et al. 2005). MRI studies have identified structural ab-normalities in children with conduct disorder, including abnormalities in temporal gray matter volume (Kruesi et al. 2004) and white matter in frontal lobes (Lyoo et al. 2002). In one study, boys with callous-unemotional conduct problems had gray matter abnormalities that suggested a delay in cortical maturation in several brain areas involved in decision-making, morality, and empathy (De Brito et al. 2009), and these boys showed less activation in the amygdala when shown slides of faces expressing fear (Jones et al. 2009).

Theoretical Integration of Neuroimaging Findings

Neuroimaging research into antisocial behavior has been underway for fewer than 15 years. At the beginning, the work was fairly a-theoretical, because scientists had never been able to look at the living brain before.

There were only good hunches about what might be found. To the uninitiated, the research may seem bewildering, involving highly complex technologies, imaging an array of bizarrely named brain structures, and finding abnormalities virtually everywhere in the brain. However, the picture for antisocial behavior is beginning to come together into a theory of individual differences in moral reasoning (Blair et al. 2006; Crowe and Blair 2008; Greene et al. 2004; Raine and Yang 2006).

One part of the theory is that among antisocial people the areas of the brain that generate strong emotion in response to input from the social environment seem to be poorly regulated by the areas of the brain that exert self-control in healthy people. Prefrontal cortical dysfunction is thought to result in diminished ability to control deeper, more primitive structures such as the amygdala, which react to perceived threat with fear and anger, emotions that feed violence. However, the theory is not limited to this story of "all gas and no brakes." A key feature of the data is the failure of connections going *both ways*, from frontal control areas down to emotion areas, and from emotion areas up to control areas. Thus, part of the theory is that impaired communication from emotional areas to reasoning areas results in deficient learning from fear-inducing punishments that would induce compliance in a healthy child. Impaired communication from emotional areas up to reasoning areas can also engender the emotional detachment, lack of empathy for the emotions of others, and callous lack of sad remorse after wrongdoing that characterizes some offenders.

If prefrontal functions are uncoupled from emotional functions, this encourages risk taking, irresponsibility, rule-breaking, emotional and aggressive outbursts, argumentative behavior, loss of self-control, immaturity, lack of tact, inability to modify and inhibit behavior appropriately, and poor social judgment, all of which predispose to violence. This uncoupling also produces loss of intellectual flexibility, weak problem-solving skills, and reduced ability to use information provided by verbal cues. These deficits impair social skills essential for formulating nonaggressive solutions to fractious encounters. Also, the poor reasoning ability and poor self-control that result from prefrontal-emotional uncoupling can lead to school failure, unemployment, and economic deprivation, thereby making young people vulnerable to a criminal and violent way of life.

INTEGRATING FINDINGS FROM BIOMARKERS, PSYCHOPHYSIOLOGY, GENETICS, AND IMAGING

Unfortunately, we do not yet have a single theory that unifies all findings on the biological correlates of crime. Biological researchers have until recently worked in their own silos, in part because it is difficult enough to master one biological research technology, let alone two or more. The result is that we lack an evidence base about how cortisol, heart rate, serotonin, birth complications, EEG arousal, genes, and the brain-imaging correlates of crime relate to each other, and how they all relate to social causes of crime such as social adversity, maltreatment, and neglect. However, this integrative work is beginning (Raine 2008a; 2008b). Here we provide two examples of studies that make interesting links between birth complications, neuroimaging findings in the brain, and the *MAOA* genotype.

Researchers in pediatric neurology have followed up infants who suffered birth complications and low birth weights, by using diffusion tensor neuroimaging when the infants reached adolescence (Skranes et al. 2007; Constable et al. 2008). The low-birth-weight adolescents, compared to controls, had abnormal white matter in the corpus callosum and other branching fibers that interconnect different parts of the brain, as we described earlier in this chapter for adults with psychopathic personalities. These studies indicate that perinatal injury of white-matter connecting tracts persists at least into adolescence, with continuing clinical significance for behavior.

Researchers in the new field of "imaging genetics" have compared individuals carrying the high- versus low-activity *MAOA* genotype on neuroimaging measures of the brain's limbic-system emotion circuitry (structures called the cingulate gyrus, amygdala, and hippocampus). This circuitry processes strong negatively valenced emotions (Buckholtz and Meyer-Lindenberg 2008). Low-*MAOA*-activity participants showed structural irregularities throughout the limbic system. Low-*MAOA*-activity participants also showed greater activation in limbic-system structures when asked to recall negative, but not neutral, visual scenes. When shown pictures of angry and fearful faces, low-*MAOA*-activity participants showed exaggerated activation in the emotional limbic system, and also weaker activation of regions of the prefrontal cortex that are involved in self-control. This pattern suggests the intriguing hypothesis that *MAOA* genotype may be involved in the cycle of violence because genetically vulnerable individuals lack the self-control to manage strong negative memories and emotions.

BIOLOGY AND THE CRIMINAL JUSTICE SYSTEM

Biological research has been moving out of the laboratory and into the courtroom, whether the findings involve genetic vulnerability to crime (Appelbaum 2005; Bernet et al. 2007) or neurological vulnerability to crime (Yang et al. 2008). Contemporary legal scholars argue that a defendant's biological characteristics such as genotype are like any other information that can legally be considered in court, and should not be excluded (Nuffield Bioethics Council, 2002). The question of whether an offender's biological vulnerability to antisocial behavior precludes free will and mitigates criminal culpability remains much more controversial (Parens et al. 2006).

The application of biological science to reforming juvenile justice is proving particularly fruitful (Scott and Steinberg 2008). In a landmark case, Roper v. Simmons, the U.S. Supreme Court held that imposing the death penalty on those under the age of 18 violates the basic precept that punishment should be proportionate to the culpability of the offender (Counsel for the APA, 543 U.S. 551, 568–575, 2005). The Court explained that youth does not excuse juveniles' crimes, but juveniles do differ from adults in ways that mitigate culpability and undermine any justification for the death penalty. This decision was based on research into brain development that shows that adolescent brains are not yet fully developed in regions related to higher-order executive functions, such as impulse control, planning ahead, risk evaluation, mature judgment, and vulnerability to negative external influences. The court was persuaded by evidence that neuroanatomical immaturity is consistent with juveniles' demonstrated psychosocial immaturity.

The following fMRI study illustrates the kind of biological evidence considered by the court (Galvan et al. 2006). Three participant groups were compared: children ages 7–11, adolescents ages 13–17, and adults ages 23–29. Using fMRI, neurological responses to changes in the value of rewards during a delayed decision-making task were measured, specifically in the orbitofrontal cortex and a brain structure called the nucleus accumbens. The accumbens is highly sensitive to rewards, such as addictive drugs, sex, and even music. Adolescents had significantly greater activation change in the accumbens than did children or adults. In contrast, juveniles showed less activation than adults in the obitofrontal cortex. The pattern of differences suggested that the accumbens (reward sensitivity) develops ahead of the orbitofrontal cortex (self-control) during adolescence. This temporarily out-of-sync brain development could explain teenagers' poor decision-making and risky behavior. Developmental neuroscience has identified several ways in which the growing adolescent brain differs from the mature adult brain, in both structure and function. Knowledge is growing about how these brain differences exacerbate criminal propensity during adolescence (Spear 2007), and developmental neuroscience is very close to explaining why the age-crime curve peaks in adolescence.

EFFECTS OF CRIME ON BIOLOGY: HARM TO OFFENDERS' HEALTH

Historically, researchers have focused on the influence of biology on crime, but very recently, attention has turned to the influence of crime on biological outcomes. The particular emphasis of this research is on pointing out that offenders' costs to society involve not just costs associated with the criminal justice system, but also major costs associated with the health care system. Researchers have tested individuals who have lived a criminal lifestyle for years, to ascertain whether they differ from comparison subjects on health measures that are known to be influenced by health behaviors in a low self-control lifestyle, such as heavy smoking, risky sexual behavior, or poor diet.

Odgers and colleagues (2007a) examined the effects of a long-term antisocial lifestyle on males' health outcomes in the Dunedin Longitudinal

Study. The researchers scored participants at ages 7, 9, 11, 13, 15, 18, 21, and 26 on antisocial conduct problems that had occurred within the last year, including fighting, bullying, property destruction, lying, truancy, and stealing. Participants were classified into four groups based on their trajectory of conduct disorder from age 7 to 26: life course persistent, adolescent onset, childhood limited, and non-antisocial. At age 32, mental and physical health measures were compared between groups. Males with life-course persistent antisocial behavior had significantly more health problems at age 32 than all other groups. Their health problems included a metabolic syndrome of risk for cardiovascular disease (for example, elevated cholesterol), elevated C-reactive protein (a blood test indicating that there is inflammation somewhere in the system of arteries), dental problems such as caries and periodontal disease, heavy cigarette smoking, drug and alcohol dependence, suicide attempts, herpes 2 virus antibodies in blood (indicating more exposure to sexually transmitted diseases), and more serious non-sport-related injuries. They had also made the most visits to a general practitioner for medical problems. The life course persistent group made up 10 percent of the total cohort of males, but accounted for 17 percent of traffic injuries, 29 percent of days spent in psychiatric facilities, 72 percent of the months spent in jail, and 42 percent of months spent homeless. The adolescent-onset group also had significantly more mental and physical health problems than the childhood limited and low groups. Poor health in life-course persistent offenders has also been reported for an American sample (Piquero et al. 2007).

Shepherd et al. (2009) found that an antisocial lifestyle and its childhood predictors are significantly associated with poor health outcomes at age 48. The researchers used data from the well-known Cambridge Study in Delinquent Development, which has followed 411 males born in working-class London from ages 8 to 48. By age 48, 34 (8 percent) of the men had died or become disabled. Multivariate analysis considering antisocial behavior at ages 8–10, parental risk factors, and convictions significantly discriminated between the 34 dead/disabled men and the remaining 377 men. Men whose family upbringing included risk factors for offending had the worst health outcomes at age 48. The study also shows that although offending rates decreased soon after adolescence, the impact of the antisocial lifestyle on health becomes most apparent in the fourth and fifth decade of life.

CONCLUSION

Biological research into antisocial behavior is a very small field, relative to biological research into other problem behaviors. Publications of primary empirical findings on the biology of antisocial behavior number in the hundreds, whereas such publications on other problem behaviors number in the hundreds of thousands. Biological research into addictions, schizophrenia, depression, anxiety, autism, attention-deficit hyperactivity, and dementia is rapidly leading toward a more complete understanding of these problems. Breakthroughs in understanding are in turn rapidly leading toward translation into treatments, and even preventions. In contrast, biological research into antisocial behavior is still very far away from translation to treatment. And yet, the costs to society of antisocial, violent, and criminal behavior arguably outweigh the costs of all other behavioral and health conditions (Anderson 1999; Ludwig 2006). Moreover, this chapter has illustrated that there is good evidence that biological vulnerabilities are involved in antisocial behavior, particularly in the lives of individuals who suffer extensive social risks for crime, and whose antisocial behavior onsets in childhood, persists for years thereafter, and involves frequent and violent victimization of others. If research led to treatments that worked, many offenders who recognize that they and their families suffer from the consequences of their violence might prefer treatment, as opposed to the options of harming their loved ones or being imprisoned. But the research is underdeveloped, and thus treatments are still beyond the horizon.

Why is the biology of crime so under-studied? There are several reasons. First, schizophrenia, attention-deficit hyperactivity disorder (ADHD), autism, and dementia have powerful advocacy groups made up of parents and family members of patients who lobby government for more funding for research, such as the National Alliance for the Mentally Ill and Autism Speaks. No comparable group of politically savvy family members advocates for antisocial criminal offenders. Second, pharmaceutical companies' market considerations drive support for biological research into ADHD, depression, anxiety, and dementia. These disorders afflict large numbers of people who seek treatment and who have health insurance to pay for medications. The antisocial population is large too, but its members generally do not seek treatment or have health insurance. Funding agencies who support biological research, such as the U.S. National Institutes of Health, tend to assume that antisocial behavior is taken care of in the funding portfolio of the U.S. National Institute of Justice (NIJ), but the NIJ funds almost exclusively social-science research into crime. Few trained criminologists undertake biological research (with some outstanding exceptions, cited in this chapter). This is in part an understandable ideological backlash against the grim history of biological ideas about crime propounded by phrenologists, eugenicists, and other "criminal anthropologists" such as Lombroso, Sheldon, Hooton, McKim, and the Gluecks, in the first half of the twentieth century (Rafter 1994). But perhaps the more pragmatic reason that criminologists have not studied biology is that most criminologists rightly favor very large community data sets to answer their questions, and collecting biological measurements in large samples has until recently been technically difficult and prohibitively costly.

Technical barriers to biological research in criminology are crumbling fast. Very large representative cohort studies with data on antisocial behavior have gathered tissue samples such as salivary cortisol, blood spots on filter paper, and of course DNA. Much of these data will be in the public domain, accessible to criminologists. Even neuroimaging technology is being applied to very large samples. Criminologists are overcoming their lack of postgraduate training in biological technology by collaborating with other kinds of scientists. Ideological barriers are crumbling fast as well. The potential for misuse of biological findings is being actively scrutinized through government funding for research into ethical, legal, and social implications (called ELSI) (Nuffield Council on Bioethics 2002; Parens et al. 2006; Singh and Rose 2009). Biological determinism is being proven wrongheaded by clear evidence that almost all biological factors' influence on antisocial behavior depends on criminogenic environmental factors, many of which are under human control (Moffitt et al. 2006). Ethnic minority scholars in the academy are beginning to call for biological research with minority samples, lest minority groups are systematically excluded and fail to garner health benefits from advances in genomic science and neuroscience (Royal and Dunston 2004). Biological research into antisocial behaviors, which has until now been carried out mainly by mental health researchers lacking in criminology training, will be hugely enhanced as more criminologists begin to take part. This chapter extends an invitation to young criminologists to do just that.

GLOSSARY OF TERMS IN THIS CHAPTER

allele—alternative variant of a gene; individuals will generally have two alleles of each gene, which may vary

antisocial personality disorder—a personality disorder characterized by amorality and lack of emotions; involves the capacity to commit violent acts without feelings of guilt

biomarker—a characteristic that is objectively measured and evaluated as an indicator of normal biologic processes (e.g., hormones, neurotransmitters, and perinatal complications)

cohort—the group of participants in a longitudinal study, generally all born in the same time period

cortisol—stress hormone

diffusion tensor imaging (DTI)—a neuroimaging method that provides quantitative visual information to examine neural pathways that connect structures in the brain of a living person **dizygotic twins (DZ)**—twins from two separately fertilized egg cells; fraternal twins

electroencephalogram (EEG)—a recording of brain waves obtained by attaching electrodes to the scalp; it shows changes in brain wave voltage and frequency

functional magnetic resonance imaging (fMRI)—a form of magnetic resonance imaging of the brain that registers blood flow to areas of the brain in a living person who is performing mental tasks

gene—the fundamental unit of inheritance; usually taken to mean a section of DNA that contains the code for a protein, but the definition is being widened to include DNA that carries other genetic instructions

genome-wide association study (GWAS)—gene-hunting technique capable of finding genes having small effects on diseases

genotype—an individual's genetic profile; can refer to one or many different alleles

genotype-by-environment interaction (GxE) study—a study technique focused on looking for effects of specific genes that depend on exposure to environmental causes of disease or behaviors

gray matter—a type of brain and nervous tissue containing cell bodies as well as fibers

haplotype—a subsection of a chromosome that tends to remain intact during recombination across many generations of inheritance

heritability—a measure of how much inheritance contributes to the variability of a disease or behavior, usually expressed as a decimal or percentage

in-utero—in the uterus; unborn

longitudinal studies—research designs in which a group of subjects is studied several different times over a period of years

monozygotic twins (MZ)—twins from a single fertilized egg cell that splits; identical twins

neurotransmitters—chemical substances that carry impulses from one nerve cell to another; found in the space that separates the transmitting neuron from the receiving neuron

perinatal—referring to the period from the 28th week of pregnancy to the 28th day after birth

phenotype—an observed characteristic of an organism, which can be influenced by either inheritance or the environment

polymorphism—a variation in the sequence of DNA among individuals

positron emission tomography (PET)—nuclear medicine imaging technique that produces a three-dimensional image of processes that use energy in the brain

psychopathy—a personality disorder indicated by a pattern of lying, exploitiveness, heedlessness, arrogance, sexual promiscuity, low self-control, and lack of empathy and remorse; violent and criminal offenses usually accompany this disorder

psychophysiological—concerned with the physiological bases of psychological processes

serotonin—a neurotransmitter involved in mood and behavior, physical coordination, appetite, body temperature, and sleep

testosterone—a potent androgenic hormone involved in aggression and
  mood disorders
white matter—a type of neural tissue in the brain and spinal cord
  composed primarily of myelin-covered axons
zygosity—a description of whether twins have identical or different
  DNA sequences

References

Anderson, David A. 1999. "The Aggregate Burden of Crime." *Journal of Law and
  Economics* 42: 611–642.
Appelbaum, Paul S. 2005. "Behavioral Genetics and the Punishment Of Crime."
  Law & Psychiatry 56: 25–27.
Arseneault, Louise, Terrie E. Moffitt, Avshalom Caspi, Alan Taylor, F. V. Rijsdijk,
  Sara R. Jaffee, J. C. Ablow, and J. R. Measelle. 2003. "Strong Genetic Effects
  on Cross-Situational Antisocial Behavior among 5-Year-Old Children
  According to Mothers, Teachers, Examiner-Observers, and Twins' Self-
  Reports." *Journal of Child Psychology and Psychiatry* 44: 832–848.
Arseneault, Louise, Richard E. Tremblay, Bernard Boulerice, and Jean-Francois
  Saucier. 2002. "Obstetrical Complications and Adolescent Violent Behaviors:
  Testing Two Developmental Pathways." *Child Development* 73: 496–508.
Baker, Laura A., Serena Bezdjian, and Adrian Raine. 2006. Behavioral Genetics:
  The Science of Antisocial Behavior." *Law and Contemporary Problems* 69:
  7–46.
Baker, Laura A., Catherine Tuvblad, Chandra Reynolds, Mo Zheng, Dora I.
  Lozano, and Adrian Raine. 2009. "Resting Heart Rate and the Development
  of Antisocial Behavior from Age 9 to 14: Genetic and Environmental
  Influences." *Development and Psychopathology* 21: 939–960.
Bauer, Lance O., and Victor M. Hesselbrock. 2003. "Brain Maturation and
  Subtypes of Conduct Disorder: Interactive Effects on P300 Amplitude and
  Topography in Male Adolescents." *Journal of American Academy of Child and
  Adolescent Psychiatry* 42: 106–115.
Beaver, Kevin M. 2009. *Biosocial Criminology: A Primer.* Dubuque, IA: Kendall/
  Hunt Publishing.
Beaver, Kevin M., J. Eagle Shutt, Brian B. Boutwell, Marie Ratchford, Kathleen
  Roberts, and J. C. Barnes. 2009a. "Genetic and Environmental Influences on
  Levels of Self-Control and Delinquent Peer Affiliation." *Criminal Justice and
  Behavior* 36: 41–60.
Beaver, Kevin M., Matthew DeLisi, Michael G. Vaughn, and J. C. Barnes. 2010.
  "*MAOA* Genotype Is Associated with Gang Membership and Weapon Use."
  Comprehensive Psychiatry 51: 130–134. Done
Beaver, Kevin M., Chris L. Gibson, Wesley Jennings, and Jeffrey T. Ward. 2009b.
  "A Gene X Environment Interaction between DRD2 and Religiosity in the
  Prediction of Adolescent Delinquent Involvement in a Sample of Males."
  Biodemography and Social Biology 55: 71–81. DONE
Beitchman, Joseph H., Lidia Baldassarra, Helene Mik, Vincenzo De Luca, Nicole
  King, Danielle Bender, Sahar Ehtesham, and James L. Kennedy. 2006.
  "Serotonin Transporter Polymorphisms and Persistent, Pervasive Childhood
  Aggression." *American Journal of Psychiatry* 163: 1103–1105.

Bernet, William, Cindy L. Vnencak-Jones, Nita Farahany, and Stephen A. Montgomery. 2007. "Bad Nature, Bad Nurture, and Testimony Regarding *MAOA* And SLC6A4 Genotyping at Murder Trials." *Journal of Forensic Science* 52: 1–10.

Blair, R. James R., K. S. Peschardt, S. Budhani, D. G. V. Mitchell, and D. S. Pine. 2006. "The Development of Psychopathy." *Journal of Child Psychology & Psychiatry* 47: 262–275.

Brennan, Patricia A., Emily R. Grekin, and Sarnoff A. Mednick. 2003. "Prenatal and Perinatal Influences on Conduct Disorder and Delinquency." In *Causes of Conduct Disorder and Delinquency*, eds. B. B. Lahey, T. E. Moffitt, and A. Caspi, 319–344. New York: Guilford Press.

Brennan, Patricia A., Adrian Raine, Fini Schulsinger, Lis Kirkegaard-Sorensen, Joachim Knop, Barry Hutchings, Raben Rosenberg, and Sarnoff A. Mednick. 1997. "Psychophysiological Protective Factors for Male Subjects at High Risk for Criminal Behavior." *American Journal of Psychiatry* 154: 853–855.

Buckholtz, Joshua W., and Andreas Meyer-Lindenberg. 2008. "*MAOA* and the Neurogenetic Architecture of Human Aggression." *Trends in Neurosciences* 31: 120–129.

Cadoret, Remi J., William R. Yates, Ed Troughton, George Woodworth, and Mark A. Stewart. 1995. "Genetic-environmental Interaction in the Genesis of Aggressivity and Conduct Disorders." *Archives of General Psychiatry* 52: 916–924.

Campbell, Jacquelyn C. 2002. "Health Consequences of Intimate Partner Violence." *The Lancet* 359: 1331–1336.

Carey, Gregory. 2003. *Human Genetics for the Social Sciences. vol. 4*. London: Sage Publications.

Caspi, Avshalom, Kate Langley, Barry Milne, Terrie E. Moffitt, Michael O'Donovan, Michael J. Owen, Monica P. Tomas, Richie Poulton, Michael Rutter, Alan Taylor, Benjamin Williams, and Anita Thapar. 2008. "A Replicated Molecular Genetic Basis for Subtyping Antisocial Behavior in Children with Attention-Deficit/Hyperactivity Disorder." *Archives of General Psychiatry* 65: 203–210.

Caspi, Avshalom, Joseph McClay, Terrie E. Moffitt, Jonathan Mill, Judy Martin, Ian W. Craig, Alan Taylor, and Richie Poulton. 2002. "Role of Genotype in the Cycle of Violence in Maltreated Children." *Science* 297: 851–854.

Caspi, Avshalom, and Terrie E. Moffitt. 2006. "Opinion—Gene-environment Interactions in Psychiatry: Joining Forces with Neuroscience." *Nature Reviews Neuroscience* 7: 583–590.

Celio, Michael, N. S. Karnik, and H. Steiner. 2006. "Early Maturation as a Risk Factor for Aggression and Delinquency in Adolescent Girls: A Review. " *International Journal of Clinical Practice* 60: 1254–1262.

Cloninger, C. Robert, and I. I. Gottesman. 1987. "Genetic and Environmental Factors in Antisocial Behavior Disorders." In *The Causes of Crime: New Biological Approaches*, eds. S. A. Mednick, T. E. Moffitt, and S. Stack. 92–109. Cambridge: Cambridge University Press.

Coker, Ann L., Keith E. Davis, Ileana Arias, Sujata Desai, Maureen Sanderson, Heather M. Brandt, and Paige H. Smith. 2002. "Physical and Mental Health Effects of Intimate Partner Violence for Men and Women." *American Journal of Preventive Medicine* 23: 260–268.

Constable, R. Todd, Laura R. Ment, Betty R. Vohr, Shelli R. Kesler, Robert K. Fulbright, Cheryl Lacadie, Susan Delancy, Karol H. Katz, Karen C. Schneider,

Robin J. Schafer, Robert W. Makuch, and Allan R. Reiss. 2008. "Prematurely Born Children Demonstrate White Matter Microstructural Differences at 12 Years of Age, Relative to Term Control Subjects: An Investigation of Group and Gender Effects." *Pediatrics* 121: 306–316.

Costa, Laura, Lance O. Bauer, Samuel Kuperman, Bernice Porjesz, Sean O'Connor, Victor M. Hesselbrock, John Rohrbaugh, and Henri Begleiter. 2000. "Frontal P300 Decrements, Alcohol Dependence, and Antisocial Personality Disorder." *Biological Psychiatry* 47: 1064–1067.

Craig, Michael C., M. Catani, Q. Deeley, R. Latham, E. Daly, R. Kanaan, M. Picchioni, P. K. McGuire, T. Fahy, and D. G. M. Murphy. 2009. "Altered Connections on the Road to Psychopathy." *Molecular Psychiatry*, E-pub: 1–8.

Crowe, Samantha L., and R. James R. Blair. 2008. "The Development of Antisocial Behavior: What Can We Learn from Functional Neuroimaging Studies?" *Development and Psychopathology* 20 (Special Issue 04): 1145–1159.

Damasio, Antonio R. 1994. *Descartes' Error: Emotion, Reason, and the Human Brain.* New York: Grosset/Putnum.

Damasio, Antonio R., D. Tranel, and H. Damasio. 1990. "Individuals with Psychopathic Behavior Caused by Frontal Damage Fail to Respond Autonomically to Social Stimuli." *Behavioral and Brain Research* 41: 81–94.

Danese, Andrea, Carmine M. Pariante, Avshalom Caspi, Alan Taylor, and Richie Poulton. 2007. "Childhood Maltreatment Predicts Adult Inflammation in a Life-Course Study." *Proceedings of the National Academy of Sciences of the United States of America* 104: 1319–1324.

Danese A, Caspi A, Williams B, Ambler A, Sugden K, Mika J, Werts H, Freeman J, Pariante CM, Moffitt TE, Arseneault L. (2010). Biological Embedding of Stress Through Inflammation Processes in Childhood. Molecular Psychiatry. 2010; epub Feb 16 (PMID: 20157309)

Davidson, Richard J., and Nathan A. Fox. 1989. "Frontal Brain Asymmetry Predicts Infants' Response to Maternal Separation." *Journal of Abnormal Psychology* 98: 127–131.

Davidson, Richard J. 1993. "Parsing Affective Space: Perspectives from Neuropsychology and Psychophysiology." *Neuropsychology* 7: 464–475.

De Brito, Stephane A., Andrea Mechelli, Marko Wilke, Kristin R. Laurens, Alice P. Jones, Gareth J. Barker, Sheilagh Hodgins, and Essi Viding. 2009. "Size Matters: Increased Grey Matter in Boys with Conduct Problems and Callous-Unemotional Traits." *Brain* 132: 843–852.

DeLisi, Matthew, Kevin M. Beaver, Michael G. Vaughn, and J. P. Wright. 2009. "All in the Family: Gene X Environment Interaction Between DRD2 And Criminal Fathers Is Associated With Five Antisocial Phenotypes." *Criminal Justice and behavior* 29: 1187-1197. DONE

Dick, Danielle M., T-K. Li, H. J. Edenberg, V. Hesselbrock, J. Kramer, S. Kuperman, B. Porjesz, K. Bucholz, A. Goate, J. Nurnberger, Jr., and T. Foroud. 2004. "A Genome-Wide Screen for Genes Influencing Conduct Disorder." *Molecular Psychiatry* 9: 81–86.

Donohue, John J., III, and Steven D. Levitt. 2001. "The Impact of Legalized Abortion on Crime." *Quarterly Journal of Economics* 116: 379–420.

Farrington, David P. 1997. "The Relationship Between Low Resting Heart Rate and Violence." In *Biosocial Bases of Violence*, eds. A. Raine, P. A. Brennan, D. P. Farrington, and S. A. Mednick. New York: Plenum.

Farrington, David P., G. C. Barnes, and S. Lambert. 1996. "The Concentration of Offending in Families." *Legal & Criminological Psychology* 1: 47–63.

Farrington, David P., Darrick Jolliffe, Rolf Loeber, Magda Stouthamer-Loeber, and Larry M. Kalb. 2001. "The Concentration of Offenders in Families, and Family Criminality in the Prediction of Boys' Delinquency." *Journal of Adolescence* 24: 579–596.

Fung, Michelle T., Adrian Raine, Rolf Loeber, Stuart R. Steinhauer, Magda Stouthamer-Loeber, Peter H. Venables, and Donald R. Lynam. 2005. "Reduced Electrodermal Activity in Psychopathy-Prone Adolescents." *Journal of Abnormal Psychology* 114: 187–196.

Galvan, Adriana, Todd A. Hare, Cindy E. Parra, Jackie Penn, Henning Voss, Gary Glover, and B. J. Casey. 2006. "Earlier development of the Accumbens Relative to Orbitofrontal Cortex Might Underlie Risk-Taking Behavior in Adolescents." *The Journal of Neuroscience* 26: 6885–6892.

Gao, Yu, and Adrian Raine. (2009). "P3 Event-Related Potential Impairments in Antisocial and Psychopathic Individuals: A Meta-Analysis". *Biological Psychology*, 82, 199–210. DONE

Gao, Yu, Adrian Raine, Peter H. Venables, and Sarnoff A. Mednick. (2010) "Poor Fear Conditioning at Age 3 Years Predisposes to Adult Crime at Age 23." *American Journal of Psychiatry, 167, 156–160.* DONE

Glenn, Andrea L., and Adrian Raine. 2008. "The Neurobiology of Psychopathy." *Psychiatric Clinics of North America* 31: 463–475.

Glenn, Andrea L., Adrian Raine, and R. Schug. 2009. "The Neural Correlates of Moral Decision-Making in Psychopathy." *Molecular Psychiatry* 14: 5–6.

Greene, Joshua D., Leigh E. Nystrom, Andrew D. Engell, John M. Darley, and Jonathan D. Cohen. 2004. "The Neural Bases of Cognitive Conflict and Control in Moral Judgment." *Neuron* 44: 389–400.

Grove, William M., Elke D. Eckert, Leonard Heston, Thomas J. Bouchard, Nancy Segal, and David T. Lykken. 1990. "Heritability of Substance Abuse and Antisocial Behavior: A Study of Monozygotic Twins Reared Apart." *Biological Psychiatry* 27: 1293–1304.

Guo, Guang, Michael E. Roettger, and Tianji Cai. 2008. "The Integration of Genetic Propensities into Social-Control Models of Delinquency and Violence among Male Youths." *American Sociological Review* 73: 543–568.

DoneHaberstick, Brett C., Andrew Smolen, and John K. Hewitt. 2006. "Family-based Association Test of the 5HTTLPR and Aggressive Behavior in a General Population Sample of Children." *Biological Psychiatry* 59: 836–843.

Handley, L., J. Lawson, and N. Perrin. 2007. "Advaces in Our Understanding of Mammalian Sex-Based Dispersal." *Molecular Ecology* 16: 1559–1578.

Haynie, Dana L., and Alex R. Piquero. 2006."Pubertal Development and Physical Victimization in Adolescence." *Journal of Research in Crime and Delinquency* 43: 3–35.

Holmes, Jane, Antony Payton, Jennifer Barrett, Richard Harrington, Peter McGuffin, Michael Owen, William Ollier, Jane Worthington, Michael Gill, Aiveen Kirley, Ziarih Hawi, Michael Fitzgerald, Philip Asherson, Sarah Curran, John Mill, Alison Gould, Eric Taylor, Lyndsey Kent, Nick Craddock, and Anita Thapar. 2002. "Association of DRD4 in Children with ADHD and Comorbid Conduct Problems." *American Journal of Medical Genetics Part B* 114: 150–153.

Hoptman, Matthew J., Debra D'Angelo, Dean Catalano, Cristina J. Mauro, Zarrar E. Shehzad, A. M. Clare Kelly, Francisco X. Castellanos, Daniel C. Javitt, and Michael P. Milham. 2009. "Amygdalofrontal Functional Disconnectivity and Aggression in Schizophrenia." *Schizophrenia Bulletin*, E-pub: 1–12.

Jones, Alice P., Kristin R. Laurens, Catherine M. Herba, Gareth J. Barker, and Essi Viding. 2009. "Amygdala Hypoactivity to Fearful Faces in Boys with Conduct Problems and Callous-Unemotional Traits." *American Journal of Psychiatry* 166: 95–102.

Kendler, Kenneth S., Po-Hsiu Kuo, B. Todd Webb, Gursharan Kalsi, Michael C. Neale, Patrick F. Sullivan, Dermot Walsh, Diana G. Patterson, Brien Riley, and Carol A. Prescott. 2006. A joint genomewide linkage analysis of symptoms of alcohol dependence and conduct disorder. *Alcoholism: Clinical and Experimental Research* 30: 1972–1977.

Kendler, Kenneth S., M. C. Neale, R. C. Kessler, A. C. Heath, and L. J. Eaves. 1994. "Parental Treatment and the Equal Environments Assumption in Twin Studies of Psychiatric Illness." *Psychological Medicine* 24: 579–590.

Kim, Myung-Sun, Jae-Jin Kim, and Jun S. Kwon. 2001. "Frontal P300 Decrement and Executive Dysfunction in Adolescents with Conduct Problems." *Child Psychiatry & Human Development* 32: 93–106.

Kruesi, Markus J. P., Manuel F. Casanova, Glenn Mannheim, and Adrienne Johnson-Bilder. 2004. "Reduced Temporal Lobe Volume in Early Onset Conduct Disorder." *Psychiatry Research* 132: 1–11.

Liu, Jianghong, Adrian Raine, Peter H. Venables, and Sarnoff A. Mednick. 2004. "Malnutrition at Age 3 Years and Externalizing Behavior Problems at Ages 8, 11 and 17 Years." *Journal of Abnormal Psychology* 114: 38–49.

Lorber, Michael F. 2004. "Psychophysiology of Aggression, Psychopathy, and Conduct Problems: A Meta-Analysis." *Psychological Bulletin* 130: 531–52.

Lyoo, In Kyoon, Ho Kyu Lee, Ji Hyun Jung, Gil G. Noam, and Perry F. Renshaw. 2002. "White Matter Hyperintensities on Magnetic Resonance Imaging of the Brain in Children with Psychiatric Disorders." *Comparative Psychiatry* 43: 361–368.

McDermott, Rose, Dustin Tingley, Jonathan Cowden, Frazzetto Giovanni, and Dominic D.P. Johnson. 2009. "Monoamine Oxidase A Gene (*MAOA*) Predicts Behavioral Aggression Following Provocation." *Proceedings of the National Academy of Sciences of the United States of America* 106: 2118–2123.

Mednick, Sarnoff A., William F. Gabrielli, and Barry Hutchings. 1984. Genetic influences in criminal convictions: Evidence from an adoption cohort. *Science* 224: 891–894.

Mednick, Sarnoff A., Terrie E. Moffitt, William F. Gabrielli, and Barry Hutchings. 1986. "Genetic Factors in Criminal Behavior: A Review." In *The Development of Antisocial and Prosocial Behavior*, eds. J. Block, D. Olweus, and M. Radke-Yarrow. New York: Pergamon Press.

Mednick, Sarnoff A., Jan Volavka, William F. Gabrielli, and Turtan M. Itil. 1981. "EEG as a Predictor of Antisocial Behavior." *Criminology* 19: 219–231.

Moffitt, Terrie E. 1990. "The Neuropsychology of Delinquency: A Critical Review of Theory and Research." In *Crime and Justice: An Annual Review of Research*, eds. N. Morris and M. Tonry. 99–196. Chicago: University of Chicago Press.

Moffitt, Terrie E. 1993a. "Adolescence-limited and Life-Course-Persistent Antisocial Behavior—A Developmental Taxonomy." *Psychological Review* 100: 674–701.

Moffitt, Terrie E. 1993b. "The Neuropsychology of Conduct Disorder." *Development and Psychopathology* 5: 135–151.

Moffitt, Terrie E. 2005a. "Genetic and Environmental Influences on Antisocial Behaviors: Evidence from Behavioral-Genetic Research." *Advances in Genetics* 55: 41–104.

Moffitt, Terrie E. 2005b. "The New Look of Behavioral Genetics in Developmental Psychopathology: Gene-Environment Interplay in Antisocial Behaviors." *Psychological Bulletin* 131: 533–554.

Moffitt, Terrie E.. 2006. Life-course Persistent Versus Adolescence-Limited Antisocial Behavior." In *Developmental Psychopathology*, 2nd ed., ed. D. J. C. D. Cicchetti, 570–598. New York: Wiley.

Moffitt, Terrie E., Avshalom Caspi, and Michael Rutter. 2006. "Measured Gene-Environment Interactions in Psychopathology: Concepts, Research Strategies, and Implications for Research, Intervention, and Public Understanding of Genetics." *Perspectives on Psychological Science* 1: 5–27.

Moffitt, Terrie E., Avshalom Caspi, Michael Rutter, and Phil A. Silva. 2001. *Sex Differences in Antisocial Behaviour: Conduct Disorder, Delinquency, and Violence in the Dunedin Longitudinal Study*. Cambridge: Cambridge University Press.

Moore, Todd M., Angela Scarpa, and Adrian Raine. 2002. "A Meta-Analysis of Serotonin Metabolite 5-HIAA and Antisocial Behavior." *Aggressive Behavior* 28: 299–316.

Naudts, Kris, and Sheilagh Hodgins. 2006. "Neurobiological Correlates of Violent Behavior Among Persons with Schizophrenia." *Schizophrenia Bulletin* 32: 562–572.

Needleman, Herbert L., Christine McFarland, Roberta B. Ness, Stephen E. Fienberg, and Michael J. Tobin. 2002. "Bone Lead Levels in Adjudicated Delinquents: A Case Study." *Neurotoxicology and Teratology* 24: 711–717.

Nelson, Randy J. 2006. *Biology of Aggression*. New York: Oxford University Press.

Neugebauer, Richard, Hans W. Hoek, and Ezra Susser. 1999. "Prenatal Exposure to Wartime Famine and Development of Antisocial Personality Disorder in Early Adulthood." *Journal of the American Medical Association* 4: 479–481.

Nigg, Joel T., and Cynthia L. Huang-Pollock. 2003. "An Early-Onset Model of the Role of Executive Functions and Intelligence in CD." In *Causes of Conduct Disorder and Juvenile Delinquency*, eds. T. E. Moffitt, B. B. Lahey, A. Caspi. New York: Guildford Press.

Nuffield, Council on Bioethics. 2002. *Genetics and Human Behaviour: The Ethical Context*. London.

Odgers, Candice L., Avshalom Caspi, Jonathan M. Broadbent, Nigel Dickson, Robert J. Hancox, HonaLee Harrington, Richie Poulton, Malcom R. Sears, W. Murray Thomson, and Terrie E. Moffitt. 2007a. "Prediction of Differential Adult Health Burden by Conduct Problem Subtypes in Males." *Archives of General Psychiatry* 64: 476–484.

Odgers, Candice L., Barry Milne, Avshalom Caspi, Raewyn Crump, Richie Poulton, and Terrie E. Moffitt. 2007b. "Predicting Prognosis for the Conduct-Problem Boy: Can Family History Help?" *Child and Adolescent Psychiatry* 46: 1240–1249.

Ortiz, Jame, and Adrian Raine. 2004. "Heart Rate Level and Antisocial Behavior in Children and Adolescents: A Meta-Analysis." *Journal of the American Academy of Child and Adolescent Psychiatry* 43: 154–162.

Parens, Erik, Audrey R. Chapman, and Nancy Press, eds. 2006. *Wrestling with Behavioral Genetics*. Baltimore: Johns Hopkins University Press.

Patrick, C. J. 2006. "Getting to the Heart of Psychopathy." In *Psychopathy: Theory, Research, and Social Implications*, eds. H. Herve and J. C. Yuille, 207–252. Hillsdale, NJ: Erlbaum.

Petersen, K. G. I., M. Matousek, S. A. Mednick, J. Volavka, and V. Pollock. 1982. "EEG Antecedents of Thievery." *Acta Psychiatrica Scandinavica* 19: 219–229.

Plomin, Robert, John C. DeFries, Gerald E. McClearn, and P. McGuffin. 2008. *Behavioral Genetics*, 5th ed. New York: Worth Publishers.

Piquero, A. and S. Tibbetts. 1999. "The Impact of Pre/Perinatal Disturbances and Disadvantaged Familial Environment in Predicting Criminal Offending." *Studies on Crime and Crime Prevention* 8: 52–70.

Piquero, Alex R., Chris L. Gibson, Leah E. Daigle, Nicole L. Piquero, and Stephen G. Tibbetts. 2007. "Are Life-Course Persistent Offenders at Risk for Adverse Health Outcomes?" *Journal of Research in Crime & Delinquency* 44: 185–207.

Rafter, Nicole. 1994. "Criminal Anthropology in the United States." In *The Criminology Theory Reader*, eds. S. Henry and W. Einstadter. New York: New York University Press.

Raine, Adrian. 1993. *The Psychopathology of Crime: Criminal Behaviors as a Clinical Disorder*. San Diego: Academic Press.

Raine, Adrian. 1997. "Psychophysiology and Antisocial Behavior." In *Handbook of Antisocial Behavior*, eds. J. B. D. Stoff and J. D. Maser, 289–304. New York: Wiley.

Raine, Adrian. 2002a. "The Biological Basis of Crime." In *Crime*, eds. cJ. Q. Wilson and J. Petersilia. Oakland: ICS Press.

Raine, Adrian. 2002b. "Biosocial Studies of Antisocial and Violent Behavior in Children and Adults: A Review." *Journal of Abnormal Child Psychology* 30: 311–326.

Raine, Adrian. 2008a. "Brain Mechanisms, Moral Decision Making and Antisocial Behaviour." *Journal of Neurology Neurosurgery and Psychiatry* 79: 969.

Raine, Adrian. 2008b. "From Genes to Brain to Antisocial Behavior." *Current Directions in Psychological Science* 17: 323–328.

Raine, Adrian, Patricia Brennan, and Sarnoff A. Mednick. 1994a. "Birth Complications Combined with Early Maternal Rejection at Age 1 Year Predispose to Violent Crime at Age 18 Years." *Archives of General Psychiatry* 51: 984–988.

Raine, Adrian, Patricia Brennan, and Sarnoff A. Mednick. 1997a. "Interaction Between Birth Complications and Early Maternal Rejection in Predisposing to Adult Violence: Specificity to Serious, Early Onset Violence." *American Journal of Psychiatry* 154: 1265–1271.

Raine, Adrian, Monte S. Buchsbaum, and Lori La Casse. 1997b. "Brain Abnormalities in Murderers Indicated by Positron Emission Tomography." *Biological Psychiatry* 42: 495–508.

Raine, Adrian, Monte S. Buchsbaum, Jill Stanley, Steven Lottenberg, Leonard Abel, and Jacqueline Stoddard. 1994b. "Selective Reductions in Pre-Frontal Glucose Metabolism in Murderers." *Biological Psychiatry* 36: 365–373.

Raine, Adrian, Todd Lencz, Susan Bihrle, Lori Lacasse, and Patrick Colletti. 2000. "Reduced Prefrontal Gray Matter Volume and Reduced Autonomic Activity in Antisocial Personality Disorder." *Archives of General Psychiatry* 57: 119–127.

Raine, Adrian, J. Reid Meloy, Susan Bihrle, Jacqueline Stoddard, Lori Lacasse, and Monte S. Buchsbaum. 1998b. "Reduced Prefrontal and Increased Subcortical Brain Functioning Assessed Using Positron Emission Tomography in Predatory and Affective Murderers." *Behavioral Sciences and the Law* 16: 319–332.

Raine, Adrian, Gavin P. Reynolds, and Charlotte Sheard. 1991. "Neuroanatomical Mediators of Electrodermal Activity in Normal Human Subjects: A Magnetic Resonance Imaging Study." *Psychophysiology* 28: 548–555.

Raine, Adrian, Peter H. Venables, and Mark Williams. 1990. "Relationships Between CNS and ANS Measures of Arousal at Age 15 and Criminality at Age 24." *Archives of General Psychiatry* 47: 1033–1007.

Raine, Adrian, Peter H. Venables, and Mark Williams. 1995. "High Autonomic Arousal and Electrodermal Orienting at Age 15 Years as Protective Factors Against Criminal Behavior at Age 29 Years." *American Journal of Psychiatry* 152: 1595–1600.

Raine, Adrian, Peter H. Venables, and Mark Williams.1996. "Better Autonomic Conditioning and Faster Electrodermal Half-Recovery Time at Age 15 Years as Possible Protective Factors Against Crime at Age 29 Years." *Developmental Psychology* 32: 624–630.

Raine, Adrian, and Yaling Yang. 2006. "Neural Foundations to Moral Reasoning and Antisocial Behavior." *Social, Cognitive, and Affective Neuroscience* 1: 202–213.

Raine, Adrian, Yaling Yang, K. Narr, and A. Toga. 2008. "Volume Reductions in Middle Frontal and Orbitofrontal Gyral Gray Matter in Antisocial Personality Disorder." *Biological Psychiatry* 63 (Supplement): 148s–149s.

Rapley, Ralph, and David Whitehouse. 2007. *Molecular Forensics.* Hoboken, NJ: Wiley.

Rhee, Soo H., and Irwin D. Waldman. 2002. "Genetic and Environmental Influences on Antisocial Behavior: A Meta-Analysis of Twin and Adoption Studies." *Psychological Bulletin* 128: 490–529.

Robins, Lee N. 1978. "Sturdy Childhood Predictors of Antisocial Behavior: Replications from Longitudinal Studies." *Psychological Medicine* 8: 611–622.

Royal, Charmaine D. M., and Georgia M. Dunston. 2004. "Changing the Paradigm from 'Race' to Human Genome Variation." *Nature Genetics* 36: 5–7.

Rutter, Michael. 2006. *Genes and Behavior: Nature-Nurture Interplay Explained.* Malden, MA: Blackwell Publishing.

Sakai, Joseph T., Susan E. Young, Michael C. Stallings, David Timberlake, Andrew Smolen, Gary L. Stetler, and Thomas J. Crowley. 2007. "Case-control and Within-Family Tests for an Association Between Conduct Disorder and 5HTTLPR." *Journal of Medical Genetics*, Part B 141: 825–832.

Scott, Elizabeth S., and Laurence D. Steinberg. 2008. *Rethinking Juvenile Justice.* Cambridge: Harvard University Press.

Shepherd, Jonathan P., Iona Shepherd, Robert G. Newcombe, and David Farrington. 2009. "Impact of Antisocial Lifestyle on Health: Chronic Disability and Death by Middle Age." *Journal Public Health*, E-pub: 1–6.

Singh, Ilina, and Nikolas Rose. 2009. Biomarkers in psychiatry. *Nature* 460: 202–207.

Skranes, Jon, T. R. Vangberg, S. Kulseng, M. S. Indredavik, K. A. I. Evensen, M. Martinussen, A. M. Dale, O. Haraldseth, and A.-M. Brubakk. 2007. "Clinical Findings and White Matter Abnormalities Seen on Diffusion Tensor Imaging in Adolescents with Very Low Birth Weight." *Brain* 130: 654–666.

Spear, Linda P. 2007. The Developing Brain and Adolescent-Typical Behavior Patterns: An Evolutionary Approach." In *Adolescent Psychopathology and the*

Developing Brain: Integrating Brain and Prevention Science, eds. E. Walker and D. Romer, 9–30. New York: Oxford University Press.

Stadler, Christina, D. Grasmann, J. M. Fegert, M. Holtmann, F. Poustka, Klaus, and K. Schmeck. 2008. "Heart Rate and Treatment Effect in Children with Disruptive Behavior Disorders." *Child Psychiatry and Human Developement* 39: 299–309.

Stadler, Christina, Philipp Sterzer, Klaus Schmeck, Annette Krebs, Andreas Kleinschmidt, and Fritz Poustka. 2006. "Reduced Anterior Cingulate Activation in Aggressive Children and Adolescents during Affective Stimulation: Association with Temperament Traits." *Journal of Psychiatric Research* 41: 410–417.

Stallings, Michael C., Robin P. Corley, Briana Dennehey, John K. Hewitt, Kenneth S. Krauter, Jeffrey M. Lessem, Susan K. Milulich-Gilbertson, Soo H. Rhee, Andrew Smolen, Susan E. Young, and Thomas J. Crowley. 2005. "A Genome-Wide Search for Quantitative Trait Loci That Influence Antisocial Drug Dependence in Adolescence." *Archives of General Psychiatry* 62: 1042–1051.

Steinberg, Laurence D., and Jay Belsky. 1996. "A Sociobiological Perspective on Psychopathology in Adolescence." In *Rochester Symposium on Developmental Psychopathology*, eds. D. Cicchetti and S. Toth. Rochester: University of Rochester Press.

Sterzer, Philipp, Christina Stadler, Annette Krebs, Andreas Kleinschmidt, and Fritz Poustka. 2005. "Abnormal Neural Responses to Emotional Visual Stimuli in Adolescents with Conduct Disorder." *Biological Psychiatry* 57: 7–15.

Stoolmiller, Mike. 1999. "Implications of the Restricted Range of Family Environments for Estimates of Heritability and Nonshared Environment in Behavior-Genetic Adoption Studies." *Psychological Bulletin* 125: 392–409.

Stuss, Dondald T., and D. Frank Benson. 1986. *The Frontal Lobes*. New York: Raven Press.

Susman, Elizabeth J. 2006. "Psychobiology of Persistent Antisocial Behavior: Stress, Early Vulnerabilities and the Attenuation Hypothesis." *Neuroscience and Biobehavioral Reviews* 30: 376–389.

Taylor, Alan, and Julia Kim-Cohen. 2007. "Meta-analysis of Gene-Environment Interactions in Developmental Psychopathology." *Development & Psychopathology* 19: 1029–1037.

Taylor, Jeanette, William G. Iacono, and Matt McGue. 2000. "Evidence for a Genetic Etiology for Early-Onset Delinquency." *Journal of Abnormal Psychology* 109: 634–643.

Thapar, Anita, Kate Langley, Tom Fowler, Frances Rice, Darko Turic, Naureen Whittinger, John Aggleton, Marianne Ven den Bree, Michael J. Owen, and Michael O'Donovan. 2005. "Catechol O-methyltransferase Gene Variant and Birth Weight Predict Early-Onset Antisocial Behavior in Children with Attention-Deficit/Hyperactivity Disorder." *Archives of General Psychiatry* 62: 1275–1278.

Van Goozen, Stephanie H. M., Graeme Fairchild, Heddeke Snoek, and Gordon T. Harold. 2007. "The Evidence for a Neurobiological Model of Childhood Antisocial Behavior." *Psychological Bulletin* 133: 149–182.

van Goozen, Stephanie H. M., Graeme Fairchild, and Gordon T. Harold. 2008. "The Role of Neurobiological Deficits in Childhood Antisocial Behavior." *Current Directions in Psychological Science* 17: 224–228.

Viding, Essi, Alice P. Jones, Paul J. Frick, Terrie E. Moffitt, and Robert Plomin. 2008. "Heritability of Antisocial Behaviour At 9: Do Callous-Unemotional Traits Matter?" *Developmental Science* 11: 17–22.

Widom, Cathy S., and Linda M. Brzustowicz. 2006. "*MAOA* and the "Cycle of Violence:" Childhood Abuse and Neglect, *MAOA* Genotype, and Risk for Violent and Antisocial Behavior." *Biological Psychiatry* 60: 684–689.

Yang, Yaling, A. L. Glenn, and Adrian Raine. 2008. "Brain Abnormalities in Antisocial Individuals: Implications for the Law." *Behavioral Sciences & the Law* 26: 65–83.

Yang, Yaling, Adrian Raine, K. L. Narr, Patrick Colletti, and A. Toga. (2009a) "Localization of Deformations within the Amygdala in Psychopaths." *Archives of General Psychiatry*, 66, 986-994. DONE

Yang, Yaling, Adrian Raine, K. L. Narr, Patrick Colletti, and A. Toga. (2009b). "Abnormal Temporal and Prefrontal Cortical Gray Matter Thinning in Psychopaths." *Molecular Psychiatry*, 14, 561–562.DONE

Zuckerman, Marvin. 2005. *Psychobiology of Personality.* New York: Cambridge University Press.

Notes

1. We understand that many social scientists may not be fully acquainted with the biological science in this chapter. To help readers, we offer here several web sites that provide some helpful background information. This web site orients readers to the parts of the brain: http://www.med.harvard.edu/AANLIB/cases/caseM/case.html. This web site is designed to teach human genetics to social science students: http://psych.colorado.edu/carey/hgss/. A catalog of human genes, describing their function and links to medical diseases and behaviors can be found at this address: http://www.ncbi.nlm.nih.gov/omim/. And these web sites contain useful information about genetics: http://www.thetech.org/genetics/ and http://learn.genetics.utah.edu/.

Chapter 4

Juvenile Crime and Juvenile Justice

Peter W. Greenwood, Susan Turner

No matter what the theory, no matter how hard we try, we come back to a few facts. The primary risk factors now known to be associated with criminal behavior, particularly serious criminal behavior, are all primarily in play during the years when the youth and his parents would fall under the jurisdiction of the juvenile or family court.

We now have scientific proof for the efficacy of a number of "brand name" family therapies as compared to treatment as usual, whether that be diversion, probation, or residential placement. A number of states have now demonstrated that investments in certain proven programs pay for themselves many times over, mostly by reducing the need for further incarceration.

After some introductory information about the patterns of juvenile crime, this chapter will primarily be a story about how well this nation's juvenile courts are grappling with this new information, and how much further they have to go. Our discussion can be summarized as follows:

- Although there are a variety of ways to measure juvenile crime, each is limited in its ability to measure juvenile crime accurately and consistently; juvenile arrests, however, are currently at a 40-year low.
- Originally conceived of as *parens patriae*, the juvenile court has evolved during the past decade of its existence into one that more closely resembles the adult justice system, with a focus on increasing punitiveness;
- Four current major themes in juvenile justice are (1) revising the criteria under which juveniles can be waived to criminal courts; (2) assessing and serving the mental health needs of juvenile offenders; (3) increasing the use of evidence-based programs; and (4) estimating the benefits of improved outcomes that are possible with evidence-based programs.
- In recent years, a number of carefully designed and rigorously tested program models have proven their ability to produce strong positive impacts on youth behavior in a variety of organizational settings, and pay for themselves in cost savings.

- The program list in this chapter can be used to train local agencies in which evidence-based programs are best suited to their local jurisdictional population needs. Effective programs include prevention (e.g., Nurse Family Partnerships, Bullying Prevention Programs, Life Skills Training), community (Multisystemtic Therapy, Functional Family Therapy) and institutional settings (Cognitive Behavioral Therapy, Aggression Replacement Training, and Family Integrated Transition).
- Funding agencies should develop the capability to hold all service providers accountable for delivering the services and outcomes they promised.

TRENDS IN JUVENILE CRIME

In the early 1990s you could not pick up a paper without finding a story about juvenile crime. Homicide and gun possession by juveniles were on the rise. From the coverage provided by the news media, one could get the strong impression that juveniles had come to represent an increasing threat of criminal violence in many communities. Not only were juveniles perceived as committing more violence, but the popular media also conveyed the impression that their violence was becoming more cal-loused and gratuitous. Many juvenile killings appeared to take place without any rational cause or purpose. Stories about juveniles killing helpless old ladies or innocent bystanders became a common feature in most urban newspapers. It was this latter characteristic of hardened malice that caused many to question the concept of protecting and rehabilitating youth upon which the juvenile justice system had historically been based. In the decade that followed, many states made it easier for prosecutors to file charges against serious juvenile offenders in adult court, and the number of youth sentenced to serve time in adult prisons grew dramatically. During this period, a number of researchers, usually with funding from the National Institute of Mental Health (NIMH) or the National Institutes of Health (NIH), began to develop and test treatment protocols that have proven to be far more cost-effective than the traditional programs offered by the juvenile system in the past. It is the reported outcomes from such programs that have led many to call for the greater use of evidence-based programming in working with juveniles.

In 2009 the number of juveniles arrested for serious crimes and the number of juveniles in custody is at an all-time low. While states are attempting to deal with the financial problems caused in part by their spending on prison construction in the 1990s, they are also attempting to find funding for the training and technical assistance that implementation of evidence-based programs require. In this chapter we will review these trends and attempt to predict where juvenile justice is headed.

Sources of Information on Juvenile Crime Trends

While many media reports may give the impression that both the amount and seriousness of juvenile crime are on the rise, we have only the most rudimentary of measures to tell whether or not this is the case. The most widely cited measure of crime, the FBI's *Uniform Crime Reports* (UCR), tells us nothing about the level of juvenile crime because it contains no information about the characteristics of offenders. The only indirect sources of information on juvenile crime rates are arrest rates and surveys of victims or high-risk youth.

Arrest rates are probably the best measure for monitoring nationwide trends in juvenile offending, although these data also reflect the shifting priorities of both the public and the police. If the public's consciousness about certain types of crime is raised, as it has been recently for so-called date rapes and child abuse, then the likelihood that any particular offense of that nature will be reported is likely to increase. On the other hand, if police resources become so strained in dealing with violent crimes or drug selling that they are unable to engage in preventive patrol or respond to calls about suspicious groups of youth, then the number of youth arrested for minor types of property crimes and antisocial behavior will probably decline, even though the number of crimes has not changed.

Victim surveys are not very useful for tracking juvenile crimes because they rely on victims' perceptions of whether offenders are over or under 18 years of age. These perceptions are often not very reliable; furthermore, victims can give age estimates only for those crimes where their assailant is seen (not for most property crimes).

Self-reporting surveys of youth, in theory, could provide a valuable means of assessing changes in delinquent behavior over time, if they were implemented in a systematic fashion. However, the self-reporting surveys that have been conducted to date are so varied in their methods and their geographic and age group focus, they provide little basis for estimating changes in prevalence and offending rates between age cohorts (Menard and Elliott 1993).

Age-Specific Arrest Rates and Crimes Attributable to Juveniles

Although crime is still a young man's game, with arrest rates peaking in the mid-to-late teens, there are considerably fewer young men around now than there were just a few decades ago. Between 1980 and 2005, the total U.S. population increased by 30.8 percent, while the number of juveniles between the ages of 10 and 17 increased by only 9.9 percent. The figures in table 4.1 show how the juvenile population and the fraction of arrests they accounted for declined over the past two decades. In 1980, as shown in table 4.1, juveniles between the ages of 10 and 17 represented 14 percent of the total U.S. population but accounted for 41 percent of all arrests for property crimes (burglary, larceny-theft, auto theft, arson) included in the FBI's *Uniform Crime Reports*[A] and 22 percent of all arrests for the four violent crimes (murder, rape, aggravated assault, robbery) included in the UCR Part I index. By 1990, this age group had shrunk to just 11 percent of the total population, where it remained for 15 years, and in 2005 accounted for only 26 percent of all index property crime arrests and just 16 percent of all index violent crime arrests.

During the late 1980s and early 1990s, the rate of juvenile involvement in violent crime, particularly homicide and assault, increased significantly, accounting for 19 percent of all arrests for Part 1 *Index* violent crimes in 1995. But since 2000, the fraction of violent crime attributable to juveniles had dropped back to the low percentage of the previous decade. Clearly, over the decades, juveniles accounted for a disproportionate but diminishing share of arrests for serious felonies. Furthermore, since juveniles are more likely than adults to commit their crimes in groups, they probably account for an even smaller percentage of actual offenses than they do arrests.

However, the declining proportion of juveniles within the general population hides some very significant changes in their rates of arrest, defined as the number of juveniles arrested divided by their number within the general population. These data are presented in table 4.2, with the arrests stated in terms of arrests per 100,000 juveniles aged 10–17. Between 1980 and 1985, while the arrest rate for adults (for all index felonies) was decreasing by 3 percent, the arrest rate for juveniles fell by 14 percent—more than 4 times as rapidly. Then, between 1985 and 1990, while the adult arrest rate for *Index* crimes increased by 15 percent, the juvenile *Index* arrest rate increased by only 9 percent. Crime rates have fallen dramatically for both youth and adults since the early 1990s. Within this downward trend, the adult arrest rate has dropped almost 30 percent from 1995 to 2005, as the youth rate has decreased almost 50 percent.

Unfortunately, more of the decline in juvenile arrest rates is accounted for by property offenses than by violent offenses. By 1990 the juvenile arrest rate for violent offenses had climbed back up to its 1980 rate, while the arrest rate for property offenses was about 6 percent lower. The same story is found in trends in juvenile arrest rates for homicide. In 1980 they accounted for just 10 percent of all arrests for homicide, but by 1990 they produced 13.6 percent of all homicide arrests. Since 2000 the percent of arrests for homicide accounted for by juveniles has ranged between about 9 and 10 percent. Thankfully, as is shown in table 4.2, in the last decade

Table 4.1. Percentage of Total Population and Index Felony Arrests Accounted for by Juveniles Aged 10–17

YEAR	1980	1985	1990	1995	2000	2005
Percent of Total U.S. Population	14%	12%	11%	11%	12%	11%
Percent Violent Index Felonies	22%	17%	16%	19%	16%	16%
Percent Property Index Felonies	41%	34%	32%	35%	32%	26%

Table 4.2. Arrest Rates for Juveniles Aged 10–17 (per 100,000 youth)*

YEAR	1980	1985	1990	1995	2000	2005
Index Violent Felonies	394	334	393	516	303	283
Index Property Felonies	2,887	2,491	2,689	2,458	1,591	1,243
Index Felonies	3,281	2,825	3,082	3,026	1,894	1,526

* Note: Only some jurisdictions, covering about half of the total U.S. population, report their arrests to the FBI broken down by age. In calculating age-specific arrest rates from these figures, it has been assumed that the age distribution in those jurisdictions reporting is the same as that for the country as a whole.

and a half, arrest rates for juveniles had declined sharply, in both the violent and property categories. Arrest rates for juveniles in 2005 were at their lowest point in over 40 years.

Possible Explanations for Trends in Juvenile Violence

The decreasing juvenile arrest rates for all types of crime, from 1980 through 1985, and then the sharp reversal and increases in arrests for violence through 1993, were mirrored by cohorts of slightly older young adults over the same time period. For both age groups, a number of analyses have shown that the increases in arrest rates were attributable to armed as opposed to unarmed crimes and disproportionately involved minority youth in large cities (Cook and Laub 1998).

Many have attributed the sharp rise in juvenile and young adult armed homicides of the latter 1980s to the introduction of crack cocaine in the mid-1980s, the disorganized street markets through which it was sold, and the recruitment of young minority males to do most of the street-level selling. They argue that increased involvement in dangerous street-level drug markets led many of these youth to arm themselves, initially for protection, which in turn led many of their peers to also engage in defensive arming. The end result of this process, particularly in large cities, was much more gun carrying and use by a population not noted for their dispute-resolution or decision-making skills (Blumstein and Rosenfeld 1998). Although the initial motive for most of these youths in carrying guns was to defend themselves, the end result was a much higher rate of homicide and aggravated assault among this population. The shift downward in juvenile violence more recently mirrors the more general shift observed for the country as a whole. There have been a number of competing claims for the overall reduction, including the role of incarceration, policing, economic opportunity, demography, and so on (Blumstein and Wallman 2006). For juveniles, reduced violence may also reflect reduced opportunities for entering the drug trade (and subsequent exposure to violence), and perhaps an attitude change among youth to reject the drug and violence lifestyle (Johnson, Golub, and Dunlap 2006). In addition, the response to juvenile offenders has become more nuanced and smarter in the last 15 or so years. The use of evidence-based programs and investment in front-end prevention programs may also have an impact. At this time, it is not clear whether the decline in juvenile arrest rates reflects a shift in cultural norms, changes in law enforcement policy, or the effects of public programs.

Juveniles are not only perpetrators of crime, they are often victims as well. The annual risk of victimization by violent crime peaks at age 16 to 19 for both sexes, and declines substantially with age thereafter (Reiss and Roth 1993). In 2006, there were 5,958 murder victims aged 10 to 24 (Centers for Disease Control and Prevention 2006). In 2007, 1,760 children under age 17 died from abuse and neglect. U.S. state and local child protective services found an estimated 794,000 children as victims of abuse or neglect, out of more than 3.2 million reports of children being neglected or abused in that same year (U.S. Department of Health and Human Services 2009). Similar to crime rates, these numbers have shown decreases over the past years. Physical abuse reports started declining in the mid-1990s, with a large decline between 1997 and 2000. From 1992 through 2004, they declined by 43 percent (Finkelhor and Jones 2006). While such statistics may be comforting, the juvenile justice system is being called upon to handle increasing numbers and severity of juvenile offenders with mental health problems, as the mental health programs in communities and schools are cut (*New York Times*, August 10, 2009).

THE JUVENILE JUSTICE SYSTEM

The juvenile court was founded at the start of the twentieth century as a specialized institution for dealing with dependent, neglected, and delinquent minors. At that time, American cities were being flooded by poor immigrants from Europe, whose values, behavior, and child-rearing practices were alien and frightening to traditionalists but represented a challenge to those who took the lead in developing the new court.

The original guiding principle of the juvenile court was *parens patriae*, a medieval English doctrine that allowed the Crown to supplant natural family relations whenever a child's welfare was at stake—in other words, to become a substitute parent. The procedures of the court were purposefully informal and its intentions were presumed to be benign. Fact-finding focused on the minor's underlying problems and special needs rather than the specific acts that brought him or her before the court. Dispositions were intended to reflect the "best interests" of the child, which were assumed to be the same as the public's interest.

The new court represented one aspect of a broad progressive movement to accommodate urban institutions to an increasingly industrial and immigrant population and to incorporate recent discoveries in the behavioral, social, and medical sciences into the rearing of children. The juvenile court was also part of another philosophical movement that has been termed "the

revolt against formalism." The new juvenile procedures reflected the ultimate pragmatic philosophy—"It's all right if it works" (Empey 1979).

In juvenile court, children were not charged with specific crimes. The
central language of the criminal law——accusation, proof, guilt, punishment——was dropped in favor of terms reflecting the social worker's
vocabulary——needs, treatment, protection, guidance, and so on. It did
not matter whether a child came into the court because of neglect or an
act of delinquency. In all cases, the court's intervention, guidance, and
supervision were presumed to be required and benevolent.

Juvenile courts have come a long way over the course of the last
century. Social scientists and juvenile advocates have demonstrated that
the "benign" intentions of the court can be just as punitive and onerous as
the sanctions inflicted by the criminal courts, often for much less serious
behavior. From an early stance of complete informality, juveniles have
now been accorded most of the procedural protections available to adults,
at least in theory if not always in practice—the two primary exceptions
being the right to a jury trial and bail.

In spite of these reforms, or perhaps encouraged by them, juvenile law
activists continue to advocate further expansion of procedural protections,
the current objective being the right to a jury trial. In somewhat the same
vein, there is a youth advocacy lobby that argues for reducing the amount
of juvenile court intervention in delinquents' lives. Diversion, deinstitutionalization, and community treatment are the current battle cries of this
group, which argues that formal sanctions and institutionalized treatment
only aggravate delinquent tendencies, and that youth are better served by
returning them to their own communities. In the 1990s, this group added
fiscal retrenchment as another reason for reducing the use of training
schools and detention centers (Schwartz and Van Vleet 1992).

No matter from what perspective you approach it, the juvenile court is an
easier target to criticize than to reform. Juvenile justice continues to remain
a troublesome public policy issue because of the competing social objectives
it involves, because our basic knowledge about how to reform troublesome
youths is so deficient, and because we have 50 different state systems, many
of which differ considerably from county to county. Other obstacles to
change include: (1) the system's heavy reliance on informal discretionary
decision-making; (2) the confidentiality that often protects its case records
from outside scrutiny and the lack of quantitative data on its operations;
(3) the unfamiliarity of most state legislators with actual juvenile court
practices and policies; and (4) a shortage of community-based programs
and services to deal with the problems of delinquency-prone youths.

The Operation of the Juvenile Court

In most states, the dividing line between the juvenile and adult systems is the
18th birthday, although a few use the 17th, 16th, or 19th birth date for this
purpose. Crimes committed before the designated birthday fall within the

jurisdiction of juvenile courts. Crimes committed after it are subject to criminal penalties and procedures. Almost all states provide for some procedure by which cases involving serious felonies (homicide, rape, aggravated assault, etc.) and older juveniles (typically 16- and 17-year-olds) can be transferred to adult criminal courts. In some jurisdictions, motions for such transfers can be initiated by the prosecutor. In others, they have been made presumptive, with juveniles so waived retaining the right to "fitness hearings" at which their attorney can argue why such a transfer should not be made.

Originally, four basic characteristics distinguished the juvenile court system from the criminal courts: (1) informality in procedures and decorum; (2) a separate detention center for juveniles; (3) contributory delinquency statutes that encouraged the judge to punish adults, primarily parents, who actively contributed to the delinquency of juveniles; and (4) probation.

Today these distinguishing features are considerably blurred. The informality is largely gone. In many jurisdictions, juveniles sit through proceedings with their counsel just like any adult defendant in criminal court, unless they have waived that right. Unfortunately, there are jurisdictions in which juveniles routinely waive that right without ever consulting with a lawyer or any other supportive adult (Feld 1989). Recent research into adolescent brain development has shown that juveniles tend to ignore long-term outcomes much more than adults and are poor decision makers when under stress (Scott and Steinberg 2008). Thus many juveniles waive their right to confer with an attorney and are much more likely to plead guilty to something they did not do. Juvenile hearings proceed along much the same lines as criminal trials. The rules of evidence and rights of the parties are about the same, except that juveniles in most states still do not have the right to a jury trial or to bail. Parents are no longer held accountable for the delinquency of their children, and in most states cannot even be compelled to participate in delinquency proceedings. Even the liability of parents for the acts of their children in civil tort litigation has been severely restricted by statute.

The separate detention centers remain. Separateness, in fact, is now the principal distinguishing characteristic of the juvenile system: separate detention, separate records, separate probation officers, separate judges, even separate funding agencies for program development and research.

And finally, probation has seeped over into the adult court. The distinguishing feature about probation in the juvenile court is its role in screening arrests made by the police. Originally, the prosecutor had no role in a juvenile hearing. A delinquency case was completely handled by a probation officer. Then, as the appellate courts became more demanding about due process considerations in juvenile proceedings and granted juveniles the right to counsel, prosecutors were brought into the process to represent the interests of the state. In most states, probation still screens all juvenile arrests and decides in which ones the prosecutor should be asked to file a petition. However, several states have eliminated this function (Washington is one) and many prosecutors would like to see it discarded completely.

Current Criticisms

In most states, interest in the juvenile justice system, on the part of elected officials and the public, is highly sporadic, usually prompted by various media-supported perceptions: that the juvenile crime rate is getting out of hand, or that serious juvenile offenders are being coddled by a system designed to serve truants and runaways, or that the system is mistreating juveniles in its custody.

Some criticisms ignore basic differences in the character of juvenile and adult crimes. Victimization data indicate that within any given crime category, crimes committed by juveniles tend to be less serious than those committed by adults. For instance, juveniles involved in robberies are less likely to be armed with a gun or to seriously injure their victims (Greenwood et al. 1983). The property losses from crimes committed by juveniles are also likely to be less than in those committed by adults. And, as we have mentioned before, juvenile crimes are more likely to involve multiple offenders than crimes by adults. A comparison of average disposition patterns between juvenile and adult criminal courts ignores the fact that the juvenile court must dispose of a much higher percentage of less serious cases, involving either minor offenses or real first-time offenders. A study that compared case outcomes between samples of older juveniles and young adults revealed that when aggravating factors were present (lengthy prior record, gun use, violent prior, etc.), juveniles were just as likely to be convicted and sentenced to state time as the young adults (Greenwood 1986).

According to the Office of Juvenile Justice and Delinquency Prevention, the number of delinquency cases has remained about the same—about 1.7 million—between 2000 and 2005; however, this period was preceded by a growth between 1985 and 1997 of over 60 percent. In 2005, the juvenile court processed almost 50 percent more cases than it did in 1985 (Sickmund 2009). The trends in offenses have changed over the last two decades, with overall increases between 1985 and 2005 in drug, crimes against persons, and public disorder crimes; contrasted with a drop in property crimes of 15 percent from 1985 to 2005. In more than half of the cases processed in 2005, a petition was filed and the case was formally handled by the system; the other half were either dismissed or handled informally. The proportion of cases handled informally rose from 46 percent in 1985 to 58 percent in the late 1990s and then fell slightly to 56 percent i2005. The vast majority of cases are not detained (79 percent in 2005) during their court processing; just over 20 percent are ordered to residential placement as their most severe outcome.

Recent Reforms

The big stories in many jurisdictions at the current time are the reduction in the use of out-of-home placements, the increased use of evidence-based interventions in the community, and the increasing per capita cost for those state training schools that still remain open.

Aside from the more general calls for increasing toughness or abolishing specialized juvenile courts altogether, the four areas of potential reform that are currently receiving the most attention are: (1) revising the criteria under which juveniles can be waived to criminal courts; (2) paying more attention to assessing and serving the mental health needs of juvenile offenders; (3) increasing the use of evidence-based programs; (4) and estimating the benefits of improved outcomes that are possible with evidence-based programs.

Waiver Criteria

In only two states (NC and NY) does the jurisdiction of the juvenile court end after the age of 15, with all 16-year-old offenders handled in criminal court. In 10 (GA, IL, LA, MA, MI, MS, NH, SC, TX, and WI) juvenile court jurisdiction applies through the 17th birthday, and in the remaining states and the District of Columbia the jurisdiction of the juvenile court ends on the 18th birthday (Griffin, Torbet, and Szymanski 1998). Connecticut was the most recent state to join the latter group, raising the age limit for juveniles from the 16th to the 18th birthday in 2008.

Yet all these states have procedures for waiving the juvenile court's jurisdiction over a serious case and transferring the matter into regular criminal courts, and many have expanded the basis for waiver in recent years, primarily by increasing the list of offenses for which waiver applies and/or lowering the age at which juveniles are eligible (Torbet and Szymanski 1998). The criteria vary from specific offense categories and age ranges to general criteria. The primary mechanisms for transferring jurisdiction from juvenile to criminal courts are judicial waiver, direct filing by prosecutors (with minimal judicial review), and statutory exclusion. In some states, the so called "fitness" or "waiver" hearings are held in juvenile court. In others, fitness hearings for juveniles who meet specified criteria are held in criminal courts, to determine in which court the proceedings should take place.

Many states are now considering a variety of proposals intended to increase the number of youth waived to the criminal courts. Colorado legislators recently passed a law that provides for 14- to 17-year-olds charged with certain violent felonies to be tried as adults, and if convicted, to serve their time in new intermediate prisons. California voters recently passed a ballot proposition that reduced the minimum age for waiver from the 16th to the 14th birthday.

The use of judicial waivers has been tracked for a number of years and was relatively constant from 1985 through 1988 with around 8,000 waivers per year, rose sharply through 1994 to a peak of approximately 12,000, and fell back to the levels of the mid-1980s by the early 2000s. It has remained at about 7,000 per year since 2001 (Sickmund 2009; Brown and Langan 1998). Analyses of waiver cases consistently show that the primary considerations in waiving a case are current offense seriousness, prior record, and the youth's current age. Studies that have looked at the impact of waiver on sanctions have found mixed results, with some finding waiver resulting in more incarceration and others not (Fagan 1995; Brown and Langan 1998). Studies of the impacts of waiver on juveniles have generally found higher recidivism rates among those waived (Fagan 1995; Redding 2008; MacArthur Research Foundation n.d.) In addition, a recent review of the evidence suggests that current laws do not have general deterrence effects (Redding 2009). A recent repeal of mandatory waivers of juveniles accused of drug crimes in Illinois showed no increase in juvenile court petitions or judicial waivers to adult court, consistent with no adverse effect on public safety (Kooy 2008).

Sentencing Structure

A number of states have reduced the dispositional discretion of juvenile court judges by moving to offense-based sentencing involving guidelines, blended sentences, mandatory minimum sentences, and extended jurisdiction. Blended sentences allow the imposition of combined juvenile and adult correctional sanctions being served in sequence. Extended jurisdiction allows a judge to commit a juvenile to the state's juvenile correctional system beyond the age of the court's jurisdiction for hearing cases. In California, Oregon, and Wisconsin the extended age is 25, and in Colorado, Connecticut, Hawaii, and New Mexico it extends to the full term of commitment, regardless of age.

Decreasing Free Rides and Increasing Accountability

As noted earlier, about half of all juvenile arrests are handled informally. For the majority of juvenile offenders who do not repeat after one or two arrests, station house adjustment and informal diversion appear to be wise and prudent actions. For the small percentage who do repeat, time and time again, this lenience appears to be seriously misguided. Simple common sense would suggest that repeated diversions lead determined offenders to believe that they will not be punished.

Some jurisdictions have responded to these concerns by attempting to develop and impose a sequence of sanctions that will ensure that no offenders get off with just a free ride. The state of Washington provides an example of how a state can modify its juvenile laws to bring more accountability to juvenile proceedings, and to more explicitly balance the competing interests of public protection and reformation of juvenile offenders. The 1977 revision, which was sponsored by the King County prosecutor, was designed to provide greater due process protection to juveniles and more protection to the community against serious juvenile crime. One key aspect of the revised law is a presumptive sentencing framework that ties dispositions to the seriousness of the current offense and the juvenile's prior criminal history.

The Washington juvenile law eliminates the role of probation officers in screening petitions and places filing decisions completely in the hands of the prosecutor. Legally sufficient cases must be either filed or diverted, a decision that is based on the seriousness of the current offense and prior record. A diversion agreement involves a written contract between the juvenile and diversionary unit whereby the juvenile agrees to fulfill certain conditions in lieu of prosecution. In theory, these conditions are supposed to be the same as would be imposed following conviction. The primary advantage of diversion to the juvenile is the avoidance of a formal conviction record. However, if the juvenile is subsequently charged with another offense, prior diversions can be counted as part of his or her prior record.

The code's sentencing scheme is semi-determinate or presumptive in nature. It is based on the concept that accountability for an offense should be determined primarily by the seriousness of the offense, the age of the offender, the offender's prior criminal history, and the recentness of that history (Greenwood at al. 1983).

Restorative justice is another strategy that communities are adopting to increase the accountability of first-time or low-level delinquents, victim reparation, and community healing. Restorative justice programs are well established in Australia, New Zealand, and more than 300 communities in the United States. These programs usually involve some form of community sentencing or accountability board and victim-offender mediation (Braithwaite 1998).

Reducing the Confidentiality of Juvenile Proceedings

Juvenile court records were traditionally sealed and offenders' names kept out of the papers in the belief that this confidentiality was required to enhance the court's efforts to identify the antecedents of each juvenile's problems, and that disclosure of the juvenile record might unfairly penalize defendants for their youthful indiscretions. However, along with increasing concerns about juvenile crime came concerns about protecting the public from youthful predators and holding the juvenile court more accountable for punishing youth. A number of states have now relaxed their restriction on what can be reported about juvenile cases in the press, and most states have some procedure for insuring that criminal courts and prosecutors have access to juvenile records, at least for some specified period, lasting for several years after the youth becomes an adult. As of the end of 1997, 30 states permitted or required open juvenile court hearings in cases involving serious offenses or repeat offenders (Torbet and Szymanski 1998). More recent statistics indicate that 14 states allow access to all hearings; another 21 to certain types of hearings (Snyder and Sickmund 2006). A number of states require notification of a juvenile's school when the youth is found guilty of particular offenses.

Finally, while the "get tough on juveniles" efforts get most of the press, a group of individuals and organizations continue to work for what were the original goals of the federal Office of Juvenile Justice and Delinquency Prevention (OJJDP): reducing or eliminating the use of large training schools; removing juveniles from adult jails and police lockups; reducing the use of detention through improved screening for risk; and increasing the number and variety of community-based alternatives. With the assistance of these individuals and organizations, a number of states and local jurisdictions have revamped their juvenile justice systems, reducing the use of "unnecessary" confinement and increasing the variety of community-based options. Utah, Pennsylvania, Oklahoma, Florida, Alabama, and Maryland have been among the leaders in instituting such reforms.

Types of Programs and Facilities

Since the disposition of juvenile cases in most states is still supposed to be tailored to the individual needs and circumstances of each juvenile, it should come as no surprise that a wide variety of programs have been developed to meet these needs. For those juveniles whose crimes or records are not very serious, and whose family is sufficiently supportive that the youth can continue to reside in their home, there are a variety of programs, such as informal or formal probation, intensive supervision, tracking and in-home supervision by private agencies, mentoring programs, after-school or all-day programs in which a youth reports to the program site for part of the day and then returns home, and community service. For those youth who must be placed out of their homes but do not represent such a risk that they must be removed from the community, many jurisdictions provide or contract for a wide variety of group homes, foster care, and other community living situations. Placements in such facilities are typically in the range of 6 to 24 months, depending on the program and seriousness of the youth's offense. For those youth who represent a more serious risk to the community, or who cannot function appropriately in an open setting, most states provide a continuum of increasingly restrictive settings ranging from isolated wilderness camps and ranches to very securely fenced and locked facilities.

The primary criticisms leveled against traditional training schools have been that they offered sterile and unimaginative programs, were inappropriate places to run rehabilitative programs, and that they fostered abuse and mistreatment of their charges (Bartollas, Miller, and Dinitz 1976; Feld 1977). At this point, the debate still goes on. A number of comparisons that set out to demonstrate that small community-based programs were more effective than traditional training schools failed to do so (Coates et al. 1979; Empey and Lubeck 1971; Greenwood and Turner 1993). Yet, several recent meta-analyses purport to demonstrate that particular types of treatment programs, primarily those employing cognitive/behavioral techniques, are more effective when run in community rather than institutional settings (Lipsey 1991).

Many states have used these results as the basis for shifting more of their youth to privately run, community-based programs; however, the vast majority of youth in custody (69 percent) are still housed in large public facilities. From 2002 to 2004, the number of youth in residential placements fell 7 percent nationally. Residential treatment centers and group homes (primarily privately run) outnumber other types of facilities, but they are smaller and house fewer youth (Livsey, Sickmund, and Sladky 2009).

It is difficult to tell whether the shift to community programs has resulted in less abuse or mistreatment of confined youth because of major efforts to cut down on mistreatment of youth in all types of programs that were underway at the same time as the deinstitutionalization movement began to have its effects. What is clear is that community programs appear to offer a much wider variety of settings and methods. Part of the reason for this difference may be due to the fact that community-based programs are more likely to be run by private (usually nonprofit) providers, rather than the county or state. In some states (Massachusetts, Pennsylvania, Maryland, and Florida), the private sector also runs a variety of secure programs for even the most serious youth. In addition to offering a greater variety in programming, surveys show that privately run programs offer more treatment services, compared to publicly run programs, and are less likely to be overcrowded (Thornberry et al. 1989).

THE CASE FOR EARLY TARGETED PREVENTION

A common piece of wisdom holds that "an ounce of prevention is worth a pound of cure." Yet in most states the current pattern of funding for juvenile justice activities concentrates most of the available resources on secure residential placements for the most serious and chronic juvenile offenders. Even though some states and the federal government are beginning to increase their funding of delinquency prevention programs, only a small fraction of the at-risk children who could benefit from such programs actually receive them.

Ten years ago the greatest impediment to the funding of delinquency prevention programs was the lack of well-tested models to serve different types of youth. However, in recent years a number of carefully designed and rigorously tested program models have proven their ability to produce strong positive impacts on youth behavior in a variety of organizational settings. Furthermore, cost-benefit studies of these programs have shown that many can virtually pay for themselves by way of the savings they produce in future law enforcement and correctional costs avoided.

In the early 2000s the greatest impediment most communities faced in attempting to build a network of effective delinquency and violence prevention programs was the reluctance of local funding agencies to adopt or to require private providers to adopt and faithfully replicate one or more of the models that have been proven effective. Now, after the cutbacks imposed in response to the 2008 recession, the problem is start-up funding. Almost everybody accepts the argument that has been successfully made in the states of Washington, Florida, Pennsylvania, New York, Connecticut, and others that wise investments in delinquency prevention programs for the proper youth can pay back large benefits in the form of reduced correctional spending (Greenwood 2006).

In the remainder of this section we will review the program models that have been shown to be most cost-effective in reducing delinquency and the organizational issues involved in getting these model programs implemented effectively.

Evidence-Based Practice in Juvenile Justice and Child Welfare

Juvenile courts are granted considerable procedural leeway and are provided with a variety of dispositional alternatives in the belief that these concessions allow them to be more effective in rehabilitating and protecting the youth who come before them. Therefore, one primary measure of the juvenile justice system is its effectiveness in protecting the youth who come before it and in decreasing the likelihood of their committing future crimes. In the past decade there has been significant progress in measuring the effectiveness of a wide a variety of programs and strategies for intervening with delinquent youth.

There are three ways to prove that a new program is more effective than customary treatment: (1) through one or more rigorous evaluations (clinical trials) of a specific model; (2) by proving that the program is a high-fidelity replication of a proven model; or (3) by demonstrating that the program fits a generic class of programs that have been found effective through meta-analysis.

Any of these three approaches can produce an evidence-based program. Anything less is just pretend. The scientific standards of proof for the kind of programs we deal with in this field are well established by such authorities as the U.S. Surgeon General, the Cochran and Campbell Collaborations (which are international groups established to systematically review what works in medicine and the social sciences, respectively), and the U.S. Government Accounting Office (GAO).

The big question for many policymakers is to discover the effectiveness of various programs' effectiveness. If you wanted to see a list of all of the programs proven effective with older runaway or homeless girls or youth from very troubled families, would you know where to look? If someone asked you about the effectiveness of programs called I Can Problem Solve or PEACE PIPE, would you know where to look?

There are now dozens of web sites where one can find various lists of promising and proven programs for reducing delinquency, drug use, and violence among at-risk and delinquent youth. At one end of the spectrum are those sites that list every program for which there is a mere glimmer of hope. At the other end are those who have only identified a very few programs because either they are very strict in their evidentiary requirements or they move very slowly in conducting their reviews.

Help in Determining Program Effectiveness

For anyone in a position to decide which programs should be continued or enhanced, which should be scrapped, and which new programs should be adopted, the ultimate questions are what works and how well does it work? The answers to these questions now come in two distinctive categories. One is "generic," including a number of generalized strategies and methods that have been tried by various investigators in different settings. Parent training, preschool, cognitive behavioral therapy, and group therapy all fall into this category. The other category includes what some have called "brand name programs" (BNPs) such as Functional Family Therapy and Multisystemic Therapy. These are programs that have been developed by a single investigator or team over a number of years and proven through careful replications, supported by millions of dollars in federal grants. The generic methods are identified by meta-analysis and represent the efforts of independent investigators, each testing particular versions of the method. The brand name programs have met the criteria established by various review groups for identifying proven programs.

These two methods overlap in an interesting way. The best of the brand name programs represent an outstanding performer within a larger generic category. Functional Family Therapy (FFT) is a brand name program that has been shown to be highly cost effective in engaging and motivating parents, increasing their parenting skills, and reducing recidivism. The four experimental trials of FFT (shown in figure 4.1) represent about 10 percent of all family therapy program evaluations. Figure 4.1 contains a histogram, showing the number of family therapy evaluations demonstrating various effect sizes. Although a number of evaluations found negative effects, the average for all is well above zero. None of the four FFT evaluations found negative effects, and three are well toward the upper end of the distribution. Figure 4.1 indicates that family therapy works as a generalized approach and that FFT works even better, when done correctly. Similarly, the other brand name programs, on average, produce larger effect sizes than the average for the generic category of which they are a part.

The most recent reviews, meta-analyses, certified lists, and cost-benefit analyses provide a variety of perspectives and a wealth of information regarding what does and does not work in preventing delinquency. At the very top of the promising program pyramid is the small group of rigorously evaluated programs that have consistently demonstrated significant positive effects and have developed effective strategies for helping others

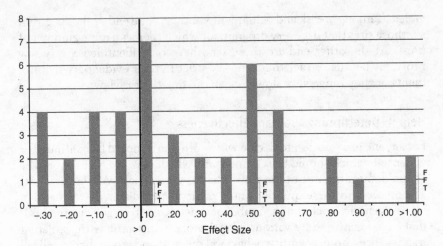

Figure 4.1 Family Therapy Effect Sizes with Functional Family Therapy Highlighted (N=43)
Source: Presentation by Mark Lipsey at meeting of the Association for the Advancement of Evidence-Based Practice, Cambridge, MD, November 2007.

to replicate their model and achieve similar results. At the bottom are the vast numbers of programs that have never been evaluated. In the middle are those for which there is some evidence to support their claims of effectiveness in at least one site.

Many of the interventions that have been shown to prevent the onset of or continued involvement in delinquency were first developed by researchers or academics outside the field of juvenile justice to deal with other problem behaviors such as child abuse, misbehavior in school, school failure, drug or alcohol abuse, or failure in foster-care placement. However, because all these targeted behaviors are closely related—and often antecedent to delinquency—programs developed to prevent them have also turned out to prevent delinquency as well.

The research is strongest and most promising for school- and community-based interventions that can be used before the demands of public safety require a residential placement. In this area a number of well-specified, proven, cost-effective programs have emerged. For youth in custodial settings there is less research to draw on, and what there is suffers from serious methodological problems. Still, some findings appear to hold up across various settings. In this section we review the evidence regarding specific programs, strategies, and principles provided by the most systematic and reliable review groups and reviewers. At this time they are:

- The Coalition for Evidence Based Policy is utilizing a review group of distinguished scientists to develop a list of effective programs whose evaluations meet the most rigorous standards. Their list is called Top Tier and is limited to brand name programs.

- The Center for the Study and Prevention of Violence at the University of Colorado in Boulder, under the leadership of Professor Delbert Elliot, has developed a systematic process (called Blueprints) for describing and evaluating prevention programs that target youth violence and substance abuse. For Blueprints to certify a program as proven, the program must: demonstrate its effects on problem behaviors with a rigorous experimental design; show that its effects persist after youth leave the program; and be successfully replicated in another site. The current Blueprints web site (www.colorado.educspvblueprints) lists 11 "model" programs and 20 "promising" programs. The design, research evidence, and implementation requirements for each model are available on the site. Promising programs have positive lasting results from one rigorous evaluation, but not a second. Compared to many other lists of recommended programs, both Top Tier and Blueprints are very strict in requiring strong evaluations, whereas many other lists contain programs for which there is no strong evaluation evidence, simply because they are interesting.
- Professor Mark Lipsey began utilizing meta-analysis to identify correlates or predictors of success in delinquency prevention programs in the early 1990s. Since that time he has published a number of articles identifying effective general (generic) intervention strategies and principles for applying them (Lipsey 2009; Lipsey and Cullen 2007).

The Washington State Institute for Public Policy (WSIPP) runs the best web site for checking out the estimated effectiveness of both brand name and generic models. A group led by Dr. Steve Aos conducts periodic reviews of program effectiveness in areas of interest to Washington's legislators. Those interests have included juvenile and criminal justice for a number of years now. For each of the program models that WSIPP reviews, whether brand name or generic, they use meta-analysis to estimate its likely effectiveness and cost-benefit analysis to estimate its likely costs and dollar benefits.

Although parts of the federal government (OMB) are adopting rigorous standards for evidence that they will consider, the federal agencies providing lists of programs that are supposed to be effective in preventing youth and gang violence have not applied such standards in putting together their lists. This lack of rigor has led to the listing of programs that are not supported by evidence meeting the most minimal standards.

A Comprehensive Rating System for Programs, Strategies, and Principles

Table 4.3 shows how information derived from the four sources listed above can be combined to provide the best possible estimates of costs and benefits for programs intended to prevent youth violence, delinquency, and substance abuse. The table is designed to provide all of the information that any local jurisdiction will need to develop its own sub-list of evidence based programs that it might support.

For purposes of categorizing the estimated impacts and strength of the evidence in support of a particular program or strategy, table 4.3 divides programs and strategies into five categories. From top to bottom they are:

Proven programs and strategies meet the three Blueprints qualifications for model programs or are found to be effective by rigorous meta-analysis.

Promising programs meet the Blueprints criteria for promising or their promise may be supported by one or more rigorous evaluations showing reductions in risk factors.

Principles are program features that have been found to be associated with more effective programs, no matter what their other characteristics.

Ineffective programs have been found to have no significant positive effects. DARE is of course the "poster program" for this category, with intensive supervision and aftercare coming in a close second and third.

The first thing one might want to know about any particular program is how it is rated by the various rating groups. If you found that it was unrated or rated ineffective, you might want to know about higher rank programs that serve the same type of youth. Both of the tasks are facilitated by the data in table 4.3.

For instance, if you were running or supporting a diversion program that provided social services to first-time offenders and you consulted table 4.3, you would see that Diversion with Services is listed as ineffective. If you looked over the programs rated as proven or preferred in table 4.3, you would discover that strategies such as Restorative Justice, Teen Court, or Family Counseling are more effective with the targeted youth than Diversion with Services, as it is usually practiced.

A Review of the Evidence

We begin this review by focusing on prevention efforts (i.e., those that aim to prevent delinquency from occurring in the first place), then discuss programs administered in the community that can be used to divert first-time offenders from deeper penetration into the justice system, as a condition of probation or parole, or to facilitate reentry for youth returning from an institutional placement, and we conclude with programs designed for the more serious youth offenders who are found in custodial settings.

All of the proven and promising programs described below are listed in table 4.3, along with the source of their rating, their effect on crime outcomes, the cost per youth, and the estimated government savings and victim benefits per youth treated.

Table 4.3. California Governor's Office of Gang and Youth Violence Policy Ranked List of Evidence-Based Crime and Violence Prevention and Intervention Practices (REVISED 9-8-09)

| PROVEN PROGRAMS | Programs in the PROVEN category are brand name programs that have been shown to reduce recidivism, substance use, and/or antisocial behavior in at least 2 trials, using strong research designs | | | | | | | Cost/Benefit Analysis (if available) | | |
| | Source of Rating | | | | | | | | | |
	Blueprints	WSIPP	Lipsey	CEBP	Description	Metric	Effect	Benefits	Costs	Benefit minus Cost
DELINQUENCY & RECIDIVISM										
Nurse Family Partnership	X	X		X	Prevention program administered by registered nurses to at-risk mothers in home	Reduction in recidivism for mothers; Reduction in recidivism for children	38.2%;15.7%	$27,092.00	$6,336	$20,756.00
Functional Family Therapy (FFT)	X	X			Intervention administered by therapist in-home focusing on family motivation, engagement & problem-solving	Reduction in recidivism	16.1%	$52,156	$2,380	$49,776.00
Multidimensional Treatment Foster Care (MTFC)	X	X		X	Intervention administered by specially trained foster parents taking teen into their home; therapy for bio-parents	Reduction in recidivism	17.3%	$95,879	$6,926	$88,953.00
Adolescent Diversion Project		X			Intervention program using mentors to provide resources & initiate behavior change	Reduction in recidivism	17.6%	$50,463	$1,975	$48,488.00

(continued)

Table 4.3. Continued

Programs in the PROVEN category are brand name programs that have been shown to reduce recidivism, substance use, and/or antisocial behavior in at least 2 trials, using strong research designs

PROVEN PROGRAMS	Source of Rating				Description	Metric	Effect	Cost/Benefit Analysis (if available)		
	Blueprints	WSIPP	Lipsey	CEBP				Benefits	Costs	Benefit minus Cost
Aggression Replacement Training (ART)		X			Intervention administered by trained staff to improve moral reasoning, aggression & anger management	Reduction in recidivism	8.3%	$23,933	$918	$23,015.00
Multisystemic Therapy (MST)	X	X		X	Intervention administered by therapist to family & provides assistance with other systems	Reduction in recidivism	7.7%	$22,058	$4,364	$17,694.00
SUBSTANCE USE										
Life Skills Training (LST)	X	X		X	Prevention of substance abuse provided in middle school classrooms	Reduction in tobacco, alcohol, & marijuana use	50%–75%			
Midwestern Prevention Project (MPP)	X				Prevention of substance abuse using community-based approach	Reduction in daily smoking and marijuana use	40.0%			
Project Toward No Drug Abuse	X				Prevention of substance abuse aimed at high-school youth	22% prevalence reduction in 30-day marijuana use 26% prevalence reduction in 30-day hard drug use				

ANTISOCIAL BEHAVIOR

	Source of Rating				Description	Outcomes
	Blueprints	WSIPP	Lipsey	CEBP		
Big Brothers/Big Sisters Mentoring	X				Prevention using volunteers as mentors for youth from single parent homes	About 33% less likely than control youth to hit someone
Olweus Anti-Bullying Program	X				Prevention administered by school staff using school-wide, classroom & individual components	Reduction in reports of bullying and victimization; Reduction in general antisocial behavior such as vandalism, fighting, theft and truancy
Promoting Alternative Thinking Strategies (PATHS)	X				Prevention promoting emotional and social competencies among elementary school children	Decreased report of conduct problems, including aggressionIncreased ability to tolerate frustration
The Incredible Years	X				Prevention administered by parents & teachers to reduce antisocial behavior	Reductions in peer aggression in the classroomReductions in conduct problems at home & school

PROVEN STRATEGIES	STRATEGIES in the PROVEN category are generic program strategies that have been found to reduce recidivism, substance use, and/or antisocial behavior in rigorous meta-analysis					

	Source of Rating				Description	Outcomes	Cost/Benefit Analysis (if available)		
	Blueprints	WSIPP	Lipsey	CEBP			Benefits	Costs	Benefit minus Cost

DELINQUENCY & RECIDIVISM

	Blueprints	WSIPP	Lipsey	CEBP	Description	Outcomes	Benefits	Costs	Benefit minus Cost
Cognitive behavioral therapy		X	X		Prevention or Intervention using structured goal setting, planning & practice	26% reduction in recidivism (Lipsey)2.6% reduction in recidivism (WSIPP)			

(continued)

Table 4.3 Continued

STRATEGIES in the PROVEN category are generic program strategies that have been found to reduce recidivism, substance use, and/or antisocial behavior in rigorous meta-analysis

PROVEN STRATEGIES	Source of Rating			Description	Outcomes	Cost/Benefit Analysis (if available)		
	Blueprints	WSIPP	Lipsey	CEBP			Benefits	Costs	Benefit minus Cost
Behavioral programs		x	X		Prevention or Intervention that awards selected behaviors	22% reduction in recidivism			
Group counseling			X		Prevention or intervention using group counseling led by a therapist	22% reduction in recidivism			
High school graduation		X			Prevention or intervention: graduation from high school	21.1% reduction in recidivism	$9,562	n/e	
Mentoring			X		Prevention or intervention using mentoring by volunteer or paraprofessional	21% reduction in recidivism			
Case management			X		Prevention or intervention using case manager or case team to develop service plan & arranges services for juvenile	20% reduction in recidivism			
Counseling / psychotherapy		X	X		Prevention or intervention: individual counseling	16.6% reduction in recidivism (WSIPP)5% reduction in recidivism (Lipsey)			

Program			Description	Outcome			
Pre-K education for low-income families	X		Prevention providing high-quality early childhood education	16.6% reduction in recidivism	$15,461	$612	$14,849.00
Mixed counseling		X	Prevention or intervention: combination of individual, group and/or family	16% reduction in recidivism			
Teen Court	X		Intervention for juvenile offenders in which they are sentenced by their peers	14% reduction in recidivism	$16,908	$937	$15,971.00
Family counseling	X		Prevention or intervention: family counseling	13% reduction in recidivism			
Social skills training		X	Prevention or intervention: teaching social skills	13% reduction in recidivism			
Challenge programs		X	Prevention or intervention: provide opportunities for experimental learning by mastering tasks	12% reduction in recidivism			
Family crisis counseling		X	Prevention or intervention: short-term family crisis counseling	12% reduction in recidivism			
Mediation		X	Intervention where offender apologizes to victim & meets under supervision	12% reduction in recidivism			
Multiple coordinated services		X	Intervention providing a package of multiple services to juveniles	12% reduction in recidivism			

(continued)

Table 4.3 Continued

STRATEGIES in the PROVEN category are generic program strategies that have been found to reduce recidivism, substance use, and/or antisocial behavior in rigorous meta-analysis

PROVEN STRATEGIES	Source of Rating			Description	Outcomes	Cost/Benefit Analysis (if available)		
	Blueprints	WSIPP	Lipsey	CEBP			Benefits	Costs	Benefit minus Cost
Skill building programs			X		Prevention or intervention aimed at developing skills to control behavior and prosocial functions	12% reduction in recidivism			
Restorative justice for low-risk offenders		X	X		Intervention using victim-offender conferences & restitution	10% reduction in recidivism (Lipsey)8% reduction in recidivism (WSIPP)	$9,609	$907	$8,702.00
Academic training			X		Prevention or intervention: tutoring, GED programs, etc.	10% reduction in recidivism			
Service broker			X		Intervention using referrals for juvenile services with minimal role afterward	10% reduction in recidivism			
Sex offender treatment		X			Intervention using a cognitive-behavioral approach specifically for juvenile sex offenders	9.7% reduction in recidivism	$57,504	$33,842	$23,662.00
Restitution			X		Intervention: offender provides financial compensation to victim and/or community service	9% reduction in recidivism			
Mixed counseling with referral			X		Intervention: supplementary referrals for other services	8% reduction in recidivism			

		Source of Rating					Cost/Benefit Analysis (if available)		
	Description	Blueprints	WSIPP	Lipsey	CEBP	Outcomes	Benefits	Costs	Benefit minus Cost
Job-related interventions	Prevention or intervention: vocational counseling, job placement, training			X		6% reduction in recidivism			
Peer counseling	Prevention or intervention: peer group plays therapeutic role			X		4% reduction in recidivism			
Diversion with services	Intervention using citizen accountability boards & counseling compared to court supervision		X			3.1% reduction in recidivism	$3,786	n/e	n/e
Multimodal regimen	Prevention or intervention: multimodal curriculum or coordinated array of services			X		3% reduction in recidivism			

PROMISING PROGRAMS Programs in the PROMISING PROGRAMS category are brand name programs that have been shown to reduce recidivism, substance use, and/or antisocial behavior in at least one trial using a strong research design

DELINQUENCY & RECIDIVISM

		Source of Rating					Cost/Benefit Analysis (if available)		
Seattle Social Development Project	Intervention administered by parents & teachers using social control & social learning	X	X			15.7% reduction in recidivism	$5,922	n/e	

(continued)

Table 4.3 Continued

PROMISING PROGRAMS	Programs in the PROMISING PROGRAMS category are brand name programs that have been shown to reduce recidivism, substance use, and/or antisocial behavior in at least one trial using a strong research design							
	Source of Rating					Cost/Benefit Analysis (if available)		
	Blueprints	WSIPP	Lipsey	CEBP	Description	Outcomes	Benefits	Costs	Benefit minus Cost
Family Integrated Transitions (FIT)		X			Intervention for the reentry of juveniles with mental illness & substance abuse	10.2% reduction in recidivism	$54,045	$9,970	$44,753.00
Guiding Good Choices	X	X			Prevention: family-focused improvement of parenting skills	7.2% reduction in recidivism	$2,586	n/e	
TeamChild		X			Intervention: Attorneys advocate on behalf of juvenile for education, treatment, housing	9.7% reduction in recidivism	$11,657	n/e	n/e
Parent-Child Interaction Therapy		X			Prevention program focusing on restructuring the parent-child bond	5.1% reduction in recidivism	$2,787	n/e	n/e
Behavioral Monitoring & Reinforcement Program	X				Prevention implemented in schools redirecting at-risk juveniles from delinquency	Less self-reported delinquency, school-based problems and unemploymentFewer county court records than peers			
Preventive Treatment Program	X				Prevention for antisocial boys and their parents	Reduction in gang involvement Reduction in delinquent acts (stealing, vandalism) Fewer friends arrested by the police			

			Description	Outcomes
SUBSTANCE USE				
CASASTART	X		Prevention combining case mgmt services, afterschool & summer activities	Less likely to report use of any drugs, gateway drugs, or stronger drugsLower levels of violent crimeLess likely to be involved in drug sales
Project Northland	X		Intervention implemented throughout the community to reduce substance abuse	Decreased tendencies to use alcoholLess alcohol, cigarette, and marijuana use
Strengthening Families	X		Prevention using a family-based apporach to improve communication & relationships	Lower rates of alcohol initiation30-60% relative reductions in alcohol use and being drunk
Strong African American Families Program	X		Prevention of substance abuse using a family-based approach in African American families	Reduced initiation of alcohol use & slowed increase in use over timeDeveloped stronger youth protective factors
Project ALERT	X		Prevention of substance abuse implemented in the classroom	30% reduction in initiation of marijuana use 60% reduction in current marijuana use
ANTISOCIAL BEHAVIOR				
Good Behavior Game	X	X	Prevention using behavior modification aimed at reducing disruptive behavior in the classroom	Less aggressive and shy behaviorsBetter peer nominations of aggressive behavior Reduction in levels of aggression for males
Brief Strategic Family Therapy (BSFT)	X		Intervention administered by a therapist improving family interactions	Significant reductions in Conduct Disorder and Socialized Aggression
FAST Track	X		Prevention to improve family & peer relationships in the classroom & at home	Better overall ratings by observers on children's aggressive, disruptive, and oppositional behavior in the classroom.

(continued)

Table 4.3 Continued

PROMISING PROGRAMS	Source of Rating					Cost/Benefit Analysis (if available)		
Programs in the PROMISING PROGRAMS category are brand name programs that have been shown to reduce recidivism, substance use, and/or antisocial behavior in at least one trial using a strong research design								
	Blueprints	WSIPP	Lipsey	CEBP	Description	Outcomes	Benefits	Costs	Benefit minus Cost
I CAN PROBLEM SOLVE	X				Prevention school-based program teaching social problem-solving skills	Less impulsive and inhibited classroom behavior Better problem-solving skills			
Linking the Interests of Families and Teachers (LIFT)	X				Prevention school-based program increasing prosocial behavior	Decrease in physical aggression on the playground Significant increase in positive social skills and classroom behavior			

PROVEN PRINCIPLES OF EFFECTIVENESS	Source of Rating					Cost/Benefit Analysis (if available)		
Each of these PRINCIPLES improves outcomes regardless of program or strategy content								
	Blueprints	WSIPP	Lipsey	CEBP	Description	Outcomes	Benefits	Costs	Benefit minus Cost
FIDELITY: Integrity of treatment implementation	X		X	X	Having procedure to ensure staff stick to protocol improves outcomes				

	Source of Rating				Description	Outcomes	Cost/Benefit Analysis (if available)		
	Blueprints	WSIPP	Lipsey	CEBP			Benefits	Costs	Benefit minus Cost
Focus on high-risk youth	X				More needs, more room for improvement, higher costs of failure				
Longer duration of treatment	X				Dosage matters: More sessions better than less				
Well established program	X				Programs improve over time: Steep learning curve for new programs				
Communities That Care (CTC)					Forming local prevention coalition, determining needs, reviewing "What Works," selecting programs				

PROVEN INEFFECTIVE Programs and strategies in the PROVEN INEFFECTIVE category are those that do not reduce recidivism or risk factors or have an adverse outcome

	Source of Rating				Description	Outcomes	Cost/Benefit Analysis (if available)		
	Blueprints	WSIPP	Lipsey	CEBP			Benefits	Costs	Benefit minus Cost
Programs									
DARE (Drug Abuse Resistance Training)				X	Prevention school-based substance abuse progarm using uniformed police officers	No significant impact on use of alcohol, tobacco, or illicit drugs			
Guided Group Interaction		X			Intervention using a peer group to promote prosocial & restructure peer interaction	No reduction in recidivism			

(continued)

Table 4.3 Continued

PROVEN INEFFECTIVE								
Programs and strategies in the PROVEN INEFFECTIVE category are those that do not reduce recidivism or risk factors or have an adverse outcome								
	Source of Rating						Cost/Benefit Analysis (if available)	
	Blueprints	WSIPP	Lipsey	CEBP	Description	Outcomes	Benefits	Costs	Benefit minus Cost
Strategies								
Boot camps		X			Intervention emphasizing drill, teamwork, etc.	No reduction in recidivism			
Court supervision		X			Intervention using court supervision compared to releasing juvenile without services	No reduction in recidivism			
Diversion with services		X			Intervention designed to treat low-risk youth outside the juvenile justice system	No reduction in recidivism			
Intensive probation		X			Intervention using more than usual contact compared to incarceration	No reduction in recidivism			
Intensive probation supervision		X			Intervention using more than the usual contacts	No reduction in recidivism	$0	$1,650	−$1,650.00
Intensive parole supervision		X			Intervention using more than the usual contacts	No reduction in recidivism	$0	$6,670	−$6,670.00
		X			Intervention involving post-release monitoring	No reduction in recidivism	$0	$1,237	−$1,237.00

Regular surveillance-oriented parole						
Wilderness Challenge	X	Intervention teaching prosocial skills through physical challenges, such as rock climbing	No reduction in recidivism	$0	$3,185	-$3,185.00
Deterrence	X	Intervention dramatizing the negative consequences of behavior	2% increase in recidivism			
Scared Straight	X	Intervention using prison inmates to confront first time offenders about the downside of criminal life	6.1% increase in recidivism	-$17,410	$60	-$17,470.00
Discipline	X	Intervention teaching discipline to succeed & avoid reoffending	8% increase in recidivism			

Prevention Programs

Primary prevention programs target the general population of youth and include those aimed at preventing smoking, drug use, or teen pregnancy. Secondary prevention efforts target those at elevated risk for a particular outcome, such as delinquency or violence, and might include youth living in disadvantaged neighborhoods, those who are struggling in school, or those who have been exposed to violence in the home.

The very first opportunity for prevention is with pregnant teens who are at risk or with at-risk children in early childhood. The preeminent program in this category is David Olds's Nurse Family Partnership, a home visitation program that trains and supervises registered nurses as the home visitors. This program is found on just about every list of promising strategies, based on the strength of its evidence regarding significant long-term effects and portability. Because of its consistent success, the program was the only prevention program selected to be part of the Obama administration's stimulus package The program attempts to identify young, poor, first-time mothers early in their pregnancy. The sequence of approximately 20 home visits begins during the prenatal period and continues over the first two years of the child's life, with declining frequency. In addition to providing transportation and linkage to other services, the nurse home visitors follow a detailed protocol that provides child-care training and social skills development for the mother.

A 15-year follow-up of the Prenatal/Early Infancy Project in Elmira, New York, showed that the nurse home visits significantly reduced child abuse and neglect in the participating families, as well as arrest rates for the children and mothers. The women who received the program also spent much less time on welfare, and those who were poor and unmarried experienced significantly fewer subsequent births.

A number of less costly and less structured home visitation models have been tested, using social workers or other types of professionals, rather than nurses, but they have not been successful in achieving the same level of success or consistency as the Olds program with nurses. The Olds model, now called the Nurse Family Partnership, has been successfully evaluated in several sites and is now replicated in over 200 counties and many foreign countries.

At a slightly older age, preschool education for at-risk three- and four-year-olds is an effective prevention strategy, particularly when they include home visits or work with parents in some other way. The Perry Preschool in Ypsilanti, Michigan, is the most well-evaluated model.

A number of school or classroom-based programs have proven effective in preventing drug use, delinquency, antisocial behavior, and early school dropout, all behaviors that can lead to further criminal behavior. These include The Incredible Years, the Olweus Bullying Prevention Program, PATHS, and Life Skills Training, The programs vary widely in their goals, although some common themes exist: collaborative planning and problem solving involving teachers, parents, students, community members, and administrators; grouping of students into small self-contained clusters; career education; integrated curriculum; and student involvement in rule setting and enforcement, and strategies to reduce dropout.

For example, the Bullying Prevention Program (BPP) was developed with elementary and junior high school students in Bergen, Norway. The program involves teachers and parents in the setting and enforcement of clear rules against bullying behavior. Two years after the intervention, bullying problems decreased by 50 percent in treated schools. Furthermore, other forms of delinquency declined as well and school climate improved. BPP is one of the 11 Blueprints "model" programs and is listed as "promising" by the Surgeon General.

Multiple evaluations of Life Skills Training (LST) have shown it to reduce the use of alcohol, cigarettes, and marijuana among participants. The reductions in alcohol and cigarette use are sustained through the end of high school. LST is listed as a model program by both Blueprints and the Surgeon General, and by most other lists of proven programs. The program has been widely disseminated throughout the United States over the past decade with funding from government agencies and private foundations.

Community-Based Interventions

Delinquency prevention programs in community settings can be created for various purposes such as: providing a means of diverting youth out of the juvenile justice system; serving youth placed on informal or formal probation; or serving youth on parole who are returning to the community after a residential placement. Settings can range from the individual home, schools, teen centers, parks, or the special facilities of private providers. They can involve anything from a one-hour monthly meeting to intensive family therapy and services.

Interestingly, programs that emphasize family interactions are the most successful, probably because they focus on providing skills to the adults who are in the best position to supervise and train the child. More traditional interventions that punish or attempt to frighten the individual youth are the least effective. For example, for youth on probation, the most effective programs are family-based interventions designated as "proven" by Blueprints and the Surgeon General: Functional Family Therapy and Multisystemic Therapy.

Functional Family Therapy (FFT) targets youth within the age range of 11–18 who have problems with delinquency, substance abuse, or violence. The program focuses on altering interactions between family members, and seeks to improve the functioning of the family unit by increasing family problem-solving skills, enhancing emotional connections between family members, and strengthening parental ability to provide appropriate structure, guidance, and limits to their children. FFT is a relatively short-term program that is delivered by individual therapists, usually in the home setting. Each team of 4 to 8 therapists works under the direct supervision and monitoring of several more experienced therapist/trainers. The effectiveness of the program has been demonstrated for a wide range of problem youth in numerous trials over the past 25 years, using different types of therapists, ranging from paraprofessionals to trainees, in a variety of social work and counseling professions. The program is well documented and readily transportable.

Multisystemic Therapy, or MST, is also a family-based program, designed to help parents deal effectively with their youth's behavior problems, including disengagement from deviant peers and poor school performance. To accomplish family empowerment, MST also addresses barriers to effective parenting and helps family members build an indigenous social support network. To increase family collaboration and treatment generalization, MST is typically provided in the home, school, and other community locations. Master-level counselors provide 50 hours of face-to-face contact, spread over four months.

MST takes about as long to work with an individual family as FFT, but it is more intensive and more expensive. In addition to working with parents, MST will locate and attempt to involve other family members in supervising the youth, as well as involving teachers, school administrators, and other adults who interact with the youth. MST therapists are also on call for emergency services, whereas FFT therapists are not. Evaluations of the program demonstrate that the therapy is effective in reducing re-arrest rates and out-of-home placements for a wide variety of problem youth enmeshed in both the juvenile justice and social service systems.

Much less effective than family-based programs are community-based programs that focus on the individual offender. For example, intensive supervision, surveillance, extra services, and early release programs have not been found to be effective. Ineffective probation programs and strategies include intensive supervision, early release, vocational training, bringing younger offenders together for programming, and deterrence approaches such as Scared Straight.

Institutional Programs

Juvenile courts, like criminal courts, function as a screening agent for the purpose of sanctions and services. The need for treatment must be balanced against the demands of accountability (punishment) and community safety. Only a fraction of the cases reaching any one stage of the process are passed on to the next stage. Out of all the juveniles arrested in 1999, only 26 percent were adjudicated delinquent and only 6.3 percent were placed out of their homes. Even in the cases of those arrested for one of the more serious UCR Part I *Index* offenses, only 35 percent were adjudicated delinquent and only 10 percent were placed out of their homes. This pattern of case dispositions reflects the juvenile court's preference for informal dispositions and its interest in child protection.

Nevertheless, juvenile courts will place youth in more structured or secure settings because of the inappropriateness of the current home setting or the public safety risk posed by the youth. In these two instances, placement in a group or institutional setting is more likely to occur.

Those who are placed out of their homes are referred to a wide variety of group homes, camps, and other residential or correctional institutions. Extensive meta-analyses of evaluations of these identify several principles that appear to increase effectiveness. The more effective programs focus on dynamic or changeable risk factors—low skills, substance abuse, defiant behavior, relationships with delinquent peers. Additionally, those that support mental health issues are more successful than those that focus on punishment.

Programs that are individually tailored to clients' needs using evidence-based methods are more successful than large generic programs. Also, focusing intervention efforts on the higher-risk youth, where the opportunity for improvement and consequences of failure are both the largest, also improves outcomes.

Finally, one of the most important characteristics of successful programs is the integrity with which they are implemented—the degree to which they follow all the prescribed protocols of the program design, their fidelity to the original.

Specific types of programs that work well with institutionalized youth include Cognitive-Behavioral Therapy, Aggression Replacement Training, and Family Integrated Transition.

Cognitive-Behavioral Therapy (CBT) is a time-limited approach to psychotherapy that utilizes skill building—through instruction and homework assignments—to achieve its goals. CBT is based on the concept that it is our thoughts about what happens to us that cause particular feelings, rather than the events themselves. The goal of CBT is to change thinking processes. CBT uses a variety of techniques to learn what goals clients have for their lives and to improve skills that can help them achieve those goals.

Aggression Replacement Training also emphasizes focusing on risk factors that can be changed. It is a cognitive-behavioral intervention that has three components: (1) "anger control," in which the participants learn what triggers their anger and how to control their reactions; (2) "behavioral skills," which teaches a series of pro-social skills through modeling, role playing, and performance feedback; and (3) and "moral reasoning", which seeks to increase youth awareness of others' points of view and. increase awareness of fairness and justice.

Family Integrated Transition program is designed to help youth with mental health and substance abuse problems return to the community after a residential stay. It integrates several forms of therapy, including MST, into a model that begins with the youth still in custody.

HOW THIS INFORMATION COULD BE USED

Training and Technical Assistance

The information in table 4.3 could be used to train practitioners in the kinds of programs that are available, and how they differ regarding resources required, impacts, reliability, and so on. The training might begin with a review of all the "proven" programs: the population they were designed to serve; their basic components; and their estimated start-up costs. These 13 programs run the gamut from very early childhood up through older, more serious delinquents, who may soon be living on their own. For each one of these programs the following questions should be asked:

- Do we have a population to serve that is like the one targeted by this program?
- How large is this population?
- How are we serving it now?
- Could we be doing a more cost-effective job?

After the group has reviewed all of the programs, they should then consider whether there are any underserved or poorly served populations that were not considered during the proven program review. If there are, then the group should consider the list of proven strategies and promising programs that might need their needs.

An Evidence-Based Approach to Disposition Planning

Evidence-Based Practice (EBP) in disposition planning uses scientific principles to make the best use of all the information available to the court at the time of disposition. The basic steps in this process, no matter how serious the case or how far it has progressed in the system, include:

- Assessment
- Identification and development of disposition options
- Comparison and evaluation of options
- Implementation planning
- Execution
- Quality assurance
- Sustainability.

The first step in disposition planning should always be an **assessment** of the youth, the offense with which he or she is charged, his or her record, his or her family, and the community in which he or she lives. An assessment should assist the decision-maker in identifying key factors that should be considered in fashioning a youth's disposition; including the risk factors that contribute to the youth's delinquent behavior and the resources available to support the youth.

A number of risk-and-needs assessment instruments have been developed and validated on various populations. They sort youth into high, medium-, and low-risk groups, identifying their risk factors that need attention. Many instruments are now commercially available, with appropriate training and technical assistance, online data entry, and vendor-provided scoring of results. It is critical that juvenile justice practitioners avail themselves of training and technical assistance when using such instruments, to ensure that the results are correctly interpreted and appropriately applied in decision-making regarding an individual youth. Such instruments are but one component of a more comprehensive assessment process that should be undertaken for each adjudicated youth. Assessments of first-time offenders or offenders involved in minor delinquency can be fairly short and abbreviated. Unless a youth's home situation is extremely deficient, diversion from the formal system is generally an appropriate option.

Assessments of older offenders with longer records, multiple placements, or those who represent a serious safety risk to the community need to be more extensive and consider issues of mental health and living arrangements. If the youth is found guilty and represents a serious risk to the community, there will probably be significant resources expended on the case. More extensive assessments probing mental health and family issues will help insure that these resources are used appropriately.

Disposition options depend on how far the case has progressed, the risk posed by and the needs of the juvenile, and the available resources. Any **evaluation of disposition options** needs to consider public safety, the interests of the child, the relative effectiveness of the options in preventing future delinquency, and their costs. Expensive interventions cannot be justified for low-risk youth. Public safety considerations may require secure placement of a youth, while a community-based intervention would be more effective in reducing recidivism. The larger the share of resources devoted to proven and promising interventions, as opposed to supervision and custodial services, the larger the expected impact on recidivism.

Any significant intervention will require some degree of **planning**, including answering the following questions:

- Who is to deliver the services? Are they culturally competent to work with this particular youth?
- Where and how will they connect with the service provider?
- How will the youth and family be engaged?
- What is supposed to happen when the intervention is completed?
- If the youth is in custody, where will he live next?
- What supportive services will be arranged to help with reentry and aftercare?
- Is this the least-restrictive option that meets the interests of the child and serves public safety?

These are all details that need to be worked through before the intervention begins.

Effective **execution** of the placement or service order requires highly competent provider and service personnel. If the trainers, therapists, and counselors to whom the youth is exposed do not perform their assigned roles with a high degree of competence, the intervention will probably not achieve its intended impact.

Quality assurance involves various means of checking to ensure that the intervention is being delivered as intended. Quality assurance may involve auditing a sample of cases and service plans, including interviews with the youth and family, or it may involve observation of training or counseling sessions. The objective of such practices is to identify and weed out incompetent or inattentive personnel and fix glitches in the delivery system.

At the individual case level, **sustainability** refers to the ability of the youth to sustain the new patterns of behavior that the youth developed during the intervention. One reason that training schools and similar institutions do not work is that the positive peer culture developed in those environments are not sustainable in the outside world.

The political and institutional changes needed to bring about evidence-based practice require champions in every organization to make them happen. Those in positions of authority for juvenile justice policy must be informed about the evidence-based programs now available to them and about how those programs can help them reduce delinquency rates, ensure safer communities, and reduce government spending

Policymakers will have to be assisted by experts in evidence-based practices in designing and implementing the reforms required. States will have to create financial incentives for local communities to invest in effective prevention programs, most likely by returning some share of the savings in future corrections costs to counties or local communities. Requests for proposals will have to require evidence-based programming and services, and those buying the services must be able to distinguish evidence-based proposals and programs from other proposals and programs. Providers will eventually be held accountable for the results they achieve.

Practitioners who are going to work with juvenile offenders and at-risk youth will have to be trained and monitored to ensure that they are delivering services in the most appropriate and prescribed manner. Achieving the consistency and fidelity that effective programs appear to require will necessitate new ways of supervising and managing those who have direct contact with youth and their families. Shifting from a management focus on preventing abuse or infractions to one that empowers employees to provide effective services to their clients is going to be a major struggle.

Those who wish to develop or promote new methods of intervention will have to learn how to play by the new set of rules and protocols that have made possible the programming advances of the past decade. Programs can no longer be promoted for wide-scale dissemination until they have been proven effective by a rigorous evaluation.

None of these challenges is impossible. Efforts to expand the use of Blueprints programs in Florida, Pennsylvania, and Washington have been under way for several years now, with considerable success. Both North Carolina and Arizona have undertaken efforts in collaboration with Mark Lipsey to evaluate all their programs. Hundreds of communities have adopted and implemented proven program models and are reaping the benefits of reduced delinquency and lower system costs. The challenge now is to move beyond these still relatively few early adopters and push these reforms into the mainstream of juvenile justice.

CONCLUSIONS

Following a sharp increase in violent offense rates in the early 1990s, juvenile arrest rates for both property and violent offenses have declined substantially in the latter half of the decade. Today juveniles are making less of a contribution to our national crime problem than they have in the past 30 years.

Meanwhile, over the past 20 years, the emphasis of the juvenile justice system has been shifting away from rehabilitation and the "best interests" of the child toward greater accountability and harsher sanctions for serious offending—in spite of the fact that we have much better information about the type of interventions that work in reducing recidivism. Many more youth are being handled in adult courts, and proceedings in juvenile courts are much more open to public inspection. Whether these changes in the juvenile justice system can be given any of the credit for recent declines in juvenile offending is difficult to say. In all likelihood, the increase in sanction severity for the more serious offenders, the improved knowledge about effective intervention strategies, and the renewed interest in prevention programs have all made their contributions to reducing juvenile crime rates, along with the booming economy of the late 1990s and the improvements it brought to the impoverished neighborhoods where many high-risk youth are raised.

References

Bartollas, Clemens, Stuart. J. Miller, and Simon Dinitz. 1976. *Juvenile Victimization: The Institutional Paradox*. New York: John Wiley and Sons.

Blumstein, Alfred, and Richard Rosenfeld. 1998. "Explaining Recent Trends in U.S. Homicide Rates." *The Journal of Criminal Law and Criminology* 88 (4): 1175–1216.

Blumstein, Alfred, and Joel Wallman. 2006. "The Recent Rise and Fall of American Violence." In *The Crime Drop in America*, eds. A. Blumstein and J. Wallman. New York: Cambridge University Press.

Braithwaite, John. 1998. "Restorative Justice: Assessing an Immodest Theory and a Pessimistic Theory." In *Crime and Justice: A Review of Research*, ed. M. Tonry. Chicago: University of Chicago Press.

Brown, J. M., and Patrick A. Langan. 1998. *State Court Sentencing of Convicted Felons*. Washington, DC: Bureau of Justice Statistics, U.S. Department of Justice.

Centers for Disease Control and Prevention. (Web-based Injury Statistics Query and Reporting System (WISQARS) [online]. 2006. National Center for Injury Prevention and Control, Centers for Disease Control and Prevention (producer). Available at www.cdc.govinjury.

Coates, Robert B., Alden D. Miller, and Lloyd B. Ohlin. 1979. *Diversity in a Youth Correctional System: Handling Delinquents in Massachusetts*. New York: HarperCollins.

Cook, Philip J., and John H. Laub. 1998. "The Unprecedented Epidemic in Youth Violence." In *Crime and Justice: A Review of Research*, eds. M. Tonry and M. H. Moore. Chicago: University of Chicago Press.

Empey, Lamar T. 1979. *American Delinquency: The Future of Childhood and Juvenile Justice*. Charlottesville: University Press of Virginia.

Empey, Lamar, and Steven G. Lubeck. 1971. *The Silverlake Experiment: Testing Delinquency Theory and Community Intervention*. Chicago: Aldine.

Fagan, Jeffrey. 1995. "Separating the Men from the Boys: The Comparative Advantage of Juvenile versus Criminal Court Sanctions on Recidivism among Adolescent Felony Offenders." In *A Sourcebook: Serious, Violent and Chronic Juvenile Offenders*, eds. J. C. Howell, B. Krisberg, J. D. Hawkins and J. J. Wilson. Thousand Oaks, CA: Sage.

Feld, Barry. 1977. *Neutralizing Inmate Violence: Juvenile Offenders in Institutions*. Cambridge, MA: Ballinger.

Feld, Barry C. 1989. "The Right to Counsel in Juvenile Court: An Empirical Study of When Lawyers Appear and the Difference They Make." *Journal of Criminal Law and Criminology* 79: 1185–1346.

Finkelhor, David, and Lisa Jones. 2006. "Why Have Child Maltreatment and Child Victimization Declined?" *Journal of Social Issues* 62 (4): 685–716.

Greenwood, Peter W. 1986. "Differences in Criminal Behavior and Court Response among Juvenile and Young Adult Defendants." In *Annual Review of Criminal Justice Research*, eds. M. Tonry and N. Morris. Chicago: University Press.

Greenwood, Peter. 2006. *Changing Lives: Delinquency Prevention as Crime Control Policy*, Chicago: University of Chicago Press.

Greenwood, Peter W., Albert Lipson, Allan Abrahamse, and Franklin Zimring. 1983. *Youth Crime and Juvenile Justice in California: A Report to the Legislature*, R-3016-CSA, Santa Monica, CA: RAND.

Greenwood, Peter W., and Susan Turner. 1993. "Evaluation of the Paint Creek Youth Center: A Residential Program for Serious Delinquents." *Criminology* 31 (2): 263–279.

Griffin, Patrick, Patricia Torbet, and Linda Szymanski. 1998. *Trying Juveniles in Adult Courts: An Analysis of State Transfer Provisions*. Washington, DC: Office of Juvenile Justice and Delinquency Prevention, Office of Justice Programs, U.S. Department of Justice.

Johnson, Bruce D., Andrew Golub, and Eloise Dunlap. 2006. "The Rise and Decline of Hard Drugs, Drug Markets, and Violence in Inner-City New York." In *The Crime Drop in America*, eds. A. Blumstein and J. Wallman. New York: Cambridge University Press.

Kooy, Elizabeth. 2008. *Changing Course: A Review of the First Two Years of Drug Transfer Reform in Illinois*. Springfield: Illinois Juvenile Justice Initiative.

Lipsey, Mark W. 1991. "Juvenile Delinquency Treatment: A Meta-Analytic Inquiry into the Variability of Effects." In *Meta-Analysis for Explanation: A Casebook*, eds. T. Cook et al. New York: Russell Sage Foundation.

Lipsey, Mark W. 2009. "The Primary Factors That Characterize Effective Interventions with Juvenile Offenders: A Meta-analytic Overview." *Victims and Offenders* 4: 124–147.

Lipsey, Mark W., and Francis T. Cullen. 2007. "The Effectiveness of Correctional Rehabilitation: A Review of Systematic Reviews." *Annual Review of Law and Social Sciences* 3: 297–320.

Livsey, Sarah, Melissa Sickmund, and Anthony Sladky. 2009. *Juvenile Residential Facility Census, 2004: Selected Findings, Juvenile Offenders and Victims National Report Series Bulletin.* Washington, DC: Office of Justice Programs.

MacArthur Foundaton Research Network. *The Changing Borders of Juvenile Justice: Transfer of Adolescents to the Adult Criminal Court.* Issue Brief no. 5. N.d.

Menard, Scott, and Delbert S. Elliott. 1993. "Data Set Comparability and Short-Term Trends in Crime and Delinquency." *Journal of Criminal Justice* 21: 433–445.

New York Times. August 10, 2009. "Mentally Ill Offenders Strain Juvenile System."

Redding, Richard E. 2008. *Juvenile Transfer Laws: An Effective Deterrent to Delinquency?* Washington, DC: Office of Juvenile Justice and Delinquency Prevention Office of Justice Programs, U.S. Department of Justice.

Reiss, Albert, and J. A. Roth. 1993. *Understanding and Preventing Violence.* Washington, DC: National Academy Press.

Schwartz, Ira M., and Russell Van Vleet. 1992. "Public Policy and the Incarceration of Juveniles: Directions for the 1990s." In *Juvenile Justice and Public Policy*, eds. I. M. Schwartz. New York: Lexington Books.

Scott, Elizabeth, and Laurence Steinberg. 2008. "Adolescent Development and the Regulation of Youth Crime." *The Future of Children* 18(2), 15–33.

Sickmund, Melissa. 2009. *Delinquency Cases in Juvenile Court.* Washington, DC: Office of Juvenile Justice and Delinquency Prevention, Office of Justice Programs, U.S. Department of Justice.

Snyder, Howard N., and Melissa Sickmund. 2006. *Juvenile Offenders and Victims: 2006 National Report.* National Report Series. Washington, DC: Office of Justice Programs.

Thornberry, Terence, Stewart E. Tolnay, Timothy J. Flanagan, and Patty Glynn. 1991. *Office of Juvenile Justice and Delinquency Prevention Report on Children in Custody, 1987: A Comparison of Public and Private Juvenile Custody Facilities.* New York: State University at Albany.

Torbet, Patricia, and Linda Szymanski. 1998. *State Legislative Responses to Violent Juvenile Crime: 1996–97 Update.* Washington, DC: Office of Juvenile Justice and Delinquency Prevention, Office of Justice Programs, U.S. Department of Justice.

U.S. Department of Health and Human Services, Administration on Children, Youth and Families. 2009. *Child Maltreatment 2007.* Washington, DC: U.S. Government Printing Office. Available at: http: www.childwelfare.gov

Chapter 5

Families and Crime

David P. Farrington

Many features of family life predict children's offending. Carolyn Smith and Susan Stern(1997, 383–384) concluded in their review that:

> We know that children who grow up in homes characterized by lack of warmth and support, whose parents lack behavior management skills, and whose lives are characterized by conflict or maltreatment will more likely be delinquent, whereas a supportive family can protect children even in a very hostile and damaging external environment.... Parental monitoring or supervision is the aspect of family management that is most consistently related to delinquency.

In agreement with this, Alan Leschied and his colleagues (2008) found that parental management that was coercive, inconsistent, or lacking in supervision during mid-childhood was a strong predictor of adult criminality, as were parental separation and marital status.

Mark Lipsey and Jim Derzon (1998) reviewed the predictors at age 6–11 of serious or violent offending at age 15–25. The best explanatory predictors (i.e., predictors not measuring some aspect of the child's antisocial behavior) were antisocial parents, male gender, low socioeconomic status of the family, and psychological factors (daring, impulsiveness, poor concentration, etc.). Other moderately strong predictors were minority race, poor parent-child relations (poor supervision, discipline, low parental involvement, low parental warmth), other family characteristics (parent stress, family size, parental discord), antisocial peers, low intelligence, and low school achievement. In contrast, abusive parents and broken homes were relatively weak predictors. It is clear that some family factors are at least as important in the prediction of offending as are gender and race.

More recently, Jim Derzon (2010) carried out a meta-analysis of family factors as predictors of criminal and violent behavior (as well as aggressive and problem behavior). The meta-analysis was based on longitudinal studies, but many predictions were over short time periods (less than four years in 55 percent of cases), many outcome variables were measured at relatively young ages (up to 15 in 40 percent of cases), and many studies were relatively small (less than 200 participants in 43 percent of cases). The strongest predictors of criminal or violent behavior were parental education (r = .30 for criminal behavior), parental supervision (r = .29 for violent behavior), child-rearing skills (r = .26 for criminal behavior), parental discord (r = .26 for criminal behavior), and family size (r = .24 for violent behavior). Notably weak predictors were young parents, broken homes, and socioeconomic status.

Reviewing these results reveals the bewildering variety of family constructs that have been studied, and also the variety of methods used to classify them into categories. In this chapter, family factors are grouped into six categories: (1) criminal and antisocial parents and siblings; (2) large family size; (3) child-rearing methods (poor supervision, poor discipline, coldness and rejection, low parental involvement with the child); (4) abuse (physical or sexual) or neglect; (5) parental conflict and disrupted families; and (6) other parental features (young age, substance abuse, stress, or depression). These groupings are somewhat arbitrary and reflect the organization of topics of investigation within the field. For example, harsh discipline is usually studied along with poor supervision but, at the extreme, it could shade into physical abuse. Physical neglect is usually grouped with physical abuse, but of course it usually coincides with emotional neglect (cold and rejecting parents). Socioeconomic aspects of the family (e.g. family poverty) are excluded.

The best method of establishing that a family factor predicts later offending is to carry out a prospective longitudinal survey, and the emphasis in this chapter is on results obtained in such surveys. The best surveys follow community samples of at least several hundreds from childhood to adulthood, with repeated face-to-face interviews as well as data from records (for a review, see Farrington and Welsh 2007, 29–36). They avoid retrospective bias (e.g., where the recollections of parents about their child-rearing methods are biased by the knowledge that their child has become a delinquent) and help in establishing causal order. Also, offenders emerge naturally in community surveys, avoiding the problem of how to choose a control group of non-offenders. Most longitudinal surveys focus on family risk factors, but information about family protective factors is also needed (see Lösel and Bender 2003).

CRIME RUNS IN FAMILIES

Criminal and antisocial parents tend to have delinquent and antisocial children, as shown in the classic longitudinal surveys by Joan McCord (1977) in Boston and Lee Robins (1979) in St. Louis. The most extensive research on the concentration of offending in families was carried out in the Cambridge Study in Delinquent Development, which is a prospective longitudinal survey of 400 males from age 8 to age 48 (Farrington et al.

2006). Having a convicted father, mother, brother, or sister predicted a boy's own convictions, and all four relatives were independently important as predictors (Farrington et al. 1996). For example, 63 percent of boys with convicted fathers were themselves convicted, compared with 30 percent of the remainder. Same-sex relationships were stronger than opposite-sex relationships, and older siblings were stronger predictors than younger siblings. Only 6 percent of the families accounted for half of all the convictions of all family members.

Similar results were obtained in the Pittsburgh Youth Study, which is a prospective longitudinal survey of 1,500 males from age 7 to age 30 (Loeber et al. 2008). Arrests of fathers, mothers, brothers, sisters, uncles, aunts, grandfathers, and grandmothers all predicted the boy's own delinquency (Farrington et al. 2001). The most important relative was the father; arrests of the father predicted the boy's delinquency independently of all other arrested relatives. Only 8 percent of families accounted for 43 percent of arrested family members.

In the Cambridge study, a convicted parent or a delinquent older sibling by the 10th birthday were consistently among the best age 8–10 predictors of the boy's later offending and antisocial behavior. Apart from behavioral measures such as troublesomeness and daring, they were the strongest predictors of juvenile convictions (Farrington 1992). A convicted parent up to age 10 was the strongest predictor of convictions up to age 50 (Farrington et al. 2009b): 62 percent of boys with convicted parents were themselves convicted, compared with 34 percent of the remainder. A convicted parent or a delinquent older sibling were also the best predictors, after poor parental supervision, of juvenile self-reported delinquency. Furthermore, the strength of intergenerational transmission of offending was similar between the fathers and the Study males and between the Study males and their sons (Farrington et al. 2009a). Parental imprisonment predicted a boy's offending over and above parental convictions (Murray and Farrington 2005).

There are six possible explanations (which are not mutually exclusive) for why offending tends to be concentrated in certain families and transmitted from one generation to the next (Farrington et al. 2001). First, there may be intergenerational continuities in exposure to multiple risk factors. For example, each successive generation may be entrapped in poverty, have disrupted family lives, may experience single and teenage parenting, and may live in the most deprived neighborhoods. Parents who use physical punishment may produce children who use similar punitive methods when they grow up, as indeed Leonard Eron and his colleagues (1991) found in New York State. One of the main conclusions of the Cambridge study is that a constellation of family background features (including poverty, large family size, parental disharmony, poor child-rearing, and parental criminality) leads to a constellation of antisocial features when children grow up, among which criminality is one element (West and Farrington 1977, 161). According to this explanation, the intergenerational transmission of offending is part of a larger cycle of deprivation and antisocial behavior.

A second explanation focuses on assortative mating, since female offenders tend to cohabit with or get married to male offenders (and vice versa). Children with two criminal parents are disproportionally antisocial (West and Farrington 1977, 122). There are two reasons why similar people tend to get married, cohabit, or become sexual partners (Rowe and Farrington 1997). The first is called "social homogamy." Convicted people tend to choose each other as mates because of physical and social proximity; they meet each other in the same schools, neighborhoods, clubs, pubs, and so on. The second process is called "phenotypic assortment." People examine each other's personality and behavior and choose partners who are similar to themselves. In the Dunedin study in New Zealand, which is a follow-up of over 1,000 children from age 3 to age 32, Robert Krueger and his colleagues (1998) found that sexual partners tended to be similar in their self-reported antisocial behavior.

The third explanation focuses on direct and mutual influences of family members on each other. For example, perhaps younger male siblings tend to imitate the antisocial behavior of older male siblings or perhaps older siblings encourage younger ones to be antisocial. There is considerable sibling resemblance in delinquency (Fagan and Najman 2003). In the Cambridge study, co-offending by brothers was surprisingly common; about 20 percent of boys who had brothers close to them in age were convicted for a crime committed with their brother (Reiss and Farrington 1991, 386). However, intergenerational mutual influences on offending seem less plausible, since co-offending by parents with their children was very uncommon in the Cambridge study. There was no evidence that parents directly encouraged their children to commit crimes or taught them criminal techniques; on the contrary, a criminal father usually disapproved of his son's offending (West and Farrington 1977, 116).

A fourth explanation suggests that the effect of a criminal parent on a child's offending is mediated by environmental mechanisms. In the Pittsburgh Youth Study, it was suggested that arrested fathers tended to have delinquent sons because they tended to impregnate young women, to live in bad neighborhoods, and to use child-rearing methods that did not develop a strong conscience in their children (Farrington et al. 2001). In the Cambridge study, it was suggested that poor parental supervision was one link in the chain between criminal fathers and delinquent sons (West and Farrington 1977, 117), and authoritarian parenting and parental conflict were mediating variables between parental antisocial behavior and child conduct problems (Smith and Farrington 2004). In the Glueck study in Boston, Robert Sampson and John Laub (1993, 92) found that maternal and paternal deviance (criminality or alcoholism) did not predict a boy's delinquency after controlling for family factors such as poor supervision, harsh or erratic discipline, parental rejection, low attachment, and large family size. Similarly, in their New York State study, Jeffrey Johnson and his colleagues (2004) concluded that problematic parenting mediated the link between parent and child antisocial behavior.

A fifth explanation suggests that the effect of a criminal parent on a child's offending is mediated by genetic mechanisms. In agreement with this, twin studies show that identical twins are more concordant in their offending than are fraternal twins (Raine 1993). Also in agreement with genetic mechanisms, adoption studies show that the offending of adopted children is significantly related to the offending of their biological parents (Brennan et al. 1993). However, an objection to adoption studies is that some children may have had contact with their biological parents, so again it is difficult to dismiss an environmental explanation of this finding. In a more convincing design comparing the concordance of identical twins reared together and identical twins reared apart, William Grove and his colleagues (1990) found that heritability was 41 percent for childhood conduct disorder and 28 percent for adult antisocial personality disorder. This design shows that the intergenerational transmission of offending is partly attributable to genetic factors. An important question is how the genetic potential (genotype) interacts with the environment to produce the offending behavior (phenotype).

A sixth explanation suggests that criminal parents tend to have delinquent children because of official (police and court) bias against known criminal families, who also tend to be known to official agencies because of other social problems. At all levels of self-reported delinquency in the Cambridge study, boys with convicted fathers were more likely to be convicted themselves than were boys with unconvicted fathers (West and Farrington 1977, 118). However, this was not the only explanation for the link between criminal fathers and delinquent sons, because boys with criminal fathers had higher self-reported delinquency scores and higher teacher and peer ratings of bad behavior. It is not clear which of these six explanations is the most important.

LARGE FAMILY SIZE

Large family size (a large number of children in the family) is a relatively strong and highly replicable predictor of delinquency. Studies relating family size (and many other factors) to offending are summarized in the massive *Handbook of Crime Correlates* by Lee Ellis and his colleagues (2009). Large family size was similarly important in the Cambridge and Pittsburgh studies, even though families were on average smaller in Pittsburgh in the 1990s than in London in the 1960s (Farrington and Loeber 1999). In the Cambridge study, if a boy had four or more siblings by his 10th birthday, this doubled his risk of being convicted as a juvenile (West and Farrington 1973, 31). Large family size at age 10 also predicted convictions up to age 50; 61 percent of boys from large families were convicted, compared with 35 percent of the remainder (Farrington et al. 2009b). Large family size also predicted self-reported delinquency (Farrington 1992).

There are many possible reasons why a large number of siblings might increase the risk of a child's delinquency. It may be that more antisocial parents have more children and also tend to have delinquent children. Generally, as the number of children in a family increases, the amount of parental attention that can be given to each child decreases. Also, as the number of children increases, the household tends to become more overcrowded, possibly leading to increases in frustration, irritation, and conflict. In the Cambridge study, large family size did not predict delinquency for boys living in the least crowded conditions, with two or more rooms than there were children (West and Farrington 1973, 33). This suggests that household overcrowding might be an important intervening factor between large family size and delinquency.

David Brownfield and Ann Sorenson (1994) reviewed several possible explanations for the link between large families and delinquency, including those focusing on features of the parents (e.g., criminal parents, teenage parents), those focusing on parenting (e.g., poor supervision, disrupted families), and those focusing on economic deprivation or family stress. Another interesting theory suggested that the key factor was birth order: large families include more later-born children who tend to be more delinquent. Based on an analysis of self-reported delinquency in a Seattle survey, they concluded that the most plausible intervening causal mechanism was exposure to delinquent siblings. Consistent with social learning theory, large families contained more antisocial models.

CHILD-REARING METHODS

Many different types of child-rearing methods predict a child's delinquency. The most important dimensions of child-rearing are supervision or monitoring of children, discipline or parental reinforcement, warmth or coldness of emotional relationships, and parental involvement with children. Unlike family size, these constructs are difficult to measure, and there is some evidence that results differ according to methods of measurement. In their extensive review of parenting methods in relation to childhood antisocial behavior, Fred Rothbaum and John Weisz (1994) concluded that the strength of associations between parent and child measures was greater when parenting was measured by observation or interview than when it was measured using questionnaires.

Parental supervision refers to the degree of monitoring by parents of the child's activities, and the degree of parental watchfulness or vigilance. Of all these child-rearing methods, poor parental supervision is usually the strongest and most replicable predictor of offending (Farrington and Loeber 1999; Smith and Stern 1997). In the Cambridge study, 61 percent of boys who were poorly supervised at age 8 were convicted up to age 50, compared with 36 percent of the remainder (Farrington et al. 2009b). Many studies show that parents who do not know where their children are when they are out, and parents who let their children roam the streets unsupervised from an early age, tend to have delinquent children. For example, in the classic Cambridge-Somerville study in Boston, Joan McCord (1979) found that poor parental supervision in childhood was the best predictor of both violent and property crimes up to age 45.

Parental discipline refers to how parents react to a child's behavior. It is clear that harsh or punitive discipline (involving physical punishment) predicts a child's delinquency, as the review by Jaana Haapasalo and Elina Pokela (1999) showed (see also Gershoff 2002). In the Cambridge Study, poor child-rearing (harsh or erratic discipline and cold or rejecting attitude) at age 8 predicted convictions up to age 50 (Farrington et al. 2009b). In the Seattle Social Development Project, which is a follow-up of over 800 children from age 10 to age 30, poor family management (poor supervision, inconsistent rules, harsh discipline) in adolescence predicted violence in young adulthood (Herrenkohl et al. 2000). In the Columbia County (New York State) follow-up of over 850 children from age 8 to age 48, Leonard Eron and his colleagues (1991) reported that parental punishment at age 8 predicted not only arrests for violence up to age 30, but also the severity of the man's punishment of his child at age 30 and also his history of spouse assault.

Family factors may have different effects on African American and Caucasian children in the United States. It is clear that African American children are more likely to be physically punished, and that physical punishment is more related to antisocial behavior for Caucasian children than for African American children (see, e.g., Deater-Deckard et al. 1996; Kelley et al. 1992). In the Pittsburgh Youth Study, 21 percent of Caucasian boys who were physically punished (slapped or spanked) by their mothers were violent, compared with 8 percent of those not physically punished. In contrast, 32 percent of African American boys who were physically punished were violent, compared with 28 percent of those not physically punished (Farrington et al. 2003). It was suggested that physical punishment may have a different meaning in African American families. Specifically, in these families it may indicate warmth and concern for the child, whereas in Caucasian families it tends to be associated with a cold and rejecting parental attitude.

Erratic or inconsistent discipline also predicts delinquency (West and Farrington 1973, 51). This can involve either erratic discipline by one parent, sometimes turning a blind eye to bad behavior and sometimes punishing it severely, or inconsistency between two parents, with one parent being tolerant or indulgent and the other being harshly punitive. It is not clear whether unusually lax discipline predicts delinquency. Just as inappropriate methods of responding to bad behavior predict delinquency, low parental reinforcement (not praising) of good behavior is also a predictor (Farrington and Loeber 1999).

Cold, rejecting parents tend to have delinquent children, as Joan McCord (1979) found 30 years ago in the Cambridge-Somerville study in Boston. More recently, she concluded that parental warmth could act as a protective factor against the effects of physical punishment (McCord 1997). Whereas 51 percent of boys with cold physically punishing mothers were convicted in her study, only 21 percent of boys with warm physically punishing mothers were convicted, similar to the 23 percent of boys with warm nonpunitive mothers who were convicted. The father's warmth was also a protective factor against the father's physical punishment.

Low parental involvement in the child's activities predicts delinquency, as John and Elizabeth Newson found in their Nottingham survey of 700 children (Lewis et al. 1982). In the Cambridge study, having a father who never joined in the boy's leisure activities doubled his risk of conviction (West and Farrington 1973, 57), and this was the most important predictor of persistence in offending after age 21, as opposed to desistance (Farrington and Hawkins 1991). Similarly, poor parent-child communication predicted delinquency in the Pittsburgh Youth Study (Farrington and Loeber 1999), and low family cohesiveness was the most important predictor of violence in the Chicago Youth Development Study follow-up of over 350 boys (Gorman-Smith et al. 1996).

Most explanations of the link between child-rearing methods and delinquency focus on social learning or attachment theories. Social learning theory suggests that children's behavior depends on parental rewards and punishments and on the models of behavior that parents represent (see, e.g., Patterson 1995). Children will tend to become delinquent if parents do not respond consistently and contingently to their antisocial behavior and if parents behave in an antisocial manner. Attachment theory was inspired by the work of John Bowlby (discussed later) and suggests that children who are not emotionally attached to warm, loving, and law-abiding parents will tend to become delinquent (see, e.g., Carlson and Sroufe 1995). The sociological equivalent of attachment theory is social bonding theory, which suggests that delinquency depends on the strength or weakness of a child's bond to society (see, e.g., Catalano et al. 2005).

Another possibility is that the link between child-rearing methods and delinquency merely reflects the genetic transmission of offending, as David Rowe (1994) argued. This idea was tested in the Cambridge study. The specific hypothesis was that child-rearing factors (supervision, discipline, and warmth/coldness) would not predict offending after controlling for parental criminality. This was confirmed in a structural equation modeling analysis but not in a regression analysis (Rowe and Farrington 1997). Thus, genetic factors could explain only part of the link between child-rearing factors and delinquency. Michael Rutter (2002) also concluded that family factors had an influence over and above genetic factors.

CHILD ABUSE AND NEGLECT

Children who are physically abused or neglected tend to become offenders later in life (Malinosky-Rummell and Hansen 1993), although Alan Leschied and his colleagues (2008) concluded that child maltreatment (and witnessing family violence) were only modest predictors of adult crime. The most famous study of child abuse and neglect was carried out by Cathy Widom (1989) in Indianapolis. She used court records to identify over 900 children who had been abused or neglected before age 11 and compared them with a control group matched on age, race, gender, elementary school class, and place of residence. A 20-year follow-up showed that the children who were abused or neglected were more likely to be arrested as juveniles and as adults than were the controls, and they were more likely to be arrested for juvenile violence (Maxfield and Widom 1996). Child abuse predicted later violence after controlling for other predictors such as gender, ethnicity, and age, and predictability was greater for females than for males (Widom and White 1997). Child sexual abuse and child physical abuse and neglect predicted adult arrests for sex crimes (Widom and Ames 1994).

Similar results have been obtained in other studies. In the Cambridge-Somerville study in Boston, Joan McCord (1983) found that about half of the abused or neglected boys were convicted for serious crimes, became alcoholics or mentally ill, or died before age 35. In the Rochester Youth Development Study follow-up of over 1,000 children, Carolyn Smith and Terence Thornberry (1995) showed that recorded child maltreatment under age 12 (physical, sexual, or emotional abuse or neglect) predicted later self-reported and official delinquency. Furthermore, these results held up after controlling for gender, race, socioeconomic status, and family structure. However, in the same study, Terence Thornberry and his colleagues (2001) concluded that maltreatment persisting into adolescence was the most damaging.

Possible environmental causal mechanisms linking childhood victimization and later violence were reviewed by Cathy Widom (1994). First, childhood victimization may have immediate but long-lasting consequences (e.g., shaking may cause brain injury). Second, childhood victimization may cause bodily changes (e.g., desensitization to pain) that encourage later violence. Third, child abuse may lead to impulsive or dissociative coping styles that, in turn, lead to poor problem-solving skills or poor school performance. Fourth, victimization may cause changes in self-esteem or in social information-processing patterns that encourage later violence. Fifth, child abuse may lead to changed family environments (e.g., being placed in foster care) that have deleterious effects. Sixth, juvenile justice practices may label victims, isolate them from prosocial peers, and encourage them to associate with delinquent peers.

Numerous theories have been put forward to explain the link between child abuse and later offending. Timothy Brezina (1998) described three of the main ones. Social learning theory suggests that children learn to adopt the abusive behavior patterns of their parents through imitation, modeling, and reinforcement. Attachment or social bonding theory proposes that child maltreatment results in low attachment to parents and hence to low self-control. Strain theory posits that negative treatment by others generates negative emotions such as anger and frustration, which in turn lead to a desire for revenge and increased aggression. Based on the Youth in Transition study, Brezina found limited support for all three theories.

PARENTAL CONFLICT AND DISRUPTED FAMILIES

John Bowlby (1951) popularized the theory that broken homes cause delinquency. He argued that mother love in infancy and childhood was just as important for mental health as were vitamins and proteins for physical health. He thought that it was essential that a child should experience a warm, loving, and continuous relationship with a mother figure. If a child suffered a prolonged period of maternal deprivation during the first five years of life, this would have irreversible negative effects, including becoming a cold "affectionless character" and a delinquent.

Most studies of broken homes have focused on the loss of the father rather than the mother, because the loss of a father is much more common. In general, it is found that children who are separated from a biological parent are more likely to offend than children from intact families. For example, in the Newcastle (UK) Thousand Family birth cohort study, Israel Kolvin and his colleagues (1988b) discovered that boys who experienced divorce or separation in their first five years of life had a doubled risk of conviction up to age 32 (53 percent as opposed to 28 percent). In the Cambridge study, 60 percent of boys who had been separated from a parent by their 10th birthday were convicted up to age 50, compared with 36 percent of the remainder (Farrington et al. 2009b). In the Dunedin study in New Zealand, Bill Henry and his colleagues (1996) found that boys from single-parent families were particularly likely to be convicted. In the National Longitudinal Survey of Adolescent Health, Stephen Demuth and Susan Brown (2004) concluded that single-parent families predicted delinquency because of their lower levels of parental supervision, closeness, and involvement.

Joan McCord (1982) in Boston carried out an innovative study of the relationship between homes broken by loss of the biological father and later serious offending by boys. She found that the prevalence of offending was high for boys from broken homes without affectionate mothers (62 percent) and for those from unbroken homes characterized by parental conflict (52 percent), irrespective of whether they had affectionate mothers. The prevalence of offending was low for those from unbroken homes without conflict (26 percent) and—importantly—equally low for boys from broken homes with affectionate mothers (22 percent). These results suggest that it might not be the broken home that is criminogenic but the parental conflict that often causes it. They also suggest that a loving mother might in some sense be able to compensate for the loss of a father.

The importance of the cause of the broken home was also shown in the UK National Survey of Health and Development by Michael Wadsworth (1979), in which over 5,000 children were followed up from birth. Illegitimate children were excluded from this survey, so all the children began life with two married parents. Boys from homes broken by divorce or separation had an increased likelihood of being convicted or officially cautioned up to age 21 (27 percent) in comparison with those from homes broken by death of the mother (19 percent), death of the father (14 percent), or from unbroken homes (14 percent). Homes broken while the boy was between birth and age 4 especially predicted delinquency, while homes broken while the boy was between ages 11 and 15 were not particularly criminogenic. Remarriage (which happened more often after divorce or separation than after death) was also associated with an increased risk of delinquency, suggesting an undesirable effect of stepparents. This undesirable effect was confirmed in the Montreal longitudinal study (Pagani et al. 1998) and in the National Longitudinal Study of Adolescent Health (Manning and Lamb 2003). The meta-analysis by Edward Wells and Joseph Rankin (1991) also shows that broken homes are more strongly related to delinquency when they are caused by parental separation or divorce rather than by death, and a more recent meta-analysis confirmed the undesirable effects of divorce (Price and Kunz 2003).

There is no doubt that parental conflict and interparental violence predict antisocial behavior by a child (see, e.g., Buehler et al. 1997; Ireland and Smith 2009). In the Christchurch (New Zealand) Health and Development Study follow-up of over 1,300 children, David Fergusson and John Horwood (1998) found that children who witnessed violence between their parents were more likely to commit both violent and property offenses according to their self-reports. The importance of witnessing father-initiated violence held up after controlling for other risk factors such as parental criminality, parental substance abuse, parental physical punishment, a young mother, and low family income. Parental conflict also predicted delinquency in both the Cambridge and Pittsburgh studies (Farrington and Loeber 1999).

Much research suggests that frequent changes of parent figures predict offending by children (e.g., Krohn et al 2009; Thornberry et al. 1999). For example, in a longitudinal survey of a birth cohort of over 500 Copenhagen males, Birgitte Mednick and her colleagues (1990) found that divorce followed by changes in parent figures predicted the highest rate of offending by children (65 percent), compared with divorce followed by stability (42 percent) and no divorce (28 percent). In the Dunedin study in New Zealand, Bill Henry and his colleagues (1993) reported that both parental conflict and many changes of the child's primary caretaker predicted the child's antisocial behavior up to age 11. However, in the Christchurch study in New Zealand, David Fergusson and his colleagues (1992) showed that parental transitions in the absence of parental conflict did not predict an increased risk of the child offending. Also, in the Oregon Youth Study follow-up of over 200 boys, Deborah Capaldi and Gerald Patterson (1991) concluded that antisocial mothers caused parental transitions, which in turn caused child antisocial behavior. In the Woodlawn longitudinal study of over 1,200 children in Chicago, the diversity and fluidity of children's living arrangements were remarkable (see, e.g., Hunter and Ensminger 1992).

Explanations of the relationship between disrupted families and delinquency fall into three major classes. Trauma theories suggest that the loss of a parent has a damaging effect on a child, most commonly because of the effect on attachment to the parent. Life course theories focus on separation as a sequence of stressful experiences, and on the effects of multiple stressors such as parental conflict, parental loss, reduced economic circumstances, changes in parent figures, and poor child-rearing methods. Selection theories argue that disrupted families produce delinquent children because of preexisting differences from other families in risk factors such as parental conflict, criminal or antisocial parents, low family income, or poor child-rearing methods.

Hypotheses derived from the three theories were tested in the Cambridge Study (Juby and Farrington 2001). While boys from broken homes (permanently disrupted families) were more delinquent than boys from intact homes, they were not more delinquent than boys from intact high-conflict families. Interestingly, this result was replicated in Switzerland (Haas et al. 2004). Overall, the most important factor was the post-disruption trajectory. Boys who remained with their mother after the separation had the same delinquency rate as boys from intact low conflict families. Boys who remained with their father, with relatives or with others (e.g., foster parents) had high delinquency rates. It was concluded that the results favored life course theories rather than trauma or selection theories.

OTHER PARENTAL FEATURES

Numerous other parental features predict delinquency and antisocial behavior of children. For example, early child-bearing or teenage pregnancy is a risk factor. Merry Morash and Lila Rucker (1989) analyzed results from four surveys in the United States and England (including the Cambridge Study) and found that teenage mothers were associated with low-income families, welfare support, and absent biological fathers, that they used poor child-rearing methods, and that their children were characterized by low school attainment and delinquency. However, the presence of the biological father mitigated many of these adverse factors and generally seemed to have a protective effect. Similarly, a large-scale study in Washington State showed that children of teenage or unmarried mothers had a significantly increased risk of offending (Conseur et al. 1997). Boys born to unmarried mothers aged 17 or less had an 11-fold increased risk of chronic offending compared to boys born to married mothers aged 20 or more.

In the Cambridge and Pittsburgh studies, the age of the mother at her first birth was only a moderate predictor of the boy's later delinquency (Farrington and Loeber 1999). In the Cambridge study, 55 percent of sons of teenage mothers were convicted up to age 50, compared with 37 percent of the remainder (Farrington et al. 2009b). More detailed analyses in this study showed that teenage mothers who went on to have large numbers of children were especially likely to have convicted children (Nagin et al. 1997). It was concluded that the results were concordant with a diminished resources theory: the offspring of adolescent mothers were more crime prone because they lacked not only economic resources but also personal resources such as attention and supervision. Of course, it must be remembered that the age of the mother is highly correlated with the age of the father; having a young father may be just as important as having a young mother. Also, since juvenile delinquency predicts causing an early pregnancy (Smith et al. 2000), the link between teenage parents and child delinquency may be one aspect of the link between criminal parents and delinquent children.

Several researchers have investigated factors that might mediate the link between young mothers and child delinquency. In the Dunedin study in New Zealand, Sara Jaffee and her colleagues (2001) concluded that the link between teenage mothers and violent children was mediated by maternal characteristics (e.g., intelligence, criminality) and family factors (e.g., harsh discipline, family size, disrupted families). In the Rochester Youth Development Study, Greg Pogarsky and his colleagues (2003) found that the most important mediating factor was the number of parental transitions (frequent changes in caregivers). Interestingly, the link between young mothers and child delinquency was stronger for Caucasian and Hispanic families than for African-American families. Pogarsky and his colleagues suggested that early child-bearing was less harmful when it was more common.

Substance use of parents predicts delinquency of children, as found in the Pittsburgh Youth Study (Loeber et al. 1998a). Smoking by the mother during pregnancy is a particularly important risk factor (e.g., McGloin et al. 2006; Wakschlag et al. 2002). The Northern Finland Birth Cohort Study of over 5,600 males showed that maternal smoking during pregnancy doubled the risk of violent or persistent offending by their sons, after controlling for other biopsychosocial risk factors (Rasanen et al. 1999). When maternal smoking was combined with a teenage mother, a single-parent family, and an unwanted pregnancy, risks of offending increased 10-fold. Comparable results were obtained in a Copenhagen birth cohort study of over 4,100 males by Patricia Brennan and her colleagues (1999).

In the Pittsburgh Youth Study, parental stress and parental depression were only moderate predictors of the boy's delinquency (Loeber et al. 1998a). In the Cambridge study, a depressed mother up to the boy's tenth birthday was a weak but significant predictor of convictions up to age 50; 50 percent of boys with depressed mothers were convicted, compared with 36 percent of the remainder (Farrington et al. 2009b). Rand Conger and his colleagues (1995) carried out an interesting study of parental stress (caused by negative life events) and delinquency, based on two surveys in Iowa and Oregon. They concluded that parental stress produced parental depression, which in turn caused poor discipline, which in turn caused childhood antisocial behavior.

KEY METHODOLOGICAL ISSUES

It is difficult to determine what are the precise causal mechanisms linking family factors—such as parental criminality, young mothers, family size, parental supervision, child abuse, or disrupted families—to the delinquency of children. This is because these factors tend to be related not only to each other but also to other risk factors for delinquency such as low family income, poor housing, impulsiveness, low intelligence, and low school attainment. Just as it is hard to know what are the key underlying family constructs, it is equally hard to know what are the key underlying constructs in other domains of life. It is important to investigate which family factors predict delinquency independently of other family factors, independently of genetic and biological factors, and independently of other factors (e.g., individual, peer, neighborhood, and socioeconomic). In the Oregon Youth Study, Lew Bank and Bert Burraston (2001) found that child maltreatment predicted arrests for violent crimes after controlling for unskilled discipline, academic performance, and deviant peers.

Another important question focuses on the interactions between family and other factors in the prediction of delinquency. There are many examples of interactions between family and biological factors. For example, Adrian Raine and his colleagues (1997, 5) found that maternal rejection interacted with birth complications in predicting violence in a large birth cohort of Copenhagen males. The prevalence of violence was only high when both maternal rejection and birth complications were present. Family factors are likely to have different effects on children of different ages (Frick et al. 1999). Similarly, family and other risk factors may have different effects on offending in different neighborhoods (Wikström and Loeber 2000).

It might be expected that family factors would have different effects on boys and girls, since there are well-documented gender differences in child-rearing experiences. In particular, boys are more likely to receive physical punishment from parents (see, e.g., Lytton and Romney 1991; Smith and

Brooks-Gunn 1997). There are some indications of gender differences in effects of family risk factors (e.g., family size: see Pagani et al. 2006). However, in their extensive review of gender differences in antisocial behavior, Terrie Moffitt and her colleagues (2001) concluded that boys were more antisocial essentially because they were exposed to more risk factors or a higher level of risk. Family risk factors did not seem to have different effects on antisocial behavior for boys and girls. It might also be expected that family factors would have different effects at different ages, and in the Rochester Youth Development Study, Terence Thornberry and his colleagues (2001) found that maltreatment during adolescence was more strongly related to delinquency than maltreatment during childhood.

While family influences are usually investigated as risk factors for delinquency, it is important also to investigate their effects as protective factors. In the Pittsburgh Youth Study, the most important factors that predicted a low likelihood of violence and serious theft were an older mother and low physical punishment (Loeber et al. 2008). In the Newcastle Thousand Family Study, Israel Kolvin and his colleagues (1988a) studied high-risk boys (from deprived backgrounds) who nevertheless did not become offenders. The most important protective factors included good maternal care and good maternal health for children under age 5 and good parental supervision at ages 11 and 15.

It is important to investigate sequential effects of risk factors on offending. Several researchers have concluded that socioeconomic factors have an effect on offending through their effects on family factors (see, e.g., Bor et al. 1997; Fergusson et al. 2004; Larzelere and Patterson 1990; Stern and Smith 1995). In the Pittsburgh Youth Study, it was proposed that socioeconomic and neighborhood factors (e.g., poor housing) influenced family factors (e.g., poor supervision) which in turn influenced child factors (e.g., lack of guilt), which in turn influenced offending (Loeber et al. 1998a, 10). There may also be sequential effects of some family factors on others, for example, if young mothers tend to use poor child-rearing methods (see Conger et al. 1995). There may also be effects of family factors on other risk factors; for example, if antisocial parents tend to have low incomes and choose to live in poor neighborhoods.

Just as parental child-rearing methods influence characteristics of children, so child characteristics may influence parenting (see, e.g., Crouter and Booth 2003). For example, an antisocial child may provoke more punishment from a parent than a well-behaved child. In their New York State longitudinal study, Patricia Cohen and Judith Brook (1995) found that there were reciprocal influences between parental punishment and child behavior disorder. Similarly, in the Rochester Youth Development Study, Sun Joon Jang and Carolyn Smith (1997) concluded that there was a reciprocal relationship between parental supervision and delinquency.

It is also important to investigate the cumulative effects of family risk factors (and indeed of all risk factors) on delinquency. Rex Forehand and his colleagues (1998) showed how the probability of conduct disorder and delinquency increased with the number of family risk factors. A logical implication of the clustering of risk factors is that boys with multiple risk factors should be studied. In the Pittsburgh Youth Study, Rolf Loeber and his colleagues (1998b) investigated how multiple risk factors were related to multiple types of child problems (including delinquency, substance use, hyperactivity, and depression). Relationships were general rather than specific. Many types of risk factors predicted many types of problems, and the number of risk factors predicted the number of problems, rather than specific risk factors predicting specific problems.

These results are in agreement with the hypothesis that delinquency is one element of a larger syndrome of antisocial behavior, and hence that predictors of one type of offending (e.g., violence) are similar to predictors of another (e.g., theft). Nevertheless, it is still useful to search for specific relationships between types of family factors and types of antisocial behavior.

FAMILY-BASED CRIME PREVENTION

To the extent that ineffective methods of child-rearing cause delinquency, it should be possible to prevent delinquency by educating or training parents to use more effective methods (for reviews, see Farrington and Welsh 2007; Piquero et al. 2009). Effective intervention programs can save a great deal of money. For example, Mark Cohen and Alex Piquero (2009) estimated that saving a high-risk youth at birth from a life of crime would save society between $2.6 and $4.4 million.

The behavioral parent management training developed by Gerald Patterson (1982) in Oregon is one of the most hopeful approaches. His careful observations of parent-child interaction showed that parents of antisocial children were deficient in their methods of child rearing. These parents failed to tell their children how they were expected to behave, failed to monitor their behavior to ensure that it was desirable, and failed to enforce rules promptly and unambiguously with appropriate rewards and penalties. The parents of antisocial children used more punishment (such as scolding, shouting, or threatening), but failed to make it contingent on the child's behavior.

Patterson attempted to train these parents in effective child-rearing methods, namely noticing what a child is doing, monitoring behavior over long periods, clearly stating house rules, making rewards and punishments contingent on behavior, and negotiating disagreements so that conflicts and crises did not escalate. His treatment was shown to be effective in reducing child stealing and antisocial behavior over short periods in small-scale studies (Dishion et al. 1992; Patterson et al. 1982, 1992). Other types of parent training, such as that devised by Carolyn Webster-Stratton (1998) in Seattle, and by Matthew Sanders and his colleagues (2000) in Brisbane, Australia, are also effective in reducing child antisocial behavior.

It is common to use parent training in conjunction with other prevention techniques. For example, the Montreal longitudinal experimental study combined child skills training and parent management training. Richard Tremblay and his colleagues (1995) identified disruptive (aggressive/hyperactive) boys at age 6 and randomly allocated over 300 of these to experimental or control conditions. Between ages 7 and 9, the experimental group received training designed to foster social skills and self-control. Coaching, peer modeling, role playing, and reinforcement contingencies were used in small group sessions on such topics as "how to help," "what to do when you are angry," and "how to react to teasing." Also, their parents were trained using Patterson's parent management training techniques.

This prevention program was quite successful. By age 12, the experimental boys committed less burglary and theft, were less likely to get drunk, and were less likely to be involved in fights than the controls (according to self-reports). Also, the experimental boys had higher school achievement. At every age from 10 to 15, the experimental boys had lower self-reported delinquency scores than the control boys. Interestingly, the differences in antisocial behavior between experimental and control boys increased as the follow-up progressed. A later follow-up showed that fewer experimental boys had a criminal record by age 24 (Boisjoli et al. 2007).

As another example of the use of parent training in conjunction with other techniques, David Hawkins and his colleagues (1991) combined parent management training, teacher training, and child skills training. About 500 first grade children (aged 6) in 21 classes in 8 schools were randomly assigned to be in experimental or control classes. The children in the experimental classes received special treatment at home and at school that was designed to increase their attachment to their parents and their bonding to the school. Also, they were trained in interpersonal cognitive problem-solving. Their parents were trained to notice and reinforce socially desirable behavior in a program called "Catch Them Being Good." Their teachers were trained in classroom management, for example to provide clear instructions and expectations to children, to reward children for participation in desired behavior, and to teach children prosocial (socially desirable) methods of solving problems.

This program had long-term benefits. In the follow-up at age 18, the full intervention group (those who received the intervention from grades 1–6) admitted less violence, less alcohol abuse, and fewer sexual partners than the late intervention group (grades 5–6 only) or the controls (Hawkins et al. 1999). According to Steve Aos and his colleagues (2001), over $4 were saved for every $1 spent on this program. In the latest follow-up at age 27, the full intervention group had better outcomes on educational attainment, socioeconomic status, mental health, and sexual health, but they were not better on crime or substance use (Hawkins et al. 2008).

General parent education, especially in the context of home visiting programs, is also effective in reducing delinquency. In the most famous intensive home-visiting program, David Olds and his colleagues (1986) in Elmira, New York, randomly allocated 400 mothers either to receive home visits from nurses during pregnancy, or to receive visits both during pregnancy and during the first two years of life, or to a control group who received no visits. Each visit lasted about one and a quarter hours, and the mothers were visited on average every two weeks. The home visitors gave advice about child-rearing, about prenatal and postnatal care of the child, about infant development, and about the importance of proper nutrition and avoiding smoking and drinking during pregnancy.

The results of this experiment showed that the postnatal home visits caused a decrease in recorded child physical abuse and neglect during the first two years of life, especially by poor unmarried teenage mothers; 4 percent of visited versus 19 percent of non-visited mothers of this type were guilty of child abuse or neglect (Olds et al. 1986). In a 15-year follow-up, the main focus was on lower-class unmarried mothers. Among these mothers, those who received prenatal and postnatal home visits had fewer arrests than those who received prenatal visits or no visits (Olds et al. 1997). Also, children of these mothers who received prenatal and/or postnatal home visits had less than half as many arrests as children of mothers who received no visits (Olds et al. 1998). According to Steve Aos and his colleagues (2001), the financial benefits of this program outweighed its financial costs for the lower-class unmarried mothers; $3 were saved for every $1 spent on this program.

Ideally, the results of prevention experiments should help to draw conclusions about which family factors have causal effects (see, e.g., Farrington 2000; Robins 1992). However, causal conclusions can only be drawn from experiments that study the effects of targeting each risk factor separately. In practice, experimenters are very concerned to use intervention programs that work. Consequently, they use multiple component interventions, which tend to be more effective than single component interventions (Wasserman and Miller 1998). There is a clear tension between maximizing the effectiveness of programs and drawing causal conclusions by disentangling the effects of different components.

CONCLUSIONS

It is clear that many family factors predict offending, but it is less clear what are the key underlying family dimensions that should be measured. The strongest predictor is usually criminal or antisocial parents. Other quite strong and replicable predictors are large family size, poor parental supervision, parental conflict, and disrupted families. In contrast, child abuse and young mothers are relatively weak predictors. Family-based prevention methods such as parent training and general parent education are effective in reducing later delinquency.

Many theories have been proposed to explain these results. The most popular are selection, social learning, and attachment theories. Selection theories argue that relationships between large family size, poor parental supervision, disrupted families (etc.) and delinquency are driven by the fact that antisocial people tend to have large families, poor parental supervision, disrupted families (etc.) as well as antisocial children. An extreme version of this theory suggests that all results reflect the genetic transmission of antisocial behavior from parents to children. Social learning theories argue that children fail to learn law-abiding behavior if their parents provide antisocial models and/or fail to react to their transgressions in an appropriate, consistent, and contingent fashion. Attachment theories argue that low attachment to parents (created, for example, by cold, rejecting parents or by separation from a parent) produces cold, callous children who tend to commit delinquent acts. These and other theories, and competing hypotheses about intervening mechanisms, need to be tested more effectively.

Most studies focus on family influences on the child's early onset of offending, rather than family influences on later criminal careers. More research is needed on family influences on adult onset or on the persistence or desistance of offending (see Farrington et al. 2009c; Zara and Farrington 2009) and on the effects of a person getting married or becoming separated on that person's own offending (see Laub and Sampson 2003; Theobald and Farrington 2009).

In order to advance knowledge about causal effects of family factors on offending, new prospective longitudinal studies are needed. Such studies should aim to estimate genetic influences and should measure a wide range of risk factors (individual, family, peer, school, neighborhood, etc.). They should aim to establish independent, interactive, sequential, and reciprocal effects of family factors on offending. They should study protective factors as well as risk factors. Systematic observation as well as interviews and questionnaires should be used to measure family factors. Ideally, intervention experiments targeting family factors should be included in longitudinal studies in order to establish causal effects more securely. A new generation of longitudinal studies should go beyond demonstrating that family factors predict offending and should seek to determine the key causal mechanisms that are involved. This should help greatly in designing family-based prevention programs to reduce crime.

References

Aos, Steve, P. Phipps, Robert Barnoski, and Roxanne Lieb. 2001. "The Comparative Costs and Benefits of Programs to Reduce Crime: A Review of research Findings with Implications for Washington State." In *Costs and Benefits of Preventing Crime*, ed. Brandon C. Welsh, David P. Farrington and Lawrence W. Sherman, 149–175. Boulder, CO: Westview Press.

Bank, Lew, and Bert Burraston. 2001. "Abusive Home Environments as Predictors of Poor Adjustment during Adolescence and Early Adulthood." *Journal of Community Psychology* 29: 195–217.

Boisjoli, Rachel, Frank Vitaro, Eric Lacourse, E. D. Barker, and Richard E. Tremblay. 2007."Impact and Clinical Significance of a Preventive Intervention for Disruptive Boys." *British Journal of Psychiatry* 191: 415–419.

Bor, William, Jake M. Najman, Margaret J. Andersen, Michael O'Callaghan, Gail M. Williams, and Brett C. Behrens. 1997. "The Relationship Between Low Family Income and Psychological Disturbance in Young Children: An Australian Longitudinal Study." *Australian and New Zealand Journal of Psychiatry* 31: 664–675.

Bowlby, John. 1951. *Maternal Care and Mental Health.* Geneva, Switzerland: World Health Organization.

Brennan, Patricia A., Emily R. Grekin, and Sarnoff A. Mednick. 1999. "Maternal Smoking during Pregnancy and Adult Male Criminal Outcomes." *Archives of General Psychiatry* 56: 215–219.

Brennan, Patricia A., Birgitte R. Mednick, and Sarnoff A. Mednick. 1993. "Parental Psychopathology, Congenital Factors, and Violence." In *Mental Disorder and Crime,* ed. Sheilagh Hodgins, 244–261. Newbury Park, CA: Sage.

Brezina, Timothy. 1998. "Adolescent Maltreatment and Delinquency: The Question of Intervening Processes." *Journal of Research in Crime and Delinquency* 35:71–99.

Brownfield, David, and Ann M. Sorenson. 1994. "Sibship Size and Sibling Delinquency." *Deviant Behavior* 15: 45–61.

Buehler, Cheryl, Christine Anthony, Ambika Krishnakumar, Gaye Stone, Jean Gerard, and Sharon Pemberton. 1997. "Interparental Conflict and Youth Problem Behaviors: A Meta-Analysis." *Journal of Child and Family Studies* 6: 233–247.

Capaldi, Deborah M., and Gerald R. Patterson. 1991. "Relation of Parental Transitions to Boys' Adjustment Problems." *Developmental Psychology* 27: 489–504.

Carlson, Elizabeth A., and L. Alan Sroufe. 1995. "Contribution of Attachment Theory to Developmental Psychopathology." In *Developmental Psychopathology, vol. 1: Theory and Methods,* ed. Dante Cicchetti and Donald J. Cohen, 581–617. New York: Wiley.

Catalano, Richard F., Jisuk Park, Tracy W. Harachi, Kevin P. Haggerty, Robert D. Abbott, and J. David Hawkins. 2005. "Mediating the Effects of Poverty, Gender, Individual Characteristics, and External Constraints on Antisocial Behavior: A Test of the Social Development Model and Implications for Developmental Life-Course Theory." In *Integrated Developmental and Life-Course Theories of Offending,* ed. David P. Farrington, 93–123. New Brunswick, NJ: Transaction.

Cohen, Mark A., and Alex R. Piquero. 2009. "New Evidence on the Monetary Value of Saving a High Risk Youth." *Journal of Quantitative Criminology* 25: 25–49.

Cohen, Patricia, and Judith S. Brook. 1995. "The Reciprocal Influence of Punishment and Child Behavior Disorder." In *Coercion and Punishment in Long-Term Perspectives,* ed. Joan McCord, 154–164. Cambridge, UK: Cambridge University Press.

Conger, Rand D., Gerald R. Patterson, and Xiaojia Ge. 1995. "It Takes Two to Replicate: A Mediational Model for the Impact of Parents' Stress on Adolescent Adjustment." *Child Development* 66: 80–97.

Conseur, Amy, Frederick P. Rivara, Robert Barnoski, and Irvin Emanuel. 1997. "Maternal and Perinatal Risk Factors for Later Delinquency." *Pediatrics* 99: 785–790.

Crouter, Ann C., and Alan Booth. eds. 2003. *Children's Influence on Family Dynamics.* Hillsdale, NJ: Lawrence Erlbaum.

Deater-Deckard, Kirby, Kenneth A. Dodge, John E. Bates, and Gregory S. Pettit. 1996. "Physical Discipline among African American and European American Mothers: Links to Children's Externalizing Behaviors." *Developmental Psychology* 32: 1065–1072.

Demuth, Stephen, and Susan L. Brown. 2004. "Family Structure, Family Processes, and Adolescent Delinquency: The Significance of Parental Absence Versus Parental Gender." *Journal of Research in Crime and Delinquency* 41: 58–81.

Derzon, James H. 2010. "The Correspondence of Family Features with Problem, Aggressive, Criminal, and Violent Behavior: A Meta-Analysis." *Journal of Experimental Criminology* 6: 263–292.

Dishion, Thomas, J., Gerald R. Patterson, and Kathryn A. Kavanagh. 1992. "An Experimental Test of the Coercion Model: Linking Theory, Measurement and Intervention." In *Preventing Antisocial Behavior: Interventions from Birth Through Adolescence*, ed. Joan McCord and Richard E. Tremblay, 253–282. New York: Guilford Press.

Ellis, Lee, Kevin Beaver, and John Wright. 2009. *Handbook of Crime Correlates*. Oxford, UK: Academic Press.

Eron, Leonard D., L. Rowell Huesmann, and Arnaldo Zelli. 1991. "The Role of Parental Variables in the Learning of Aggression." In *The Development and Treatment of Childhood Aggression*, ed. Debra J. Pepler and Kenneth J. Rubin, 169–188. Hillsdale, NJ: Lawrence Erlbaum.

Fagan, Abigail A., and Jake M. Najman. 2003. "Sibling Influences on Adolescent Delinquent Behavior: An Australian Longitudinal Study." *Journal of Adolescence* 26: 547–559.

Farrington, David P. 1992. "Juvenile Delinquency." In *The School Years*, ed. John C. Coleman, 2nd ed., 123–163. London: Routledge.

Farrington, David P. 2000. "Explaining and Preventing Crime: The Globalization of Knowledge—The American Society of Criminology 1999 Presidential Address." *Criminology* 38: 1–24.

Farrington, David P., Geoffrey Barnes, and Sandra Lambert. 1996. "The Concentration of Offending in Families." *Legal and Criminological Psychology* 1: 47–63.

Farrington, David P., Jeremy W. Coid, Louise Harnett, Darrick Jolliffe, Nadine Soteriou, Richard Turner, and Donald J. West. 2006. *Criminal Careers up to Age 50 and Life Success up to Age 48: New Findings from the Cambridge Study in Delinquent Development*. London: Home Office (Research Study No. 299).

Farrington, David P., Jeremy W. Coid, and Joseph Murray.2009a. "Family Factors in the Intergenerational Transmission of Offending." *Criminal Behaviour and Mental Health* 19: 109–124.

Farrington, David P., Jeremy W. Coid, and Donald J. West. 2009b. "The Development of Offending from Age 8 to Age 50: Recent Results from the Cambridge Study in Delinquent Development." *Monatsschrift fur Kriminologie und Strafrechtsreform (Journal of Criminology and Penal Reform)* 92: 160–173.

Farrington, David P., and J. David Hawkins. 1991. "Predicting Participation, Early Onset, and Later Persistence in Officially Recorded Offending." *Criminal Behaviour and Mental Health* 1: 1–33.

Farrington, David P., Darrick Jolliffe, Rolf Loeber, Magda Stouthamer-Loeber, and Larry M. Kalb. 2001. "The Concentration of Offenders in Families, and Family Criminality in the Prediction of Boys' Delinquency." *Journal of Adolescence* 24: 579–596.

Farrington, David P., and Rolf Loeber. 1999. "Transatlantic Replicability of Risk Factors in the Development of Delinquency." In *Historical and Geographical Influences on Psychopathology*, eds. Patricia Cohen, Cheryl Slomkowski, and Lee N. Robins, 299–329. Mahwah, NJ: Lawrence Erlbaum.

Farrington, David P., Rolf Loeber, and Magda Stouthamer-Loeber. 2003. "How Can the Relationship Between Race and Violence be Explained?" In *Violent Crime: Assessing Race and Ethnic Differences*, ed. Darnell F. Hawkins, 213–237. Cambridge, UK: Cambridge University Press.

Farrington, David P., Maria M. Ttofi, and Jeremy W. Coid. 2009c. "Development of Adolescence Limited, Late-Onset and Persistent Offenders from Age 8 to Age 48." *Aggressive Behavior* 35: 150–163.

Farrington, David P., and Brandon C. Welsh. 2007. *Saving Children from a Life of Crime: Early Risk Factors and Effective Interventions*. Oxford, UK: Oxford University Press.

Fergusson, David M., and L. John Horwood. 1998. "Exposure to Interparental Violence in Childhood and Psychosocial Adjustment in Young Adulthood." *Child Abuse and Neglect* 22: 339–357.

Fergusson, David M., L. John Horwood, and Michael T. Lynskey.1992. "Family Change, Parental Discord and Early Offending." *Journal of Child Psychology and Psychiatry* 33: 1059–1075.

Fergusson, David, Naomi Swain-Campbell, and L. John Horwood. 2004. "How Does Childhood Economic Disadvantage Lead to Crime?" *Journal of Child Psychology and Psychiatry* 45: 956–966.

Forehand, Rex, Heather Biggar, and Beth A. Kotchick. 1998. "Cumulative Risk across Family Stressors: Short and Long Term Effects for Adolescents." *Journal of Abnormal Child Psychology* 26: 119–128.

Frick, Paul J., Rachel E. Christian, and Jane M. Wootton. 1999. "Age Trends in the Association Between Parenting Practices and Conduct Problems." *Behavior Modification* 23: 106–128.

Gershoff, E. T. 2002. "Corporal Punishment by Parents and Associated Child Behaviors and Experiences: A Meta-Analytic and Theoretical Review." *Psychological Bulletin* 128: 539–579.

Gorman-Smith, Deborah, Patrick H. Tolan, Arnaldo Zelli, and L. Rowell Huesmann. 1996. "The Relation of Family Functioning to Violence among Inner-City Minority Youths." *Journal of Family Psychology* 10: 115–129.

Grove, William M., Elke D. Eckert, Leonard Heston, Thomas J. Bouchard, Nancy Segal, and David T. Lykken. 1990. "Heritability of Substance Abuse and Antisocial Behavior: A Study of Monozygotic Twins Reared Apart." *Biological Psychiatry* 27: 1293–1304.

Haapasalo, Jaana, and Elina Pokela. 1999. "Child-Rearing and Child Abuse Antecedents of Criminality." *Aggression and Violent Behavior* 4: 107–127.

Haas, Henriette, David P. Farrington, Martin Killias, and Ghazala Sattar. 2004. "The Impact of Different Family Configurations on Delinquency." *British Journal of Criminology* 44: 520–532.

Hawkins, J. David, Richard F. Catalano, Rick Kosterman, Robert Abbott, and Karl G. Hill. 1999. "Preventing Adolescent Health Risk Behaviors by Strengthening Protection during Childhood." *Archives of Pediatrics and Adolescent Medicine* 153: 226–234.

Hawkins, J. David, Elizabeth von Cleve, and Richard F. Catalano. 1991. "Reducing Early Childhood Aggression: Results of a Primary Prevention Program." *Journal of the American Academy of Child and Adolescent Psychiatry* 30: 208–217.

Hawkins, J. David, Rick Kosterman, Richard F. Catalano, Karl G. Hill, and Robert D. Abbott. 2008. "Effects of Social Development Intervention in Childhood 15 Years Later." *Archives of Pediatrics and Adolescent Medicine* 162: 1133–1141.

Henry, Bill, Avshalom Caspi, Terrie E. Moffitt, and Phil A. Silva. 1996. "Temperamental and Familial Predictors of Violent and Nonviolent Criminal Convictions: Age 3 to Age 18." *Developmental Psychology* 32: 614–623.

Henry, Bill, Terrie Moffitt, Lee Robins, Felton Earls, and Phil Silva. 1993. "Early Family Predictors of Child and Adolescent Antisocial Behavior: Who Are the Mothers of Delinquents?" *Criminal Behavior and Mental Health* 3: 97–118.

Herrenkohl, Todd I., Eugene Maguin, Karl G. Hill, J. David Hawkins, Robert D. Abbott, and Richard F. Catalano. 2000. "Developmental Risk Factors for Youth Violence." *Journal of Adolescent Health* 26: 176–186.

Hunter, Andrea G., and Margaret E. Ensminger. 1992. "Diversity and Fluidity in Children's Living Arrangements: Family Transitions in an Urban Afro-American Community." *Journal of Marriage and the Family* 54: 418–426.

Ireland, Timothy O., and Carolyn A. Smith. 2009. "Living in Partner-Violent Families: Developmental Links to Antisocial Behavior and Relationship Violence." *Journal of Youth and Adolescence* 38: 323–339.

Jaffee, Sara, Avshalom Caspi, Terrie E. Moffitt, Jay Belsky, and Phil A. Silva. 2001. "Why Are Children Born to Teen Mothers at Risk for Adverse Outcomes in Young Adulthood? Results from a 20-year Longitudinal Study." *Development and Psychopathology* 13: 377–397.

Jang, Sung Joon, and Carolyn A. Smith. 1997. "A Test of Reciprocal Causal Relationships among Parental Supervision, Affective Ties, and Delinquency." *Journal of Research in Crime and Delinquency* 34: 307–336.

Johnson, Jeffrey G., Elizabeth Smailes, Patricia Cohen, Stephanie Kasen, and Judith S. Brook. 2004. "Antisocial Parental Behaviour, Problematic Parenting and Aggressive Offspring Behaviour During Adulthood." *British Journal of Criminology* 44: 915–930.

Juby, Heather, and David P. Farrington. 2001. "Disentangling the Link between Disrupted Families and Delinquency." *British Journal of Criminology* 41: 22–40.

Kelley, Michelle L., Thomas G. Power, and Dawn D. Wimbush. 1992. "Determinants of Disciplinary Practices in Low-income Black Mothers." *Child Development* 63: 573–582.

Kolvin, Israel, Frederick J. W. Miller, Mary Fleeting, and Philip A. Kolvin. 1988a. "Risk/Protective Factors for Offending with Particular Reference to Deprivation." In *Studies of Psychosocial Risk: The Power of Longitudinal Data*, ed. Michael Rutter, 77–95. Cambridge, UK: Cambridge University Press.

Kolvin, Israel, Frederick J. W. Miller, Mary Fleeting, and Philip A. Kolvin. 1988b. "Social and Parenting Factors Affecting Criminal-Offence Rates: Findings from the Newcastle Thousand Family Study (1947–1980)." *British Journal of Psychiatry* 152: 80–90.

Krohn, Marvin D., Gina P. Hall, and Alan J. Lizotte. 2009. "Family Transitions and Later Delinquency and Drug Use." *Journal of Youth and Adolescence* 38: 466–480.

Krueger, Robert F., Terrie E. Moffitt, Avshalom Caspi, April Bleske, and Phil A. Silva. 1998. "Assortative Mating for Antisocial Behavior: Developmental and Methodological Implications." *Behavior Genetics* 28: 173–186.

Larzelere, Robert E., and Gerald R. Patterson. 1990. "Parental Management: Mediator of the Effect of Socioeconomic Status on Early Delinquency." *Criminology* 28: 301–324.

Laub, John H., and Robert J. Sampson. 2003. *Shared Beginnings, Divergent Lives: Delinquent Boys to Age 70.* Cambridge, MA: Harvard University Press.

Leschied, Alan, Debbie Chiodo, Elizabeth Nowicki, and Susan Rodger. 2008. "Childhood Predictors of Adult Criminality: A Meta-Analysis Drawn from the Prospective Longitudinal Literature." *Canadian Journal of Criminology and Criminal Justice* 50: 435–467.

Lewis, C., Elizabeth Newson, and John Newson. 1982. "Father Participation Through Childhood and Its Relationship with Career Aspirations and Delinquency." In *Fathers: Psychological Perspectives*, eds. N. Beail and J. McGuire, 174–193. London: Junction.

Lipsey, Mark W., and James H. Derzon. 1998. "Predictors of Violent or Serious Delinquency in Adolescence and Early Adulthood: A Synthesis of Longitudinal Research." In *Serious and Violent Juvenile Offenders: Risk Factors and Successful Interventions*, eds. Rolf Loeber and David P. Farrington, 86–105. Thousand Oaks, CA: Sage.

Loeber, Rolf, David P. Farrington, Magda Stouthamer-Loeber, and Welmoet van Kammen. 1998a. *Antisocial Behavior and Mental Health Problems: Explanatory Factors in Childhood and Adolescence.* Mahwah, NJ: Lawrence Erlbaum.

Loeber, Rolf, David P. Farrington, Magda Stouthamer-Loeber, and Welmoet van Kammen. 1998b. "Multiple Risk Factors for Multi-Problem Boys: Co-occurrence of Delinquency, Substance Use, Attention Deficit, Conduct Problems, Physical Aggression, Covert Behavior, Depressed Mood and Shy/Withdrawn Behavior." In *New Perspectives on Adolescent Risk Behavior*, ed. Richard Jessor, 90–149. Cambridge, UK: Cambridge University Press.

Loeber, Rolf, David P. Farrington, Magda Stouthamer-Loeber, and Helene R. White. 2008. *Violence and Serious Theft: Development and Prediction from Childhood to Adulthood.* New York: Routledge.

Lösel, Friedrich, and Doris Bender. 2003. "Protective Factors and Resilience." In *Early Prevention of Adult Antisocial Behaviour*, eds. David P. Farrington and Jeremy W. Coid, 130–204. Cambridge, UK: Cambridge University Press.

Lytton Hugh, and David M. Romney. 1991. "Parents' Differential Socialization of Boys and Girls: A Meta-Analysis." *Psychological Bulletin* 109: 267–296.

McCord, Joan. 1977. "A Comparative Study of Two Generations of Native Americans." In *Theory in Criminology*, ed. Robert F. Meier, 83–92. Beverly Hills, CA: Sage.

McCord, Joan. 1979. "Some Child-Rearing Antecedents of Criminal Behavior in Adult Men." *Journal of Personality and Social Psychology* 37: 1477–1486.

McCord, Joan. 1982. "A Longitudinal View of the Relationship Between Paternal Absence and Crime." In *Abnormal Offenders, Delinquency, and the Criminal Justice System*, eds. John Gunn and David P. Farrington, 113–128. Chichester, UK: Wiley.

McCord, Joan. 1983. "A Forty Year Perspective on Effects of Child Abuse and Neglect." *Child Abuse and Neglect* 7: 265–270.

McCord, Joan. 1997. "On Discipline." *Psychological Inquiry* 8: 215–217.

McGloin, Jean M., Travis C. Pratt, and Alex R. Piquero. 2006. "A Life-Course Analysis of the Criminiogenic Effects of Maternal Cigarette Smoking During Pregnancy." *Journal of Research in Crime and Delinquency* 43: 412–426.

Malinosky-Rummell, R. and David J. Hansen. 1993. "Long-Term Consequences of Childhood Physical Abuse." *Psychological Bulletin* 114: 68–79.

Manning, Wendy D., and Kathleen L. Lamb.2003. "Adolescent Well-Being in Cohabiting, Married, and Single-Parent Families." *Journal of Marriage and the Family* 65: 876–893.

Maxfield, Michael G., and Cathy S. Widom. 1996. "The Cycle of Violence Revisited 6 Years Later." *Archives of Pediatrics and Adolescent Medicine* 150: 390–395.

Mednick, Birgitte R., Robert L. Baker, and Linn E. Carothers. 1990. "Patterns of Family Instability and Crime: The Association of Timing of the Family's Disruption with Subsequent Adolescent and Young Adult Criminality." *Journal of Youth and Adolescence* 19: 201–220.

Moffitt, Terrie E., Avshalom Caspi, Michael Rutter, and Phil A. Silva. 2001. *Sex Differences in Antisocial Behaviour*. Cambridge, UK: Cambridge University Press.

Morash, Merry, and Lila Rucker. 1989. "An Exploratory Study of the Connection of Mother's Age at Childbearing to her Children's Delinquency in Four Data Sets." *Crime and Delinquency* 35: 45–93.

Murray, Joseph, and David P. Farrington. 2005. "Parental Imprisonment: Effects on Boys' Antisocial Behavior and Delinquency through the Life-Course." *Journal of Child Psychology and Psychiatry* 46: 1269–1278.

Nagin, Daniel S., Greg Pogarsky, and David P. Farrington. 1997. "Adolescent Mothers and the Criminal Behavior of their Children." *Law and Society Review* 31: 137–162.

Olds, David L., John Eckenrode, Charles R. Henderson, Harriet Kitzman, Jane Powers, Robert Cole, Kimberly Sidora, Pamela Morris, Lisa M. Pettitt, and Dennis Luckey. 1997. "Long-Term Effects of Home Visitation on Maternal Life Course and Child Abuse and Neglect: Fifteen-Year Follow-up of a Randomized Trial." *Journal of the American Medical Association* 278: 637–643.

Olds, David L., Charles R. Henderson, Robert Chamberlin, and Robert Tatelbaum. 1986. "Preventing Child Abuse and Neglect: A Randomized Trial of Nurse Home Visitation." *Pediatrics* 78: 65–78.

Olds, David L., Charles R. Henderson, Robert Cole, John Eckenrode, Harriet Kitzman, Dennis Luckey, Lisa Pettitt, Kimberly Sidora, Pamela Morris, and Jane Powers. 1998. "Long-Term Effects of Nurse Home Visitation on Children's Criminal and Antisocial Behavior: 15-Year Follow-up of a Randomized Controlled Trial." *Journal of the American Medical Association* 280: 1238–1244.

Pagani, Linda S., Christa Japal, A. Girard, A. Farhat, S. Cote, and Richard E. Tremblay. 2006. "Middle Childhood Life-Course Trajectories: Links Between Family Dysfunction and Children's Behavioral Development." In *Developmental Contexts in Middle Childhood*, eds. A. Huston and M. N. Ripke, 130–149. New York: Cambridge University Press.

Pagani, Linda, Richard E. Tremblay, Frank Vitaro, Margaret Kerr, and Pierre McDuff. 1998. "The Impact of Family Transition on the Development of Delinquency in Adolescent Boys: A 9-year Longitudinal Study." *Journal of Child Psychology and Psychiatry* 39: 489–499.

Patterson, Gerald R. 1982. *Coercive Family Process*. Eugene, OR: Castalia.

Patterson, Gerald R. 1995. "Coercion as a Basis for Early Age of Onset for Arrest." In *Coercion and Punishment in Long-Term Perspectives*, ed. Joan McCord, 81–105. Cambridge, UK: Cambridge University Press.

Patterson, Gerald, R., Patricia Chamberlain, and John B. Reid. 1982. "A Comparative Evaluation of a Parent Training Program." *Behavior Therapy* 13: 638–650.

Patterson, Gerald R., John B. Reid, and Thomas J. Dishion. 1992. *Antisocial Boys*. Eugene, OR: Castalia.

Piquero, Alex R., David P. Farrington, Brandon C. Welsh, Richard E. Tremblay, and Wesley Jennings. 2009. *Effects of Early Family/Parent Training Programs on Antisocial Behavior and Delinquency*. Journal of Experimental Criminology 5: 83–120.

Price, C., and J. Kunz. 2003. "Rethinking the Paradigm of Juvenile Delinquency as Related to Divorce." *Journal of Divorce and Remarriage* 39: 109–133.

Pogarsky, Greg, Alan J. Lizotte, and Terence P. Thornberry. 2003. "The Delinquency of Children Born to Young Mothers: Results from the Rochester Youth Development Study." *Criminology* 41: 1249–1286.

Raine, Adrian. 1993. *The Psychopathology of Crime: Criminal Behavior as a Clinical Disorder*. San Diego, CA: Academic Press.

Raine, Adrian, Patricia A. Brennan, and David P. Farrington. 1997. "Biosocial Bases of Violence: Conceptual and Theoretical Issues." In *Biosocial Bases of Violence*, ed. Adrian Raine, Patricia A. Brennan, David P. Farrington, and Sarnoff A. Mednick, 1–20. New York: Plenum.

Rasanen, Pirkko, Hilina Hakko, Matti Isohanni, Sheilagh Hodgins, Marjo-Riitta Jarvelin, and Jari Tiihonen. 1999. "Maternal Smoking during Pregnancy and Risk of Criminal Behavior among Adult Male Offspring in the Northern Finland 1966 Birth Cohort." *American Journal of Psychiatry* 156: 857–862.

Reiss, Albert J., and David P. Farrington. 1991. "Advancing Knowledge about Co-offending: Results from a Prospective Longitudinal Survey of London Males." *Journal of Criminal Law and Criminology* 82: 360–395.

Robins, Lee N. 1979. "Sturdy Childhood Predictors of Adult Outcomes: Replications from Longitudinal Studies." In *Stress and Mental Disorder*, eds. J. E. Barrett, R. M. Rose, and Gerald L. Klerman, 219–235. New York: Raven Press.

Robins, Lee N. 1992. "The Role of Prevention Experiments in Discovering Causes of Children's Antisocial Behavior." In *Preventing Antisocial Behavior: Interventions from Birth through Adolescence*, eds. Joan McCord and Richard E. Tremblay, 3–18. New York: Guilford Press.

Rothbaum, Fred, and John R. Weisz. 1994. "Parental Caregiving and Child Externalizing Behavior in Nonclinical Samples: A Meta-Analysis." *Psychological Bulletin* 116: 55–74.

Rowe, David C. 1994. *The Limits of Family Influence: Genes, Experience, and Behavior*. New York: Guilford Press.

Rowe, David C., and David P. Farrington. 1997. "The Familial Transmission of Criminal Convictions." *Criminology* 35: 177–201.

Rutter, Michael. 2002. "Nature, Nurture, and Development: From Evangelism Through Science toward Policy and Practice." *Child Development* 73: 1–21.

Sampson, Robert J, and John H. Laub. 1993. *Crime in the Making: Pathways and Turning Points Through Life*. Cambridge, MA: Harvard University Press.

Sanders, Matthew R., C. Markie-Dadds, L. A. Tully, and W. Bor. 2000. "The Triple P-Positive Parenting Program: A Comparison of Enhanced Standard and Self-directed Behavioral Family Intervention for Parents of Children with Early Onset Conduct Problems." *Journal of Consulting and Clinical Psychology* 68: 624–640.

Smith, Carolyn A. and David P. Farrington. 2004. "Continuities in Antisocial Behavior and Parenting across Three Generations." *Journal of Child Psychology and Psychiatry* 45: 230–247.

Smith. Carolyn A., Marvin D. Krohn, Alan J. Lizotte, Cynthia P. McCluskey, Magda Stouthamer-Loeber, and Anne Weiher. 2000. "The Effect of Early Delinquency and Substance Use on Precocious Transitions to Adulthood among Adolescent Males." In *Families, Crime and Criminal Justice*, ed. Greer L. Fox and Michael L. Benson, *vol. 2*, 233–253. Amsterdam: JAI Press.

Smith, Carolyn A., and Susan B. Stern. 1997. "Delinquency and Antisocial Behavior: A Review of Family Processes and Intervention Research." *Social Service Review* 71: 382–420.

Smith, Carolyn A., and Terence P. Thornberry. 1995. "The Relationship Between Childhood Maltreatment and Adolescent Involvement in Delinquency." *Criminology* 33: 451–481.

Smith, Judith R., and Jeanne Brooks-Gunn. 1997. "Correlates and Consequences of Harsh Discipline for Young Children." *Archives of Pediatrics and Adolescent Medicine* 151: 777–786.

Stern, Susan B., and Carolyn A. Smith. 1995. "Family Processes and Delinquency in an Ecological Context." *Social Service Review* 69: 705–731.

Theobald, Delphine, and David P. Farrington. 2009. "Effects of Getting Married on Offending: Results from a Prospective Longitudinal Survey of Males." *European Journal of Criminology* 6: 496–516.

Thornberry, Terence P., Timothy O. Ireland, and Carolyn A. Smith. 2001. "The Importance of Timing: The Varying Impact of Childhood and Adolescent Maltreatment on Multiple Problem Outcomes." *Development and Psychopathology* 13: 957–979.

Thornberry, Terence P., Carolyn A. Smith, Craig Rivera, David Huizinga, and Magda Stouthamer-Loeber. 1999. *Family Disruption and Delinquency*. Washington, DC: Office of Juvenile Justice and Delinquency Prevention.

Tremblay, Richard E., Linda Pagani-Kurtz, Louise C. Masse, Frank Vitaro, and Robert O. Pihl. 1995. "A Bimodal Preventive Intervention for Disruptive Kindergarten Boys: Its Impact Through Mid-Adolescence." *Journal of Consulting and Clinical Psychology* 63: 560–568.

Wadsworth, Michael. 1979. *Roots of Delinquency*. London: Martin Robertson.

Wakschlag, Lauren S., Kate E. Pickett, Edwin Cook, Neal L. Benowitz, and Bennett L. Leventhal. 2002. "Maternal Smoking During Pregnancy and Severe Antisocial Behavior in Offspring: A Review." *American Journal of Public Health* 92: 966–974.

Wasserman, Gail A., and Laurie S. Miller. 1998. "The Prevention of Serious and Violent Juvenile Offending." In *Serious and Violent Juvenile Offenders: Risk Factors and Successful Interventions*, eds. Rolf Loeber and David P. Farrington, 197–247. Thousand Oaks, CA: Sage.

Webster-Stratton, Carolyn. 1998. "Preventing Conduct Problems in Head Start Children: Strengthening Parenting Competencies." *Journal of Consulting and Clinical Psychology* 66: 715–730.

Wells, L. Edward, and Joseph H. Rankin. 1991. "Families and Delinquency: A Meta-Analysis of the Impact of Broken Homes." *Social Problems* 38: 71–93.

West, Donald J., and David P. Farrington. 1973. *Who Becomes Delinquent?* London: Heinemann.

West, David J., and David P. Farrington. 1977. *The Delinquent Way of Life.* London: Heinemann.

Widom, Cathy S. 1989. "The Cycle of Violence." *Science* 244: 160–166.

Widom, Cathy S. 1994. "Childhood Victimization and Adolescent Problem Behaviors." In *Adolescent Problem Behaviors*, eds. Robert D. Ketterlinus and Michael E. Lamb, 127–164. Hillsdale, NJ: Lawrence Erlbaum.

Widom, Cathy S., and M. Ashley Ames. 1994. "Criminal Consequences of Childhood Sexual Victimization." *Child Abuse and Neglect* 18: 303–318.

Widom, Cathy S., and Helene R. White. 1997. "Problem Behaviors in Abused and Neglected Children Grown Up: Prevalence and Co-occurrence of Substance Use, Crime, and Violence." *Criminal Behaviour and Mental Health* 7: 287–310.

Wikström, Per-Olof, and Rolf Loeber. 2000. "Do Disadvantaged Neighborhoods Cause Well-Adjusted Children to Become Adolescent Delinquents? A Study of Male Juvenile Serious Offending, Individual Risk and Protective Factors, and Neighborhood Context." *Criminology* 38: 1109–1142.

Zara, Georgia, and David P. Farrington. 2009. "Childhood and Adolescent Predictors of Late Onset Criminal Careers." *Journal of Youth and Adolescence* 38: 287–300.

Chapter 6

Street Gangs

Cheryl Maxson

Many people believe that, beginning in the mid-1980s, street gangs from cities such as Los Angeles and Chicago appeared in previously unaffected cities and towns. According to this view, Crips and Bloods, Latin Kings and Black Gangster Disciples fanned out across the nation to establish drug sales franchises, particularly cocaine crack distribution networks. These gangs are considered to be highly organized and focused on the lucrative proceeds from new markets established in environments where law enforcement is less sophisticated in recognizing and responding to gang activity. The recruitment of youth into these newly established satellites of big-city gangs, as well as the spread of gang culture and violence, is considered a by-product of a drug distribution strategy that requires violence in order to establish turf and provide security for drug operations. A recent example of this depiction is the portrayal of Central American immigrant gangs such as the Mara Salvatrucha (MS13) spawning cells across the United States, Mexico, and Central America in the transnational export of guns, drugs, human smuggling, violence, and gang culture.

This depiction of the growth of gangs and gang migration, the organizational forms that gangs develop, the group dynamics that occur within them, and the patterns of criminal activity engaged in by gang members have been critical to the development of public policy about gangs. But scholars are not convinced that the account given above is entirely or even largely correct. Studies of gangs and gang crime conducted over the past three decades challenge these misconceptions and point us in a different policy direction. It is critical that programs and policy responses be based on a firm foundation of research-based information about gangs and patterns of gang activity, rather than on the conventional wisdom derived from anecdotal accounts and media depictions of rare and sensationalized crime incidents.

This chapter begins with a review of the current research on the growth, migration, and proliferation of gangs in the United States and elsewhere. I then describe the characteristics of youth who join gangs and discuss the growing body of research that examines the risk factors for gang membership. Next, I summarize the research on gang crime, with particular attention to patterns of criminal offending. Moving from individuals to groups, I note that gangs take different forms and offer a typology that appears to capture most of the variation in structures among gangs in the United States and Europe. I weave the theme of policy implications throughout this chapter, but the final section records some of the lessons learned from failed gang programs and points to areas where research can inform directions for gang responses.

The major findings of this chapter include:

- Over the past 25 years, street gangs have emerged in cities and towns across North America and Europe. Gang proliferation is more likely the result of local community conditions and the diffusion of gang culture through the media than the migration of gangs or gang members.
- In places with gangs, between 6 and 30 percent of youth may join street gangs at some point during adolescence, typically between the ages of 13 and 15 years, usually participating for a year or less. Males and members of racial/ethnic minority groups are more likely to become involved with gangs, but substantial numbers of females and white youth join as well. Youth likely to join gangs are denotable by several gang risk factors, reflecting individual, family, and peer characteristics.
- Youth who join gangs commit a disproportionate share of most types of crime, and this pattern is most evident during the active period of gang engagement. The dynamics within gangs that contribute to elevated crime and violence include an oppositional culture, group identity and cohesion, and status processes that encourage violent responses to signs of disrespect or challenges to the group.
- Efforts to effectively control gang crime and violence and to reduce rates of joining gangs have been stymied by program models based on misconceptions about gang contours and dynamics, the failure to adequately implement programs as designed, and the lack of systematic, independent evaluations that could generate sufficient documentation of what works and what does not. Some recent, highly visible programs have generated mixed outcomes. Preventive efforts that target clients based on research-derived gang risk factors and that seek to revamp proven youth violence reduction strategies for the gang setting are currently underway and represent a positive direction in evidence-based programming.

GANG PROLIFERATION AND MIGRATION

Research confirms the common perception of gang proliferation in the 1980s, but diverges regarding the role and nature of gang migration.

During the latter part of the 1980s, I noted a steady stream of media inquiries and accounts of the emergence of gangs in small cities and towns that were far from the urban centers that were traditionally associated with gang activity. Malcolm Klein and I conducted a national survey of law enforcement with the goal of identifying the scope of gang problems, patterns of gang emergence, and the role of gang migration, if any. We surveyed police in more than 1,000 agencies—all cities with a population of over 100,000 and several hundred smaller locations that had indicators of gang activity. We asked respondents whether their jurisdictions had gangs (defined as a group of youth who see themselves as a group, that is recognized as such in the community, and whose criminal activity precipitates a response by the community or law enforcement). If they responded affirmatively, we asked in what year gangs were first recognized, and, for purposes of the migration study component, whether or not individuals that had joined gangs in other places had relocated to their jurisdictions. By this process, we identified 58 cities that had gangs by 1960, 101 by 1970, 179 by 1980, and 769 gang cities by 1992. This study provided early documentation of the proliferation of street gangs; a more current, systematic assessment of the growth of gang problems is available from the National Youth Gang Center (NYGC).

Since 1996, the NYGC has conducted annual surveys of a nationally representative sample of law enforcement agencies (city police and county sheriff's departments) regarding gang presence and the date of gang onset as well as the number of gangs and gang members in the jurisdiction. The NYGC defines youth gangs as groups recognized as gangs by law enforcement in that location.[1] Based on the 2007 survey, the NYGC estimates that there are 3,550 jurisdictions that experienced gang problems, with 788,000 gang members and 27,000 gangs active in the United States (Egley and O'Donnell 2009). Other analyses of the gang onset dates suggest that patterns of gang proliferation vary somewhat by the size of city population (Klein and Maxson 2006; Egley, Howell, and Major 2004). Most large (100,000 population and above) cities reported gang problems by 1990. The proliferation of gangs in mid-sized (50,000 to 99,000) cities was most notable between 1986 and 1990; this occurred later (1991 to 1995) in smaller cities.

By 1997, the proliferation trend reversed, with noteworthy declines in the proportion of locales reporting gang problems in all the population categories except large cities. When respondents from all city and county jurisdictions are grouped together, 1996—the first year of the nationally representative NYGC survey—appears to be the time when there were the most cities with gang problems, as well as for the annual estimates that NYGC issues on the national counts of gangs and gang members. As shown in figure 6.1, 40 percent of the survey sample reported gangs in 1996 and 1997. This proportion steadily declined until 2001, when 24 percent indicated gang activity on the survey. This decline is most evident among small cities and towns and rural counties. Since 2001, the percent of law enforcement agencies reporting active gangs in their jurisdictions has risen to 35 in 2007. These patterns of gang prevalence in cities and counties, along with the trends in gang onset dates, illustrate the shifting nature of gang activity, even in as blunt an indicator as whether or not a location has gangs (see Klein 1995a for a description of gang activity cycles). Gangs have been noted in isolated circumstances in Europe for some time (Patrick 1973), but are now widely recognized in dozens of locations. Following a systematic review of nine European cities, Klein concludes that compared with the United States, the two gang situations are variations on "a similar theme attributable to common group processes and similar combinations of societal variables that produce marginalization of some youth populations" (Klein 2002, 253).

When a spurt of gang growth occurs, the migration of gang members from traditional gang centers is often identified in the media as the culprit, often with accompanying quotes from local politicians or law enforcement supporting this claim. But research in the early 1990s made a strong case that migration was not the cause of gang proliferation (Maxson 1998; Maxson, Woods, and Klein1996). Interviews with law enforcement gang experts in over 200 cities with gang migration revealed that the majority had indigenous, local gangs at least one year prior to the first arrival of gang migrants. In contrast to the depictions in the media, fully four out of five police officers in our study felt that the city would have a gang problem with or without gang migration.

The collective migration of gang members from the same gang also appears to be quite rare: a lot of gang members move, but gangs do not. Gang members move for the same reasons that other folks do: for better

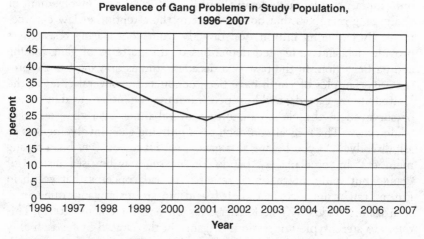

Prevalence of Gang Problems in Study Population, 1996–2007

Figure 6.1. The proportion of cities and counties with gang problems in the National Youth Gang Survey

Source: Egley and O'Donnell (2009), used with permission.

jobs, better housing, and to be closer to family and friends. Just one out of five of these police respondents told us that drug market expansion was the primary reason that most gang migrants moved to their city. This pattern of social rather than drug trafficking motives for relocation has been confirmed by several NYGC surveys, most recently in 1999.

We also interviewed about three dozen gang migrants in three cities and discovered variation in the types of gang involvement. After relocation, many migrants maintained social ties with at least some members of their original gang; some even "commuted to gang turf" if they lived close enough. Others established new cliques of their old gang, joined an existing gang in the new location, or stopped gang activity altogether. The police gang officers often noted that migrants had a substantial impact on local gang culture and activities, but the diffusion of gang culture through the popular media was pervasive. We heard about many gangs with notorious Los Angeles–based Crips and Blood gang names whose members had virtually no contact with the original (see also Decker and Van Winkle 1996, for a description of this process in St. Louis). The image of satellite gangs under the control of big-city leadership rarely holds up to research scrutiny: it was refuted in our migration study, even with Chicago gang influences, which are thought to be more organized than elsewhere. I see little evidence of tight gang connections or control in the "transnational" gangs like the Mara Salvatrucha (MS-13) that I am currently studying.

PATTERNS OF GANG PARTICIPATION

The NYGC survey describes the number of gangs in cities and counties but cannot provide much detail about the nature of gang involvement or about gang members that do not come to the attention of law enforcement. By gathering information directly from youth, gang researchers provide rich and variegated depictions of the patterns of gang joining and participation. In the past two decades, studies drawing from representative samples of youth have been conducted in several cities in the United States, Canada, and Europe. Youth may be interviewed in person or surveyed in the classroom, often several times over the course of adolescence. The typical approach to identifying gang involvement is to ask directly: "Do you belong to a gang?" or "Have you ever been a gang member?" In some places, "bande" or "posse" may be used instead of "gang," but some international researchers had concerns that youth in Europe might not recognize their friendship groups as gangs due to the "Eurogang Paradox" (Klein, Kerner, Maxson, and Weitekamp 2001). This refers to stereotypic impressions of gangs in the United States as highly organized and violent, and therefore quite unlike the informal youth groups that appear in Europe. In fact, most street gangs in the United States are more like the latter than the former. To address this concern, the Eurogang Research Program developed a series of questions that capture the individual elements of the definition of gangs that they adopted: "A street gang is any durable, street-oriented youth group whose own identity includes involvement in illegal activity" (see the Euro-gang web site, http://www.umsl.edu/~ccj/eurogang/euroganghome.htm). Accordingly, researchers may categorize a respondent as a gang member if the group of close friends qualifies with these features of durability, age composition, street orientation, and crime identity. One virtue of this method is that it permits comparison of gang participation rates in places with very different linguistic conventions.

In a review of 19 studies that queried youth on gang membership, I found that membership varied from about 6–8 percent (current members in general population samples) to as high as 20–30 percent (gang membership at any point during adolescence in high-risk samples). There is not much evidence that the proportion of people in gangs varies by geographic location; the few studies that have performed direct comparisons between the United States and European sites find little difference in the proportion of youth that joined gangs (Esbensen and Weerman 2005; Huizinga and Schumann 2001). The only available national estimate for the United States finds that 8 percent of youth join gangs by age 17 (Snyder and Sickmund 2006). Taken as a whole, these prevalence rates challenge some popular notions of gang participation. Some consider all youth who live in neighborhoods with gang activity to be at risk for joining gangs. While these participation rates are disturbing and certainly reveal sufficient membership to make it desirable to attach importance to gang programs, the strong message within these data is that, even using broad definitions and risky samples, most youth—7 or 8 out of 10—do not join gangs at any point in their adolescence.

Another surprising finding from these studies that follow youth for several years is that the majority of gang members retain their affiliation for a year or less. It is hard to convince Los Angelenos of this finding, and it should be noted that none of these studies has been conducted in notorious gang cities like Los Angeles or Chicago. Typically, study sites are places where gangs emerged during the growth spurt of the late 1980s or early 1990s. Still, the assumption that "once you're a Crip, you're a Crip for life" is challenged by these studies. At some point, all gang members separate themselves from gang activity, and most probably do so earlier rather than later. Many youth appear to leave gangs quickly and easily.

Depictions of youth who join gangs vary radically according to whether information is gathered from law enforcement or directly from youth. The NYGC periodically reports the age, race/ethnicity and gender distributions among gang members. In 1999, the NYGC reported that just 37 percent of gang members were under the age of 18 years—nearly two-thirds are adults. While the studies of youth samples typically do not follow subjects into adulthood, they suggest a very different pattern. The typical age of joining gangs is between 13 and 15 years of age. Coupled with the relatively brief periods of gang participation revealed in these studies, it is difficult to conceive of a ratio of two adult gang members for every youth member.

The two sources of data produce different sex distributions as well. The NYGC 2000 survey finds that just 6 percent of gang members are female. In contrast, youth studies typically report that girls represent one-fourth to one-third of all gang members. In these studies, there is an intriguing suggestion that girls join at younger ages and quit gang participation earlier than boys. If this is true, it may be that girl gang members are less likely to come to the attention of police.

Comparisons between the two data sources on race and ethnicity of gang membership are difficult because site-specific youth studies reflect the ethnic distributions of the location. A comparison between NYGC and the evaluation of the Gang Resistance Education and Training (GREAT) program that surveyed about 6,000 eighth grade students in 11 U.S. cities is instructive. Among the students, 25 percent of gang members were white, 31 percent black and 25 percent were Latino (Esbensen and Winfree 1998). The 1999 NYGC survey distributions were 13 percent white, 31 percent black, and 47 percent Latino.

These demographic comparisons reveal that our understanding of who participates in street gangs would vary substantially according to whether information is derived from law enforcement surveys or from studies of youth. The NYGC provides a national picture on an annual basis and is based on police estimates or records on the gang members they encounter. The use of different definitions also complicates the picture. It has been suggested that law enforcement comes into contact with—and records—a quite different segment of the gang population—older, males and racial/ethnic minorities—than that captured by youth survey researchers (Curry 2000).

The youth studies have produced a rich literature on risk factors for gang joining that extends far beyond demographic characteristics. I reviewed 20 recent studies from the United States, Canada, and Europe and identified six broad categories of individual, family and peer characteristics that most consistently distinguished those who joined gangs from other youth (Klein and Maxson 2006). These six, listed in table 6.1, are a subset of 21 individual, family, school, peer, and neighborhood risk factors that have been tested in this broad range of studies.

Three individual-level factors emerged among the most consistently supported predictors of gang membership. Youth who have recently experienced the stress of critical life events, such as a serious injury or parental divorce, are more likely to join gangs. A range of non-delinquent problem behaviors, such as risk-taking, impulsivity, and antisocial tendencies, are associated with gang membership. Another individual gang risk factor is embracing delinquent beliefs, for example feeling that committing crime is acceptable. The effect of peers was expected to be strong, but it is surprising that the only family characteristic to meet the criteria

Table 6.1. The Most Consistently Supported Risk Factors for Joining Gangs

1. Critical life events, such as a serious illness or injury; disruption in intimate social relationships
2. Non-delinquent problem behaviors, such as risk-taking, impulsivity, and antisocial tendencies
3. Delinquent beliefs, such as acceptance of antisocial behavior and neutralization of guilt over offending
4. Weak parental monitoring
5. Peer delinquency
6. Negative peer influence

of support I set was parental monitoring. Having friends who engage in delinquent behavior and get the youth into trouble (i.e., negative peer influence) are two peer risk factors that a variety of studies link to gang involvement. No school or neighborhood characteristics met the standard of consistent support.

Many of the risk categories generated mixed support. Some of the factors that received little or no support in the gang risk research are surprising and informative for the development of gang response programs. For example, gang and non-gang youth do not vary in levels of self-esteem. Neither family structure (e.g., two parents in the home) nor feelings of warmth and attachment among family members distinguish gang youth from their non-gang counterparts. These features might help to identify youth at risk for delinquency, but consistent empirical support exists only for the six risk factors listed in table 6.1. These gang risk factors provide a strong foundation for targeting clients in gang prevention programs, a topic to which I will return in a later section.

One other research finding regarding gang risk factors is important to note before I turn to a discussion of gang crime patterns. Despite consistent support in different studies, each risk factor is not a particularly strong predictor of gang joining. The accumulation of multiple risks appears to be important, and particularly so when these factors span different domains (e.g., school, family, peer, etc.) Thornberry and colleagues (Thornberry, Krohn, Lizotte, Smith, and Tobin2003) determined that 61 percent of youth in the Rochester study with risk markers in seven different domains joined gangs.[2]

GANG CRIME PATTERNS

One media-driven image about gangs is accurate: gang-involved youth commit a lot of crime and violence—far more than their non-gang counterparts. Gang crime produces enormous costs to victims and their families, to the public health and criminal justice systems, and strains the fabric of communities. There are also considerable costs to gang members in the loss of future opportunities, as they are more likely to drop out of school, be teenage parents, have unstable employment well into adulthood and higher rates of welfare receipt (Krohn and Thornberry 2008). Another study finds that gang members released from prison are more likely to recidivate and be reconvicted more quickly (Huebner, Varano, and Bynum 2007). The authors remark that gang members entered prison with substantial deficits that upon release interrupt positive community integration.

The gang/crime relationship is the single most robust finding over many decades of research. Youth who are gang members at some point in their adolescence commit a disproportionate share of virtually every type of crime. For example, in the Rochester longitudinal study, the 30 percent of youth who participated in gangs committed more than two-thirds of property and violent offenses reported by all youth throughout adolescence and a whopping 86 percent of all serious crimes (Thornberry 1998). This pattern is evident in Denver (the 14 percent of the sample who were gang members committed 79 percent of all serious violent crimes) and Seattle (85 percent of all robberies were by gang members). In reviewing a wide range of longitudinal and cross-sectional studies, I determined that this pattern of higher offending among gang members is evident (1) in different countries, including Canada and Europe, (2) regardless of definitions of gang membership, (3) among self-report offending and arrests, (4) whether offending in the year prior to interview or lifetime is considered, and (5) in comparing gang members to all other sampled youth, to non-gang but highly delinquent youth, or to non-gang youth with delinquent friends (Klein and Maxson 2006).

The gang/non-gang crime differentials are highest among the most serious and violent crime types, but gang members do not specialize in violence. Gang youth engage in the diverse array of offending that characterizes most youth crime patterns. Even though it is gang violence such as drive-by shootings and inter-gang retaliations that engages public attention, it is important for policy purposes that reductions in all types of crime would accrue if programs were effective in reducing gang participation.

At least that would be true if these accelerated crime patterns were the result of gang membership rather than an individual propensity to commit crime. Thornberry and colleagues (Thornberry, Krohn, Lizotte, and Chard-Wierschem 1993) observed that this strong gang/crime relationship might be explained by two different mechanisms. Youth with strong tendencies to commit crime might gravitate toward gangs or be valued targets for gang recruitment. Evidence for this *selection* model would be indicated by consistently higher levels of offending by gang members before, during, and after gang membership, as compared with other youth. Conversely, a strong group *facilitation* effect would be reflected by low levels of offending among youth prior to joining a gang, strong increases during active gang participation, and then sharp reductions in offending levels. Facilitation advocates view the gang itself as a major cause of offending, whereas the selection perspective would see the gang as a by-product of offending, ("birds of a feather, flocking together"). A third pattern of *enhancement* predicts that both selection and facilitation from the group context will be evident in offending comparisons between gang and non-gang youth.

The analytic approaches to examine these models become quite complex as researchers consider individual offending trajectories over the course of adolescence, make comparisons to non-gang youth, and assess differential patterns by type of offense. Krohn and Thornberry (2008) review the wealth of such studies that include different sites, in different countries, with different sample characteristics, over different time periods, and with different approaches to gang measurement and analysis, to conclude:

> Overall, perhaps the safest conclusion to draw is that there is a minor selection effect, a major facilitation effect, and no evidence consistent with a pure selection model. The weight of the evidence suggests that street gangs do facilitate or elicit increased involvement in delinquency, violence and drugs. There is no evidence to the contrary and abundant evidence in support of this view. (2008, 147)

GANGS AS GROUPS

This stream of research clarifies that gang membership is criminogenic but fails to reveal what it is about gangs and their group dynamics that sparks this dramatic increase in offending. Decades of ethnographic research provide tantalizing hints about that which makes gangs *qualitatively* different from other forms of delinquent youth groups. Moore and Vigil (1989) note that gangs reflect an "oppositional culture" that sets the group apart from the larger community and against major social institutions like the police, schools, and other authority figures. As this process of mutual rejection occurs, group cohesiveness and intra-dependency increases. Identification with neighborhood territory is a logical, but not required, outgrowth of this process, and its defense becomes one catalyst for the reinforcement of group identity. Members respond to perceived slights and signs of disrespect in ways that solidify members' identification with the gangs and contribute to gang-generated violence. We (Klein and Maxson 2006) described the evolution of gang identity through an intricate process that revolves around a group orientation toward crime and violence:

> Crime and group identity are not merely fellow travelers in the gang world: they are mutual reinforcers. As a group becomes more gang-like, with an increasing orientation to illegality or to intergroup rivalries, it recognizes this in itself. Even the police, school officials, and family members note and comment on the process. The gang reaches a tipping point beyond which its identity becomes entwined with its community. It is no longer just a play group, a team, a peer group, a rowdy crowd—it is a *street gang*. It is the

advancement into a delinquent or criminal or retaliatory mentality that brings the gang into its self-realization. (2006, 205–206)

Thus, violence is a unifier within gangs and attains a special symbolic value (Decker 1996). The offending profiles evident in youth surveys show that violence is a relatively small segment of an overall versatile offending pattern, but critical to reinforcing gang cohesion and fending off threats to status either within or outside the gang (Short and Strodtbeck 1965). Violence can also be a catalyst for youth to join gangs, as seeking "protection" is one of the common reasons offered (Decker and Curry 2000; Esbensen and Lynsky 2001; Maxson and Whitlock 2002). It has long been recognized by researchers that joining gangs leads to more, rather than less, violence victimization (Decker and Van Winkle 1996; Miller 2001; Taylor, Peterson, Esbensen, and Freng 2007; Vigil 1988). A recent analysis suggests that gang members also perceive a higher risk of violent victimization but associate gang membership with a reduction in fear of victimization (Melde, Taylor, and Esbensen 2009).

Group cohesion is an important dimension because crime levels appear to fluctuate with group attachments: as cohesiveness increases, so does criminal activity (Klein 1971). Gang programs and law enforcement operations must avoid activities that might inadvertently increase gang cohesiveness, as this will undermine crime reduction goals. At the same time, in the face of these strong group dynamics, it is unlikely that ratcheting up prison sentences for gang members will serve a deterrence function since oppositional culture, identification with the group, the status potential from violence engagement, and the spontaneous nature of much inter-gang violence would counteract threats of long sentences (Maxson, Matsuda, and Hennigan 2009; Watkins, Huebner, and Decker 2008).

While much law enforcement practice focuses on perceived gang leaders, scholars of gangs generally find leadership to be unstable, shifting and shared among many gang members. Decker and Van Winkle (1996, 275) note from interviews with gang members in St. Louis that "the values of the street also prohibit a leader from effectively assuming control of gang members. The autonomy from authority so highly prized on the street inhibits effective leadership." Street gangs with hierarchical, stable leadership and strong formal organization that operate with quasi-militaristic discipline are either pure fiction or exceedingly rare. Chicago gangs are thought to be among the most organized, but even here, there appears to be great variation (Decker, Bynum, and Weisel 1998; Block and Block 1993).

Scholars have attempted to depict the variation between gangs with different typologies. Early researchers proposed types based on perceived crime patterns (e.g., Cloward and Ohlin 1960: criminal, conflict, and retreatist subcultures); more recently, Fagan (1989) identified social, party, conflict, and delinquent gangs. We developed a typology with five gang forms based on six structural elements that emerged in interviews conducted with 60 police gang experts: group size, age range, duration, territoriality, subgroup/clique structure, and crime versatility (Klein and Maxson 2006; Maxson and Klein 1995). The *traditional gang* is the type most often depicted in the media: it is a large, enduring, territorial gang with a wide age range and several internal cliques based on age or area. We were surprised to find from further interviews with police in more than 200 cities that this form was among the least common and appears to produce the least amount of crime per member. Members of *specialty gangs* (small size, narrow age range, short duration, and crime-focused) commit more crime. This type is the only one of the five that did not reflect crime versatility; some speciality gangs focus on drugs, while others commonly engaged in graffiti or assault. *Compressed gangs* appear to be the most common form. They have relatively short histories, small size, and narrow age range and may or may not be territorial. The remaining two forms are *neo-traditional*, which differ from traditional in their shorter duration and smaller size, and *collective*. The collective form is an amorphous mass of medium size, age range, and duration, yet they do not form subgroups. Most cities have multiple types of gangs. Other researchers have applied this structural typology successfully in diverse gang settings, and it appears to hold up in descriptions of gangs in Europe as well as the United States (Weitekamp 2001).

We do not yet know enough about these gang structures to determine their relevance to programming, but two points seem appropriate. First, examination of structural elements over time suggests that groups often change by, for example, transforming from neo-traditional to traditional, compressed, or collective. As expected, the collective form is the most transitional of all. Even as individuals are constantly moving in and out of gangs, the shape and characteristics of the group are in flux as well. Second, the nature of the group structure should inform intervention strategies for both social service and police practitioners. For example, reducing affiliation to multigenerational, traditional gangs requires different attention to gang ties among family and friends than, for example, the specialty type.

PROGRAMS AND POLICIES

There are a variety of goals that programs might try to accomplish. Programs might attempt to prevent youth from joining gangs, encourage youth to exit gangs, or try to reduce criminal activity during gang membership. Alternatively, program goals might target groups rather than individuals, attempting to reduce the size of gangs or eliminate them entirely. Group-level efforts also target gang crime and violence, for example by intervening to prevent retaliation and reducing violence between gangs. At the community level, neighborhood features that foster gang emergence and maintenance (Klein 1995b) might be addressed or community capacities, like informal social control, strengthened.

The proliferation of gang problems in the United States has spawned a profusion of gang control efforts. Malcolm Klein and I gathered documents from all the gang programs we could locate and reviewed 59 gang response efforts (Klein and Maxson 2006). We arrayed these programs along several dimensions. We first categorized them as prevention, intervention, and/or law enforcement suppression programs. A second dimension that we considered was targeting, at various levels: individual, group (whether process or structure), and/or community. Finally, the focus on individual versus group change was considered. I expected that law enforcement suppression efforts would dominate (Greene and Pranis 2007), but instead we found that programs were fairly evenly distributed across prevention, intervention, and suppression. However, very few programs spanned these categories, attempting both prevention and intervention, both intervention and suppression, or all three. Most programs are narrow in both scope and the issues that they address. Group process and structure are virtually ignored, and the community context of gangs is rarely a central focus. It is far more common to target individuals than to attempt group change. Very few programs are truly comprehensive, such that they engage in prevention, intervention, and/or suppression at multiple levels (i.e., individual, group, and/or community).

One exception is the Comprehensive Community-wide Approach to Gang Prevention, Intervention and Suppression, also known as the Spergel Model or the Comprehensive Strategy, which has been promoted by the U.S. Department of Justice, Office of Juvenile Justice and Delinquency Prevention. This is a highly complex strategy, involving multiple agency partners in delivering a variety of services. The program model was developed by Irving Spergel (2007), based on his earlier formulations of the integration of a five-prong strategy (i.e., social intervention, community mobilization, provision of social opportunities, suppression, and organizational change). These services are delivered by a consortium of social service, justice, educational and community agencies. Five test sites were funded to implement the program and Spergel conducted a long-term and thorough evaluation. Due to the complexity of the model and the multi-agency approach and several other factors, implementation was difficult and uneven. The results were mixed, with some positive outcomes in some sites and negative or null results in others. The evaluation accounts clearly illustrate the challenges of keeping diverse agency partners focused upon implementing multiple strategies in a way that is faithful to a program model.

Conversely, the evaluation of the school-based universal gang prevention GREAT program revealed faithful implementation, but no effect on gang participation rates was evident in a four-year follow-up of the students (Esbensen, Osgood, Taylor, Peterson, and Freng 2001). The program's sponsor asked the evaluators to spearhead a revision of the program, and the preliminary, one-year results indicate less gang joining among youth exposed to GREAT (Esbensen 2008).

Chicago's CeaseFire program attempts to change community norms about violence, promote alternatives to violent dispute resolution, and increase perceived risks and costs of violence involvement among high-risk youth (Skogan, Hernett, Bump, and Dubois 2008). The CeaseFire strategy includes community mobilization and public education campaigns, outreach workers, community partners who provide job and educational services, and "violence interrupters" who intervene in gang-related conflicts to reduce violence escalation and retaliation. The evaluators attributed positive trends in actual or attempted shootings, as well as decreases in the size and intensity of shooting "hot spots" to the program in four of the eight CeaseFire neighborhoods examined with extended time series of police data. Gang violence reductions were indicated by declines in: (1) the proportion of killings attributed to gang members in two CeaseFire sites; (2) the proportion of gang homicides that were retaliatory in four program areas; and (3) average gang involvement in homicide in three neighborhoods, relative to comparison areas. It is not clear why these positive effects were achieved in some neighborhoods and not others, but the CeaseFire approach holds promise for other urban areas with long-standing gang issues.

Chicago's CeaseFire program should not be confused with an earlier program implemented in Boston in 1996, Operation CeaseFire, also known as "the Boston Gun Project" or "the Boston model." Building on a variety of public health, law enforcement suppression, and social service efforts initiated in the mid-1980s, Operation CeaseFire incorporated a targeted deterrence, or "pulling levers," approach to youth violence. Fliers and forums informed gang members that further gun violence would be met with heightened levels of enforcement and serious penalties. The enforcement message was supported by service providers from the faith-based Ten Point Coalition, the Boston Streetworker Program, and public health practitioners (McDevitt, Braga, Nurge, and Buerger 2003). While gang-specific outcomes were not reported, the rates of homicides of all youth under 25 years of age and incidents of gun violence fell precipitously in the years immediately following implementation of Operation CeaseFire, and evaluators attribute these positive trends to the program (Braga, Kennedy, Waring, and Piehl 2001). More recently, researchers have noted resurgence in youth gun violence, attributed to a growth in gang activity among new groups of males and females rather than the gang members targeted by the original Operation CeaseFire (McDevitt et al. 2003). The "pulling levers" strategy has been adopted in many other cities, but the impact on gang outcomes remains unknown (Braga, Kennedy, and Tita 2002).

These are among the very few gang programs that have been independently and systematically evaluated in a manner that might determine whether or not the effort is effective at accomplishing any of the goals discussed earlier. Unfortunately, none of the evaluations thus far has uniformly supported the efficacy of these efforts, although there is reason to be optimistic about the revised GREAT gang prevention program. Our review of gang prevention programs and evaluations suggested that program models are often poorly implemented and program goals are displaced or not adequately articulated in the first place (Klein and Maxson 2006). The massive proliferation of gang problems in the United States and the clear evidence of the deleterious consequences of gang participation demand greater scientific scrutiny of our current responses. Addressing the absence of proven programs, the remainder of this chapter presents a discussion of three areas in which gang research can inform the development of more efficacious responses.

Gang Prevention Targeting

Confronting the lack of gang prevention programs with a proven track record, researchers have recommended targeting gang members and youth at risk for joining gangs with programs that have established success in reducing youth violence or juvenile delinquency more generally (Thornberry et al. 2003). This suggestion has considerable merit: while we continue to experiment with innovative programs and evaluate gang response efforts, let us get the best services to the youth who arguably need them the most. Setting aside the issue of the content of these programs for the moment, accurate targeting of youth at risk for gang involvement is easier said than done, as I learned in my recent foray into the gang practice terrain in Los Angeles.

Despite Los Angeles's position at the epicenter of street gang activity in the United States for many decades, the city's response to gangs has fairly been characterized as uncoordinated and chaotic (Advancement Project 2007). A series of failed programs (see descriptions of the L.A. Plan and L.A. Bridges in Klein and Maxson 2006, chapter 3), high-profile killings, city council task forces, and damning government audit reports provided the momentum to remove funding from existing gang programs for lack of any evidence of effectiveness. These monies and centralized control for the distribution of resources and monitoring of programs was moved to the auspices of a newly created Gang Reduction and Youth Development (GRYD) division in the Office of the Mayor (and away from the Los Angeles City Council).

Relevant data were scrutinized to identify 12 communities with demonstrably high gang problems and socio-demographic disadvantage, and the GRYD office issued a request for proposals (RFP) to provide gang prevention services. The mandate to service providers was clearly stated: primary outcome goals were reduction of numbers of youth who join gangs, level of gang association, and gang risk factors evidenced in youth served. Moreover, candidates for the program would be selected by a "standardized gang assessment tool" to determine the level of risk for joining gangs. Specifically listed in the RFP were the six categories of risk that recent empirical research most strongly supported. This direct

translation of the latest and best science to inform gang prevention practices was very heady stuff, but there was a problem: there was no "standardized gang assessment tool" for agency practitioners to use to identify
youth at high risk for joining gangs. Studies used different measures to
capture these risk indicators. There is no discussion in the research regarding the point along a dimension (for example, parental monitoring) at
which a youth becomes at risk (i.e., "cut points"), nor do we know the
number of areas of risk that youth should experience before they are
deemed appropriate for prevention services. Researchers approach risk
as a continuum, but in practice, youth must be identified as eligible for a
program or not. The GRYD director approached Karen Hennigan, David
Sloane, Malcolm Klein, and me to develop a practical tool for practitioners that would serve this purpose.

We first obtained the various measures that scholars had used to
capture each of the six strongest risk factors (see table 6.1). We selected
those measures that derived from studies with samples most appropriate
to the Los Angeles program targets (i.e., younger adolescents from diverse
racial and ethnic backgrounds) that offered available data to establish
norms for the types of cut points we would need. During this process,
we decided that one of the risk categories, non-delinquent problem
behaviors, was more appropriately captured by separate measures of
risk-taking, impulsivity and antisocial behaviors. Further, our prior review
of risk studies had omitted the important indicators of self-reported
delinquency and substance abuse, so these were now added to the gang
risk factor brew. We then examined the distributions of scale scores for
gang and non-gang youth in several study data sets to identify the cut
points on each factor that would exclude most non-gang youth while
capturing most gang youth. Comparable analyses revealed the number
of risk factors that best differentiated youth who participated in gangs
from those that did not.

The resulting Gang Risk Entry Factors (GREF) inventory has now been
used to screen over 4,000 youth by service providers in the 12 GRYD
zones. The implementation of the assessment tool has been challenging.
It is a departure for practitioners who customarily draw from their experience and insight to select clients. When providers feel that youth could
benefit from service resources, it is both difficult and frustrating to turn
youth away (and in practice, such youth often receive services through
a different path).

The pressing political need to get the GRYD agencies funded and services
initiated eclipsed the possibility of developing and validating this tool on an
independent population. We are now in the process of conducting a validation study so that we can learn how well the GREF predicts which youth will
join gangs. While the GRYD program model is still in a state of flux, we have
established that a systematic gang risk assessment tool can be used—if not
warmly embraced—by practitioners in the service of a better match between
prevention services and the gang risk level of clients.

Gang Intervention Targeting

There is a need for a comparable assessment tool to determine the appropriate clients for the GRYD intervention services. Knowing that there was little information available on what programs are effective for what types of gang members, I turned to the gang research that draws distinctions among gang members in ways that might be helpful in thinking about client targeting. The three distinctions are: core versus fringe gang members, stable versus intermittent gang members, and former versus current gang members.

Core versus Fringe Gang Members

This label connotes centrality of gang identification, time spent with other gang members, and involvement in gang activity. Klein's studies in Los Angeles (1995b; 1971) in the 1960s used intervention workers' observations to make this assessment. Core members were distinct in their scores on a factor of individual "deficient-aggressiveness" (i.e., lower scores in school performance, judged intelligence, impulse control, desire for rehabilitation, and outside interests; and higher recorded delinquency, likelihood to get others in trouble, truancy, psycho- or sociopathic, group dependency, need for help, and willingness to fight). A less important but significant factor that distinguished the two groups was labeled "group involvement" (i.e., more participation in spontaneous activities, clique involvement, contribution to the group, desire to lead and acceptance by core members). Importantly, cores were not distinct from fringe members in regards to socio-demographics like age, residential origin, family structure, family education, or family income.

Alternatively, Finn Esbensen, along with his colleagues in the GREAT evaluations, have used the target or bull's eye diagram to ask individual respondents to locate themselves in one of five numbered concentric circles: "How far from the center of the gang are you?" In one analysis, the most important predictor of gang centrality was low self-control, an index of measures of impulsivity, risk-taking, and physicality (Peterson-Lynsky, Winfree, Esbensen, and Clason 2000). A different analysis of the same data set compared demographic, attitudinal, and criminal offending characteristics among differently defined gang groups, including subjects who identified themselves as core (i.e., two inner circles), current members of delinquent gangs (Esbensen, Winfree, He, and Taylor 2001). In comparison to a group composed of all other gang members (i.e., non-core, members of non-delinquent gangs, and all former gang members), core members were significantly different on all attitudinal and behavioral measures, but not on the demographic characteristics of age, sex, race, family structure, or parents' education. In the more sophisticated, multivariate analysis of the demographic and attitudinal measures, just three characteristics distinguish current, core delinquent gang members: lower guilt at engaging in delinquent acts; more delinquent peers; and more acceptance of physical violence as a suitable response to conflict. Neither demographics nor self-control variables significantly differentiated core members from other gang members in this analysis.

This research suggests that core versus fringe is a meaningful distinction, although the optimal approach to measuring it requires further investigation. Perhaps one-quarter to one-half of gang members might be core members. Demographic characteristics do not seem to be good markers of core versus marginal gang members, but delinquent peers and antisocial attitudes about crime, like low guilt and acceptance of violence, appear to be important dimensions. Self-control indicators such as impulsivity and risk-taking produce mixed results, but they are likely less important than antisocial attitudes and peers.

Stable versus Intermittent Gang Members

As noted earlier, studies of representative youth samples reveal that the majority of youth who say they are gang members in an interview remain gang members for a year or less. This condition has permitted researchers to compare those who identify as gang members for multiple, consecutive years with short-term members, including those who identify as gang members in a later interview ("restarters"). Like core gang members, those who have been active in gangs for longer periods may be more difficult to intervene with successfully, but the ultimate payoff might be greater. These studies find that few risk factors on the order of those included in the GREF distinguish between stable and transient gang members. For example, Thornberry and colleagues (2003; table 4.3) tested 40 characteristics and found just six to differentiate transient from stable male gang members in Rochester: parent education, family disadvantage, poverty, changes in parent figures, early dating and early drug use. Assessments used to determine risk for joining would not be useful in predicting which gang members have short versus long-term involvement.

Former versus Current Gang Members (Desistance)

Studies have systematically compared surveys of youth who report that they are current gang members with those who say they have been gang members in the past but are no longer, and some qualitative researchers observe differences in the former gang members they encounter. If former gang members have special characteristics, these might be markers of good program candidates in which to encourage desistance, although we cannot know whether these differences in attitudes and behaviors were the result of leaving the gang. Also, some studies ask former gang members why they left and these might be clues to good intervention candidates. Finally, several researchers speak to the issue of the process of leaving.

Esbensen and colleagues observe from their comparison of various definitions of gang membership in the GREAT study that:

> although it is the case that the largest distinction in this study is that between those youths who claim to never have been a gang member and those who claim gang affiliation at some time, it is vital to note that those gang members who no longer claim gang status are substantially more pro-social in both attitudes and behavior than are those persisting in their membership, a finding consistent with longitudinal results from the Denver and Rochester studies (e.g., Esbensen & Huizinga, 1993; Thornberry et al., 1993). (reprint in Esbensen et al. 2004, 70)

In a multivariate analysis of survey responses from eighth graders across the United States, Esbensen and colleagues find that current gang members have more delinquent peers, more commitment to negative peers, less guilt in engaging in criminal activity, and more acceptance of violence.

Researchers conducting qualitative or observational gang research offer insight on why youth leave gangs. Decker and Lauritsen (1996) draw from interviews with 24 former gang members in St. Louis to identify violence victimization as the most common reason that members quit. Most current gang members knew others who had quit due to violence, along with family concerns and jobs. Huizinga, Cunningham, and Elliott (2005) use both quantitative and qualitative data from the Denver Youth Study to identify maturation (including "grew up," "had a family") as the most frequently cited reason (43 percent of former gang members in the survey sample) for leaving. About half as frequently offered were concerns for safety (19 percent) (confirming Decker and Lauritsen) and an expression that gang participation was "not worth the trouble" (22 percent).

Medina, Aldridge, and Ralphs (2009) studied several gangs in an English city and describe a gradual process of desistance, beginning with a cognitive element (wanting to leave), experiencing turning points like parenthood or new romantic relationships and pro-social opportunities like jobs. They note that leaving involved a "renegotiation" of involvement in gang activities to exclude criminality but also a lot of "drift" back into criminal involvement and varying attitudes toward gang membership over time. Reputation and embeddedness in the gang appeared to create obstacles to breaking away; these researchers offer examples of other gang members' requests for conflict mediation and opportunities for illegal activities as enticements. They also warn that rival gang members and law enforcement authorities can represent obstacles to desistance. Vigil (1988) notes that gang desisters had developed increased ties to other social institutions and found jobs or family connections as replacements for the social ties of the gang.

In summary, the gang desistance research points to the importance of relationships and engagement with gang peers as juxtaposed against the positive effects of pro-social opportunities and alternatives like jobs and family responsibilities. Decker's work identifies the exposure to violence as a potential catalyst to beginning the process of desistance, and it appears that the fostering of social ties outside the gang network is important.

These findings resonate with the distinctions found between marginal and core gang members. Core gang members spend more time engaged with gang peers, including in delinquent activities, express less guilt associated with committing crime, and accept violence as a conflict-resolution technique. Marginal/core gang status can be identified by self-report (i.e., placement away from the center of concentric circles meant to represent the gang) or by individuals very familiar with a particular gang's social network. Alternatively, program candidates may be assessed by attention to the attitudes and behaviors found to be associated with the differences between core and marginal gang members and between current and former gang members. In general, the known risk factors for gang joining do not appear helpful in predicting gang stability or desistance.

If providers could adequately draw the distinction between core and marginal members, it remains to be seen which group would benefit the most from services or should be the designated target for intervention services. The rationale for targeting more marginal members would be that they are likely more malleable and amenable to services, and are easier to wean from gang involvement. On the other hand, findings from program evaluations for youthful offenders often find positive effects for the highest risk, most criminally involved targets. Ultimately, we want to reduce crime with our interventions, so effectively intervening with the most criminally active, core members is likely to yield the most benefit. I recently posed this issue of targeting to a group of more than a dozen gang intervention workers and learned that the vast majority felt that core members should be the target. One stated, "I want the most knucklehead, hardest core gang member—not the goody two-shoes...the most active, shot callers or leaders in the violence are the most vulnerable. They don't know the alternatives and I can help them."

Modifying Successful Delinquency or Violence Programs

Until effective gang prevention and intervention programs are identified, Thornberry and colleagues (2003) recommend providing the programs that have a proven record of success in reducing youth violence and juvenile crime to gang members and youth at high risk for joining gangs. However, if gangs are qualitatively different from other types of law-violating youth groups, then general delinquency or violence programs may be less effective with gang members and may even backfire (Klein 1995b). Thornberry (2008) has proposed that a review of the Blueprints for Violence Prevention programs be conducted to identify which might be promising for gang-specific outcomes, such as prevention of gang joining or reducing levels of gang activity). Using high standards, the Blueprints effort has identified 11 "model" programs and 18 "promising" programs that produce significant and sustained deterrent effects on delinquency and violence (Elliott and Mihalic 2004). Intervention points in the Blueprint programs span infancy to late adolescence and include a broad range of prevention and treatment strategies. Thornberry has impaneled a team of experts to consider the types of modifications needed to make these programs more appropriate to gang settings. Ultimately, the modified programs could be tested in a demonstration trial and thoroughly evaluated for gang outcomes.

Judging from the patterns of gang proliferation and the NYGC national surveys, there are plenty of candidates for intervention. The studies on patterns of criminal activity demonstrate that there is much to be gained in crime and violence reduction if effective prevention and intervention programs were launched. Programs should be sited in neighborhoods and communities that demonstrate the greatest need, either by the current level of gang activity or evidence that they appear to be on the cusp of developing a gang problem. Even in those communities, most youth will not join gangs, so we need to be careful not to interrupt the natural processes for gang prevention already in place. The gang prevalence rate in smaller cities and rural areas is lower than in more populated areas, and gang problems are far less established. Thus, some types of programs may be more appropriate to urban, inner-city neighborhoods and others for rural communities. Special programs for gang migrants do not appear to be necessary, at least in the vast majority of places.

Programs should include the full range of individuals who join gangs, including girls and nonminority youth. Except for universal prevention programs, it will be important to consider the established strongest risk factors when selecting clients for prevention strategies. Prevention should be targeted to the ages of 10 to 14 years, just before youth enter the peak period of joining gangs. The research is less useful in providing guidance for gang intervention client targeting. Programs should use validated measures for determining gang membership and should probably consider the core/fringe status and length of participation in the gang.

The modality of service delivery is crucial for gang intervention. Programs need to be scrupulous in avoiding the contamination effects of bringing together gang members or youth not in gangs with gang members. Activities that might reinforce the status of gangs and gang membership should be eliminated. Gang programmers should be aware that the period of gang membership is often quite brief; we want to avoid doing anything that would interrupt the processes of desistance that are apparently already in place.

The content of gang programs is an open question. Spergel and Curry (1993) observed that most law enforcement respondents in their survey of 45 cities identified opportunities provision and community mobilization as the most effective gang strategies, even while the vast majority of these cities emphasized suppression in practice. Until we have solid tests of effective strategies, we should experiment with efforts that reduce crime and delinquency and innovate new ways to fulfill the developmental needs that gangs seem to meet for some youth.

Finally, in the domain of public policy, we should recognize that vast resources have been expended in law enforcement efforts to suppress gang crime and increase penalties for gang membership. These programs have no more evidence to suggest their effectiveness than do prevention and treatment strategies. We need to invest our scare resources in responses that are independently evaluated so that we might finally learn what programs and policies are effective in addressing the social costs of gang membership.

References

Advancement Project. 2007. "Citywide Gang Activity Reduction Strategy: Phase III." Report to the Los Angeles City Council. Los Angeles: Advancement Project.

Barrows, Julie, and C. Ronald Huff. 2009. "Gangs and Public Policy: Constructing and Deconstructing Gang Databases." *Criminology and Public Policy* 8(4): 675–703.

Block, Carolyn Rebecca, and Richard Block. 1995. "Street Gang Crime in Chicago." In *The Modern Gang Reader*, eds. Malcolm W. Klein, Cheryl L. Maxson, and Jody Miller. Los Angeles: Roxbury.

Braga, Anthony A., David M. Kennedy, and George E. Tita. 2001. "New Approaches to the Strategic Prevention of Gang and Group-Involved Violence." In *Gangs in America*, 3rd ed., ed. C. Ronald Huff, 271–286. Thousand Oaks, CA: Sage.

Braga, Anthony A., David M. Kennedy, Ellin J. Waring, and Anne M. Piehl. 2001. "Problem-Oriented Policing, Deterrence, and Youth Violence: An Evaluation of Boston's Operation-Ceasefire." *Journal of Research in Crime and Delinquency* 38: 195–225.

Cloward, Richard A., and Lloyd E. Ohlin. 1960. *Delinquency and Opportunity: A Theory of Delinquent Gangs*. New York: Free Press.

Curry, G. David. 2000. "Self-reported Gang Involvement and Officially Recorded Delinquency." *Criminology* 38: 1253–1274.

Decker, Scott H. 1996. "Collective and Normative Features of Gang Violence." *Justice Quarterly* 13: 243–264.

Decker, Scott H., Tim Bynum, and Deborah Weisel. 1998. "A Tale of Two Cities: Gangs as Organized Crime Groups." *Justice Quarterly* 15: 395–425.

Decker, Scott H., and G. David Curry. 2000. "Addressing Key Features of Gang Membership: Measuring The Involvement of Young Members." *Journal of Criminal Justice* 28: 473–482.

Decker, Scott H., and Janet L. Lauritsen. 2002. "Leaving the Gang." In *Gangs in America*, 3rd ed., ed. C. Ronald Huff, 51–67. Thousand Oaks, CA: Sage.

Decker, Scott H., and Barrik Van Winkle. 1996. *Life in the Gang: Family, Friends, and Violence*. Cambridge: Cambridge University Press.

Egley, Arlen, Jr., James C. Howell, and Aline K. Major. 2004. "Recent Patterns of Gang Problems in the United States: Results from the 1996–2002 National Youth Gang Survey." In *American Youth Gangs at the Millennium*, eds. Finn-Aage Esbensen, Stephen G. Tibbetts, and Larry Gaines, 90–108. Long Grove, IL: Waveland Press.

Egley, Arlen, Jr., and Christina O'Donnell. 2009. "Highlights of the 2007 National Youth Gang Survey." Washington DC: Office of Juvenile Justice Delinquency and Prevention.

Elliott, Delbert S., and Sharon Mihalic. 2004. "Blueprints for Violence Prevention." Boulder: University of Colorado, Institute of Behavioral Science, Center for the Study and Prevention of Violence.

Esbensen, Finn-Aage. 2008. "Preliminary Short-Term Results from the Evaluation of the G.R.E.A.T. Program." Online. Available at http://www.iir.com/nygc/publications/2008-12-esbensen.pdf. Retreived 9/14/09.

Esbensen, Finn-Aage, and David Huizinga. 1993. "Gangs, Drugs, and Delinquency in a Survey of Urban Youth." Criminology 31 (4): 565–587.

Esbensen, Finn-Aage, and Dana Peterson Lynskey. 2001. "Youth Gang Members in a School Survey." In The Eurogang Paradox: Street Gangs and Youth Groups in the U.S. and Europe, eds. Malcolm W. Klein, Hans-Juergen Kerner, Cheryl L. Maxson, and Elmer G. M. Weitekamp, 93–114. Dordrecht: Kluwer Academic Publishers.

Esbensen, Finn-Aage, D. Wayne Osgood, Terence. J. Taylor, Dana Peterson, and Adrienne Freng. 2001. "How Great is G.R.E.A.T.? Results from the Longitudinal Quasi-Experimental Design." Criminology and Public Policy 1: 87–118.

Esbensen, Finn-Aage, and Frank M. Weerman. 2005. "Youth Gangs and Troublesome Youth Groups in the United States and the Netherlands: A Cross-National Comparison." European Journal of Criminology 2: 5–37.

Esbensen, Finn-Aage, and L. Thomas Winfree, Jr. 1998. "Race and Gender Differences Between Gang and Non-Gang Youth: Results from a Multisite Survey." Justice Quarterly 15: 505–526.

Esbensen, Finn-Aage, L. Thomas Winfree, Jr., Ni He, and Terence J. Taylor.2001. "Youth Gangs and Definitional Issues: When Is a Gang a Gang, and Why Does It Matter?" Crime and Delinquency 47: 105–130. Cited version appears in Esbensen, Finn-Aage, Stephen Tibbetts, and Larry Gaines, eds. 2004. American Youth Gangs at the Millennium. Long Grove, IL: Waveland Press.

Fagan, Jeffrey. 1989. "The Social Organization of Drug Use and Dealing among Urban Gangs." Criminology 27: 633–669.

Greene, Judith, and Kevin Pranis. 2007. Gang Wars: The Failure of Enforcement Tactics and the Need for Effective Public Safety Strategies. Washington, DC: Justice Policy Institute.

Huebner, Beth M., Sean P. Varano, and Timothy S. Bynum. 2007. "Gangs, Guns, and Drugs: Recidivism among Serious, Young Offenders." Criminology and Public Policy 6: 187–222.

Huizinga, David, Linda Cunningham, and Amanda Elliott. 2005. "How Do I Get In? What Have I Joined? And, How Do I Get Out? Joining, Leaving and the Structure Of Gangs." Presentation to the annual meeting, American Society of Criminology.

Huizinga, David, and Karl F. Schumann. 2001. "Gang Membership in Bremen and Denver: Comparative Longitudinal Data." In The Eurogang Paradox: Street Gangs and Youth Groups in the U.S. and Europe, edited by Malcolm W. Klein, Hans-Juergen Kerner, Cheryl L. Maxson, and Elmar G. M. Weitekamp. Dordrecht: Kluwer Academic Publishers.

Klein, Malcolm W. 1971. Street Gangs and Street Workers. Englewood Cliffs, NJ: Prentice-Hall.

Klein, Malcolm W. 1995a. "Street Gang Cycles." In *Crime*, eds. James Q. Wilson and Joan Petersilia, 217–236. San Francisco: Institute for Contemporary Studies.

Klein, Malcolm W. 1995b. *The American Street Gang: Its Nature, Prevalence, and Control*. New York: Oxford University Press.

Klein, Malcolm W. 2002. "Street Gangs: A Cross-National Perspective." In *Gangs in America*, 3rd ed., ed. C. Ronald Huff, 237–254. Thousand Oaks, CA: Sage Publications.

Klein, Malcolm W., Hans-Juergen Kerner, Cheryl L. Maxson, and Elmar G. M. Weitekamp, eds. 2001. *The Eurogang Paradox: Street Gangs and Youth Groups in the U.S. and Europe*. Dordrecht: Kluwer Academic Publishers.

Klein, Malcolm W., and Cheryl L. Maxson. 2006. *Street Gang Patterns and Policies*. New York: Oxford University Press.

Krohn, Marvin D., and Terenc e P. Thornberry. 2008. "Longitudinal Perspectives on Adolescent Street Gangs." In *The Long View Of Crime: A Synthesis of Longitudinal Research*, ed. Akiva M. Liberman. New York: Springer.

Maxson, Cheryl L. 1998. *Gang Members on the Move*. Washington, DC: U.S. Department of Justice, Office of Juvenile Justice and Delinquency Prevention.

Maxson, Cheryl L., and Malcolm W. Klein. 1995. "Investigation Gang Structures." *Journal of Gang Research* 3: 33–40.

Maxson, Cheryl L., Kristy N. Matsuda, and Karen Hennigan. 2009. " 'Deterrability' among Gang and Nongang Juvenile Offenders: Are Gang Members More (or Less) Deterrable Than Other Juvenile Offenders?" *Crime and Delinquency* Available online: OnlineFirst published on 8/20/09 as doi:10.1177/0011128709343137. Xxxxxx still not published!

Maxson, Cheryl, and Monica L. Whitlock. 2002. "Joining the Gang: Gender Differences in Risk Factors for Gang Membership." In *Gangs in America*, 3rd ed., ed. C. Ronald Huff, 19–36. Thousand Oaks, CA: Sage Publications.

Maxson, Cheryl L., Kristi J. Woods, and Malcolm W. Klein. 1996. *Street Gang Migration: How Big a Threat?* Washington, DC: U.S. Department of Justice, Office of Juvenile Justice and Delinquency Prevention.

McDevitt, Jack, Anthony A. Braga, Dana Nurge, and Michael Buerer. 2003. "Boston's Youth Violence Prevention Program: A Comprehensive Community-Wide Approach." In *Policing Gangs and Youth Violence*, ed. Scott H. Decker, 53–76. Toronto: Wadsworth.

Medina, Juanjo, Judith Aldridge, and Robert Ralphs. 2009. " 'Chimera' or "Super Gangs"? Studying Youth Gangs in an English City." Unpublished manuscript. Manchester: University of Manchester, Centre for Criminological and Socio-Legal Research.

Melde, Chris, Terence J. Taylor, and Finn-Aage Esbensen. 2009. " 'I Got Your Back' An Examination of the Protective Function of Gang Membership in Adolescence." *Criminology* 47: 565–594.

Miller, Jody. 2001. *One of the Guys: Girls, Gangs, and Gender*. New York: Oxford University Press.

Moore, J. and Vigil, J. D. 1989. "Chicano Gangs: Group Norms and Individual Factors Related to Adult Criminality." *Aztlan* 18: 31–42.

Patrick, James. 1973. *A Glascow Gang Observed*. London: Eyre Methuen.

Peterson-Lynsky, Dana, L. Thomas Winfree, Finn-Aage Esbensen, and Dennis Clason. 2000. "Linking Gender, Minority Group Status and Family Matters to Self-Control Theory: A Multivariate Analysis of Key Self-Control Concepts in a Youth-Gang Context." *Juvenile and Family Court Journal* 51: 1–19.

Short, James F., Jr., and Fresc L. Strodbeck. 1965. *Group Process and Gang Delinquency.* Chicago: University of Chicago Press.

Skogan, Wesley G., Susan M. Harnett, Natalie Bump, and Jill Dubois. 2008. "Evaluation of CeaseFire-Chicago." Online. Available at www.northwestern. edu/ipr/publications/ceasefire.html.

Snyder, Howard N., and Melissa Sickmund. 2006. "Juvenile Offenders and Victims: 2006 National Report." Washington, DC: U.S. Department of Justice, Office of Justice Programs, Office of Juvenile Justice and Delinquency Prevention[C2].

Spergel, Irving A. 2007. *Reducing Youth Gang Violence.* Lantham, MD: AltaMira Press.

Spergel, Irving A., and G. David Curry. 1993. "The National Youth Gang Survey: A Research and Development Process." In *The Gang Intervention Handbook*, eds. Arnold P. Goldstein and C. Ronald Huff, 359–392. Champaign, IL: Research Press.

Taylor, Terence J., Dana Peterson, Finn-Aage Esbensen, and Adrienne Freng. 2007. "Gang Membership as a Risk Factor for Adolescent Violent Victimization." *Journal of Research in Crime and Delinquency* 44: 351–380.

Thornberry, Terence. 1998. "Membership in Youth Gangs and Involvement in Serious and Violent Offending." In *Serious and Violent Offenders: Risk Factors and Successful Interventions*, eds. Rolf Loeber and David P. Farrington. Newbury Park, CA: Sage Publications.

Thornberry, Terence. 2008. "Blueprints for Gang Prevention: A Concept Paper." Boulder, CO: Institute of Behavioral Science, University of Colorado.

Thornberry, Terence, Marvin D. Krohn, Alan J. Lizotte, and Deborah Chard-Wierschem. 1993. "The Role of Juvenile Gangs in Facilitating Delinquent Behavior." *Journal of Research in Crime and Delinquency* 30: 55–87.

Thornberry, Terence, Marvin D. Krohn, Alan J. Lizotte, Carolyn A. Smith, and Kimberly Tobin. 2003. *Gangs and Delinquency in a Developmental Perspective.* Cambridge: Cambridge University Press.

Vigil, James D. 1998. *Barrio Gangs: Street Life and Identity in Southern California.* Austin: University of Texas Press.

Watkins, A., Beth Huebner, and Scott Decker. 2008. "Patterns of Gun Acquisition, Carrying and Use among Juvenile and Adult Arrestees: Evidence from a High-Crime City." *Justice Quarterly* 25: 674–700.

Weitekamp, Elmar G.M. 2001. "Gangs in Europe: Assessments at the Millennium." In *The Eurogang Paradox: Street Gangs and Youth Groups in the U.S. and Europe*, eds. Malcolm W. Klein, Hans-Juergen Kerner, Cheryl L. Maxson, and Elmar G. M. Weitekamp, 309–322. Dordrecht: Kluwer Academic Publishers.

Notes

1. The NYGC defines a gang as "a group of youths or young adults in your jurisdiction that you or other responsible persons in your agency or community are willing to identify as a 'gang.'" Motorcycle gangs, hate groups, prison gangs, or "exclusively adult gangs" are excluded. A recent review of gang definitions in state legislation by Barrows and Huff (2009) finds that just two states share the same gang definition.

2. The seven domains were area characteristics, family socio-demographic characteristics, parent-child relations, school factors, peer relationships, individual characteristics, and early delinquency. Each subject was classified as above or below the median number of risk factors in each domain. A total of 40 risk characteristics were assessed in this study.

Chapter 7

Labor Markets and Crime

Shawn D. Bushway

The sustained and substantial drop in the crime rates in the second half of the 1990s coincided with the longest economic expansion since 1945. This co-occurrence, which most scholars conclude has at least some causal connection (Grogger 2000), refocused attention on the exciting possibility that crime can be reduced by increasing legitimate economic opportunities (Bernstein and Houston 2000). In the third edition of this book, Bushway and Reuter (2002) assessed the current state of knowledge on the impact of labor market–oriented programs on crime prevention. The labor market is made up of employers who demand labor, and people who supply labor. Bushway and Reuter (2002) divided programs into demand-side programs that focused on either creating new jobs or incentivizing employers to hire at-risk workers, and supply-side programs designed to increase the job skills and job readiness of potential employees who might otherwise become involved in crime. Bushway and Reuter (2002) concluded that demand-side programs had shown no significant crime reduction potential, while supply-side programs had shown some potential, particularly for a few subgroups, such as older males and low-risk populations.

This finding is consistent with the academic research that has consistently found a significant but weak causal relationship between individual employment and crime (Sampson and Laub 1993; Thornberry and Christenson 1984; Farrington et al. 1986; Needels 1996). New research has continued to reach the same conclusion. For example, Uggen and Thompson (2003) showed that legal earnings had a significant and negative effect on illegal earnings, using data from a contemporary sample of Minnesota youth in a fairly strong causal model. But the magnitude is small—a one dollar increase in legitimate earnings in a month leads to a seven cent decrease in illegal earnings. A successful labor market program such as Job Corps (Schochet, Burghardt, and McConnell 2006) that can increase earnings by 10 percent (about $100 a month) would only decrease monthly illegal earnings by seven dollars. In the same vein, Steve Raphael and David Weiman (2007) estimate that having a job reduces the probability that the average parolee returns to prison within three years by at most 3 percent.

Finding that the average criminal is not very responsive to work incentives is consistent with the strong consensus from the deterrence literature that the bulk of serious criminals are not "rational," meaning that they are not responsive to changing incentives at the margin (Cook 1980; Pogarsky 2002; Tonry 2008). Why would individuals who are demonstrably unresponsive to large changes in potential punishment be responsive to small changes in earnings?

But work programs can, and perhaps should, be developed to serve the specialized and (small) groups of at-risk individuals who are likely to be most responsive to work incentives. Chris Uggen (2000) found that Supported Work, a subsidized work program for ex-offenders, had no impact overall, but did reduce re-arrest by 20 percent for participants over 26 years old. Lattimore, Witte, and Baker (1990) describe the Vocational Delivery System, a program unapologetically focused only on young adults identified by staff as having the most potential to benefit from work programs. This specialized subgroup (with an average IQ of 100, high for an offender population) showed a 20 percent reduction in re-arrest in a two-year follow-up study. Such creaming might not be popular among those looking for programs to serve large numbers of at risk individuals, but it represents a realistic response to the research literature on labor market programs aimed at crime prevention (Bushway and Reuter 2003).

While realistic, the conclusion that labor market crime prevention programs should be focused on motivated or marginal offenders runs the risk of putting too much emphasis on the immediate causal relationship between legitimate work and crime populations; in addition, places with a high prevalence of crime are detached from the labor market. Detachment from the legal labor market is a cause of crime, *and* a signal for substantial structural problems that will not be solved by relatively inexpensive programs focused only on getting an individual employed. Dramatic changes in incentives *and* attitudes, akin to what happened during welfare reform in the late 1990s (Blank 2002), are needed to reattach individuals to the labor market. This chapter focuses on three recent developments in the research literature that have reenergized the research on work and crime and led to important new insights for policy. Each development starts from the belief that the labor market is more than a legitimate alternative to income-generating crime. Rather, the legal labor market provides the normative social context for most of adult life, particularly for males. According to the American Time Use survey, the average employed American between the ages of 15 and 54 spends more time during a work day working than on any other activity, including sleeping (Bureau of Labor Statistics 2009). Changes in this social context caused by macro changes in the economy could plausibly have a major effect on the behavior of individuals, including on their criminal behavior, simply by changing the landscape in which they live.

The next section reviews new research on the relationship between work and crime for adolescents. Starting in the 1980s, the prevailing opinion has been that work, particularly intense work, is bad for adolescents (for a review, Cauffman and Steinberg 1995). This research created the curious situation in which attachment to work during adolescence is considered criminogenic, but attachment to work during adulthood is prophylactic. The changing causal nature of work is consistent with a life-course view that early transitions to adult roles can be problematic for adolescents. However, this conclusion raises serious policy questions. Exactly when should policymakers start to attach adolescents to the labor market—when does work start to become "good" and stop being "bad"?

New research starting with Paternoster and colleagues (2003) has suggested that the earlier conclusion that intense work leads to crime was driven by selection bias. Delinquent kids were both more likely to work earlier and to work more than non-delinquent kids. Once selection is properly controlled for, intense adolescent work does not lead to crime (that is, is not criminogenic, Apel et al. 2007, 2008) and does not affect school grades (Rothstein 2007; Apel et al. 2007), although it may lead to increased dropout (Apel et al. 2008; Staff and Mortimer 2007; Lee and Staff 2007).

A bigger problem for youth is the lack of stable attachment to work. Adolescence is a time when youth move from a world of school to a world of work. Youth who are unattached to work in late adolescence will be unattached to work in young adulthood, and recent research has shown that unstable work patterns in adolescence are associated with elevated risks for crime (Mortimer 2002; Paternoster et al. 2009). Young adults who are unattached to work are exactly those who are most at risk for crime. Caspi and colleagues (1998) show that factors such as intelligence, family structure, and difficult temperament measured at age three can significantly predict the amount of unemployment during young adulthood. Caspi and colleagues (1998) argue that failure to control for these individual differences on the impact of unemployment can lead to overestimates of the role of unemployment on factors such as crime. Whatever the causal reasons, there is now growing evidence that lack of attachment to the workplace during adolescence *and* adulthood is associated with crime.

Although attachment to the labor market is at least partially dependent on individual characteristics, it is also true that involvement in the labor market is dependent on economic activity, or the demand for labor. Even the most motivated worker, youth or adult, cannot work if there are no jobs. Therefore, the next section moves to explore new research on the relationship between economic trends and crime. This research explicitly moves away from focusing on the relationship between unemployment and crime at the national level, and moves to a theoretically grounded relationship between the business cycle, economic trends, and crime. The business cycle is a dynamic feature of the national economy, and is not measured well by changes in the unemployment rate. A new focus on the business cycle and long-term economic trends has led to stronger evidence of a link between the economy and crime. It also provides a new emphasis on how broad social changes that lead to detachment from the labor market can affect crime.

The final section discusses the growing literature on mass incarceration and employment. The incarceration rate in state and federal prisons in 2007 was 506 people per 100,000, 3.5 times as high as the rate in 1980. To put this in perspective, there were more people serving time in American prisons in 2007 than there were serving on active duty in the U.S. military (West and Sabol 2009; U.S. Department of Defense 2008). Prison and jail now "compete" with employment for the time of low-skilled men. Moreover, prison and felony convictions can serve as barriers to employment. The cost to the individual has gone up in the last 30 years as computerized criminal history records have made background checks easier at the same time that a criminal history record has joined teenage pregnancy as a (more) common life experience. Researchers and policy-makers need to more fully come to grips with the role that the criminal justice system plays as a competitor to, and an impediment in, the labor market for the time of adult men.

YOUTH WORK AND STABILITY

The classroom and the workplace are two of the most important developmental contexts for youth in American society. Until well into the early twentieth century, adolescents were likely to mix school attendance and employment on the family farm, inside the home, or in factories, with employment generally taking up at least as much time as their schooling (Bremner et al. 1971; Kett 1977, 1978). Even children whose primary "occupation" was attending school were likely to have jobs in close proximity to the home, for example, running errands, selling papers, shining shoes, or other forms of informal work. Although the relative importance of education in the lives of America's youth grew with compulsory attendance laws, employment and schooling were always closely interwoven and have historically competed for the time and energy of young people. While concern was expressed about the working conditions of children, there was little doubt that, like schooling, employment was good for them.

Demand for reform grew slowly over the years, and the U.S. Congress finally passed the Fair Labor Standards Act (FLSA) in 1938, which established a minimum age of 16 years for non-agricultural employment but did allow 14- and 15-year-olds to work, as long as their employment did not interfere with their schooling and was not under conditions that proved detrimental to their health and well-being. Efforts to further restrict adolescent access to work characterized both federal and state legislation until the 1970s. In 1974, however, the Panel on Youth of the President's Science Advisory Committee (Coleman et al. 1974) signaled a change in thinking about adolescent employment. This and other blue-ribbon commissions, such as the National Commission on the Reform of Secondary Education (1973), the National Panel on High School and Adolescent Education (1976), the Work-Education Consortium of the National Manpower Institute (1978), the Carnegie Council on Policy Studies in Higher Education (1979), and the National Commission on Youth (1980), were highly critical of the age-segregated nature of American high schools and noted that youth in school were too far removed from work. With minor variations, each of these commissions maintained that working would enhance youths' education rather than detract from it, would better prepare them for the future, and therefore urged the relaxation of rules imposing limits on youth entering the workforce while still in school.

Beginning in the mid-1980s, the pendulum shifted again. Critics of the youth work movement, armed with empirical data to support their position, advocated careful consideration of the dangers and risks of adolescent employment. The first empirical studies of the effect of adolescent work indicated that employment during the school year, particularly what was called "intensive work" (an average of more than 20 hours per week), was related to poor school performance and involvement in a host of antisocial and "pseudo-adult" behaviors. Renewed skepticism about adolescent employment was given full expression in 1986 with the publication of Ellen Greenberger and Laurence Steinberg's *When Teenagers Work: The Psychological and Social Costs of Adolescent Employment*. Based on their extensive research on youth who worked during the school year, especially those who worked intensively, Greenberger and Steinberg found that adolescents often paid a high developmental price for working. The areas where youth were at greatest risk were their performance in school as well as participation in antisocial and "pseudo-mature" behaviors (e.g., smoking, drinking, using drugs, early sexuality). In rejecting the notion that high-school employment should be encouraged, Greenberger and Steinberg suggest that adolescents need a space for "daydreaming, fantasy and harmless irresponsibility" (Greenberger and Steinberg 1986, 167–173).

A voluminous amount of research published from the 1980s onward, reviewed by Paternoster and colleagues (2003), Apel and colleagues (2008), and Uggen and Wakefield (2008), only confirmed the conclusion of these developmental scholars that adolescent employment comes with high psychological and social costs and should be discouraged. Working too much during the school year appeared to lead to higher dropout rates, poorer school performance, lower educational aspirations, and an elevated risk for delinquency and other problem behaviors such as early smoking, drinking, and illicit drug use. It was in large measure due to this growing consensus in the social science literature that intensive working during the school year was potentially harmful for adolescents that the National Research Council (NRC) proposed stricter limits on the hours that high-school students should be allowed to work during the school year. Specifically, the NRC recommended (1998, 226) that the federal government limit school-year work for young people ages 16 and 17—a group presently allowed to work as many hours as they choose under the federal child labor law—to no more than 20 hours per week.

Despite the large body of literature, the NRC conclusion was not built on a strong causal foundation. Intense workers are more delinquent than non-intense workers even before they begin to work. To deal with this real possibility of selection bias, researchers prior to the NRC report used cross-sectional comparisons with multiple control variables. After the NRC report, researchers have used panel data with fixed effects and propensity scoring techniques,[1] both of which provide stronger controls for selection. A general pattern emerged in these results, nicely demonstrated by Paternoster and colleagues (2003) and Apel and colleagues (2007), in which the positive correlation between intense work and delinquency is first weakened and then eliminated by stronger controls for selection in the National Longitudinal Study of Youth, 1997 Cohort, a nationally representative sample of youth who were ages 12 through 16 in 1997. Furthermore, research has shown that much of the negative associations of work and crime are driven by informal work and summer-only work, not the type of formal employer jobs that are the subject of legal restrictions (Apel et al. 2006). While not everyone agrees (Uggen and Wakefield 2008), the research is now clear that the conclusion of the NRC was premature—intense work is not criminogenic. On crime prevention grounds, there is little support for the notion that policymakers should discourage youth who are often detached from school and moving toward delinquency to stunt their growing attachment to the labor market.

Another serious flaw with the literature that informed the NRC recommendation is that no study actually looked at the impact of the federal laws governing work on adolescent delinquency. These federal laws seriously limit the non-agricultural employment and work hours of adolescents younger than 16 years of age. Starting at age 16, state rules take over. The state rules vary from restricting 16-year-olds to 20 hours of work to imposing no restrictions at all, essentially treating 16-year-olds as adults. In an important paper, Apel and colleagues (2008) look at the treatment effect of moving from the federal regime at age 15 to the different state regimes that exist at age 16. The results are unambiguous. The different state laws have a dramatic impact on the formal labor market involvement of 16-year-old workers, and that change is associated with a decrease in delinquency. The opportunity for "harmless irresponsibility" afforded by tight labor restrictions on 16- and 17-year-olds might not be so harmless.

Youth who are allowed to work more, do work more, and commit fewer delinquent acts as a result.

Working more has no impact on school performance (see also Rothstein 2007), but it does appear to increase school dropout. This latter result is troubling, and points to the competing nature of work and school. From a crime-prevention perspective, however, this trade-off does not appear to lead to increased crime, at least in the short run. It is also consistent with research that shows that dropout for economic reasons is associated with a drop in delinquency, while dropout motivated by a dislike of school, with no subsequent movement into the labor market, may be criminogenic (Sweeten et al. 2009; Jarjoura 1993).

The use of the state labor laws to statistically identify the causal impact of work also has the important advantage of beginning to move the discussion to the process by which people move into the labor market. The data from National Longitudinal Survey of Youth (1997) show quite clearly how the change in work rules leads to a doubling in the percentage of workers from 20 percent to 40 percent in the first six months after the individual's sixteenth birthday. But very little research has been done on describing the nature of the transition into work.

While working during the school year is normal for American teenagers, it might be developmentally disruptive if it is initiated too early or if attachment to the labor force occurs at too young an age. Further, while it is normative for workers who have finished their schooling to engage in a certain amount of developmentally healthy "job-shopping" as they try to better match their interests and skills with their jobs, "floundering" or "churning" during high school may be developmentally disruptive (Neumark 2002; Yates 2005). Sampson and Laub (1993) suggest that the *stability* of one's work is particularly important in inhibiting criminal offending because it could increase social control. The stable accumulation of work experience may also allow for the development of the kinds of human capital (hard skills, such as fluency with numbers or writing ability, and soft skills, such as punctuality and dependability) that can be called upon later as a resource for youth either in their transition to a full-time job after high school or post-secondary education (Staff and Mortimer 2007; Mortimer et al. 2008).

There are a number of empirical studies which suggest that work timing and stability may be important correlates of delinquent and criminal offending. Sampson and Laub's (1993) reanalysis of the Glueck data on the development of young boys in Boston provides some support for the importance of work stability (length of time in present or most recent job), though their interest was not in adolescent but young adult job stability. They found that those with low job stability between the ages of 17 and 25 were more likely to be involved with crime, more likely to be arrested, and more likely to have problems with alcohol than those with greater job stability. Job stability between the ages of 17 and 25 was one of the most important predictors of successful adjustment up to age 45.

Mortimer (2002) combined the dimensions of work intensity and work duration and found that a consistent pattern of low-intensity employment during school was beneficial (see also Mortimer and Johnson 1998). In a follow-up study that directly appealed to a life-course perspective, Staff and Mortimer (2007) found that steady low-intensity work over the high school years was positively related to educational attainment, particularly for a group that they called "low-promise" youth.

Although not related to crime, Alon and colleagues (2001) investigated the relationship between the timing and volatility of work experience for young women and their subsequent labor force attachment. They found that the more labor force experience that a woman acquires, the more likely she is to be attached to the labor force as an adult. With respect to whether the timing of that experience matters, they also found that high-school work experience increases the chance that a woman would attach to the labor market as an adult. With respect to volatility, Alon and colleagues found that the greater the number of work to non-work transitions, the less likely a woman was to be attached to the labor force as an adult.

Paternoster and colleagues (2009) have also studied the stability of adolescent work with the National Longitudinal Survey of Youth 1997 data set. They found that those adolescents with more job transitions were at greater risk of young adult crime. In contrast, they found no evidence that youth who enter work or attach to work at an earlier age than "normal" during the years 14–18 are at any greater risk of crime in young adulthood (ages 18–20).

These results dovetail with earlier results suggesting that working may actually lead to less, rather than more, delinquency for adolescents (Apel et al. 2008). Although adolescents are at a different developmental stage from adults, the same work-crime relationship that exists for adults is also applicable to youth. Youth and adults who work more commit less crime than they would otherwise, and at the very least, an unstable work history for adolescents is a risk factor for young adult criminal involvement. Attachment to and involvement in pro-social activities appears to be the key factor, regardless of the age of the individual. In a nutshell, "*work is work*" regardless of when it occurs, and what matters for both adolescents and adults is stable accumulation of work-related capital.

This commitment is at least partially dependent on the demand for workers. At-risk and low-skill youth are at the end of the line when it comes to jobs, and therefore should be particularly sensitive to changes in the labor market (Gould et al. 2002). Although there may be little that governments can do to increase demand for labor in ways that reduce the crime rate (Bushway and Reuter 2002), macro-level changes in the economy nonetheless have the potential to affect employment (and thus the crime rate) (Apel et al. 2008). The next section reviews research documenting the relationship between the economy and crime at the aggregate level.

THE BUSINESS CYCLE AND CRIME

Researchers have long wanted to know if the national crime rate depends in any substantial way on the national labor market (e.g., Thomas 1927). The labor market is typically measured by the unemployment rate, which is the percentage of those individuals in the labor market (either working or looking for work) who do not have a job. A large number of ambiguous results in the aggregate unemployment and crime literature has led to what Chiricos (1987, 188) referred to as the "consensus of doubt."

In a seminal series of papers, Cantor and Land (1985, 1991; Land et al. 1995) argued that the generally null and/or inconsistent findings between unemployment and crime that have characterized previous empirical work is due to the fact that the basic relationship is the result of two competing forces. In the standard rational choice explanation, unemployment has a positive effect on crime by increasing the criminal motivation of both unemployed and employed persons. The unemployed are more highly motivated to commit crimes because they are out of work and have financial needs. The employed are also at greater risk of crime during periods of high unemployment because periods of high joblessness are indicative of a poorly performing economy. When unemployment levels are high in a sluggish economy, even the employed are in a precarious economic position because they often are underemployed, have to remain in jobs they are unsuited for or dissatisfied with, and often feel that they will be the next one to be laid off.

Cantor and Land (1985) further argue that this motivational effect of unemployment is not expected to be immediate, but should be lagged by some time period. This is because those recently made jobless have a stock of resources (savings, unemployment, welfare) that they can immediately draw upon and first must exhaust before feeling the financial costs of unemployment. The motivational shift from conformer to offender is gradual, becoming more acute as one's economic resources become depleted.

Cantor and Land also argue that there is a contemporaneous negative relationship between unemployment on crime that is based on routine activities theory. This argument hypothesizes that an immediate consequence of unemployment is to reduce crime because the unemployed generally find themselves in routine activities that are more home-based. As a result of their unemployment, the argument goes, those without jobs are less likely, at least in the short term, to be in public places where the risk of being victimized is greater and are more likely to be guardians for their residences. Cantor and Land refer to these crime-reducing immediate consequences of unemployment as the guardianship and system activity effect, respectively. This introduction of the routine activities explanation (Cohen and Felson 1979) for the relationship between employment and crime represents an important theoretical contribution to the debate, by suggesting that the relationship between labor markets and crime need not operate strictly through economic need. Labor markets can also change how people live, creating and destroying opportunities for crime.

Cantor and Land's re-specification of the problem spurred a whole new body of empirical research on the unemployment and crime relationship, although it also generated a continuing debate about the proper specification and the identification strategy (Rosenfeld and Fornango 2007; Greenfield 2001; Cantor and Land 2001; O'Brien 2001; Britt 2001; Paternoster and Bushway 2001). The results point to a weak motivation effect, particularly for property crime, with even weaker or nonexistent opportunity effects (Arvanites and Defina 2006). Paternoster and Bushway (2001) report that a 1 percentage point increase in the unemployment rate will lead to a 2 percent increase in property crime (see also Freeman 1999; Piehl 1998; Levitt 2001), a small effect size. Not all reviewers are willing to discount the opportunity effect based on the current evidence. Uggen and Wakefield conclude that "unemployment has a lagged and contemporaneous effect on crime" (2008, 204), suggesting support for both the rational choice and routine activities mechanisms for a relationship between the labor market and crime.

Alternatively, Paternoster and Bushway (2001) suggested that aggregate research on the national-level time series[2] has failed to show the expected strong relationship between the business cycle and crime because the research has not studied business cycle fluctuations. On average, business cycles have lasted 5.5 years since 1945 (NBER 2009). Table 7.1 provides the National Bureau of Economic Research data on U.S. business cycle expansions and contractions. According to this data, the average contraction since 1945 has lasted 10 months, while the average expansion has lasted 57 months, leading to an average cycle of 67 months. One-year changes do not adequately capture the change described by the business cycle.

Cook and Zarkin (1985), in contrast to Cantor and Land (1985), present an analysis that focuses explicitly on the business cycle using U.S. data covering roughly the same period as Cantor and Land's research (1933–1981). They perform two analyses. The first is a clever non-parametric test based on the changes in criminal activity during the entire business cycle. They show that robbery and burglary increase more during economic contractions than expansions, indicating evidence for a motivational theory of crime. There is no observed motivational effect for homicide. More auto theft occurs during expansions relative to contractions, suggesting that opportunity might be an especially important factor for auto theft (Paternoster and Bushway 2001). An expansion of this approach to include the most recent business cycles has been able to replicate these results—business cycle booms correspond with declines in burglary and robbery, and increases of auto theft. Booms and busts appear to have no relationship with violent crime (Bushway, Cook, and Phillips 2009).

Cook and Zarkin (1985) also try to quantify this analysis using trends in the unemployment rate, and these results are supportive of the more

Table 7.1. U.S. Business Cycle Expansions and Contractions (1945 to 2001)

| Peak Date | Trough Date | Length (months) | | |
		Contraction (peak to trough)	Expansion (prev. trough to this peak)	Cycle (trough from prev. trough)
Feb. 1945	Oct. 1945	8	80	88
Nov. 1948	Oct. 1949	11	37	48
July 1953	May 1954	10	45	55
Aug. 1957	Apr. 1958	8	39	47
Apr. 1960	Feb. 1961	10	24	34
Dec. 1969	Nov. 1970	11	106	117
Nov. 1973	Mar. 1975	16	36	52
Jan. 1980	July 1980	6	58	64
July 1981	Nov. 1982	16	12	28
July 1990	Mar. 1991	8	92	100
Mar. 2001	Nov. 2001	8	120	128
Average (10 Cycles)		10	57	67

http://www.nber.org/cycles/cyclesmain.html

descriptive analysis. The problem, as noted by Greenberg (2001), Arvanites and Defina (2006), and Rosenfeld and Fornango (2007), is that unemployment is not a good measure of the business cycle. The National Bureau of Economic Research determines the timing of the business cycle primarily by the gross domestic product, with input from measures of income and employment. Specifically, the NBER states on its web site that:

> Unemployment is generally a lagging indicator, particularly after the trough in economic activity determined by the NBER. For instance, the unemployment rate peaked 15 months after the NBER trough month in the 1990–91 recession and 19 months after the NBER trough month in the 2001 recession. The unemployment rate (which the committee does not use) tends to lag behind employment (which the committee *does* use) on account of variations in labor-force participation. (http://www.nber.org/cycles/recessions_faq.html)

Arvanites and Defina (2006) try to construct a more realistic quantitative model of the business cycle by redoing Cantor and Land (1985) using state-level measures of gross domestic product and a panel data structure from 1986 to 2001. They find a strong and negative lagged relationship between gross state product and property crime rates, and no contemporaneous effect. Their results support motivational theory over opportunity theory and highlight the potential power of moving to a truer measure of the business cycle.

Rosenfeld and Fornango (2007) replicate these results for robbery and larceny over a longer time period (1970 to 2003) using regional rather than state measures. But Rosenfeld and Fornango (2007) also suggest using a measure of consumer sentiment rather than a measure of gross domestic product. The argument here is similar to the question about perceptual deterrence. What matters is not the objective experience of the economy, but people's perceptions of that experience. Consumer sentiment is not used to identify business cycles by the NBER, but it has proven predictive ability (Gelper et al. 2007) and it is explicitly used by banks, manufacturers, and the government to gain real-time insight into the direction and current state of the economy.

Rosenfeld and Fornango (2007) find strong evidence for a negative relationship between consumer sentiment and property crime, even when controlling for GDP and unemployment. Indeed, they conclude that improvement in consumer sentiment can explain a third of the drop in robbery during the 1990s. This conclusion contrasts sharply with Levitt's (2004) dismissal of economic explanations of the crime drop, and serves as an upper bound on the estimates provided by others such as Grogger (2000). Moreover, they begin to tell an important theoretical story, continued by Rosenfeld (2009), for how opportunity theory can also explain how crime increases during recessions, as the underground demand for stolen goods increases.

There are at least two reasons to be excited by this renewed discussion about the relationship between the business cycle and crime. First, it reflects a renewed belief in the existence of a national time trend in crime. There is undoubtedly local variation in crime, and local factors matter for both crime and the economy (Levitt 2001). But routine activity theory (Cohen and Felson 1979; Felson 2002) relies on large-scale social changes that facilitate and impede criminal opportunities. Large-scale social factors—such as the loss of high paying U.S. manufacturing jobs, the increase in incarceration as a policy choice, the increase in female labor supply, and the rise of illegal markets such as crack—all affect the mix of motivated offenders, suitable targets, and available guardians in such a way that might affect crime. The absence of a meaningful national trend in crime would necessarily put the lie to such national level theories. Yet actually identifying a national trend is no simple matter, and it is relatively easy to show that there is substantial variation in crime trends across cities (Brownstein 1996).

McDowall and Loftin (2009) take on this challenge using 45 years of annual data on 134 U.S. cities with populations of more than 100,000 people. Using a variety of techniques, they find conservatively that the national trend can explain at least 20 percent of the overall variation of crime rates across places over time. At least in theory, this national trend can be explained by other national-level trends, such as the national business cycle.

The second reason to get more excited about explaining national trends comes from the movement to other measures of the economy besides unemployment. The focus on unemployment rates raised a difficult conceptual problem. Crime rates and unemployment rates are the products of fundamentally different stochastic or probabilistic processes (McDowall and Loftin 2005). Aggregate crime rates follow a random walk process, which means that crime does not return to a common mean, or equilibrium position (McDowall and Loftin 2009). Crime goes up or down in response to shock, and it stays up or down, without necessarily returning to the previous level. It is inherently unpredictable and tends to follow long meandering paths. Unemployment, however, is stationary—moving up and down in a rhythmic or cyclical way. Unemployment rates are more predictable than crime rates—simply checking where the unemployment rate is relative to its historical average provides a reasonable prediction about what will happen in the next year.

This difference in process implies that crime and unemployment do not track, or move together. Their relationship, if it exists, must be more complicated, perhaps with changes in unemployment affecting changes in crime in a non-linear way, or with structural breaks (meaning that the causal relationship changes over time).[3] In contrast, the economic evidence suggests that both consumer sentiment (Gelper et al. 2007) and GDP (Rapach 2002) also do not move around a common mean (like unemployment), even after taking into account the standard upward trend in measures such as GDP.[4] The key insight here is that the processes generating GDP and consumer sentiment are similar in structure to the processes generating crime (unlike unemployment). Beyond resolving some of the confusion dealing with trends that follow different processes (Paternoster and Bushway 2001), this result means that national crime trends could legitimately be caused, in the conventional sense, by these large-scale economic forces. This could also explain the apparently stronger relationship between crime and GDP and consumer sentiment in standard regressions relative to unemployment and crime.[5]

It may also help that these models (Rosenfeld and Fornango 2007; Arvanites and Defina 2006) are estimated using data from after 1970, a period that contains what is the arguably the most important macro-level trend in the United States with respect to the labor market and crime: the shift away from the heavy dependence on less-educated male workers that began in the 1970s.[6] From the early 1900s through the 1960s, the real earnings of less-educated male workers grew markedly (Mishel, Bernstein, and Boushey 2003). Increased productivity gains, relative shortages of less-educated workers, as well as expanding unionization and the federal minimum wage legislation all seemed to ensure decade by decade increases in the economic fortunes of less-educated male workers in the United States over this period.

But a shift in this trend began to occur in the 1970s and 1980s as the wages paid to less-educated male workers began to decline in both real terms and relative to the earnings of more educated (i.e., college trained) workers. These declines accelerated during the 1980s, especially for young males with a high school degree or less (Blackburn, Bloom, and Freeman 1990). These trends were especially pronounced for young black men. Not only did the earnings and employment of less-educated young men decline more generally over the late 1970s and 1980s, but less-educated young black men's outcomes also fell relative to those of comparable whites (Bound and Freeman 1992).

The declining labor market fortunes of less-educated male workers and the growing concentration of the poor in urban areas, especially the black poor, over the 1980s could clearly have influenced criminal activity in the United States over a long period. This is especially true, given recent research on the long-term earnings shocks of layoffs during recessions (von Wachter et al. 2009). The effect on earnings for the individuals directly affected is long term, and it outlasts the recession itself. But, if the changing economic conditions faced by less-educated young men influenced their propensity to engage in criminal activities over the 1980s, then surely the relative improvements in earnings and employment that were observed during the economic boom of the mid-1990s for this age group should have reduced crime as well. While there is some evidence that the economic boom did benefit less-educated young black men by modestly increasing the wages of those who were in the labor market (Freeman and Rodgers 2001), the secular downward trend in their employment and labor force participation continued over this period.[7]

Male labor force participation in the 16–24 age group, the peak age group for criminal activity, has declined 18 percentage points from 83 percent since 1989 (BLS 2009). Only half of the men in this age group worked during July 2009, and only 36 percent of blacks worked during this month, the peak month of work for this age group. These numbers would be even worse if blacks in prison and jail were counted as part of the population (Petit 2009). This unprecedented level of detachment from the labor market should raise red flags about the potential for crime. Even if one does not believe that these potential workers will change their criminal behavior in response to changes in the economy, the fact that almost two-thirds of the non-institutionalized population of blacks in the United States did not work in July 2009 raises important questions about their "routine activities." Is this population "working" in the drug markets, or off the books in the informal economy? Have these workers, particularly the men, been displaced by welfare reform, which successfully moved thousands of women into the workforce (Blank 2002)? What is clear is that the United States has experienced a fundamental shift in the degree to which individuals in the country, particularly populations at risk for crime, are attached to the formal labor market. At the same time, the United States has experienced an unprecedented and well-documented growth in the prison population. On any given day, more black male high school dropouts aged 20–35 are incarcerated than employed (Western and Pettit 2000). Given that incarceration is now a major factor of life for large numbers of people and communities, the next section examines ways in which incarceration and employment interact.

INCARCERATION

A fundamental fact of incarceration is that people who are incarcerated are not employed. But, the causal impact of incarceration on employment depends on whether new inmates come from the population who are in the workforce itself. The exact answer is difficult to determine definitely, since incarcerated people are either not counted or counted poorly in most official counts of the U.S. population (Pettit 2009). Such an undercount would lead to an overestimate of the percent of people in the workforce, and an underestimate of the impact of incarceration on the labor force participation rate.[8]

Despite these challengers, Holzer and colleagues (2005) create a credible estimate that every one percentage point increase in the incarceration rate for black men leads to a one percentage point decline in labor force attachment. If the imprisonment rate for black men has increased from 2 percent to 5 percent from 1979 to 1999, then incarceration can account for, at most, 4 percentage points of the overall 13 percentage point decline in labor force attachment among young black men during this same period. This estimate suggests that the increased incarceration in the United States has not included employed men, but rather, the unemployed and detached workers who were marginalized by the economic restructuring of the 1970s and who were most susceptible to the lures of the drug markets that grew up around crack cocaine in the 1980s.

This interpretation is supported by a description of the average incarcerated offender. Close to 70 percent are high school dropouts, for example, and most are unemployed at the time they are arrested (Petersilia 2001). Studies of employment for incarcerated offenders using official data find only 30 percent employed in the quarter before incarceration (far below the 57 percent self-reported rate), a figure that includes part-time (but not informal) work, with yearly earnings among those employed of less than $8,000 (Holzer 2009).

This low starting point means that it is also difficult for incarceration to have a dramatic impact on the earnings and employment on those who are incarcerated. The question of the impact of incarceration on earnings and unemployment was reviewed extensively and competently by Holzer (2009). He concluded that "while the credible empirical evidence is quite mixed, the preponderance of it points to *negative effects of incarceration on the subsequent employment and earnings of offenders*" (2009, 2).

Holzer makes it clear that not everyone agrees with this conclusion. A reasonable person could conclude on the basis of this evidence that incarcerating someone (rather than putting them on probation) has no causal impact on employment and earnings for the average offender after they are released (white collar offenders are a noteworthy exception; Nagin and Waldfogel 1996).[9] Individuals convicted of felonies are in the secondary labor market with unstable employment and flat wage trajectories before they are incarcerated (Bushway 1998, 2004).

It is possible, however, to put too much weight on the causal impact of incarceration on employment and earnings after release. Even if the incarcerated offender is not in the labor market before the spell of incarceration, the incarcerated offender spends yet more time out of the formal labor market while he or she is incarcerated. Or, to put it another way, prison unquestionably has a causal impact on the lifetime earning and employment of people who are incarcerated. This is a dead weight loss to society and to this individual, which may or may not be compensated by the corresponding drop in crime associated with his or her prison sentence.[10]

Prison work industries can try to mimic employment, but employment inside and outside a prison will always be fundamentally different enterprises. Prison is not work—and it is telling that for key demographic groups, incarceration is a more common experience than is work. Prison work programs have promise (Wilson et al. 2001; Jensen and Read 2006), but few rigorous evaluations have shown positive outcomes. Mostly what criminologists know is that there are some people in prison who want to participate in vocational programs—and these people do better in both the labor market and commit less crime when released.

As prison sentences become longer (Raphael and Stoll 2009), there are more and more people reentering society at older ages with little real experience in the labor market, meaning that even these motivated offenders face bigger challenges than in years past. Bushway, Tsao, and Smith (2009) show that the median age of the average prisoner has increased by about 8 years from 1974 to 2004, and the median age of released prisoners increased 5 years from 1984 to 1994 (Langan and Levin 2002). Twenty-seven-year-olds with no job experience have a better chance of attaching to the labor market than do 34-year-olds with no job experience. Mass incarceration has taken a group of people who were detached from the labor market and extended that detachment. Even if one doubts the evidence supporting the claim that incarceration causally increases employment problems after release from incarceration, it is hard to argue that incarceration is a solution to the problem of growing detachment of adults from the labor market. Policymakers should be particularly concerned about any policy that further isolates individuals and communities from the labor market.

Mass incarceration is not the only such policy. An even more prevalent problem is the use of criminal history records by employers. It is absolutely indisputable that employers are using criminal history records to bar offenders from employment at ever higher rates (Stoll and Bushway 2008; Holzer 2009; Pager 2003; Bushway 1998; Uggen et al. 2006; Travis 2002). There is a strong consensus in the literature that a criminal history record showing a conviction of a felony, independent of an arrest or criminal activity, has a sizable, causal, negative impact on employment and earnings. The debate in this literature centers on what to do about the problem given the tension between protecting the public against the threat of ex-felons and the rights (and possible rehabilitation) of ex-felons.

Ex-felons are at a higher risk of crime, and while change can and does happen, the reality is that the social science evidence in support of work, for example, as a change agent for ex-offenders is relatively weak (Bushway and Reuter 2002; Raphael and Weiman 2007; Fagan and Freeman 1999). The last time SEARCH, the consortium of state criminal history records, reviewed its standards for conduct by the repositories, they did not choose to restrict employer access to even arrest records because social science research "suggest(s) that even where employers do use arrest information as a bar to or a restriction on employment opportunities, this may not be significant from a rehabilitation standpoint because recidivism statistics suggest that rehabilitation is seldom achieved regardless of offenders' employment prospects" (SEARCH 1988 29). Recent reviews on desistance (Laub and Sampson 2001) reach a different conclusion regarding the power of work to aid recidivism, but there is still no strong consensus about the causal mechanisms underlying the desistance process (NRC 2008).

Of course, governments could simply ban background checks. Yet employers and other policy agents clearly believe that information on criminal history records is valuable for making informed decisions about future risk. The widespread proliferation of private criminal history record checks in the last 15 years is a testimony to the demand for this information, as are the steps that agents will take to circumvent restrictions on access to official repository data (Bushway et al. 2007). Agents who believe that this information might be relevant could also resort to statistical discrimination on the basis of race, which is highly correlated to criminal history records (Bushway 2004; Holzer, Raphael, and Stoll 2005). This type of discrimination not only hurts minority ex-offenders, it also hurts minority non-offenders. For example, Pager's (2003) audit study in Milwaukee revealed that race is as salient as criminal history record among employers who do not check for a criminal history record. All things equal, it might make more sense to develop rational guidelines for the use of criminal history records than advocate a policy that could well lead to much wider employment problems for non-felons (SEARCH 2006).

One standard would limit the use of old criminal history records and eliminate lifetime bans on the basis of risk of recidivism (Kurlychek et al. 2006, 2007; Blumstein and Nakamura 2009; Bushway and Sweeten 2007). Recent research has shown that ex-offenders eventually "look like" non-offenders in terms of recidivism after 7 to 10 years. Good policy could include sunset clauses for individuals who meet certain standards of conduct, like staying "straight" for 7 to 10 years. It is possible that this sunset clause could be conditioned on age or other factors correlated with recidivism. For example, perhaps older offenders need not stay straight for that long before they can claim that they have desisted (Bushway et al. 2009).

Other policy experiments include the "ban the box" movement, in which employers are not allowed to ask about criminal history records at the beginning of the process (Henry and Jacobs 2007). This policy—which has been implemented for local government jobs in San Francisco, Chicago, Boston and statewide in Minnesota—moves the background check to a later step in the process, essentially preventing employers from asking about a criminal history record on the application. The belief is that the information will matter less when taken in the larger context of the employee's qualifications, essentially forcing employers to evaluate the record relative to other job qualifications and the characteristics of the job. No evaluations have yet been completed of this policy, but it represents an innovative attempt to encourage employers to avoid using the criminal history record as the only measure of risk.

Private employers, however, have not followed the lead of public employers in cities with "ban the box" initiatives (Gebo and Norton-Hawk 2009). The primary reason appears to be concerns about liability. Negligent hiring lawsuits allow claimants to hold companies liable if they hire someone who does harm to the claimant if the act was "reasonably forseeable." The key is the meaning of the phrase "reasonably forseeable," which is usually interpreted in layman's terms by juries. This concept is usually not applied in a statistical sense.

But, statistically, violent acts committed on the job are rare, and therefore hard to foresee, even by people who have done such acts before. Suppose that the chance of serious harm by an employee is .1 percent, meaning that one out of every 1,000 employees will commit a serious violent act on the job in the coming year. Predicting this outcome is incredibly difficult, and even a good predictor might only identify people that are two or three times more likely to commit a crime (.3 percent rather than .1 percent) (Gottfredson and Gottfredson 1994; Gottfredson and Moriarity 2006). Using such predictors will result in the exclusion of many people who were in fact never going to commit any such crime. Legislatures and courts must decide whether this small reduction in risk is worth the further detachment and isolation of a large subset of the population from work. Even if such exclusion does not directly cause crime by the person excluded, it seems inevitable that such exclusion will heighten the detachment from work in that person's family and community. Employment exclusion, unlike incarceration, seems unlikely to prevent much crime—yet, the potential for further harm by continuing to weaken the link to employment in populations already detached from the legal labor market might swamp any harm caused by ex-offenders.

CONCLUSION

Only 55.6 percent of youth aged 16 to 24 were working in July 2008. The percentage of blacks who were working, 41.3 percent, is even lower. These numbers reflect the steady decline in labor force participation since July 1989. These trends for the most crime-prone age group are startling, and particularly alarming for a chapter on labor markets and crime. The current recession only makes the problem worse, leaving attachment to the workforce at all time lows.

This trend is worrisome on many levels. The second section of this chapter made it clear that detachment from the labor market is associated with crime for all people, including youth. Work competes with school, but attachment to both work and school lowers crime and should be encouraged for youth who lack a pro-social major life activity that leads to non-crime-centric routine activities. More research needs to focus on the reasons for and the possible solutions to this secular decline in work attachment among young adults.

Perhaps this secular decline, however, need not concern criminologists given that the United States has experienced a substantial decline in crime starting roughly around 1990. This decline has occurred mainly in violent crime, which historically has had the weakest connection to the labor market, though property crime has also declined somewhat during this same period (Levitt 2004; Rosenfeld 2009). The third section of this chapter reviewed the existing research on the relationship between the economy and crime and pointed to new research that suggests that the negative relationship between property crime and the economy is stronger than previously suggested, particularly if researchers use techniques and measures that allow them to focus both on the business cycle and secular trends such as the growing detachment of at-risk groups from work.

A discussion of crime and employment since 1989 would be deficient without a discussion of the massive increase in the prison population that accelerated starting in the 1990s. Most analysts agree that this increase in incarceration is responsible in part for the resulting decline in crime during this time period (Rosenfeld 2009; Levitt 2004; Donohue 2009). But this policy of incarceration, in combination with the increased concern about criminal history records checks by employers, has exacerbated the detachment from the labor market. The fourth section of this paper discussed the mechanisms by which this might occur.

As the United States begins a national discussion about de-incarceration, researchers and policymakers need to come to grips with the low levels of labor-market participation among young adult men. Communities in which the majority of young men are either in prison or are unemployed are not healthy places. The Welfare Reform Act of 1996 showed that a governmental and societal commitment to work could create positive outcomes for women who were detached from work (Blank 2002). Future work needs to focus on finding equally effective strategies for men who are detached from work.

References

Abbott, A. 2001. *Time Matters: On Theory and Method.* Chicago: University of Chicago Press.

Alon, S., D. Donahoe, and M. Tienda. 2001. "The Effects of Early Work Experience on Young Women's Labor Force Attachment." *Social Forces* 79: 1005–1035.

Apel, R., S. Bushway, R. Brame, A. Hayiland, D. Nagin, and R. Paternoster. 2007. "Unpacking the Relationship Between Adolescent Employment and Antisocial Behavior: A Matched Samples Comparison." *Criminology* 45: 67–97.

Apel, R., S. Bushway, R. Paternoster, R. Brame, and G. Sweeten. 2008. "Using State Child Labor Laws to Identify the Causal Effect of Youth Employment on Deviant Behavior and Academic Achievement." *Journal of Quantitative Criminology* 24 (4): 337–363.

Arvanites, T., and R. Defina. 2006. "Business Cycles and Street Crime." *Criminology* 44 (1): 139–164.

Bernstein, L., and E. Houston. 2000. *Crime and Work: What We Can Learn from the Low-Wage Labor Market.* Washington, DC: Economic Policy Institute.

Blackburn, M. L., D. Bloom, and R. B. Freeman. 1990. "The Declining Economic Position of Less Skilled American Men." In *A Future Of Lousy Jobs: The Changing Structure of U.S. Wages*, ed. Gary Burtless. Washington, DC: Brookings Institution.

Blank, R. M. 2002. "Evaluating Welfare Reform in the United States." *Journal of Economic Literature* 40 (4): 1105–1166.

Blumstein, A., and K. Nakamura. 2009. "Redemption in the Presence of Widespread Criminal Background Checks." *Criminology* 47 (2): 327–359.

Bound, J., and R. B. Freeman. 1992. "What Went Wrong? The Erosion of the Relative Earnings and Employment among Young Black Men in the 1980s." *Quarterly Journal of Economics* 107: 201–232.

Bremner, R. J., J. Barnard, T. Hareven, and R. Mennel, eds. 1971. *Children and Youth in America: A Documentary History, Vol 2., 1866–1932.* Cambridge, MA: Harvard University Press.

Britt, C. L. 2001. "Testing Theory and the Analysis of Time Series Data." *Journal of Quantitative Criminology* 17 (4): 343–357.

Brownstein, H. H. 1996. *The Rise and Fall of a Violent Crime Wave: Crack Cocaine and the Social Construction of a Crime Problem.* New York: Criminal Justice Press, Monsey.

Bureau of Labor Statistics. 2009. *Economic News Release: American Time Use Survey Summary.* Washington, DC: United States Department of Labor.

Bushway, S. 1998. "The Impact of an Arrest on the Job Stability of Young White American Men." *Journal of Research in Crime and Delinquency* 35 (4): 454–479.

Bushway, S. 2004. "Labor Market Effects of Permitting Employer Access to Criminal History Records." *Journal of Contemporary Criminal Justice* (Special Issue on Economics and Crime) 20: 276–291.

Bushway, S., P. Cook., and M. Phillips. 2009. "Youth Crime and Violence over the Business Cycle." Presentation at CDC working group on youth crime.

Bushway, S., P. Nieuwbeerta, and A. Blokland. 2009. "The Predictive Value of Criminal Background Checks: Do Age and Criminal History Affect Time to Redemption?" Working paper.

Bushway, S., and P. Reuter. 2002. "Labor Markets and Crime." In *Crime: Public policies for Crime Control*, 2nd ed., eds. J. Q. Wilson and J. Petersilia. San Francisco: Institute for Contemporary Studies Press.

Bushway, S., and G. Sweeten. 2007. "Abolish Lifetime Bans for Ex-Felons." *Criminology and Public Policy* 6 (4): 697–706.

Bushway, S., H. Tsao, and H. Smith. 2009. "Has the U.S. Prison Boom Changed the Age Distribution of the Prison Population?" Working paper.

Cantor, D., and K. C. Land. 1985. "Unemployment and Crime Rates in the Post-World War II United States: A Theoretical and Empirical Analysis." *American Sociological Review* 50: 317–332.

Cantor, D., and K. C. Land. 1991. "Exploring Possible Temporal Relationships of Unemployment and Crime: A Comment of Hale and Sabbagh." *Journal of Research in Crime and Delinquency* 28: 418–425.

Caspi, A., B. R. Entner Wright, T. E. Moffitt, and P. A. Silva. 1998. "Early Failure in the Labor Market: Childhood and Adolescent Predictors of Unemployment in the Transition to Adulthood." *American Sociological Review* 63 (3): 424–451.

Cauffman, E., and L. Steinberg. 1995. "The Cognitive and Affective Influences on Adolescent Decision-Making." *Temple Law Review* 68: 1763–1789.

Chiricos, T. 1987. "Rates of Crime and Unemployment: An Analysis of Aggregate Research Evidence." *Social Problems* 34: 187–212.

Cohen, L. E., and M. Felson. 1979. "Social Change and Crime Rate Trends: A Routine Activity Approach." *American Sociological Review* 44: 588–608.

Coleman, J. S., R. H. Bremner, B. R. Clark, J. B. Davis, D. H. Eichorn, Z. Griliches, J. F. Kett, N. B. Ryder, Z. B. Doering, and J. M. Mays. 1974. *Youth: Transition to Adulthood. Report of the Panel on Youth of the President's Science Advisory Committee.* Chicago: University of Chicago Press.

Cook, P. 1980. "Research in Criminal Deterrence: Laying the Groundwork for the Second Decade." In *An Annual Review of Research, vol. 2*, eds. N. Morris and M. Tonry, 211–268. Chicago: University of Chicago Press.

Cook, P., and G. A. Zarkin. 1985. "Crime and the Business Cycle." *Journal of Legal Studies* 14: 115–128.

Donohue, J. J. 2009. "Assessing the Relative Benefits of Incarceration: The Overall Change over the Previous Decades and the Benefits on the Margin." In *Do Prisons Make Us Safer? The Benefits and Costs of the Prison Boom*, eds. S. Raphael and M. A. Stoll, 269–341. New York: Russell Sage Foundation.

Elder, G. H. 1985. *Life Course Dynamics: Trajectories and Transitions, 1968–1980.* Ithaca, NY: Cornell University Press.

Elder, G. H. 1998. "The Life Course as Developmental Theory." *Child Development* 69 (1): 1–12.

Fagan, J., and R. B. Freeman. 1998. "Crime and Work." In *Crime and Justice: A Review of Research*, ed. M. Tonry, 113–178. Chicago: University of Chicago Press.

Farrington, D. P., ed. 2005. *Integrated Developmental and Life-Course Theories of Offending.* New Brunswick, NJ: Transaction Publishers.

Farrington, D. P., B. Gallagher, L. Morley, R. J. St. Ledger, and D. J. West. 1986. "Unemployment, School Leaving, and Crime." *British Journal of Criminology* 6: 335–356.

Felson, M. 2002. *Crime and Everyday Life.* Thousand Oaks, CA: Sage.

Freeman, R. B. 1999. "The Economics of Crime." In *The Handbook of Labor Economics, vol. 3*, eds. O. Ashenfelter and D. Card, 3529–3571. New York: Elsevier Science.

Freeman, R. B., and W. Rodgers. 2003. "Crime and the Labor Market Outcomes of Young Men in the 1990s Expansion." Presented at the Association for Public Policy and Management Meetings, Oct 31–Nov 2.

Gebo, E., M. Norton-Hawk. 2009. "Criminal Record Policies and Private Employers." *Justice Policy Journal* 6: 1.

Gelper, S., A. Lemmens, and C. Croux. 2007. "Consumer Sentiment and Consumer Spending: Decomposing the Granger Causality Relationship in the Time Domain." *Applied Economics* 39: 1–11.

Gottfredson, S. D., and D. Gottfredson. 1994. "Behavioral Prediction and the Problem of Incapacitation." *Criminology* 32: 441–474.

Gottfredson, S. D., and L. J. Moriarty. 2006. "Statistical Risk Assessment: Old Problems and New Applications." *Crime and Delinquency* 52 (1): 178–200.

Gould, E. D., B. A. Weinberg, and D. B. Mustard. 2002. "Crime Rates and Local Labor Market Opportunities in the United States: 1977–1997." *The Review of Economic and Statistics* 84 (1): 45–61.

Greenberg, D. 2001. "Time Series Analysis of Crime Rates." *Journal of Quantitative Criminology* 17 (4): 291–327.

Greenberger, E., and L. Steinberg. 1986. *When Teenagers Work: The Psychological and Social Costs of Adolescent Employment*. New York: Basic Books.

Greenfield, L. 2001. *The Spirit of Capitalism: Nationalism and Economic Growth*. Cambridge, MA: Harvard University Press.

Grogger, J. 2000. "An Economic Model of Recent Trends in Violence." In *The Crime Drop*, eds. A. Blumstein and J. Wallman. Cambridge: Cambridge University Press.

Henry, J., S. James, and B. Jacobs. 2007. "Ban the Box to Promote Ex-Offender Employment." *Criminology and Public Policy* 6 (4): 755–762.

Holzer, H. J. 2009. "Collateral Costs: The Effects of Incarceration on the Employment and Earnings of Young Workers." In *Do Prisons Make Us Safer? The Benefits and Costs of the Prison Boom*, eds. S. Raphael and M. A. Stoll, 119–150. New York: Russell Sage Foundation.

Holzer, H. J., P. Offner, and E. Sorenson. 2005. "Declining Employment among Young Black Men: The Role of Incarceration and Child Support." *Journal of Policy Analysis and Management* 24: 329–350.

Holzer, H. J., S. Raphael, and M. A. Stoll. 2006. "Perceived Criminality, Criminal Background Checks, and the Racial Hiring Practices of Employers." *Journal of Law and Economics* 49: 451–480.

Jarjoura, G. R. 1993. "Does Dropping Out of School Enhance Delinquent Involvement? Results from a Large-Scale National Probability Sample." *Criminology* 31: 149–172.

Jensen, E., and G. Reed. 2006. "Adult Correctional Education Programs: An Update on Current Status Based on Recent Studies." *Journal of Offender Rehabilitation* 44 (1): 81–98.

Kett, J. F. 1977. *Rites of Passage: Adolescence in America, 1970 to the Present*. New York: Basic Books.

Kett, J. F. 1978. "Curing the Disease of Precocity." In *Turning Points: Historical and Sociological Essays on the Family*, eds. J. Demos and S. S. Boocock, 183–211. Chicago: University of Chicago Press.

Kurlychek, M. C., R. Brame, and S. Bushway. 2006. "Scarlet Letters and Recidivism: Does an Old Criminal Record Predict Future Offending?" *Criminology and Public Policy* 5 (3): 483–522.

Kurlychek, M. C., R. Brame, and S. Bushway. 2007. "Enduring Risk: Old Criminal Records and Prediction of Future Criminal Involvement." *Crime and Delinquency* 53 (1): 64–83.

Land, K. C., D. Cantor, and S. T. Russell. 1995. "Unemployment and Crime Rate Fluctuations in the Post-World War II United States: Statistical Time Series

Properties and Alternative Analysis of Time Series Data." In *Crime and Inequality*, eds. J. Hagan and R. Peterson, 55–79. Palo Alto, CA: Stanford University Press.

Langan, P. A., and D. Levin. 2002. *Recidivism of Prisoners Released in 1994*. Bureau of Justice Statistics Special Report. Washington, DC: United States Department of Justice, Bureau of Justice Statistics.

Lattimore, P. K., A. D. Witte, and J. R. Baker. 1990. "Experimental Assessment of the Effect of Vocational Training on Youthful Property Offenders." *Evaluation Review* 14 (2): 115–133.

Lee, J. C., and J. Staff. 2007. "When Work Matters: The Varying Impact of Adolescent Work Intensity on High School Drop-Out." *Sociology of Education* 80: 158–178.

Levitt, S. D. 2001. "Alternative Strategies for Identifying the Link Between Unemployment and Crime." *Journal of Quantitative Criminology* 17 (4): 377–390.

Levitt, S. D. 2004. "Understanding Why Crime Fell in the 1990s: Four Factors That Explain the Decline and Six That Do Not." *Journal of Economic Perspectives* 18 (1): 163–190.

Lewontin, R. C. 2000. *The triple Helix: Gene, Organism, and Environment*. Cambridge, MA: Harvard University Press.

Ludwig, J. 1999. Information and inner city educational attainment. *Economics of Education Review* 18 (1):17–30.

McDowall, D., and C. Loftin. 2005. "Are United States Crime Rate Trends Historically Contingent?" *Journal of Research in Crime and Delinquency* 42 (35): 359–383.

McDowall, D., and C. Loftin. 2009. "Do United States City Crime Rates Follow a National Trend? The Influence of Nationwide Conditions on Local Crime Patterns." *Journal of Quantitative Criminology* 25 (3): 307–324.

Mishel, L., J. Bernstein, and H. Boushey. *The State of Working America 2002/2003*. Ithaca, NY: ILR Press.

Mortimer, J. T. 2002. *Working and Growing Up in America*. Cambridge, MA: Harvard University Press.

Mortimer, J. T., and M. K. Johnson. 1998. "Adolescent Part-Time Work and Educational Achievement." In *The Adolescent Years: Social Influences and Educational Challenges*, ed. K. Borman and B. Schneider, 183–206. Chicago: University of Chicago Press.

Mortimer, J. T., M. C. Vuolo, J. Staff, S. Wakefield, and W. Xie. 2008. "Tracing the Timing of a "Career" Acquisition in a Contemporary Youth Cohort." *Work and Occupations* 35 (1): 44–84.

Nagin, D., and J. Waldfogel. 1995. "The Effects of Criminality and Conviction on the Labor Market Status of Young British Offenders." *International Review of Law and Economics* 15: 109–126.

National Research Council. 1998. *Protecting Youth at Work: Health, Safety, and Development of Working Children and Adolescents in the United States*. Washington, DC: National Academy Press.

Needels, K. 1996. "Go Directly to Jail and Not Collect? A Long-Term Study of Recidivism, Employment, and Earnings Patterns among Prison Releases." *Journal of Research in Crime and Delinquency* 33: 471–496.

Neumark, D. 2002. "Youth Labor Markets in the United States: Shopping Around vs. Staying Put." *Review of Economics and Statistics* 84 (3): 462–482.

O'Brien, R. M. 2001. "Theory, Operationalization, Identification, and the Interpretation of Different Differences in Time Series Models." *Journal of Quantitative Criminology* 17 (4): 359–375.

Pager, D. 2003. "The Mark of a Criminal Record." *American Journal of Sociology* 108 (5): 937–975.

Pager, D. 2006. "Evidence-Based Public Policy for Successful Prisoner Reentry." *Crime and Public Policy* 5 (3): 501–511.

Paternoster, R., R. Apel, and S. Bushway. 2009. "The Effect of Adolescent Work Timing and Stability on Young Adult Crime." Working paper.

Paternoster, R., and S. Bushway. 2001. "Theoretical and Empirical Work on the Relationship Between Unemployment and Crime." *Journal of Quantitative Criminology* 17 (4): 391–407.

Paternoster, R., S. Bushway, R. Brame, and R. Apel. 2003. "The Effect of Teenage Employment on Delinquency and Problem Behaviors." *Social Forces* 82: 297–335.

Petersilia, J. 2001. "Prisoner Reentry: Public Safety And Reintegration Challenges." *Prison Journal* 81 (3): 360–375.

Pettit, B. 2009. "Enumerating Inequality: The Constitution, the Census Bureau, and the Criminal Justice System". *University of Connecticut Public Interest Law Journal.* http://www.law.uconn.edu/connecticut-public-interest-law-journal/current-issue

Piehl, A. 1998. "Economic Conditions, Work, and Crime." In *Handbook on Crime and Punishment,* ed. M. Tonry, 302–319. New York: Oxford University Press.

Pogarsky, G. 2002. "Identifying Deterrable Offenders: Implications for Deterrence Research." *Justice Quarterly* 19: 431–452

Rapach, D. E. 2002. "Are Real GDP Levels Nonstationary? Evidence from Panel Data Tests." *Southern Economic Journal* 68 (3): 473–495.

Raphael, S., and D. Weiman. 2007. "The Impact of Local Labor Market Conditions on the Likelihood That Parolees Are Returned to Custody." In *Barriers to Reentry: The Labor Market for Released Prisoners in Post-Industrial America,* ed. S. Bushway, M. Stoll, and D. Weiman. New York: Russell Sage Foundation.

Rondeaux, C., and D. Morse. 2007. "For Thieves, Copper Is Gold in the Gutter." *The Washington Post,* July 25, 2007.

Rosenfeld, R. 2009. "Crime Is the Problem: Homicide, Acquisitive Crime, and Economic Conditions." *Journal of Quantitative Criminology* 25: 287–306.

Rosenfeld, R., and R. Fornango. 2007. "The Impact of Economic Conditions on Robbery and Property Crime: The Role of Consumer Sentiment." *Criminology* 45: 735–770.

Rothstein, D. S. 2007. "High School Employment and Youths' Academic Achievement." *Journal of Human Resources* 42: 194–213.

Sampson, R., and J. Laub. 1993. *Crime in the Making.* Cambridge, MA: Harvard University Press.

Schochet, P. Z., J. Burghardt, and S. McConnell. 2006. *National Job Corps Study and Longer-term Follow-Up Study: Impact and Benefit-Cost Findings Using Survey and Summary Earnings Records Data.* Princeton, NJ: Mathematic Policy Research.

SEARCH. 1998. Report of the National Task Force on the Criminal Background of America. SEARCH Group. The National Consortium for Justice Information and Statistics. Sacramento, CA.

SEARCH. 2006. Report of the National Task Force on the Criminal Background of America. SEARCH Group. The National Consortium for Justice Information and Statistics. Sacramento, CA.

Staff, J., and J. T. Mortimer. 2007. "Educational and Work Strategies from Adolescence to Early Adulthood: Consequences for Educational Attainment." *Social Forces* 85: 1169–1194.

Stoll, M. A., and S. Bushway. 2008. "The Effect of Criminal Background Checks on Hiring Ex-Offenders." *Criminology and Public Policy* 7 (3): 371–404.

Sweeten, G., S. Bushway, and R. Paternoster. 2009. "Does Dropping Out of School Mean Dropping into Delinquency?" *Criminology* 47 (1): 47–91.

Thomas, D. 1927. "Social Aspects of the Business Cycle." NY: E. P. Dutton.

Thornberry, T., and R. L. Christenson. "Unemployment and Criminal Involvement: An Investigation of Reciprocal Causal Structures." *American Sociological Review* 49: 397–411.

Tonry, M. A. 2008. "Learning from the Limitations of Deterrence Research." In *Crime and Justice: A Review of Research, vol. 37*, ed. M. A. Tonry. Chicago: University of Chicago Press.

Travis, J. 2002. "Invisible Punishment: An Instrument of Social Exclusion." In *Invisible Punishment: The Collateral Consequences of Mass Imprisonment*, eds. M. Mauer and M. Chesney-Lind. New York: The Free Press.

U.S. Department of Defense. 2008. *Department of Defense Active Duty Military Personnel by Rank/Grade*. Washington, DC: United States Department of Defense.

Uggen, C. 2000. "Work as a Turning Point in the Life Course of Criminals: A Duration Model of Age, Employment, and Recidivism." *American Sociological Review* 65: 529–546.

Uggen, C., J. Manza, and M. Thompson. 2006. "Citizenship, Democracy, and the Civic Reintegration of Criminal Offenders." *The Annals of the American Academy of Political and Social Science* 605: 281–310.

Uggen, C., and M. Thompson. 2003. "The Socioeconomic Determinants of Ill-Gotten Gains: Within-Person Changes in Drug Use and Illegal Earnings." *American Journal of Sociology* 109: 146–185.

Uggen, C., and S. Wakefield. 2007. "What Have We Learned from Longitudinal Studies of Adolescent Employment and Crime?" In *The Long View of Crime: A Synthesis of Longitudinal Research*, ed. A. Liberman. New York: Springer.

Von Wachter, T., J. Manchester, and J. Song. 2009. Long-term Earnings Losses Due to Mass-Layoffs during the 1982 recession: An Analysis Using Longitudinal Administrative Data from 1974 to 2004.

Weiman, D. F., M. A. Stoll, and S. Bushway. 2007. "The Regime of Mass Incarceration: A Labor Market Perspective." In *Barriers to Reentry? The Labor Market for Released Prisoners in Post-Industrial America*, eds. D. Weiman, M. A. Stoll, and S. Bushway, 29–79. New York: Russell Sage Foundation.

West, H. C., and W. J. Sabol. *Prison Inmates at Midyear 2008*. U.S. Department of Justice: Office of Justice Programs. Washington, DC: Bureau of Justice Statistics.

Western, B. 2002. "The Impact of Incarceration on Wage Mobility and Inequality." *American Sociological Review* 67: 526–546.

Western, B., and B. Pettit. 2000. "Incarceration and Racial Inequality in Men's Employment." *Industrial and Labor Relations Review* 54: 3–16.

Wilson, D. B., C. A. Gallagher, and D. L. MacKenzie. 2001. "A Meta-Analysis of Corrections-Based Education, Vocation, and Work Programs for Adult Offenders." *Journal of Research in Crime and Delinquency* 37: 347–368.

Yates, J. A. 2005. "The Transition from School to Work: Education and Work Experiences." *Monthly Labor Review* 128 (2): 21–32.

Notes

Many of the themes in this chapter are extensions and reflections of themes in my research with several different sets of co-authors with whom I have been fortunate to work over the last 10 years. Special thanks belong to Robert Apel, Arjan Blokland, Robert Brame, Phil Cook, Megan Kurlychek, Daniel Nagin, Paul Nieuwbeerta, Raymond Paternoster, Herb Smith, Michael Stoll, Gary Sweeten, Hui-shien Tsao, and David Weiman. Special thanks also belong to Peter Reuter, with whom I had the privilege of writing on this topic in an earlier edition of this volume. Please address all correspondence to Shawn Bushway at 219 Draper Hall, School of Criminal Justice; University at Albany; Albany, NY 12222.

1. Fixed-effect models control for all unobserved, time stable differences that might exist between people, which represents an improvement over controls for observable differences only. Propensity score models try to mimic an experiment by matching people who look otherwise similar on observable variables, but differ on work status. They have the conceptual advantage of comparing similar people.

2. A one percentage point increase in the unemployment rate when the unemployment rate is 6 percent represents a 17 percent increase in unemployment. The corresponding 2 percent increase in crime rates reflects a low elasticity of .11.

3. But see McDowall and Loftin (2005) for evidence against the possibility of structural breaks.

4. There is a substantial literature on this question of the stationarity of macroeconomic trends. The basic tests are relatively low power, making it hard to reject the null hypothesis of non-stationarity. New tests are constantly being invented with more power, so that there is some controversy about whether or not these trends are truly non-stationary. See Fleissig and Strauss (1999) for a paper that claims that GDP is stationary. This ambiguity does not surround unemployment rates, which are clearly stationary, even with low power tests.

5. A reasonable person might begin to question whether a movement to these broader economic indicators reflects an abandonment of labor markets, the ostensible focus on this chapter. Does consumer sentiment really reflect labor market outcomes? Rosenfeld (2009) provides a partial answer by focusing on the relationship between consumer sentiment and consumer choices rooted in the rational choice or economic model of behavior. People with less income or with real concerns about the future might buy fewer legal goods, and begin to look for illegal goods to buy. This boost in demand leads to increased demand for thieves, which should result in an increase in theft, in much the same way that an increase in copper prices has led to a spike in scrap copper theft (Rondeaux and Morse 2007). The discouragement reflected in the consumer sentiment could also be reflective of a loss of income, perhaps through detachment from the legal labor market, as employment becomes more difficult to find and maintain. In other words, consumer sentiment can predict both the demand for and the supply of labor in both the legal and illegal markets—and these factors could well influence crime.

6. For a more complete treatment of this trend, see Weiman et al. 2007.

7. It is also worth noting that the crime drop during this period was concentrated in violent crime. Property crime, which has a stronger tie to the labor market, has stayed relatively constant (Levitt 2004).

8. In fact, numbers used in Western and Pettit (2005) suggests that labor market participation among black males has stayed constant. The BLS numbers reported in the last section using alternative sources raise serious questions about these numbers. See also Weiman et al. 2007.

9. Much of the disagreement hinges on the weight one is willing to give a prominent article by Bruce Western (2002), which, unlike other studies, relies on self-reported employment data. Because of the lack of information on conviction, arrest, or criminal activity, Western's work compares incarcerated offenders to all other individuals, including those who are not convicted. This strategy makes it hard to isolate the impact of incarceration over and above that of criminal activity or conviction and probation. The same problem limits demand-side studies such as the well-known audit study by Pager (2003).

10. See an excellent article by Donohue (2009) on the cost and benefits of prison for a discussion of whether lost wages should be included in the cost-benefit equation.

Chapter 8

The Community

Robert J. Sampson

Public crime policy at the dawn of the twenty-first century was dominated by the ever-greater use of penal control—especially in the form of mandatory sentences and imprisonment. The results were dramatic, as rates of incarceration in the United States skyrocketed to unprecedented historical levels (Western 2006). With the costs of incarceration rising and municipal resources for police services stretched thin after 9/11, community-based policy alternatives became widely debated across the political spectrum. Most prisoners usually return home, after all (Travis 2005), so whether in the context of the etiology of committing crime in the first place or the reintegration of offenders upon release, the role of local communities has assumed increasing importance.

In this chapter, I advance a community-level approach as a promising way to think about explaining and preventing crime, with a specific focus on urban neighborhoods. It is not the only or necessarily most effective approach, of course, but it has the advantage of being an intellectually distinctive one. Namely, instead of seeking to predict or change *individual* behavior—the traditional criminological approach—the neighborhood level of social inquiry asks how *community structures and cultures produce differential rates of crime*. What characteristics of neighborhoods are associated with high rates of violence? Are communities safe or unsafe because of the persons who reside in them or because of community properties themselves? Perhaps most important, by changing communities can we bring about changes in crime rates? As implied by these questions, the goal of community-level research is to explain variations in rates of crime across neighborhoods and other social-ecological units of analysis. A community-level perspective also aims to uncover how federal, state, and local governmental policies not directly concerned with crime may nonetheless bear indirectly on crime rates through their influence on neighborhood structures and cultures.

My argument synthesizing research on neighborhood social characteristics, crime rates, and policy implications may be summarized as follows:

- There is substantial inequality between neighborhoods in terms of economic status and correlated social resources. There is particularly strong evidence that links concentrated poverty, unemployment, and family disruption to the geographical isolation of racial minority groups—what is called *concentrated disadvantage*.
- Crime, violence, arrest, and incarceration are all spatially clustered in the same neighborhoods that are characterized by severe concentrated disadvantage. There are neighborhood "hot spots"of crime *and* criminal justice intervention, in other words.
- Although neighborhoods are constantly in flux, with individuals moving in and out, there is simultaneously a general durability or stability in the relative social positions that neighborhoods hold; disadvantage is both concentrated and cumulative in nature.
- In turn, mechanisms such as informal social control, trust, moral cynicism, network ties, and organizational capacity are hypothesized to explain violence rates, mediating in part neighborhood structural characteristics and durable concentrated disadvantage.
- A community-level approach to crime prevention implies intervening in neighborhoods, changing places not people. I outline ten strategies, focusing on: neighborhood "hot spot" policing, reducing disorder, building collective efficacy, housing-based stabilization, deconcentration of poverty, municipal services, child development, increasing organizational capacity, community-based prisoner reentry, and an "eco-metrics" for evaluation.

In short, a long tradition of research yields important clues about why communities matter for crime. I begin by highlighting the broad continuities that characterize research to the present day, and I then turn to the implications of a community-level approach to crime policy.

DEFINITIONS AND PATTERNS

Although there are many types of communities that one could define in terms of shared values or primary group ties, I define neighborhoods and local communities in spatial terms, letting properties of social organization vary. Sometimes neighborhoods make a community in the traditional sense of shared values, but often they do not—neighborhoods are *variable* in the nature and content of social ties, and they are nested within successively larger communities.

This conception is consistent with the classic view that a neighborhood is a collection of both people and institutions occupying a spatially defined area influenced by ecological, cultural, market, and political forces (Park 1915). Suttles (1972) refined this view by arguing that neighborhoods do not form their identities or composition as the result of free-market competition or internal dynamics only, the usual emphasis. Instead, some neighborhoods and local communities have their identity and boundaries imposed on them by outsiders.

Virtually all empirical studies of neighborhoods employ operational definitions that depend on geographic boundaries set by the government (e.g., the Census Bureau) or other administrative agencies (e.g., school districts, police districts). Although administratively defined units such as census tracts are reasonably consistent with the notion of nested ecological structures and permit the analysis of rich sources of linked data, researchers have become increasingly interested in strategies to define neighborhoods that respect the logic of street patterns and the social networks of neighbor interactions (Grannis 1998). Still, there is no one correct definition of neighborhood that enjoys universal support, nor should there be—definitions vary according to the research question and theory, just as they do for other social phenomena.

Research conducted in Chicago in the early part of the twentieth century provided the impetus for modern American studies of neighborhoods and crime. In their classic work—*Juvenile Delinquency and Urban Areas*—Shaw and McKay (1969 [1942]) argued that low economic status, ethnic heterogeneity, and residential instability led to the disruption of local community social organization, which in turn accounted for variations in crime and delinquency. They also demonstrated that high rates of delinquency in Chicago persisted in certain areas over many years, regardless of population turnover. More than any other, this finding led Shaw and McKay to question individualistic explanations of delinquency and to focus on the processes by which criminal patterns of behavior, especially group-related, were transmitted across generations in areas of poverty, instability, and weak social controls (Bursik 1988).

Neighborhood Stratification

Neighborhood research in the post—Shaw and McKay era has tended to focus on the socially structured dimensions of disadvantage, especially the geographic isolation of the poor, and, in the United States, the racial isolation of African Americans in concentrated poverty areas (Massey and Denton 1993; Wilson 1987). The range of outcomes associated with concentrated disadvantage extends well beyond crime and violence to include infant mortality, low birth weight, teenage childbearing, dropping out of high school, and child maltreatment (Brooks-Gunn et al. 1997; Sampson et al. 2002). The evidence thus suggests that there are geographic hot spots for crime and problem behaviors, and that such hot spots are characterized by the concentration of multiple forms of disadvantage that are surprisingly stable over time (Sampson 2009b).

To a lesser extent, research has considered aspects of neighborhood social differentiation other than concentrated disadvantage, including life-cycle status, residential stability, home ownership, population density, and ethnic heterogeneity. The evidence on these factors is mixed, especially for density and ethnic heterogeneity (Morenoff et al. 2001). Perhaps the most extensive area of ecological inquiry about disadvantage, dating back to the early Chicago school, concerns residential stability and home ownership. There is research showing that residential instability and low rates of home ownership are durable correlates of many problem behaviors (Brooks-Gunn et al. 1997), but also that residential stability interacts with poverty. In contexts of deprivation and poverty, residential stability has been shown to correlate with negative rather than positive outcomes (Ross et al. 2000), which makes theoretical sense if long-term exposure to concentrated disadvantage is a risk factor. Another object of inquiry is concentrated affluence. Brooks-Gunn and colleagues (1993) argue that it is the positive influence of concentrated socioeconomic resources and educated neighbors, rather than the presence of low-income neighbors, that matters most for adolescent behaviors. According to this view, the common tactic of focusing on disadvantage may obscure the potential protective effects of affluence and education.

In brief, empirical research on neighborhood differentiation has established a reasonably consistent set of facts relevant to crime. First, there is considerable social inequality between neighborhoods in terms of socioeconomic resources and their link to racial/ethnic segregation. Second, a number of social problems tend to come bundled together at the neighborhood level, including, but not limited to crime, adolescent delinquency, social and physical disorder, low birth weight, infant mortality, school dropout and child maltreatment. Third, these two sets of clusters are themselves related—neighborhood predictors common to many child and adolescent outcomes include the concentration of poverty, racial isolation, single-parent families, and, to a lesser extent, rates of home ownership and length of tenure. Fourth, these results tend to persist over time, and the empirical results have not varied much with the operational unit of analysis. Stratification of local communities with respect to crime and disadvantage is a robust phenomenon that emerges at multiple levels of geography (Sampson et al. 2002).

SOCIAL MECHANISMS AND PROCESSES

The empirical evidence points to a number of durable neighborhood-level correlates of crime rates but it does not answer what is potentially the most important question: *Why* does community structure matter? Put differently, what are the mechanisms and social processes that help explain why factors such as concentrated poverty lead to increases in crime and violence? It is to these questions that criminologists have increasingly turned their attention.

The most famous approach to mechanism-based theory can be traced back to those working in the Chicago-school tradition of *social disorganization theory*, including Shaw and McKay. Social disorganization has been defined as the inability of a community structure to realize the common interests of its residents in maintaining effective social controls (Sampson and Groves 1989). The social disorganization approach views local communities and neighborhoods as a complex system of friendship, kinship, and acquaintanceship networks, and formal and informal associational ties rooted in family life and ongoing socialization processes. From this view, both social organization and social *dis*organization are inextricably tied to systemic networks that facilitate or inhibit social control.[1] When formulated in this way, social disorganization is analytically separable not only from the processes that may lead to it (e.g., poverty, residential mobility), but from the degree of criminal behavior that may be a result. This conceptualization also goes beyond the traditional account of community as a strictly geographical phenomenon by focusing on social networks and voluntary associations.

A major emphasis in social disorganization is the ability of a community to supervise and control peer groups—especially adolescent gangs. Delinquency is primarily a group phenomenon, suggesting that the capacity of the community to control group-level dynamics is a key theoretical mechanism linking community characteristics with crime. Cultural heterogeneity is another, related mechanism. A venerable finding is that the majority of gangs develop from unsupervised, spontaneous play-groups (Thrasher 1963 [1927]). Shaw and McKay thus argued that residents of cohesive communities with greater agreement on normative rules were better able to control the teenage behaviors that set the context for gang violence. Examples of such controls include the supervision of leisure-time youth activities, intervention in street-corner congregation (Thrasher 1963, 339; Shaw and McKay 1969, 176–185), and challenging youth "who seem to be up to no good" (Skogan 1986, 217). Socially disorganized communities with extensive street-corner peer groups are also expected to have higher rates of adult violence, especially among younger adults who still have ties to youth gangs.

A different dimension of community social organization is the density or "connectivity" of local friendship and acquaintanceship networks. Systemic theory holds that locality-based social networks constitute the core social fabric of human ecological communities (Bursik 1988). When residents form local social ties, their capacity for social control is in theory increased because they are better able to recognize strangers and are more apt to engage in guardianship behavior against victimization (Taylor et al. 1984, 307; Skogan 1986, 216). The greater the density and overlapping nature of interpersonal networks in a community, therefore, the greater the constraint on deviant behavior within the network, according to disorganization theory.

The social networks among adults and children in a community are particularly important in fostering the capacity for collective socialization and supervision. In a system involving parents and children, communities characterized by an extensive set of obligations, expectations, and social networks connecting the adults are better able to facilitate the control and supervision of children. The notion of intergenerational closure helps us to understand parent-child relations that extend beyond the household. For example, when closure is present through the relationship of a child to two adults whose relationship transcends the household (e.g., friendship, work-related acquaintanceship), the adults have the potential to "observe the child's actions in different circumstances, talk to each other about the child, compare notes, and establish norms" (Coleman 1990, 593; Coleman 1988). This form of relation can also provide reinforcement for disciplining the child, as found when parents in communities with dense social networks and high stability assume responsibility for the supervision of youth that are not their own (Coleman 1990, 320). The closure of local networks can therefore provide the child with norms and sanctions that could not be brought about by a single adult alone, or even married-couple families in isolation.

Collective Efficacy

Social networks and closure are not sufficient to understand local communities, however. Networks are differentially invoked, and dense, tight-knit networks may impede social organization if they are isolated or weakly linked to collective expectations for rules of action. At the neighborhood level, the willingness of local residents to intervene on behalf of public safety depends, in large part, on conditions of mutual trust and shared expectations among residents. In particular, one is unlikely to intervene in a neighborhood context where the rules are unclear and people mistrust or fear one another. It is the linkage of mutual trust and the shared willingness to intervene for the common good that defines the neighborhood context of what Sampson et al. (1997) term *collective efficacy*. Just as individuals vary in their capacity for efficacious action, so too do neighborhoods vary in their capacity to achieve common goals. Moreover, just as self-efficacy is situated rather than global (one has self-efficacy relative to a particular task or type of task), neighborhood efficacy exists relative to collective tasks such as maintaining public order. Collective efficacy with respect to crime is thus a task-specific construct that refers to shared expectations and mutual engagement by residents in local social control.

Moving from a focus on private ties to social efficacy signifies an emphasis on shared beliefs in neighbors' joint capability for action to achieve an intended effect, and hence an active sense of engagement on the part of residents. As Bandura (1997) argues, the meaning of efficacy is captured in expectations about the exercise of control, elevating the "agentic" aspect of social life over a perspective centered on the accumulation of "stocks" of social resources. Distinguishing between the resource potential represented by personal ties, on the one hand, and the shared expectations among neighbors for engagement in social control represented by collective efficacy, on the other, helps clarify the systemic model: social networks foster the conditions under which collective efficacy may flourish, but they are not sufficient for the exercise of control. In this way, collective efficacy may be seen as a logical extension of systemically based social disorganization theory. The difference is mainly one of emphasis: locality-based networks may enhance neighborhood social organization, but the collective capacity for social action, even if rooted in weak personal ties, constitutes the more proximate social mechanism for understanding between-neighborhood variation in crime rates.

A theory of social organization and collective efficacy can ill afford to ignore institutions or the wider political environment in which local communities are embedded. Indeed, many neighborhoods exhibit intense private ties (e.g., among friends, kin) and yet still lack the institutional capacity to achieve social control (Hunter 1985). The institutional component is thus crucial and refers to the resource stock of neighborhood organizations and their linkages with other organizations both within *and* outside the community. Kornhauser (1978, 79) argues that when the horizontal links among institutions within a community are weak, the capacity to defend local interests is weakened. Bursik and Grasmick (1993) highlight vertical links, or the capacity of local community organizations to obtain extra-local resources (police, fire services, block grants) that help sustain neighborhood social stability and local controls.

Empirical Evidence

I focus in this section on research that examines neighborhood social mechanisms and collective processes linked theoretically to crime. There is a large research on land use and other aspects of the physical environment that I do not address because of space constraints.

In one of the first "social process" studies of its kind, Taylor and colleagues (1984) examined variations in violent crime (e.g., mugging, assault, murder, rape) across street blocks in Baltimore. They constructed block-level measures of the proportion of respondents who belonged to an organization to which co-residents also belonged, and the proportion of respondents who felt responsible for what happened in the area surrounding their home. Both dimensions of informal social control were significantly and negatively related to rates of violence, exclusive of other ecological factors (1984, 320). These results support the hypothesis that organizational participation and informal social control of public space depress criminal violence. Around the same time, Simcha-Fagan and Schwartz (1986) collected survey-based information on over 500 residents of 12 different neighborhoods in New York City. Although the number of neighborhoods was small, they found a significant negative relationship between delinquency and rates of organizational participation by local residents. A multivariate analysis provided further support for this pattern—"level of organizational participation and residential stability have unique effects in predicting survey-reported delinquency" (1986, 683).

In a study conducted in Great Britain in 1982 and 1984, Sampson and Groves (1989) showed that the prevalence of unsupervised teenage peer-groups in a community had the largest effect on rates of robbery and violence by strangers. The density of local friendship networks also had a significant negative effect on robbery rates, while the level of organizational participation by residents had significant inverse effects on both robbery and stranger violence (1989, 789). Central to present concerns, variations in these structural dimensions of community social (dis)organization transmitted in large part the effects of community socioeconomic status, residential mobility, ethnic heterogeneity, and family disruption in a theoretically consistent manner. Notably, socioeconomic status significantly predicted organizational participation.

Elliott and colleagues (1996) examined survey data from neighborhoods in Chicago and Denver. A multilevel analysis revealed that a measure of "informal control" was significantly and negatively related to adolescent problem behavior in both sites. Like the British results, informal control mediated the prior effects of neighborhood structural disadvantage—declining poor neighborhoods displayed less ability to maintain social control, and they in turn suffered higher delinquency rates. Similarly, several studies have used survey data from over 5,000 Seattle residents living within 100 census tracts to investigate the connection between social control processes and crime. Warner and Rountree (1997) found a significant negative association between assault rates and the proportion of respondents in white neighborhoods who engaged in neighboring activities with one another—including borrowing tools or food, having lunch or dinner, or helping each other with problems. In a subsequent study, Bellair (2000) approached the neighboring question from a somewhat different perspective on mediating processes. He assumed that neighboring activities affect crime rates only indirectly, by increasing the likelihood that neighbors will engage in informal surveillance of one another's property. These causal paths were consistent with the empirical results he obtained.

A large-scale research program in Chicago (Project on Human Development in Chicago Neighborhoods, or PHDCN) proposed as a primary objective the study of criminal behavior in community context. A major component of this study was a community survey of 8,782 residents of 343 Chicago neighborhoods in 1995. Sampson and colleagues (1997) developed a two-part scale from this survey to examine rates of violence. One component was shared expectations about "informal social control," represented by a five-item Likert-type scale. Residents were asked about the likelihood ("Would you say it is very likely, likely, neither likely nor unlikely, unlikely, or very unlikely?") that their neighbors could be counted on to take action if: (1) children were skipping school and hanging out on a street corner, (2) children were spray-painting graffiti on a local building, (3) children were showing disrespect to an adult, (4) a fight broke out in front of their house, and (5) the fire station closest to home was threatened with budget cuts. The second component was "social cohesion," measured by asking respondents how strongly they agreed (on a five-point scale) that "People around here are willing to help their neighbors"; "This is a close-knit neighborhood"; "People in this neighborhood can be trusted"; and (reverse coded): "People in this neighborhood generally don't get along with each other"; "People in this neighborhood do not share the same values." Social cohesion and informal social control were closely associated across neighborhoods, suggesting that they tapped aspects of the same latent construct. Sampson et al. (1997) combined the two scales into a summary measure termed "collective efficacy."

The PHDCN study found that collective efficacy varied widely across Chicago neighborhoods and was associated with lower rates of violence measured by independent methods, all the time controlling for concentrated disadvantage, residential stability, immigrant concentration, and a comprehensive set of individual-level characteristics (e.g., age, sex, SES, race/ethnicity, home ownership) as well as indicators of personal ties and the density of local organizations. Whether measured by homicide events or violent victimization reported by residents, neighborhoods high in collective efficacy consistently had significantly lower rates of violence. Even after adjusting for prior violence, a two standard-deviation elevation in collective efficacy was associated with a 26 percent reduction in the expected homicide rate (Sampson et al. 1997, 922). In addition, the association of concentrated disadvantage and residential instability with higher violence declined after collective efficacy was controlled, suggesting a potential causal pathway at the community level. This pathway is presumed to operate over time, wherein collective efficacy is undermined by the concentration of disadvantage, racial segregation, family disruption, and residential instability, which in turn fosters more crime. A later study in Chicago using the same PHDCN collective efficacy scale found that robbers were less likely to choose high efficacy neighborhoods to carry out robberies, controlling for racial and economic composition (Bernasco and Block 2009). Morenoff et al. (2001) also used PHDCN to show that the density of personal ties was associated with higher collective efficacy but did not translate directly into lower crime rates—the association of dense ties with lower crime was entirely indirect.

We must bear in mind that social ties are neutral in the sense that they can be drawn upon for negative as well as positive goals. With this in mind, Browning and colleagues (2004) found that dense networks attenuate the effect of collective efficacy on crime, adding a twist to the idea that strong ties are not necessarily a good thing. In what is termed a *negotiated coexistence* model, collective efficacy is negatively associated with the prevalence of violent crime in urban neighborhoods, but the density of exchange networks interacts with collective efficacy such that as network density increases, the regulatory effect of collective efficacy on violence declines. However, adding to the complexity, another study by Browning (2002) showed a direct association between collective efficacy and lower partner violence.

What are the kinds of structural and normative contexts that promote (or undermine) collective efficacy and non-exclusive social networks other than those already considered? This is a question that cannot be answered easily, but there is evidence that the civic infrastructure of local organizations and voluntary associations helps sustain capacity for social action in a way that transcends traditional personal ties. Organizations are equipped to foster collective efficacy, often through strategic networking of their own or by creating tasks that demand collective responses (Small 2009). Whether disorder removal, school improvements, or police responses, a continuous stream of challenges faces contemporary communities, challenges that no longer can be met by relying solely on individuals. Effective action can thus be conceived as depending in part on organizational settings and connections that are not necessarily reflective of the density of personal ties in a neighborhood. PHDCN-related research supports this position by showing that the density of local organizations as reported by residents, along with their involvement in voluntary associations, predicts higher levels of both collective efficacy and collective civic events, controlling for poverty, social composition, and prior crime rates (Morenoff et al. 2001).

There is evidence from beyond Chicago that supports these general observations on collective efficacy. Rather than provide a review of the evidence from individual studies, I rely on an independent review of more than 200 empirical studies from 1960 to 1999 using meta-analysis (Pratt and Cullen 2005). Collective efficacy emerged with an overall correlation of −.303 with crime rates across studies (95 percent confidence interval of −.26 to −.35). By meta-analysis standards this is a robust finding, and the authors' rank collective efficacy number 4 when weighted by sample size, ahead of traditional suspects such as poverty, family disruption, and race. Although the number of studies and hence the empirical base is limited, and while there is considerable variability in units of analysis across studies, the class of mechanisms associated with social disorganization theory and its offspring, collective efficacy theory, shows a robust association with lower crime rates (Kubrin and Weitzer 2003; Sampson et al. 2002). Moreover, comparative research in Stockholm using similar measures suggests a general mechanism is at work in the collective efficacy—crime rate relationship (Sampson and Wikström 2008).

Recent studies have also shown a direct link between violence and heterogeneity in age-appropriate cultural scripts (Harding 2010) and moral cynicism about whether laws or collective moral rules are considered binding. For example, PHDCN respondents were asked to report their level of agreement with statements such as "Laws were made to be broken"; "It's okay to do anything you want as long as you don't hurt anyone"; and "To make money, there are no right and wrong ways anymore, only easy ways and hard ways." In communities with high levels of cynicism and a perceived lack of legitimacy of normative and legal rules, violent offending was significantly higher after controlling for demographic composition (Sampson et al. 2005). These findings bear on the larger theoretical assertion of social disorganization theory: Where there is greater normative heterogeneity and moral skepticism or legal cynicism, violence is higher.

Summarized briefly, I would argue that the cumulative results of research support the theory that neighborhoods characterized by (a) mistrust, (b) perceived lack of shared expectations and cultural heterogeneity, (c) sparse acquaintanceship and exchange networks among residents, (d) attenuated social control of public spaces, (e) a weak organizational and institutional base, (f) low participation in local voluntary associations, and (g) moral/legal cynicism are associated with an increased risk of interpersonal crime and public disorder within their borders. Moreover, the data suggest that key dimensions of social organization and collective action are influenced (although not determined) by neighborhood structural differentiation. Collective efficacy in particular appears to be undermined by concentrated poverty that is coupled with long-term patterns of racial subjugation, family disruption, and residential instability.

Effects of Crime on Social and Economic Organization

It is important to recognize that crime and its consequences may themselves have important reciprocal effects on community structure and process. Skogan (1990) has provided an overview of some of the "feedback" processes that may further increase levels of crime. These include:

- physical and psychological withdrawal from community life because of fear
- weakening of the informal social control processes that inhibit crime
- decline in the organizational life and mobilization capacity of the neighborhood
- deteriorating business conditions
- importation and domestic production of delinquency and deviance
- further dramatic changes in the composition of the population.

For example, if people shun their neighbors and local facilities out of fear of crime, fewer opportunities exist for local networks and organizations to take hold. Street crime may be also accompanied by residential out-migration and business relocation from inner-city areas. As a result, crime can lead to simultaneous demographic "collapse" and a weakening of the informal control structures and mobilization capacity of communities, which in turn fuels further crime.

Although the number of empirical studies is relatively small, the evidence is consistent that crime can undermine the social and economic fabric of urban areas. One of the most important findings is that crime generates fear of strangers and a general alienation from participation in community life (Skogan 1986, 1990). Besides weakening neighborhood social organization, high crime rates and concerns about safety may trigger population out-migration. For example, delinquency rates are not only one of the outcomes of urban change; they are an important part of the process of urban change. Studying Chicago neighborhoods, Bursik (1986, 73) observes that "although changes in racial composition cause increases in the delinquency rate, this effect is not nearly as great as the effect that increases in the delinquency rate have in minority groups being stranded in the community." In a study of 40 neighborhoods in eight cities, Skogan (1990) found that high rates of crime and disorder were associated with higher rates of fear, neighborhood dissatisfaction, and intentions to move out. Using the PHDCN, Morenoff and colleagues (2001) found a dynamic process where prior violence depressed collective efficacy (presumably because of fear or cynicism), even as collective efficacy helped stave off later crime. Similarly, Sampson and Raudenbush (1999) found a reciprocal negative relationship between collective efficacy and rates of violence in Chicago neighborhoods. While businesses may be less sensitive to crime than individual residents, they too are not immune from the social disorganization, fear, and social incivilities associated with street violence (Skogan 1990).

Although the empirical base is limited, the overall picture painted by prior research on the effects of crime is one of population abandonment of urban neighborhoods, business relocation to the suburbs, loss of economic revenue, a decrease in economic status and property values, and escalating levels of fear in central cities. Consider that many cities in the North and Midwest that lost population in the 1970s and 1980s became increasingly poorer and racially isolated (Wilson 1987). An important part of this racially selective decline in population and economic status apparently stems from violent crime. Interestingly, however, many of these same cities recovered and even thrived during the most recent era of the great crime decline (Blumstein and Wallman 2000). New York City is perhaps the "poster city" for how low crime rates serve as a leading indicator of urban vitality. As Skogan (1990) has emphasized, crime is a salient event that has important symbolic consequences for perceptions of the inhabitability and civility of city life. Breaking the cycle of violence in communities and maintaining the declines in crime that have blessed many central cities in recent years is thus crucial to a general strategy for urban policy.

LIMITATIONS OF THE COMMUNITY APPROACH

Like any complex phenomenon, numerous challenges confront research on neighborhoods and crime. Among other limitations, the use of administrative and sometimes highly aggregated units of analysis, potentially biased sources of information on violence (e.g., police data), indirect measures of key social mechanisms, feedback or reciprocal effects from crime, widely varying analytical techniques, selection effects, and high correlations among ecological variables all hinder the attempt to draw causal inferences about the unique explanatory power of neighborhood characteristics (Sampson and Lauritsen 1994, 75–85; Sampson et al.

2002). "Selection bias" has drawn the most concern: if area differences in violence rates result from the characteristics of individuals selectively located in those communities, the findings derived from community-level research may be confounded and thus hard to interpret. For example, is the correlation of concentrated poverty with rates of violence caused by an aggregation of individual-level effects of poverty, a causal community-level effect, or is it a differential selection of individuals into communities based on some prior (e.g., antisocial) behavior? Or do common third factors cause individuals to both commit violence and end up in poverty? And if violent and antisocial tendencies are formed in childhood, what plausible roles can community labor markets and economic stratification play in understanding violence?

Simply put, the level at which a causal relation occurs is a complex issue that is not solved simply by the nature of how variables are measured or the unit for which they are measured. To make matters more complicated, the concrete actions of individuals feed back to shape the collective environment itself. Thus the unit of analysis does not define the level of causal explanation, and social processes do not necessarily generate the information contained in aggregate data. But it is likewise true that individual-level data are not necessarily produced by individual level causal processes. The difference is that the assumptions embodied in individual-level research are usually accepted at face value. Consider that many individual or group-level correlates of crime (e.g., race, family supervision) may in fact stem from community-related processes (Sampson and Wilson 1995). The "individualistic fallacy" and individual reductionism are just as problematic as the so-called selection bias in neighborhood research.

Even if the analytic problems of neighborhood research were solved, there seems to be a consensus in evaluation research that community crime-prevention programs have achieved only limited success. Probably the most common crime-prevention approach has been the "neighborhood watch," where attempts are made to increase residents' participation in local efforts at social control (e.g., community meetings, neighborhood patrols). Other interventions have tried to increase social interaction among neighbors and instill concern for the public welfare of local residents. There have also been even more general efforts to change neighborhood opportunity structures, such as the classic Chicago Area Project patterned after Shaw and McKay's original theory. Yet evaluations of these programs are for the most part pessimistic about concrete reductions in crime (Bursik and Grasmick 1993, 148–175; Hope 1995; Rosenbaum 1986).

Although disappointing results from evaluation research could mean that neighborhood-level theories are wrong, another possibility is that programs were not implemented correctly. We know, for example, that community crime prevention is especially hard to implement in the areas that need them the most—poor, unstable neighborhoods with high crime rates—and that participation levels tend to fall off quickly once interventions are removed. Efforts to reduce crime are most likely to succeed if they are embedded in more comprehensive programs for neighborhood stabilization that local residents support. "One shot" interventions that are externally imposed and simply try to reduce crime in the short run without confronting durable aspects of a neighborhood's vulnerability are, not surprisingly, highly susceptible to failure (Hope 1995). Whether the poor track record of community interventions (not dissimilar from the poor track record of individual interventions) is due to a failure of theory or a programmatic failure of implementation is thus unknown. It is perhaps most likely that neighborhood-level interventions have pulled the wrong levers of change or targeted non-essential mechanisms.

A confluence of factors—selective decisions to live in different communities, potential misspecification due to population composition effects, overlap among ecological variables, a static conceptualization of community structure, the early onset of individual criminal careers, the indirect measurement of neighborhood social processes, and weak intervention results—combine to warrant caution in the interpretation of community-level research. Nevertheless, I believe that a community-level perspective not only improves our understanding of the etiology of crime and violence, but that it expands our conceptual apparatus to think about fresh policies for the public agenda on crime. Indeed, what seem most promising are policies that embed a concern for crime reduction in larger, more systemic efforts to improve the social organizational capacities of the neighborhood. The following section builds on this general idea.

PUBLIC POLICY IMPLICATIONS: CHANGING PLACES, NOT PEOPLE

Having outlined both the strengths and weaknesses of a community-level perspective on crime and social organization, I now examine some policy-related implications that attempt to move beyond past efforts. I focus primarily on community-level mechanisms reviewed above that are theoretically related, whether directly or indirectly, to the policy decisions of public officials. For the most part, these are policy domains that focus on crime prevention and the enhancement of community social organization from other than criminal justice agencies. Initiatives that rely on the police, prisons, and other agencies of social control have been reviewed at length many times, and hence I do not cover them here, except as they interface with community-level efforts. For example, I do not cover the traditional literature on neighborhood watch and community crime prevention. Rather, my discussion focuses on alternative neighborhood-level policies most directly related to crime and justice concerns, along with more comprehensive strategies that attack "root causes" of crime but that I argue are still amenable to community-level policy.

Identify Neighborhood "Hot Spots" for Crime

One area of promise is simple yet powerful. Research has long demonstrated that crimes are not randomly distributed in space. Rather, they are disproportionately concentrated in certain neighborhoods and "places" (e.g., taverns, parking lots). Ecologically oriented criminologists have dubbed these areas "hot spots" of crime (Sherman et al. 1989). Drawing on community theory and advances in computer mapping technology, my argument is that policing strategies can be more effective if they are implemented using information on neighborhood hot spots.

Consider, for example, a pilot program in Chicago that instituted an "early warning system" for gang homicides. By plotting each homicide incident and using state-of-the-art mapping and statistical clustering procedures, the early warning system allowed the police to identify potential neighborhood crisis areas at high risk for suffering a "spurt" of gang violence (Block 1991). Places may also be mapped and then modified so as to reduce the opportunities for crime to occur. Sherman and colleagues (1989, 48) advocated place-based interventions whereby hot spot data are used to study the effects of differential patrol allocations, selective revocation of bar licenses, and removal of vacant "crack" houses. Recent experimental-based research shows that policing and situational crime-prevention strategies targeted to small ecological areas (about two blocks in size) reduces crime. Moreover, crime is not simply displaced elsewhere—instead, there is a spatial diffusion of safety (Braga and Bond 2008; Braga et al. 1999; Weisburd et al. 2006).

The evidence on hot spots thus suggests that a neighborhood-level response may be more effective than policies that simply target individuals or even families. By proactively responding to neighborhoods (and smaller places within them) that disproportionately generate crimes, policing strategies can more efficiently stave off epidemics of crime and its spatial diffusion.

Reduce Social Disorder and Physical "Incivilities"

Both the logic of social disorganization theory and the extant evidence suggest that "incivilities" such as broken windows, trash, public drinking, and prostitution increase fear of crime (Skogan 1986, 1990). Incivilities and signs of disorder may increase not just fear but crime itself. One possibility is that potential offenders recognize such deterioration and assume that residents are so indifferent to what goes on in their neighborhood that they will not be motivated to confront strangers, intervene in a crime, or call the police (Wilson and Kelling 1982). Another possibility is that physical and social elements of disorder comprise highly visible cues to which all neighborhood observers respond, potentially influencing migration patterns, investment by businesses, and overall neighborhood viability (Sampson and Raudenbush 1999; Taylor 2001). Thus if disorder operates in a cascading fashion by encouraging people to move (increasing residential instability) or discouraging efforts at building collective responses, it would indirectly have an effect on crime (Sampson 2009a). To foster a climate of safety, public order, and social organization, policy should consider collective strategies that would:

- clean up graffiti, trash, needles, vials, and the like
- stagger bar closing times; enact strict zoning/licensing
- organize against public drinking, open drug use, and street prostitution
- form walking, sports, and other groups for collective activities in public areas.

Although limited in frequency, there is evidence to support the idea that neighborhood-based cleanup and disorder interventions increase perceptions of safety and potentially reduce crime (Braga and Bond 2008; Keizer et al. 2008; Rosenbaum 1986). The Police Foundation also conducted a study in which a specially trained group of officers performed disorder-reduction tasks within a Newark experimental area (Skogan 1990). The results were mixed, but they did indicate that crime was lower under conditions of aggressive field interrogations.

The optimal strategies for reducing disorder would appear to be those that involve both the police *and* community residents in the definition of the specific disorder problem to be solved and the planning of any interventions. The reason is that disorder is not a unitary concept, and people living in the same neighborhoods do not always agree on whether disorder is in fact a problem. Moreover, the evaluation of disorder depends on the racial and economic status of the neighborhood (Sampson 2009a). It follows that citizen perceptions or input about the meanings of disorder and the legitimacy of police efforts are ignored at potentially large cost.

3. Build Informal Social Control and Collective Efficacy

As described earlier, a major dimension of social organization is the ability of a community to supervise and control teenage peer-groups. Communities characterized by an extensive set of obligations, expectations, and social networks connecting the adults are better able to facilitate this task. For example, when the parents' friends or acquaintances are the parents of their children's friends, the adults have the potential to observe the child's actions in different circumstances, talk to each other about the child, compare notes, and establish norms (Coleman 1988). This form of relation can provide reinforcement for inculcating positive youth outcomes, as found when parents in communities with dense or overlapping social networks assume responsibility for the supervision of youth that are not their own. Closure of local networks provides the child with social resource of a collective nature—a social good that is created when relations among persons facilitate action. One can extend this model to closure among networks involving parents and teachers, religious and recreational leaders, businesses that serve youth, and even agents of criminal justice.

Programs that might foster informal social controls and collective efficacy include:

- organized supervision of leisure-time youth activities
- monitoring/reduction of street-corner congregation in high crime areas
- staggered school closing times to reduce peer-control system
- parent surveillance/involvement in after-school and nighttime youth programs
- adult-youth mentoring systems; create forums for parent acquaintanceship.

The key here is to increase positive connections among youth and adults in the community. Stricter sanctions such as curfews for adolescents in public areas may be necessary, but my focus is on informal social controls that arise from ongoing social interactions and community support. Consider as a possibility what Meares and Kahan (1998) describe as the emergence of a "working trust" between the police and residents of Chicago's poverty-stricken West Side in the co-creation of zones of safety. Policies including juvenile curfews and policing of minor disorders were supported by residents largely because of the leadership role of the local police commander, who was a longtime resident. In fact, the police commander led a prayer vigil to protest the occurrence of drug dealing and crime in the community. Over 1,000 residents participated, and in groups of ten they marched and reclaimed street corners where drug dealers had previously dominated. Following the prayer vigil, over 7,000 residents retired to a local park for a celebration. Such a coalition is surely controversial, but from the perspective of collective efficacy theory, coupled with the strength of the black church as a site for collective-action strategies, the Chicago alliance is a fascinating development that bears watching. Indeed, it appears that participation by residents in a newly constituted and legitimized community policing effort was in itself an action that increased community solidarity and collective efficacy.

Promote Housing-Based Neighborhood Stabilization

A more general option for enhancing social organization is to focus on joint public/private intervention programs to help stabilize and revitalize deteriorating neighborhoods. My focus is primarily on investment in the housing structure of declining but still-reachable communities. As noted above, a long history of community-based research shows that population instability and housing decay are linked to crime and social problems among youth. This research becomes more salient in the era of housing foreclosures brought on by the 2008 economic collapse. The implication is that community-based policy interventions may help to reverse the tide of vacancies and deterioration in many neighborhoods across America, not just the concentrated poverty areas of our large cities. These policies might include:

- resident management of public housing
- tenant buyouts
- rehabilitation of existing low-income housing
- strict code enforcement
- low-income and vacancy reduction tax credits.

Inner-city neighborhoods have historically suffered from severe population and housing loss of the sort that is disruptive of the social and institutional order. Bursik (1989) has shown that the planned construction of new public housing projects in Chicago's poor communities in the 1970s was associated with increased rates of population turnover, which in turn were related to increases in crime independent of racial composition. More generally, Skogan (1990) has noted how urban renewal and forced migration contributed to the wholesale uprooting of many urban black communities, especially the extent to which freeway networks, driven through the hearts of many cities in the 1950s, destroyed viable, low-income communities. In Atlanta one in six residents were dislocated through urban renewal, and the great majority of these were poor blacks (Logan and Molotch 1987, 114). Nationwide, fully 20 percent of all central city housing units occupied by blacks were lost in the period 1960–1970 alone.

Recognizing these patterns, housing policies should focus more on stabilization of existing areas—especially those at risk of a tipping point to widespread vacancy. When considered with the practices of redlining and disinvestments by banks and "block-busting" by real estate agents (Massey and Denton 1993), local policies toward code enforcement—which on the surface are far removed from crime—have nonetheless contributed to crime through neighborhood deterioration, forced migration, and instability. By acting to reduce population flight, residential anonymity, and housing deterioration, the hope is that neighborhood stabilization and ultimately a more cohesive environment for youth socialization will emerge.

Deconcentrate Poverty; Scattered-Site New Housing

This strategy is linked to that above, but it is more focused on promoting certain forms of class and race integration. As Wilson (1987) argued, the social transformation of the inner city in the late twentieth century resulted in the disproportionate concentration and segregation of the most disadvantaged segments of the urban black population—especially poor, female-headed families with children. This social transformation was fueled by macro structural economic changes related to the de-industrialization of central cities where disadvantaged minorities are concentrated (e.g., shift from goods-producing to service-producing industries; increasing polarization of the labor market into low-wage and high-wage sectors). But perhaps more important, the steady out-migration of middle and upper-income black families from core inner-city areas may have removed a former source of institutional supports. Consistent with a social organizational approach, Wilson (1987, 56; 1996) theorized that the basic institutions of a neighborhood (e.g., churches, schools, stores, recreational facilities) were more likely to remain viable if the core of their support came from more economically stable families.

An understanding of concentration effects must also recognize not just voluntary migration decisions but the negative consequences of policy decisions to concentrate minorities and the poor in public housing. Opposition from organized community groups to the building of public housing in their "backyard," de facto federal policy to tolerate segregation against blacks in urban housing markets, and decisions by local governments to neglect the rehabilitation of existing residential units led to massive, segregated housing projects, which became ghettos for the minorities and disadvantaged (Massey and Denton 1993). The great American crime decline and the economic boom of the 1990s offered new opportunities to reverse these changes, and in fact growing evidence shows real progress on the health of many U.S. cities. Building on the previous strategy, community-level approaches that merit further investigation are:

- dispersing concentrated public housing
- scattered-site, new, low-income housing
- mixed-income housing development and incentives for mixed-income neighborhoods.

The evidence that dispersion policies and scattered-site and mixed-income housing can work is small but encouraging (Cisneros and Engdahl 2009; Popkin and Cove 2007). In a major example, the Chicago Housing Authority embarked on an ambitious plan to "scatter" tens of thousands of units of high-rise public housing in the city's ghetto as a means to break down the severe segregation that was firmly in place. The infamous Robert Taylor Homes that became a national symbol of urban despair no longer exists—in its place, a black middle class is now emerging. There is also quasi- and experimental evidence that offering poor mothers on welfare the opportunity to relocate to more thriving neighborhoods improves their mental health and many of the outcomes of their children (Kling et al. 2007; Turner and Rawlings 2005). Safety and fear reduction appear to be key (see also Popkin and Cove 2007). These results suggest the positive outcomes of housing policies that incentivize or promote increased integration by class and race. To these I would add immigrant status. Counter to public perceptions, increases in the foreign-born population have revitalized many inner-city neighborhoods while concentrated immigration has contributed to lower rates of violence (Sampson 2009b; Sampson et al. 2005).

Maintain and Build Municipal Service Base

The provision of city municipal services for public health and fire safety—decisions presumably made with little if any thought to crime and violence—appear to be salient in the social (dis)integration of poor communities. As Wallace and Wallace (1990) argue based on an analysis of the "planned shrinkage" of New York City fire and health services: "The consequences of withdrawing municipal services from poor neighborhoods, the resulting outbreaks of contagious urban decay and forced migration which shred essential social networks and cause social disintegration, have become a highly significant contributor to decline in public health among the poor" (1990, 427). The loss of social integration and networks from planned shrinkage of services may increase behavioral patterns of violence, which cause further social disintegration (1990, 427). This pattern of destabilizing feedback (see Skogan 1986) is central to an understanding of the role of municipal service policies in fostering the downward spiral of low-income, high-crime areas, and by implication, *their turnaround and stabilization*. Housing and community-based policies in the previous two categories should thus be coordinated with local policies regarding fire, sanitation, and other municipal services.

Integrate Community and Child Development/Health Policy

Research has demonstrated a substantial connection between structural disadvantage and childhood development. One link comes in the form of physical abuse and maltreatment. In a study of 20 sub-areas and 93 census tracts within a city, Garbarino and Crouter (1978) found that poverty, residential mobility, and single-parent households accounted for over 50 percent of the variation in rates of child abuse. Coulton and colleagues' (1995) analysis of Cleveland showed that children who live in neighborhoods characterized by poverty, population turnover, and the concentration of female-headed families are at highest risk of abuse. The influence of concentrated poverty extended to adolescent risk factors as well, including the teen birth rate, delinquency, and high-school dropout rate. Similar to Shaw and McKay (1969 [1942]), they suggest that child maltreatment is a manifestation of community disorganization and that its occurrence is related to the same underlying social conditions that foster other urban problems.

Additional evidence consistent with social disorganization theory is found in a series of studies by Wallace and colleagues of community-level variations in low-birth-weight babies and infant mortality (Wallace and Wallace 1990). These authors document the strong upsurge in infant mortality and low birth weight in the late 1970s in New York City, especially in devastated areas of the Bronx. In particular, they found that poverty, overcrowded housing, and rapid population change were the main predictors of increased rates of low birth weight starting in 1974. Community instability, coupled with concentrated poverty, predicted increased infant mortality beyond what was expected based on migration. There is thus evidence that concentrated urban poverty and social disorganization combine to increase child abuse/neglect, low birth,weight, cognitive impairment, and other adjustment problems, which in turn constitute risk factors for later crime and violence. For these reasons, community-based interventions are needed to foster prenatal health care, infant/child health, and support programs for effective family management (e.g., child-rearing skills; conflict resolution).

The science is clear that human capital interventions are important for children, the earlier the better (Heckman 2006). I would argue the same for community-level interventions. The good news is that these formerly disconnected ideas are being combined in innovative programs such as the Harlem Children's Zone, with encouraging early results. The initiative of President Obama to create "Promise Neighborhoods" and "Choice Neighborhoods" in multiple cities is a concrete affirmation of the goal of safe, educationally intensive communities with a commitment to the human and social capital development of the next generation.[2]

Increase Community Organizational Base

Stable interlocking organizations form a major linchpin of building social capital, collective efficacy, and effective social control (Small 2009). When local organizations are unstable and isolated, and when the vertical links of community institutions to the outside are weak, the capacity of a community to defend its local interests is thus weakened. As Bursik and Grasmick (1993) argue, along similar lines, public control refers to the regulatory capacities that develop from the networks among neighborhoods and between neighborhoods and public/private agencies. More specifically, this dimension "refers to the ability to secure public and private goods and services that are allocated by groups and agencies located outside of the neighborhood" (1993, 19). It follows that interventions promoting public control might:

- increase local involvement in community organizations
- promote the vertical integration of local institutions with extra local resources
- promote collective civic action and awareness of resource allocation strategies.

Although it cannot be said with certainty that large changes will result from this type of mobilization, success at the margins produces cumulative changes that may ultimately promote a more stable and long-lasting social organization.

Community Justice and Re-entry

As I noted in the introduction, imprisonment rates have soared, but most prisoners return to a home community (Travis 2005). The logic of this chapter is consistent with recent calls for a community-level approach that seeks to reintegrate offenders and help counteract the hardships that already disadvantaged neighborhoods face when unemployed ex-felons return home. Not only might concentrated incarceration have the unintended consequence of increasing crime rates through its negative impact on the labor market and social capital prospects of former prisoners (Clear et al. 2001; Western 2006), there is evidence that neighborhood context plays a major role in the recidivism rates of ex-prisoners (Hipp et al. 2010). It follows that a policy of integrating prisoner release programs with efforts to build community capacity and achieve community justice is an important step for policy (Clear and Karp 1999; Clear et al. 2001). I think of this as "collective efficacy meets prisoner re-entry."

"Ecometrics"—Toward a National Strategy of Community Monitoring

Finally, community-based policy is not complete without a rigorous system of measurement and evaluation. One of the most important "first-order" findings from recent research is that community-based surveys can yield reliable and valid measures of neighborhood social and institutional processes. However, unlike individual-level measurements, which are backed up by decades of psychometric research into their statistical properties, the methodology needed to evaluate neighborhood mechanisms is not widespread. Raudenbush and Sampson (1999) thus proposed moving toward a science of ecological assessment, which they call "ecometrics," by developing systematic procedures for directly measuring neighborhood mechanisms, and by integrating and adapting tools from psychometrics to improve the quality of neighborhood-level measures. Leaving aside statistical details, the important procedural point is that neighborhood processes can and should be treated as ecological or collective phenomena, rather than as stand-ins for individual-level traits. A national or codified system of measurement, with standard protocols for evaluation, would enhance the science behind any community-based policy. Furthermore, local communities could use standardized measures for benchmarking or monitoring their progress or capacities in meeting stated goals.

CONCLUSION

What seem to be "non-crime" policies—that is, where or if to build a housing project, enforcement of municipal codes, reduction in essential municipal services, rehabilitation of existing residential units, the breakdown of concentrated poverty, building social connections among adults and youth, increasing collective efficacy to achieve common goals, and community monitoring through "ecometrics"—may nonetheless have important bearing on assessing communities and preventing crime. As detailed above, for example, residential instability and the concentration of poor, female-headed families with children appear to have been shaped by planned governmental policies at local, state, and federal levels. This conceptualization diverges from the natural market assumptions of the early Chicago school theorists by considering the role of political decisions in shaping local community structure. Crime also generates a reciprocal feedback effect by undermining social and economic organization, which in turn leads to further increases in crime. Even decisions to relocate businesses appear to be shaped in part by the corrosive impact of serious crime on the quality of life for workers and customers alike. Hence policies on urban development can ill afford to ignore the symbolic and economic consequences of crime for the habitability, civility, and economic vitality of city life.

On the positive side, the implication of this paper's community-level perspective is that realistic policy options may help reverse the tide of social disorganization in concentrated poverty areas and maintain the crime declines in communities that are now well underway. The unique value of a community-level perspective is that it cautions against a simple "kinds of people" analysis by suggesting a focus on how social characteristics of collectivities are interrelated with crime. Based on the theory and research reviewed here, it seems that policymakers should pay special attention to integrating crime-targeted interventions (e.g., early-warning systems, "hot spot" identification; reduction of social disorder; community prisoner re-entry) with more general "non-crime" policies that address mediating processes of social organization (e.g., intergenerational closure, control-of-street-corner peer groups, organizational participation and mobilization, collective efficacy), the political economy of place (e.g., how concentrated poverty and vacancy rates are influenced by housing policy and municipal services), and community investments in early child development. Only then can we expect a more lasting effect of neighborhood-based interventions on the reduction of crime and disorder and the enhancement of community social infrastructure. The widespread return migration to U.S. cities and the broad crime reductions of the early twenty-first century suggest that community-level approaches are not utopian and may even be responsible for some of the observed gains.

References

Bandura, Albert. 1997. *Self Efficacy: The Exercise of Control*. New York: W. H. Freeman.

Bellair, Paul E. 2000. "Informal Surveillance and Street Crime: A Complex Relationship." *Criminology* 38: 137–167.

Bernasco, Wim, and Richard Block. 2009. "Where Offenders Choose to Attack: A Discrete Choice Model of Robberies in Chicago." *Criminology* 47: 93–130.

Block, Carolyn. 1991. *Early Warning System for Street Gang Violence Crisis Areas: Automated Hot Spot Identification in Law Enforcement*. Chicago: Illinois Criminal Justice Information Authority.

Blumstein, A., and J. Wallman. 2000. *The Crime Drop in America*. New York: Cambridge University Press.

Braga, Anthony, and Brenda J. Bond. 2008. "Policing Crime and Disorder Hot Spots: A Randomized Controlled Trial." *Criminology* 46: 577–607.

Braga, Anthony, David L. Weisburd, Elin J. Waring, Lorraine Green Mazerolle, William Spelman, and Francis Gajewski. 1999. "Problem-Oriented Policing in Violent Crime Places: A Randomized Controlled Experiment." *Criminology* 37: 541–580.

Brooks-Gunn, Jeanne, Greg Duncan, and Lawrence Aber, eds. 1997. *Neighborhood Poverty: Policy Implications in Studying Neighborhoods*. New York: Russell Sage Foundation.

Brooks-Gunn, Jeanne, Greg Duncan, Pamela Kato, and Naomi Sealand. 1993. "Do Neighborhoods Influence Child and Adolescent Behavior? " *American Journal of Sociology* 99: 353–395.

Browning, Christopher R. 2002. "The Span of Collective Efficacy: Extending Social Disorganization Theory to Partner Violence." *Journal of Marriage and the Family* 64: 833–850.

Browning, Christopher R., Seth L. Feinberg, and Robert Dietz. 2004. "The Paradox of Social Organization: Networks, Collective Efficacy, and Violent Crime in Urban Neighborhoods." *Social Forces* 83: 503–534.

Bursik, Robert J. 1988. "Social Disorganization and Theories of Crime and Delinquency: Problems and Prospects." *Criminology* 35: 677–703.

Bursik, Robert J. 1989. "Political Decision-Making and Ecological Models of Delinquency: Conflict of Consensus." In *Theoretical Integration in the Study of Deviance and Crime*, eds. S. Messner, M. Krohn, and A. Liska. Albany: State University of New York Press.

Bursik, Robert J., and Harold Grasmick. 1993. *Neighborhoods and Crime: The Dimensions of Effective Community Control*. New York: Lexington Books.

Cisneros, Henry G., and Lora Engdahl, eds. 2009. *From Despair to Hope: Hope VI and the New Promise of Public Housing in America's Cities*. Washington, DC: Brookings Institution Press.

Clear, Todd, and David Karp. 1999. *The Community Justice Ideal: Preventing Crime and Achieving Justice*. Boulder, CO: Westview.

Clear, Todd R., Dina R. Rose, and Judith A. Ryder. 2001. "Incarceration and Community: The Problem of Removing and Returning Offenders. "*Crime and Delinquency* 47: 335–351.

Coleman, James. 1990. *Foundations of Social Theory*. Cambridge, MA: Harvard University Press.

Coleman, James S. 1988. "Social Capital in the Creation of Human Capital." *American Journal of Sociology* 94: S95–120.

Coulton, Claudia, Jill Korbin, Marilyn Su, and Julian Chow. 1995. "Community Level Factors and Child Maltreatment Rates." *Child Development* 66: 1262–1276.

Elliott, Delbert, James Q. Wilson, David Huizinga, Robert J. Sampson, Amanda Elliott, and Bruce Rankin. 1996. "Effects of Neighborhood Disadvantage on Adolescent Development." *Journal of Research in Crime and Delinquency* 33: 389–426.

Garbarino, James, and A. Crouter. 1978. "Defining the Community Context for Parent-Child Relations: The Correlates of Child Maltreatment." *Child Development* 49: 604–616.

Grannis, Rick. 1998. "The Importance of Trivial Streets: Residential Streets and Residential Segregation." *American Journal of Sociology* 103: 1530–1564.

Harding, David J. 2010. *Living the Drama: Community, Conflict, and Culture among Inner-City Boys*. Chicago: University of Chicago Press.

Heckman, James J. 2006. "Skill Formation and the Economics of Investing in Disadvantaged Children." *Science* 312: 1900–1902.

Hipp, John R., Joan Petersilia, and Susan Turner. 2010. "Parolee Recidivism in California: The Effect of Neighborhood Context and Social Service Agency Characteristics." *Criminology:* Forthcoming.

Hope, Tim. 1995. "Community Crime Prevention." In *Building a Safer Society*, eds. M. Tonry and D. Farrington, 21–89. Chicago: University of Chicago Press.

Hunter, Albert. 1985. "Private, Parochial and Public Social Orders: The Problem of Crime and Incivility in Urban Communities." In *The Challenge of Social Control*, edds. G. Suttles and M. Zald. Norwood, NJ: Ablex.

Keizer, Kees, Siegwart Lindenberg, and Linda Steg. 2008. "The Spreading of Disorder." *Science* 322: 1681–1685.

Kling, Jeffrey, Jeffrey Liebmanm and Lawrence Katz. 2007. "Experimental Analysis of Neighborhood Effects." *Econometrica* 75: 83–119.

Kornhauser, Ruth Rosner. 1978. *Social Sources of Delinquency: An Appraisal of Analytic Models*. Chicago: University of Chicago Press.

Kubrin, Charis E., and Ronald Weitzer. 2003. "New Directions in Social Disorganization Theory." *Journal of Research in Crime and Delinquency* 40: 374–402.

Logan, John, and Harvey Molotch. 1987. *Urban Fortunes: The Political Economy of Place*. Berkeley: University of California Press.

Massey, Douglas S., and Nancy Denton. 1993. *American Apartheid: Segregation and the Making of the Underclass*. Cambridge, MA: Harvard University Press.

Meares, Tracey, and Dan Kahan. 1998. "Law and (Norms of) Order in the Inner City." *Law and Society Review* 32: 805–838.

Morenoff, Jeffrey D., Robert J. Sampson, and Stephen Raudenbush. 2001. "Neighborhood Inequality, Collective Efficacy, and the Spatial Dynamics of Urban Violence." *Criminology* 39: 517–560.

Park, Robert E. 1915. "The City: Suggestions for the Investigations of Human Behavior in the Urban Environment." *American Journal of Sociology* 20: 577–612.

Popkin, Susan, and Elizabeth Cove. 2007. "Safety Is the Most Important Thing: How Hope VI Helped Families." Washington, DC: Urban Institute, Metropolitan Housing and Communities Center.

Pratt, Travis, and Frances Cullen. 2005. "Assessing Macro-Level Predictors and Theories of Crime: A Meta-Analysis." In *Crime and Justice: A Review of Research*, ed. M. Tonry, 373–450. Chicago: University of Chicago Press.

Raudenbush, Stephen W., and Robert J. Sampson. 1999. "'Ecometrics': Toward a Science of Assessing Ecological Settings, with Application to the Systematic Social Observation of Neighborhoods." *Sociological Methodology* 29: 1–41.

Rosenbaum, Dennis P., ed. 1986. *Community Crime Prevention: Does It Work?* Beverly Hills, CA: Sage.

Ross, Catherine E., J. R. Reynolds, and Karlyn J. Geis. 2000. "The Contingent Meaning of Neighborhood Stability for Residents' Psychological Well-Being." *American Sociological Review* 65: 581–97.

Sampson, Robert J. 2009a. "Disparity and Diversity in the Contemporary City: Social (Dis)Order Revisited." *British Journal of Sociology* 60: 1–31.

Sampson, Robert J. 2009b. "Racial Stratification and the Durable Tangle of Neighborhood Inequality." *Annals of the American Academy of Political and Social Science* 621: 260–280.

Sampson, Robert J., and W. B. Groves. 1989. "Community Structure and Crime: Testing Social-Disorganization Theory." *American Journal of Sociology* 94: 774–802.

Sampson, Robert J., and Janet L. Lauritsen. 1994. *Violent Victimization and Offending: Individual-, Situational-, and Community-Level Risk Factors.* Washington, DC: National Academy Press.

Sampson, Robert J., Jeffrey D. Morenoff, and Thomas Gannon-Rowley. 2002. "Assessing 'Neighborhood Effects': Social Processes and New Directions in Research." *Annual Review of Sociology* 28: 443–78.

Sampson, Robert J., Jeffrey D. Morenoff, and Stephen W. Raudenbush. 2005. "Social Anatomy of Racial and Ethnic Disparities in Violence." *American Journal of Public Health* 95: 224–232.

Sampson, Robert J., and Stephen W. Raudenbush. 1999. "Systematic Social Observation of Public Spaces: A New Look at Disorder in Urban Neighborhoods." *American Journal of Sociology* 105: 603–651.

Sampson, Robert J., and Per-Olof Wikström. 2008. "The Social Order of Violence in Chicago and Stockholm Neighborhoods: A Comparative Inquiry." In *Order, Conflict, and Violence,* eds. S. N. Kalyvas, I. Shapiro, and T. Masoud, 97–119. New York and Cambridge, UK: Cambridge University Press.

Sampson, Robert J., and William Julius Wilson. 1995. "Toward a Theory of Race, Crime, and Urban Inequality." In *Crime and Inequality,* eds. J. Hagan and R. D. Peterson, 37–56. Stanford, CA: Stanford University Press.

Shaw, Clifford R., and Henry D. McKay. 1969 [1942]. *Juvenile Delinquency and Urban Areas.* Chicago: University of Chicago Press.

Sherman, Lawrence, Patrick Gartin, and M. Buerger. 1989. "Hot Spots of Predatory Crime: Routine Activities and the Criminology of Place." *Criminology* 27: 27–56.

Simcha-Fagan, O., and J. E. Schwartz. 1986. "Neighborhood and Delinquency: An Assessment of Contextual Effects." *Criminology* 24: 667–703.

Skogan, Wesley. 1986. "Fear of Crime and Neighborhood Change." In *Communities and Crime,* eds. J. Albert J. Reiss and M. Tonry, 203–229. Chicago: University of Chicago Press.

Skogan, Wesley. 1990. *Disorder and Decline: Crime and the Spiral of Decay in American Cities.* Berkele: University of California Press.

Small, Mario. 2009. *Unanticipated Gains: Origins of Network Inequality in Everyday Life.* New York: Oxford University Press.

Suttles, Gerald D. 1972. "The Defended Community." In *The Social Construction of Communities,* ed. G. D. Suttles, 21–43. Chicago: University of Chicago Press.

Taylor, Ralph B. 2001. *Breaking Away from Broken Windows: Baltimore Neighborhoods and the Nationwide Fight against Crime, Grime, Fear, and Decline.* Boulder, CO: Westview.

Taylor, Ralph B., Stephen D. Gottfredson, and Sidney Brower. 1984. "Block Crime and Fear: Defensible Space, Local Social Ties, and Territorial Functioning." *Journal of Research in Crime and Delinquency* 21: 303–331.

Thrasher, Frederick. 1963 [1927]. *The Gang: A Study of 1.313 Gangs in Chicago.* Chicago: University of Chicago Press.

Travis, Jeremy. 2005. *But They All Come Back: Facing the Challenges of Prisoner Reentry*. Washington, DC: Urban Institute Press.

Turner, Margery Austin, and Lynette A. Rawlings. 2005. "Overcoming Concentrated Poverty and Isolation: Ten Lessons for Policy and Practice." Washington, DC: Urban Institute.

Wallace, Rodrick, and Deborah Wallace. 1990. "Origins of Public Health Collapse in New York City: The Dynamics of Planned Shrinkage, Contagious Urban Decay and Social Disintegration." *Bulletin of the New York Academy of Medicine* 66: 391–434.

Warner, Barbara, and Pamela Rountree. 1997. "Local Social Ties in a Community and Crime Model: Questioning the Systemic Nature of Informal Social Control." *Social Problems* 44: 520–536.

Weisburd, David, Laura Wyckoff, Justin Ready, John Eck, J. Hinkle, and F. Gajewski. 2006. "Does Crime Just Move around the Corner? A Controlled Study of Spatial Displacement and Diffusion of Crime Control Benefits." *Criminology* 44: 549–1592.

Western, Bruce. 2006. *Punishment and Inequality in America*. New York: Russell Sage Foundation.

Whyte, William F. 1943. *Street Corner Society: The Social Structure of an Italian Slum*. Chicago: University of Chicago Press.

Wilson, James Q., and George Kelling. 1982. "Broken Windows: The Police and Neighborhood Safety." *Atlantic*, 29–38.

Wilson, William Julius. 1987. *The Truly Disadvantaged: The Inner City, the Underclass, and Public Policy*. Chicago: The University of Chicago Press.

Notes

1. This conceptualization of community addresses the early criticism that Chicago-school social ecologists over-emphasized disorganization and dysfunction. In *Street Corner Society*, W. F. Whyte (1943) argued that what looks like social disorganization from the outside is actually an intricate internal organization. That is, he maintained that the real problem of slums was that their social organization failed to mesh with the structure of the society around it. However, public and parochial dimensions of informal social control (e.g., collective supervision of youth; density and strength of local organizations) may be weak even when certain forms of internal social organization (e.g., dense primary group relations; organized crime) are present. Social disorganization theory thus does not assume that there is no organization in high crime areas. It assumes variability in the ability of residents to achieve a crime-free environment.

2. As of late 2009, Congress has signed legislation to spend over $65 million to replicate the Harlem Children's Zone in 20 neighborhoods across the United States. This represents a major opportunity for criminologists who are interested in child development and neighborhood context. See also http://www.alliance1. org/Public_Policy/Neighborhoods/Tipping_neighborhoods.pdf.

Chapter 9

Race and the Administration of Criminal Justice in the United States

Randall Kennedy

Racial politics have made a deep imprint on the administration of criminal justice in the United States. From the founding of the nation until Reconstruction, there existed virtually no legal constraints on the authority of the central government or the states to discriminate invidiously on racial grounds against blacks and other peoples of color. Officials at every level availed themselves of this power. States that permitted Negro slavery typically created separate laws and institutions to govern those deemed to be mere human chattel (Flanigan 1987; Morris 1996). In many contexts, slaves were subjected to a separate judicial system and regime of punishments. Long after branding, ear cropping, whipping, and castration had been retired as modes of correction for whites deemed to be criminals, they remained available for use against blacks deemed to be criminals. Even more telling than the way in which the legal system subjected people of color to hyper-punishment was the way in which it subjected them to under-protection. In *State v. Mann* (13 NC 263 [1829]), for example, the North Carolina Supreme Court reversed the conviction of a white man who had wantonly shot and injured an enslaved woman. Noting the absence of a statute expressly prohibiting such conduct, the Court held that the shooting posed no violation of common law. In *George v. the State* (37 Miss 316 [1859]), a state supreme court reversed the conviction of a male slave convicted of raping a female slave under the age of ten, observing that there existed no statute that criminalized the rape or attempted rape of a female slave. Addressing what it perceived to be a deficiency highlighted by this ruling, the Mississippi legislature enacted a law criminalizing the rape or attempted rape of "a female negro or mulatto"—but only if the victim was under twelve years of age and only if the perpetrator was also "a negro or mulatto."

Although virtually all slaves in the antebellum United States were "black" (a designation capable of various meanings but typically denoting a person with apparent African ancestry), not all blacks were slaves. Yet free blacks, like those enslaved, were pervasively subjected to invidious racial distinctions. In many locales, laws created "Negro crimes" that punished blacks for conduct in which whites could freely engage. Examples include laws that prohibited blacks from being in public after certain hours, possessing firearms, walking in certain areas, or strolling with canes (Berlin 1974).

Many jurisdictions in antebellum America excluded peoples of color from participation as jurors, police, prosecutors, judges, or even witnesses. In *Hall v. California* (4 Cal. 399 [1854]) the validity of a murder conviction turned on whether a trial court had properly admitted the testimony of a Chinese man against a white defendant. California law expressly barred testimony from "Negroes, mulattoes, and Indians." The defendant argued that this prohibition should be interpreted to exclude Chinese witnesses. The California Supreme Court agreed, overturning his conviction, maintaining that justice required protecting trials against testimony from a race of people "whose mendacity is proverbial" and "whom nature has marked as inferior."

Reconstruction wrought major changes. The Thirteenth Amendment to the federal constitution abolished slavery, and the Fourteenth Amendment imposed upon the states a requirement that they offer to all persons "the equal protection of the laws." As a formal matter, officials could no longer lawfully treat people of color as inferior to whites. Hence, in *Strauder v. West Virginia* (100 U.S. 303 [1880]), the first Supreme Court decision to interpret the Fourteenth Amendment in a race relations context, a majority of the Justices invalidated a state law that expressly excluded blacks on a racial basis from eligibility for jury service. More specifically, the Court reversed the conviction of a black man convicted of murder by a jury selected pursuant to a state law limiting jury service to "all white male persons." Observing that blacks were in special need of protection against "unfriendly action in the States," the Court insisted that the Fourteenth Amendment "was designed to assure to the colored race the enjoyment of all the civil rights that under the law are enjoyed by White persons." What this means, the Court maintained, was that "the law of the States shall be the same for the black as for the white; that all persons . . . shall stand equal before the laws;" that no discrimination shall be made against anyone because of race.

For a brief period, the reforms of Reconstruction injected a degree of racial equality into the administration of criminal justice. In some jurisdictions, blacks (actually black *men*) participated in law enforcement as sheriffs, jurors, lawyers, and even judges. Jonathan Jasper Wright of South Carolina became, in 1870, the first black to sit on a state Supreme Court.

In the final decades of the nineteenth century, however, Reconstruction was destroyed, and white supremacist policies reasserted themselves, especially in locales where colored peoples were numerous. Consider the case of jury service. Although *Strauder* prohibited racial exclusion in the selection of juries, many officials in the decades after Reconstruction openly defied the new federal constitutional regime. In 1910 an enterprising student of race relations wrote jury commissioners throughout the South to ask them about the extent to which blacks actually served on juries (Stephenson 1910). He received scores of replies in which commissioners confided that they never knowingly called blacks for jury service. Among the conditions that facilitated widespread nullification of antidiscrimination norms was widespread hostility or complacency on the part of local and federal judges. From the 1880s until the 1960s, in numerous cases, judges at various levels declined to recognize even obvious instances of blatant illicit racial discrimination (Kennedy 1997).

During this era of unembarrassed white supremacy, courts did occasionally intervene in especially egregious episodes of racial mistreatment. A conspicuous instance is the case of the Scottsboro Boys—nine black youths convicted and sentenced to death in Alabama in the 1930s for allegedly raping two white women. In *Norris v. Alabama* (254 U.S. 587 [1935]) the Supreme Court reversed the conviction of one of the defendants on the ground that, on a racial basis, blacks had been excluded from consideration as potential jurors. Describing the racial demographics of jury service in the area in which the trial took place, the Court observed that no black within memory had served on any jury. Attempting to rebut the allegations of racial exclusion, state officials made two claims. The first was that officials had in fact included on lists of potential jurors the names of some blacks. The second was that the absence of black jurors was attributable not to racial discrimination but to the paucity of blacks reputed to be of good character and sound judgment. The defense revealed, however, that local officials had fraudulently added the names of Negroes to the jury rolls *after* jury selection was completed. The defense also showed that among the blacks passed over for jury service were people who were far better educated than whites who had been selected for jury service. *Norris* thus involved more than racial discrimination; it also involved fraudulence on the part of law enforcement personnel.

Several of the foundational cases that created minimal federal constitutional standards of procedural decency arose from racially biased criminal prosecutions of black defendants. *Moore v. Dempsey* (261 U.S. 86 [1923]), which involved black workers who did nothing but defend themselves against violence, gave rise to judicial recognition of the right to trial free of intimidation by mob violence. *Powell v. Alabama* (287 U.S. 45 [1932]), another case stemming from the prosecution of the Scottsboro Boys, established the proposition that due process of law requires that defendants in capital cases be assigned counsel in circumstances allowing for effective representation. *Brown v. Mississippi* (297 U.S. 278 [1936]), which involved the conviction of innocent black defendants convicted on the basis of confessions elicited by beatings, gave rise to judicial recognition of a right to freedom from torture.

These intermittent interventions, however, failed to affect substantially the day-to-day administration of law enforcement. Almost everywhere whites monopolized decision-making as police, prosecutors, and judges. This monopolization reflected and reinforced sharply etched patterns of racial mistreatment. One pattern involved under-protection—the willful failure of governments to protect citizens of color against racially motivated violence perpetrated by whites. Between 1882 and 1968, at least 4,743 people were lynched in the United States, about 73 percent of whom were blacks lynched by mobs of whites (Zangrando 1980). Although several states enacted anti-lynching legislation, enforcement was, in most places, virtually nonexistent (Chadbourn 1933). Although numerous efforts were made to enact federal anti-lynching legislation, all were thwarted by white supremacists in the United States Senate, several of whom championed the deployment of extra-legal violence against blacks suspected of certain offenses, particularly the crime of rape, or more specifically, the crime of raping a white woman (Williamson 1984).

Law enforcement did attempt, in some circumstances, to respond to racially motivated crimes committed against blacks. In 1955 in Money, Mississippi, two white men killed a black youngster, Emmett Till, because he had whistled at the wife of one of the men. Although local officials initially seemed intent upon winning a conviction, their enthusiasm waned when "outside agitators" placed a national spotlight on the murder and the attendant prosecution. Addressing the all-white jury, defense counsel asserted that he was sure that, despite outside pressure, "every last Anglo-Saxon one of you has the courage to free [the defendants]." After deliberating for little more than an hour, the jury voted for acquittal, despite overwhelming evidence of guilt. One juror remarked, "If we hadn't stopped to drink pop, it wouldn't have taken that long" (Whitfield 1988).

A second pattern involved continued discrimination against black suspects or defendants. Jury discrimination was such an entrenched feature of courthouse culture throughout the Jim Crow era that attorneys were loathe to challenge it. In 1964 the United States Court of Appeals candidly acknowledged that when attorneys for black defendants raised the exclusion issue in jurisdictions suffused by white supremacist sentiments, the attorneys and their clients became targets of extreme hostility (*Whitus v. Balkom*, 333 F.2d. 496 [CA5 1964], cert. denied, 379 U.S. 931 [1964]).

The civil rights revolution, sometimes referred to as the Second Reconstruction, generated reforms that substantially affected the racial context in which criminal law is administered. Strongly supported by public opinion, federal and state law enforcement officials began to act against violent white supremacists. In 1964, for example, an all-white jury in Meridian, Mississippi, convicted several defendants, including lawmen, of criminal civil rights violations stemming from the murders of three civil rights activists. That the convictions constituted a landmark occasioning surprise is itself sobering insofar as the incriminating evidence was overwhelming. Still, as the *New York Times* noted, the verdicts, issued by an all-white jury, were indicative of a "quiet revolution . . . a slow, still faltering but inexorable conversion to the concept that a single standard of justice must cover whites and Negroes alike" (Belknap 1987).

Suppression of racially motivated violence lessened fear of racist terror—a development that allowed for increased black political participation, which, in turn, led to increased demands for racially fair provision of law enforcement services. Simultaneously, judges and other officials educated by revelations of denial and recalcitrance, and prompted by a willingness to act on that knowledge, became increasingly insistent upon actual as opposed to mere nominal compliance with anti-discrimination norms.

CONTEMPORARY ISSUES

Despite changes wrought by the Second Reconstruction, allegations of racial mistreatment continue to haunt the administration of criminal justice. One is that police racially mistreat colored minorities commonly in street-level, low-visibility, highly discretionary decisions involving stops, searches, and arrests (Hagan et al. 2005). A second complaint is that racial prejudice infects the administration of punishment. Some observers maintain, for example, that the racial demographics of the death penalty and mass incarceration stemming from the war on drugs are products of racially selective animus or indifference (Loury 2007). Whether these allegations are accurate is hotly and widely disputed.

Police and Racial Suspicion

Many people of color have long viewed law enforcement officials with deep distrust. The destructive race riots that erupted during the "long hot summers" of the 1960s were typically precipitated by altercations involving white police and black civilian. (Report of the National Advisory Committee on Civil Disorders 1968). The Miami race riot of 1980, which claimed 18 lives, stemmed from the acquittal of police officers prosecuted for murdering a black man (Porter and Dunn 1984). The Los Angeles race riot of 1992, which claimed 52 lives, stemmed from the acquittal of police officers prosecuted for using excessive force against a black suspect, the now-famous Rodney King (Report of the Independent Commission of the Los Angeles Police Department 1991).

Writing in 1995, the eminent black scholar Henry Louis Gates, Jr., observed that black men "swap their experiences of police encounters like war stories, and there are few who don't have more than one story to tell" (Gates 1995). Fourteen years later, a white police officer arrested Gates for disorderly conduct during the course of an investigation prompted by a civilian report of suspicious activity (Harcourt 2009). As it turned out, the "suspicious activity" was Gates's labored effort to enter his own home. A passerby had alerted the police to the possibility of a robbery in progress—an impression primed in part by a spate of recent break-ins in the area. A series of misperceptions fueled by angry resentments escalated into shouting that prompted the officer to arrest Gates. The spectacle of a black Harvard professor being arrested outside his own home by a white policeman became a leading news story that even ensnared the president of the United States when Barak Obama initially criticized the officer's decision.

Gates's arrest was, on one level, rather trivial; within days, municipal authorities had dismissed the charges filed against him. On another level, though, Gates's arrest and the controversy surrounding it were significant in that the episode displayed an alienation between blacks and police authorities (including African American police authorities) that is an entrenched feature on the American social landscape. For many onlookers, the Gates affair provided yet more substantiation for journalist Don Wycliff's assertion that "a dangerous, humiliating... encounter with the police is almost a rite of passage for a black man in the United States" (Wycliff 1987).

The perception that racial discrimination in policing is widespread is a social phenomenon with important consequences. For one thing, it affects the way in which many civilians of color interpret their interactions with police. A given event can be viewed in different ways, depending on the disposition of the interpreter. A person who is positively disposed toward the police, upon being stopped and questioned by an officer in an ambiguous circumstance, might view the intrusion as an effort to protect the community. By contrast, a person subject to the same action who is negatively disposed toward the police might well attribute bad motives to the police conduct in question. In light of ingrained suspicion toward the police—especially in minority communities—commentators, activists, and law enforcement consultants are increasingly urging that police authorities take concerted action to minimize the sense of racial grievance that constitutes a major problem for police-civilian relations in many jurisdictions across the United States..

Apart from perception, to what extent, if any, is there racial discrimination in policing? The range of topics potentially embraced by this subject is large. The one that has garnered the most attention for social scientists, statisticians, legal academics, police authorities, and the courts is referred to as "racial profiling." A consequence of the popularization of this term is conceptual fuzziness. Sometimes racial profiling is defined as the deployment of scrutiny upon a person *solely* on the basis of that person's perceived race. Ironically, those most likely to define racial profiling in this way are frequently the most extreme antagonists in struggles surrounding the issue. On the one hand, police authorities often advocate this restrictive definition. One reason they probably do so is that this definition entails far less encroachment upon police conduct than other definitions prohibiting "racial profiling." Rarely do police officers act "solely" on the basis of race. By identifying for purposes of regulation or prohibition such a narrowly delimited action, authorities burden only the most egregious instances of race-dependent decision-making, thereby leaving unburdened the much more prevalent type of behavior—conduct arising from mixed motives, decisions that stem from other factors as well as racial considerations. On the other hand, civil liberties organizations, such as the American Civil Liberties Union (ACLU), also frequently define racial profiling restrictively as police investigation undertaken solely on account of a person's race. They do so for the purpose of better mobilizing public opinion against racial profiling; it is, after all, difficult to justify a police investigation that is prompted *only* because of a person's race (Banks 2003). Some jurisdictions that have banned "racial profiling" have done so using the restrictive definition (Ky St.s 15A.195 (2007); Okla Stat. tit. 22, § 34.3 [2001]).

An alternative, less restrictive way of defining "racial profiling" is to deem it as any practice that takes race into account at all in placing individuals under special scrutiny. Whereas the restrictive definition noted above identifies racial profiling as investigations prompted *solely* on a racial basis, the less restrictive definition identifies racial profiling as investigations that are prompted *at all*, even minimally, by racial considerations. The California Peace Officers and the United States Department of Justice are among the agencies that embrace the less restrictive definition (Ramirez, McDevitt, and Farrell 2000).

To determine whether racial profiling is being deployed, one must first clarify the operative definition. After that, one must determine whether or to what extent police are pursuing investigations on a racial basis solely (the restrictive definition) or on a racial basis in part (the less restrictive definition). Ferreting out this information when police deny that they are engaging in racial profiling (however defined) is a difficult, contentious endeavor. The most highly publicized studies are those that have both animated and justified movements to ban racial profiling. These studies typically reveal a disproportionality between the percentage of people of color in a given jurisdiction and the percentage of people of color who are subjected to police stops, searches, or arrests; people of color are investigated in numbers beyond their share of the population. The more sophisticated of these studies then proceeded to take into account variables, such as varying rates of criminality in different locales, to determine whether they, as opposed to racial discrimination by the police, explain the disproportionality (Ayres 2008). Those who contend that racial profiling is a major presence in law enforcement are especially enthusiastic about studies which show that "hit rates"—the rate at which contraband is seized from those who are stopped and searched—between people of color and whites are strikingly less dissimilar than the rates at which people of color and whites are stopped and searched. These studies are widely viewed as negating the principal alternative to the theory that racially disproportionate stops and searches stem from and signal illicit racial selectivity on the part of police. That alternative theory is that racially disproportionate stops, searches, and arrests stem from and signal racially differential rates of involvement in crime. But, according to those, like David Cole and John Lamberth, who believe that racial profiling is a major presence, the "hit rates" studies indicate that claims of racially differential rates of criminality are inaccurate. "If blacks are carrying drugs more often than whites, police should find drugs on the blacks they stop more often than on the whites they stop. But they don't" (Cole and Lamberth 2001).

Claims that racial profiling is widespread, ineffective, and unfair have been influential. They have prompted leading politicians and law enforcement officials to disavow the practice, numerous jurisdictions to ban it (albeit with exceptions), and scores of agencies to embark upon expensive regulatory regimes, including information-gathering and training protocols, to dissuade officers from engaging in racial profiling.

There are students of racial profiling, however, who criticize on methodological grounds the literature that portrays racial profiling as a major phenomenon. They maintain that, when used without rigorous controls (which, in their view, is all too often the case), the measurement used to derive the all-important signal of racial disproportionality is misleading. They contend that the studies which purport to discover large amounts of racial profiling fail to consider adequately explanations for racial disproportionality other than racial discrimination by the police. They also argue that when variables other than police racial discrimination are satisfactorily assimilated into comprehensive analyses, what appear at first to be ominous signs of illicit racial selectivity are shown, upon reflection, to be the outgrowth of other factors, such as increased exposure to the police and increased levels of criminality by racial minorities. In 2006 in New York City, for example, 55 percent of the pedestrian stops by police involved blacks, a figure twice the representation of blacks in the local population, according to the 2000 U.S. Census. Greg Ridgeway concluded, however, that upon deeper scrutiny the disproportionality was mainly attributable to racial differences in criminal, or at least suspicious, activity. He noted the striking racial disproportionality of crime-suspect descriptions—descriptions generated not by police but by civilians. According to Ridgeway, the percentage of descriptions featuring blacks far exceeded the percentage of blacks subjected to pedestrian stops. Indeed, according to his calculations, black pedestrians were stopped at a rate that was 20 to 30 percent *lower* than their representation in crime suspect descriptions.

Ridgeway did not contend that racial profiling was wholly absent in New York. He examined the records of individuals officers who patrolled the same territory and found that a few officers stopped notably larger percentages of black pedestrians than their peers. This anomaly, he argued, signaled a potential problem, since the discrepancy could not be attributed to significant differences in the time, place, or context of the law enforcement activities in question. Even if these officers were engaged in racial profiling, however, Ridgeway's main point is that they were few in number, the proverbial "bad apples," and did not represent the norm (Ridgeway 2009).

Additional studies that offer a predicate for racial-profiling skepticism are those that seek to determine whether there is a change in the racial demographics of police stops contingent on the ability of police to discern the race of drivers. Jeffrey Grogger and Greg Ridgeway designed a study that compared the racial demographics of traffic stops during daylight, when racial identification is presumably easier, as opposed to nighttime, when racial identification is presumably more difficult. Applying this model to data gathered from Oakland, California, Grogger and Ridgeway found little evidence of racial profiling in traffic stops (Grogger and Ridgeway 2006). Applying a similar methodology to data generated by the Cincinnati, Ohio, Police Department, Ridgeway again saw little evidence of racial profiling and indeed found that black drivers were less likely to be stopped during daylight, contrary to what would be expected if racial profiling were indeed being deployed. The debate over the prevalence of profiling is that unsettled. Methodological disputes are rife. Conclusions vary, depending on the models used and the jurisdictions studied.

Apart from the sociological issue is the normative question whether, or in what circumstances, racial profiling is ever morally or legally justifiable. A strong consensus condemns racial profiling to express racial prejudice; no court would tolerate scrutinizing blacks or Latinos or Arabs more closely than others for the purpose of harassing these visible, vulnerable groups. Some influential commentators do contend, however, that racial profiling, intelligently deployed, advances the mission of efficient law enforcement (Kinsley 2001; ; Risse and Zeckhauser 2004; Taylor 2001). They contend that, insofar as patterns of criminality are sometimes distinguishable along racial lines, it sometimes makes sense to count race as a variable in making quick investigatory calculations in the shadow of uncertainty.

Critics counter that this argument for "rational" racial profiling constitutes a paradigmatic example of the self-fulfilling prophecy. They maintain that the data profilers rely upon to justify their racial distinctions is itself often infected by racial bias, contending that if police start off investigating blacks more rigorously than others, it is altogether likely that they will uncover more criminality among blacks—not because blacks are, in fact, perpetrating more crime but because the police, primed by their initial racially discriminatory intuition, simply found more criminal activity within a subgroup in which they expected to find more criminality. Opponents of racial profiling also advance other arguments against racially discriminatory assessments of criminal risk, asserting that such practices alienate potential allies, fail to advance the cause of efficient law enforcement, and, most fundamentally, are simply unfair to those subjected to what amounts to a racial tax (Kennedy 1997; Cole 1999).

Conflict over racial profiling is much in evidence in the court of public opinion. Prior to the attacks against the United States on September 11, 2001, public opinion was turning decisively against racial profiling. In the wake of 9/11, however, the idea that racial profiling could be put to legitimate purposes—for instance, thwarting future terroristic attacks by focusing special scrutiny on people of apparent Arab ancestry at airports—gained new currency (Gross and Livington 2002). In 2003 the Bush administration promulgated regulations governing federal law enforcement agencies that were notably ambivalent: they prohibited racial profiling for the deterrence or detection of regular crime but expressly permitted it (up to constitutional limitations) for the purpose of fighting crimes that posed risks to national security (U.S. Department of Justice, Civil Rights Division, Guidance Regarding the Use of Race by Federal Law Enforcement Agencies, June 2003).

The legal status of racial profiling is unsettled. On the one hand, courts are haunted by the specter of *Korematsu v. United States* (323 US 214 [1944]), the Supreme Court ruling that upheld the legitimacy of the largest and most intrusive exercise of racial profiling in American history: the removal and detention of all persons of Japanese ancestry in certain designated areas of the United States after the Japanese attack on Pearl Harbor during World War II. The Court justified the government's policy as a reasonable prophylactic in wartime in defense of national security. The policy and the judiciary's affirmation of it, however, have been widely condemned. In 1989 federal legislation apologized for the nation's conduct and offered reparations to Japanese Americans who had been subject to removal and detention. (Civil Liberties Act of 1988, codified at 50 U.S.C. 1989 [1988]; Commission on Wartime Relocation and Interment of Civilians, Personal Justice Denied [1982]) On the other hand, courts have also upheld police conduct based on racially discriminatory calculations of suspicion. In the past, the United States Border Patrol has conceded that its agents used apparent Mexican ancestry as a basis for subjecting certain motorists to investigatory stops in an effort to fight trafficking in illegal alien workers. In the 1970s the Supreme Court upheld the constitutionality of this practice (*United States v. Martinez-Fuerte*, 428 U.S. 543 [1976]; Harcourt 2006). Whether it would do so currently is unclear.

Punishment and Allegation of Racial Discrimination

Punishment is another area in which opinions bitterly clash. There is consensus that blacks are disproportionately represented among those subjected to the supervision of the criminal justice apparatus (Blumstein 1993; Western 2006). Although blacks constitute only about 13 percent of the general population, they represent nearly half of the prison inmates and about 40 percent of the inmates on death row. Although the disparity is nationwide, its severity varies in a surprising way, with disproportionality being relatively high in the states of the Northeast and upper Midwest (e.g., Minnesota and New Jersey) and relatively low in southern states (e.g., Georgia and South Carolina). The racial disparity is nothing new; the disproportionate presence of black men within the ranks of the imprisoned is a phenomenon that was witnessed before the Civil War. What is some-what new, however, is the appalling extent of that disproportionality. As Glenn Loury notes, "the extent of racial disparity in imprisonment rates is greater than in any other major arena of American social life: at eight to one, the black-white ratio of incarceration rate drawfs the two-to-one ratio of unemployment rates, the three-to-one ratio of non-marital childbearing, the two-to-one ratio of infant mortality rates, and the one-to-five ratio of net worth" (Loury 2007). Notable, too, is the timing of this burgeoning dispari-ty: it grew dramatically in the decades *after* the Second Reconstruction.

Criminologists offer competing explanations for the racial demo-graphics of punishment in America. One camp that generally stresses the sociocultural deficiencies of black communal life, maintains that, to the extent that racial discrimination in the administration of criminal justice exists at all, it is only of marginal significance (Wilbanks 1987; Langan 1994). A second camp emphasizes racially selective indifference or animus in shaping law enforcement policies and strategies that fore-seeably disadvantage historically oppressed racial minorities (Tonry 1995; Wacquant, 2002); Alexander 2010). To the proponents of this perspec-tive, racial discriminations of various sorts—purposeful, unconscious, structural—largely explain the conspicuously disproportionate presence of blacks and, to a lesser extent, Latinos in the ranks of arrestees, defen-dants, and convicts.

These camps have clashed over scores of issues but with particular vehemence over capital punishment and the war on drugs, especially the singling out of crack cocaine trafficking as a key target of suppression.

Race and Capital Punishment

The first rigorous effort to convince a court of the presence of an illicit racial discrimination in capital sentencing did not occur until the late 1940s in the neglected case of *Hampton v. Commonwealth of Virginia* (58 S.E.2d 288 [1950]). *Hampton* involved a group of seven black men condemned to death for raping a white woman in Martinsville, Virginia. The defendants argued that they were punished more harshly by state officials because of their race. Defense attorneys showed that between 1908 and 1949 no white man had been executed for rape, while during that same period for the same crime 45 black men had been executed. During those same years almost twice as many blacks as whites convicted for rape were sentenced to life imprisonment. The Supreme Court of Virginia rebuffed the defendants' allegation of racial discrimination, aver-ring that there was "not a scintilla of evidence" to support it. The Court offered, however, no counter-explanation to account for why, for over four decades, ^forty-two period, 45 forty-five of the 46 men sentenced to death in Virginia for rape were black. Rather than attempting to explain the arresting racial pattern disclosed by the defense, the Virginia Supreme Court upbraided the defense attorneys for even raising the issue, asserting that doing so had represented "an abortive attempt to inject into the proceedings racial prejudice."

To the Virginia Supreme Court, what happened in other prosecutions was irrelevant to what transpired in the immediate case. In its view, the dispositive facts were first the absence of direct evidence of racial bias in the instant sentencing decision and, second, the presence of a non-racial reason for the jury to sentence these defendants to death. After all, the Court observed, "[o]ne can hardly conceive of a more atrocious, a more beastly crime."

Although the defendants in *Hampton* were executed, the argument pioneered by their attorneys did not die. Other defense counsel, often using social scientists as expert witnesses or research associates, deployed that argument in other jurisdictions (Dorin 1981). In several cases in Florida, for example, defense attorneys challenged death sentences with racial discrimination claims based on evidence that, for a 20-year period between 1935 and 1955, 23 blacks but only one white person were executed for rape. These challenges, too, however, proved unavailing. Characteristic was the following response by the Florida Supreme Court. The defendant's statistical evidence, the Court declared,

> is not shown to have any bearing on or relation to the case at bar.... To a sociologist or psychologist in some fields of research [the racial demographics of the historical pattern] would no doubt have value, but in a court of law as presented they are devoid of force or effect. (*State ex rel. Copeland v. Mango* 87 So.2d 501, 503 [1956])

The Court insisted, in brief, that, as a legal matter, sentencing in other cases shed no light on whether racial prejudice had infected the punishment meted out in the case at hand.

In 1987, in *McCleskey v. Kemp* (481 U.S. 279 [1987]), the Supreme Court of the United States ratified the uniform judgments of state and lower federal courts by once again rejecting a challenge to a death sentence on grounds of racial discrimination. *McCleskey* involved a black defendant convicted and sentenced to death for killing a white policeman during the course of a robbery. Supported by the most comprehensive statistical analysis ever done on the racial demographics of capital punishment in a single state, McCleskey's attorneys argued that their client's death sentence should be invalidated because of a constitutionally impermissible risk that his race, or the race of his victim (or both), played a role in the decision to sentence him to death. The claim was mainly predicated on a study devised and administered by David C. Baldus (Baldus 1983, 1985. 1990). Derived from records documenting more than two thousand murder cases between 1973 and 1979, the Baldus study found that among the variables that might plausibly influence capital sentencing— age, level of education, criminal record, military record, method of killing, motive for killing, relationship of defendant to victim, strength of evidence and so forth—the race of the victim emerged as the most salient factor. After taking into account some 230 non-racial variables that might have influenced the pattern of sentencing, Baldus found that the race of the victim continued to have a statistically significant correlation with the imposition of capital sentences. He concluded that the odds of being condemned to death were 4.3 times greater for defendants who killed whites than for defendants who killed blacks, a variable nearly as influential as a prior conviction for armed robbery, rape, or even murder.

A closely divided (5 to 4) Supreme Court assumed, *arguendo*, the validity of the Baldus Study. Echoing the rulings discussed previously, however, the Court insisted that the constitutionality of the defendant's sentence must be determined by asking whether it had been established that officials in *his* case purposefully discriminated on the basis of race. The Court ruled that no such inference could be drawn from the Baldus study statistics. Demanding "exceptionally clear proof" before inferring that a sentencing authority had abused its discretion, Justice Lewis F. Powell maintained that, in the Court's view, the racial correlations revealed by the Baldus study did not meet that standard. "At most," Powell averred," the Bladus study indicates a discrepancy that appears to correlate with race."

Justice Powell mentioned several reasons of policy that influenced the Court's decision. One was the need to give ample latitude for sentencers to use their discretion in determining whether to end a person's life as a punishment. Another was that ruling in favor of McCleskey would open a pandora's box of litgation. "McCleskey's claim, taken to its logical conclusion," Powell remarked with alarm, "throws into serious question the principles that underlie our entire criminal justice system, because, if accepted, the Court could soon be faced with similar claims as to other types of penalty from members of other groups alleging bias." Finally, Powell invoked an institutional consideration as a reason to stay judicial intervention. "McCleskey's arguments," he declared, "are best presented to legislative bodies. . . . It is the elected representatives of the people that are constituted to respond to the will and consequently the moral values of the people."

Several features of the *McCleskey* ruling bear noting. One is that the way the Supreme Court resolved the case left unsettled the legal status of the Baldus study. The Court did not accept, in fact, the study's conclusions. The Court only accepted the study's conclusions for the sake of argument, maintaining that even *if* the conclusions were true the petitioner's claim would still fail. Indeed, the only court that adjudicated the evidentiary merit of the Baldus research—the United States District Court that denied McCleskey's plea for habeas corpus relief—rejected the study. There is good reason to doubt the validity of the court's assessment (Gross and Mauro 1984). Still, there is more controversy surrounding the Baldus study than is often recognized.

Second, the decision as to whether to annul McCleskey's death sentence did not necessarily turn on whether courts believed that racial prejudice had infected the proceedings against him. At least one Supreme Court Justice seems to have believed, at least during one phase of the deliberations, that it was appropriate to reject McCleskey's plea even if his allegations of racial discrimination were true. In an unpublished memorandum to his colleagues, Justice Antonin Scalia stated that he believed that racial discrimination did affect capital sentencing but that he would nonetheless vote to uphold it. He wrote that he did not "share the view, implicit in [Justice Powell's draft opinion] that an effect of racial factors upon sentencing, if it could be shown by sufficiently strong statistical evidence, would require reversal. Since it is my view," he continued, "that the unconscious operation of irrational sympathies, including racial, upon jury decision and (hence) upon prosecutorial [ones] is real, acknowledged by the [cases] of this court and ineradicable, I cannot honestly say that all I need is more proof" (Dorin 1994). Justice Scalia is not alone. John C. McAdams, a proponent of capital punishment, lauds Baldus, calling him "the preeminent scholar" of decision-making in capital sentencing. McAdams concedes that "there is a general and quite robust bias against black victims." This is, in his view, regrettable. Yet he also deems it "peculiar" to contend that if the death penalty is not administered with racial fairness, it must be abolished.

> Nobody [he declares] would even think of trying to apply this principle in a consistent way. If we find that black neighborhoods get less police protection than white neighborhoods, would we withdraw cops from both white and black neighborhoods? If banks are discriminating against black home buyers in mortgage lending, would we demand they stop all mortgage lending? (McAdams 1998)

Those, like McAdams, who perceive capital punishment to be a public good, see abolishing the death penalty on account of racial bias as equivalent to reducing to darkness a town in which lighting has been provided on a racially unequal basis; the norm of equality would be enforced but at the cost of reducing services to all.

Third, while many commentators continue to discuss the Baldus study in *McCleskey* as if it mainly revealed racial discrimination based on the identity of alleged perpetrators, its authors maintained that the patterns it uncovered mainly revealed racial discrimination based on the identity of *victims*. Baldus states that he found "neither strong nor consistent" evidence of discrimination directed against black defendants. Rather, his key finding was that among the variables that might plausibly influence capital sentencing—age, level of education, criminal record, method of killing, motive for killing, and so forth—the race of the victim emerged as the most powerful factor. He concluded that the odds of being condemned to death in Georgia were about four times greater for defendants who killed whites than for defendants who killed blacks. He determined that killing a white as opposed to a black victim was nearly as influential a variable in prompting a sentence of death as a prior conviction for armed robbery, rape, or even murder.

The race-of-the-victim analysis complicates the story of race and the death penalty. While much of the commentary on race and capital punishment focuses upon the danger of racial animus against black defendants, a race-of-the-victim perspective points towards an alternative source: racially selective empathy for victims. One theory posits that the racial patterns revealed by the Baldus study and similar findings reflect a tendency by jurors, judges, and prosecutors to be more viscerally moved by the murders of white victims than black victims. Proponents of this theory suggest that, perhaps unconsciously, key administrators of criminal justice care more about white victimization than black victimization and thus respond more forcefully to the former (Carter 1988; Kennedy 1988). An offshoot of this theory, congenial to stalwart supporters of the death penalty, is the contention that, for purposes of making capital punishment more racially just, the legal system should punish with death more murderers of blacks (Dissenting Views on Racial Justice Act, Report 103–458, House Committee on the Judiciary 1994; Kennedy 1988). Such a policy, however, would immediately confront a paradox: to condemn to death more murderers of blacks would entail sending more blacks to death row since criminality, like so many activities in American life, is highly segmented racially. Most murderers of blacks are other blacks. Punishing more murderers of blacks with death would thus inevitably exacerbate still further racial disparities in the demographics of those most harshly punished by the criminal justice system.

Race and the War on Drugs

Charges of racial discrimination have also been aimed at virtually every aspect of "the war on drugs." Michael Tonry and Matthew Melewski contend, for instance, that police officials have gone about their business of apprehending drug users and traffickers in a fashion that forseeably disadvantages black offenders. They maintain that police officials pursue their mission in ways that are least expensive financially and politically, which means targeting impoverished, urban, predominantly black communities as opposed to middle-class, suburban, predominantly white communities.

> The reason why so many more blacks than whites are arrested . . . is well known. . . . They are much easier to arrest. Much white drug dealing occurs behind closed doors and in private. Much black drug dealing occurs in public or semi-public, on the streets and in open-air drug markets. And much black drug dealing occurs between strangers. . . . Undercover drug agents can penetrate black urban drug markets relatively easily. . . . Most white drug dealing, by contrast, occurs within existing social networks in which people know one another, and in private. Undercover agents have to invest much more time in establishing their bona fides; the arrest yield from a fixed amount of time or effort is much lower when pursuing white than when pursuing black sellers. (Tonry and Melewski 2008)

By deploying certain tactics over others—strategies that foreseeably yield different "catches" in terms of racial demographics—police decide, according to Tonry and Melewski, "to invest more energy and effort in arresting blacks." Their own theory, however, offers the predicate for an alternative interpretation that is non-racial, at least in terms of motivation. That interpretation would emphasize that police decisions are prompted by *considerations of cost*. In terms of outcome, it might not matter whether the choice of tactics is animated by considerations of cost as opposed to considerations of race. As a legal issue, however, the characterization of motive matters greatly. In the eyes of American constitutional law, it is one thing—a permissible thing—for public officials to follow a policy that has the incidental effect of disadvantaging a racial group—so long as officials do not do so for a racial purpose. It is another thing entirely—an impermissible thing—for public officials to act to the detriment of a person or group for a racial purpose (Kennedy 1988; Sklansky 1995).

The significance of the way that the federal judiciary has come to administer this rule is underscored by the controversy surrounding allegations that punishments for involvement with crack cocaine are racially discriminatory. These allegations are largely based on the confluence of three factors. The first is the severity of the punishments in question. Until relatively recently, federal law mandated that a person convicted of possession with intent to distribute 50 grams or more of crack cocaine had to be sentenced to no less than 10 years in prison. In contrast, only if a person was convicted of possession with intent to distribute at least 5,000 grams of powder cocaine was he subject to a mandatory minimum of 10 years—a 100:1 ratio in terms of intensity of punishment. Federal law also mandated that a person caught merely possessing one to five grams of crack cocaine was subject to a mandatory minimum sentence of five years in prison. The second factor is the apparent similarity between powder cocaine offenses and crack cocaine offenses. All involve cocaine, yet, as noted above, the law imposed—and continues to impose—notably more severe punishments on crack than powder cocaine offenses. The third factor is the difference in the racial demographics of those arrested, prosecuted, and imprisoned for various drug offenses. Blacks predominate dramatically among those subject to the draconian anti-crack statutes.

In light of these factors, many observers have concluded that the anti-crack laws are racially discriminatory. A notable judicial declaration of this perspective is a ruling by U.S. District Judge Clyde S. Cahill, who refused to apply the law's punishment provisions to an 18-year-old black man with no prior convictions. Judge Cahill concluded that

> racially discriminatory influences, at least unconsciously, played an appreciable role in promulgating the enhanced statutory scheme for possession and distribution of crack. Legislators' unconscious racial aversion towards blacks, sparked by unsubstantiated reports of the effects of crack, reaction-

ary media prodding, and an agitated constituency, motivated the legislators. (United States v. Clary, 846 F.Supp. 768 [E.D.Mo. 1994], rev'd, 34 F.3d 709 [CA8 1994], cert. denied, 513 U.S. 1182 [1995])

According to the judge, while racially discriminatory "intent per se may not have entered Congress' enactment of the crack statute, its failure to account for a foreseeable disparate impact which would affect black Americans in grossly disproportionate numbers would nonetheless violate the spirit and letter of equal protection." Congress would have acted differently, he charged, if legislators knew that it was mainly whites rather than blacks who stood to suffer such harsh and communally destructive penalties. "If young white males were being incarcerated at the same rate as young black males," he declared, "the statute would have been amended long ago."

Judge Cahill's ruling was reversed on appeal; the federal judiciary has uniformly rejected allegations that the crack cocaine laws are racially discriminatory. (United States v. Butler, 41 F.3d 1435 [CA11 1995]; United States v. Thompson 27 F.3d 671 [D.C. CA] cert. denied 115 S. Ct. 650 [1994]; United States v. Frazier 981 F.2d 92 [CA 3] cert. denied 113 S.Ct. 1661 [1993]) Defenders of the constitutionality of the law point to a legislative record that is free of any unambiguous sign of racial prejudice. They point, as well, to the fact that leading black figures in Congress were in the forefront of the effort to "crack down on crack," believing that crack posed an unprecedented danger to already-weakened urban minority communities because of its relative inexpensiveness and pharmacological properties. Defenders concede that the conclusions reached by Congress are controversial. But they insist that, in the absence of evidence proving racially discriminatory purpose, majoritarian politics should govern (Kennedy 1994; Kennedy 1997).

Despite the unwillingness of federal courts to invalidate the crack laws on constitutional grounds, those attacking these laws have won significant victories. The Supreme Court of Minnesota struck down that state's ana-logue to the federal crack statute, holding that that law violated the Minne-sota constitution's equal protection clause (State v. Russell, 477 N.W. 2d 886 [1971]). The United States Sentencing Commission, moreover, has revis-ited the crack-powder distinction and, largely because of racial disparities, concluded that punishments for crack offenses ought to be lessened, though they remain considerably harsher than penalties stemming from other drug offenses (United States Sentencing Commission 2007).

CONCLUSION

Race relations in the criminal justice system remain vexed. Suspicion erodes the trust upon which an efficient and fair system of law enforcement depends. One way in which scholars can contribute to the betterment of law enforcement as well as the enlargement and deepening of knowledge is by continuing to examine, as rigorously as possible, allegations of wrongful racial discrimination in the administration of criminal justice.

References

Alexander, Michelle. 2010. The New Jim Crow: Mass Incarceration in the Age of Colorblindness.

Ayres, Ian. 2008. Racial Profiling and the LAPD: A Study of Racially Disparate Outcomes in the Los Angeles Police Department. On-line at http://www.aclu-sc.org/lapdracialprofiling.

Baldus, David, George Woodward and Charles Pulaski, 1990. Equal Justice and the Death Penalty: A Legal and Empirical Analysis. Boston: Northeastern University Press.

Banks, R. Richard, 2003. Beyond Profiling: Race, Policing, and the Drug War, 56 Stanford Law Review 71–604.

Belknap, Michael V., 1998. Federal Law and the Southern Order: Racial Violence and Constitutional Conflict in the Post-Brown South. Athens: University of Georgia Press.

Berlin, Ira, 1975. Slaves Without Masters: The Free Negro in the Antebellum South. New York: Pantheon Books.

Blumstein, Alfred, 1993. Racial Disproportionality of U.S. Prison Populations Revisited, Colorado Law Review 64, 743–760.

Bright, Stephen B., 1995. "Discrimination, Death and Denial: The Tolerance of Racial Discrimination in the Infliction of the Death Penalty" 35 Santa Clara Law Review 433–484.

Carter, Dan T., 1979. Scottsboro: A Tragedy of the American South (Rev. ed.). Baton Rouge: Louisiana University Press.

Carter, Stephen L., 1988. "When Victims Happen to Be Black" 97 Yale Law Journal 420–447.

Chadbourn, James Harmon. 1933. Lynching and the Law Chapel Hill: University of North Carolina Press.

Cole, David. 1999. No Equal Justice: Race and Class in the American Criminal Justice System. New York: The New Press.

Cole, David. Lamberth, John. May 13, 2001. The Fallacy of Racial Profiling. New York Times.

Dorin, Dennis, 1981. "Two Different Worlds: Criminologists, Justices and Racial Discrimination in the Imposition of Criminal Punishment in Rape Cases" 72 Journal of Criminal Law and Criminology 1667–1698.

Flanigan, Daniel J., 1987. The Criminal Law of Slavery and Freedom, 1800–1868. New York: Garland Publishing.

Gates, Henry Louis. 1997. Thirteen Ways of Looking at a Black Man. New York: Random House.

Grogger, Jeffrey. Ridgeway, Greg. 2006. Testing for Racial Profiling in Traffic Stops from Behind a Veil of Darkness, 101 (475) Journal of the American Statistical Association 878–887.

Gross, Samuel R. Mauro, Robert. 1984. Patterns of Death: An Analysis of Racial Disparities in Capital Sentencing and Homicide Victimization. 37 Stanford Law Review 27.

Gross, Samuel R. and Debra Livingston, 2002. Racial Profiling Under Attack, 102 Columbia Law Review 1413–1438.

Hagan, John. (with Carla Shedd and Monique Payne). 2005. Race, Ethnicity and Youth Perceptions of Criminal Injustice. 70 American Sociological Review 381–407.

Harcourt, Bernard. 2009. Henry Louis Gates and racial Profiling: What's The Problem? The Law School: The University of Chicago. Public Law and Legal Theory Working Paper No. 277. On-line at http://www.law.uchicago.edu-academics/publiclaw-index.html.

Independent Commission on the Los Angeles Police Department. (Warren Commission). 1991. Report of the Independent Commission on the Los Angeles Police Department. Los Angeles, Cal: The Commission.

Kennedy, Randall, 1997. Race, Crime and the Law New York: Pantheon Books.

Kennedy, Randall. 1994. The State, Criminal Law, and Racial Discrimination: A Comment. 107 Harvard Law Review 1255–1278.

Kinsley, Michael. September 30, 2001. When is Racial Profiling Okay? Washington Post.

Langan, Patrick, 1994. No Racism in the Justice System, 117 Public Interest 48–51.

Litwack, Leon F., 1961. North of Slavery: The Negro in the Free States, 1790–1860. University of Chicago Press.

Loury, Glenn. 2008. Race, Incarceration and American Values. Cambridge: Mass: MIT Press.

McAdams, John C. 1988. Racial Disparity and the Death Penalty. 61 (4) Law and Contemporary Problems 153–170.

Morris, Thomas D. 1996. Southern Slavery and the Law. Chapel Hill: University of North Carolina Press.

Porter, Bruce, and Marvin Dunn, 1984. The Miami Riot of 1980: Crossing the Bounds Lexington, MA: Lexington Books.

Ramirez, Deborah. McDevitt, Jack. Ferrell, Amy. 1999. A Resource Guide on Racial Profiling Data Collection Systems: Promising Practices and Lessons Learned. U. S. Department of Justice.

Ridgeway, Greg. 2007. Analysis of Racisl Disparities in the New York Police Department's Stop, Question, and Frisk Practices. The RAND Corp.

Ridgeway et al. 2006. Police-Community Relations in Cincinnati: Year Two Evaluation Report. The RAND Corp.

Rise, Eric W. 1995. The Martinsville Seven: Race, Rape, and Capital Punishment Charlottesville: University of Virginia Press.

Risse, Mathias. Zeckhauser, Richard. 2004. Racial Profiling. 32 (2) Philosophy and Public Affairs 131–170.

Sklansky, David A. 1995. "Cocaine, Race, and Equal Protection" 47 Stanford Law Review 1283–1322.

Stephenson, Gilbert Thomas. 1910. Race Distinctions in American Law. New York: Appleton and Co.

Taylor, Stuart, Jr. September 22, 2001. The Case for Using Racial Profiling at Airports. National Journal.

Tonry, Michael, 1995. Malign Neglect: Race, Crime, and Punishment in America. New York: Oxford University Press.

Tonry, Michael. Melewski, Matthew. 2008. The Malign Effects of drugs and Crime Control policies on Black Americans. 37 Crime and Justice: A Review of Research 1–44.

U.S. Congress, 1994. Dissenting Views on Racial Justice Act, Report 103–458, House Committee on the Judiciary, 103 Congress, 2d Sess., March 24, 1994.

U.S. Commission on Wartime Relocation and Internment of Civilians. 1982.: Personal Justice Denied.

U.S. Department of Justice, Civil Rights Division. 2003. Guidance Regarding the Use of Race by Federal Law Enforcement Agencies.

U.S. Riot Commission. 1968. Report of the National Advisory Commission on Civil Disorders. (The Kerner Report) New York: Bantam Books.

U.S. Sentencing Commission. 2007. U.S. Sentencing commission Votes to Amend Guidelines for terrorism, Sex Offenses, Intellectual Property Offenses, and Crack Cocaine Offenses.

Wacquant, Loic 2002. From Slavery to Mass Incarceration, 13 New Left Review 41–60.

Western, Bruce. 2006. Punishment and Inequality in America. New York: Russell Sage Foundation.

Whitfield, Stephen J., 1988. A Death in the Delta: The Story of Emmett Till. New York: Free Press.

Wilbanks, William. 1987. The Myth of a Racist Criminal Justice System. Monterey, Cal: Brooks/Cole.

Williamson, Joel. 1984. The Crucible of Race: Black/White Relations in the American South Since Emancipation. New York: Oxford University Press.

Wolfgang, Marvin E., and Marc Riedel, 1976. "Rape, Racial Discrimination, and the Death Penalty" In Capital Punishment in the United States, edited by Hugo Adam Bedau and Chester M. Pierce New York: AMS Press.

Wycliff. Don. February 8, 1987. Blacks and Blue Power. New York Times.

Zangrando, Robert L. 1980. The NAACP Crusade Against Lynching, 1909–1950. Philadelphia: Temple University Press.

Chapter 10

Gun Control

Philip J. Cook, Anthony A. Braga & Mark H. Moore

In the search for public safety, establishing more stringent controls on gun commerce and use has the broad support of the American public. Thousands are killed by gunfire each year (including almost 12,800 homicides in 2006) and hundreds of thousands more are threatened or injured in robberies and assaults. Developing and implementing government programs to make guns less readily available, especially to those inclined toward violence, deserve a high priority in the quest to save lives and reduce the burden of crime on our society.

But not everyone accepts this perspective on guns. Some argue that guns are the mere instruments of criminal intent, with no more importance than the brand of shoes the criminal wears. If the weapon used by assailants does not matter, then policy interventions focused on guns are futile. Another path leading to the same conclusion of futility posits that in a society already saturated with guns, it is simply not feasible to prevent a determined criminal from obtaining a gun if he or she wants one. Furthermore, if guns provide law-abiding citizens with an important means of self-defense against crime, then government attempts to restrict gun availability may be perverse rather than merely futile. Of course, each of these assertions about the actual or potential consequences of gun control has been extensively debated.

But the debate over gun control is not only concerned with factual issues. If this were true, empirical research might, in principle at least, resolve the matter, and the proper choice of gun-control measures would become clear. In reality, however, there are important value conflicts as well, conflicts concerning the proper relationship between the individual, the community, and the state. Even a definitive empirical demonstration that a gun-control measure would save lives will not persuade someone who believes in an absolute individual right to keep and bear arms. The U.S. Supreme Court has recently weighed in on this matter, finding for the first time that the Second Amendment to the Constitution does provide an individual right to keep a handgun in the home for self-defense (*Heller v. District of Columbia* 2008), at least in a federal jurisdiction.

The purpose of this essay is to provide a foundation for understanding the "Great American Gun War" and to consider the next steps that could be taken in the search for an effective gun-control policy. We begin with a review of the more-or-less uncontroversial facts about patterns in gun ownership and use, and the reasons why Americans are inclined to arm themselves. A discussion follows of the more contentious issues—whether and how guns influence levels or seriousness of crime. We then summarize existing firearms regulations and identify the important values at stake when it comes to future gun-control policy. Looking to the future, we provide a policy analysis organized around three broad arenas of regulation. The last section concludes.

Our main conclusions can be briefly summarized:

- Guns were used in 500,000 robberies and assaults in 2006 and accounted for 28,000 deaths (mostly murder or suicide). They were also used in self-defense in an unknown number of cases.
- Case-fatality rates are much higher in assaults with guns than with other weapons. Although guns are used only in a minority of robberies, gun robberies are more lucrative, successful, and deadly than robberies with other weapons.
- The prevalence of gun ownership differs widely among communities in the United States, and the prevalence has a direct positive effect on the likelihood that a criminal assailant uses a gun rather than another weapon. However, the prevalence of gun ownership has no discernible effect on the overall volume of violent crime.
- Commerce in guns and the possession and use of guns are regulated by state, federal, and sometimes local government. The public interest in firearms regulations depends on value judgments that are only partially informed by empirical evidence.
- Gun-control measures are usefully classified into three categories: those that are intended to reduce overall gun ownership; those that are intended to keep guns away from particularly dangerous people; and those that are intended to influence choices about how guns are used and to what effect. All three approaches have some merit.
- One important proximate goal for policy (both regulations and criminal justice response) is to make guns a liability to criminals by increasing the likelihood that they will be arrested and punished if they use a gun rather than another weapon.

GUN OWNERSHIP, USE, AND MISUSE

Guns are versatile tools, useful in providing meat for the table, eliminating varmints and pests, providing entertainment for those who have learned to enjoy the sporting uses, and protecting life and property against criminal predators. They are an especially common feature of rural life, where wild animals provide both a threat and an opportunity for sport. As America has become more urban, however, the demand for guns has become increasingly motivated by the felt need for protection against other people.

Patterns of Gun Ownership

The annual General Social Survey, conducted by the National Opinion Research Center, has long included questions on gun ownership. In 1999 just 36 percent of American households owned at least one firearm, down from nearly 50 percent in 1980 (Smith 2000, 55). The drop in household ownership in part reflects the trend in household composition during this period; households are less likely to include a gun because they have become smaller and, in particular, are less likely to include a man.

The *number* of guns in private hands is unknown, since there is little information on the average number of guns kept by gun-owning households. The most detailed national survey on the subject (the National Firearms Survey) found that gun-owning households average 5.2 guns in 2004, up substantially from the 1970s (Hepburn et al. 2007). The alternative to survey data are the administrative data on manufacturing and net imports, but these provide no guidance as to the rate of disposal of existing guns through breakage, confiscation, and off-the-books imports and exports.

One addition for many gun-owning households has been a handgun. The significance of this trend toward increased handgun ownership lies in the fact that while rifles and shotguns are acquired primarily for sporting purposes, handguns are primarily intended for use against people, either in crime or self-defense. The increase in handgun prevalence corresponds to a large increase in the relative importance of handguns in retail sales: In 2007, the Bureau of Alcohol, Tobacco, and Firearms and Explosives (ATF) reported that handguns represented nearly 42 percent of new firearms manufactured in the United States (http://www.atf.gov/firearms/stats/afmer/afmer2007.pdf). Just 23 percent of manufactures were handguns during the first half of the twentieth century (ATF 2000a).

Some of the increased handgun sales have been to urban residents who have no experience with guns but are convinced they need one for self-protection, as suggested by the surges in handgun sales after the Los Angeles riots and other such events (Kellermann and Cook 1999). But while the prevalence of handgun ownership has increased substantially over the past three decades, it remains true now, as earlier, that most who possess a handgun also own one or more rifles and shotguns. The 2004 survey found that just 17 percent of gun-owning individuals have only handguns, while 30 percent have only long guns and 44 percent have both.

These statistics suggest that people who have acquired guns for self-protection are for the most part also hunters and target shooters. Indeed,

77 percent of long-gun owners say that their one most important reason for owning the long gun was sport shooting (Hepburn et al. 2007).

The demographic patterns of gun ownership are no surprise: most owners are men, and the men who are most likely to own a gun reside in rural areas or small towns and were reared in such places (Kleck 1991). Blacks are less likely to own guns than whites, in part because the black population is more urban.[1] The likelihood of gun ownership increases with income and peaks in middle age.

The fact that guns fit much more comfortably into rural life than urban life raises a question. In 1940, 49 percent of teenagers were living in rural areas; by 2000, that had dropped to 22 percent. What will happen to gun ownership patterns as new generations with less connection to rural life come along? Hunting is already on the decline: the absolute number of hunting licenses issued in 2003 (14.7 million) was smaller than in 1970 (15.6 million) despite the growth in population, indicating a decline in the percentage of people who hunt (http://wsfrprograms.fws.gov/Sub-pages/LicenseInfo/HuntingLicCertHistory.pdf). Confirming evidence comes from the National Survey of Wildlife-Associated Recreation, which found that 5 percent of adults age 16 and over were hunters in 2006, compared with 9 percent in 1970.[2] This trend may eventually erode the importance of the rural sporting culture that has dominated the gun "scene." In its place is greater focus on the criminal and self-defense uses of guns.

Uses of Guns Against People

A great many Americans die by gunfire. The gun-death counts from suicide, homicide, and accident have totaled over 28,000 for every year from 1972 to 2006. In that year there were approximately 30,900 firearms deaths, a rate of 10.2 per 100,000 U.S. residents. All but 862 were either suicides or homicides. While homicides make the headlines, there were actually 4,100 more gun suicides than homicides. The remainder were classified as accidents, legal interventions, or unknown (http://we-bappa.cdc.gov/sasweb/ncipc/mortrate.html). Various points of reference help calibrate these numbers. In terms of numbers of Americans killed, a year of gun killing in the United States is the equivalent of American deaths during the Korean War. Another familiar reference is the highway fatality rate, which is about 50 percent higher nationwide.

It is criminal homicide and other criminal uses of guns that cause the greatest public concern. There are relatively few gun accidents,[3] and suicide seems more a private concern than a public risk. Fortunately, the homicide rate (both gun and non-gun) has been dropping rapidly in recent years, from twentieth-century highs in 1980 and 1991 of over 10 per 100,000. The rate was just 6.2 in 2006. Nearly 70 percent of homicides are committed with guns, most of which (80 percent) are handguns. Both with respect to the percentage and the rate of firearm homicides, the

United States is extraordinarily high by the standards of other industrialized countries (Zimring and Hawkins 1997). Overall violence rates in the United States are also above average, though not to nearly the same extent. The overall homicide rate in Canada is about the same as the non-gun homicide rate in the United States (Cook, Cukier, and Krause 2009).

Homicide is not a democratic crime. Both victims and perpetrators are vastly disproportionately male, black, and quite young. With respect to the victims, homicide is the leading cause of death for black male youths. The gun homicide rate in 2006 for Hispanic men ages 18 to 29 was five times the rate for non-Hispanic white men of the same age; the gun homicide rate for black men 18 to 29 was 109 per 100,000, 18 times the rate for white males in that age group. (Most male victims in the high-risk category are killed by people of the same race, sex, and age group [Cook and Laub 1998].) About 85 percent of the homicide victims in this group were killed with firearms. The disparity between the demography of gun sports and of gun crime is telling: sportsmen are disproportionately older white males from small towns and rural areas, while the criminal misuse of guns is concentrated among young urban males, especially minorities.[4]

Of course, most gun crimes are not fatal. For every gun homicide victim, there are roughly six gun-crime victims who receive a less-than-mortal wound (Cook 1985) and many more who are not wounded at all. Indeed, the most common criminal use of guns is to threaten, with the objective of robbing, raping, or otherwise gaining the victim's compliance; relatively few of these victims are physically injured, but the threat of lethal violence

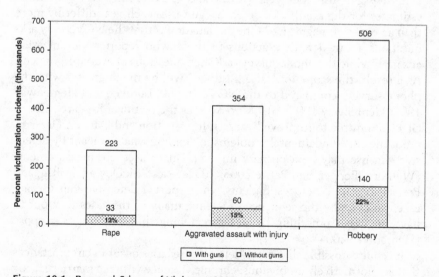

Figure 10.1. Personal Crimes of Violence, 2006
Source: National Crime Victimization Survey http://www.ojp.usdoj.gov/bjs/pub/pdf/cvus05.pdf

and the potential for escalation necessarily make these crimes serious. According to the 2006 National Crime Victimization Survey (NCVS), there were 140,000 gun robberies, 325,000 aggravated assaults (of which 60,000 caused injury) and 33,000 rapes in that year, for a total estimated volume of gun crimes of about 500,000 (http://www.ojp.usdoj.gov/bjs/pub/pdf/cvus0604.pdf). And these gun crimes are only a fraction of all robberies, aggravated assaults, and rapes, as shown in figure 10.1. When a gun is used, it is most likely (85 percent) a handgun.

While guns do enormous damage in crime, they also provide some crime victims with the means of escaping serious injury or property loss. The National Crime Victimization Survey is generally considered the most reliable source of information on predatory crime, since it has been in the field since 1973 and incorporates the best thinking of survey methodologists. From this source it would appear that use of guns in self-defense against criminal predation occurs approximately 100,000 times per year (Cook, Ludwig, and Hemenway 1997).[5] Of particular interest is the likelihood that a gun will be used in self-defense against an intruder. Cook (1991), using the NCVS data for the mid-1980s, found that only 3 percent of victims were able to deploy a gun against someone who broke in (or attempted to do so) while they were at home. Since about 45 percent of all households possessed a gun during that period, we conclude that it is relatively unusual for victims to be able to deploy a gun against intruders, even when they have one nearby.

In contrast are the results of several smaller one-time telephone surveys, which provide a basis for asserting that there are millions of defensive gun uses per year (Kleck and Gertz 1995). Why do these estimates for the number of defensive gun uses each year differ by more than an order of magnitude? One explanation is that the NCVS only asks questions about defensive actions to those who report a victimization attempt, while the phone surveys ask such questions of every respondent. As a result, the scope for "false positives" will be much greater with the phone surveys compared to the NCVS (Cook, Ludwig, and Hemenway 1997; Hemenway 1997a,b).[6] Moreover, as the National Research Council's Committee to Improve Research Information and Data on Firearms report notes, "fundamental problems in defining what is meant by defensive gun use may be a primary impediment to accurate measurement" (Wellford, Pepper, and Petrie 2005, 103; see also McDowall, Loftin, and Presser 2000). When respondents who report a defensive gun use are asked to describe the sequence of events, many of the cases turn out to have involved something far less threatening than one might suppose (Hemenway 2004).

It is quite possible that most "self-defense" uses occur in circumstances that are normatively ambiguous: chronic violence within a marriage, gang fights, robberies of drug dealers, encounters with groups of young men who simply *appear* threatening. Indeed, drug dealers and predatory criminals do face extraordinarily high risks of being assaulted (Levitt and

Venkatesh 2000; Cook and Ludwig 2000). In one survey of convicted felons in prison, the most common reason offered for carrying a gun was self-defense (Wright and Rossi 1994); a similar finding emerged from a study of juveniles incarcerated for serious criminal offenses (Smith 1996). Self-defense conjures up an image of the innocent victim using a gun to fend off an unprovoked criminal assault, but in fact many "self-defense" cases are not so commendable.

EFFECTS OF GUN POSSESSION AND USE

Do "guns kill people" or do "people kill people"? In murder trials the killer's motivation and state of mind are explored thoroughly, while the type of weapon—usually some type of gun—is often treated as an incidental detail. Yet there is compelling evidence that the type of weapon matters a lot in determining whether the victim lives or dies. If true, then depriving potentially violent people of guns would save lives, an essential tenet of the argument for restricting gun availability. But then a second question arises. How can we use the law to deprive violent people of guns if such people are not inclined to be law abiding? The saying "If guns are outlawed, only outlaws will have guns" may ring true.[7] There is also some evidence on this matter, suggesting that some "outlaws'" decision of what weapon to use is indeed influenced by the difficulty and legal risks of obtaining and using a gun (Wright and Rossi 1994).

In this section we develop the evidence on these two issues, designated "instrumentality" and "availability." The same two issues should also be raised in an assessment of the self-defense uses of guns, and we do so in the third part of this section.

Instrumentality

In some circumstances the claim that the type of weapon matters seems indisputable. There are very few drive-by knifings, or people killed accidentally by stray fists. When well-protected people are murdered, it is almost always with a gun; over 90 percent of lethal attacks on law enforcement officers are with firearms, and all assassinations of U.S. presidents have been shootings. When lone assailants set out to kill as many people as they can in a commuter train, business, or campus, the only readily available weapon that will do the job is a gun. But what about the more mundane attacks that make up the vast bulk of violent cases?

The first piece of evidence is that robberies and assaults committed with guns are more likely to result in the victim's death than are similar violent crimes committed with other weapons. In the public health jargon, the "case-fatality rates" differ by weapon type. Take the case of robbery, a crime that includes holdups, muggings, and other violent confrontations motivated by theft. The case-fatality rate for gun robbery is three times as high as for robberies with knives, and ten times as high as for robberies with other weapons (Cook 1987). For aggravated (serious) assault, it is more difficult to come up with meaningful case-fatality estimates, since the crime itself is in part *defined* by the type of weapon used. (A threat delivered at gunpoint is likely to be classified as an aggravated assault, while the same threat delivered while shaking a fist would be classified as a simple assault.) We do know that for assaults where the victim sustains an injury, the case-fatality rate is closely linked to the type of weapon (Zimring 1968, 1972; Kleck and McElrath 1991), as is also the case for family and intimate assaults known to the police (Saltzman et al. 1992).

Case-fatality rates do not by themselves prove that the type of weapon has an independent causal effect on the probability of death. It is possible that the type of weapon is simply an indicator of the assailant's intent and that it is the intent, rather than the weapon, that determines whether the victim lives or dies. In this view—which has been offered as a reasonable possibility by Wolfgang (1958); Wright, Rossi, and Daly (1983); and others—the gun makes the killing easier and is hence the obvious choice if the assailant's intent is indeed to kill. But if no gun were available, then most would-be killers would still find a way. Fatal and nonfatal attacks form two distinct sets of events with little overlap, at least regarding the assailant's state of mind.

Perhaps the most telling response to this argument is due to Franklin Zimring (1968, 1972), who concluded that there is actually a good deal of overlap between fatal and nonfatal attacks: even in the case of earnest and potentially deadly attacks, assailants commonly lack a clear or sustained intent to kill. Whether the victim lives or dies then depends importantly on the lethality of the weapon with which the assailant strikes the first blow or two. For evidence on this perspective, Zimring notes that in a high percentage of cases the assailant is drunk or enraged, unlikely to be acting in a calculating fashion. Zimring's studies of wounds inflicted in gun and knife assaults demonstrate that the difference between life and death is evidently just a matter of chance, determined by whether the bullet or blade found a vital organ. It is relatively rare for assailants to administer the *coup de grace* that would ensure their victim's demise. For every homicide inflicted with a single bullet wound to the chest, there are two survivors of a bullet wound to the chest, and similarly for knife attacks.

Zimring's argument in a nutshell is that robbery murder is closely related to robbery, and assaultive homicide is closely related to aggravated assault; death is in effect a probabilistic by-product of violent crime. While the law determines the seriousness of the crime by whether the victim lives or dies, the outcome is not a reliable guide to the assailant's intent or state of mind. One logical implication of this perspective is that there should be a close link between the overall volume of violent crimes and the number of murders. Confirmatory evidence is provided by a study that demonstrated by use of data on changes in crime rates in 44 cities that an increase of 1,000 gun robberies is associated with three times as many additional murders as an increase of 1,000 non-gun robberies (Cook 1987). "Instrumentality" provides a natural explanation for this pattern.

Zimring's reasoning can be extended to a comparison of different types of guns. In the gun-control debate, the prime target has been the handgun, since handguns are used in most gun crimes. But rifles and shotguns tend to be more lethal than handguns: a rifle is easier to aim, and the bullet travels with higher velocity than for a short-barreled weapon, while a shotgun blast spreads and may cause a number of wounds when it strikes. To the extent that assailants substitute rifles and shotguns for handguns in response to handgun-control measures, the result may be to increase the death rate (Kleck 1984).[8] Unfortunately, there is little systematic evidence on the question of whether effective handgun control would lead robbers and other violent people to substitute long guns (more lethal) or knives (less).[9] "Instrumentality effects" are not limited to differences in case-fatality rates. The type of weapon also appears to matter in other ways. For example, gun robbers are far less likely to attack and injure their victims than robbers using other weapons, and are less likely to incur resistance (Conklin 1972; Cook 1976, 1980; Skogan 1978). (In cases in which the victim is attacked and injured, the likelihood of death in gun robberies is far higher than with knives or blunt objects, which accounts for the relatively high case-fatality rate in gun robbery.) We also have evidence that aggravated assaults follow similar weapon-specific patterns (Kleck and McElrath 1991). The most plausible explanation for this pattern of outcomes is simply that a gun gives the assailant the power to intimidate and gain his victim's compliance without use of force, whereas with less lethal weapons the assailant is more likely to find it necessary to back up the threat with a physical attack.

The intimidating power of a gun may also help explain the effectiveness of using one in self-defense. According to one study of NCVS data, in burglaries of occupied dwellings only 5 percent of victims who used guns in self-defense were injured, compared with 25 percent of those who resisted with other weapons.[10] Other studies have confirmed that victims of predatory crime who are able to resist with a gun are generally successful in thwarting the crime and avoiding injury (Kleck 1988; McDowall, Loftin, and Wiersema 1992a). But the interpretation of this result is open to some question. Self-defense with a gun is a relatively unusual event in crimes like burglary and robbery, and the cases in which the victim does use a gun differ from others in ways that help account for the differential success of gun defense. In particular, other means of defense usually are attempted after the assailant threatens or attacks the victim, whereas those who use guns in self-defense are relatively likely to be the first to threaten or use force (McDowall, Loftin, and Wiersema 1992b). Given this difference in the sequence of events, and the implied difference in the competence or intentions of the perpetrator, the proper interpretation of the statistical evidence concerning weapon-specific success rates in self-defense is unclear (Cook 1986, 1991).

Instrumentality plays a more subtle role in robbery, where the choice of victim and technique to some extent reflect strategic considerations. The robber (or group of robbers) chooses the victim, the weapon, and the technique, while the victim must decide whether to cooperate or resist. Based on interviews with robbers and other evidence, it is safe to say that robbers' choices reflect a desire to preempt resistance, secure as much loot as possible, and then make a safe getaway, although actual behavior in these fraught encounters is not necessarily rational (Conklin 1972; Wright and Decker 1997; Jacobs 2000). One useful concept is the "power" of the robber to gain the victim's compliance (Cook 1976). Power depends on the weapon used by the robber; a gun, by creating a lethal threat at a distance, is most powerful, enough for a single robber to control several victims at once. Accomplices also enhance power, as does skill and experience. A solo offender who lacks a gun or accomplices is more likely to select a woman or older person as a victim—a majority of gun robberies, on the other hand, are directed against relatively robust commercial targets (Cook 1980).

A multivariate analysis of NCVS data for 2000–2005 (all robberies committed by an adult male) confirms that the chances of successful theft are greatly enhanced when a gun is used or the robber has accomplices (Cook 2009).[11] A gun also enhances the amount of loot in those robberies that are successful, in part because gun robbers are able to choose more lucrative targets (couples, males age 25–54), who might otherwise be in a position to defend themselves. This analysis of the payoff to robbery technique can be used to compute the value of using a gun as opposed to, say, a knife. Other things being equal, the likelihood of successful theft increases by 12.5 percentage points, and the average value of loot in successful robberies almost doubles, when compared to using a knife (the second-best weapon alternative from the robber's perspective).

Robbers use different methods for gaining compliance, depending in part on the circumstances. The standard technique in both gun and knife robberies is to threaten without actually attacking (78 percent and 64 percent of gun and knife noncommercial cases, respectively), which is usually sufficient to gain compliance. The standard technique in unarmed robberies or robberies utilizing sticks and clubs is to attack physically (over 60 percent of cases) and then attempt to take the valuables by force. The chances of injury follow the same pattern, ranging from just 11 percent for gun robberies to 36 percent for robberies with clubs.[12] Of course, when a gun is present and fired, the resulting injury is far more likely to be fatal, and the chances that the victim will be killed are highest for gun robberies.

In sum, we postulate that the type of weapon deployed in violent confrontations appears to matter in several ways. Because guns provide the power to kill quickly, at a distance, and without much skill or strength, they also provide the power to intimidate other people and gain control of a violent situation without an actual attack. When there is a physical attack, then the type of weapon is an important determinant of whether the victim survives, with guns far more lethal than other commonly used weapons.

Availability

Perhaps the question of primary interest to individual citizens is whether guns make the owners and members of their household more or less safe. Several studies have demonstrated that a gun in the home is far more likely to end up being used to kill a member of the household (including suicide) than to kill or injure an intruder (Hemenway 2004, chap. 5). But that comparison is not exactly on point: the number of intruders who are shot understates the total number of instances in which an intruder is repelled or scared off. If guns in the home are dangerous to its occupants on balance, then we would predict that people who are victimized in their homes would be more likely to have a gun than non-victims, other things equal. This prediction has been tested by use of case-control studies that compare gun ownership rates of homicide victims with those of neighbors who share similar sociodemographic characteristics (Kellermann et al. 1993). But it is not clear that these studies have really controlled for other relevant factors. Another problem is that the indicators of gun ownership used in these studies (reports by neighbors or others) may be confounded by what people know about the lethal event itself.

A more subtle concern with case-control studies is that they ignore the possibility that individual gun ownership affects other people in the community. These external effects could be salutary, if widespread gun ownership deters criminals; or negative, if widespread ownership facilitates diversion to criminal use through theft and secondary sales. Hence it is important to assess the effects of overall rates of gun ownership within a community.

One way to learn about the effects of community gun prevalence on crime is to compare crime rates across jurisdictions that have different rates of gun ownership. Because there are no administrative data on gun owner-ship rates, small-area estimates must utilize a proxy. The best generally available proxy for gun prevalence is the fraction of suicides that involve a firearm (FSS), which is highly correlated with survey-based measures of gun ownership rates in cross-section data (at both the state and county level) and also tracks movements over time at the regional and state levels (Azrael, Cook, and Miller 2004; Kleck 2004; Cook and Ludwig 2006a).

Several studies report a strong positive correlation between the FSS proxy and homicide rates across counties (Cook and Ludwig 2002; Miller, Azrael, and Hemenway 2002).[13] However, the fundamental problem with cross-sectional studies is that gun-rich jurisdictions, such as Mississippi, are systematically different in various ways from jurisdictions with relatively few guns, such as Massachusetts. The usual approach for addressing this "apples and oranges" problem has been to statistically control for measured local-area characteristics, such as population density, poverty, and the age and racial composition of the population. But these variables never explain very much of the cross-sectional variation in crime rates (Glaeser, Sacerdote, and Scheinkman 1996), suggesting that the list of control variables is inadequate to the task. Also unclear is whether widespread gun ownership is cause or effect of an area's crime problem, since high crime rates may induce residents to buy guns for self-protection. These same concerns are arguably even more severe with cross-sectional comparisons across countries.

Some of the problems with cross-sectional studies can be overcome by using panel data—repeated cross-sections of city, county, or state data measured at multiple points in time—to compare *changes* in gun ownership with *changes* in crime. Compared with Massachusetts, the state of Mississippi may have much higher homicide rates year after year for reasons that cannot be fully explained by standard socio-demographic or other variables. But by comparing changes across areas, we implicitly control for any unmeasured differences across areas that are relatively fixed over time, such as a "Southern culture of violence" (see Butterfield 1996; Loftin, McDowall, Wiersema, and Cottey 1991). The best available panel-data evidence suggests that more guns lead to more homicides, which is driven entirely by a relationship between gun prevalence and homicides committed with firearms; there is little association of gun prevalence with non-gun homicides or other types of crimes (Duggan 2001; Cook and Ludwig 2006b). We should note that recent empirical estimates are not unanimous on this point: John Lott (2000) comes to the opposite conclusion, although we put more weight on the other studies because of problems with Lott's data and methods (see Cook and Ludwig 2006b).

An alternative approach for learning about the effects of gun availability on public health and safety is to examine the effects of policy changes that influence overall gun ownership rates. While these policy experiments have commanded a great deal of public attention, they are not very informative about the effects of widespread gun availability on violence, primarily because even outright bans on handguns have surprisingly modest effects on gun ownership rates (Cook and Ludwig 2006b).

One important question remains. While the general availability of guns appears to influence the choice of weapons in violent crime, and the likelihood that a violent crime will result in the victim's death, does gun availability influence the overall *volume* of violent crime? The available evidence provides little reason to believe that robbery and assault rates are much affected by the prevalence of gun ownership (Cook 1979; Kleck and Patterson 1993). The fact that the United States is such a violent country[14] does not have much to do with guns; the fact that our violent crimes are so deadly has much to do with guns (Zimring and Hawkins 1997).

THE VALUES AT STAKE

A gun provides recreation, food, and, arguably, a way of learning a sense of responsibility. When kept behind the counter of a small grocery in a high-crime neighborhood, a gun may help stiffen the owner's resolve to stay in business while serving as part of the informal social-control system for local youth. When used as an instrument of gang warfare, a gun becomes part of the nation's nightmare of crime that terrorizes urban residents and cuts short far too many lives.

These different uses of guns all have value to those who use them in these ways. Society as a whole, however, values some uses less highly than do the individual owners. The "Great American Gun War" is an ongoing debate and political struggle to determine which uses will be protected, and which sacrificed to achieve some greater social good. There is widespread consensus that disarming the gangs would be a step in the right direction (a conclusion that the gang members themselves may or may not agree with), but the social value of preserving current opportunities for self-defense and sporting use is far more controversial.

Gun control advocates typically argue their case both by pointing to the reductions in fatalities engendered by the proposed reform and by insisting that gun owners, as a matter of principle, should be willing to relinquish some of their rights to own guns in the interests of achieving these benefits. The opponents of gun control argue that gun ownership serves to reduce crime rather than increase it, and that in any event they have a constitutional right to own guns.

The Public Health Perspective

Public health advocates are primarily concerned with the loss of life and limb caused by the use of guns against people. They are not much concerned with whether any particular shooting is criminal or not; all loss of life is equally serious. Thus lives lost to gun accident, suicide, and criminal homicide are of equal public concern (Moore et al 1994).

Assigning suicide the same importance as homicide is profoundly important in evaluating the gun "problem." There are more gun deaths from suicide than homicide, and the demographic incidence of suicide is quite different than homicide.[15] Looking at homicide statistics, we conclude that guns are a far greater problem in cities than elsewhere, especially in minority communities, and we are led to focus gun-control efforts there. But including suicide as an equally important prevention target suggests that guns are a major problem in suburban and rural areas as well, posing a considerable threat to older whites as well as to black and Hispanic youths (Cook and Ludwig 2000).

The public-health argument is that a proposed control measure should reduce the incidence of injury and death. There is little concern with the value of sporting uses of guns. From this perspective, the modest pleasures associated with recreational shooting and the dubious benefits from self-defense should yield to society's overwhelming interest in reducing gun deaths. Preserving life is the paramount value in this scheme.[16]

The Welfare Economics Framework

Welfare economists argue that the gun "problem" involves harm inflicted on others, with much less attention to suicides and self-inflicted accidents. There is no presumption that punishing criminal uses is an adequate response, and there remains the possibility that the benefits of preemptive controls on guns, such as a ban on carrying concealed weapons, would outweigh the costs (Cook and Leitzel 1996). The costs of such controls include the public costs of enforcement and the private costs of compliance (or evasion) of these regulations.

In principle we could determine whether a particular gun-oriented measure is worthwhile by comparing the cost with the benefits stemming from whatever reductions in gun crime are accomplished. A direct comparison requires that benefits be expressed in monetary terms, and since much of the value of living in a safer community is subjective, this translation requires an assessment of preferences. In that spirit, Cook and Ludwig (2000) asked respondents from a national sample how much they would be willing to pay for a reduction in their community's gun-violence rate of 30 percent. Based on their responses, the authors estimated that such a reduction would be worth about $24 billion nationwide.

In this calculus of cost and benefit, where does self-defense fit in? For most gun owners, the possibility that the gun will prove useful in fending off a robber or burglar is one source of its value.[17] Indeed, if guns had no value in self-protection, a ban on possession of guns in the home would quite likely be worthwhile, since other, sporting uses of guns could be preserved by allowing people to store firearms in shooting clubs and use them under regulated conditions. This arrangement would be akin to the military policy for controlling the use of rifles and ammunition by servicemen on military bases, and is somewhat more liberal than the current policy governing fireworks in most states (and far looser than policies regulating the distribution of high explosives). We believe that the self-defense uses of guns are more important than sporting uses in assessing the costs of restrictions on home possession and carrying in urban areas. Note that the home defense use figured centrally in the *Heller v. District of Columbia* (2008) decision of the U.S. Supreme Court.

The "Rights and Responsibilities" Perspective

The welfare-economics framework helps organize the arguments pro and con for gun controls, and suggests a procedure for assigning values. But for those who believe in the "right" to bear arms, it is not a completely satisfactory approach. The debate over gun control can and should be conducted, at least in part, in the context of a framework that defines the appropriate relationship between the individual, the community, and the state.

Very much in the foreground of this debate lies the Second Amendment, which states, "A well regulated Militia, being necessary to the security of a free State, the right of the people to keep and bear Arms, shall not be infringed." The proper interpretation of this statement has been contested in recent years. Some scholars focus on the militia clause, and conclude that this is a right given to state governments (Henigan 1991; Wills 1995). Others assert that the right is given to "the people" rather than to the states, just as are the rights conferred in the First Amendment, and that the Founding Fathers were committed to the notion of an armed citizenry as a defense against both tyranny and crime (Kates 1983, 1992; Halbrook 1986; van Alstyne 1994).[18] The Supreme Court ruled in limited support of this latter view in the case of *Heller v. District of Columbia* (2008). This ruling found that trustworthy citizens had the right to keep a handgun in their home for the purpose of self-defense against crime. The focus on crime rather than tyranny creates a "demilitarized" reading of the Second Amendment (Cook, Ludwig, and Samaha 2009) with limited application.

In any event, the newly minted individual right to bear arms, like the right of free speech, is not absolute, but subject to reasonable restrictions, as spelled out by the majority in *Heller* (Cook, Ludwig and Samaha 2009). The appropriate extent of those restrictions, however, remains an unresolved issue.

A POLICY ANALYSIS

Commerce in guns and the possession and use of guns are regulated by federal, state, and local governments. To assess the options for reform, it is first helpful to understand the current array of controls and why they fail to achieve an acceptably low rate of gun violence.

The Current Array of Policies

The primary objective of federal law in this area is to insulate the states from one another, so that the stringent regulations on firearms commerce adopted in some states are not undercut by the greater availability of guns in other states. The citizens of rural Wyoming understandably favor a more permissive system than those living in Chicago, and both can be accommodated if transfers between them are effectively limited. The Gun Control Act of 1968 established the framework for the current system of controls on gun transfers. All shipments of firearms (including mail-order sales) are limited to federally licensed dealers who are required to obey applicable state and local ordinances, and to observe certain restrictions on sales of guns to out-of-state residents.[19]

Federal law also seeks to establish a minimum set of restrictions on acquisition and possession of guns. The Gun Control Act specifies several categories of people who are denied the right to receive or possess a gun, including illegal aliens, convicted felons and those under indictment, people ever convicted of an act of domestic violence, users of illicit drugs, and those who have at some time been involuntarily committed to a mental institution. Federally licensed dealers may not sell handguns to people younger than 21, or long guns to those younger than 18. And dealers are required to ask for identification from all would-be buyers, have them sign a form indicating that they do not have any of the characteristics that would place them in the "proscribed" category, and initiate a criminal-history check. Finally, dealers are required to keep a record of each completed sale and to cooperate with authorities who seek to trace the sequence of ownership of guns used in crime.

In addition to these federal requirements, states have adopted significant restrictions on commerce, possession, and use of firearms. A number of states require that handgun buyers obtain a permit or license before taking possession of a handgun, a process that may entail payment of a fee and some waiting period. All but a few state transfer-control systems are "permissive," in the sense that most people are legally entitled to obtain a gun. In a few jurisdictions, however, it is very difficult to obtain a handgun legally. In Chicago, only law enforcement officers and security guards are eligible to obtain a handgun. A variety of more modest restrictions on commerce have been enacted as well: for example, several states have limited dealers to selling no more than one handgun a month to any one buyer.

State and local legislation tends to make a sharp distinction between keeping a gun in one's home or business and carrying a gun in public. Every state except Vermont and Alaska either bans carrying a concealed firearm or requires a special license or permit. Local ordinances typically place additional restrictions on carrying and discharging guns inside city limits.

Some types of firearms are regulated more stringently than others in federal and state law. The National Firearms Act of 1934 mandated registration and a $200 tax on all transfers of gangster-style firearms, including sawed-off shot-guns and automatic weapons (such as the Tommy gun); more recently, Congress has prohibited the manufacture of such weapons. The Gun Control Act of 1968 banned the import of small, cheap handguns,[20] and subsequent legislation banned the importation and manufacture of certain "assault" weap-ons (Roth and Koper 1997)—although that ban was allowed to expire in 2004. States typically regulate handguns more closely than long guns, since the former account for most of the firearms used in crime.

In searching for worthwhile reforms, we find it useful to classify alternative gun-control measures into three generic strategies (cf., Zimr-ing 1991; Wintemute 2000):

1. Those designed to raise the price of guns and reduce general availability
2. Those designed to influence who has these weapons
3. Those designed to affect how the guns are used and with what effect.

We offer a general assessment of each of these strategies below.

Strategy 1: Raising the Price, Reducing Availability

Many gun-control measures have an effect on the overall supply of guns or ammunition. If guns (or ammunition) become less readily available, or more expensive to purchase, then some violence-prone people will arguably decide to rely on other weapons instead, and gun violence will be reduced.

Commentators have suggested that this strategy is doomed by the huge arsenal of guns currently in private hands. How can we discourage dangerous people from obtaining guns when there are already enough in circulation to arm every teenager and adult in the country (Wilson 1994; Polsby 1994; Wright 1995)? In response, we note that the number of guns in circulation is only indirectly relevant to whether supply restrictions can hope to succeed; of direct consequence is the price and difficulty of obtaining a gun.

Basic economic reasoning suggests that if the price of new guns is increased by raising the federal tax or other means, the effects will ripple through all the markets in which guns are transferred, including the black market for stolen guns (Cook and Leitzel 1996). If the average prices of guns go up, some people—including some violence-prone people—will decide that there are better uses for their money. Others will be discouraged if, in addition to raising the money price, the amount of time or risk required to obtain a gun increases. While there are no reliable estimates of the elasticity of demand for guns by violence-prone people, we submit that they are likely to be more responsive to price than to more remote costs (such as the possibility of arrest and punishment). Those who argue that offenders will do whatever is necessary to obtain their guns may have some hard-core group of violent gang members and drug dealers in mind, but surely not the much larger group who get into fights from time to time (Sheley and Wright 1995; Smith 1996; Cook et al. 2007).[21]

The discussion in the previous section on the effects of availability noted the strong evidence indicating that the prevalence of gun ownership in a jurisdiction differs widely across regions, states, and local jurisdictions. This variation is highly correlated to gun carrying, weapon choice in violent crime, and homicide rates (Cook and Ludwig 2004, 2006). More telling with respect to causality, intertemporal variation in gun prevalence is closely followed by variation in homicide rates. But are there feasible methods for reducing prevalence or for raising prices and reducing prevalence?

Some jurisdictions have adopted regulations that are intended to reduce the overall prevalence of handguns, either through a ban on acquiring such guns (Chicago, District of Columbia) or by restrictive licensing (New York City). Ordinances of this sort are being litigated under the theory that Second Amendment protections (as defined in the *Heller* decision) should extend to the states and localities. In any event, it is not clear that they have been effective in reducing overall prevalence (Cook and Ludwig 2006b).

An indirect approach to raising prices is to impose safety requirements on gun manufacturers (Cook 1981). Proposals in this area include "child-proofing" guns so that they are inoperable by children; requiring that domestically manufactured guns meet the same safety requirements as imports, including protections against accidental discharge; and requiring safety devices such as trigger locks and loaded chamber indicators (Teret and Wintemute 1993). Under current laws, firearms manufacturers are remarkably free of safety regulation, in part because the Consumer Product Safety Commission has no authority over personal firearms. While safety regulations may be welcomed by gun buyers worried about gun accidents, they would have little direct effect on suicide and criminal misuse of firearms. To the extent that such regulations made guns more costly, however, there could be some indirect effect, comparable to raising the federal tax (Cook and Leitzel 1996).

The argument against requiring that new guns meet minimum design standards follows from the fact that such standards would take the cheapest guns off the market, thus making it more costly for poor households to enjoy whatever protection a gun conveys. Since it is the poorest households that generally face the greatest threat from predatory crime, this argument is not easily dismissed.

Finally, both government and nonprofit groups have shown enthusiasm for reducing availability through gun buy-back programs. Research on these programs, which are typically short-duration offers of cash or goods in exchange for guns, has suggested that these approaches are not effective at reducing gun violence (Kennedy, Piehl, and Braga 1996a; Romero, Wintemute, and Vernick 1998; Rosenfeld 1996). There is even a theoretical possibility that a permanent gun buy-back policy might increase the prevalence of gun ownership because by increasing the resale value of the gun, it would reduce the cost of owning one for a while (Mullin 2001). But a note of caution is in order. The effects of a gun buy-back will likely depend on the circumstances. Australia's 1997 buy-back of semi-automatic rifles may constitute a best-case scenario; in that case, the buy-back was a prelude to a near-comprehensive ban on private ownership of these weapons. Thus owners could not exploit the buy-back to exchange their old gun for a new one, nor were the sellers to the buy-back limited to those who had no further use for the weapon. There is some evidence that in this ideal case, the buy-back saved lives (Reuter and Mouzos 2003).

Strategy 2: Restricting Access

The second broad class of gun-control policy instruments are those designed to influence who has access to different kinds of weapons. The intuitive notion here is that if we could find a way to keep guns out of the hands of the "bad guys" without denying access to the "good guys," then gun crimes would fall without infringing on the legitimate uses of guns. The challenges for this type of policy are, first, to decide where to draw the line and, second, to develop effective barriers to prevent guns from crossing this line.

Who should be trusted with a gun? Federal law is guided by the premise that owning a gun is a right granted to all adults[22] who are legal residents of the United States, unless they do something to disqualify themselves, such as committing a serious crime. A quite different approach would be to treat gun ownership as a privilege, as is the case, say, with driving a vehicle on public highways.[23] And as in the case of the driving privilege, one requirement for those who seek to acquire a gun is that they demonstrate knowledge of how to use it safely and legally.[24] It is an intriguing possibility that such a requirement would engender considerable growth in the National Rifle Association's safety training programs, since many of those wishing to qualify for a license would need to enroll in such a course (Moore 1983).

Wherever the line is drawn, there is the serious problem of defending it against illegal transfers. That task is currently being done very poorly indeed. There is mounting evidence that illegal gun transfers in the United States not only arm our domestic criminals, but also arm drug traffickers, violent gangs, and other criminals in Mexico, Canada, and other foreign countries (see, e.g., Cook, Cukier, and Krause 2009). The major gun market loopholes stem from scofflaw dealers, the difficulty in screening out ineligible buyers, and, most important, a vigorous and largely unregulated secondary market in which used guns change hands. We discuss each of these three areas in turn.

Scofflaw and Negligent Dealers.   Licensed dealers' access to large numbers of firearms makes them a particular threat to public safety when they fail to comply with the law (Braga, Cook, Kennedy, and Moore 2002; Wachtel 1998). A review of ATF firearms-trafficking investigations revealed that corrupt licensed dealers were involved in under 10 percent of the trafficking investigations but were responsible for the illegal diversion of nearly half of the total number of firearms trafficked in the ATF investigations (ATF 2000b). The average number of guns trafficked by a corrupt licensed dealer in any one case was over 350. These dealers were engaged in an assortment of violations, including making false entries in their record books, selling firearms "off the books," knowingly transferring firearms to convicted felons, conducting illegal out-of-state sales, and illegally selling National Firearms Act weapons such as machine guns, grenades, and sawed-off shotguns.

ATF's efforts are now guided in part by the results of systematic data on the origins of guns used in crime. Police departments submit confiscated guns to ATF for tracing. The tracing process is cumbersome since there is no central database on gun sales, and only about half of all trace requests are successful to the point of identifying the dealer who first sold the gun at retail (Cook and Braga 2001). Nonetheless these trace data have proven useful in pinpointing targets for investigation. Analysis of trace data has determined that some dealers are greatly overrepresented as a source of crime guns—in 1998, for example, just 1.2 percent of dealers accounted for 57 percent of all traced firearms. This concentration is explained only in part by differences in sales volume (Bureau of Alcohol, Tobacco and Firearms, 2000a).

Screening. The Brady Handgun Violence Prevention Act, implemented in 1994, required that anyone seeking to buy a handgun from a dealer submit to a criminal-history background check. (Beginning in 1998 the background-check requirement was expanded to include transfers of rifles and shotguns.) A number of states also impose more stringent require-ments for handgun transfers, including a waiting period and a more thorough check of records. If the dealer complies with this requirement, there is some chance that disqualified buyers will be identified and screened out. But the reliability of the screening process in identifying proscribed applicants is limited by the generally poor quality of criminal history records and inaccessibility of mental health records, and by the fact that in most jurisdictions would-be buyers are identified only through a driver's license or other document that is readily forged.

Nonetheless, studies of California data suggest that the screening pro-cess in that state has been effective in keeping guns out of the hands of some violent criminals (Wright et al. 1999; Wintemute et al. 1999). And our experience with Brady background checks certainly demonstrates that a considerable number of proscribed people do attempt to buy hand-guns from licensed dealers without concealing their identity: between 1994 and 1998, Brady background checks resulted in about 320,000 requests for purchase being denied, with 220,000 of the rejections due to prior felony convictions or pending indictments (Bureau of Justice Statistics 1999). Other would-be handgun purchasers may have been discouraged from trying, knowing that they would be blocked as a result of the background check.

Realistically, however, there is no guarantee that those who were prevented from purchasing a handgun from a dealer remained unarmed. They could buy one in the secondary market from an acquaintance or unlicensed dealer. Alternatively, they can buy from a licensed dealer by use of a qualified "straw man" purchaser, or perhaps find a licensed dealer who is willing to sell guns off the books. According to one evaluation, the direct effect of the Brady Act on homicide rates was statistically negligible (Ludwig and Cook 2000). Closing the secondary-market loophole may be a necessary precondition for effective screening.

Laws that prohibit certain individuals from owning firearms also per-tain to ammunition. Whereas retail sales of firearms to criminals are regularly disrupted by instant background checks, sales of ammunition are essentially unchecked, and the rate at which criminals acquire ammu-nition is largely unknown. However, a recent study conducted criminal background checks on individuals purchasing ammunition in the City of Los Angeles in April and May 2004 (Tita, Braga, Ridgeway, and Pierce

2006). Nearly 3 percent of ammunition purchasers had a prior felony conviction or another condition that prohibited them from possessing ammunition. During the study period, prohibited possessors purchased more than 10,000 rounds of ammunition in Los Angeles. These estimates suggest that monitoring ammunition transactions may help reduce the supply of ammunition to criminals and the frequency of injuries from felonious gun assaults. Such a record can also provide information for generating leads on illegal firearm possession.

Secondary Markets.   There is a remarkably active and open market for used guns, which is largely unregulated, a market where buyers and sellers find each other through word of mouth, the Internet, classified ads, or gun shows. These transactions, constituting 30 to 40 percent of all firearms transactions (Cook and Ludwig 1996), are often entirely legal—someone who sells a gun or two on occasion is not subject to any federal requirements except that they not knowingly sell to a felon, a minor, or other person prohibited from possessing a gun.

This legal loophole could be closed by a requirement that all transactions be processed through a licensed dealer (or a law-enforcement agency) and include the same record-keeping and background-check requirements as the sale of a gun by a dealer. However, compliance with this requirement would likely be low unless there were some incentive to sellers or buyers. In the case of motor vehicles, the registration requirement coupled with liability serves that purpose (Cook, Molliconi, and Cole 1995), and could conceivably be applied to firearms, although there are a number of practical concerns about this arrangement (Jacobs and Potter 1995, 1998). A requirement that sellers at gun shows conduct background checks of would-be buyers is a modest step in the right direction, recently adopted by several states.

The importance of licensed dealers in supplying crime guns has been established on the basis of analyses of firearms trace data. The rather surprising finding is that guns recovered by the police are not representative of the stock of guns in private hands; a relatively large percentage are quite new, although rarely in the hands of the person who is recorded as the original buyer (Zimring 1976; Cook and Braga 2001; ATF 1997). That, together with other information, suggests that many of the guns used in crime may have moved rather directly from dealer to criminal user, by way of a straw purchase or trafficker. That evidence suggests that the supply of guns to crime can be curtailed by closer regulation of dealers (as explained above), as well as such measures as requiring that dealers report multiple purchases, and the prohibition adopted by several states on selling more than one handgun to a customer per month. Indeed, "one gun a month" laws in Virginia and Maryland caused the number of guns recovered in Washington, D.C., with Virginia and Maryland origins to drop dramatically, though the number of crime guns recovered from other source states increased (Weil and Knox 1996; Teret et al. 1998).

Reducing theft may be more difficult, yet with over 500,000 guns a year being transferred this way each year (Cook and Ludwig 1996), it is just as important. To shrink this source of crime guns, it may be possible to impose some obligation on gun dealers and gun owners to store their weapons securely (as we now do on pharmacists who sell abusable drugs), or to step up enforcement against "fences" who happen to deal in stolen guns.

There is evidence that some of the thefts supplying criminal use are organized (Braga, Cook, Kennedy, and Moore 2002). More than a quarter of ATF gun-trafficking investigations involved the theft of firearms from residences, licensed dealers, and common carriers (such as the United Parcel Service) (ATF 2000b). Organized rings of thieves that specialized in stealing firearms often characterized these cases. To the extent that stolen guns are channeled to the street through theft rings and fences, law enforcement agencies can work to identify these criminal networks (through informants, proffers to criminals caught in the possession of stolen guns, and the like) and disrupt these supply lines.

A technological "fix" for gun theft may be feasible. If guns were designed so that they were "personalized," then their value to thieves would be reduced to an extent that depends on the cost of "re-keying" them. If the personalization device is readily replaced, as is the case, say, for motor vehicles today, then theft would remain an important source of guns to proscribed users. But if the device were costly to re-key, or the re-keying process were only accessible through specially authorized dealers, then theft of new guns would cease to be a problem (Cook and Leitzel 2002).

Interdicting transfers *within* the illicit sector has been a low-priority mission for most police departments. Because there has been so little experience with local investigations directed at stopping the redistribution of guns among youths, drug dealers, and others in the illicit sector, it is not clear what can be accomplished in this arena. The analogy to drug enforcement may provide some guidance (Koper and Reuter 1996). But gun markets appear quite different from heroin and cocaine markets for several reasons.

First, the supply of guns to this market is diffuse, involving myriad potential sellers who enter the market when they happen to have an extra gun or two, rather than the more concentrated illicit supply system that characterizes the cocaine and heroin markets. Every burglar who steals a gun then has the opportunity to become a dealer for the purpose of disposing of the gun, selling to other youth they know. Alternatively, they may sell to middlemen, including drug dealers. And police investigations occasionally turn up a licensed dealer who has been active in making illicit sales. But it appears that the bulk of the sales in the black market are by people who have no commitment to this line of business.

Second, because guns are a durable good, and are both purchased and used less frequently than drugs, the total number of transactions in the market is much smaller than in the illicit drug market (Koper and Reuter 1996). There are also fewer repeat buyers. This means that the illicit gun markets are less visible than drug markets in local communities, but relatively easy to penetrate by the police informants and undercover agents.

Third, because in most areas there is a large legal market standing alongside the illicit market, the prices that can be charged in the illicit market are typically lower than in other markets for guns, just as is true for stolen jewelry or televisions. The exception may be in very tight control jurisdictions, such as New York and Boston, where prices are apparently high enough to motivate a good deal of gun running from jurisdictions with weaker controls. There is some evidence that these gun-running operations tend to be small (Moore 1981). More than 40 percent of ATF gun-trafficking investigations involved the illegal diversion of 10 guns or less (ATF 2000b).

Thus, the illicit gun market appears to be made up for the most part of relatively small and unspecialized enterprises, with easy entry and exit. While shutting down particular trafficking operations may be of little consequence in such a regime, law-enforcement efforts directed at illicit trafficking can be effective to the extent that they discourage entry by creating a general deterrent. The potential for attacking the secondary market in guns has scarcely been tested, and until it is tested in systematic fashion, no firm conclusions are warranted.[25]

Strategy 3: Controlling Uses

The third broad class of gun-control-policy instruments is concerned with limiting unsafe and criminal uses of guns. These include both design regulation and law enforcement.

Design regulation has been discussed at several points above; federal law currently limits commerce in sawed-off shotguns, fully automatic guns, and some types of "assault" weapons, and the list could be extended in various ways (Wintemute 1996; Teret et al. 1998). For example, certain small cheaply made guns, often called "Saturday night specials," are banned from importation by the federal Gun Control Act of 1968, but domestic manufacturers have been free to make such guns. Maryland has banned a list of such domestic guns since 1988, apparently with substantial effect (Vernick, Webster, and Hepburn 1999), and other states are now considering legislation of this sort.

A number of commentators have pointed out the logic in treating guns the same as most other consumer products, which are subject to ongoing review and regulation by federal agencies including the Consumer Product Safety Commission and the National Highway Traffic Safety Administration (Bonnie, Fulco, and Liverman 1999). Again, by analogy to other products, it seems appropriate that this type of design regulation be supplemented by the threat of civil liability for unsafe design.

The criminal law and enforcement do play a prominent role in deterring the misuse of firearms. Most prominent are sentencing-enhancement provisions for the use of a gun in crime. One clear advantage of this approach as compared with other gun policies is that it does not impinge on legitimate uses of guns. One analysis of crime trends in jurisdictions that adopted such sentencing provisions provides evidence that they can be effective in reducing the homicide rate, although there is no consensus on this matter (McDowall, Loftin, and Wiersema 1992b).[26]

Another and more controversial tactic is to focus local law-enforcement efforts on illegal possession and carrying. This sort of gun enforcement typically requires proactive policing, and police departments differ widely in how much effort they direct to halting illegal possession and gun carrying (Moore 1980). The controversy over enforcement stems in part from the concern that police, if sufficiently motivated, may conduct illegal searches in the effort to get guns off the street. Nonetheless, gun-oriented patrol tactics have the potential to reduce gun violence (Sherman and Rogan 1995; Fagan, Zimring, and Kim 1998; Sherman 2000).

It turns out that illegal gun use is highly concentrated in crime "hot spots" (Sherman, Gartin, and Buerger 1989) spread across city landscapes. For instance, Braga, Hureau, and Winship (2008) found that gun violence hot spots covered only 5 percent of Boston's 48.4 square miles, but generated nearly 53 percent of fatal and non-fatal shootings in 2006. The spatial concentration of gun violence remained remarkably stable over time; only 5 percent of street corners and block faces in Boston accounted for 74 percent of all shootings in the city between 1980 and 2008 (Braga, Papachristos, and Hureau, 2010).

The best scientific evidence suggests that taking a focused approach to high-crime places works. A systematic review of randomized controlled experiments and quasi-experiments on concentrating police resources on criminally active places found the approach was effective in preventing crime without simply displacing crime to nearby locations (Braga 2001, 2005). The National Research Council's Committee to Review Research on Police Policy and Practices concluded that taking a focused geographic approach to crime problems can increase policing effectiveness in reducing crime and disorder (Skogan and Frydl 2004).[27]

The best known of the deterrence-based strategies to reduce illicit gun use is the Boston Gun Project. Beginning in 1995, an interagency working group composed of Harvard University researchers, members of the Boston Police Department, and other criminal justice agencies conducted research and analysis on Boston's youth violence problem, designed a problem-solving intervention to reduce youth violence, and implemented the intervention. The research showed that the problem of youth violence in Boston was concentrated among a small number of serially offending gang-involved youth (Kennedy, Piehl, and Braga 1996b; Kennedy, Braga, and Piehl, 1997). The key problem-solving intervention that arose from the research diagnoses was known as the "pulling levers" focused deterrence strategy. This approach involved deterring violent behavior by chronic gang offenders by reaching out directly to gangs, saying explicitly that violence would no longer be tolerated, and backing that message by "pulling every law enforcement lever" legally available when violence occurred (Kennedy 1997, 1998).

The "pulling levers" approach attempted to prevent gang violence by making gang members believe that gun use by any one member of the gang would result in legal problems for all members. The intent was to create an incentive for gang members to discourage each other from gunplay, thus reversing the usual group norm in support of violence. A key element of the strategy was the delivery of a direct and explicit "retail deterrence" message to a relatively small target audience regarding what kind of behavior would provoke a special response and what that response would be. The deterrence message was delivered by talking to gang members on the street, handing out fliers in the hot spot areas explaining the enforcement actions, and organizing forums between violent gang members and members of the interagency working group (Kennedy 1997, 1998). An evaluation of the Boston strategy to prevent youth violence found it to be associated with significant decreases in youth homicides, shots fired, and gun assaults (Braga et al. 2001; Piehl et al. 2003).[28]

A number of cities have begun to experiment with these analytic frameworks, and a very promising body of evaluation evidence is accumulating. Consistent with the problem-solving approach, these cities have tailored the strategy to fit their violence problems and operating environments. Including the Boston experience, six quasi-experimental evaluations have now been completed that support the gun violence reduction benefits associated with these focused approaches. These cities include: Chicago (Papachristos et al. 2007); Indianapolis (McGarrell et al. 2006); Los Angeles (Tita et al. 2004); Lowell, Massachusetts (Braga et al. 2008); and Stockton, California (Braga 2008).

Finally, several jurisdictions have implemented specialized courts for firearms-related offenses, based on the premise that deterrence is enhanced when punishment is administered soon after the offense is committed and with a high degree of certainty.

CONCLUSION: WHAT'S TO BE DONE?

Given the important value conflicts and empirical uncertainties surrounding gun-control policies, some caution in recommending public or governmental action is warranted. But recommending caution is far from recommending inaction. Indeed, we think that it is time to get on with the business of actively exploring alternative gun-control initiatives to develop more effective interventions than those we now rely upon. Exploration and experimentation are urgent for several reasons.

It is only through trying alternative approaches that we can hope to develop confident conclusions about what works. Learning from experience is not automatic, but it can happen if reforms are coupled with systematic evaluation. With additional evidence may come a shift in the politics of gun control as well. Currently, advocates on both sides mix value statements concerning rights or social welfare with factual claims concerning potential efficacy. For example, those who assert an individual right to bear arms usually also claim that widespread private ownership of guns reduces crime, implying that the value at stake here (freedom from government interference) can be preserved without social cost. If the factual claims were sufficiently robust that advocates had to accept the fact that their position entailed real costs, we would begin to learn something about how strongly these values are actually held.

Our suggestions are organized according to level of government.

The challenge of finding the best portfolio of gun-control measures is daunting in the face of our considerable uncertainty about what works and the profound disagreements about which values should be paramount. But with continuing attention to the evidence generated by the state and local innovations, and a vigorous public dialogue on the importance of both rights and responsibilities in this arena, there is every hope of doing better.

References

Azrael, Deborah, Philip J. Cook, and Matthew Miller. 2004. "State and Local Prevalence of Firearms Ownership: Measurement, Structure, and Trends" *Journal of Quantitative Criminology* 20: 43–62.

Blackman, Paul H. 1997. "A Critique of the Epidemiologic Study of Firearms and Homicide." *Homicide Studies* 1: 169–89.

Block, Richard. 1993. "A Cross-Section Comparison of the Victims of Crime: Victim Surveys of Twelve Countries." *International Review of Criminology* 2: 183–207.

Bonnie, Richard J., Carolyn E. Fulco, and Catharyn T. Livermore, eds. 1999. *Reducing the Burden of Injury.* Washington, DC: National Academy Press.

Braga, Anthony A. 2001. "The Effects of Hot Spots Policing on Crime." *Annals of the American Academy of Political and Social Science* 578: 104–125.

Braga, Anthony A. 2005. "Hot Spots Policing and Crime Prevention: A Systematic Review of Randomized Controlled Trials." *Journal of Experimental Criminology* 1: 317–342.

Braga, Anthony A. 2008. "Pulling Levers Focused Deterrence Strategies and the Prevention of Gun Homicide." *Journal of Criminal Justice* 36: 332–343.

Braga, Anthony A., Philip J. Cook, David M. Kennedy, and Mark H. Moore. 2002. "The Illegal Supply of Firearms." In *Crime and Justice: A Review of Research*, ed. Michael Tonry, *vol. 29.* Chicago: University of Chicago Press.

Braga, Anthony A., David Hureau, and Christopher Winship. 2008. "Losing Faith? Police, Black Churches, and the Resurgence of Youth Violence in Boston." *Ohio State Journal of Criminal Law* 6: 141–172.

Braga, Anthony A., David M. Kennedy, Elin J. Waring, and Anne M. Piehl. 2001. "Problem-Oriented Policing, Deterrence, and Youth Violence: An Evaluation of Boston's Operation Ceasefire." *Journal of Research in Crime and Delinquency* 38: 195–225.

Braga, Anthony, Andrew V. Papachristos, and David Hureau. (2010). "The Concentration and Stability of Gun Violence at Micro-Places in Boston, 1980–2008," *Journal of Quantitative Criminology*, 26, 1: 33–53.

Braga, Anthony A. and Glenn L. Pierce. 2005. "Disrupting Illegal Firearms Markets in Boston: The Effects of Operation Ceasefire on the Supply of New Handguns to Criminals." *Criminology & Public Policy* 4: 717–748.

Braga, Anthony A., Glenn L. Pierce, Jack McDevitt, Brenda J. Bond, and Shea Cronin. 2008. "The Strategic Prevention of Gun Violence among Gang-Involved Offenders." *Justice Quarterly* 25: 132–162.

Bureau of Alcohol, Tobacco, and Firearms (ATF). 1997. *Crime Gun Trace Analysis Reports: The Illegal Youth Firearms Market in 17 Communities.* Washington, DC: U.S. Department of the Treasury.

Bureau of Alcohol, Tobacco, and Firearms (ATF). 2000a. *Commerce in Firearms in the United States.* Washington, DC: U.S. Department of the Treasury.

Bureau of Alcohol, Tobacco, and Firearms (ATF). 2000b. *Following the Gun: Enforcing Federal Laws Against Firearms Traffickers.* Washington, DC: U.S. Department of the Treasury.

Bureau of Justice Statistics. 1999. *Presale Handgun Checks, the Brady Interim Period, 1994–1998.* Washington, DC: Bureau of Justice Statistics, U.S. Department of Justice.

Butterfield, Fox. 1996. *All God's Children: The Bosket Family and the American Tradition of Violence.* New York: Avon Books.

Conklin, John E. 1972. *Robbery and the Criminal Justice System.* Philadelphia: Lippincott.

Cook, Philip J. 1976. "A Strategic Choice Analysis of Robbery." In *Sample Surveys of the Victims of Crimes,* ed. Wesley Skogan. Cambridge, MA: Ballinger.

Cook, Philip J. 1979. "The Effect of Gun Availability on Robbery and Robbery Murder: A Cross-Section Study of Fifty Cities." *Policy Studies Review Annual* 3. Beverly Hills: Sage.

Cook, Philip J. 1980. "Reducing Injury and Death Rates in Robbery." *Policy Analysis* (Winter): 21–45.

Cook, Philip J. 1981. "The Effect of Gun Availability on Violent Crime Patterns." *Annals of the American Academy of Political and Social Science* 455: 63–79.

Cook, Philip J. 1985. "The Case of the Missing Victims: Gunshot Woundings in the National Crime Survey." *Journal of Quantitative Criminology* 1: 91–102.

Cook, Philip J. 1986. "The Relationship Between Victim Resistance and Injury in Noncommerical Robbery." *Journal of Legal Studies* 15 (1): 405–416.

Cook, Philip J. 1987. "Robbery Violence." *Journal of Criminal Law and Criminology* 78: 357–376.

Cook, Philip J. 1991. "The Technology of Personal Violence." In *Crime and Justice: A Review of Research,* ed. Michael Tonry, *vol. 14.* Chicago: University of Chicago Press.

Cook, Philip J. 2009. "Robbery." In *The Oxford Handbook of Crime and Public Policy,* ed. Michael Tonry. New York: Oxford University Press.

Cook, Philip J., and Anthony A. Braga. 2001. "Comprehensive Firearms Tracing: Strategic and Investigative Uses of New Data on Firearms Markets." *Arizona Law Review* 43 (2): 277–309.

Cook, Philip J., Wendy Cukier, and Keith Krause. 2009. "The Illicit Firearms Trade in North America." *Criminology and Criminal Justice* 9: 265–286.

Cook, Philip J., and John Laub. 1998. "The Unprecedented Epidemic of Youth Violence." In *Youth Violence,* eds. Mark H. Moore and Michael Tonry. Chicago: University of Chicago Press.

Cook, Philip J., and James Leitzel. 1996. "Perversity, Futility, Jeopardy: An Economic Analysis of the Attack on Gun Control." *Law and Contemporary Problems* 59: 91–118.

Cook, Philip J., and James Leitzel. 2002. "'Smart Guns': A Technological Fix for Regulating the Secondary Gun Market." *Contemporary Economic Problems* 20: 38–49.

Cook, Philip J., and Jens Ludwig. 1996. *Guns in America: Results of a Comprehensive National Survey on Firearms Ownership and Use.* Washington, DC: Police Foundation.

Cook, Philip J., and Jens Ludwig. 2000. *Gun Violence: The Real Costs.* New York: Oxford University Press.

Cook, Philip J., and Jens Ludwig. 2002. "Litigation as Regulation: The Case of Firearms." In *Regulation Through Litigation,* ed. W. Kip Viscusi. Washington, DC: Brookings Institution.

Cook, Philip J., and Jens Ludwig. 2003. "Guns and Burglary." In *Evaluating Gun Policy,* eds. Jens Ludwig and Philip J. Cook. Washington, DC: Brookings Institution Press.

Cook, Philip J., and Jens Ludwig. 2004. "Does Gun Prevalence Affect Teen Gun Carrying After All?" *Criminology* 42: 27–54.

Cook, Philip J., and Jens Ludwig. 2006a. "The Social Costs of Gun Ownership." *Journal of Public Economics* 90: 379–391.

Cook, Philip J., and Jens Ludwig. 2006b. "Aiming for Evidence-Based Gun Policy." *Journal of Policy Analysis and Management* 25: 691–735.

Cook, Philip J., Jens Ludwig, and David Hemenway. 1997. "The Gun Debate's New Mythical Number: How Many Defensive Gun Uses Per Year?" *Journal of Policy Analysis and Management* 16: 463–469.

Cook, Philip J., Jens Ludwig, and Adam Samaha. 2009. "Gun Control after *Heller:* Threats and Sideshows from a Social Welfare Perspective." *UCLA Law Review* 56: 1041–1093.

Cook, Philip J., Jens Ludwig, Sudhir Venkatesh, and Anthony A. Braga. 2007. "Underground Gun Markets." *The Economic Journal.* 117 (524) Nov.: 558–588.

Cook, Philip J., Stephanie Molliconi, and Thomas Cole. 1995. "Regulating Gun Markets." *Journal of Criminal Law and Criminology* 86: 59–92.

Duggan, Mark. 2001. "More Guns, More Crime." *Journal of Political Economy* 109: 1086–1114.

Fagan, Jeffrey. 2002. "Policing Guns and Youth Violence." *The Future of Children* 12: 133–151.

Fagan, Jeffrey, Franklin Zimring, and J. Kim. 1998. "Declining Homicide in New York City: A Tale of Two Trends." *Journal of Criminal Law and Criminology* 88: 1277–1323.

Fingerhut, Lois A. 1993. "Firearm Mortality among Children, Youth, and Young Adults 1–34 Years of Age, Trends, and Current Status: United States, 1985–90." *Advance Data from Vital and Health Statistics.* No. 231. Hyattsville, MD: National Center for Health Statistics.

Glaeser, Edward L., Bruce Sacerdote, and Jose Scheinkman. 1996. "Crime and Social Interactions." *Quarterly Journal of Economics* 111: 507–548.

Halbrook, Stephen P. 1986. "What the Framers Intended: A Linguistic Analysis of the Right to 'Bear Arms.'" *Law and Contemporary Problems* 49: 151–62.

Hemenway, David. 1997a. "The Myth of Millions of Self-Defense Gun Uses: An Explanation of Extreme Overestimates." *Chance* 10: 6–10.

Hemenway, David. 1997b. "Survey Research and Self-Defense Gun Use: An Explanation of Extreme Overestimates." *Journal of Criminal Law and Criminology* 87: 1430–1445.

Hemenway, David. 2004. *Private Guns, Public Health.* Ann Arbor: University of Michigan Press.

Henigan, Dennis A. 1991. "Arms, Anarchy and the Second Amendment" *Valparaiso University Law Review* 26: 107–29.

Hepburn, L. M. Miller, D. Azrael and D. Hemenway. 2007. "The US Gun Stock: Results from the 2004 National Firearms Survey." *Injury Prevention* 13: 15–19.

Jacobs, Bruce A. 2000. *Robbing Drug Dealers: Violence Beyond the Law.* Hawthorne, WI: Aldine de Gruyter.

Jacobs, James B., and Kimberly A. Potter. 1995. "Keeping Guns out of the Wrong Hands: The Brady Law and the Limits of Regulation." *Journal of Criminal Law and Criminology* 86: 101–130.

———. 1998. "Comprehensive Handgun Licensing and Registration: An Analysis and Critique of Brady II, Gun Control's Next (and Last?) Step." *Journal of Criminal Law and Criminology* 89: 81–110.

Kates, Don B., Jr. 1983. "Handgun Prohibition and the Original Meaning of the Second Amendment." *Michigan Law Review* 82: 204–273.

Kates, Don B., Jr. 1992. "The Second Amendment and the Ideology of Self-Protection." *Constitutional Commentary* 9: 87–104.

Kellermann, Arthur L. and Philip J. Cook. 1999. "Armed and Dangerous: Guns in America Homes." In *Lethal Imagination: Violence and Brutality in American History*, ed. M.A. Bellesiles. New York: New York University Press.

Kellermann, Arthur L., Frederick P. Rivara, Norman B. Rushforth, Joyce G. Banton, Donald T. Reay, Jerry T. Francisco, Ana B. Locci, Janice Prodzinski, Bela B. Hackman, and Grant Somes. 1993. "Gun Ownership as a Risk Factor for Homicide in the Home." *New England Journal of Medicine* 329: 1084–1091.

Kennedy, David M. 1997. "Pulling Levers: Chronic Offenders, High-Crime Settings, and a Theory of Prevention." *Valparaiso University Law Review* 31: 449–484.

Kennedy, David M. 1998. "Pulling Levers: Getting Deterrence Right." *National Institute of Justice Journal* (July): 3–8.

Kennedy, David M., Anthony A. Braga, and Anne M. Piehl. 1997. "The (Un) Known Universe: Mapping Gangs and Gang Violence in Boston." In *Crime Mapping and Crime Prevention*, eds. David Weisburd and J. Thomas McEwen. New York: Criminal Justice Press.

Kennedy, David. M., Anne M. Piehl, and Anthony A. Braga. 1996a. "Gun Buy-Backs: Where Do We Stand and Where Do We Go?" In *Under Fire: Gun Buy-back, Exchanges, and Amnesty Programs*, ed. Martha Plotkin. Washington, DC: Police Executive Research Forum.

Kennedy, David. M., Anne M. Piehl, and Anthony A. Braga. 1996b. "Youth Violence in Boston: Gun Markets, Serious Youth Offenders, and a Use-Reduction Strategy." *Law and Contemporary Problems* 59: 147–196.

Kennett, Lee B., and James LaVerne Anderson. 1975. *The Gun in America: The Origins of a National Dilemma* Westport, CT: Greenwood Press.

Kleck, Gary. 1984. "Handgun-only Control: A Policy Disaster in the Making." In *Firearms and Violence: Issues of Public Policy*, ed. Don B. Kates, Jr. Cambridge, MA: Ballinger.

Kleck, Gary. 1988. "Crime Control Through the Private Use of Armed Force." *Social Problems* 35: 1–22.

Kleck, Gary. 1991. *Point Blank: Guns and Violence in America*. New York: Aldine de Gruyter.

Kleck, Gary. 2004. "Measures of Gun Ownership Levels for Macrolevel Crime and Violence Research." *Journal of Research in Crime and Delinquency* 41: 3–36.

Kleck Gary, and Marc Gertz. 1995. "Armed Resistance to Crime: The Prevalence and Nature of Self-Defense with a Gun." *Journal of Criminal Law and Criminology* 86: 150–187.

Kleck, Gary, and Karen McElrath. 1991. "The Effects of Weaponry on Human Violence." *Social Forces* 69: 669–692.

Kleck, Gary, and E. Britt Patterson. 1993. "The Impact of Gun Control and Gun Ownership Levels on Violence Rates." *Journal of Quantitative Criminology* 9 (3): 249–287.

Koper, Christoper S., and Peter Reuter. 1996. "Suppressing Illegal Gun Markets: Lessons from Drug Enforcement." *Law and Contemporary Problems* 59: 119–143.

Levitt, Steven D., and Sudhir Alladi Venkatesh. 2000. "An Economic Analysis of a Drug-Selling Gang's Finances." *Quarterly Journal of Economics* 115: 755–790.

Loftin, Colin, David McDowall, Brian Wiersema, and Talbert Cottey. 1991. "Effects of Restrictive Licensing of Handguns on Homicide and Suicide in the District of Columbia." *New England Journal of Medicine* 325: 1625–1630.

Lott, John. 2000. *More Guns, Less Crime*, 2nd ed. Chicago: University of Chicago Press.

Ludwig, Jens, and Philip J. Cook. 2000. "Homicide and Suicide Rates Associated with Implementation of the Brady Handgun Violence Prevention Act." *Journal of the American Medical Assn* 284 (5): 585–591.

Marvell, Thomas, and Carlisle Moody. 1995. "The Impact of Enhanced Prison Terms for Felonies Committed with Guns." *Criminology* 33: 247–281.

McDowall, David, Colin Loftin, and Stanley Presser. 2000. "Measuring Civilian Defensive Firearm Use: A Methodological Experiment." *Journal of Quantitative Criminology* 16: 1–19.

McDowall, David, Colin Loftin, and Brian Wiersema. 1992a. "The Incidence of Civilian Defensive Firearm Use." Institute of Criminology and Criminal Justice, University of Maryland, College Park.

McDowall, David, Colin Loftin, and Brian Wiersema. 1992b. "A Comparative Study of the Preventive Effects of Mandatory Sentencing Laws for Gun Crimes." *Journal of Criminal Law and Criminology* 83 (2): 378–394.

McGarrell, Edmund, Steven Chermak, Jeremy Wilson, and Nicolas Corsaro. 2006. "Reducing Homicide through a 'Lever-Pulling' Strategy." *Justice Quarterly* 23: 214–229.

Milller, Matthew, Deborah Azrael, and David Hemenway. 2002. "Household Firearm Ownership Levels and Homicide Rates Across U.S. Regions and States, 1988–1997." *American Journal of Public Health* 92: 1988–1993.

Monkkonen, Eric H. 2000. *Homicide in New York City*. Berkeley: University of California Press.

Moore, Mark H. 1980. "Police and Weapons Offenses." *Annals of the American Academy of Political and Social Science* 452: 22–32.

Moore, Mark H. 1981. "Keeping Handguns from Criminal Offenders." *Annals of the American Academy of Political and Social Science* 455: 92–109.

Moore, Mark H. 1983. "The Bird in Hand: A Feasible Strategy for Gun Control." *Journal of Policy Analysis and Management* 2 (2): 185–195.

Moore, Mark H., Deborah Prothrow-Stith, Bernard Guyer, and Howard Spivak. 1994. "Violence and Intentional Injuries: Criminal Justice and Public Health Perspectives on an Urgent National Problem." In *Understanding and Preventing Violence*, Vol. 4: *Consequences and Control*, eds. Albert J. Reiss, Jr., and Jeffrey A. Roth. Washington, DC: National Academy Press.

Mullin, Wallace P. 2001. "Will Gun Buyback Programs Increase the Quantity of Guns?" *International Review of Law & Economics* 21: 87–102.

Papachristos, Andrew, Tracey Meares, and Jeffrey Fagan. 2007. "Attention Felons: Evaluating Project Safe Neighborhoods in Chicago." *Journal of Empirical Legal Studies* 4: 223–272.

Piehl, Anne M., Suzanne J. Cooper, Anthony A. Braga, and David M. Kennedy. 2003. "Testing for Structural Breaks in the Evaluation of Programs." *Review of Economics and Statistics* 85: 550–558.

Pierce, Glenn L., Anthony A. Braga, Raymond R. Hyatt, and Christopher S. Koper. 2004. "The Characteristics and Dynamics of Illegal Firearms Markets: Implications for a Supply-Side Enforcement Strategy." *Justice Quarterly* 21: 391–422.

Polsby, Daniel D. 1994. "The False Promise of Gun Control." *The Atlantic Monthly* (March): 57–60.

Reuter, Peter, and Jenny Mouzos. 2003. "Australia: A Massive Buyback of Low-Risk Guns." In *Evaluating Gun Policy*, eds. Jens Ludwig and Philip J. Cook. Washington, DC: Brookings Institution Press.

Romero, Michael, Garen Wintemute, and Jon Vernick. 1998. "Characteristics of a Gun Exchange Program, and an Assessment of Potential Benefits." *Injury Prevention* 4: 206–210.

Rosenfeld, Richard. 1996. "Gun Buy-Backs: Crime Control or Community Mobilization?" In *Under Fire: Gun Buy-back, Exchanges, and Amnesty Programs*, ed. Martha Plotkin. Washington, DC: Police Executive Research Forum.

Rosenfeld, Richard, Robert Fornango, and Eric Baumer, E. 2005. "Did Ceasefire, Compstat and Exile Reduce Homicide?" *Criminology & Public Policy* 4: 419–450.

Roth, Jeffrey A., and Christopher S. Koper. 1997. *Impact Evaluation of the Public Safety and Recreational Firearms Use Protection Act of 1994*. Washington, DC: The Urban Institute.

Saltzman, Linda E., James A. Mercy, Patrick W. O'Carroll, Mark L. Rosenberg, and P.H. Rhodes. 1992. "Weapon Involvement and Injury Outcomes in Family and Intimate Assaults." *Journal of the American Medical Association* 267: 3043–3047.

Sheley, Joseph F., and James D. Wright. 1995. *In the Line of Fire: Youth, Guns, and Violence in Urban America*. New York: Aldine de Gruyter.

Sherman, Lawrence. 2000. "Gun Carrying and Homicide Prevention." *Journal of the American Medical Association* 283: 1193–1195.

Sherman, Lawrence, Patrick Gartin, and Michael Buerger. 1989. "Hot Spots of Predatory Crime: Routine Activities and the Criminology of Place." *Criminology* 27: 27–55.

Sherman, Lawrence and Dennis Rogan. 1995. "Effects of Gun Seizures on Gun Violence: 'Hot Spots' Patrol in Kansas City." *Justice Quarterly* 12: 673–694.

Skogan, Wesley. 1978. "Weapons Use in Robbery: Patterns and Policy Implications." Center for Urban Affairs, Northwestern University. Unpublished.

Skogan, Wesley, and and Kathleen Frydl, eds. 2004. *Fairness and Effectiveness in Policing: The Evidence.* Washington, DC: The National Academies Press.

Smith, M. Dwayne. 1996. "Sources of Firearms Acquisition among a Sample of Inner-City Youths: Research Results and Policy Implications." *Journal of Criminal Justice* 24: 361–367.

Smith, Tom W. 1997. "A Call for a Truce in the DGU War." *Journal of Criminal Law and Criminology* 87: 1462–1469.

Smith, Tom W. 2000. "1999 National Gun Policy Survey of the National Opinion Research Center: Research Findings." University of Chicago, NORC. Unpublished.

Teret, Stephen P., Susan DeFrancesco, Stephen W. Hargarten, and Krista Robinson. 1998. "Making Guns Safer." *Issues in Science and Technology* (Summer): 37–40.

Teret, Stephen, Daniel Webster, Jon Vernick, Tom Smith, Deborah Leff, Garen Wintemute, Philip Cook, Darnell Hawkins, Arthur Kellerman, Susan Sorenson, and Susan DeFrancesco. 1998. "Support for New Policies to Regulate Firearms: Results of Two National Surveys." *New England Journal of Medicine* 339: 813–818.

Tita, George E., Anthony A. Braga, Greg Ridgeway, and Glenn L. Pierce. 2006. "The Criminal Purchase of Firearm Ammunition." *Injury Prevention* 12: 308–311.

Tita, George E., Kevin Jack Riley, Greg Ridgeway, C. Grammich, Allan Abrahamse, and Peter Greenwood. 2004. *Reducing Gun Violence: Results from an Intervention in East Los Angeles.* Santa Monica, CA: RAND Corporation.

Teret, Stephen P., and Garen J. Wintemute. 1993. "Policies to Prevent Firearm Injuries." *Health Affairs* (Winter): 96–108.

Van Alstyne, William. 1994. "The Second Amendment and the Personal Right to Arms." *Duke Law Journal* 43: 1236–1255.

Vernick, Jon S., Daniel W. Webster, and Lisa M. Hepburn. 1999. "Effects of Maryland's Law Banning Saturday Night Special Handguns on Crime Guns." *Injury Prevention* 5: 259–263.

Wachtel, Julius. 1998. "Sources of Crime Guns in Los Angeles, California." *Policing: An International Journal of Police Strategies and Management* 21 (2): 220–239.

Weil, David, and R. Knox. 1996. "Effects of Limiting Handgun Purchases on Interstate Transfers of Firearms." *Journal of the American Medical Association* 275: 1759–1761.

Wellford, Charles, John V. Pepper, and Carol V. Petrie, eds. 2005. *Firearms and Violence: A Critical Review.* Washington, DC: National Academies Press.

Wills, Garry. 1995. "To Keep and Bear Arms." *New York Review of Books,* September 21.

Wilson, James Q. 1994. "Just Take Their Guns Away: Forget About Gun Control." *New York Times Magazine* (March 20): 46–47.

Wintemute, Garen J. 1996. "The Relationship Between Firearm Design and Firearm Violence: Handguns in the 1990s." *Journal of the American Medical Association* 275: 1749–1753.

Wintemute, Garen J. 2000. "Guns and Gun Violence." In *The Crime Drop in America,* eds. Alfred Blumstein and Joel Wallman. New York: Cambridge University Press.

Wintemute, Garen J., Philip J. Cook, and Mona Wright. 2005. "Risk factors among Handgun Retailers for Frequent and Disproportionate Sales of Guns Used in Violent and Firearm Related Crimes." *Injury Prevention* 11: 357–363.

Wintemute, Garen J., Mona Wright, Carrie Parham, Christina Drake, and James Beaumont. 1999. "Denial of Handgun Purchase: A Description of the Affected Population and a Controlled Study of Their Handgun Preferences." *Journal of Criminal Justice* 27: 21–31.

Wolfgang, Marvin E. 1958. *Patterns in Criminal Homicide.* Philadelphia: University of Pennsylvania.

Wright, James D. 1995. "Ten Essential Observations on Guns in America." *Society* (March/April): 63–68.

Wright, James D., and Peter H. Rossi. 1994. *Armed and Considered Dangerous: A Survey of Felons and Their Firearms,* 2nd ed. Hawthorne, New York: Aldine de Gruyter.

Wright, James D., Peter H. Rossi, and Kathleen Daly. 1983. *Under the Gun: Weapons, Crime, and Violence in America.* Hawthorne, NY: Aldine de Gruyter.

Wright, Mona, Garen Wintemute, and Frederick Rivara. 1999. "The Effectiveness of Denial of Handgun Purchase to Persons Believed to be at High Risk for Firearms Violence." *American Journal of Public Health* 89: 88–90.

Wright, Richard, and Scott H. Decker. 1997. *Armed Robbers in Action.* Boston, MA: Northeastern University Press.

Zimring, Franklin E. 1968. "Is Gun Control Likely to Reduce Violent Killings?" *University of Chicago Law Review* 35: 21–37.

Zimring, Franklin E. 1972. "The Medium Is the Message: Firearm Caliber as a Determinant of Death from Assault." *Journal of Legal Studies* 1: 97–124.

Zimring, Franklin E. 1976. "Street Crime and New Guns: Some Implications for Firearms Control." *Journal of Criminal Justice* 4: 95–107.

Zimring, Franklin E. 1991. "Firearms, Violence, and Public Policy." *Scientific American* 265 (5): 48–54.

Zimring, Franklin E., and Gordon Hawkins. 1997. *Crime Is Not the Problem: Lethal Violence in the United States.* New York and London: Oxford University Press.

Notes

Previous versions of this chapter has been much improved by suggestions from a number of people, including Mark Duggan, Dennis Henigan, James Jacobs, Jens Ludwig, Eric Monkkonen, Jeremy Travis, and Franklin Zimring.

1. It should be kept in mind that these patterns are based on surveys and are subject to potential biases induced by the sensitivity of the topic and the difficulty of contacting a representative sample of young urban males.

2. This survey is conducted annually by the Fish and Wildlife Service of the U.S. Department of the Interior.

3. Much has been made of the unintentional firearm deaths of children; but, tragic as such cases are, it should be noted they are quite rare. Between 1985 and 1990 the annual average number of deaths for children less than 10 years old was 94 (Fingerhut 1993).

4. On the other hand, the demography of gun suicide looks much more like that of gun sports, with victims coming disproportionately from the ranks of older white males.

5. The NCVS may lead to a modest underestimate of the self-defense uses of guns. It only provides respondents an opportunity to say that they used a gun in self-defense if they first say that they were the victims of an assault, robbery, rape, or other crime in which they were present. Respondents may fail to report instances in which they used a gun to scare off a person who intended to steal something from them or attack them, simply because they would not consider themselves as "victims" in that instance. For a further discussion, see Smith (1997).

6. The possibility of false negatives is also increased. But given the rarity of gun use in self-defense, the effect of the two types of error is not symmetric. Even a small false positive rate will have a large effect proportional effect on self-defense uses.

7. It is, after all, a tautology.

8. Kleck, like Wright, Rossi, and Daly (1983), claims that Zimring and others have not succeeded in demonstrating that guns are more lethal than knives, but accept with confidence the claim that long guns are more lethal than handguns. See Cook (1991) for a discussion of this paradox.

9. It does appear that in jurisdictions that have banned or strictly limited private possession of handguns, such as Chicago, Washington, D.C., Massachusetts, and Canada, it remains true that most gun crimes are still committed with handguns.

10. The source is unpublished data provided by the Bureau of Justice Statistics. See Cook (1991) for details.

11. The logit-regression specification also includes indicators for whether the offender and victim are strangers, for the number of victims, for race and age of the victim, and whether the robbery occurred during the night time. The coefficient estimates for most of these variables are not significantly different from zero. Significantly positive coefficients were estimated for "at home" and "female victim."

12. In a multivariate analysis the likelihood of attack and injury is increased when there are several robbers, the robber is black, and the robbery occurs in a residence.

13. Kleck and Patterson (1993) use a similar proxy with city-level data and find no statistically significant cross-section relationship between gun ownership rates and homicide or other crime rates. However, rather than relying on a simple cross-section regression-adjusted comparison of crime rates across areas with different rates of gun ownership, they attempt to isolate variation in gun ownership rates that will be arguably unrelated to the unmeasured determinants of local crime rates. Their choice of "instrumental variable" to explain variation in gun prevalence—per capita rates of hunting licenses and subscriptions to gun magazines—are likely to be biased in the direction of overstating the net deterrent effect of guns on crime (see, for example, the discussion in Cook and Ludwig 2003).

14. One comparison of victim survey estimates found that the U.S. robbery rate was substantially higher than that of England, Germany, Hungary, Hong Kong, Scotland, and Switzerland. On the other hand, Canada's robbery rate was nearly twice as high as that of the United States (Block 1993).

15. The notable exception is sex. Male victims predominate in both homicide and suicide.

16. For a highly critical review of the public health literature on firearms and homicide, see Blackman 1997.

17. This is true not just for law-abiding citizens but is felt even more keenly by drug dealers and other criminals who are frequently threatened by the bad company they keep (Wright and Rossi 1994).

18. Kennett and Anderson (1975) argues that the arming of American households did not begin in earnest until 40 or 50 years after ratification of the U.S. Constitution. At the time the Second Amendment was being debated, guns were expensive, unreliable, and rare. See Monkkonen (2000) for further evidence on gun ownership in the nineteenth century.

19. The McClure-Volkmer Amendment of 1986 eased the restriction on out-of-state purchases of rifles and shotguns. Such purchases are now legal as long as they comply with the regulations of both the buyer's state of residence and the state in which the sale occurs.

20. An important loophole allowed the import of parts of handguns that could not meet the "sporting purposes" test of the Gun Control Act. This loophole was closed by the McClure-Volkmer Amendment of 1986.

21. There is good evidence on other unsafe behaviors by youth. In particular, youthful consumption of cigarettes and beer has been shown to be highly responsive to price. It should be noted that there is a possibility that higher prices of guns will stimulate gun theft somewhat; if so, that might have the good effect of encouraging owners to store their guns more securely.

22. While federal law does not prohibit gun possession by youth, a number of states have placed limits on when youth can carry guns in public.

23. An example of this restrictive approach was until quite recently embodied in the North Carolina pistol permit requirement: permit applicants were required to satisfy their sheriff that they were of "good moral character" and needed the gun to defend their homes.

24. One distinction may be deemed important here. Drivers licenses are required only for operating a vehicle on the public highways, and not on one's own land. By analogy, a licensing requirement for guns could be limited to those who wish to carry the gun in public.

25. There is some evidence that strategic partnerships between ATF and local police departments can quite possibly be effective at disrupting local illegal gun markets, but only if they concern themselves with gathering the necessary intelligence and acting on it. Key in these partnerships is the comprehensive tracing of all firearms recovered in a jurisdiction to their first sale at retail source and the strategic analysis of trace information to identify suspicious purchase and sales patterns indicative of illegal gun trafficking (Cook and Braga 2001; Pierce, Braga, Hyatt, and Koper 2004). Based on an analysis of the local illegal gun market in Boston, the resulting enforcement strategy was appropriately focused on the illegal diversion of new handguns from retail outlets in Massachusetts, southern states along Interstate 95, and elsewhere (Kennedy et al. 1996b). The results of a Department of Justice—funded evaluation found that the strategy was associated with significant decreases in the percentage of handguns recovered by the Boston Police that were new (Braga and Pierce 2005).

26. Marvell and Moody (1995) find that such policies have no discernible effect.

27. Improving the ability of the police to find guns in hot spot areas through portable gun detectors would greatly aid these efforts (Wilson 1994). Unfortu-

nately, the technology has not been developed to the point where its portability is suitable for use by police in field conditions.

28. Other researchers, however, have observed that some of the decrease in homicide may have occurred without the Ceasefire intervention in place as violence was decreasing in most major U.S. cities (Fagan 2002; Rosenfeld et al. 2005). The National Research Council's Panel on Improving Information and Data on Firearms (Wellford et al. 2005) concluded that the Ceasefire evaluation was compelling in associating the intervention with the subsequent decline in youth homicide. However, the Panel also suggested that many complex factors affect youth homicide trends and it was difficult to specify the exact relationship between the Ceasefire intervention and subsequent changes in youth offending behaviors. While the U.S Department of Justice—sponsored evaluation controlled for existing violence trends and certain rival causal factors, such as changes in the youth population, drug markets, and employment in Boston, there could be complex interaction effects among these factors not measured by the evaluation that could account for some meaningful portion of the decrease. The evaluation was not a randomized, controlled experiment. Therefore, the non-randomized control group research design cannot rule out these internal threats to the conclusion that Ceasefire was the key factor in the youth homicide decline. For a more recent account of Operation Ceasefire in Boston, see Braga, Hureau, and Winship, 2008.

Chapter 11

Rehabilitation and Treatment Programs

Francis T. Cullen, Cheryl Lero Jonson

"Is rehabilitation dead?" The voicing of this question, which occurred repeatedly in the mid-1970s (see, e.g., Halleck and Witte 1977; Serrill 1975), signaled the collapse of the paradigm of "individualized treatment" that had dominated correctional thinking throughout the twentieth century (Rothman 1980; Rotman 1990). Shortly before this time, it was taken for granted that the chief purpose of state intervention was to treat offenders. We were the nation, after all, that had *invented the penitentiary*, built *reformatories*, created a juvenile court to *save wayward children*, and transformed prisons into *correctional* institutions where *therapeutic communities* could envelop offenders. Writing in 1972, Judge Marvin Frankel (7) captured the hegemony of the treatment paradigm when he observed that it is "fashionable nowadays to say that only rehabilitation can justify confinement." Indeed, criminologists believed that treatment was the logical extension of the scientific study of crime: find the causes of persistent criminality and then develop interventions to cure offenders of their criminogenic influences. As Gibbons (1999, 32) suggests, "It seemed to many criminologists that they were about to become 'scholar princes' who would lead a social movement away from punitive responses to criminals and delinquents and toward a society in which treatment, rehabilitation, and reintegration of deviants and law-breakers would be the dominant cultural motif" (see Toby 1964).

A sea change in thinking, however, ended such delusions of grandeur. Scarcely at the end of the 1970s, Gottfredson (1979, 39) would observe that "the conventional wisdom in criminology is that rehabilitation has been found to be ineffective." In fact, criminologists' antipathy toward rehabilitation had become so intense that Gottfredson was able to document the "treatment destruction techniques"—the biased methodological critiques, the ex post facto arguments—that scholars would unfairly invoke to scuttle evaluation studies showing program effectiveness.

Criminologists, it seems, were politicized by the events of that day—by a civil rights movement that did not achieve all its goals and left racial inequality intact, by the waging of the Vietnam War, by the shootings at

Kent State and Attica, by the Watergate scandal, and so on. Confidence in government plummeted generally in society during this time (Lipset and Schneider 1983), but mistrust in academia was so feverish that many scholars became "enemies of the state." Because rehabilitation justified giving "the state"—judges and correctional officials—near unfettered discretion to individualize interventions, criminologists took special aim at rehabilitation. Their intellectual project thus turned from the science of rehabilitation to the deconstruction of rehabilitation. Where once rehabilitation was seen as reflecting "good intentions," now the appearance of "benevolence was really a mask for coercion" and the pursuit of class interests; correctional counselors, probation officers, and parole boards became "state agents of control"; extending services to troubled youths was portrayed as "net widening"; the ideal of "individualized treatment" was transformed into "state-enforced therapy"; and prison programs became an insidious attempt to "discipline the minds" of inmates (Binder and Geis 1984; Cullen and Gendreau 1989, 2001).

Outside criminology, elected officials and policymakers hardly embraced the view that rehabilitation was an instrument of state repression; if they had, they might have been more supportive of it! Instead, "treatment" was seen as yet another social welfare program that undermined individual responsibility and that separated bad behavioral choices (in this case, criminal acts) from unpleasant consequences (in this case, punishment). Rehabilitation "coddled offenders" by making life inside prison comfortable; it also allowed inmates to escape the full sting of a stiff prison sentence by conning a parole board that they were "cured" and deserving of an early release. Criminals, they argued, needed to be disciplined and punished (Cullen and Gilbert 1982; see also Garland 1990).

Much to the chagrin of offenders, criminologists did not become "scholar princes," and they wielded less power than elected officials. As result, the well-being of offenders receded in importance as one "get tough" law after another was passed to inflict more discomfort on "career criminals" and "super-predators." After a while, criminologists came to blame this "penal harm movement" (Clear 1994)—especially the sevenfold increase in the prison population—on elected officials and not on rehabilitation (see, e.g., Beckett 1997; Gottschalk 2006; Simon 2007). Still, their affection for treating offenders had passed, and they remained convinced that nothing they could ever do would make rehabilitation "work."

Given these developments, one might have expected that rehabilitation would, in fact, have "died." Over three decades later, however, it is now clear that the requiem planned for rehabilitation proved premature. To be sure, the legitimacy once enjoyed by the treatment paradigm is shaky and must be constantly reinforced. Virtually every state has changed its sentencing system to be more punitive and mindful of public safety; many probation departments place a priority on the surveillance of offenders, what one officer called the "pee 'em and see 'em" approach to supervision (drug testing and monitoring); and many jurisdictions have cut back on treatment services. Even so, virtually every prison also continues to have an array of rehabilitation programs—perhaps to keep inmates busy, perhaps because it would have been too much effort to get rid of them; probation officers continue to deliver or broker services when they can; and public support for treatment, especially for juveniles, remains high (Applegate, Cullen, and Fisher 1997; Cullen, Fisher, and Applegate 2000; Cullen and Moon 2002; Cullen et al. 2002; Cullen et al. 2007; Moon et al. 1999; Nagin et al. 2006). Indeed, recently, some jurisdictions seem to have recognized the limits and inordinate expense of punitive corrections and are experimenting anew with treatment interventions (Listwan et al. 2008).

The key issue, however, is what the future will hold for the rehabilitative ideal and for treatment programs. Although the handiwork of a limited number of criminologists, one exciting development is the emergence of a much clearer idea, based on empirical evidence, of "what works" to inhibit offender recidivism. These insights on effective correctional intervention were largely produced by a new statistical technique called *meta-analysis*, and by a number of Canadian psychologists who liked their government and never became "enemies of the state." This story of how rehabilitation was "saved," so to speak, will be told below (see also Cullen 2005). An effort will also be made, however, to detail the special challenge facing corrections: how to use this emergent knowledge and implement effective treatment programs. This essay concludes with some thoughts about the broader issue of whether we *should* retain rehabilitation as an integral part of our correctional system.

Before proceeding, it is necessary to convey how the concept of "rehabilitation" or "treatment" will be defined in this essay: *a planned correctional intervention that targets for change internal and/or social criminogenic factors with the goal of reducing recidivism and, where possible, of improving other aspects of an offender's life.* Rehabilitation may be conducted in conjunction with different types of criminal sanctions (e.g., imprisonment versus probation) and in different correctional settings (e.g., in an institution versus in the community). The type of sanction or setting, however, does not define whether treatment is being delivered. Instead, the key ingredient to rehabilitation is that a conscious effort is made to design an intervention whose expressed purpose is to provide some service to offenders that will change them in such a way as to make recidivism less likely. Typically, then, we speak of placing offenders in "programs." But it also is possible that treatment may be a "component" of a correctional program, such as a "boot camp" or "intensive supervision," whose goals include but are not limited to rehabilitation (i.e., they may include "control" or "deterrence") (MacKenzie 2006; Taxman 1999). Finally, unlike the punishment-oriented goals of retribution, deterrence, and incapacitation, which seek to inflict pain on or cage lawbreakers, rehabilitation attempts to cure, fix, or otherwise improve offenders.

Palmer (1992) has captured the essential features of rehabilitation in the following way:

> [Treatment] usually tries to reach its socially centered and offender-centered goals by focusing on such factors and conditions as the offender's *adjustment techniques, interests, skills, personal limitations, and/or life circumstances*. It does so in order to affect his or her future behavior and adjustment. That is, treatment efforts focus on any of several factors or conditions and are directed at particular future events. These efforts may be called treatment programs or approaches insofar as they involve specific components and inputs (e.g., counseling or skill development) that are organized, interrelated, and otherwise planned so as to generate changes in the above factors and conditions—changes which, in turn, may help generate the desired future events (e.g., reduced illegal behavior). (1992, 22–23; emphasis in original)

BEYOND MARTINSON

"With few and isolated exceptions," wrote Robert Martinson, "the rehabilitation efforts that have been reported so far have had no appreciable effect on recidivism" (1974a, 25). This technical-sounding conclusion would soon come to be known as the "nothing works" doctrine in corrections—that is, that "nothing works" in treatment to change the law-breaking into law-abiding. It would also have enormous ramifications. Two years following Martinson's declaration, Adams (1976, 76) captured its impact when he observed that the "Nothing Works doctrine...has shaken the community of criminal justice to its root...widely assorted members of the criminal justice field are briskly urging that punishment and incapacitation should be given much higher priority among criminal justice goals" (see Blumstein 1997). Even today, some commentators continue to offer Martinson's findings as solid evidence that treatment programs are ineffective—that their "record for repairing and reconstructing souls has been abysmal" (Reynolds 1996, 7; see also Farabee 2005).

Martinson (1974a) presented his assessment of rehabilitation programs in his classic essay, published in *The Public Interest*, entitled "What Works?—Questions and Answers About Prison Reform." This work was a provocative precursor to a more judicious 736-page coauthored book published the next year, *The Effectiveness of Correctional Treatment* (Lipton, Martinson, and Wilks 1975). This project involved an analysis of 231 studies, conducted between 1945 and 1967, which evaluated the effectiveness of rehabilitation programs. Although almost half the studies surveyed showed reductions in recidivism (Palmer 1975), Martinson suggested that no category or modality of treatment—such as counseling, skill development, or psychotherapy—reliably "worked" to cut criminal involvement. In practical terms, correctional interventions were unlike medical treatment where, for example, diseases were combated with proven cures. Instead, the extant research could give no advice to correctional officials on specific treatment programs that could, with any certainty, diminish recidivism.

Martinson recognized that the pessimistic results from his analysis might be due to poorly conducted research studies or to treatment programs that were sound in principle but inadequately implemented. But he was moved to ask, "whether all these studies lead irrevocably to the conclusion that *nothing works*, that we haven't the faintest clue about how to rehabilitate offenders and reduce recidivism" (48; emphasis added). He then suggested that the treatment enterprise might be inherently futile. "It may be," he warned, "that there is a radical flaw in our present strategies—that education at its best, or that psychotherapy at its best, cannot overcome, or even appreciably reduce, the powerful tendency, for offenders to continue in criminal behavior." Martinson stopped short in the essay of explicitly saying that "nothing works," but this was the message being conveyed. Indeed, Martinson soon clarified that he believed that "rehabilitation was a myth. That is a conclusion I have come to . . . based on the evidence made available by this volume" (1974b, 4).

For its time, the Martinson study was credible and not inconsistent with contemporary reviews of the treatment-evaluation literature (see, e.g., Bailey 1966; Greenberg 1977; Logan 1972; Robison and Smith 1971). Most noteworthy, a panel of scholars commissioned by the National Academy of Sciences examined research on rehabilitation generally and, in particular, conducted a detailed analysis of a 10 percent random sample of the studies assessed by Martinson. The panel concluded that Martinson and his colleagues, Lipton and Wilks, were "reasonably accurate and fair in the appraisal of the rehabilitation literature" (Sechrest, White, and Brown 1979, 31). Based on the existing body of studies, they shared his view that it was not possible to make "recommendations about ways of rehabilitating offenders . . . with any warranted confidence" (102). However, given the methodological problems of many evaluation studies and the failure of agencies to implement programs as designed, the panel also cautioned that "neither could one say with justified confidence that rehabilitation cannot be achieved, and, therefore, no drastic cutbacks in rehabilitative effort should be based on that proposition" (102–103). This judicious assessment—that is, the panel's call for more rigorous research before prematurely jumping to conclusions and scuttling treatment programs—would not be heeded by the many criminologists who came to embrace the "nothing works" doctrine.

In any case, Martinson's study was formidable in its scope, and it would be unfair to characterize his account of the status of treatment programs as based on a gross misreading of the extant evaluation studies. Even so, as is the case with social science research on virtually any topic, Martinson's conclusions were hardly definitive or the "last word" on treatment effectiveness.

First, as noted, many of the studies he reviewed reduced recidivism (Palmer 1975), a finding that is inconsistent with a "nothing works" conclusion. This was true as well of the other reviews at this time that, on grounds similar to Martinson, also questioned the value of treatment programs (Andrews and Bonta 2006; Gottfredson 1979).

Second, Martinson's research is commonly believed to have assessed 231 studies. What is less known, however, is that the analysis covered only 138 measures of recidivism, of which fewer than 80 measures were linked to interventions that could legitimately be categorized as a "treatment program" as opposed to a "sanction" such as imprisonment or probation (Cullen and Gendreau 2000; Gottfredson 1979). Accordingly, only a limited number of studies fell into any of the treatment categories created by Martinson, and often they were a mixed bag of interventions that had little in common with one another (Klockars 1975).

Third, his study did not contain a category for behavioral or cognitive-behavioral interventions. This omission is especially telling because research now shows that this treatment modality is associated with meaningful reductions in recidivism (Andrews and Bonta 2006; Gendreau 1996; Landenberger and Lipsey 2005; Lipsey and Cullen 2007; Lipsey, Landenberger, and Wilson 2007; MacKenzie 2000, 2006; MacKenzie and Hickman 1998; McLaren 1992; Pearson et al. 2002; Tong and Farrington 2006; Wilson, Bouffard, and MacKenzie 2005).

Now more than three decades after Martinson's essay, we should recognize his study for what it was: an important and sobering reminder that correctional treatment is a difficult enterprise fraught with many failures. It was not, however, a project that was flawless or capable of fully settling the issue of treatment effectiveness. We might have expected, in fact, that scholars would have greeted the publication of his essay with "organized skepticism," a core norm of science that prescribes that provocative findings be subjected to careful scrutiny by the discipline's community of scholars (Merton 1973). Instead, with the exception of a few lonely voices (e.g., Cullen and Gilbert 1982; Gendreau and Ross 1979; Palmer 1975), Martinson's study was readily accepted by criminologists as incontrovertible proof that "nothing works" in correctional treatment (see Martinson 1979). This doctrine thus became a "conventional wisdom," and contrary views either were dismissed out of hand or, when addressed at all, were rejected as "obviously" based on methodologically flawed evidence (Gottfredson 1979). In short, it became standard operating procedure in the discipline to discredit correctional treatment, not to conduct a value-free assessment of its effectiveness (however, see Sechrest, White, and Brown 1979).

The willingness to accept the "nothing works" view and the withering scrutiny given to positive research findings on treatment were not based on fair-minded scientific criteria but were ideologically inspired (Cullen and Gendreau 2001). By the time Martinson's essay appeared, many criminologists already had rejected or, at the least, had serious doubts about correctional programs. As noted previously, their suspicions were rooted in the fact that the "state" was administering these interventions. In the rehabilitative ideal, which emerged in the early 1900s in the Progressive Era (Rothman 1980), government officials were accorded the discretion to "individualize treatment," much as a physician does with medical interventions. Judges were given wide latitude in whether to sentence offenders to prison and, if so, for how long; for offenders in the community, probation and parole officers were to help those amenable to rehabilitation but also were expected to pick out which "bad apples" should be "revoked" and sent to prison; once in prison, release was to depend on being cured, and a parole board would determine who would, or would not, be granted their freedom.

But what if this "ideal" was nothing but a "noble lie" (Morris 1974)—a benevolent set of good intentions that masked the disquieting practices that really went on in the justice system? Or, still worse, what if rehabilitation was, underneath its cloak of benevolence, an insidious system of power used by the state to discipline deviants and the disadvantaged (Foucault 1977)? And this is precisely what many scholars were prepared to believe at this historical juncture. A series of cataclysmic sociopolitical events and the continuing turbulence in the 1960s and early 1970s had coalesced to diminish Americans' confidence in their government (Lipset and Schneider 1983). Affected by this social context, many criminologists lost their trust in the state and feared the power that it exercised over offenders.

They were prepared to believe that judges were using their discretion not to individualize treatments but to discriminate against poor and minority defendants; that parole was a lottery—run by a board of political appointees with no criminological expertise—in which release from prison was unrelated to the risk of recidivating; and that treatment programs were used not to cure inmates but to coerce them to behave while incarcerated, lest they "rot" in prison until they buckled under to institutional rules. They mistrusted the motives of judges and correctional officials, now seeing them as "state agents of social control" who used their discretionary power to reinforce an unequal and unjust social order that benefited the rich, not the poor (Binder and Geis 1984). They embraced policy positions that minimized control over offenders, mindlessly favoring, for example, community sanctions over imprisonment and "radical nonintervention" over any type of state penalty (Schur 1973). Not surprisingly, Martinson's findings of "no appreciable" treatment effects were hardly an occasion for dispute but rather were easily interpreted as showing what they already knew: that "nothing works" in state-enforced therapy (Cullen and Gendreau 1989; Cullen and Gilbert 1982).

Criminologists had good reasons to be concerned about the reality of correctional rehabilitation programs. State officials often had virtually unfettered discretion over offenders' lives, often had little or no expertise in rehabilitation, and often made decisions based on ignorance, hunch, or bias (Kittrie 1971; Rothman 1980). Still, the collateral argument that "nothing works" in rehabilitation did not follow from these legitimate concerns about how rehabilitation was being implemented. Most unfortunate, criminologists closed their minds to the possibility that treatment programs—or other interventions carried out by the criminal justice system—could reduce crime. As a discipline, criminologists were more committed to showing that nothing that the state did could diminish crime rates than to building knowledge on what could work to limit offenders' criminality (Cullen and Gendreau 2001; more generally, see Maruna 2001).

In any case, it is time for criminologists—and others concerned about corrections—to move beyond Martinson's view of rehabilitation. His study's exalted status was never deserved and has served to stifle debate and scientific progress in the study of treatment effectiveness. If we have learned anything over the past three decades, it is that rehabilitating offenders, while a daunting challenge, is feasible. Revisionist scholars engaged in the study of correctional rehabilitation have rejected the "nothing works" doctrine and are hard at work in discerning "what works" to change offenders. It is to this exciting development that we now turn.

BIBLIOTHERAPY FOR CYNICS: LESSONS FROM META-ANALYSIS

In 1979, Gendreau and Ross furnished a systematic review of effective treatment programs (see also Gendreau and Ross 1987). They hoped, in their words, that this review would provide "bibliotherapy for cynics" who endorsed the "nothing works" doctrine. Although some scholars took notice, most criminologists resisted the "bibliotherapy." In part, their resistance stemmed from their ideology—from their mistrust of the state and its supposed attempt to "coerce" offenders into treatment. But the failure to take seriously Gendreau and Ross's assessment also was made easier by the type of review they conducted: a "narrative review" or a qualitative summary and discussion of what the "research shows."

Until relatively recently, scholars reviewed research in an area in one of two ways. First, in the narrative review, the scholar compiled studies, analyzed them, and then—like Gendreau and Ross—drew conclusions. Second, in the "ballot box" or "vote counting" review, the scholar would find all relevant studies and then would count, one by one, whether a study showed that a treatment program worked or did not work to reduce recidivism. At least with regard to rehabilitation, the difficulty with these approaches was that they often provided mixed results. The question of whether the glass was half empty or half full inevitably emerged. Whereas Gendreau and Ross could identify a host of programs that reduced recidivism, critics could point to a host of programs that were ineffective. The imprecision of the review technique thus encouraged competing interpretations that would be difficult to falsify. In short, the notion that "treatment works" could be dismissed as Gendreau and Ross's "opinion" about what the studies meant.

Research on the accuracy and consistency of narrative or qualitative reviews of scholarly studies reveals that such assessments can draw erroneous conclusions of the extant empirical evidence. In such reviews, authors analyzing the same set of studies are prone to classify these studies differently and to reach contrasting conclusions (Glass, McGraw, and Smith 1981). In such a situation, "conclusions are influenced by prejudice and stereotyping to a degree that would be unforgivable in primary research itself" (18). It might be argued that this interpretive divergence is simply a by-product of the nature of social science research—that is, that methodological imprecision and the inability to replicate findings makes the accumulation of research knowledge difficult and the interpretation of studies more art than science. In an illuminating analysis of research findings in physics and psychology, however, Hedges (1987, 443) contends that "the results of physical experiments may not be strikingly more consistent than those of social and behavioral experiments." Even with the inherent limitations of social science methodology taken into account, the problem in understanding what a cumulative body of research shows may lie not in the sample of studies conducted but in the method used to organize and analyze them (Gendreau, Goggin, and Smith 2000, 2001; Glass, McGraw, and Smith 1981; Hedges 1987).

In this regard, beginning in the 1990s, a new way of "making sense" of a body of research emerged: the *meta-analysis* or a *quantitative* synthesis of studies. In this approach, each study is coded to determine the statistical relationship—the *effect size*—between the treatment intervention and recidivism. The researcher then computes what is analogous to a batting average across all studies, or what is known as an *average effect size*. This is a precise point estimate of the impact of treatment on recidivism. To make sense of the statistics, most analysts assume a base rate of recidivism of 50 percent for the control group. They then compute, based on the meta-analysis, what the recidivism rate would be for the treatment group. In a recent study, for example, Lipsey (2009) found that the mean *phi* coefficient or "effect size" for cognitive-behavioral programs was .13. This would compute to a recidivism rate of .37, or a 26 percent reduction in recidivism for the treatment group versus the control group (13 percent/ 50 percent base rate). Finally, in a meta-analysis, it is possible to introduce *moderators*, or factors that might be seen as influencing the effect size. For example, one might see if the effect size varies by the quality of a study's methodology or by the quality of the treatment delivered (see, e.g., Lipsey 2009).

Meta-analysis is not without its own limitations, the largest one being the "garbage in, garbage out" problem: that is, that the quality of the review will be shaped by the quality of the studies that are quantitatively synthesized. Even the most sophisticated meta-analysis studies cannot derive sound conclusions from a set of methodologically unsound studies. There is also the possibility of selection bias to the extent that the studies reviewed are not representative of all existing programs or of all evaluations that have been conducted (e.g., evaluations tend to be performed on innovative programs, or published studies tend to report statistically significant findings). Nonetheless, meta-analysis largely eliminates the bias that often emerges when two scholars differentially interpret what a study "really found." Further, because coding criteria and decisions are made public, any given meta-analysis is open to replication.

Overall Treatment Effects

Importantly for the debate over the effectiveness of rehabilitation, meta-analysis has provided a way out of the "half-empty or half-full" assessment of the extant literature. Again, as a quantitative approach, it can provide an "effect size" estimate of the relationship between rehabilitation—or different types of treatment interventions—and recidivism. It is noteworthy that, although not beyond dispute, these favorable results have been far more influential than previous narrative and vote-counting reviews in persuading criminologists that "rehabilitation works."

On a broad level, it is perhaps useful to begin by asking whether planned interventions are able to improve a range of behaviors, including mental health problems, educational performance, and developmental difficulties. If not, then one might conclude that human conduct, once deeply ingrained, cannot be changed. But if interventions can be beneficial, then one would have to wonder why criminal behavior, among all human problems, would be unique in its resistance to reformation. In a review of 302 meta-analyses, Lipsey and Wilson (1993, 1181) discovered that across a variety of psychological, educational, and behavioral outcomes, the interventions had "a strong, dramatic pattern of overall effects." The average difference in success rates between the treatment groups and control groups was 24 percentage points. It seems that human conduct, including that deemed as an unfortunate affliction or as a wayward choice, is amenable to alteration. "The number and scope of effective treatments covered by this conclusion are impressive," concluded Lipsey and Wilson, "and the magnitude of the effects for a substantial portion of those treatments is in a range of practical significance by almost any reasonable criteria" (1199).

We should note that in this review, Lipsey and Wilson included 10 meta-analyses that were conducted on offenders. They did find that the effect sizes for meta-analyses on treatment programs for criminal conduct were lower than for other problem behaviors. Still, consistent with their more general findings, there was no evidence that offenders cannot be rehabilitated.

In this regard, in a review of 13 meta-analyses of offender rehabilitation programs published between 1985 and 1995, Losel (1995) reported that the mean effect size varied from a low of .05 to a high of .18 (see also

Lipsey and Cullen 2007; Lipsey, Landenberger, and Wilson 2007; McGuire 2002; McLaren 1992; Redondo, Sanchez-Meca, and Garrido 1999). He estimated that the "mean effect size of all assessed studies probably has a size of about .10" (1995, 89; see also Andrews et al. 1990; Lipsey 1992; Losel 2001; McGuire 2002). In practical terms, this would mean that the recidivism rate for the treatment group would be 45 percent, compared to 55 percent for the control group.More recently, Lipsey and Cullen (2007) conducted "a review of systematic reviews" of correctional interventions on subsequent criminal behavior and reached similar conclusions. Summarizing across eight "meta-analyses of the effects of rehabilitation treatment generally on recidivism," they showed that treatment programs were consistently associated with reductions in reoffending (2007, 303). In fact, they discovered that none of the meta-analyses "found less than a 10 percent reduction in recidivism," and that "most of their mean effect sizes represent recidivism reductions in the 20 percent range, varying upward to nearly 40 percent" (303; see also Lipsey 2009).

It is possible, moreover, that the figures in these overall assessments may underestimate the true influence of treatment programs, for two reasons. First, treatment groups are not always compared to control groups who receive "no intervention." Because some criminal justice sanctions might include a rehabilitation component, members of the control group might experience an unmeasured treatment effect (Losel 1995; MacKenzie 2006). Second, most studies rely on official and dichotomous measures of recidivism (e.g., either were or were not arrested). According to Lipsey (1992, 98), this measurement strategy may attenuate the effect size of treatment because "it is largely a matter of chance whether a particular delinquent act eventuates in an official recorded contact with an agent of law enforcement or the juvenile justice system." He estimates that when this fact is taken into account, the true effect size for treatment interventions may double. We should note that some commentators suggest that other methodological considerations may diminish the treatment effects reported thus far (Gaes et al. 1999; Losel 2001). Nonetheless, even when a range of methodological and research design factors are taken into account, it appears that the positive effects of treatment found in the extant meta-analyses are sustained (Landenberger and Lipsey 2005; Lipsey 1992, 1999a, 1999b, 2009; Lipsey, Chapman, and Landenberger 2001; Lipsey and Cullen 2007; Lipsey and Wilson 1998; Losel and Schmucker 2005; Pearson et al. 2002; Wilson, Bouffard, and MacKenzie 2005; Wilson, Gallagher, and MacKenzie 2000).

Heterogeneity of Treatment Effects

Thus far, we have been reviewing the impact of rehabilitation on recidivism across a panoply of programs. If we might use a medical analogy, this would be akin to testing whether it was possible to cure strep throat by giving ill patients such diverse interventions as penicillin, aspirin, mouthwash, and bloodletting. Across all of these "treatments," one might find a small positive treatment effect when compared with doing nothing with the patients. Clearly, though, calculating the overall treatment effect would mask the potent impact of some interventions (e.g., penicillin and its derivatives) and the impotence of other interventions (e.g., aspirin, mouthwash, bloodletting). In other words, the treatment effects would, in this case, be *heterogeneous*—some would be strong, others weak. Further, it would seem that searching for "strong effects" would be necessary if one wished to avoid medical quackery, in which useless interventions were dispensed regardless of their failure to cure patients.

It is inadvisable to assume that correctional treatment will ever be as precise as medical treatments of this sort, unless, of course, some crime-curing pills are suddenly invented! If we were to draw a more appropriate medical analogy, it might be to the search for treatments for cancer. This search has made important advances, but it is still plagued by substantial failure rates and by the need for ongoing research to do better in saving patients' lives. In a similar manner, correctional interventions will invariably be beset by higher than desired recidivism rates and by the need for continuing experimentation in what really works to divert offenders from criminal conduct. However, in both cases—the treatment of cancer and of criminality—the standard of success is not high cure rates but rather doing better than alternative interventions that are available.

In any event, meta-analyses of treatment programs have moved into a "second generation." Beyond computing an effect size across all interventions, scholars are now documenting heterogeneity in effect sizes—that is, they are seeking to differentiate treatment programs that work from those that do not. This enterprise seems commonsensical, but systematic research in this direction remains in the beginning stages (Losel 2001). Making strides is hindered by three considerations.

First, many evaluations do not describe or measure the intervention with enough specificity to know what exactly was done. In particular, unless process evaluations are conducted, "what went on" in the course of the treatment delivery is difficult to assess with any certainty. Second, the categories used to create homogeneous treatment types or modalities are often not theoretically derived (see Andrews et al. 1990). Instead, treatment types are grouped by labels that have long existed, such as "individual counseling" or "life skills." Although not without some value, the weakness of this approach is that a modality such as "individual counseling" may have as much within-group or within-category variation as between-group variation. For example, individual counseling that is behaviorally oriented may have more in common with a token economy than with other types of psychological counseling (e.g., psychoanalytic or client-centered therapy). Third, although hundreds of evaluation studies are now available for meta-analysis, when divided up into specific categories, the number of studies in any one category can become limited.

Drawing firm conclusions on the effects of a few evaluations—especially when they are of varying methodological quality—can be risky (Lipsey and Cullen 2007).

With these caveats in mind, the meta-analytic evidence is reasonably clear about what treatment programs are most successful in reducing recidivism: interventions that are based on social learning or behavioral principles, are structured rather than nondirective, seek to build human capital in offenders, and use more than one treatment modality to address the multiple problems that offenders may be experiencing. In contrast, interventions that are loosely structured, are based on psychoanalytic or client-centered therapy, and/or that target for change factors unrelated or weakly related to recidivism (e.g., self-concept) do not have meaningful effects on recidivism (Andrews and Bonta 2006; Gendreau et al. 2006; MacKenzie 2006; McGuire 2002; Sherman et al. 1997).

Thus, as Losel (1995, 91) notes, based on his review of existing meta-analyses, "it is mostly cognitive-behavioural, skill-oriented and multi-modal programmes that yield the best effects" (see also Garrett 1985; Izzo and Ross 1990; Landenberger and Lipsey 2005; Lipsey 1992; Lipsey, Chapman, and Landenberger 2001; Lipsey and Cullen 2007; Lipsey, Landenberger, and Wilson 2007; MacKenzie 2006; McGuire 2002; Pearson et al. 2002; Redondo, Sanchez-Meca, and Garrido 1999; Wilson, Bouffard, MacKenzie 2005). Echoing these views, MacKenzie concludes that meta-analyses "have supported the finding that effective programs are structured and focused, use multiple treatment components, focus on developing skills, and use behavioral (including cognitive-behavioral) methods (with reinforcements for clearly identified, overt behaviors as opposed to nondirective counseling focusing on insight, self-esteem, or disclosure)" (2000, 464). She also observes that "effective programs... must be designed to address the characteristics of offenders that are associated with criminal activities and can be changed" (see also MacKenzie 2006). Similarly, in a more recent review of the literature, Smith, Gendreau, and Swartz show that "meta-analyses of the offender treatment literature have *consistently* favored cognitive-behavioral interventions over the other treatment modalities" (2009, 8; emphasis in original). Not only were these programs more effective than other treatment modalities, but also the majority of cognitive-behavioral programs examined were associated with at least a 15 percent reduction in recidivism. Based on these results and on a priori theoretical views, some criminologists have derived "principles of effective intervention"—an issue we return to below (Andrews 1995; Gendreau 1996).

It might also be useful to pause for a moment to define "cognitive-behavioral" programs—another topic we will revisit in this essay (see Spiegler and Guevremont 1998). These programs are based on the view that cognitions—what and how we think—are learned and affect behavioral choices, including the choice to break the law. As Van Voorhis and Lester (2004) point out, cognitive-behavioral programs fall into two categories, although interventions may include both types of approaches (see also Andrews and Bonta 2006). "Cognitive restructuring" programs attempt to change the content of what offenders believe, such as their procriminal attitudes and rationalizations for why law violations are acceptable (e.g., externalizing blame). "Cognitive skills" programs attempt to change the structure or the way that offenders reason, such as how to cope with and control anger or impulsive urges. Cognitive-behavioral treatments often involve the reinforcement of prosocial attitudes and behavior and efforts to show prosocial coping strategies through modeling, role-playing, and structured group learning (e.g., anger management classes).

Equally salient from a policy standpoint, meta-analysis research also reveals that deterrence-oriented and "character building" interventions—such as "scared straight" programs, shock incarceration ("boot camps"), and "wilderness" programs—do not blunt criminality and might, in fact, be associated with slight increases in recidivism (Austin 2000; Andrews et al. 1990; Bottcher and Ezell 2005; Cullen, Wright, and Applegate 1996; Gendreau et al. 2000; Lipsey 1992; Lipsey and Wilson 1998; MacKenzie 2000, 2006; MacKenzie, Wilson, and Kider 2001; Parent 2003; Petrosino, Turpin Petrosino, and Buehler 2004; Stinchcomb and Terry 2001; Wilson, MacKenzie, and Mitchell 2003; see also Finckenauer and Gavin 1999). Similar results have been found for "intermediate sanctions"—punishments that lie "between prison and probation" (Morris and Tonry 1990). In the 1980s, an array of community-based programs were introduced to exert control over and presumably deter offenders free in society—programs such as intensive supervision, drug testing, and electronic monitoring/home incarceration. A meta-analysis of these programs by Gendreau et al. (2000) reported an effect size of zero. This result confirms the conclusions based on the best experimental studies (see, e.g., Petersilia and Turner 1993) and on narrative reviews of the literature (Byrne and Pattavina 1992; Cullen, Wright, and Applegate 1996; Fulton et al. 1997; Gendreau, Cullen, and Bonta 1994; MacKenzie 1997, 2000, 2006; Marion 2002; McGuire 2002; Petersilia 1998). Finally, it is noteworthy that, although suggestive, the evidence also indicates that control-oriented programs only reduce recidivism when they include a treatment component (Bonta, Wallace-Capretta, and Rooney 2000; Cullen, Wright, and Applegate 1996; MacKenzie 2006; Mitchell, MacKenzie, and Perez 2005; Petersilia and Turner 1993).

ASSESSING COMMONLY USED TREATMENT PROGRAMS

The section after this one will present an attempt by Canadian criminologists to develop a research-based theory of effective correctional intervention. The value of their theoretical enterprise is that it endeavors to move beyond empirical descriptions of treatment effectiveness to provide both a rationale for why certain interventions reduce recidivism and a blueprint for future program development. An exclusive focus on this undertaking, however, would be misleading, in that it would ignore the wealth of interventions that occur every day within the correctional system. Some of these programs manifest principles of effective treatment; some do not. In any event, they are the kinds of treatment that offenders most often receive, and thus it seems incumbent to consider their effectiveness. In this section, we consider three types of treatment programs that are found in virtually every state correctional system: (1) education and work programs, (2) drug programs, and (3) sex-offender programs.

Education and Work Programs

"Education and work programs," observe Gaes and colleagues (1999, 398), "are the cornerstones of correctional intervention" (see also Lin 2000; Silverman and Vega 1996). Each year, prisons in the United States spend an estimated $493 million on educational programs (*Corrections Compendium* 2008b). These programs are potentially consequential, given that roughly 68 percent of state prison inmates are high school dropouts (Harlow 2003). Indeed, Harlow (2003) observes that, while incarcerated, over 50 percent of state prison inmates report taking at least one education course. A survey of 44 state correctional systems conducted in 2007 revealed that roughly one-quarter of those incarcerated were currently enrolled in some type of educational program (*Corrections Compendium* 2008b). Further, when assessing the specific education programs offered, all 44 state agencies surveyed stated that they provide the General Equivalency Development (GED) program, with 16 states requiring all or certain groups of inmates (e.g., those without a high school education, those under age 65 in Missouri, those under age 22 in Washington) to obtain their GED in some of their institutions (*Corrections Compendium* 2008b). Additionally, about 98 percent of state correctional departments offer adult basic education in some of their prisons, which involves learning in such core areas as mathematics, literacy, language arts, and social studies, and 93 percent give special education programs (*Corrections Compendium* 2008b).

Due to 1994 federal legislation that excluded inmates from securing Pell Grants to fund more advanced study, participation in college degree programs is declining (Tewksbury, Erickson, and Taylor 2000). Still, college education courses are available in many correctional institutions, with 61 percent of state systems offering two-year degree programs, 41 percent having four-year degree programs, and 25 percent running post-graduate degree programs in some of their facilities. In the 2003–2004 academic year, over 85,000 prisoners were enrolled in post-secondary education. In that same period, 2,191 college degrees and 24,627 certificates were awarded to inmates participating in post-secondary correctional education (Erisman and Contardo 2005).

Vocational education programs are also found in about half of all correctional institutions. More specifically, 56 percent of state prisons, 94 percent of federal prisons, 44 percent of private prisons, and 7 percent of local jails offer vocational training to their inmates (Harlow 2003). These programs include a plethora of services, ranging from classroom-based education to apprenticeships (MacKenzie 2006). In the 2007 survey of 44 state correctional systems, 84 percent of the states reported providing job readiness programs, while 50 percent said that they offered apprenticeship programs in some of their institutions (*Corrections Compendium* 2008b). Approximately one-third of state and federal prisoners were enrolled in training programs aimed at equipping them with vocational skills that would enhance post-release job prospects (Harlow 2003).

It also is estimated that roughly one-half of all inmates have a work assignment while incarcerated (Stephan 2008). A 2005 survey indicated that 88 percent of adult correctional facilities operated work programs. The most common type of work offered was facility support (e.g., office administration, food service, and building maintenance), with 74 percent of the state and federal institutions providing such employment (Stephan 2008). Approximately 300,000 inmates work in food and laundry services (Stone 2006). An assignment to public works, which includes road and park maintenance, was the second most common work program provided by institutions. Another 31 percent of state and federal institutions offered prison industry programs (*Corrections Compendium* 2002) with an additional 16 percent of facilities supplying work on prison farms (Stephen 2008). A 2002 survey of 44 state correctional systems found that over 54,000 inmates were assigned to prison industry programs (*Corrections Compendium* 2002). Not only do these prison industry programs "employ" large numbers of inmates, but they also require large amounts of money to run smoothly. In 2002, the prison industry budget across states ranged from $2.4 million in Delaware and Vermont to $163 million in California; the budget for the nation exceeded $1 billion (*Corrections Compendium* 2002; Wunder 1994). This means that between 0.1 percent (in Vermont) and 9.19 percent (in Montana) of states' annual adult correctional budgets were allocated to correctional industries (*Corrections Compendium* 2008a).

Inmates work an average of seven hours daily, with wages ranging from 22 cents per hour in Idaho to $5.71 per hour in North Dakota (*Corrections Compendium* 2002). Further, inmates' wages can be garnished in 34 states. Garnished wages are most likely to be used to fund room and board costs, victim restitution, child/family support, and court fines and fees. State correctional systems manufacture or provide a multitude of prison industry products and services. These include wood products (e.g., furniture, picnic tables) in 98 percent of U.S. state correctional systems, garments (e.g., clothing, flags) in 93 percent, metals (e.g., license plates) in 91 percent, printing in 86 percent, data entry in 49 percent, agriculture (e.g., beef, milk) in 60 percent, foods in 44 percent, construction in 33 percent, and electronics (e.g., computers) in 19 percent of state correctional systems. Other goods and services include vehicular repair, laundry, optical or dental labs, dog training, cement products, market research, groundskeeping, and mailing/product fulfillment (*Corrections Compendium* 2002). In a 2002 survey of 42 state systems, it was estimated that the income generated from prison industry sales exceeded $1 billion, with 32 systems making a profit (*Corrections Compendium* 2002).

Most institutions have a unique combination of education and work programs. A sample of program offerings at three correctional facilities in the state of Ohio illustrates this point. At the state's main maximum-security institution, the 1,347-inmate Southern Ohio Correctional Facility at Lucasville, program options are comparatively restricted. Prison industries are limited to the shoe shop, while the lone vocational training program available is a building maintenance apprenticeship. Academic alternatives include only adult basic education and the GED (see http://www.drc.ohio.gov/Public/socf.htm). In contrast, at the 2,921-inmate Chillicothe Correctional Institution, industrial programs include the chair and mattress factories, vehicle modification, Ohio Prison Industry asbestos removal, and YUSA (a truck company). Vocational programs include carpentry, building maintenance, welding, and heating/cooling/air conditioning. The academic options encompass not only basic education and the GED—as at the Lucasville prison—but also literacy education and classes from a technical college (see http://www.drc.ohio.gov/Public/cci.htm). Finally, the 2,537-offender Ohio Reformatory for Women in Marysville has industrial programs in the optical shop and sewing shop, which manufactures socks as well as Ohio and U.S. flags. Additionally, there is vocational training in building trades, landscaping and horticulture, general office systems, and cosmetology, as well as apprenticeships in operating boilers and in steam engineering. Academically, the offerings range from literacy and basic education to the GED and then to technical college courses (http://www.drc.ohio.gov/Public/orw.htmm).

Beyond programs within adult institutions, prison inmates also have access to work-release and education-release programs in the community. The goal of these release programs is to ease the transition of offenders from the institution into the community while simultaneously promoting stable employment after release (MacKenzie 2006). In a 2005 survey, 28 percent of state and federal facilities reported having work-release programs, with roughly 25,000 inmates leaving the institution each day to participate in these programs (Stephan 2008; see also Turner and Petersilia 1996). Similarly, 7 percent of state and federal institutions stated that they offered a study-release program that allowed inmates to depart the facility to attend educational classes in the community (Stephan 2008).

For offenders on probation, there are also programs aimed at providing career counseling, job placement, and general "job development" (Bushway and Reuter 1997). Academic programs and vocational education are commonplace as well in juvenile facilities (*Corrections Compendium* 2002, 2006; Lillis 1994). In a 2002 and a 2005 survey of state correctional systems, all states surveyed reported having at least one academic program, and a majority of states indicated that they offered either vocational counseling or vocational training in their juvenile facilities (*Corrections Compendium* 2002, 2006). In the community, there also have been programs aimed at diverting at-risk youths from crime by improving their labor-market prospects (Burghardt et al. 2001; Bushway and Reuter 1997). One such program is Job Corps. In the 1994–1995 randomized National Job Corps Study, Job Corps participants were found to have increased skill and educational attainment. The program also resulted in a 12 percent increase in occupational earnings and a 16 percent decrease in the arrest rate for individuals participating in the program (Burghardt et al. 2001).

Why, however, should education, improving vocational skills, and/or actual work experiences reduce criminal involvement? In part, Americans have long believed that the discipline inherent in diligent study and, in particular, hard work builds sound character and instills appropriate social habits (Phillips and Sandstrom 1990). For example, when correctional leaders met in Cincinnati for the now-famous 1870 National Congress on Penitentiary and Reformatory Discipline, one of the core "principles" they formally adopted was that "education is a vital force in the reformation of fallen men" (Wines 1871, 542). Likewise, they encouraged "industrial training" because "work is no less an auxiliary to virtue, than it is a means of support. Steady, active, honorable labor is the basis of all reformatory discipline" (543). In more contemporary times, the idea of character formation has been complemented with the sense that, in modern society, a conventional life is not possible without adequate education and a good job. Virtually every criminological theory has an explanation for why this is so (Cullen et al. 2001; Piehl 1998; Uggen 1999, 2000). Education and work are seen to prevent crime because they provide legitimate opportunities (strain theory), foster commitment and informal social control (social bond theory), are conduits for prosocial learning (differential association theory), blunt stigma and enhance reintegration (labeling/shaming theory), make the choice of "going straight" more beneficial (rational choice theory), and so on. Added to these ruminations is the stubborn reality that offenders earn fewer years of education and have poorer work histories than members of the general public (Andrews and Bonta 2006; Harlow 2003; Saylor and Gaes 1996; Silverman and Vega 1996; Wilson et al. 1999; Wilson, Gallagher, and MacKenzie 2000).

In this context, it seems only a matter of "common sense" that access to education and work would diminish criminal participation. Complexity, however, is often the victim of common sense, and how crime is shaped by schooling and jobs is, if anything, complex. Indeed, numerous considerations caution against the facile assumption that equipping offenders with human capital and occupational opportunities will invariably diminish their criminal involvement: the roots (or "early predictors") of serious criminality emerge before or are coterminous with entry into school (and surely before the age of adult employment); associations between education/job problems and crime may, due to preexisting individual differences, be partially, or wholly, spurious; educational attainment and employment, though not unimportant, are generally not the strongest predictors of recidivism; many offenders are employed at the time of their crimes; and jobs can furnish opportunities to commit crimes and to develop antisocial friendships that amplify offending outside the workplace (Andrews and Bonta 2006; Bachman and Schulenberg 1993; Fagan and Freeman 1999; Gendreau, Little, and Goggin 1996; Hirschi and Gottfredson 1995; Lipsey and Derzon 1998; Piehl 1998; Uggen 1999; Wright and Cullen 2000).

Despite the long-standing prevalence of work and education programs, the research evidence on whether this treatment modality reduces recidivism is limited and of low quality. A number of useful reviews are now available, but they generally conclude by cautioning against drawing definitive conclusions and by calling for more well-designed studies (Bouffard, MacKenzie, and Hickman 2000; Bushway and Reuter 1997; Cecil et al. 2000; Gaes 2008; Gaes et al. 1999; Gerber and Fritsch 1995; MacKenzie 2006; MacKenzie and Hickman 1998; Pearson and Lipton 1999a; Wilson, Gallagher, and MacKenzie 2000; Wilson et al. 1999). The main difficulty is that the research designs used typically cannot rule out "selection bias"—that is, that positive treatment results may be due not to the impact of the intervention but to preexisting differences that make members of the treatment less likely to recidivate than those in the control group (e.g., more motivated to change, unmeasured, pro-social, psychological traits). However, some attempts have been made to control for selection bias (Chappell 2004; Harer 1995; Steurer, Smith, and Tracy 2001).

Four main conclusions are suggested by the existing evaluation literature. First, there is evidence that participation in education and work education programs may decrease inmates' disciplinary problems while incarcerated. By contributing to social order, programs thus may also serve as a management resource (Lin 2000). Second, although less clear, involvement in these prison programs may increase prosocial activities in the community such as employment and increased schooling (Gaes et al. 1999; Gerber and Fritsch 1993; Harer 1995; Steurer, Smtih and Tracy 2001; see also Steurer and Smith 2003). Third and most salient, it appears that across existing studies, education and work programs reduce recidivism (Batiuk et al. 2005; Chappell 2004; Coley and Barton 2006; Drake, Aos, and Miller 2009; Harer 1995; Steurer and Smith 2003; Steurer, Smith, and Tracy 2001; Wilson, Gallagher, and MacKenzie 2000). Again, this finding is qualified by the dearth of experimental randomized studies that would rule out selection bias. Raising this methodological concern, however, does not obviate the fact that more evidence exists that these programs "work" than exists that they are inconsequential. As

MacKenzie (2006, 84) notes, "notwithstanding, these methodological flaws in the extant research, there is sufficient evidence ... to conclude that correctional education programs work to reduce recidivism" (see also Gaes 2008).

Wilson, Gallagher, and MacKenzie's (2000) meta-analysis of 33 educational, vocational, and work programs is most instructive (see also MacKenzie 2006; Wilson et al. 1999). They calculated that "assuming a 50 percent recidivism rate for nonparticipants, [program] participants recidivate, on average, at a rate of 39 percent" (361). They also concluded that education programs appeared to achieve a larger reduction in recidivism than work programs. Insights can also be drawn from a systematic review of this literature by Bouffard, MacKenzie, and Hickman (2000). Although cautious about the methodological limitations of the extant research, they suggest that three interventions likely reduce recidivism: (1) vocational education; (2) "multi-component" correctional industry programs that combine employment with other "components," such as vocational education and job search assistance; and (3) community employment programs, such as work-release or job search assistance outside the prison.

Additionally, in a release cohort study of 3,170 inmates in three states (Ohio, Maryland, and Minnesota), Steurer, Tracy, and Smith (2001; see also Steurer and Smith 2003) found that education programs are effective in achieving a reduction in recidivism. In each state, rearrest, reconviction, and reincarceration were lower for individuals participating in correctional education programs. When all three states' data were combined, of the individuals in educational programs, 48 percent (versus 57 percent of non-participants) were rearrested, 27 percent (versus 35 percent) were reconvicted, and 21 percent (versus 31 percent) were reincarcerated. In light of these findings, Steurer, Smith, and Tracy (2001, 49) conclude that "education provides a real payoff to the public in terms of crime reduction ... investments in correctional education programs have been confirmed as a wise and informed public policy."

Finally, the research suggests a fourth conclusion: treatment effects may be modified by offender and program characteristics. Thus, in a study of more than 14,000 Texas inmates released from prison in 1991 and 1992, Adams et al. (1994) found that prison education programs tended to be most effective in reducing recidivism for inmates who initially had low levels of educational achievement. They also uncovered a treatment "dose" effect: education only began to diminish reoffending once inmates had spent a minimum of 200 hours in the program. Uggen (2000) also found that characteristics of the offender had a moderating effect. In his study, educational programs led to a significant reduction in recidivism only for those over age 26. For younger offenders, no differences were found between participants and non-participants. On a broader level, it also seems likely that programs aimed at creating human capital will be more effective if they are able to link offenders not merely with employment but also with *quality* jobs. There is at least some evidence that, while merely having a job does not foster desistance, quality employment is related—net of individual differences—to lower recidivism (Uggen 1999; see also Currie 1985; Laub and Sampson 2003; Sampson and Laub 1993).

Drug Treatment Programs

Drug use and crime are behaviors that often co-occur in the same individuals. The precise causal relationship of involvement in drugs and other illegal conduct is debated, but it appears that drug use amplifies criminality (De Li, Priu, and MacKenzie 2000; Hough 2002; Huebner and Cobbina 2007; Lurigio 2000; Olson and Lurigio 2000). There also is evidence that offenders are more likely to ingest drugs, especially heroin and cocaine, than the general population (Bureau of Justice Statistics 1992; Lurigio 2000; Lurigio et al. 2003). For example, probationers in Illinois were found to be two and a half times more likely to report illicit drug use during their lifetime when compared to a sample of Illinois residents (Lurigio et al. 2003).

As might be anticipated, a high proportion of the offenders under correctional supervision have a history of drug use and/or related criminal activity (Karberg and James 2005; Maruna 2001; West and Sabol 2008). Thus, about one in five state prison inmates (253,300 offenders), one in two federal inmates (95,446 prisoners), and one-quarter of jail inmates (typically serving sentences for under a year in local county facilities) are incarcerated for drug-related offenses (Karberg and James 2005; West and Sabol 2008). Equally illuminating, in a 2004 survey of state and federal prison inmates, 1.2 percent of both state and federal prisoners met the criteria for drug dependence, 17.3 percent of state and 16.8 percent of federal prisoners met the criteria for drug abuse, and 34.9 percent of state and 27.5 percent of federal inmates met the criteria for both drug dependence and abuse in the 12 months prior to admission (Mumola and Karberg 2006).

Self-report surveys of offenders in prison, in jail, and on probation also show the prevalence of drug use among correctional populations (Glaze and Bonczar 2009; James 2004; Karberg and James 2005; Lurigio et al. 2003; Mumola 1998; Mumola and Bonczar 1998; Mumola and Karberg 2006; Wilson 2000). For example, in a 2004 survey of inmates in state and federal prisons, approximately eight in ten reported using drugs at some point in their lives (Mumola and Karberg 2006). More instructive, among state prisoners, 56 percent used drugs in the month before being arrested for their current offense, while 32 percent were using drugs at the time of the offense. Similar figures were found for convicted jail inmates, with 55 percent reporting taking drugs in the month before their offense and 29 percent using at the time of the crime (James 2004). For offenders in federal prisons, the percentages were lower but still substantial: 50 percent used drugs the month before being arrested, and 26 percent used at the time of arrest (Mumola and Karberg 2006). Drug use is also prevalent in the community correctional population. In 2005, roughly one-quarter of probationers were convicted of a drug offense (Glaze and Bonczar 2009). These figures, moreover, do not include offenders' involvement with alcohol. Thus, to take but one statistic, over one-half of state prison inmates were using drugs or alcohol when they were arrested (see Mumola 1998; Mumola and Bonczar 1998; Wilson 2000).

In response, jurisdictions have increasingly subjected convicted offenders, including those incarcerated, to drug tests. In a 1995 survey, about half of all offenders on probation reported being tested for drugs during their current period of supervision (Mumola and Bonczar 1998). In 2002, prison inmates in 44 state systems were subjected to more than 1.9 million drug tests, with 3.14 percent testing positive (*Corrections Compendium* 2003). Analyses of existing studies reveal that drug testing, even in conjunction with threats of punishment (e.g., revocation), generally fail to decrease offenders' risk of recidivating (see, e.g., Cullen, Wright, and Applegate 1996; Gendreau, Goggin, and Smith 2000; MacKenzie and Hickman 1998). As Prendergast, Anglin, and Wellisch note, "supervision is not enough. For offenders with serious drug problems, it is treatment, not merely supervision, however intensive, that is needed" (1995, 72).

Reflecting this reality, drug treatment programs are found throughout the correctional system. Among probationers, for example, 17.4 percent report participating in a drug treatment or drug abuse program during their current sentence. This figure, however, rises to 42.2 percent for offenders who reported using drugs in the month prior to being arrested (Mumola and Bonczar 1998). Similarly, among state prisoners who used drugs in the month prior to admission, approximately 40 percent had participated in a drug-related program while incarcerated; this figure was similar for those who met the criteria for drug dependence or abuse (Mumola and Karberg 2006). Forty-five percent of federal inmates who used drugs in the month prior to their admission took part in a drug-related treatment program, while 49 percent of drug dependent or abusing federal inmates participated in a substance abuse treatment program (Mumola and Karberg 2006). In raw numbers, 258,900 state and 269,200 federal inmates were participating in drug treatment programs in 2004 (Mumola and Karberg 2006). Still, the need for drug treatment seems to outstrip the supply (Lurigio 2000). Of offenders in prison, seven in ten who reported using drugs "regularly" before institutionalization were receiving no drug-related programming (Mumola 1998).

Within corrections, common forms of treatment include self-help/peer counseling (e.g., Narcotics/Cocaine Anonymous), drug and alcohol awareness and education classes, counseling by a professional, peer counseling, detoxification, maintenance drug programs, and a residential facility or unit (Karberg and James 2005; Mumola 1998; Mumola and Bonczar 1998; Mumola and Karberg 2006; Wilson 2000). A residential unit devoted solely to the treatment of drug and substance abuse is commonly called a "therapeutic community" or "TC" (Wexler, Falkin, and Lipton 1990). The state of Ohio, which has several of these units in its prisons, describes therapeutic communities in this way:

> ...long-term (6–12 months) residential Alcohol and Other Drug (AOD) treatment programs. The Therapeutic Community approach views AOD abuse as a reflection of chronic deficits in social, vocational, familial, economic, and personality development. The aim of the Therapeutic Community is to promote prosocial behavior, attitudes, and values as a method to attain abstinence from alcohol and other drugs and eliminate antisocial behaviors. (http://www.drc.ohio.gov/Public/BECI.htm)

Again, the critical issue is whether drug treatment programs in the correctional system are effective in reducing drug/criminal recidivism. The results seem, in the least, to be promising (Aos et al. 2001; Gaes et al. 1999; Lurigio 2000; MacKenzie 2006; Mitchell, Wilson, and MacKenzie 2007; Prendergast, Anglin, and Wellisch 1995; Taxman 1999). There is a growing consensus that intervention is likely to be successful when it adheres to certain "principles": the program is intensive, long-term, structured, backed up by penalties for non-participation (including criminal sanctions); multimodal, so as to deal with other problems that offenders have; and followed by aftercare services (Latessa 1999; Lurigio 2000; MacKenzie 2006; Mitchell, Wilson, and MacKenzie 2007; Prendergast, Anglin, and Wellisch 1995; Taxman 1999).

These principles are met most fully in prison-based "therapeutic communities." A meta-analysis by Pearson and Lipton (1999b) found that across seven "TC" studies, the treatment effect size was .133, which can be interpreted in practical terms as a success rate for the experimental group versus the control group of 56.7 percent versus 43.4 percent (see also Gaes et al. 1999). Although based on a limited number of studies, they also suggested that treatment options deserving of further study include methadone maintenance for offenders addicted to heroin, cognitive-behavioral therapy, and 12-step programs (similar to Alcoholics Anonymous programs). In contrast, Pearson and Lipton's meta-analysis revealed no support for the effectiveness of boot camps for drug offenders and for group counseling. Finally, MacKenzie and Hickman (1998, 58) conclude that currently there is "little evidence" that "community-based outpatient programs" reduce recidivism among drug offenders.

A more recent review of substance abuse programs reached similar conclusions concerning incarceration-based drug treatment. In 2007, Mitchell, Wilson, and MacKenzie conducted a meta-analysis of 66 evaluations assessing the impact of five types of drug treatment programs: therapeutic communities (TC), residential substance abuse treatment (RSAT), group counseling, boot camps exclusively for drug offenders, and narcotic maintenance programs. Overall, drug treatment programs were found to be associated with an 8 percent reduction in post-release offending; however, there was no general treatment effect on subsequent drug use. When examining each individual type of treatment modality, it was evident that some treatments are more effective than others in reducing post-release criminal behavior and drug use. Specifically, like Pearson and Lipton (1999b), Mitchell and colleagues reported that TC programs significantly reduce both the recidivism and drug use of its participants. However, unlike Pearson and Lipton (1999b), counseling programs were also found to significantly decrease post-release offending; even so, this treatment modality did not have a significant effect on drug use. Additionally, RSAT programs were associated with a reduction in recidivism, but the results were mixed concerning drug use. Finally, both narcotic maintenance and boot camp programs had no significant effects on either post-release criminal behavior or on drug use, thus suggesting that control-based programs are ineffective with substance abusing offenders.

Sex-Offender Programs

It is estimated that approximately a quarter of a million sex offenders are under the supervision of the correctional system (MacKenzie 2006). Of these, more than 180,000 are incarcerated (*Corrections Compendium* 2008c). In a 2008 survey of 44 state correctional systems, the most common types of treatment programs found in prison include group counseling (95 percent of systems), relapse prevention (88 percent), cognitive-behavioral therapy (83 percent), individual counseling (80 percent), offender-specific counseling (65 percent), and inmate support groups (60 percent). Less prevalent are medical interventions, family and spousal counseling, sexual reconditioning, and short-term crisis intervention programs. Just over half (55 percent) had special facilities for sex offenders (e.g., therapeutic communities, diagnostic centers) (*Corrections Compendium* 2008c). One residential sex-offender program in Virginia is described in this way:

> The SORT [Sex Offender Residential Treatment] Program utilizes a Transtheoretical Model to assess an offender's readiness for change and determine appropriate interventions. Most of the treatment provided is cognitive behaviorally based and emphasizes the use of the Relapse Prevention Model to deter reoffending behavior. Other types of treatment may be used based on the individual needs of the offender. Offenders accepted into the SORT program will typically be engaged in treatment for approximately two to three years. Length of involvement may vary based on the following factors: Time remaining on the offender's sentence, how quickly the inmate progresses, and whether or not the inmate is terminated from the program based on his behavior or other conflicting issues. (http://www.vadoc.virginia.gov/offenders/institutions/program/sort.shtm)

Reviews of research are now showing that modest, but meaningful, reductions in recidivism can be achieved by sex-offender programs (Gallagher et al. 1999; Hanson et al. 2002, Hanson et al. 2009; Losel and Schmucker 2005; MacKenzie 2006). According to MacKenzie (2006, 163), for example, there is evidence that "treatment programs using cognitive-behavioral therapy/relapse prevention and chemical castration/ psychotherapy" reduce sex-offender recidivism. Additionally, MacKenzie concludes that "treatment in hospital-based settings is more effective than treatment provided in prisons" (163). A meta-analysis reviewed by MacKenzie (2006) showed that across 28 studies, sexual reoffending was, on average, 12 percent for the treatment group and 22 percent for the control group. More specifically, the meta-analysis had two main conclusions. First, it appears that hormonal injections in conjunction with psychotherapy—an intervention that is typically used outside justice agencies—reduced recidivism among samples of exhibitionists and non-institutionalized pedophiles. Second, cognitive-behavioral programs that include relapse prevention—an intervention common in the correctional system—reduced recidivism among samples of rapists and institutionalized pedophiles.

In 2002, a comprehensive evaluation of the effectiveness of psychological treatment for sex offenders—mostly cognitive-behavioral programs— was completed (Hanson et al. 2002). In Hanson and colleagues' meta-analysis, 43 studies were assessed, including 15 that they judged to have "credible research designs" for sexual recidivism outcomes and 7 "credible" studies for general recidivism outcomes. Based on this latter subset of studies, they concluded that the psychological treatments were effective. Compared to control groups, offenders receiving treatment had only about half the recidivism rate for sex offenses (9.9 percent versus 17.4 percent) and a lower overall recidivism rate for any offense (32.3 percent versus 51.3 percent). Treatments delivered in the community and prison had similar effects for sex reoffending, but there was a tendency for community-based programs to achieve greater reductions in recidivism for crime in general.

Most recently, Hanson and colleagues (2009) completed another meta-analysis of 23 studies examining the effectiveness of sex-offender treatment. Similar to Hanson's earlier review, sex-offender treatment was found to be associated with a decrease in both sexual (10.9 percent versus 19.2 percent) and general (31.8 percent versus 48.3 percent) recidivism. They also discovered that programs that followed the principles of effective intervention (risk, need, and responsivity) were more effective than those that did not. (We discuss these principles below.) Furthermore, in both reviews by Hanson and colleagues, the findings are consistent with those found in the largest review of sex-offender treatment to date.

Thus, in a meta-analysis of 69 studies with 80 comparisons, Losel and Schmucker (2005) discovered that the treated group had a sexual recidivism rate of 11.1 percent compared to a rate of 17.5 percent for the comparison group. Although this seems like a small reduction in recidivism (only 6 percent), they argue that, when the low base-rate of sexual recidivism is taken into account, this reduction is equivalent to a 37 percent decrease in post-release sexual offending. Consequently, Losel and Schmuker (2005, 138) conclude that "cognitive-behavioral and hormonal treatments are most promising" in reducing subsequent criminal behavior among sex offenders.

BUILDING A THEORY OF EFFECTIVE REHABILITATION

Although criminology is rich in contemporary theories of crime (Akers and Sellers 2008; Cullen and Agnew 2011; Paternoster and Bachman 2001), true theories of correctional intervention are in short supply. One can find descriptions of successful programs and attempts to show how various counseling approaches apply to offenders (Cullen and Applegate 1997; MacKenzie 2006; Van Voorhis, Braswell, and Lester 2004). Even so, one searches in vain in mainstream criminology journals and textbooks for new *systematic* theories of intervention and for empirical tests of these perspectives. Why is this so?

Discussions of how criminologists think about rehabilitation cannot yet escape Martinson's "nothing works" legacy. Martinson framed the debate over offender treatment as an *empirical* issue: does rehabilitation work or not? Developing theories of effective intervention seemed ill-advised if there was, in essence, no "treatment effect" to be explained. Believing that rehabilitation was a euphemism for punishment and a hoax to boot, criminologists had no compelling reason to embark on theoretical inquiry.

Beyond Martinson, however, the politicization of criminology resulted in theories of crime that were not conducive to uncovering the proximate causes of crime—the kinds of factors that treatment programs might change. Again, for criminologists in the Martinson era, the state was transformed from an instrument of good into an instrument of oppression. Theories that blamed the state for "criminalizing" the wayward and "creating criminals"—labeling and conflict theories, for example—suddenly flourished. Explanations of crime not based in the unanticipated consequences of state control focused on the "evils" of American society, especially such structures as capitalism, patriarchy, and inequality. Theories of individual differences were dismissed as "blaming the victim" and as "pathologizing" people whose only crime was being born into an unjust society. Campaigning for social justice, not theorizing and designing effective treatment programs, was seen as the solution for the crime problem.

It is perhaps not surprising, then, that the most prominent effort to build a theory of effective correctional intervention came from a group of scholars—most notably Don Andrews, James Bonta, Paul Gendreau, and Robert Ross—who are not American criminologists. Instead, they are Canadians; at some point in their career, they either worked for or consulted with the government; and they are psychologists by training who saw the contention that behavior—including criminal behavior—could not be changed as inconsistent with a wealth of scientific evidence to the contrary. For them, rehabilitation was still a means to humanize corrections, improve offenders, and protect public safety. American criminologists' views on treatment struck them as ideological, as unscientific, and as bad social policy. Instead, free from the constraints imposed by the professional ideology of U.S. criminology (Cullen and Gendreau 2001), they sought to develop a coherent theory of rehabilitation that they typically have labeled the "principles of effective correctional treatment" (Andrews 1995; Andrews and Bonta 2006; Andrews et al. 1990; Cullen and Gendreau 1989; Gendreau 1996; Ross, Antonowicz, and Dhaliwal 1995; Ross and Fabiano 1985).

The Canadians' Theory of Rehabilitation

This perspective starts with the assumption that a theory of rehabilitation should be based on the social psychology of offending (Andrews 1995; Andrews and Bonta 2006). In this approach, individual and social/situational factors intersect to create in offenders values, cognitions, and personality orientations that foster crime. To a large extent, these ways of thinking and responding are learned and reinforced, and thus become, in effect, individual differences in criminal propensity. This social-psychological approach rejects psychodynamic and psychoanalytical theories of behavior as being too asocial and inconsistent with the empirical literature on crime (a point we will revisit shortly). It also rejects structural theories that link crime to "root causes" whose origins lie in the organization of society; after all, root causes are not amenable to change by correctional programming (see also Wilson 1975). Indeed, from the Canadians' standpoint, structural factors can only have effects to the extent that they produce, within individuals, the antisocial values, cognitions, and orientations that are the proximate causes of criminal conduct. Accordingly, while broader reforms may alleviate the distal structural sources of crime, treatment interventions must target those criminogenic factors that are within, or close to, offenders and thus within the reach of the kinds of programs the correctional system can undertake.

The Canadians also readily embraced positivist criminology, arguing that correctional interventions must be rooted in empirical knowledge about the sources of criminal conduct. It has long been asserted that, similar to medicine, rehabilitation programs should seek to change what causes crime (Cullen and Gendreau 2001). Taking this commonsensical insight seriously, these scholars used reviews of the evidence, including meta-analyses, to document the major *known predictors of recidivism* (Andrews 1995; Andrews and Bonta 2006; Gendreau, Little, and Goggin 1996; Gendreau, Smith, and French 2006). This research revealed that the major predictors include (1) "antisocial/procriminal attitudes, values, beliefs and cognitive-emotional states (that is, personal cognitive supports for crime)"; (2) "procriminal associates and isolation from anticriminal others (that is, interpersonal supports for crime)"; and (3) antisocial personality orientations such as low self-control, impulsiveness, risk-taking, and egocentrism (Andrews 1995, 37). Recidivism also is predicted by a history of antisocial conduct extending to childhood, by families that lack proper parenting (e.g., inadequate support and supervision of children), and by "low levels of personal, educational, vocational or financial achievement," including an "unstable employment record" (Andrews 1995, 37).

Importantly, the Canadians noted that some predictors of crime are "static" and cannot be changed, such as a past history of misconduct. However, other predictors, such as antisocial values, are "dynamic" and thus are theoretically amenable to change. If most predictors were static, then there would be nothing to change, and rehabilitation would be impossible. As it turns out, the most important predictors of recidivism are dynamic and thus might conceivably be treated or "cured." The Canadians called these dynamic risk factors "criminogenic needs." They also argued that instruments used to classify the "risk level" of offenders should measure not only static risk factors but also these criminogenic needs (Bonta 1996). If so, these classification instruments could be employed in treatment programs to assess whether interventions had altered criminogenic needs. In short, these instruments could serve both a public safety function (estimating risk) and a treatment function (helping to diagnose offender needs and change).

These considerations lead to the question: What, precisely, should treatment programs target for change? This issue is critical because the Canadians' theory of rehabilitation argues that offender behavior will not change if factors weakly related or unrelated to recidivism are the main focus of an intervention (e.g., self-esteem). In fact, a major reason that treatment programs fail is because they either target the wrong factors for intervention or are unspecific as to what is to be altered (i.e., they have no underlying theory of crime guiding the program). In contrast, interventions should focus on the known predictors of recidivism (listed above). If they did, then "promising targets" for change would include "changing antisocial attitudes; changing antisocial feelings; reducing antisocial peer associations; promoting familial affection/communication; promoting familial monitoring and supervision; promoting identification/association with anticriminal role models; increasing self-control, self-management and problem solving skills..." (Andrews 1995, 55).

The next step is to determine what type or modality of treatment would be most effective in changing the factors that a program targets for rehabilitation. In the Canadians' scheme, "general responsivity" is the use of a treatment modality that is "responsive to" or capable of changing the major known predictors of recidivism. Given their social psychological theory of crime, which emphasizes social learning and antisocial values/cognitions, they hypothesized that the "best modes of service are *behavioural*" (Andrews 1995, 56; emphasis in original). These programs thus should "employ the cognitive-behavioural and social learning techniques of modeling, graduated practice, role playing, reinforcement, extinction, resource provision, concrete verbal suggestions (symbolic modeling, giving reasons, prompting), and cognitive restructuring" (Andrews 1995, 56; see also Ross, Antonowicz, and Dhaliwal 1995; Van Voorhis, Braswell, and Lester 2004; more generally, see Spiegler and Guevremont 1998). In these programs, it is also advised that positive reinforcements outweigh negative reinforcements by a four-to-one ratio (Gendreau 1996).

This theory of rehabilitation has the advantage of predicting not only what does work but also what does not work to reform offenders. According to Andrews (1995, 56), these include "programs designed according to the . . . principles of deterrence and labeling, innovative alternative intermediate punishments, non-directive, client-centered counseling, and unstructured psychodynamic therapy." Again, these interventions would be ineffective either because they do not target the appropriate factors for change and/or they are unresponsive to—incapable of altering—the major criminogenic needs.

Beyond general responsivity, the Canadians' model proposes that treatment will be more effective if it pays attention to "specific responsivity." Depending on their characteristics (e.g., intelligence, levels of anxiety), offenders may have different learning styles and thus respond more readily to some techniques than others (e.g., more or less structure in a program, the method through which program information is relayed) (Andrews 1995; Andrews and Bonta 2006; Gendreau 1996). For example, offenders with lower IQs might be more amenable to treatment if a program was less verbal, relied on tangible reinforcers, and conveyed content in a repeated, gradual way. Notably, specific responsivity does not mean—as some commentators are prone to say—that "some forms of treatment work for some types of offenders some of the time." Rather, it only means that the degree to which interventions based on the principle of general responsivity will be effective can be further increased if specific responsivity considerations are taken into account. This situation is analogous to one in which a certain drug is effective in combating an infection, but its impact will be stronger if the physician considers the specific characteristics of the patient in prescribing the frequency and dose with which the medicine is given. In any event, specific responsivity is a way of fine-tuning treatment delivery. It is not meant to make the matching of treatments to offenders so individualized as to render the delivery of effective intervention unfeasible within the context of the resources available to correctional agencies.

The Canadian scholars have argued as well that interventions will be more effective if they are directed to offenders that a risk-needs classification instrument categorizes as "high risk" (Andrews and Bonta 2006). This principle both violates and is explained by "common sense," showing that common sense can account for both sides of most empirical relationships! Thus, common sense would suggest that low-risk offenders are more amenable to treatment because they are less "hardened" in their criminality. But common sense would also suggest that high-risk offenders are more amenable to treatment because they are in a sense "sicker" and thus have more about them that potentially can be changed. The Canadians contend that the latter version is accurate and thus recommend devoting most resources to the treatment of high-risk offenders. Low-risk offenders, they argue, may be made more criminogenic by intrusive interventions.

Finally, the Canadian model makes a number of other recommendations for increasing treatment effectiveness (see Andrews 1995; Andrews and Bonta 2006; Gendreau 1996). These include staff delivering treatment in an authoritative way (warm but restrictive, firm but fair); structured aftercare to give offenders a treatment "booster shot"; program "therapeutic integrity" that involves the use of detailed training manuals, the training and supervision of staff, adherence to the prescribed treatment modality, and a treatment dosage of sufficient duration and intensity to affect the criminogenic needs targeted for change; and a host agency that is supportive of the program's implementation and operation.

In brief, the Canadians' theory of rehabilitation involves the following principles: (1) use a social psychological perspective to focus on the proximate causes of crime; (2) based on empirical data, target for change known predictors of recidivism that are dynamic, not static—that is, focus on "criminogenic needs"; (3) use cognitive-behavioral treatment programs, because these are "generally responsive" to changing the major criminogenic needs; (4) where possible, develop programs that can be "specifically responsive" to the learning styles and characteristics of offenders; (5) focus interventions on high-risk offenders, with risk level determined by classification instruments that measure static risk and dynamic risk factors; and (6) ensure that intervention programs have therapeutic integrity.

Testing the Canadians' Theory of Rehabilitation

The Canadian scholars have not simply constructed a theory of rehabilitation but also have dared to test it through meta-analyses of the existing program evaluation literature. In an initial effort, Andrews et al. (1990) categorized 80 studies in terms of whether the intervention conformed to the principles of effective treatment. If the treatment intervention adhered to these principles, it was defined as providing "appropriate service" (see Andrews et al. 1990, 379).

Across all studies in the sample, they found that the effect size was .10, a result consistent with other meta-analyses (Lipsey and Cullen 2007; Losel 1995, 2001; McGuire 2002). When they examined "appropriate" treatments, however, the effect size rose to .30 or the equivalent of a 30 percentage-point difference in the recidivism rate between the treatment and control groups. This assessment was later extended to include 230 studies, with similar results. Programs conforming to the principles of the theory of effective intervention had an effect size of .26 (Andrews and Bonta 2006; Andrews, Dowden, and Gendreau 1999; see also Antonowicz and Ross 1994). Although based on a smaller number of studies, these results also are found for programs involving female offenders (Dowden and Andrews 1999; Hubbard and Pratt 2002).

The Canadians' theory is important because it organizes much knowledge about treatment effectiveness. In particular, it tells us not only what works and why but also what does not work and why. Most salient, it makes strong predictions about the *ineffectiveness* of control-oriented interventions that seek to specifically deter offenders through surveillance and threats of punishment. Because these control-oriented programs do not target for change the known predictors of recidivism and do not conform to the principle of general responsivity (i.e., do not use cognitive-behavioral treatments), they will not reduce recidivism. As noted previously, the existing literature shows that control-oriented programs are ineffective (see, e.g., Byrne and Pattvina 1992; Cullen and Gendreau 2000; Cullen, Wright, and Applegate 1996; Fulton et al. 1997; Gendreau, Cullen, and Bonta 1994; Gendreau et al. 2000; Lipsey and Cullen 2007; MacKenzie 1997, 2000, 2006; Marion 2002; McGuire 2002; Petersilia 1998; Sherman et al. 1997).

The Canadians' theory of rehabilitation would gain added credence if it were systematically tested by other scholars (Gaes et al. 1999). Further, some contrary results have emerged. For example, studies do not uniformly show that treatment interventions are more effective with high-risk offenders (Dowden and Andrews 2000; Dowden, Antonowicz, and Andrews 2003; Gaes et al. 1999; Ross, Antonowicz, and Dhaliwal 1995; Smith, Gendreau, and Swartz 2009; see, however, Lipsey 2009). Still, the evidence from existing meta-analyses largely support the principles of effective treatment outlined by the Canadians. "It is interesting," observes Lipsey (1992, 123), "that the treatment types that show this larger order of effects are, with few exceptions, those defined as most 'clinically relevant' in the Andrews et al. review" (see also Lipsey 1995, 77–78). Similarly, in a replication of the Andrews et al. study, Pearson, Lipton, and Cleland's (1996) meta-analysis found that programs that delivered "appropriate correctional services" were more effective in reducing recidivism than "unspecified" and "inappropriate" programs. The effect size for appropriate programs was not as high as that reported by Andrews et al. (1990), but the results were in the same direction. Additionally, Smith, Gendreau, and Swartz (2009, 163) conclude that "as the results have been replicated with remarkable consistency, it is clear that treatments adhering to the principles of effective intervention are effective in reducing offender recidivism." Further, consistent with the theory of rehabilitation, there is growing evidence that cognitive-behavioral treatment is efficacious in lowering reoffending (see Landenberger and Lipsey 2005; Lipsey 1992; Lipsey, Chapman, and Landenberger 2001; Lipsey and Cullen 2007; Lipsey, Landenberger, and Wilson 2007; Losel 1995; MacKenzie 2000, 2006; McGuire 2002; Pearson et al. 2002; Redondo, Sanchez-Meca, and Garrido 1999; Wilson, Bouffard, and MacKenzie 2005).

In closing, Andrews, Bonta, Gendreau, Ross, and their fellow Canadian coauthors have made an impressive contribution to the study of offender treatment (Ogloff and Davis 2004). They have constructed a model of rehabilitation that is rooted in theoretical and empirical criminology, that organizes much of what is known about effective interventions, and that is largely supported by existing meta-analyses of the treatment literature. As with any social science paradigm, this theory warrants our organized skepticism and rigorous empirical scrutiny (see Gaes et al. 1999; Duguid 2000; Whitehead and Lab 1989). Even so, few criminological perspectives have been developed with such clarity as to their core assumptions and with such respect for the extant data. Until rival perspectives meet these standards, it seems likely that the Canadians' theory of rehabilitation will serve as a Kuhnian (1962) paradigm that shapes how treatment research and, potentially, practice are undertaken.

THE CHALLENGE OF TECHNOLOGY TRANSFER

Technology transfer refers to the transmission of scientific knowledge from the producers to the potential consumers of this information. In the social sciences, technology transfer typically involves the dissemination of research findings to practitioners and policymakers so as to improve the effectiveness of service delivery and the soundness of policy initiatives (Backer, David, and Soucy 1995; Cullen, Myer, and Latessa 2009). In some fields, such as medicine, technology transfer is institutionalized through professional training, continuing education, and expectations that scientific journals will be consulted (Blumstein and Petersilia 1995, 470). In fact, the failure to receive current scientific knowledge and to incorporate it into medical decision-making can expose physicians to legal liability and professional sanctions for malpractice.

In human service fields, however, scientific "technology" is often not transmitted. Take, for example, the treatment of alcohol problems. A review of existing research led Hester and Miller (1995, xi) to conclude that "a number of treatment methods were consistently supported by controlled scientific research." However, they were "dismayed to realize that virtually none of these treatment methods was in common use within alcohol treatment programs in the United States."

This situation is commonplace in the delivery of correctional rehabilitation. Criminologists share much of the blame, because they have been substantially in the grips of a "nothing works" ideology for 25 years and thus lax in developing treatment-program technology that could be transferred (Cullen and Gendreau 2001). Indeed, if not for the research of scholars—mostly psychologists—outside traditional criminology, it is not clear that we would have any meaningful body of scientific knowledge on rehabilitation to share (see, e.g., Andrews and Bonta 2006; Henggeler et al. 1998; Loeber and Farrington 1998; Palmer 1992; see also Cullen and

Applegate 1997). Still, much of the blame for the lack of technology transfer must be shouldered by policymakers and practitioners. They have often been skeptical of research findings and prepared to privilege "personal experience" over scientific knowledge in deciding which programs to implement (Blumstein and Petersilia 1995). The result has been a form of correctional malpractice or quackery in which ineffective, if not harmful, interventions have been embraced (Cullen and Gendreau 2000; Gendreau, Smith, and Theriault 2009; Latessa, Cullen, and Gendreau 2002). Meanwhile, calls for "evidence-based corrections" have too often fallen on deaf ears (Andrews and Bonta 2006; Cullen and Gendreau 2000; Cullen, Myer, and Latessa 2009; Gendreau 1996; Gendreau et al. 2002; Latessa, Cullen, and Gendreau 2002; MacKenzie 2000, 2006).

The saga of "boot camps" is a recent case in point (for another example, see Latessa and Moon 1992, on the use of acupuncture with drug offenders). An invention of the 1980s, boot camps proposed to expose offenders to a military-style boot camp in hopes of "breaking them down and building them back up." This intervention built on the long-standing narrative in American culture, often represented in films such as *An Officer and a Gentleman*, in which rag-tag, irresponsible young men are inculcated with backbone and maturity under the watchful tough love of a gruff drill sergeant. These programs appealed in particular to elected officials who had, in their minds, been transformed by the discipline of boot camps and believed that their personal experience of being whipped into shape would generalize to offenders (Cullen et al. 2005; Cullen, Myer, and Latessa 2009; Cullen, Wright, and Applegate 1996; Listwan et al. 2008; Selcraig 2000; Stinchcomb 2005). One classic example of this way of thinking is provided by former Georgia Governor Zell Miller. Describing his boot camp experience in the Marines as a "molding experience," Miller argued in his 1990 campaign that boot camps would be an effective way to reform offenders. He contended that boot camp programs can shape and transform undisciplined offenders into disciplined and law-abiding individuals (Erwin 1996, 163). Even when faced with evidence of the ineffectiveness of boot camps, Miller's spokesman quipped back "we don't care what the study shows" while Georgia's Commissioner of Corrections argued that academics were too quick to ignore the knowledge of the people who actually work in the system (Vaughn 1994, 2).

Millions of dollars were spent to implement boot camps without any thought given to the existing criminological technology on program effectiveness. No one involved in the boot camp movement seemed to question the amorphous, if not ridiculous, notion that offender change involved "breaking people down" and then "building them back up"—whatever that means. In fact, as shown above, advocates were adamantly supportive of these programs even in light of contradictory evidence. No one asked what known predictors of recidivism the program was targeting. No one wondered whether such a program, which involved threatening confrontations and punishment in the name of discipline, was a "responsive" treatment for the population to which it was directed—low-risk offenders. No one paused to consult the literature showing that military service has, at best, a modest and complex impact on criminal propensities, with no evidence that boot camps per se have any ameliorative effects (Cullen et al. 2005; Cullen, Wright, and Applegate 1996; Listwan et al. 2008; Stinchcomb 2005). And no one raised the opportunity costs of building boot camps instead of using resources to initiate rehabilitation programs rooted in the principles of effective intervention. In fact, there is no evidence that anyone did any library research on "what works" with offenders or picked up the phone and called Canada to see if they had any scholars that knew anything about changing lawbreakers for the better!

Fortunately, there are signs that the field of corrections is becoming more open to technology transfer. Although boot camps are still operating in many states, two main factors have caused other states (i.e., Alabama, Arizona, California, Colorado, Georgia, Maryland, New Hampshire, Oregon, and South Dakota) to abandon these programs (Leary 2006; Listwan et al. 2008). First, there is now near incontrovertible evidence showing the failure of boot camps to achieve large reductions in recidivism (Austin 2000; Bottcher and Ezell 2005; Cullen, Wright and Applegate 1996; Cullen et al. 2005; Drake, Aos, and Miller 2009; MacKenzie 1997, 2006; MacKenzie, Wilson, and Kider 2001; Parent 2003; Stinchcomb and Terry 2001; Wilson, MacKenzie, and Mitchell 2003). Second, claims of physical and emotional abuse of boot camp participants have led to a public outcry and lawsuits (Listwan et al. 2008; Leary 2006; Newborn 2006; Selcraig 2000). In light of these issues, major professional organizations in corrections have embraced the value of technology transfer. The International Community Corrections Association, for example, now regularly sponsors annual "what works" conferences, where "keynote speeches presenting state of the art research findings highlight evidence-based best practices in the field" and "an array of workshops focus on implementing best practices in a wide variety of topic areas and related publications" (http://www.iccaweb.org/conferences.html; see, e.g., Harland 1996; Latessa 1999). Similarly, the American Correctional Association publishes a variety of resources describing the "best bets" for effective intervention (Rhine 1998) and how to put the empirical "research into practice" (Rhine and Evans 2008). Still, much work remains to be done.

To assess the quality of programming delivered by agencies, or therapeutic integrity, the Canadian scholars designed the Correctional Program Assessment Inventory, or CPAI (Gendreau and Goggin 1997; Gendreau, Goggin, and Smith 2001), which was subsequently revised into the CPAI-2000 (Gendreau and Andrews 2001). Developed on the basis of their theory of rehabilitation, the CPAI is a 131-item instrument that can be used to assess eight features of an agency delivering a treatment program: (1) organizational culture, (2) program implementation/ maintenance,

(3) management/staff characteristics, (4) client risk-need practices, (5) program characteristics, (6) core correctional practices (e.g., relationship and skill factors), (7) inter-agency communication, and (8) evaluation (see also Latessa and Holsinger 1998; Smith, Gendreau, and Goggin 2004). The CPAI can be employed to judge whether agencies are marked by major programming deficits or by the effective delivery of services.

Multiple studies using the CPAI have assessed, in combination, more than 400 programs in Canada and the United States (Lowenkamp 2004; Smith, Gendreau, and Swartz 2009). The results have not been encouraging. According to Gendreau, Goggin, and Smith (2001), "the blunt truth is that 70 percent of all programs... 'failed' according to the CPAI" (see also Lipsey 1999a). Similarly, Matthews, Hubbard, and Latessa (2001) and Lowenkamp, Latessa, and Smith (2006) also found that a large percentage of programs scored in the failing or needs improvement categories (over 60 percent of programs). Latessa and Holsinger summarize common problems found by the CPAI in the area of "characteristics of the program":

Since programs are rarely designed around a theoretical model, it was not surprising to find a lack of a consistently applied treatment model in place. In general, the major shortcomings... include lack of programmatic structure; incomplete or nonexistent treatment manuals; few rewards to encourage program participation and compliance; the ineffective use of punishment; staff being allowed to design their own interventions regardless of the treatment literature base; and a host of very obvious and definable, yet ineffective, treatment models.... Finally, many programs failed to provide aftercare services or booster sessions. (1998, 26)

The CPAI findings are troubling because they show how much correctional practice is doomed to failure because it is based on incorrect "technology." But these results also offer some basis for optimism. It is clear that a number of programs in the "real world" are being conducted largely in accordance with the principles of effective treatment. Lipsey (1999a) reports similar findings in an analysis of "practical" juvenile interventions—programs conducted in agency settings that were not designed and/or operated by researchers. Although still in the minority, these programs supply important evidence that well-designed and effective programs can be administered in correctional agencies (see also Lipsey 2009).

Additionally, since the CPAI measures adherence to the principles of effective intervention, treatment programs that have high therapeutic integrity (e.g., a high score on the CPAI) should be associated with a reduction in recidivism. The research has confirmed this relationship between program integrity and program outcomes (Holsinger 1999; Lowenkamp 2004; Lowenkamp, Latessa, and Smith 2006; Nesovic 2003). Conducting a meta-analysis of 173 studies, Nesovic (2003) found that high CPAI scores were associated with lower recidivism rates. Similarly, in an assessment of 38 community-based residential programs in Ohio, Lowenkamp, Latessa, and Smith (2006) showed that the total CPAI score has a fairly strong, nearly linear negative relationship with recidivism. Those programs that adhered most closely to the principles of effective intervention achieved the highest reductions in returns to prison. Compared to a matched sample of parolees/post-release control releases, the reduction in recidivism was 22 percent for the one program rated as satisfactory, 8.1 percent for programs rated as satisfactory but in need of improvement, and 1.7 percent for programs rated as unsatisfactory.

Lipsey (1999a) reminds us, however, that having an effective program is not an easy task. He argues that "such beneficial effects do not come automatically—a concerted effort must be made to configure the programs in the most favorable manner and to provide the types of services that have been shown to be effective, and avoid those shown to be ineffective" (1999a, 641; see also Lin 2000). Again, motivating correctional agencies to make such an effort will require, at least in part, persuading staff that doing so makes good sense. In this context, technology transfer is important in showing clearly why certain correctional practices are almost certain to fail and in pointing out how other intervention strategies can achieve meaningful reductions in recidivism. As Van Voorhis (1987) points out, there is a "high cost to ignoring success" in offender treatment—an observation that gives technology transfer an inherent rationality.

In this exchange, the challenge for criminologists will be to construct a knowledge base—likely built off the Canadians' theory of rehabilitation—that provides clearer guidance both on "what works" and on strategies to implement such principles in the real world. The challenge for policymakers and practitioners will be to become more willing partners with criminologists in the development of effective programs, both receiving and helping to create new offender-treatment "technology."

CONCLUSION: REAFFIRMING REHABILITATION

This essay has been informed by the assumption that treatment programs and the goal of rehabilitation are integral to the correctional enterprise. In the face of various attacks on offender treatment—especially the "nothing works" doctrine—it has been argued, in essence, that rehabilitation should not be abandoned but rather "reaffirmed" (Cullen 2007; Cullen and Gilbert 1982; Cullen and Moon 2002). This view rests on three contentions, which will be shared—albeit briefly—as a way of concluding our discussion on offender treatment.

First, rehabilitation programs reduce recidivism overall and, when implemented according to the principles of effective treatment, potentially reduce reoffending substantially. In short, "rehabilitation works." This is not to say that correctional treatment is a panacea or easily accomplished. We need to be far more judicious than the early advocates of the rehabilitative ideal who often were naive about the difficulty of changing wayward behavior (Rothman 1980). Effective intervention must be based on more than good intentions; it must reflect good science, good policy, and good practice. Still, the empirical evidence is fairly convincing—and growing stronger as time passes—that treatment interventions are capable of decreasing recidivism. The influence of these programs is also likely to be "general." That is, with some variation in effects, they work with serious offenders, drug offenders, and sex offenders; with juveniles and with adults; with males and with females; in the community and in prison. In contrast, correctional programs based on the principles of specific deterrence are notoriously ineffective. In the end, the utility of rehabilitation argues for its retention as a core goal of corrections.

Second, the public supports rehabilitating offenders and expanding treatment programs. There is little doubt that there is an ample reservoir of punitive sentiments among the American public to prompt citizens' support for a range of "get tough" policies. Public opinion polls, for example, regularly show that upwards of three-fourths of Americans believe that the courts in their area do not "deal harshly enough with criminals" (Cullen, Fisher, and Applegate 2000). Even so, there is another side of public opinion about corrections. Study after study shows that Americans support rehabilitation as a central goal of imprisonment. In forced-choice questions. a substantial minority selects treating offenders as their preferred goal. When asked to rate the role of treatment in prisons, four in five see rehabilitation as "important" or "very important." A high percentage of citizens also endorses expanding treatment services. Support for rehabilitation is especially pronounced for juvenile offenders. Early intervention programs are strongly advocated, with citizens preferring to spend tax funds on these programs as opposed to building more prisons (Applegate, Cullen, and Fisher 1997; Cullen, Fisher, and Applegate 2000; Cullen and Moon 2002; Cullen et al. 2007; Cullen et al. 1998; Moon et al. 1999; Nagin et al. 2006). In short, the "public will" is not only to punish offenders but also to rehabilitate them.

Third, attempting to rehabilitate offenders is the right thing to do. Admittedly, sustaining this argument is more difficult because ultimately it reflects the choice of a particular moral compass and is based less on data and more on speculation. A different view is defensible. Thus, those rejecting rehabilitation are often troubled by its paternalism and by its implicit message—broadcast to the larger community—that the harmful behavior of offenders is to be understood, if not excused. In contrast, punishment unadulterated by utilitarian goals is held to clearly demarcate right from wrong, thus setting firm moral boundaries. Punishment also affirms the dignity of offenders, because it treats them "as responsible human beings who must accept the consequences of their actions" (Logan and Gaes 1993, 258).

Our difficulty with this line of reasoning is twofold (Cullen and Applegate 1997). First, the "messages" offender rehabilitation broadcasts are, at the least, in the eye of the beholder. Where other commentators see paternalism and the excuse of wrongdoing, others might well see rehabilitation as reflecting not the attenuation of moral values but a shared social purpose—"a society in which the dominant groups possess high confidence in their definitions of character and their standards of good behavior" (Allen 1981, 11). Or perhaps they might see the call for treatment as showing a legitimate concern for social justice—as evidence that the poor and minority offenders concentrated in the nation's prisons are not to be treated as human refuse but as people with dignity who deserve the opportunity for self-improvement.

Second and more important, we are troubled by what transpires when the correctional system starts to forfeit the rehabilitative ideal and embrace starkly punitive principles—much as has occurred in various jurisdictions in the United States over the past quarter century. We find it difficult to sustain the view that the absence of a firm commitment to offender treatment fosters more justice and dignity for offenders. Indeed, if anything, the contemporary historical record is disquieting in showing that in recent decades, elected officials gave short shrift to the ideals of justice and instead competed to see who could make sentences longer and prison life harsher (Clear 1994). In contrast, by showing concern for the welfare of offenders—with the exchange being that investing in the wayward advances public safety by reducing their risk of recidivating—rehabilitation provides one of the few rationales for not imposing unnecessary pains on those under correctional supervision. In the current context, we suggest that whatever humanity the practice of rehabilitation brings to the correctional enterprise is much needed. And if reaffirming rehabilitation makes corrections a bit more paternalistic and kindhearted, we are all for it.

References

Adams, Kenneth, Katherine J. Bennett, Timothy J. Flanagan, James W. Marquart, Steven J. Cuvelier, Eric Fritsch, Jurg Gerber, Dennis R. Longmire, and Velmer S. Burton, Jr. 1994. "A Large-Scale Multidimensional Test of the Effect of Prison Education Programs on Offenders' Behavior." *The Prison Journal* 74: 433–449.

Adams, Stuart. 1976. "Evaluation: A Way Out of Rhetoric." In *Rehabilitation, Recidivism, and Research*, eds. Robert Martinson, Ted Palmer, and Stuart Adams, 75–91. Hackensack, NJ: National Council on Crime and Delinquency.

Akers, Ronald L., and Christine S. Sellers. 2008. *Criminological Theories: Introduction, Evaluation, and Application*, 5th ed. New York: Oxford University Press.

Allen, Francis A. 1981. *The Decline of the Rehabilitative Ideal: Penal Policy and Social Purpose*. New Haven, CT: Yale University Press.

Andrews, D. A. 1995. "The Psychology of Criminal Conduct and Effective Treatment." In *What Works: Reducing Reoffending*, ed. James McGuire, 35–62. West Sussex, UK: John Wiley.

Andrews, D. A., and James Bonta. 2006. *The Psychology of Criminal Conduct*, 4th ed. Cincinnati, OH: Anderson.

Andrews, D. A., Craig Dowden, and Paul Gendreau. 1999. "Clinically Relevant and Psychologically Informed Approaches to Reduced Reoffending: A Meta-Analytic Study of Human Service, Risk, Need, Responsivity, and Other Concerns in Justice Contexts." Unpublished manuscript, Carleton University, Ottawa, Ontario, Canada.

Andrews, D. A., Ivan Zinger, Robert D. Hoge, James Bonta, Paul Gendreau, and Francis T. Cullen. 1990. "Does Correctional Treatment Work? A Clinically Relevant and Psychologically Informed Meta-Analysis." *Criminology* 8: 369–404.

Antonowicz, Daniel H., and Robert R. Ross. 1994. "Essential Components of Successful Rehabilitation Programs for Offenders." *International Journal of Offender and Comparative Criminology* 38: 97–104.

Aos, Steve, Polly Phipps, Robert Barnoski, and Roxanne Lieb. 2001. *The Comparative Costs and Benefits of Programs to Reduce Crime*. Olympia: Washington State Institute for Public Policy.

Applegate, Brandon K., Francis T. Cullen, and Bonnie S. Fisher. 1997. "Public Support for Correctional Treatment: The Continuing Appeal of the Rehabilitative Ideal." *The Prison Journal* 77: 237–258.

Austin, James. 2000. *Multi-Site Evaluation of Boot Camp Programs: Final Report*. Washington, DC: George Washington University, The Institute on Crime, Justice, and Corrections.

Bachman, Jerald G., and John Schulenberg. 1993. "How Part-Time Work Intensity Relates to Drug Use, Problem Behavior, Time Use, and Satisfaction among High School Seniors: Are These Consequences Merely Correlates?" *Developmental Psychology* 29: 220–235.

Backer, Thomas E., Susan L. David, and Gerald Soucy, eds. 1995. *Reviewing the Behavioral Science Knowledge Base on Technology Transfer*. Rockville, MD: National Institute on Drug Abuse, U.S. Department of Health and Human Services.

Bailey, Walter C. 1966. "Correctional Outcome: An Evaluation of 100 Reports." *Journal of Criminal Law, Criminology and Police Science* 57: 153–160.

Batiuk, Mary Ellen, Karen F. Lahm, Matthew Mckeever, Norma Wilcox, and Pamela Wilcox. 2005. "Disentangling the Effects of Correctional Education: Are Current Policies Misguided? An Event History Analysis." *Criminal Justice* 5 (5): 55–74.

Beckett, Katherine. 1997. *Making Crime Pay: Law and Order in Contemporary American Politics*. New York: Oxford University Press.

Binder, Arnold, and Gilbert Geis. 1984. "*Ad Populum* Argumentation in Criminology: Juvenile Diversion as Rhetoric." *Crime and Delinquency* 30: 624–647.

Blumstein, Alfred. 1997. "Interaction of Criminological Research and Public Policy." *Journal of Quantitative Criminology* 12: 349–361.

Blumstein, Alfred, and Joan Petersilia. 1995. "Investing in Criminal Justice Research." In *Crime*, eds. James Q. Wilson and Joan Petersilia, 465–487. San Francisco: ICS Press.

Bonta, James. 1996. "Risk-Needs Assessment and Treatment." In *Choosing Correctional Interventions That Work: Defining the Demand and Evaluating the Supply*, ed. Alan T. Harland, 18–32. Thousand Oaks, CA: Sage.

Bonta, James, Suzanne Wallace-Capretta, and Jennifer Rooney. 2000. "A Quasi-Experimental Evaluation of an Intensive Supervision Rehabilitation Program." *Criminal Justice and Behavior* 27: 312–329.

Bottcher, Jean, and Michael E. Ezell. 2005. "Examining the Effectiveness of Boot Camps: A Randomized Experiment with a Long-Term Follow-Up." *Journal of Research in Crime and Delinquency* 43: 309–332.

Bouffard, Jeffrey A., Doris Layton MacKenzie, and Laura J. Hickman. 2000. "Effectiveness of Vocational Education and Employment Programs for Adult Offenders: A Methodology-Based Analysis of the Literature." *Journal of Offender Rehabilitation* 31: 1–41.

Bureau of Justice Statistics. 1992. *Drugs, Crime, and the Justice System: A National Report.* Washington, DC: Bureau of Justice Statistics, U.S. Department of Justice.

Burghardt, John, Peter Z. Schochet, Sheena McConnell, Terry Johnson, R. Mark Gritz, Steven Glazerman, John Homrighausen, and Russell Jackson. 2001. *Does Job Corp Work? Summary of the National Job Corps Study.* Washington, DC: U.S. Department of Labor.

Bushway, Shawn, and Peter Reuter. 1997. "Labor Markets and Crime Risk Factors." Chapter 6 in *Preventing Crime: What Works, What Doesn't, What's Promising,* eds. Lawrence W. Sherman, Denise Gottfredson, Doris Layton MacKenzie, John Eck, Peter Reuter, and Shawn Bushway. Washington, DC: National Institute of Justice, U.S. Department of Justice.

Bynre, James M., and April Pattavina. 1992. "The Effectiveness Issue: Assessing What Works in the Adult Corrections System." In *Smart Sentencing: The Emergence of Intermediate Sanctions,* eds. James M. Byrne, Arthur J. Lurigio, and Joan Petersilia, 281–303. Newbury Park, CA: Sage.

Chappell, Cathryn. 2004. "Post-Secondary Correctional Education and Recidivism: A Meta-Analysis of Research Conducted 1990–1999." *Journal of Correctional Education* 55: 148–169.

Cecil, Dawn K., Daniella A. Drapkin, Doris Layton MacKenzie, and Laura J. Hickman. 2000. "The Effectiveness of Adult Basic Education and Life-Skills Programs in Reducing Recidivism: A Review and Assessment of the Research." *Journal of Correctional Education* 51: 207–226.

Clear, Todd R. 1994. *Harm in American Penology: Offenders, Victims, and Their Communities.* Albany: State University of New York Press.

Coley, Richard J., and Paul E. Barton. 2006. *Locked Up and Locked Out: An Educational Perspective on the U.S. Prison Population.* Princeton, NJ: Educational Testing Service, Policy Information Center.

Corrections Compendium. 2002. "Prison Industries: Survey Summary." 27 (September): 8–19.

Corrections Compendium. 2003. "Drug Testing." 28 (April): 10–22.

Corrections Compendium. 2006. "Juvenile Offenders." 31 (January–February): 10–6.

Corrections Compendium. 2008a. "Adult Correctional Budgets, 2007–2008: Survey Summary." 33 (November–December): 13–23.

Corrections Compendium. 2008b. "Inmate Education Programs: Survey Summary." 33 (May–June): 9–25.

Corrections Compendium. 2008c. "Sex Offenders in the Correctional System." 33 (March–April): 12–27.

Cullen, Francis T. 2005. "The Twelve People Who Saved Rehabilitation: How the Science of Criminology Made a Difference—The American Society of Criminology 2004 Presidential Address." *Criminology* 43: 1–42.

Cullen, Francis T. 2007. "Make Rehabilitation Corrections' Guiding Paradigm." *Criminology and Public Policy* 6: 717–728.

Cullen, Francis T., and Robert Agnew, eds. 2011. *Criminological Theory: Past to Present*, 4th ed. New York: Oxford University Press.

Cullen, Francis T, and Brandon Applegate, eds. 1997. *Offender Rehabilitation: Effective Correctional Intervention*. Aldershot, UK: Ashgate/Dartmouth.

Cullen, Francis T., Kristie R. Blevins, Jennifer S. Trager, and Paul Gendreau. 2005. "The Rise and Fall of Boot Camps: A Case Study in Common-Sense Corrections." *Journal of Offender Rehabilitation* 40: 53–70.

Cullen, Francis T., Bonnie S. Fisher, and Brandon K. Applegate. 2000. "Public Opinion About Punishment and Corrections." In *Crime and Justice: A Review of Research*, vol. 27, ed. Michael Tonry, 1–79. Chicago: University of Chicago Press.

Cullen, Francis T., and Paul Gendreau. 1989. "The Effectiveness of Correctional Treatment: Reconsidering the 'Nothing Works' Debate." In *The American Prison: Issues in Research and Policy*, eds. Lynne Goodstein and Doris L. MacKenzie, 23–44. New York: Plenum.

Cullen, Francis T., and Paul Gendreau. 2000. "Assessing Correctional Rehabilitation: Policy, Practice, and Prospects." In *Criminal Justice 2000: Volume 3—Policies, Processes, and Decisions of the Criminal Justice System*, ed. Julie Horney, 109–175. Washington, DC: U.S. Department of Justice, National Institute of Justice.

Cullen, Francis T., and Paul Gendreau. 2001. "From Nothing Works to What Works: Changing Professional Ideology in the 21st Century." *The Prison Journal* 81: 313–338.

Cullen, Francis T., and Karen E. Gilbert. 1982. *Reaffirming Rehabilitation*. Cincinnati, OH: Anderson.

Cullen, Francis T., and Melissa M. Moon. 2002. "Reaffirming Rehabilitation: Public Support for Correctional Treatment." In *What Works: Risk Reduction Interventions for Special Needs Offenders*, ed. Harry E. Allen, 7–26. Lanham, MD: American Correctional Association.

Cullen, Francis T., Andrew J. Myer, and Edward J. Latessa. 2009. "Eight Lessons from *Moneyball*: The High Cost of Ignoring Evidence-Based Corrections." *Victims and Offenders* 4: 197–213.

Cullen, Francis T., Jennifer A. Pealer, Bonnie S. Fisher, Brandon K. Applegate, and Shannon A. Santana. 2002. "Public Support for Correctional Rehabilitation in America: Change or Consistency?" In *Changing Attitudes to Punishment: Public Opinion, Crime, and Justice*, eds. Julian V. Roberts and Mike Hough, 128–147. Devon, UK: Willian.

Cullen, Francis T., Travis C. Pratt, Sharon Levrant, Micelli, and Melissa M. Moon. 2001. "Dangerous Liaison? Rational Choice Theory as the Basis for Correctional Intervention." In *Rational Choice and Criminal Behavior*, eds. Alex R. Piquero and Stephen G. Tibbetts, 279–296. New Brunswick, NJ: Transaction.

Cullen, Francis T., Brenda A. Vose, Cheryl Lero Jonson, and James D. Unnever. 2007. "Public Support for Early Intervention: Is Child Saving a 'Habit of the Heart'?" *Victims and Offenders* 2: 109–124.

Cullen, Francis T., John Paul Wright, and Brandon K. Applegate. 1996. "Control in the Community: The Limits of Reform?" In *Choosing Correctional Interventions That Work: Defining the Demand and Evaluating the Supply*, ed. Alan T. Harland, 69–116. Newbury Park, CA: Sage.

Cullen, Francis T, John Paul Wright, Shayna Brown, Melissa M. Moon, Michael B. Blankenship, and Brandon K. Applegate. 1998. "Public Support for Early Intervention Programs: Implications for a Progressive Policy Agenda." *Crime and Delinquency* 44: 187–204.

Currie, Elliott. 1985. *Confronting Crime: An American Dilemma*. New York: Pantheon.

De Li, Spencer, Heidi D. Priu, and Doris L. MacKenzie. 2000. "Drug Involvement, Lifestyles, and Criminal Activities among Probationers." *Journal of Drug Issues* 30: 595–620.

Dowden, Craig, and D. A. Andrews. 1999. "What Works for Female Offenders: A Meta-Analysis." *Crime and Delinquency* 45: 438–452.

Dowden, Craig, and D. A. Andrews. 2000. "Effective Correctional Treatment and Violent Reoffending: A Meta-Analysis." *Canadian Journal of Criminology* 42: 449–467.

Dowden, Craig, Daniel H. Antonowicz, and D. A. Andrews. 2003. "The Effectiveness of Relapse Prevention with Offenders: A Meta-Analysis." *International Journal of Offender Therapy and Comparative Criminology* 47: 516–528.

Drake, Elizabeth K., Steve Aos, and Marna G. Miller. 2009. "Evidence-Based Public Policy Options to Reduce Crime and Criminal Justice Costs: Implications in Washington State." *Victims and Offenders* 4: 170–196.

Duguid, Stephen. 2000. *Can Prisons Work? The Prisoner as Object and Subject in Modern Corrections*. Toronto: University of Toronto Press.

Erisman, Wendy, and Jeanne Bayer Contardo. 2005. *Learning to Reduce Recidivism: A 50-State Analysis of Postsecondary Correctional Education Policy*. Washington, DC: National Institute for Higher Education Policy.

Erwin, Billie S. 1996. "Discipline in Georgia's Boot Camps." In *Correctional Boot Camps: A Tough Intermediate Sanction*, eds. Doris Layton MacKenzie and Eugene E. Hebert, 191–206. Washington, DC: National Institute of Justice, U.S. Department of Justice.

Fagan, Jeffrey, and Richard B. Freeman. 1999. "Work and Crime." In *Crime and Justice: A Review of Research, vol. 25*, ed. Michael Tonry, 225–290. Chicago: University of Chicago Press.

Farabee, David. 2005. *Rethinking Rehabilitation: Why Can't We Reform Our Criminals?* Washington, DC: AEI Press.

Finckenauer, James O., and Patricia W. Gavin. 1999. *Scared Straight: The Panacea Phenomenon Revisited*. Prospect Heights, IL: Waveland.

Foucault, Michel. 1977. *Discipline and Punish: The Birth of the Prison*. New York: Pantheon.

Frankel, Marvin E. 1972. *Criminal Sentences: Law Without Order*. New York: Hill and Wang.

Fulton, Betsy, Edward J. Latessa, Amy Stichman, and Lawrence E. Travis III. 1997. "The State of ISP: Research and Policy Implications." *Federal Probation* 61(4): 65–75.

Gaes, Gerald G. 2008. *The Impact of Prison Programs on Post-Release Outcomes*. Elkridge, MD: Correctional Education Association.

Gaes, Gerald G., Timothy J. Flanagan, Larry Motiuk, and Lynn Stewart. 1999. "Adult Correctional Treatment." In *Crime and Justice: A Review of Research, vol. 26*, ed. Michael Tonry, 85–150. Chicago: University of Chicago Press.

Gallagher, Catherine A., David B. Wilson, Paul Hirschfield, Mark B. Coggeshall, and Doris L. MacKenzie. 1999. "A Quantitative Review of the Effects of Sex

Offender Treatment on Sexual Reoffending." *Corrections Management Quarterly* 3 (Fall): 19–29.

Garland, David. 1990. *Punishment and Modern Society: A Study in Social Theory.* Chicago: University of Chicago Press.

Garrett, Carol J. 1985. "Effects of Residential Treatment on Adjudicated Delinquents: A Meta-Analysis." *Journal of Research in Crime and Delinquency* 22: 287–308.

Gendreau, Paul. 1996. "The Principles of Effective Intervention with Offenders." In *Choosing Correctional Interventions That Work: Defining the Demand and Evaluating the Supply,* ed. Alan T. Harland, 117–130. Newbury Park, CA: Sage.

Gendreau, Paul, and D. A. Andrews. 2001. *Correctional Program Assessment Inventory (CPAI-2000).* St. John, NB: New Brunswick.

Gendreau, Paul, Francis T. Cullen, and James Bonta. 1994. "Intensive Rehabilitation Supervision: The Next Generation in Community Corrections?" *Federal Probation* 58 (1): 72–78.

Gendreau, Paul, and Claire Goggin. 1997. "Correctional Treatment: Accomplishments and Realities." In *Correctional Counseling and Rehabilitation,* 3rd ed., eds. Patricia Van Voorhis, Michael Braswell, and David Lester, 271–279. Cincinnati, OH: Anderson.

Gendreau, Paul, Claire Goggin, Francis T. Cullen, and D. A. Andrews. 2000. "The Effects of Community Sanctions and Incarceration on Recidivism." *Forum on Corrections Research* 12 (2): 10–13.

Gendreau, Paul, Claire Goggin, Francis T. Cullen, and Mario Paparozzi. 2002. "The Common Sense Revolution and Correctional Policy. In *Offender Rehabilitation and Treatment: Effective Programs and Policies to Reduce Re-offending,* ed. James McGuire, 360–386. Chichester, UK: Wiley.

Gendreau, Paul, Claire Goggin, Sheila French, and Paula Smith. 2006. "Practicing Psychology in Correctional Settings: 'What Works' in Reducing Criminal Behavior." In *The Handbook of Forensic Psychology,* 3rd ed., eds. Allen K. Hess and Irving B. Weiner, 722–750. New Brunswick, N.J.: Transaction.

Gendreau, Paul, Claire Goggin, and Paula Smith. 2000. "Generating Rational Correctional Policies: An Introduction to Advances in Cumulating Knowledge." *Corrections Management Quarterly* 4 (Spring): 52–60.

Gendreau, Paul, Claire Goggin, and Paula Smith. 2001. "Implementation Guidelines for Correctional Programs in the 'Real World.'" In *Offender Rehabilitation in Practice: Implementing and Evaluating Effective Programs,* ed. Gary A. Bernfeld, Alan Leischied, and David P. Farrington, 247–268. Scarborough, Ont.: Wiley.

Gendreau, Paul, Tracy Little, and Claire Goggin. 1996. "A Meta-Analysis of the Predictors of Adult Offender Recidivism: What Works!" *Criminology* 34: 575–607.

Gendreau, Paul, and Robert R. Ross. 1979. "Effective Correctional Treatment Bibliotherapy for Cynics." *Crime and Delinquency* 25: 463–489.

Gendreau, Paul, and Robert R. Ross. 1987. "Revivification of Rehabilitation: Evidence from the 1980s." *Justice Quarterly* 4: 349–407.

Gendreau, Paul, Paula Smith, and Sheila French. 2006. "The Theory of Effective Correctional Intervention: Empirical Status and Future Directions." In *Taking Stock: The Status of Criminological Theory—Advances in Criminological Theory,* vol. 15 eds. Francis T. Cullen, John Paul Wright, and Kristie R. Blevins, 419–446. New Brunswick, NJ: Transaction.

Gendreau, Paul, Paula Smith, and Yvette L. Theriault. 2009. "Chaos Theory and Correctional Treatment: Common Sense, Correctional Quackery, and the Law of Fartcatchers." *Journal of Contemporary Criminal Justice* 25: 384–396.

Gerber, Jurg, and Eric J. Fritsch. 1993. *Prison Education and Offender Behavior: A Review of the Scientific Literature*. Huntsville, TX: Criminal Justice Center, Sam Houston State University.

Gerber, Jurg, and Eric J. Fritsch. 1995. "Adult Academic and Vocational Correctional Education Programs: A Review of Recent Research." *Journal of Offender Rehabilitation* 22: 119–142.

Gibbons, Don C. 1999. "Review Essay: Changing Lawbreakers—What Have We Learned since the 1950s?" *Crime and Delinquency* 45: 272–293.

Glass, Gene V., Barry McGraw, and Mary Lee Smith. 1981. *Meta-Analysis in Social Research*. Beverly Hills, CA: Sage.

Glaze, Lauren E., and Thomas P. Bonczar. 2009. *Probation and Parole in the United States, 2007: Statistical Tables*. Washington, DC: Bureau of Justice Statistics, U.S. Department of Justice.

Gottfredson, Michael R. 1979."Treatment Destruction Techniques." *Journal of Research in Crime and Delinquency* 16: 39–54.

Gottschalk, Marie. 2006. *The Prison and the Gallows: The Politics of Mass Incarceration in America*. New York: Cambridge University Press.

Greenberg, David F. 1977. "The Correctional Effects of Corrections: A Survey of Evaluations." In *Corrections and Punishment*, ed. David F. Greenberg, 111–148. Beverly Hills, CA: Sage.

Halleck, Seymour L., and Anne D. Witte. 1977. "Is Rehabilitation Dead?" *Crime and Delinquency* 23: 372–382.

Hanson, R. Karl, Guy Bourgon, Leslie Helmus, and Shannon Hodgson. 2009. *A Meta-Analysis of the Effectiveness of Treatment for Sexual Offenders: Risk, Need, and Responsivity*. Ottawa, ON Public Safety Canada.

Hanson, R. Karl, Arthur Gordon, Andrew J. R. Harris, Janice K. Marques, William Murphy, Vernon L. Quinsey, and Michael C. Seto. 2002. "First Report of the Collaborative Outcome Data Project on the Effectiveness of Psychological Treatment for Sex Offenders." *Sexual Abuse* 14: 169–194.

Harer, Miles D. 1995. *Prison Education Program Participation and Recidivism: A Test of the Normalization Hypothesis*. Washington, DC: Office of Research and Evaluation, Federal Bureau of Prisons.

Harland, Alan T., ed. 1996. *Choosing Correctional Options That Work: Defining the Demand and Evaluating the Supply*. Thousand Oaks, CA: Sage.

Harlow, Caroline Wolf. 2003. *Education and Correctional Populations*. Washington, DC: Bureau of Justice Statistics, U.S. Department of Justice.

Hedges, Larry V. 1987. "How Hard Is Hard Science, How Soft Is Soft Science? The Empirical Cumulativeness of Research." *American Psychologist* 42: 443–455.

Henggeler, Scott W., Sonja K. Schoenwald, Charles M. Borduin, Melisa D. Rowland, and Phillippe B. Cunningham. 1998. *Multisystemic Treatment of Antisocial Behavior in Children and Adolescents*. New York: Guilford Press.

Hester, Reid K., and William R. Miller, eds. 1995. *Handbook of Alcoholism Treatment Approaches: Effective Alternatives*, 2nd ed. Boston: Allyn and Bacon.

Hirschi, Travis, and Michael R. Gottfredson. 1995. "Control Theory and the Life-Course Perspective." *Studies in Crime and Crime Prevention* 4: 131–142.

Holsinger, Alexander M. 1999. *Opening the "Black Box": Assessing the Relationship Between Program Integrity and Recidivism*. University of Cincinnati: Doctoral Dissertation.

Hough, Mike. 2002. "Drug User Treatment Within a Criminal Justice Context." *Substance Use and Misuse* 37: 985–996.

Hubbard, Dana Jones, and Travis C. Pratt. 2002. "A Meta-Analysis of the Predictors of Delinquency among Girls." *Journal of Offender Rehabilitation* 34 (3): 1–13.

Huebner, Beth M., and Jennifer Cobbina. 2007. "The Effect of Drug Use, Drug Treatment Participation, and Treatment Completion on Probationer Recidivism." *Journal of Drug Issues* 37: 619–641.

Izzo, Rhena L., and Robert R. Ross. 1990. "Meta-Analysis of Rehabilitation Programs for Juvenile Delinquents." *Criminal Justice and Behavior* 17: 134–142.

James, Doris J. 2004. *Profile of Jail Inmates, 2002*. Washington, DC: Bureau of Justice Statistics, U.S. Department of Justice.

Karberg, Jennifer C., and Doris J. James. 2005. *Substance Dependence, Abuse, and Treatment of Jail Inmates, 2002*. Washington, DC: Bureau of Justice Statistics, U.S. Department of Justice.

Kittrie, Nicholas N. 1971. *The Right To Be Different: Deviance and Enforced Therapy*. Baltimore, MD: Penguin.

Klockars, Carl B. 1975. "The True Limits of the Effectiveness of Correctional Treatment." *The Prison Journal* 55: 53–64.

Kuhn, Thomas S. 1962. *The Structure of Scientific Revolutions*. Chicago: University of Chicago Press.

Landenberger, Nana A., and Mark W. Lipsey. 2005. "The Positive Effects of Cognitive-Behavioral Programs for Offenders: A Meta-Analysis of Factors Associated with Effective Treatment." *Journal of Experimental Criminology* 1: 451–476.

Latessa, Edward J. 1999. *Strategic Solutions: The International Community Corrections Association Examines Substance Abuse*. Lantham, MD: American Correctional Association.

Latessa Edward J., Francis T. Cullen, and Paul Gendreau. 2002. "Beyond Correctional Quackery: Professionalism and the Possibility of Effective Treatment." *Federal Probation* 66 (3): 43–49.

Latessa, Edward J., and Alexander Holsinger. 1998. "The Importance of Evaluating Correctional Programs: Assessing Outcome and Quality." *Corrections Management Quarterly* 2 (Fall): 22–29.

Latessa, Edward J., and Melissa M. Moon. 1992. "The Effectiveness of Acupuncture in an Outpatient Drug Treatment Program." *Journal of Contemporary Criminal Justice* 8: 317–331.

Laub, John H., and Robert J. Sampson. 2003. *Shared Beginnings, Divergent Lives: Delinquent Boys to Age 70*. Cambridge, MA: Harvard University Press.

Leary, Alex. 2006. "Boot Camps Losing Favor Nationally." *St. Petersburg Times* March 5. Retrieved August 2, 2009 from http://www.sptimes.com/2006/03/05/State/Boot_camps_losing_fav.shtml.

Lillis, Jamie. 1994. "Survey Summary: Education in U.S. Prisons-Part Two." *Corrections Compendium* 19 (April): 10–16.

Lin, Ann Chih. 2000. *Reform in the Making: The Implementation of Social Policy in Prison*. Princeton, NJ: Princeton University Press.

Lipset, Seymour Martin, and William Schneider. 1983. *The Confidence Gap: Business, Labor, and Government in the Public Mind.* New York: The Free Press.

Lipsey, Mark W. 1992. "Juvenile Delinquency Treatment: A Meta-Analytic Inquiry into the Variability of Effects." In *Meta Analysis for Explanation: A Casebook*, eds. Thomas D. Cook, Harris Cooper, David S. Cordray, Heidi Hartmann, Larry V. Hedges, Richard J. Light, Thomas A. Lewis, and Frederick Mosteller, 83–127. New York: Russell Sage.

Lipsey, Mark W. 1995. "What Do We Learn from 400 Research Studies on the Effectiveness of Treatment with Juvenile Delinquency?" In *What Works: Reducing Reoffending*, ed. James McGuire, 63–78. West Sussex, UK: John Wiley.

Lipsey, Mark W. 1999a. "Can Rehabilitative Programs Reduce the Recidivism of Juvenile Offenders? An Inquiry into the Effectiveness of Practical Programs." *Virginia Journal of Social Policy and Law* 6: 611–641.

Lipsey, Mark W. 1999b. "Can Intervention Rehabilitate Serious Delinquents?" *The Annals of the American Academy of Political and Social Science* 564: 142–166.

Lipsey, Mark W. 2009. "The Primary Factors That Characterize Effective Interventions with Juvenile Offenders: A Meta-Analytic Review." *Victims and Offenders* 4: 124–147.

Lipsey, Mark W., Gabrielle L. Chapman, and Nana A. Landenberger. 2001. "Cognitive-Behavioral Programs for Offenders." *The Annals of the American Academy of Political and Social Science* 578: 144–157.

Lipsey, Mark W., and Francis T. Cullen. 2007. "The Effectiveness of Correctional Rehabilitation: A Review of Systematic Reviews." *Annual Review of Law and Social Science* 3: 297–320.

Lipsey, Mark W., and James H. Derzon. 1998. "Predictors of Violent and Serious Delinquency in Adolescence and Early Adulthood." In *Serious and Violent Juvenile Offenders: Risk Factors and Successful Interventions*, eds. Rolf Loeber and David P. Farrington, 86–105. Thousand Oaks, CA: Sage.

Lipsey, Mark W., Nana A. Landenberger, and Sandra J. Wilson. 2007. *Effects of Cognitive-Behavioral Programs for Criminal Offenders.* Philadelphia: The Campbell Collaboration.

Lipsey, Mark W, and David B. Wilson. 1993. "The Efficacy of Psychological, Educational, and Behavioral Treatment." *American Psychologist* 48: 1181–1209.

Lipsey, Mark W, and David B. Wilson. 1998. "Effective Intervention for Serious Juvenile Offenders: A Synthesis of Research." In *Serious and Violent Juvenile Offenders: Risk Factors and Successful Interventions*, eds. Rolf Loeber and David P. Farrington, 313–45. Thousand Oaks, CA: Sage.

Lipton, Douglas, Robert Martinson, and Judith Wilks. 1975. *The Effectiveness of CorrectionalTreatment: A Survey of Treatment Evaluation Studies.* New York: Praeger.

Listwan, Shelley Johnson, Cheryl Lero Jonson, Francis T. Cullen, and Edward J. Latessa. 2008. "Cracks in the Penal Harm Movement: Evidence from the Field." *Criminology and Public Policy* 7: 423–465.

Loeber, Rolf, and David P. Farrington, eds. 1998. *Serious and Violent Juvenile Offenders: Risk Factors and Successful Interventions.* Thousand Oaks, CA: Sage.

Logan, Charles H. 1972. "Evaluation Research in Crime and Delinquency: A Reappraisal." *Journal of Criminal Law, Criminology and Police Science* 63: 378–387.

Logan, Charles H., and Gerald Gaes. 1993. "Meta-Analysis and the Rehabilitation of Punishment." *Justice Quarterly* 10: 245–263.

Losel, Friedrich. 1995. "The Efficacy of Correctional Treatment: A Review and Synthesis of Meta-Evaluations." In *What Works: Reducing Reoffending*, ed. James McGuire, 79–111. West Sussex, UK: John Wiley.

Losel, Friedrich. 2001. "Evaluating the Effectiveness of Correctional Programs: Bridging the Gap Between Research and Practice." In *Offender Rehabilitation in Practice: Implementing and Evaluating Effective Programs*, eds. Gary A. Bernfeld, Alan Leischied, and David P. Farrington, 67–96. Scarborough, Ont.: Wiley.

Losel, Friedrich, and Martin Schmucker. 2005. "The Effectiveness of Treatment for Sexual Offenders: A Comprehensive Meta-Analysis." *Journal of Experimental Criminology* 1: 117–146.

Lowenkamp, Christopher T. 2004. *Correctional Program Integrity and Treatment Effectiveness: A Multi-Site Program-Level Analysis*. University of Cincinnati: Doctoral Dissertation.

Lowenkamp, Christopher T., Edward J. Latessa, and Paula Smith. 2006. "Does Correctional Program Integrity Really Matter? The Impact of Adhering to the Principles of Effective Intervention 2006." *Criminology and Public Policy* 5: 201–220.

Lurigio, Arthur J. 2000. "Drug Treatment Availability and Effectiveness: Studies of the General and Criminal Justice Populations." *Criminal Justice and Behavior* 27: 495–528.

Lurigio, Arthur J., Young Ik Cho, James A. Swartz, Timothy P. Johnson, Ingrid Graf, and Lillian Pickup. 2003. "Standardized Assessment of Substance-Related, Other Psychiatric, and Comorbid Disorders among Probationers." *International Journal of Offender Therapy and Comparative Criminology* 47: 630–652.

MacKenzie, Doris Layton. 1997. "Criminal Justice and Crime Prevention." Chapter 9 in *Preventing Crime: What Works, What Doesn't, What's Promising*, eds. Lawrence W. Sherman, Denise Gottfredson, Doris Layton MacKenzie, John Eck, Peter Reuter, and Shawn Bushway. Washington, DC: National Institute of Justice, U.S. Department of Justice.

MacKenzie, Doris Layton. 2000. "Evidence-Based Corrections: Identifying What Works." *Crime and Delinquency* 46: 457–471.

MacKenzie, Doris Layton. 2006. *What Works in Corrections: Reducing the Criminal Activities of Offenders and Delinquents*. New York: Cambridge University Press.

MacKenzie, Doris Layton, and Laura J. Hickman. 1998. *What Works in Corrections? An Examination of the Effectiveness of the Type of Rehabilitation Programs Offered by Washington State Department of Corrections*. College Park, MD: University of Maryland.

MacKenzie, Doris Layton, David B. Wilson, and Suzanne B. Kider. 2001. "Effects of Correctional Boot Camps on Offending." *The Annals of American Academy Political and Social Science* 588: 126–143.

Marion, Nancy. 2002. "Effectiveness of Community-Based Correctional Programs: A Case Study." *The Prison Journal* 82: 478–497.

Martinson, Robert. 1974a. "What Works? Questions and Answers About Prison Reform." *The Public Interest* 35 (Spring): 22–54.

Martinson, Robert. 1974b. "Viewpoint." *Criminal Justice Newsletter* 5 (November 18): 4–5.

Martinson, Robert. 1979. "New Findings, New Views: A Note of Caution Regarding Sentencing Reform." *Hofstra Law Review* 7: 243–258.

Maruna, Shadd. 2001. *Making Good: How Ex-Convicts Reform and Rebuild Their Lives.* Washington, DC: American Psychological Association.

Matthews, Betsy, Dana Jones Hubbard, and Edward J. Latessa. 2001. "Making the Next Step: Using Evaluability Assessment to Improve Correctional Programming." *The Prison Journal* 81: 454–472.

McGuire, James. 2002. "Integrating Findings from Research Reviews." In *Offender Rehabilitation and Treatment: Effectiveness of Programmes and Policies to Reduce Re-Offending,* ed. James McGuire, 3–18. West Sussex, UK: John Wiley.

McLaren, Kaye. 1992. *Reducing Reoffending: What Works Now.* Wellington, New Zealand: Penal Division, Department of Justice.

Merton, Robert K. 1973. *The Sociology of Science: Theoretical and Empirica Investigations.* Chicago: University of Chicago Press.

Mitchell, Ojmarrh, Doris Layton MacKenzie, and Deanna M. Perez. 2005. "A Randomized Evaluation of the Maryland Correctional Boot Camp for Adults: Effects on Offender Anti-Social Attitudes and Cognitions." *Journal of Offender Rehabilitation* 40 (3): 71–86.

Mitchell, Ojmarrh, David B. Wilson, and Doris L. MacKenzie. 2007. "Does Incarceration-Based Drug Treatment Reduce Recidivism? A Meta-Analytic Synthesis." *Journal of Experimental Criminology* 3: 353–375.

Moon, Melissa M., Jody L. Sundt, Francis T. Cullen, and John Paul Wright. 1999. "Is Child Saving Dead? Public Support for Rehabilitation." *Crime and Delinquency* 46: 38–60.

Morris, Norval. 1974. *The Future of Imprisonment.* Chicago: University of Chicago Press.

Morris, Norval, and Michael Tonry. 1990. *Between Prison and Probation: Intermediate Punishments in a Rational Sentencing System.* New York: Oxford University Press.

Mumola, Christopher J. 1998. *Substance Abuse and Treatment: State and Prisoners 1997.* Washington, DC: Bureau of Justice Statistics, U.S. Department of Justice.

Mumola, Christopher, with the assistance of Thomas P. Bonczar. 1998. *Substance Abuse and Treatment of Adults on Probation, 1995.* Washington, DC: Bureau of Justice Statistics, U.S. Department of Justice.

Mumola, Christopher J., and Jennifer C. Karberg. 2006. *Drug Use and Dependence, State and Federal Prisoners, 2004.* Washington, DC: Bureau of Justice Statistics, U.S. Department of Justice.

Nagin, Daniel S., Alex R. Piquero, Elizabeth S. Scott, and Laurence Steinberg. 2006. "Public Preferences for Rehabilitation Versus Incarceration for Juvenile Offenders: Evidence from a Contingent Valuation." *Criminology and Public Policy* 5: 627–651.

Newborn, Steve. 2006. "Polk County Gives the Boot to Juvenile Boot Camp." June 19. Tampa, FL: WUSF Public Broadcasting. Retrieved August 2, 2009, from http://www.publicbroadcasting.net/wusf/news.newsmain?action=article&ARTICLE_ID=930246&sectionID=1.

Nesovic, Aleksandra. 2003. *Psychometric Evaluation of the Correctional Program Assessment Inventory (CPAI).* Carleton University: Doctoral Dissertation.

Ogloff, James R. P., and Michael R. Davis. 2004. "Advances in Offender Assessment and Rehabilitation: Contribution of the Risk-Needs-Responsivity Approach." *Psychology, Crime and Law* 10: 229–242.

Olson, David E., and Arthur J. Lurigio. 2000. "Predicting Probation Outcomes: Factors Associated with Probation Rearrest, Revocations, and Technical Violations during Supervision." *Justice Research and Policy* 2:7 3–86.

Palmer, Ted. 1975. "Martinson Revisited." *Journal of Research in Crime and Delinquency* 12: 133–152.

Palmer, Ted. 1992. *The Re-Emergence of Correctional Intervention*. Newbury Park, CA: Sage.

Parent, Dale G. 2003. *Correctional Boot Camps: Lessons Learned from a Decade of Research*. Washington, DC: National Institute of Justice, U.S. Department of Justice.

Paternoster, Raymond, and Ronet Bachman, eds. 2001. *Explaining Criminals and Crime: Essays in Contemporary Criminological Theory*. Los Angeles: Roxbury.

Pearson, Frank S., and Douglas S. Lipton. 1999a. "The Effectiveness of Educational and Vocational Programs: CDATE Meta-Analyses." Paper presented at the Annual Meeting of the American Society of Criminology, November, Toronto.

Pearson, Frank S., and Douglas S. Lipton. 1999b. "A Meta-Analytic Review of the Effectiveness of Corrections-Based Treatment for Drug Abuse." *The Prison Journal* 79: 384–410.

Pearson, Frank S., Douglas S. Lipton, and Charles M. Cleland. 1996. "Some Preliminary Findings from the CDATE Project." Paper presented at the annual meeting of the American Society of Criminology, November, Chicago.

Pearson, Frank, Douglas S. Lipton, Charles M. Cleland, and Dorline S. Yee. 2002. "The Effects of Behavioral/Cognitive Behavioral Programs on Recidivism." *Crime and Delinquency* 48: 476–496.

Petersilia, Joan. 1998. "A Decade of Experimenting with Intermediate Sanctions: What Have We Learned?" *Federal Probation* 62 (2): 3–9.

Petersilia, Joan, and Susan Turner. 1993. "Intensive Probation and Parole." In *Crime and Justice: An Annual Review of Research, vol. 17*, ed. Michael Tonry, 281–335. Chicago: University of Chicago Press.

Petrosino, Anthony, Carolyn Turpin Petrosino, and John Buehler. 2004. *"Scared Straight" and Other Juvenile Awareness Programs for Preventing Juvenile Delinquency*. Philadelphia: The Campbell Collaboration.

Phillips, Sarah, and Kent L. Sandstrom. 1990. "Parental Attitudes Toward Youth Work." *Youth and Society* 22: 160–183.

Piehl, Anne Morrison. 1998. "Economic Conditions, Work, and Crime." In *The Handbook of Crime and Punishment*, ed. Michael Tonry, 302–319. New York: Oxford University Press.

Prendergast, Michael L., M. Douglas Anglin, and Jean Wellisch. 1995. "Treatment for Drug-Abusing Offenders under Community Supervision." *Federal Probation* 59 (4): 66–75.

Redondo, Santiago, Julio Sanchez-Meca, and Vincente Garrido. 1999. "The Influence of Treatment Programmes on the Recidivism of Juvenile and Adult Offenders: A European Meta-Analytic Review." *Psychology, Crime and Law* 5: 251–278.

Reynolds, Morgan O. 1996. *Crime and Punishment in Texas: An Update*. Dallas: National Center for Policy Analysis.

Rhine, Edward E., ed. 1998. *Best Practices: Excellence in Corrections*. Lanham, MD: American Correctional Association.

Rhine, Edward E., and Donald G. Evans. 2008. *Research into Practice: Bridging the Gap in Community Corrections*. Lanham, MD: American Correctional Association.

Robison, James, and Gerald Smith. 1971. "The Effectiveness of Correctional Programs." *Crime and Delinquency* 17: 67–80.

Ross, Robert R., Daniel H. Antonowicz, and Gurmeet K. Dhaliwal. 1995. "Something Works." In *Going Straight: Effective Delinquency Prevention and Offender Rehabilitation*, eds. Robert R. Ross, Daniel H. Antonowicz, and Gurmeet K. Dhaliwal, 3–28. Ottawa, ON: Air Training and Publications.

Ross, Robert R., and Elizabeth A. Fabiano. 1985. *Time to Think: A Cognitive Model of Delinquency Prevention and Offender Rehabilitation*. Johnson City, TN: Institute of Social Sciences and Arts.

Rothman, David J. 1980. *Conscience and Convenience: The Asylum and Its Alternatives in Progressive America*. Boston: Little, Brown.

Rotman, Edgardo. 1990. *Beyond Punishment: A New View on the Rehabilitation of Offenders*. New York: Greenwood.

Sampson, Robert J., and John H. Laub. 1993. *Crime in the Making: Pathways and Turning Points Through Life*. Cambridge, MA: Harvard University Press.

Saylor, William G., and Gerald G. Gaes. 1996. *PREP: Training Inmates Through Industrial Work Participation and Vocational and Apprenticeship Instruction*. Washington, DC: Federal Bureau of Prisons.

Schur, Edwin M. 1973. *Radical Non-Intervention: Rethinking the Delinquency Problem*. Englewood Cliffs, NJ: Prentice-Hall.

Sechrest, Lee, Susan O. White, and Elizabeth D. Brown, eds. 1979. *The Rehabilitation of Criminal Offenders: Problems and Prospects*. Washington, DC: National Academy of Sciences.

Selcraig, Bruce. 2000. "Camp Fear." *Mother Jones* November-December: 64–71.

Serrill, Michael S. 1975. "Is Rehabilitation Dead?" *Corrections Magazine* 1 (May–June): 21–32.

Sherman, Lawrence W., Denise Gottfredson, Doris MacKenzie, John Eck, Paul Reuter, and Shawn Bushway. 1997. *Preventing Crime: What Works, What Doesn't, What's Promising*. Washington, DC: National Institute of Corrections, U.S. Department of Justice.

Silverman, Ira J., and Manuel Vega. 1996. *Corrections: A Comprehensive Review*. Minneapolis, MN: West.

Simon, Jonathan. 2007. *Governing Through Crime: How the War on Crime Transformed American Democracy and Created a Culture of Fear*. New York: Oxford University Press.

Smith, Paula, Paul Gendreau, and Claire Goggin. 2004. "Correctional Treatment: Accomplishments and Realities." In *Correctional Counseling and Rehabilitation*, 5th ed., eds. Patricia Van Voorhis, Michael Braswell, and David Lester, 285–294. Cincinnati, OH: Anderson.

Smith, Paula, Paul Gendreau, and Kristin Swartz. 2009. "Validating the Principles of Effective Intervention: A Systematic Review of the Contributions of Meta-Analysis in the Field of Corrections." *Victims and Offenders* 4: 148–169.

Spiegler, Michael D., and David C. Guevremont. 1998. *Contemporary Behavior Therapy*, 3rd ed. Pacific Grove, CA: Brooks/Cole.

Stephan, James J. 2008. *Census of State and Federal Correctional Facilities, 2005* Washington, DC: Bureau of Justice Statistics, U.S. Department of Justice.

Steurer, Stephen J., and Linda G. Smith. 2003. *Education Reduces Crime: Three-State Recidivism: Executive Summary*. Lanham, MD: Correctional Education Association.

Steurer, Stephen J., Linda G. Smith, and Alice Tracy. 2001. *Three State Recidivism Study*. Washington, DC: Office of Correctional Education, U.S. Department of Education.

Stinchcomb, Jeanne B. 2005. "From Optimistic Policies to Pessimistic Outcomes: Why Won't Boot Camps Either Succeed Pragmatically or Succumb Politically?" *Journal of Offender Rehabilitation* 40: 26–52.

Stinchcomb, Jeanne B., and W. Clinton Terry III. 2001. "Predicting the Likelihood of Rearrest among Shock Incarceration Graduates: Moving Beyond Another Nail in the Boot Camp Coffin." *Crime and Delinquency* 47: 221–242.

Stone, William. 2006. "Industry, Agriculture, and Education." In *Prisons: Today and Tomorrow*, 2nd ed., ed. Joycelyn M. Pollock, 124–157. Sudbury, MA: Jones and Bartlett Publishers.

Taxman, Faye S. 1999. "Unraveling 'What Works' for Offenders in Substance Abuse Treatment Services." *National Drug Court Institute Review* 2: 93–134.

Tewksbury, Richard, David John Erickson, and Jon Marc Taylor. 2000. "Opportunities Lost: The Consequences of Eliminating Pell Grant Eligibility for Correctional Education Students." *Journal of Offender Rehabilitation* 31: 43–56.

Toby, Jackson. 1964. "Is Punishment Necessary?" *Journal of Criminal Law, Criminology and Police Science* 55: 332–337.

Tong, L. S. Joy, and David P. Farrington. 2006. "How Effective is the 'Reasoning and Rehabilitation' Program in Reoffending? A Meta-Analysis of Evaluations in Four Countries." *Psychology, Crime and Law* 12: 3–24.

Turner, Susan, and Joan Petersilia. 1996. *Work Release: Recidivism and Corrections Costs in Washington State*. Washington, DC: National Institute of Justice, U.S. Department of Justice.

Uggen, Christopher. 1999. "Ex-Offenders and the Conformist Alternative: A Job Quality Model of Work and Crime." *Social Problems* 46: 127–151.

Uggen, Christopher. 2000. "Work as a Turning Point in the Life Course of Criminals: A Duration Model of Age, Employment, and Recidivism." *American Sociological Review* 65: 529–546.

Van Voorhis, Patricia. 1987. "Correctional Effectiveness: The High Cost of Ignoring Success." *Federal Probation* 51 (1): 59–62.

Van Voorhis, Patricia, Michael Braswell, and David Lester, eds. 2004. *Correctional Counseling and Rehabilitation*, 5th ed. Cincinnati, OH: Anderson.

Van Voorhis, Patricia, and David Lester. 2004. "Cognitive Therapies." In *Correctional Counseling and Rehabilitation*, 5th ed., ed. Patricia Van Voorhis, Michael Braswell, and David Lester, 183–208. Cincinnati, OH: Anderson.

Vaughn, Mark. 1994. "Boot Camps." *The Grapevine* 2: 2.

West, Heather C., and William J. Sabol. 2008. *Prisoners in 2007*. Washington, DC: Bureau of Justice Statistics, U.S. Department of Justice.

Wexler, Harry K., Gregory P. Falkin, and Douglas P. Lipton. 1990. "Outcome Evaluation of a Prison Therapeutic Community for Substance Abuse Treatment." *Criminal Justice and Behavior* 17: 71–92.

Whitehead, John T., and Steven P. Lab. 1989. "A Meta-Analysis of Juvenile Correctional Treatment." *Journal of Research in Crime and Delinquency* 26: 276–295.

Wilson, David B., Leanna A. Bouffard, and Doris L. MacKenzie. 2005. "A Quantitative Review of Structured, Group-Oriented, Cognitive-Behavioral Programs for Offenders." *Criminal Justice and Behavior* 32: 172–204.

Wilson, David B., Catherine A. Gallagher, Mark B. Coggeshall, and Doris L. MacKenzie. 1999. "A Quantitative Review and Description of Corrections-Based Education, Vocation, and Work Programs." *Corrections Management Quarterly* 3 (Fall): 8–18.

Wilson, David B., Catherine A. Gallagher, and Doris L. MacKenzie. 2000. "A Meta-Analysis of Corrections-Based Education, Vocation, and Work Programs for Adult Offenders." *Journal of Research in Crime and Delinquency* 37: 347–368.

Wilson, David B., Doris L. MacKenzie, and Fawn Ngo Mitchell. 2003. *Effects of Correctional Boot Camps on Offending.* Philadelphia: The Campbell Collaboration.

Wilson, James Q. 1975. *Thinking about Crime.* New York: Vintage Books.

Wilson, James. 2000. *Drug Use, Testing and Treatment in Jails.* Washington, DC: Bureau of Justice Statistics, U.S. Department of Justice.

Wines, E. C., ed. 1871. *Transactions of the National Congress on Penitentiary and Reformatory Discipline.* Albany, NY: Weed Parsons.

Wright, John Paul, and Francis T. Cullen. 2000. "Juvenile Involvement in Occupational Delinquency." *Criminology* 38: 863–892.

Wunder, Amanda. 1994. "Working for the Weekend: Prison Industries and Inmate-Employees." *Corrections Compendium* 19 (October): 9–22.

Chapter 12

Sex Offenders and Sex Offender Policy

Eric Beauregard, Roxanne Lieb

The term *sex offender* designates different types of offenders (MacKenzie 2006). The criminal justice system typically classifies sex offenders into two categories:individuals who have committed forcible rape and individuals who have committed sexual assault (which includes statutory rape, sodomy, incest, offenses against chastity, common decency and morals, unwanted sexual contacts, and fondling). In 2008 in the United States, the rate of forcible rape/sexual assault was of 0.8/1,000 persons age 12 or older (Rand 2009). Sex offenders are treated as exceptions in the criminal justice systems of virtually every state in the United States as well as many common law countries. Numerous policies and laws unique to sex offenders cover all aspects of the criminal justice system, including pre- and post-sentencing policies, civil commitment for sexually violent predators, and post-release controls such as registration and community notification. The practice of distinguishing sex offenders in the United States can be traced back over 70 years (Freedman 1987, 83). In the most recent decade, this tide of exceptionalism has risen dramatically.

Why have policymakers in the United States, at all levels of government, chosen to single out this group of offenders for special considerations? This chapter will explore this topic through three questions:

- What rationales are used by policymakers to distinguish sex offenders; does research support these arguments?
- What is known about how sex offenders commit their crimes?
- Have current laws and policies caused a reduction in sex crimes?

The results suggest the following conclusions:

- Sex offenders are treated as exceptions in the criminal justice systems of virtually every state in the United States as well as many common law countries. This policy of exceptionalism is typically justified by the impact of sexual abuse on its victims and society and the high rates of recidivism by sex offenders.
- Victims of sexual assault often suffer serious psychological harm.

- o Sex offender recidivism rates vary, depending on the study population, the diverse definitions of recidivism, data sources, follow-up periods, and sample characteristics.
- o Because of the sexual nature of their crime, sex offenders use specific strategies to offend that may appear different from other criminals; however, studies examining their modus operandi suggested that sex offenders are influenced by factors similar to those that influence other criminals.
- o After about 15 years of steady increases, sex crimes against children began to decline in the early 1990s. From 1992 through 2007, substantiated sexual abuse cases in the child welfare system declined by 52 percent.
- o Efforts to prevent sexual crimes have focused on multiple fronts: incapacitation of convicted sex offenders, changing social norms, situational crime prevention, in addition to treatment of offenders.

WHAT RATIONALES ARE USED BY POLICYMAKERS TO DISTINGUISH SEX OFFENDERS; DOES RESEARCH SUPPORT THESE ARGUMENTS?

Two principal arguments are used by lawmakers to justify special laws for sex offenders:the impact of sexual abuse on its victims and society, and the high rates of recidivism by sex offenders. We will cover each argument and discuss the relevant research findings related to this justification.

The Impact of Sexual Abuse on Its Victims and Society

Sexual assault is associated with greater psychological harm than other crimes; extensive research evidence has demonstrated serious consequences for victims of both rape and child sexual assault. People typically experience fear and terror-related symptoms following a violent experience that may result in post-traumatic stress disorder (PTSD), a diagnosis characterized by intrusive recollections, avoidance responses, and hyperarousal (American Psychiatric Association 2000). In clinical samples, almost all rape victims meet symptom criteria for this disorder immediately following an attack, and 46 percent still meet diagnostic criteria three months later (Rothbaum, Foa, Riggs, Murdock, and Walsh 1992). In contrast, the rates are lower and the symptoms resolve faster for nonsexual assault victims:71 percent of women and 50 percent of men meet PTSD criteria, and at three months, only 21 percent of women and no men continue to meet the criteria (Riggs, Rothbaum, and Foa 1995). Similarly for children, sexual abuse is more likely to result in PTSD than is physical abuse (Deblinger, Steer, and Lippmann 1999).

Child sexual abuse has been empirically associated with additional negative short- and long-term outcomes. Children with sexual abuse histories, as compared with those without, have been found to suffer increased anxiety and depression, somatic complaints, social withdrawal, anger and aggression, substance abuse disorders, along with sexual behavior problems (e.g., Kendall-Tackett, Williams, and Finkelhor 1993; Kendler, Bulik, Silberg, Hettema, Myers, and Prescott 2000). A 1995 meta-analysis examining the effects of child sexual abuse on adult adjustment connected this abuse to impaired adult psychological adjustment (Jumper 1995).

Fears about being sexually victimized are an influential component of women's psychology and often lead women to adjust their routine activities (Gordon and Riger 1989). This consequence is described as the "shadow of sexual assault," in which the possibility of sexual assault exists in non-sexual crimes that include face-to-face contact such as burglary and robbery (Ferraro 1995). In terms of child sexual assault, apprehension about this crime underlies the widespread popularity of sexual abuse prevention programs for children. A 1995 survey of children and parents found that more than two-thirds of children had received abuse education (Finkelhor, Asdigian, and Dziuba-Leatherman 1995).

How many people experience sexual assault? Sexual crimes are probably the most underreported crimes to the criminal justice system. Data from the 2008 National Crime Victimization Survey (NCVS), which randomly selected respondents across the country aged 12 and older, revealed that 59 percent of rapes/sexual assaults were not reported to a law enforcement agency (Rand 2009, 6). A similar degree of underreporting in official statistics has been documented in numerous sources (e.g., Kilpatrick, Saunders, Veronen, Best, and Von 1987; Finkelhor and Ormrod 1999). In the mid-1990s, the National Violence Against Women Survey (NVAW) used random digit dialing of households across the United States and interviewed 8,000 women and 8,005 men aged 18 and over; using precise definitions of rape,[1] the surveyors found that 17.6 percent of women and 3 percent of men who were surveyed experienced a rape at some point in their lives (14.8 percent of women and 2.1 percent of men reported completed as opposed to attempted rapes). The overall finding translates to a rate of 1 in 6 women and 1 in 33 men (Tjaden and Thoennes 2000). In terms of the timing of these rapes, more than half of the females and nearly three-quarters of the male victims were younger than 18 when the events occurred (Tjaden and Thoennes 2000).

High Rates of Recidivism by Sex Offenders

Sex crime legislation frequently includes an intent section that references the high likelihood and frequency of sex offender recidivism rates (Logan 2000). The 1997 Tennessee Legislature's intent section for sex offender registration, for example, reads as follows:"sexual offenders pose a high rate of engaging in further offenses after release ... and protection from these offenders is a paramount public interest" (Tenn. Code Ann. 40–39–201[b]).

The commonly accepted notion that sex offenders have high recidivism rates has its roots in highly publicized cases of sexual murder and mutilation by individuals with extensive histories of sexual offending. Some of the victims' names have been memorialized into legislation (e.g., the Jacob Wetterling Act, Megan's Law, Jessica's Law) and have led to significant policy changes in state and federal policy. Clearly, some sex offenders who commit horrendous crimes have a long history of offending with sexual and other crimes. What is known about the recidivism rates of typical sex offenders, if there is such a thing?

Looking across the research literature on sex offender recidivism, one finds wide-ranging rates depending on the study population (juvenile sex offender, adult child molester, adult rapist). In addition, rate differences can be traced to the diverse definitions of recidivism (arrests, convictions, returns to prison), data sources (self-reports, arrest records, convictions), follow-up periods (a few months to 25 years), and sample characteristics (persons receiving treatment in the community, persons released from prison, those released from mental hospitals; see Lussier 2005). Two studies that examine recidivism, both for sex and non-sex offenders, are particularly interesting because of their large sample sizes. Langan, Schmitt, and Durose (2003) compared the recidivism rate for sex offenses following the release of sexual (n = 9,691) and non-sexual (n = 262,420) offenders across 15 United States states. Nonsexual offenders showed a recidivism rate for sex crimes of 1 percent, compared with 5 percent for sex offenders. When looking at rearrest rate for any type of crime (not just sex crimes), the study found that 43 percent of the released sex offenders were rearrested, compared to 68 percent of the non-sex offenders. The rearrest offense was a felony for 75 percent of the rearrested sex offenders, compared to 84 percent for the non-sex offenders. The second study, by Sample and Bray (2003), looked at the recidivism rates of individuals arrested between 1990 and 1997 (n = 146,918). After a follow-up period of five years, the sexual recidivism rate was about 6 percent for sexual offenders, compared with 0 to 3 percent for non-sexual offenders. As a comparison, when considering other crimes, findings showed that 17.9 percent of robbers were rearrested for robbery and 23.1 percent of burglars were rearrested for burglary. "Homicide (5.7 percent), kidnapping (2.8 percent), and stalking (5 percent) were the only categories with lower offense-specific rearrest rates within five years than sex offending, and those differences are very small" (Sample and Bray 2003, 73). However, there are problems related to the use of official statistics:they are limited to those persons who come to official attention; they sometimes more accurately reflect police procedures than actual criminal occurrences; and finally, many sexual assaults are not reported to police (Sample and Bray 2003).

Some researchers have studied recidivism rates by examining sex offenders' victim preferences; here again we see significant differences in rates. For instance, Quinsey, Lalumiere, Rice, and Harris (1995) found a sexual reconviction rate of about 23 percent for offenders against women, 18 percent for heterosexual child molesters, and 35 percent for homosexual child molesters. Alexander (1999) reported similar rates for untreated sex offenders: 24 percent for sexual aggressors against women, 16 percent for heterosexual child molesters, and 34 percent for homosexual child molesters. When subjects are followed for longer time periods, the identified recidivism rates rise considerably. For instance, Prentky, Lee, Knight, and Cerce's 1997 study of repetitive and/or aggressive sex offenders found that 26 percent of aggressors against women and 32 percent of aggressors against children committed another sexual offense over a period of 25 years following their release.

As these studies reveal, the common perception that all or most sex offenders reoffend is not supported by the research; within the population of sex offenders, however, some subpopulations pose high risks of reoffending. To that end, risk assessment instruments have been developed to estimate the likelihood of reoffending (Doren 2004). Risk prediction has been an element of criminal justice decision-making for several decades (Monahan 1981; Morris and Miller 1985). Critics in the 1980s assailed the first generation of instruments designed to assess risk as vastly inaccurate; they argued that the best one can hope for "is one true prediction of danger for two false positives" (Morris 1982, 519). Since that time, however, technological innovations have allowed researchers to create a second generation of what are known as "actuarial prediction instruments." These instruments are exceptionally stable when subject to cross validation (e.g. Bonta, Harman, Hann, and Cormier 1996; Rice and Harris 1997) and have been shown to be highly superior to clinical prediction. For adult sex offenders, the most commonly used risk-prediction instruments are the STATIC 99 (Hanson and Thornton 1999), the SORAG (Quinsey, Harris, Rice, and Cormier 1998), and the MnSOST-R (Epperson, Kaul, and Hesselton 1998).

Probably the most commonly used actuarial instruments for the assessment of risk of sexual recidivism is the STATIC-99 (Hanson and Thornton, 1999). The STATIC-99 is a risk-assessment instrument used to evaluate the likelihood of a convicted sexual offender committing subsequent sexual offenses. It was developed by Hanson and Thornton, who combined two previously existing risk assessment instruments, the Rapid Risk Assessment for Sexual Offense Recidivism (RRASOR; Hanson 1997) and the Structured Anchored Clinical Judgment—Minimum (SACJ-Min; Grubin 1998). Both the RRASOR and the SACJ-Min were intended to be brief screening instruments for risk of sexual offense recidivism that utilize only case file data and do not require a face-to-face interview by the screener.

These two instruments, however, have different emphases, and they assess related but different constructs. The RRASOR focuses almost exclusively on factors related to sexual deviance, whereas the SACJ-Min incorporates also non-sexual criminal history factors. The STATIC-99 is a 10-item prediction scale, scored by combining both types of data and using information collected solely from individual case file information. These 10 items are:(1) any male victims, (2) never married, (3) any noncontact sex offenses, (4) any unrelated victims, (5) any stranger victims, (6) any prior sexual offenses, (7) any current nonsexual violence, (8) prior nonsexual violence, (9) four or more prior sentencing occasions, (10) age less than 25 years. These 10 risk factors are scored and summated, producing a single numeric score (maximum total score of 12). The summated score is then categorized into one of 4 risk groups: low (0–1), moderate-low (2–3), moderate-high (4–5), and high (6+). It has been reported that the STATIC-99 is a "robustly predictive instrument with moderate predictive accuracy" ($r = .33$, Receiver Operating Characteristics [ROC] Area Under the Curve [AUC] $= .71$) (de Vogel et al. 2004; Doren 2002; Hanson and Thornton 2000). Doren (2004) identified at least 22 studies testing the STATIC-99's predictive validity concerning sexual recidivism across different countries (e.g., Barbaree, Seto, Langton, and Peacock 2001; Beech, Friendship, Erikson, and Hanson 2002; McGrath, Cumming, Livingston, and Hoke 2003; Nunes, Firestone, Bradford, Greenberg, and Broom 2002). Of the 22 studies, 20 support the instrument's predictive validity, whereas two were less clear in that regard (Doren 2004).

Do these specialized actuarial instruments for sex offenders work better than those instruments for regular offenders (e.g., LSI-R)? The research that is currently available does not permit to answer this question. However, a study compared risk classifications made using the STATIC-99 and the LSI-R (Level of Service Inventory-Revised). Interestingly, findings revealed significant differences between the two instruments, the STATIC-99 identifying higher risk classifications than the LSI-R (Gentry, Dulmus, and Theriot 2005). Such discrepancy between a specialized instrument for sex offenders and instruments used for general offenders might be explained by the fact that specialized instruments are designed to assess those factors empirically associated to sexual recidivism, whereas the more general instruments such as the LSI-R look at general recidivism and do not assess certain risk factors associated to sexual reoffending (e.g., prior male victims, prior sexual offense).

WHAT IS KNOWN ABOUT HOW SEX OFFENDERS COMMIT THEIR CRIMES?

Because of the sexual nature of their crimes, sex offenders use very specific strategies to commit their crimes; specifically, these appear different from other offenders. However, we have learned by examining their modus operandi, that is, "the pattern of behaviors that perpetrators display in the periods prior to, during, and following illicit sexual contact" (Kaufman, Hilliker, and Daleiden 1996, 18), that sex offenders are influenced by factors similar to those that influence other criminals.

Offenders who sexually offend against children are mostly male, know the victim (Snyder 2000), and have been found to use common strategies to gain access and compliance (Leclerc, Proulx, and Beauregard 2009). For instance, sex offenders gradually desensitize the child victim to physical contact before moving to sexual touch (Berliner and Conte 1990), an approach frequently referenced as "grooming" (Elliott, Browne, and Kilcoyne 1995). This group of sex offenders may also use some type of coercion and threats (Budin and Johnson 1989; Conte, Wolf, and Smith 1989; Lang and Frenzel 1988), particularly when manipulation fails (Christiansen and Blake 1990; Leclerc and Tremblay 2007). However, these strategies are influenced by situational factors common to other forms of crime as well. For instance, findings show that younger offenders (adolescents) use a broader range of strategies as well as more violence than adult offenders to gain victims' compliance and maintain their silence following the abuse (Kaufman et al. 1998). This finding can be explained by the use of more sophisticated strategies (e.g., manipulation) with age and/or the special status (e.g. social, parental) of adult offenders, which does not require them to adopt coercive strategies as often as adolescent offenders (Kaufman, Orts, Holmberg, McCrady, Daleiden, and Hilliker 1996). Moreover, the age of the victim influences offenders' patterns of access and offending (Leclerc, Proulx, Lussier, and Allaire 2009), as adult offenders who sexually abuse older children are more likely to use a manipulative, rather than a non-persuasive strategy (Leclerc, Carpentier, and Proulx 2006). The offender-victim relationship is another contextual factor influencing the modus operandi. Intrafamilial offenders more often expose victims to pornography, as well as using gift-giving and threats, to gain cooperation, whereas extrafamilial offenders more frequently use alcohol and drugs (Kaufman et al. 1996; Kaufman et al. 1998). Finally, the type of location—for example, the offender's home when no one else is home—is likely to be the place and situation for offenders who rely on manipulative strategies (Leclerc, Beauregard, and Proulx 2008). However, it is important to stress the fact that what is known about these aspects of offending are derived from profiles of those who are caught, which may be a selective sample of all sex offenders.

Similar situational or contextual factors have been found to also influence the target selection process in sex offenders. Beauregard and colleagues (Beauregard and Leclerc 2007; Beauregard, Proulx, Rossmo, Leclerc, and Allaire 2007; Beauregard, Rossmo, and Proulx 2007) studied the complete sequence leading to the target selection in sexual assault cases.

The majority of sex offenders are sexually polymorphous—that is, displaying crime-switching patterns along several dimensions, such as victim's age (Abel and Rouleau 1990; Bradford, Boulet, and Pawlak 1992; Heil, Ahlmeyer, and Simons 2003; Lussier, Leclerc, Healey, and Proulx 2007). Researchers in this field of situational crime analyzed sexual assault events involving both children and adult women and identified three target selection scripts, that is, the complete sequence of instrumental decisions and actions prior to, during, and following the criminal act (Cornish and Clarke 2002).

The *coercive script* includes the *home-intrusion* track (tracks are considered variants of a more generic script and enable the individual to deal with differences in procedures under specific circumstances; see Cornish 1994) and the *outdoor* track. In the home-intrusion track, the aggressor uses the victim's residence as the base of his search. The encounter, attack, crime, and victim-release site are the same, most often the victim's residence or somewhere in the building in which the victim resides. The aggressor employs physical violence when approaching the victim and committing the crime. In the outdoor track, the aggressor ambushes the victim in a public outdoor place that is familiar to both. Unlike the home-intrusion track, the aggressor uses physical violence to bring the victim to the crime scene and commit the crime.

The *manipulative script* includes the *sophisticated* track as well as the *family-infiltrator* track. The characteristic feature of the sophisticated track is a search that is based in a prostitution market or workplace (employment, volunteer work, management of activities, etc.). Contact with the victim occurs outdoors, in a public place familiar to both aggressor and victim. Unlike aggressors who use the coercive script, the aggressor here uses manipulation, game-play, or the offer of money and gifts to lead the victim to the scene where he commits the assault. He does not kidnap the victim, even if the attack takes place in an indoor or private location known to him (most often his own residence). The assailant meets the victim opportunistically, during his non-predatory activities, and attacks only when the victim is attracted to a place—such as a residence or work-place—where he is in power. In the family-infiltrator track, the aggressor mostly seeks victims within a family setting or through his occupation. He uses money and gifts, or alcohol and drugs, to approach the victim, to lead the victim to the crime scene, and to commit the crime. The locations are typically private and indoors, most often the aggressor's residence.

Finally, the *non-persuasive script* includes only the *direct action* track, which describes an aggressor who pursues his victims in a public place and makes contact directly (i.e., with no particular strategy), taking the victim to the crime site, and committing the crime. Most often this type of aggression takes place in indoor public places such as bars and malls.

The identified scripts show how environmental factors (e.g., indoor versus outdoor locations, site familiarity, etc.) are important in the target-selection process of sex offenders. Thus, the types of location are related to the selected strategies that offenders use during the selection process and vice versa. Such results are congruent with the environmental criminology perspective, which states that the spatial and temporal distribution of offenders and victims are patterned (Brantingham and Brantingham 1993), and that target selection is highly dependent on the physical environment (Canter and Larkin 1993).

Although previous studies have shown the importance of the environment on the modus operandi of sex offenders, technological innovations have created a new environment for sex offenders:the Internet. However, far from the media portrayal of Internet sex crimes, where violence and threats are depicted, most of these crimes fit a model that has been called statutory rape—that is, "adult offenders who meet, develop relationships with, and openly seduce underage teenagers" (Wolak, Finkelhor, Mitchell, and Ybarra 2008, 111). Online child molesters often use the Internet to get access to youth, establish trust, introduce discussion of sex, and arrange for face-to-face encounters for sexual purposes (Wolak, Finkelhor, and Mitchell 2004). For instance, chat rooms represent a virtual environment where offenders can communicate directly with potential victims. In their extensive survey, Wolak and colleagues (2004) found that the majority of offenders met their victims in chat rooms (76 percent) but also communicated online in multiple ways (77 percent). Interestingly, the offender spoke on the phone (79 percent), sent pictures (48 percent), and/or offered money or gifts to the victim (47 percent). More than half of the offenders used deception to some extent, and the majority (80 percent) used the Internet to bring up sexual topics with the victim. This "virtual" environment provides new opportunities for offenders to get access to victims, therefore creating a need to adapt and develop new strategies to commit sexual crimes.

HAVE CURRENT LAWS AND POLICIES CAUSED A REDUCTION IN SEX CRIMES?

In recent decades, many calls for legal reforms regarding sex offenses have emphasized a sudden acceleration of incidents—often referred to as a "sex-crime wave" (Freedman 1987, 83). While official statistics showed an increase in sex crimes through the mid-1980s, these rates stabilized in the early 1990s; starting in 1993, the trend has been very different.

Criminologists have paid close attention to the drop in violent crime in the last decade; the 2008 violent crime rate was 41 percent lower than in 1998. Rape and sexual assault victimizations followed this trend, dropping by 53 percent during this decade (Rand 2009). Data from the child welfare system reveals similar declines for substantiated child sexual abuse. After about 15 years of steady increases, these crimes against children began to decline in the early 1990s. From 1992 through 2007, substantiated sexual abuse cases in the child welfare system declined by 52 percent (Jones and Finkelhor 2007).

Explanations for the drop in violent crime typically focus on factors such as an aging population, stronger economy, increased incarceration patterns, more police, and decline in risky behaviors, among others (Blumstein and Wallman 2005; Mishra and Lalumiere 2009). Researchers have dedicated significant attention to potential explanations for the drop in sex offenses against children; Finkelhor and Jones's 2006 review

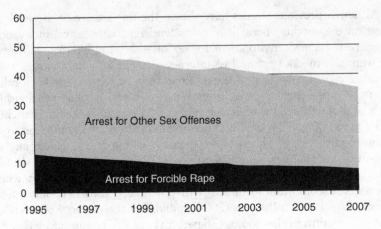

Figure 12.1. Trends in Sex Crime Arrests, 1995–2007
Source: FBI Sex Offense Data

concluded that multiple explanations are the most likely, including a combination of "economic prosperity, increasing numbers of agents of social intervention, and psychiatric pharmacology" (707). In terms of the role of pharmacology, effective treatment of depression is theorized to lead to fewer individuals acting out aggressively and sexually.

During this period in which the incidence of sex crimes has been reduced, public concern has risen. In 2005, a national poll found that two out of three Americans described themselves as "very concerned" about sexual molestation of children, rating concerns about this crime higher than violent crime and acts of terrorism in their communities (Carroll 2005). Legislative responses have included significant increases in sentence length; at least half the states require mandatory minimum prison terms of 25 years for first-time felony sex offenders against children (National Council of State Legislators 2008). Approximately 20 states have authorized indefinite civil commitment of highly dangerous sex offenders (Gookin 2007). Both state and federal laws have created special provisions for sex offenders after their release from incarceration. These post-release provisions are aimed at decreasing the anonymity of sex offenders and restricting their access to victims. A key strategy in this regard requires sex offenders to register with law enforcement following their release from incarceration; in 2009, there were 687,000 people listed on sex offender registries (National Center for Missing and Exploited Children 2009).

Registration ordinances were first introduced in the United States in the 1930s; they originally focused on habitual violators of criminals laws (Logan 2009). These ordinances had modest use until the 1990s, when they were resurrected as a means of decreasing sex crimes. Starting in 1990 in Washington State, authorities required convicted sex offenders, upon release from custody or after sentencing, to register with local law enforcement.

The 1990 law also authorized officials to notify the public when dangerous sex offenders were released into the community. These measures were intended to "restrict the access of known sex offenders to vulnerable populations, and also to improve law enforcement's ability to identify convicted offenders" (Task Force on Community Protection 1989, II-27).

Following Washington State, numerous states passed similar legislation through the mid-1990s. The federal government entered this field with the 1994 Jacob Wetterling Act, requiring states to implement a sex offender registry or face a financial penalty. With amendments in 1996, community notification also became a requirement. In July 2006, Congress passed the Adam Walsh Child Protection and Safety Act, further standardizing state laws. Since the federal government commonly leaves criminal matters to the states' discretion, Congress's significant role in sex offender policies is unusual and speaks to the political popularity of this category of laws (Logan 2008b). Several studies have demonstrated that citizens are very supportive of these law (Lieb and Nunlist 2008; Levenson, Brannon, Fortney, and Baker 2007; Proctor, Badzinski, and Johnson 2002); a 2005 Gallup Poll found that 94 percent of Americans were in favor of the law; interestingly, only one-quarter reported that they checked the available registries (Gallup News Service 2005). Because registration laws require the compliance of sex offenders, they have been frequently found to be inaccurate (e.g., Peterson 1995; Ballard 2005). Courts have grappled with the constitutionality of both registration and notification laws, with most courts to date finding that these policies are a reasonable exercise of regulatory power with any potential rights' infringements outweighed by the contribution to public safety (Terry and Ackerman 2009).

Two studies have analyzed multiple states and relied on aggregate-level data to determine whether registration and notification laws have changed crime rates. Prescott and Rockoff (2008) analyzed National Incidence Based Reporting System data to examine the effects in 15 states, taking account of the timing and scope of state laws. For registration laws, the authors found evidence that registration reduces the frequency of sex offenses because law enforcement is knowledgeable about the location of registered offenders. Notification laws were found to deter first-time sex offenders, but to increase the recidivism rates of registered sex offenders. The authors speculate that this increase is caused by the "heavy social and financial costs associated with the public release of their information" (34). The overall net effect is a 10 percent reduction because registration has a greater effect than notification. Shao and Li (2006) used Uniform Crime Report panel data for all 50 states from 1970 to 2002 and estimated that registration led to a 2 percent reduction in rapes reported to police. Researchers have documented numerous other effects of registration/notification laws, including labor and equipment costs to law enforcement (Zevitz and Farkas 2000a), declines in property values for households close to registered offenders (Linden and Rockoff 2006; Pope

2008), and disruptions to offenders and their families (Levenson and Cotter 2005; Tewksbury and Lees 2007; Zevitz and Farkas 2000b).

In addition to registration and notification laws, electronic monitoring has been used in 34 states with sex offenders released to the community (Interstate Commission for Adult Offender Supervision 2007). One form of these devices relies on Global Positioning System (GPS) technology, which allows real-time monitoring of geographical locations of individuals. A majority of the jurisdictions that use GPS technology for this purpose apply it to high-risk, violent, or aggressive sex offenders (Nieto and Jung 2006). In terms of GPS systems and their use with high-risk sex offenders, the most rigorous study to date did not find any recidivism reduction in a preliminary report (Turner and Janetta 2007). In 2009, a woman kidnapped 18 years earlier was found living in the backyard of a registered sex offender who was on electronic monitoring and subject to monthly visits; this discovery led to debates about the value of registries and electronic monitoring (Davey 2009). In past decades, decisions about where sex offenders could live when they were released from custody were either made by individual offenders or, if the person was under the authority of a parole officer, in conjunction with the paroling authority. This decision-making apparatus continues, but is significantly restricted by the recent proliferation of state and municipal laws restricting where sex offenders can live (Meloy, Miller, and Curtis 2008). These laws are intended to restrict the access of sex offenders to victims and force them to live outside populated areas and away from children. Two types of laws have been passed:"child safety zones," where offenders are not allowed to loiter, and "distance marker" laws that give specific space restrictions where offenders cannot live—typically, 1,000 to 2,500 feet from schools, playgrounds, and other areas where children congregate (Nieto and Jung 2006). Some communities have passed ordinances restricting registered sex offenders from living there (Fonce-Olivas 2006); some developers are building "sex offender—free subdivisions" (Axtman 2006).

It is unclear whether residency restrictions are effective in reducing sex offenses. A Minnesota study examined new offenses committed by released sex offenders and identified residential locations for these offenders and victims. The authors concluded that "none of the 224 incidents of sex offender recidivism fit the criteria of a known offender making contact with a child victim at a location within the distances typically covered by residential restriction laws" (Duwe, Donnay, and Tewksbury 2008, 498). One consequence of these restrictions has been increased homelessness among released sex offenders. In 2008, California reported that over 3,000 released sex offenders registered as transient, a 60 percent increase from 2005 (California Sex Offender Management Board 2008). Although there are no studies linking increased homelessness among sex offenders with higher rates of recidivism, the criminological literature links stability and support with successful community reentry for offenders (Petersilia 2003).

In spite of controversy about its effectiveness, treatment for sex offenders continues to be a relatively common component of the criminal justice system response. Sex offenders, especially offenders against children, stand a fair chance of receiving a sentence that involves treatment, often in the community, instead of a legislatively mandated period of incarceration (Cross, Walsh, Simone, and Jones 2003; Berliner, Schram, Miller, and Milloy 1995). The Safer Society Press identified more than 1,500 programs across the United States in a survey conducted in 1994 (Knopp, Freeman-Longo, Bird, Stevenson, and Fiske 1994).

A key rationale for the treatment focus with sex offenders, particularly for cases with child victims, has been to encourage victim reporting and cooperation with the criminal justice system. The other argument is that sex offender recidivism can be reduced with specialized treatment (Berliner et al. 1995).

The debate in the scientific literature on the effectiveness of sex offender treatment has been extensive. Depending on which studies are given weight and the methods of analysis, researchers have concluded that treatment reduces recidivism (Hall 1995; Hanson, Bourgon, Helmus, and Hodgson 2009; Losel and Schmucker 2005; MacKenzie 2006), whereas others have determined that the research evidence is still insufficient to draw a firm conclusion (Furby, Weinrott, and Blackshaw 1989; Harris, Rice, and Quinsey 1998; Kenworthy, Adams, Bilby, Brooks-Gordon, and Fenton 2004; Rice and Harris 2003). In reviewing sex offender programming along with the prior assessments and the meta-analyses, MacKenzie (2006) found that sex offender treatment programs using cognitive-behavioral therapy (such as the relapse prevention model) and chemical castration/psychotherapy were the most effective in reducing recidivism. Moreover, her analysis revealed that treatment in hospital-based settings was more effective than treatment provided in prison.

How Can We Prevent Sexual Crimes?

Efforts to prevent sexual crimes have focused on multiple fronts:incapacitation of convicted sex offenders, changing social norms, situational crime prevention, in addition to treatment of offenders. Although relatively new and unexplored, situational crime prevention principles can be applied to sexual crimes. Situational prevention aims to make the offender decide not to commit a crime by targeting the "precriminal situation" and reducing crime opportunities (Cusson 1992). This approach is likely to make crime more difficult and risky or less rewarding by managing, designing, or manipulating the environment (Clarke 1997). Referencing the broad situational crime prevention literature (Cornish and Clarke 2003), Wortley and Smallbone (2006) suggest four techniques as having potential value in preventing child sexual abuse:

- Increasing effort:This strategy consists of making it harder for the offender to commit his crime and be successful. One of the most widely known of these techniques is *target hardening* (i.e., teaching of self-protective behaviors). School-based programs for young children have been a primary force of this type of intervention. Other techniques consist of *controlling tools/weapons* (e.g., controlling what appears on Internet sites, setting up web sites to lure persons interested in child pornography; see Smallbone, Marshall, and Wortley 2008), and *controlling access to facilities* (i.e., excluding potential offenders from places where children congregate such as youth-oriented organizations, requiring visitors to schools to report to the office before they enter the property, etc.).

- Increasing risk: This general strategy consists of improving surveillance at possible crime sites. Specific techniques aim at *extending guardianship* (e.g., making sure the child is not alone, forbidding sports coaches to go to competitions or on trips alone with a group of children), *strengthening formal surveillance* (e.g., use of police patrols, security guards, or closed circuit television to watch over risky areas, setting up help lines), *utilizing place managers* (e.g., teaching pool attendants or lifeguards to identify grooming behaviors), and *assisting natural surveillance* (e.g., building public toilets in busy locations and ensuring they are well lit; see Smallbone et al. 2008).

- Controlling prompts: The goal here is to remove situational triggers (e.g., restricting observation of children in "provocative" situations or in intimate parenting roles such as giving children a bath or tucking them into bed).

- Reducing permissibility: This strategy aims at challenging distorted beliefs, excuses, or minimizations by offenders regarding the link between their behavior and its consequences (e.g., messages through public education programs, introducing explicit codes of conduct and induction procedures for staff within youth organizations that clearly mention acceptable and unacceptable behavior; see Leclerc, Proulx, and Beauregard 2009).

Smallbone and colleagues (2008) noted that, while based on well-established crime prevention principles, these strategies and techniques are speculative. However, educational programs targeted at children themselves have been evaluated. The aims of these programs are to teach skills to help children identify dangerous situations, refuse invitations, break off interactions, and ask for help (Finkelhor 2009). A series of evaluation studies has demonstrated that children were able to acquire the key concepts being taught in the program (see for instance Berrick and Barth 1992; Davis and Gidycz 2000; Finkelhor and Strapko 1992; Hebert and Tourigny 2004). In fact, a meta-analysis revealed that children who had participated in an education program were six times more likely to demonstrate protective behavior in simulated situations than children who have not (Zwi 2007). However, no studies based on strong research designs have investigated whether or not these programs helped to prevent victimization (Finkelhor 2009). Some of these approaches have been applied to college campuses in an effort to reduce sexual abuse, as sexual assault is the most common violent crime committed on campuses (Fisher, Cullen, and Turner 2000). Prevention campaigns in these settings have focused on the high prevalence of alcohol in connection to sexual assaults. Some fraternities have, for example, appointed "guardians" for inebriated women (Ehrhart and Sanders 1985). Other approaches have emphasized attitudinal changes (e.g., by-stander education; see, for instance, Banyard, Moynihan, and Plante 2007) and self-defense training programs. Despite the lack of empirical evaluations of such programs, there seems to be indirect support for their efficacy (Sochting, Fairbrother, and Koch 2004).

CONCLUSION

Sex offenders are treated as exceptions in the criminal justice system. Extensive media coverage of violent sexual crimes committed by con-victed sex offenders has intensified community outrage and fueled the public's desire for immediate solutions to a complex public policy issue (LaFond 2005). The analysis in this chapter shows that the serious psy-chological harm inflicted to the victims may justify treating sex offenders differently. When looking at recidivism rates, certain types of sex offen-ders (e.g., homosexual child molesters, sexual aggressors against women) represent a high risk to the community. However, as we have seen, the recidivism risk for sex offenders varies by the type of offense and offender characteristics. Recent policy changes for sex offenders typically target all sex offenders indiscriminately, which leads to the diffusion of scarce resources to a large pool of offenders. Knowledge about sex offenders can be used to focus application of these restrictive measures to the most dangerous offenders. For instance, having offenders convicted of statutory rape included in the sex offender registry is of little use to law enforce-ment agencies in their attempt to prioritize suspects in stranger-to-strang-er sexual assaults.

Given our increased experience in risk assessment, the criminal justice system can rely on differentiated measures for sex offenders to distinguish offenders according to their predicted future dangerousness (LaFond 2005). Such measures are already in place in several states and aim at incapacitating dangerous sex offenders. One example is using indetermi-nate sentences for dangerous sex offenders. In these cases, an individual is not released back into the community until there is strong evidence that he is no longer dangerous. Dangerous sex offenders can also be submitted to long-term parole as well as intensive supervision programs after their release to the community.

For some types of crime, a downward trend in incidences changes the focus of legislation, as policymakers turn their attention toward issues of higher public concern. To date, however, public attention toward this crime has not waned with the drop in incidence levels; it is difficult to foresee a lessening of public attention.

References

Abel, G. G., and J. L. Rouleau. 1990. "The Nature and Extent of Sexual Assault." In *Handbook of Sexual Assault: Issues, Theories and Treatment of the Offender*, eds. W. L. Marshall, D. R. Laws, and H. E. Barbaree, 9–22. New York: Plenum Press.

Alexander, M. A. 1999. "Sexual Offender Treatment Efficacy Revisited." *Sexual Abuse: A Journal of Research and Treatment* 11: 101–116.

American Psychiatric Association. 2000. Posttraumatic Stress Disorder. In *Diagnostic and Statistical Manual of Mental Disorders*, 4th ed., text revision. Washington, DC: Author.

Axtman, K. 2006. July 28. "Efforts Grow to Keep Tabs on Sex Offenders." *The Christian Science Monitor*. Retrieved from http://www.csmonitor.com&/2006/0728&/p01s02-ussc.html.

Ballard, P. 2005. October 4. "State Officials Grapple with Problems in Tracking Sex Offenders." *The Herald-Mail*. Retrieved from http://www.herald-mail.com/?module=displaystory&story_id=121167&format=html.

Banyard, V. L., M. M. Moynihan, and E. G. Plante. 2007. "Sexual Violence Prevention Through Bystander Education: An Experimental Evaluation." *Journal of Community Psychology* 35: 463–481.

Barbaree, H. E., Seto, M. C., Langton, C., and Peacock, E. 2001. "Evaluating the Predictive Accuracy of Six Risk Assessment Instruments for Adult Sex Offenders." *Criminal Justice and Behavior* 28: 490–521.

Beauregard, E., and B. Leclerc. 2007. "An Application of the Rational Choice Approach to the Offending Process of Sex Offenders: A Closer Look at the Decision-Making." *Sexual Abuse: A Journal of Research and Treatment* 19: 115–133.

Beauregard, E., J. Proulx, K. Rossmo, B. Leclerc, and J.-F. Allaire. 2007. "Script Analysis of Hunting Process in Serial Sex Offenders." *Criminal Justice and Behavior* 34: 1069–1084.

Beauregard, E., K. Rossmo, and J. Proulx. 2007. "A Descriptive Model of the Hunting Process of Serial Sex Offenders: A Rational Choice Perspective." *Journal of Family Violence* 22: 449–463.

Beech, A., C. Friendship, M. Erikson, and R. K. Hanson. 2002. "The Relationship Between Static and Dynamic Risk Factors and Reconviction in a Sample of U.K. Child Abusers." *Sexual Abuse: A Journal of Research and Treatment* 14: 155–168.

Berliner, L., and J. R. Conte. 1990. "The Process of Victimization: The Victim's Perspective." *Child Abuse and Neglect* 14: 29–40.

Berliner, L., D. Schram, L. Miller, and D. Milloy. 1995. "A Sentencing Alternative for Sex Offenders." *Journal of Interpersonal Violence* 10: 487–502.

Berrick, J., and R. Barth. 1992. "Child Sexual Abuse Prevention Training: What Do They Learn?" *Child Abuse and Neglect* 12: 543–553.

Blumstein, A., and J. Wallman. 2005. *The Crime Drop in America*. New York: Cambridge University Press.

Bonta, J., W. G. Harman, R. G. Hann, and R. B. Cormier. 1996. "The Prediction of Recidivism among Federally Sentenced Offenders: A Re-Validation of the SIR Scale." *Canadian Journal of Criminology* 38: 61–79.

Bradford, J. M., J. Boulet, and A. Pawlak. 1992. "The Paraphilias: A Multiplicity of Deviant Behaviours." *Canadian Journal of Psychiatry* 37: 104–108.

Brantingham, P. L., and P. J. Brantingham. 1993. "Environment, Routine and Situation: Toward a Pattern Theory of Crime." In *Routine Activity and Rational Choice*, eds. R. V. Clarke and M. Felson 259–294. New Brunswick, NJ: Transaction.

Budin, L. E., and C. F. Johnson. 1989. "Sex Abuse Prevention Programs: Offenders' Attitudes about Their Efficacy." *Child Abuse and Neglect* 13: 77–87.

California Sex Offender Management Board. 2008, December. *Homelessness among Registered Sex Offenders in California: The Numbers, the Risks and the Response.* Executive Summary. Sacramento, CA. Retrieved from http://www.casomb.org/docs/Housing%202008%20Rev%201%205%20FINAL.pdf.

Canter, D., and P. Larkin. 1993. "The Environmental Range of Serial Rapists." *Journal of Environmental Psychology* 13: 63–71.

Carroll, J. 2005, May 3. "Crystal Meth, Child Molestation Top Crime Concerns." *Gallup, Inc.* Retrieved from http://www.gallup.com/poll/16123/crystal-meth-child-molestation-top-crime-concerns.aspx

Christiansen, J. R., and R. H. Blake. 1990. "The Grooming Process in Father-Daughter Incest." In *The Incest Perpetrator: A Family Member No One Wants to Treat*, eds. A. L. Horton, B. L. Johnson, L. M. Rowndy, and D. Williams, 88–98. Newbury Park, CA: Sage Publications.

Clarke, R. V. 1997. "Introduction." In *Situational Crime Prevention: Successful Case Studies*, ed. R. V. Clarke, 1–43. Guilderland, NY: Harrow and Heston.

Conte, J. R., S. Wolf, and T. Smith. 1989. "What Sexual Offenders Tell Us about Prevention Strategies." *Child Abuse and Neglect* 13: 293–301.

Cornish, D. B. 1994. "Crime as Scripts." In *Proceedings of the International Seminar on Environmental Criminology and Crime Analysis*, eds. D. Zahm and P. Cromwell, University of Miami, Coral Gables, FL, 1993. Tallahassee: Florida Statistical Analysis Center, Florida Criminal Justice Executive Institute, Florida Department of Law Enforcement.

Cornish, D. B., and R. V. Clarke. 2002. "Analyzing Organized Crimes." In *Rational Choice and Criminal Behaviour: Recent Research and Future Challenges*, eds. A. R. Piquero and S. G. Tibbetts, 41–63. New York: Routledge.

Cornish, D. B., and R. V. Clarke. 2003. "Opportunities, Precipitators and Criminal Decisions: A Reply to Wortley's Critique of Situational Crime Prevention." In *Theory for Practice in Situational Crime Prevention (Crime Prevention Studies 16)*, eds. M. J. Smith and D. B. Cornish, 41–96. Monsey, NY: Criminal Justice Press.

Cross T., W. Walsh, M. Simone, and L. Jones. 2003. "Prosecution of Child Abuse." *Trauma, Violence, and Abuse* 4 (4): 323–340.

Cusson, M. 1992. "L'analyse criminologique et la prévention situationnelle." *Revue Internationale de Criminologie et de Police Technique* 2: 137–149.

Davey, M. 2009, September 2. "Case Shows Limits of Sex Offender Alert Programs." *New York Times.* Retrieved from http://www.nytimes.com/2009/09/02/us/02offenders.html.

Deblinger, E., R. Steer, and J. Lippmann. 1999. "Two-Year Follow-Up Study of Cognitive Behavioral Therapy for Sexually Abused Children Suffering Post-Traumatic Stress Symptoms." *Child Abuse and Neglect* 12: 1371–1378.

de Vogel, V., C. de Ruiter, D. van Beek, and G. Mead. 2004. "Predictive Validity of the SVR-20 and STATIC-99 in a Dutch Sample of Treated Sex Offenders." *Law and Human Behavior* 28: 235–251.

Doren, D. M. (2002).*Evaluating Sex Offenders: A Manual for Civil Commitments and Beyond.* Thousand Oaks, CA: Sage.

Doren, D. M. 2004. "Stability of the Interpretative Risk Percentages for the RRASOR and STATIC-99." *Sexual Abuse: A Journal of Research and Treatment* 16: 25–36.

Doren, D. M. 2004, September 20. *Bibliography of Published Works Relative to Risk Assessment for Sexual Offenders.* Retrieved from http://www.atsa.com/pdfs/riskAssessmentBiblio.pdf.

Duwe, G., W. Donnay, and R. Tewksbury, R. 2008. "Does Residential Proximity Matter? A Geographic Analysis of Sex Offense Recidivism." *Criminal Justice and Behavior* 35: 484–504.

Ehrhart, J. K., and B. R. Sanders. 1985. *Campus Gang Rape: Party Games?* Project on the Status and Education of Women, Association of American Colleges, Washington DC.

Elliott, M., K. Browne, and J. Kilcoyne. 1995. "Child Sexual Abuse Prevention: What Offenders Tell Us." *Child Abuse and Neglect* 19: 579–594.

Epperson, D. L., J. D. Kaul, and D. Hesselton. 1998, October. "Final Report on the Development of the Minnesota Sex Offender Screening Tool-Revised (MnSOST-R)." Paper presented at the 17th Annual Conference of the Association for the Treatment of Sexual Abusers, Vancouver, Canada.

Ferraro, K. F. 1995. *Fear of Crime: Interpreting Victimization Risk.* Albany: State University of New York Press.

Finkelhor, D. 2009. "The Prevention of Childhood Sexual Abuse." *The Future of Children* 19: 53–78. Available at www.futureofchildren.org.

Finkelhor, D., N. Asdigian, and J. Dziuba-Leatherman. 1995. "The Effectiveness of Victimization Prevention Instruction: An Evaluation of Children's Responses to Actual Threats and Assaults." *Child Abuse and Neglect* 19 (2): 141–153.

Finkelhor, D., and R. Ormrod. 1999. *Reporting Crimes Against Juveniles* (NCJ 178887). Juvenile Justice Bulletin. Washington, DC: U.S. Department of Justice, Office of Juvenile Justice and Delinquency Prevention. Retrieved from http://www.ncjrs.gov/pdffiles1/ojjdp/178887.pdf.

Finkelhor, D., and N. Strapko. 1992. "Sexual Abuse Prevention Education: A Review of Evaluation Studies." In *Child Abuse Prevention,* eds. D. Willis, E. Holden, and M. Rosenberg, 150–167. New York: Wiley.

Fisher, B., F. Cullen, and M. Turner. 2000. *The Sexual Victimization of College Women* (NCJ 182369). Washington, DC: Bureau of Justice Statistics, U.S. Department of Justice, Office of Justice Programs.

Fonce-Olivas, T. 2006, February 24. "Proposal to Ban Sex Offenders from Border May Not Be Legal." *El Paso Times,* 1A.

Freedman, E. B. 1987. "Uncontrolled Desires': The Response to the Sexual Psychopath, 1920–1960." *Journal of American History* 74: 86–106.

Furby, L., M. Weinrott, and L. Blackshaw. 1989. "Sex Offender Recidivism: A Review." *Psychological Bulletin* 105 (1): 3–30.

Gallup News Service. 2005, June 9. "Sex Offender Registries Are Underutilized by the Public" Retrieved from http://www.gallup.com/poll/16705/sex-offender-registries-underutilized-public.aspx.

Gentry, A. L., C. N. Dulmus, and M. T. Theriot. 2005. "Comparing Sex Offender Risk Classification Using The STATIC-99 and LSI-R Assessment Instruments." *Research on Social Work Practice* 15: 557–563.

Gookin, K. 2007. *Comparison of State Laws Authorizing Involuntary Commitment of Sexually Violent Predators: 2006 Update, Revised* (Document No. 07–08–1101). Olympia: Washington State Institute for Public Policy.

Gordon, M. T., and S. Riger. 1989. *The Female Fear.* New York: Free Press.

Grubin, D. 1998. *Sex Offending Against Children: Understanding the Risk.* Police Research Series Paper 99. London: Home Office.

Hall, G. C. N. 1995. "Sexual Offender Recidivism Revisited: A Meta-Analysis of Recent Treatment Studies." *Journal of Consulting and Clinical Psychology* 63: 802–809.

Hanson, R. K. 1997. *The Development of a Brief Actuarial Risk Scale for Sexual Offense Recidivism.* Ottawa, Ontario: Department of the Solicitor General of Canada.

Hanson, R. K., and D. Thornton. 1999. *STATIC-99: Improving Actuarial Risk Assessments for Sex Offenders* (User Report No. 1999–02). Ottawa: Department of the Solicitor General of Canada.

Hanson, R., G. Bourgon, L. Helmus, and S. Hodgson. 2009. *A Meta-Analysis of the Effectiveness of Treatment for Sexual Offenders: Risk, Need, and Responsivity, 2009–01.* Ottawa, Ontario: Public Safety Canada.

Harris, G., M. Rice, and V. Quinsey. 1998. "Appraisal and Management of Risk in Sexual Aggressors: Implications for Criminal Justice Policy." *Psychology, Public Policy, and Law* 4: 73–115.

Hebert, M., and M. Tourigny, 2004. "Child Sexual Abuse Prevention: A Review of Evaluative Studies and Recommendations for Program Development." *Advances in Psychology Research* 29: 123–155.

Heil, P., S. Ahlmeyer, and D. Simons. 2003. "Crossover Sexual Offenses." *Sexual Abuse: A Journal of Research and Treatment* 15: 221–236.

Interstate Commission for Adult Offender Supervision. 2007, April. ICAOS GPS Update survey April 2007. Retrieved from http://www.interstatecompact.org/LinkClick.aspx?fileticket=lU6GvRmuPwM%3D&tabid=105&mid=431.

Jones, L., and D. Finkelhor. 2007. *Updated Trends in Child Maltreatment, 2007.* Durham, NH: Crimes Against Children Research Center, University of New Hampshire.

Jumper, S. A. 1995. "A Meta-Analysis of the Relationship of Child Sexual Abuse to Adult Psychological Adjustment." *Child Abuse and Neglect* 19: 715–728.

Kaufman, K. L., D. R. Hilliker, and E. L. Daleiden. 1996. "Subgroup Differences in the Modus Operandi of Adolescent Sexual Offenders." *Child Maltreatment* 1: 17–24.

Kaufman, K. L, J. K. Holmberg, K. A. Orts, F. E. McCrady, A. L. Rotzien, E. L. Daleiden, and D. R. Hilliker. 1998. "Factors Influencing Sexual Offenders' Modus Operandi: An Examination of Victim-Offender Relatedness and Age." *Child Maltreatment* 4: 349–361.

Kaufman, K. L., K. Orts, J. Holmberg, F. McCrady, E. L. Daleiden, and D. Hilliker, D. 1996, November. "Contrasting Adult and Adolescent Sexual Offenders' Modus Operandi: A Developmental Process?" Paper presented at the 15th Annual Conference of the Association for the Treatment of Sexual Abusers, Chicago, IL.

Kendall-Tackett, K. A., L. M. Williams, and D. Finkelhor. 1993. "The Impact of Sexual Abuse on Children: A Review and Synthesis of Recent Empirical Studies." *Psychological Bulletin* 113: 164–180.

Kendler, K. S., C. M. Bulik, J. Silberg, J. Hettema, J. Myers, and C. A. Prescott. 2000. "Childhood Sexual Abuse and Adult Psychiatric and Substance Use Disorders in Women: An Epidemiological and Cotwin Control Analysis." *Archives of General Psychiatry* 57: 953–959.

Kenworthy, T., C. E. Adams, C. Bilby, B. Brooks-Gordon, and M. Fenton. (2004). *Psychological Interventions for Those Who Have Sexually Offended or Are at Risk of Offending*. Cochran Database of Systematic Reviews, University of Bristol, School for Policy Studies, Bristol, UK.

Kilpatrick, D. G., B. E. Saunders, L. J. Veronen, C. L. Best, and J. M. Von. 1987. "Criminal Victimization: Lifetime Prevalence, Reporting to Police, and Psychological Impact." *Crime and Delinquency* 33 (4): 479–489.

Knopp, F., R. Freeman-Longo, S. Bird, W. Stevenson, and J. Fiske. 1994. *Nationwide Survey of Treatment Programs and Models*. Brandon, VT: Safer Society Press.

LaFond, J. Q. 2005. *Preventing Sexual Violence: How Society Should Cope with Sex Offenders*. Washington, DC: American Psychological Association.

Lang, R. A., and R. R. Frenzel. 1988. "How Sexual Offenders Lure Children." *Annals of Sex Research* 1: 303–317.

Langan, P. A., E. L. Schmitt, and M. R. Durose. 2003. *Recidivism of Sex Offenders Released from Prison in 1994* (NCJ 198281). Washington, DC: U.S. Department of Justice, Office of Justice Programs, Bureau of Justice Statistics. Retrieved from http://www.ojp.usdoj.gov/bjs/pub/pdf/rsorp94.pdf.

Leclerc, B., E. Beauregard, and J. Proulx. 2008. "Modus Operandi and Situational Aspects in Adolescent Sexual Offenses Against Children: A Further Examination." *International Journal of Offender Therapy and Comparative Criminology* 52: 46–61.

Leclerc, B., J. Carpentier, and J. Proulx. 2006. "Strategies Adopted by Sexual Offenders to Involve Children in Sexual Activity." In *Situational Prevention of Child Sexual Abuse* (*Crime Prevention Studies*, Vol. 19), eds. R. Wortley and S. Smallbone, 251–270. Monsey, NY: Criminal Justice Press.

Leclerc, B., J. Proulx, and E. Beauregard. 2009. "Examining the Modus Operandi of Sexual Offenders Against Children and Its Practical Implications." *Aggression and Violent Behavior* 14: 5–12.

Leclerc, B., J. Proulx, P. Lussier, and J.-F. Allaire. 2009. "Offender-Victim Interaction and Crime Event Outcomes: Modus Operandi and Victim Effects on the Risk of Intrusive Sexual Offenses Against Children." *Criminology* 47: 595–618.

Leclerc, B., and P. Tremblay. 2007. "Strategic Behavior in Adolescent Sexual Offenses Against Children: Linking Modus Operandi to Sexual Behaviors." *Sexual Abuse: A Journal of Research and Treatment* 19: 23–41.

Levenson, J., and L. Cotter. 2005. "The Effect of Megan's Law on Sex Offender Reintegration." *Journal of Contemporary Criminal Justice* 21 (1): 49–66.

Levenson, J. S., Y. Brannon, T. Fortney, and J. Baker. 2007. "Public Perceptions about Sex Offenders and Community Protection Policies." *Analyses of Social Issues and Public Policy* 7 (1): 1–25.

Lieb, R., and C. Nunlist. 2008. *Community Notification as Viewed by Washington's Citizens: A 10-Year Follow-Up* (Document No. 08–03–1101). Olympia: Washington State Institute for Public Policy.

Linden, L. L., and J. E. Rockoff. 2006. *There Goes the Neighborhood? Estimates of the Impact of Crime Risk on Property Values from Megan's Laws*. Social Science Research Network. Retrieved from http://ssrn.com/abstract=903178.

Logan, W. A. 2000. "A Study in 'Actuarial Justice': Sex Offender Classification Practice and Procedure." *Buffalo Criminal Law Review* 3: 593–637.

Logan, W. A. 2008b. "Criminal Justice Federalism and National Sex Offender Policy." *Ohio State Journal of Criminal Law* 6: 51–122.

Logan, W. A. 2009. *Knowledge as Power: Criminal Registration and Community Notification Laws in America.* Stanford, CA: Stanford University Press.

Losel, F., and M. Schmucker. 2005. "The Effectiveness of Treatment for Sexual Offenders: A Comprehensive Meta-Analysis." *Journal of Experimental Criminology* 1 (1): 117–146.

Lussier, P. 2005. "The Criminal Activity of Sexual Offenders in Adulthood: Revisiting the Specialization Debate." *Sexual Abuse: A Journal of Research and Treatment* 17: 269–292.

Lussier, P., B. Leclerc, J. Healey, and J. Proulx. 2007. "Generality of Deviance and Predation: Crime-Switching and Specialization Patterns in Persistent Sexual Offenders." In *Violent Offenders: Theory, Public Policy and Practice,* eds. M. Delisi and P. Conis, 97–140. Boston: Jones and Bartlett Publishers.

MacKenzie, D. L. 2006. *What Works in Corrections: Reducing the Criminal Activities of Offenders and Delinquents.* New York: Cambridge University Press.

McGrath, R. J., G. Cumming, J. A. Livingston, and S. E. Hoke. 2003. "Outcome of a Treatment Program for Adult Sex Offenders: From Prison to Community." *Journal of Interpersonal Violence* 18: 3–17.

Meloy, M. L., S. L. Miller, and K. M. Curtis. 2008. "Making Sense Out of Nonsense: The Deconstruction of State-Level Sex Offender Residence Restrictions." *American Journal of Criminal Justice* 33: 209–222.

Mishra, S., and M. Lalumiere. 2009. "Is the Crime Drop of the 1990s in Canada and the USA Associated with a General Decline in Risky and Health-Related Behavior?" *Social Science and Medicine* 68: 39–48.

Monahan, J. 1981. *Predicting Violent Behavior: An Assessment of Clinical Techniques.* Beverly Hills, CA: Sage.

Morris, N. 1982. *Madness and the Criminal Law.* Chicago: University of Chicago Press.

Morris, N., and M. Miller M. 1985. "Predictions of dangerousness." In *Crime and Justice: An Annual Review of Research,* eds. M. Tonry and N. Morris, Vol. 6. Chicago: University of Chicago Press.

National Center for Missing and Exploited Children. 2009. *Registered Sex Offenders in the United States per 100,000 Population,* Special Analysis Unit, July 22, 2009.

National Council of State Legislators. 2008. *State Statutes Related to Jessica's Law.* Denver, CO.

Nieto, M., and D. Jung. 2006, August. *The Impact of Residency Restrictions on Sex Offenders and Correctional Management Practices: A Literature Review.* Sacramento: California Research Bureau.

Nunes, K. L., P. Firestone, J. M. Bradford, D. M. Greenberg, and I. Broom. 2002. "A Comparison of Modified Versions of the STATIC-99 and the Sex Offender Risk Appraisal Guide." *Sexual Abuse: A Journal of Research and Treatment* 14: 253–269.

Petersilia, J. 2003. *When Prisoners Come Home: Parole and Prisoner Reentry.* New York: Oxford University Press.

Peterson, I. 1995, January 12. "Mix-ups and Worse Arising from Sex-Offender Notification." *New York Times.* Retrieved from http://www.nytimes.com/

1995/01/12/nyregion/mix-ups-and-worse-arising-from-sex-offender-notification.html.

Pope, J. C. 2008. "Fear of Crime and Housing Prices: Household Reactions to Sex Offender Registries." *Journal of Urban Economics* 64: 601–614.

Prentky, R. A., A. F. S. Lee, R. A. Knight, and D. Cerce. 1997. "Recidivism Rates among Child Molesters and Rapists: A Methodological Analysis." *Law and Human Behavior* 21: 635–659.

Prescott, J. J. and J. E. Rockoff. 2008, February 1. *Do Sex Offender Registration and Notification Laws Affect Criminal Behavior?* NBER Working Paper No. 13803; 3rd Annual Conference on Empirical Legal Studies Papers; University of Michigan Law and Economics. Retrieved from http://ssrn.com/abstract=1100663.

Proctor, J. L., D. M. Badzinski, and M. Johnson. 2002. "The Impact of Media on Knowledge and Perceptions of Megan's Law." *Criminal Justice Policy Review* 13 (4): 356–379.

Quinsey, V. L., G. T. Harris, M. E. Rice, and C. A. Cormier. 1998. *Violent Offenders: Appraising and Managing Risk.* Washington, DC: American Psychological Association.

Quinsey, V. L., M. L. Lalumiere, M. E. Rice, and G. T. Harris. 1995. "Predicting Sexual Offenses." In *Assessing Dangerousness: Violence by Sexual Offenders, Batterers, and Child Abusers*, ed. J. C. Campbell, 114–137. Thousand Oaks, CA: Sage.

Rand, Michael R. 2009. *Criminal Victimization, 2008* (NCJ-227777), Washington DC: U.S. Department of Justice, Bureau of Justice Statistics.

Rice, M. E., and G. T. Harris. 1997. "Cross Validation and Extension of the Violence Risk Appraisal Guide for Child Molesters and Rapists." *Law and Human Behavior* 21: 231–241.

Rice, M. E., and G. T. Harris. 2003. "The Size and Sign of Treatment Effects in Sex Offender Therapy." *Annals of the New York Academy of Sciences* 989: 428–440.

Riggs, D. S., B. O. Rothbaum, and E. B. Foa. 1995. "A Prospective Examination of Symptoms of Posttramautic Stress Disorder in Victims of Nonsexual Assault." *Journal of Interpersonal Violence* 10: 201–214.

Rothbaum, B. O., E. B. Foa, D. S. Riggs, T. Murdock, and W. Walsh. 1992. "A Prospective Examination of Post-Traumatic Stress Disorder in Rape Victims." *Journal of Traumatic Stress* 5: 455–475.

Sample, L. L., and T. M. Bray. 2003. "Are Sex Offenders Dangerous?" *Criminology and Public Policy* 3: 59–82.

Shao, L., and J. Li. 2006. *The Effect of Sex Offender Registration Laws on Rape Victimization.* Unpublished manuscript.

Smallbone, S., W. L. Marshall, and R. Wortley. 2008. *Preventing Child Sexual Abuse: Evidence, Policy and Practice.* Devon, UK: Willan.

Snyder, H. N. 2000. *Sexual Assault of Young Children as Reported to Law Enforcement: Victim, Incident, and Offender Characteristics* (NCJ 182990). U.S. Department of Justice, Office of Justice Programs. Retrieved from http://www.ojp.usdoj.gov/bjs/pub/pdf/saycrle.pdf.

Sochting, I., N. Fairbrother, and W. J. Koch. 2004. "Sexual Assault of Women: Prevention Efforts and Risk Factors." *Violence Against Women* 10: 73–93.

Task Force on Community Protection. 1989. *Task Force on Community Protection: Final Report to Booth Gardner, Governor, State of Washington.* Olympia, WA: Author.

Tennessee Legislature. 1997. Tennessee Sexual Offender and Violent Sexual Offender Registration, Verification, and Tracking Act, Tenn. Code Ann. 40–39–201(b).

Terry, K. J., and A. R. Ackerman. 2009. "A Brief History of Major Sex Offender Laws." In *Sex Offender Laws: Failed Policies, New Directions*, ed. R. G. Wright, 65–98. New York: Springer.

Tewksbury, R. and M. Lees. 2007. "Perceptions of Punishment: How Registered Sex Offenders View Registries." *Crime and Delinquency* 53 (3): 380–407.

Tjaden, P. and N. Thoennes. 2000. *Full Report of the Prevalence, Incidence, and Consequences of Violence Against Women* (NCJ-183781), Washington DC: U.S. Department of Justice, National Institute of Justice.

Turner, S. and J. Janetta. 2009, May 24. "Evaluating the Effectiveness of Global Positioning Devices for High Risk Sex Offenders in San Diego, California." Paper presented at the annual meeting of the American Society of Criminology, Philadelphia, PA.

Wolak, J., D. Finkelhor, and K. J. Mitchell. 2004. "Internet-Initiated Sex Crimes Against Minors: Implications for Prevention Based on Findings from a National Study." *Journal of Adolescent Health* 35: 11–20.

Wolak, J., D. Finkelhor, K. J. Mitchell, and M. L. Ybarra. 2008. "Online 'Predators' and Their Victims: Myths, Realities, and Implications for Prevention and Treatment." *American Psychologist* 63 (2): 111–128.

Wortley, R., and S. Smallbone. 2006. "Applying Situational Principles to Sexual Offenses Against Children." In *Situational Prevention of Child Sexual Abuse (Crime Prevention Studies*, Vol. 19), eds. R. Wortley and S. Smallbone, 7–35. Monsey, NY: Criminal Justice Press.

Zevitz, R. G., and M. Farkas. 2000a. "The Impact of Sex-Offender Community Notification on Probation/Parole in Wisconsin." *International Journal of Offender Therapy and Comparative Criminology* 44 (1): 8–21.

Zevitz, R. G., and M. A. Farkas. 2000b. "Sex Offender Community Notification: Managing High Risk Criminals or Exacting Further Vengeance?" *Behavioral Sciences and the Law* 18 (2–3): 375–391.

Zwi, K. J. 2007. "School-Based Education Programs for the Prevention of Child Sexual Abuse." *Cochrane Database for Systematic Reviews* 2: 1–44.

Notes

1. Rape was defined as an event that occurred without the victim's consent, that involved the use or threat of force to penetrate the victim's vagina or anus by penis, tongue, fingers, or object, or the victim's mouth by penis. The definition included both attempted and completed rape (Tjaden and Thoennes 2000).

Chapter 13

Drugs, Crime, and Public Policy

David A. Boyum, Jonathan P. Caulkins
& Mark A. R. Kleiman

Drug use and drug control policies can both cause crime. Intoxication can generate violence; otherwise, the phrase "barroom brawl" would have no meaning. Crime can also result from financial strain due to reduced earnings and the need to steal to be able to buy drugs.

When drugs are either banned or so tightly regulated or heavily taxed as to support an illicit market, the result is likely to be violence among dealers and disorderly conditions around retail markets. In addition, drug enforcement competes with predatory-crime enforcement for scarce criminal-justice resources, and contributes to hostility between police and the residents of some neighborhoods. In the United States, drug enforcement also makes a major contribution to mass incarceration, a phenomenon that rivals crime itself as a social problem.

The use of intoxicants, whatever their legal status, also carries risks (which vary greatly from drug to drug) of health damage from consuming or administering drugs and of injury or economic loss from unwise intoxicated behavior. This creates a problem: drug control policies can generate increased crime as an unwanted side effect. Therefore, some drug policy decisions involve balancing crime-control and public-health goals. The goal is to find smart policies that limit drug abuse, non-drug crime, and incarceration.

Whether, on balance, current drug laws and policies increase or decrease total non-drug crime is hard to judge, because it is hard to predict all the consequences of any profound policy shift. The question is also incomplete, since the best drug policy from a crime-control perspective alone may not be the best policy once the other costs of drug abuse have been figured in. Doubtless, higher taxes on cigarettes have generated crime through the illicit markets in smuggled cigarettes, but they have also prolonged life and prevented disease and disability.

A different question is whether increasingly stringent drug law enforcement tends to increase or reduce non-drug crime. By some measures, the

United States increased the stringency of its drug enforcement by an order of magnitude between the mid-1980s and today. A return to the enforcement practices of the early Reagan administration would be a dramatic change, but not even remotely as profound as allowing cocaine to be sold as alcohol is sold. What would be the effects of such a shift on the rate of various kinds of predatory crime?

After a long period in which policy analysts could merely shake their heads in disapproval at a set of policies that created unnecessarily bad results, suggest doing less of the obviously harmful things, and speculate about hypothetically superior but untested alternatives, the past decade has seen a sudden increase in our working knowledge of how to have less crime, less drug abuse, and fewer people behind bars. In addition to the old standby of higher alcohol taxation, we now have experience in breaking up flagrant drug markets with a minimal number of arrests and in using the power of the agencies of community supervision—probation, parole, and pre-trial release—to reduce drug abuse among those under their jurisdiction. Since criminally active heavy users account for large fractions both of total illicit drug consumption and of non-drug crime, success with that population could make a major contribution to both crime control and substance abuse control.

SUMMARY OF POLICY IMPLICATIONS

This chapter will argue that some of the popular remedies for drug-related crime—longer sentences for drug dealers, preventing cannabis initiation among schoolchildren, treatment in lieu of incarceration for drug users, shifting resources away from enforcement and toward prevention and treatment, and legalization—are less promising than they appear. The list of drug policies with a high probability of substantially reducing non-drug crime is fairly short:

- Reducing drunkenness, especially drunkenness among those who tend to behave badly when drunk, will reduce crime. Increased taxation and a campaign of persuasion to make drunkenness less fashionable both seem like good candidates; even a doubling of the current modest taxes would measurably reduce violent crime. Preventing people who commit crimes under the influence from continuing to drink would be harder to achieve, but the potential rewards would be large.
- Reducing the volume of cocaine, heroin, and methamphetamine consumed without raising their prices will also reduce crime. Making treatment more available is one way to do so. In particular, opiate maintenance therapy (methadone and buprenorphine) is a proven crime-control strategy. It needs more money and fewer regulations.

- Concentrating long sentences on violent dealers rather than large-volume dealers will tend to reduce violence in the drug markets. Crackdowns on flagrant drug dealing designed to minimize arrests by issuing specific enforcement threats directly to the dealers involved can break up those markets, protect neighborhoods, and reduce crime, even if they do little to reduce drug consumption.
- Drug testing combined with quick and reliable—but not severe—sanctions for drug use among probationers and parolees could greatly reduce crime committed to buy drugs, the violence and disorder incident to drug dealing, the number of dealers incarcerated, and the number of drug users behind bars for non-drug crimes.

While this list is short, each item on it is of potentially great significance. If drug policy were made primarily for practical reasons and primarily with an eye to the control of predatory crime, the results might be startling.

THE DRUGS-CRIME CONNECTIONS

The connections between drugs and crime are complicated and depend on circumstances. There is no universal rule that so-and-so much crime will accompany so many kilograms of drug consumption (Caulkins and Kleiman 2008; Watters, Reinarman, and Fagan 1985; Hamid 1990, 32). However, Goldstein (1985) introduced a highly influential tripartite framework for categorizing drug-related violence that can be applied equally well to all drug-related crime. In this schema, psychopharmacologic crime is caused by the short- or long-term effects of drug use (as distinct from its expense or illegality), systemic crime stems from the illicit trade, and economic-compulsive crime is driven by the need for money to acquire drugs.

Crime Related to Drug Use or Abuse (Psychopharmacologic Crime)

More crimes—and in particular, more violent crimes—are committed under the influence of alcohol than under the influence of all illegal drugs combined (U.S. Department of Justice 1999; Sharps et al. 2003). That alcohol, a legal and inexpensive drug, is implicated in so much crime suggests that substance abuse itself, and not just economic motivation or the perverse effects of illicit markets, can cause crime. Anything that weakens self-control and reduces foresight is likely to increase lawbreaking, or any risky activity that promises immediate benefits and only the possibility of future costs (Wilson and Herrnstein 1985).

That alcohol intoxication is so clearly linked to offending may distort intuition about crime related to abuse of illegal drugs, by leading people to over-estimate how much psychopharmacological crime there is. The reasoning seems to be, "Heroin is more addictive than alcohol, so it must also induce more crime." But the example of nicotine—a terribly addictive substance—shows the flaw in that reasoning. Addiction alone is not a cause of crime; any link depends on other characteristics (pharmacological, social, and economic) of the drug and of its sale and use. Indeed, of all psychoactive substances, alcohol is the only one that has been shown in behavioral experiments to commonly (not inevitably) increase aggression (Roth 1994; Reiss and Roth 1993). Heroin and marijuana, for example, seem to generate pacific rather than aggressive pharmacological effects, although short tempers are common during withdrawal from opiate addiction (Martin 1983; Dewey 1986). In general, sweeping assertions about intoxication and aggression do not withstand scrutiny; the relationship only holds for people with certain types of personalities, using certain substances, in certain settings (Fagan 1990).

On the other hand, the immediate effects of intoxication are not the only, or necessarily the most significant, effects of drug-taking on offending; chronic drug-taking can also cause crimes (Weiss and Mirin 1987; Post 1975; Rawson 1999; MacDonald et al. 2008; Murray et al. 2008; Bejerot 1970; Grinspoon and Bakalar 1985; Stretesky 2009; Satel et al. 1991; Spunt et al. 1995).

Crime Attributable to Drug Markets (Systemic Crime)

Some illicit drug markets are violent, particularly those organized around a physical place as opposed to virtual markets embedded within social networks. Business arrangements involving illegal drug distribution cannot be enforced by law. So if disagreements involving territorial disputes among dealers, employee discipline, debt collection, or disputes over the price, quantity, and quality of drugs cannot be resolved amicably, they are likely to be settled by the use or threat of force, and the victim of force is unlikely to call the police. This gives dealers an incentive to create and sustain a reputation for being at least as tough and at least as well-armed as their competitors and their customers. Thus we should expect drug dealers to be more commonly and more heavily armed than entrepreneurs and employees in other lines of work, and indeed they seem to be better-armed than other perpetrators of deadly violence (Goldstein and Brownstein 1987; (US DOJ 2008). While the presence of guns deters violent encounters, it tends to raise the lethality of incidents that do take place (Cook et al. 2002). The fear generated by gun violence among drug dealers may encourage gun acquisition among other residents of drug-involved neighborhoods (Blumstein and Cork 1996; Sheley and Wright 1993; Kennedy 1994).

Some share of the violence thought of as "drug-related"—because it takes place among dealers, between members of drug-dealing gangs, or at a known dealing location (Goldstein et al. 1990)—is not directly attributable to the drug trade itself but more to the personal characteristics of dealers and to a social setting in which apparent weakness is dangerous (Anderson 1994, 92; Fagan 1992, 117; Ferguson 1993). Conversely, some violence that is not "drug-related" in the conventional sense is attributable to the street conditions that drug dealing helps create. If drug dealing provides access to cheap crack, makes use of violence or its threat routine, and/or provides incentive and funding to acquire the guns that make routine disputes more lethal, then drug distribution could have played a causal role in some homicides that are not drug-related in the narrow sense.

Perhaps the most dramatic examples of systemic crime are the long-term pattern of violence in Colombia (Pastrana et al. 2000) and the more recent upsurge of drug-related killings in northern Mexico: 5,000 dead in 2008 alone by one count (Wilkinson 2008). Roughly speaking, there is one dealing-related death in Colombia or Mexico for every $5–10 million in illicit drug expenditure in the United States.

Economically Motivated Crimes by Users (Economic-Compulsive Crime)

Many heavy users of expensive drugs have no innocent means of raising the sums involved. Fred Goldman (1976, 1977, 1981) found that among heroin addicts, 90 cents of each criminally earned dollar was spent on heroin. In studying New York City heroin addicts, Bruce Johnson and his colleagues found a close match between criminal income and drug expenditures (Johnson et al. 1985; Johnson, Anderson, and Wish 1988). Similar correlations have been found for criminally active cocaine users (Collins, Hubbard, and Rachal 1985). Two-thirds of imprisoned property offenders met criteria indicating drug dependence or abuse (Mumola and Karberg 2006).

Most criminally active drug users have been involved in crime before starting to use drugs (Ball et al. 1981; Weisman, Marr, and Katsampes 1976; Farabee et al. 2001). But those who are both offenders and drug users commit more crime during periods of heavy use and less crime during periods of lower use or abstinence (Chaiken and Chaiken 1990). According to a 2004 survey of prison inmates, 30 percent of all property offenders in state prisons claimed to have committed their current offense to get money to buy drugs (Mumola and Karberg 2006). This version of the drugs-crime link may work in both directions: for hard-drug users, the receipt of any sort of income tends to push up drug use (Satel 1995).

Indirect Causal Linkages Between Drug Use and Crime

Goldstein's tripartite framework omits important indirect mechanisms by which drug use, drug dealing, and drug policies contribute to crime. The drug trade promotes non-drug crime by absorbing criminal justice resources. There are approximately 1.8 million drug arrests a year in the United States (US DOJ 2008); more than 50 percent of the residents of federal prisons are committed for drug offenses; in state prisons, the figure is roughly 20 percent in 2004 (ONDCP 2009). Given that criminal justice resources are limited, drug law enforcement reduces the enforcement risks associated with committing non-drug crimes (Blumstein 1993). In terms of controlling non-drug crime, the costs of arresting, prosecuting, and imprisoning the significant minority of drug offenders with little other criminal activity (e.g., couriers, users put on probation for possession and then incarcerated as probation violators for continued drug use) are pure losses.

The drug trade also contributes to crime by diverting inner-city youths away from legitimate pursuits of school and employment (Inciardi and Pottieger 1991). One mechanism at work here is that the criminal history accumulated in the course of drug dealing can greatly shrink the envelope of licit economic opportunity.

Imprisoning large numbers of drug dealers has other criminogenic effects. It can blunt the deterrent effect of any given level of non-drug imprisonment by reducing the social stigma associated with incarceration. It can increase the number of people who experience the criminogenic effects both of drug dealing and of incarceration, since in active markets an incarcerated dealer is certain to be replaced.

Both the presence of active street drug markets and the often intrusive enforcement efforts aimed at closing those markets tend to worsen relations between the police and the high-crime neighborhoods in which those markets exist. Since police work relies heavily on the cooperation of the public, this, too, is criminogenic.

Examples could be multiplied: crime by children subject to drug-related parental abuse and neglect, crime by former drug users and drug dealers as a result of having been incarcerated, and crime due to the lack of legitimate job opportunities in neighborhoods devastated by drug dealing.

DIFFERENCES AMONG DRUGS

Since illicit drugs vary in pharmacological effects and in patterns of use, price, and availability, the nature of the connection between drugs and crime can vary across drugs. There are at least four distinct categories of illegal drugs in this regard: (1) diverted pharmaceuticals, including narcotic pain relievers such as oxycodone (Percodan, Oxycontin) and hyrdocodone (Vicodin), benzodiazepine anti-anxiety and sleep-inducing drugs such as diazepam (Valium) and aprazolam (Xanax), and the stimulants prescribed for attention deficit/hyperactivity disorder and narcolepsy (amphetamine, methamphetamine, and methylphenidate [Ritalin]); (2) the minor illegal drugs (PCP, GHB, LSD, etc.); (3) the major "expensive" illegal drugs (cocaine/crack, heroin, and methamphetamine); and (4) cannabis.

Diverted pharmaceuticals account for a large share of drug-related overdoses, use by youth, and prevalence in the general population (Compton and Volkow, 2006). However, their ill-effects are largely confined to the users; there is little black-market violence. Furthermore, they merit separate analysis, because the options for interventions are so different from those relevant for the purely illicit drugs. We say nothing more about them here.

The minor illegal drugs generate little drug-related crime because of some combination of their intrinsically limited appeal and the success of current policies. Few people are dependent on one of them without also being dependent on something else, and the markets are largely social rather than commercial, thus generating few problems.

Of the major illicit drugs of abuse, one would expect marijuana to be the least implicated in crime: it is relatively cheap, dealing is compara- tively discreet, marijuana users purchase their drug less often than heroin or cocaine users, intoxication does not typically lead to aggression, and marijuana is less likely to bring its users into a criminal subculture. Accordingly, the ratios of measured drug use among arrestees to self- reported drug use in the population as a whole suggest that a cocaine or heroin user has a much higher annual chance of being arrested for a predatory crime than does a marijuana user.

The differences among cocaine, methamphetamine, and heroin are less clear. Violence is still more common in the cocaine business, and pharmacologically, cocaine and methamphetamine are more likely to trigger aggression. However, criminally active heavy users of these three very different drugs probably commit income-generating crime at roughly similar rates; in dollar terms, their drug habits appear comparable. Fur- thermore, some of these distinctions may be more contextual than intrin- sic properties of the substances.

Hence, the drugs that matter most are the "majors," but it is essential to distinguish between cannabis on the one hand and the "expensive" illegal drugs on the other. Little that one can learn or say about cannabis applies to the other drugs, and vice versa.

DRUG ABUSE CONTROL POLICIES

For purposes of taxonomy, policies can be grouped into four categories: laws, prevention and treatment, conventional law enforcement, and in- novative partnerships.

Drug Laws: Prohibition, Decriminalization, Regulation-plus-Taxation

The single most important policy choice regarding a substance is whether it will be legal or prohibited. This is not a binary choice;. the spectrum of options ranges from a draconian prohibition (more or less the situation for heroin in the United States) to little or no regulation whatsoever (as with caffeine). However, the crucial distinction is whether production, distribution, and unsupervised purchase and use are legally permissible for at least a sizable share of the population (e.g., for all adults). If so, then all other things being equal, one would expect greater use and, hence, use-related crime. If not, then there is room for a black market and the possibility of high levels of systemic and economic-compulsive crime.

For legal substances, regulations can partially control a variety of behaviors connected to drug sales and use. Laws can regulate intoxicated behavior, such as driving while intoxicated (DWI) or public drunkenness. Laws can regulate commerce by placing restrictions on potency and form and on commercial behavior by limiting the times and places of sale. Beer and whiskey are allowed to have only a certain alcohol content; cigarettes cannot be advertised on television, or used in most indoor environments. There can be limits on the purpose of use, as we now have for prescription drugs. There can be restrictions on who uses, such as the prohibition for minors, although enforcing those restrictions is harder than announcing them. Price can be manipulated via taxation.

Prohibition is less discriminating. It threatens all sellers, buyers, and users, rather than some, with criminal penalties. It also expresses a collective sentiment that drug use is dangerous, if not wrong in itself (Moore 1991). Decriminalization tries to find a middle ground. It threatens sellers of the drug but leaves users largely untouched. This regime was called Prohibition when applied to alcohol in the 1920s.

Prohibition, decriminalization, and regulation-plus-taxation will all reduce consumption compared to unrestricted commerce and thereby tend to reduce the crime attributable to the pharmacology of drug consumption. Other things being equal, decriminalization will tend to result in the largest black market; users, facing less legal risk, will tend to buy more, while supply is still from an illicit market.

Regulation-plus-modest-taxation will usually result in a smaller black market than prohibition or decriminalization, although a well-enforced prohibition could easily have a smaller illicit market than poorly enforced regulation or regulation with higher taxes.

What might happen if we changed the laws concerning one or more drugs? As examples, we analyze cannabis, PCP, and cocaine, before turning to the one drug where feasible policy changes have the clearest shot at reducing crime: alcohol.

Changing Drug Laws (I): Legalizing Marijuana

If cannabis were legally available on more or less the same terms as alcohol, the violence in the cannabis market would be substantially abolished, along with the drain on enforcement resources caused by cannabis-related enforcement and incarceration. But even now the cannabis market causes little violence in the United States (though it causes some share of the violence in northern Mexico). Cannabis offenders occupy relatively few jail and prison cells, perhaps 30,000 out of the 2.4 million people behind bars at any one time. This is a smaller tally than drunken driving. Even in its illegal state, cannabis is not so expensive as to drive many of its users to economic-compulsive crime. So the direct crime-prevention effects of legalization would be modest. By the same token, since cannabis intoxication does not lead to aggression, legalizing cannabis would not be likely to cause much additional pharmacologic crime.

Changes in the availability of a drug can influence crime indirectly by changing the consumption of other drugs. It is sometimes assumed without argument that any two drugs must be substitutes for one another, as for example two different brands of beer are substitutes. In that case, making one of the two cheaper or more available will reduce consumption of the other. But pairs of goods can also be complements, for example bread and butter, pen and paper, razors and razor blades, automobiles and gasoline, gin and tonic, and cigarettes and coffee. Lowering the price or increasing the availability of one of a pair of complementary goods tends to increase consumption of the other.

If cannabis turned out to be a substitute for alcohol, the effects on pharmacological crime could be substantial; replacing aggressive drunks with peaceful stoners would represent a gain. But the evidence is mixed, with several studies finding substitution (DiNardo 1991; Model 1991, 1994; Chaloupka and Laixuthai 1997; Cameron et al. 2001) but others finding complementarity, particularly for youth, so that greater marijuana use might lead to greater alcohol use (Pacula 1998, 2001; Farrelly et al. 1999; Williams et al. 2004). Thies and Register (1993) and Saffer and Chaloupka (1999a, b) find conflicting results within a single study. Cannabis legalization could also reduce crime if cannabis were a substitute for cocaine or heroin or methamphetamine, or if, as a result of legalization, cannabis users were less likely to go on to use the hard drugs. There is no strong evidence either way.

It would seem, then, that cannabis legalization would tend to have modest effects on crime in the United States. It would also eliminate more than half of all drug arrests, since a majority of such arrests are for simple possession of cannabis. That leaves the question of whether those gains, plus any gains accruing to Mexico, would be sufficient to offset the (non-crime) costs of the resulting increase in heavy cannabis use.

Decriminalization would reduce the number of arrests, but it would increase the size of what would remain an illicit cannabis market. Expanding the size of the market while leaving it in the hands of criminals would—if the expansion were substantial—tend to increase the level of non-drug crime; illegal dealers of a decriminalized product still cannot resolve their disputes in court and, fearing to call the police, need to defend themselves against robbery.

Changing Drug Laws (II): Legalizing PCP

Legalization of phencyclidine (PCP) would most likely increase crime. The illicit market in PCP is small, both in the number of users and in the revenues involved. (PCP, which is easily synthesized, remains cheap even as a forbidden commodity.) Thus legalizing PCP would not eliminate much illicit-market crime, avoid much economic crime by users, or free much in the way of law-enforcement resources. Even a small increase in crime related to intoxication and addiction would make PCP legalization a net crime-increaser.

PCP may not fully deserve its evil reputation as the generator of bizarrely aggressive behavior; some of that effect surely relates to the demography of its users rather than the pharmacology of the drug. Still, given that PCP today is a tiny contributor to crime, legalizing it as a crime-control measure would be a far-fetched notion.

Changing Legal Status (III): Legalizing Cocaine

The main event on the legalization fight-card is not cannabis or PCP, but cocaine. It is cocaine whose trafficking and consumption causes enormous amounts of crime and a massive hemorrhage of enforcement resources. Would legalizing cocaine reduce crime?

No one knows. Even if the details of the "legalization" (who could buy, at what price, and with what limits on quantity) were better specified than they usually are by either proponents or opponents, the effects of cocaine legalization would be so numerous, so profound, and so unpredictable that any strongly expressed opinion on the subject must reflect some mix of insufficient intellectual humility and simple bluff. No one knows, and there is no plausible way of finding out, short of actually legalizing cocaine over a wide region for a long time. Even then one could not be sure, as other factors would be changing in ways important to the drugs-crime connections. So "successful" legalization in one place would be persuasive but not definitive evidence that crime would fall if another jurisdiction were to implement the same policy.

A survey of the likely effects of cocaine legalization will serve to justify this agnostic claim. If cocaine were sufficiently legal that heavy users, who account for the vast bulk of illicit purchases, could obtain legal supplies—which would mean, in effect, selling unlimited quantities, as is now the case with alcohol—illicit cocaine dealers would be put out of business. In the short run, this might increase predatory crime, if some turned to theft as the next-best alternative to honest work and others tried to muscle into the remaining illicit drug markets (assuming that some drugs remained illegal). Also in the short run, the supply of guns already purchased for use in the cocaine trade would remain in the hands of young men with short fuses.

In the long run, smaller illicit-market revenues would translate into less illicit-market crime, and the shrinking of illicit business would tend to increase licit job-market participation in high-crime neighborhoods and decrease the number of people with prison records and expensive weapons. At the same time, about 20 percent of the nation's law enforcement, prosecution, and corrections resources would be freed up for other purposes.

Whether cocaine legalization had a beneficial effect on the income-producing crime of cocaine users would depend on its details, and especially on the price set by taxation. Legalization near current black-market prices (about $100 per gram) would require implausible levels of enforcement against illicit sales of untaxed product (Caulkins 2000). Such a legalization, if it were feasible, would presumably increase user crime, since there would be more users due to reduced stigma and enforcement risk and increased availability but no less need of money among those who did become heavy users. Moreover, some of the income needs of heavy users now satisfied by dealing would have to be satisfied by theft instead.

At prices closer to the free-market price ($1–5 per gram, or 25 cents or less per rock of crack), users would probably commit less crime to finance their use. Around current prices, the elasticity of demand for cocaine is in the neighborhood of -1, implying that 10 percent reductions in price would lead to roughly 10 percent increases in consumption and, hence, no net change in spending. However, there are probably physiological limits on how much cocaine people could consume. If prices fell to 1/20th of their current levels, we would not expect a 20-fold increase in use, so the motivation to commit crime specifically to purchase cocaine would likely fall.

In contrast, crime associated with cocaine use and the long-term effects of addiction would presumably increase. Since cocaine (as opposed to coca leaf) has never been legal in any modern, developed country, there is no compelling way to estimate the number of people who would try it if it were legal and cheap. Even if we knew that number, we would have to guess at the proportion of them who would become dependent and/or increase their criminality under the immediate influence of the drug or due to its chronic effects: probably a smaller proportion than now do so, but how much smaller?

Anyone who doubts that the horrible cocaine/crime situation of today could get worse might contemplate the alcohol/crime problem, and then recall that alcohol plus cocaine is a frequent (and highly aggression-enhancing) drug combination. Even without the nightmare scenario of developing as many cocaine addicts as there now are alcoholics, cocaine legalization could greatly increase the level of cocaine abuse and the level of alcohol abuse, thus creating a double pharmacological source of crime increase to set off against the likely decreases in economic and systemic crime.

As with cannabis, crime-related outcomes are not the only relevant issue when considering cocaine legalization. On a pharmacological level alone, putting aside the legal risks and expense, chronic heavy cocaine use can be an intense misery for the user and his or her intimates and neighbors. Any thoroughgoing legalization would almost certainly swell the number of victims of cocaine abuse disorders.

However, against this, one must offset the sheer volume of imprisonment resulting from current cocaine enforcement; imprisonment, like addiction, is a source of suffering for those immediately subject to it and those who care about them or depend on them. Also to be weighed on the pro-legalization side is the enormous damage now being done to Mexico, to some parts of Central America, and to Colombia by the illicit industry that feeds America's cocaine habit.

Thus the outcomes of legalizing cocaine would be very much a mixed bag: gains in violence prevention in Mexico to offset against losses in the form of increased domestic drug abuse, with the net effect on non-drug crime in the United States unknown even as to direction. Progress in making prohibition more effective (by putting pressure on probationers and parolees to abstain) and less costly (by eliminating pointlessly harsh sentences for drug dealing and using low-arrest crackdowns to break up flagrant street markets) would make the choice between evils somewhat less painful.

Changing Drug Laws (IV): Getting Serious about
Alcohol Supply

An observer from Mars would find the treatment of alcohol in the American drug-policy debate hard to understand. Drug policy reformers routinely cite the example of alcohol as an argument for legal access to some or all of the currently prohibited substances, pointing out how much more damage alcohol does than any of them, or for that matter all of them combined. Drug warriors tend to respond with some variation on "don't change the subject," though some have the wit to respond that observing more damage from the one legal addictive intoxicant than from all the illegal addictive intoxicants combined casts doubt on the idea that legalization minimizes aggregate harm.

Neither side shows any urgency about changing current policies toward alcohol. Since those policies produce quite miserable results, this passivity seems surprising. It would not be hard to do better. Raising the price of alcohol would clearly reduce crime, and it requires no more effort than changing a few figures in the tax code.

Current federal and state taxes on the average drink total only about 10 cents, roughly one-tenth of its total price. Both economic efficiency and fairness dictate that alcohol taxes should be high enough to cover the costs that drinkers impose on others. Current tax levels do not come close; even studies that exclude the costs of alcohol-related crime suggest that drinkers pay for only a third of their external costs (Manning et al. 1989). A good case can thus be made for alcohol taxes at the level of a dollar per drink (Kleiman 1992a). That would roughly double the price of the average drink; the effect on alcohol-related crime (including domestic violence and child abuse) would likely be substantial. "Moonshining" would be a problem, but evidence from countries where alcohol is taxed more highly than in the United States—and from the early 1950s, when U.S. alcohol taxes were, in purchasing-power terms, several times higher than they are now—suggests that the safety and convenience of legal alcohol and loyalty to legal brands limit the appeal of untaxed alcohol products.

Even much smaller increases would have a major impact on the harms related to alcohol use. Philip J. Cook estimates that doubling the current tax levels, which would increase retail prices by about 10 percent, would shrink drunken-driving deaths and alcohol-driven homicides by about 3 percent, preventing about 500 homicides per year (Cook 2008). Taxes tend to reduce drinking specifically by heavy drinkers, simply because the price of alcohol is a bigger budget item for those who drink heavily (Cook 2009).

A more radical step would be to reduce the availability of alcohol. Since the vast majority of alcohol users are not problem users, the logical goal would be to limit availability selectively. Current laws attempt such a selective limitation by age, though with only partial success. There is at least as strong a justification for limiting access according to prior conduct. It seems curious that someone who drinks and drives is deprived of his or her driving license, while the "license" to drink is treated as irrevocable.

Like the current age limit, a ban on drinking by those previously convicted of alcohol-related offenses—in effect, a selective, rather than a blanket, prohibition—would have to be enforced primarily by sellers, rather than on buyers (Kleiman 1992b). Naturally, compliance would be well short of perfect, though both sellers of alcohol and law enforcement personnel might be willing to treat violations of such a ban somewhat more seriously than they do the widespread adolescent practice of buying alcohol with false identification documents. A certain amount of incon-venience would be imposed on all drinkers by the need to show a driver's license before buying. (Those who had lost their drinking privileges as a result of a conviction would carry driver's licenses with different mark-ings, as minors currently do in some states.) Such a program, even with its imperfections, would almost certainly be crime-reducing, perhaps sub-stantially so through a combination of deterrence and incapacitation; in addition, it might free police resources by reducing the population of chronic inebriates repeatedly arrested for minor public order offenses.

PREVENTION AND TREATMENT

Prevention and treatment, albeit linked together as "demand-side" pro-grams, are very different interventions. Prevention is usually the province of K–12 education, the mass media, and community groups; treatment is a medical, psychiatric, or social work program. Prevention is targeted at children, usually thought of as relatively innocent and "at risk"; treatment is primarily targeted at adults whose lives have become chaotic.

Yet prevention and treatment share one common advantage when compared to enforcement. While eliminating a drug dealer creates a niche that another dealer can fill, eliminating a current user tends to reduce rather than increase initiation rates, simply because most new users are initiated by existing users rather than by the mythical "drug pusher" who entices the innocent.

Prevention

Even modestly successful drug-prevention programs are unambiguously beneficial in reducing crime. They offer the benefit of reduced drug use and reduced drug dealing without any of the unwanted side effects of enforcement. Unfortunately, even modestly successful drug-prevention programs are hard to find (Faggiano et al. 2005); positive results demonstrated in pilot programs have often proven difficult to replicate (Haaga and Reuter 1995).

Chronic use of the expensive illegal drugs is relatively rare and generally develops long after the ages at which typical prevention programs are run. Hence, experimental trials that directly measure effects on these outcome variables would have to involve very large numbers of subjects and follow them up for a decade or more, making for prohibitively expensive study design. As a result, the most common measure of primary prevention effectiveness is a program's effect on early initiation to tobacco, alcohol, and cannabis use. Some may view those outcomes as important in and of themselves, but their relevance to the control of non-drug crime depends on the strong historical correlation between early initiation and subsequent problems of all sorts, including participation in crime. However, no one knows the extent to which that correlation is causal and therefore exploitable for policy purposes.

By those measures, results from the top tier of programs are worthwhile, though not spectacular: reductions of about 25 percent in rates of early initiation. Since even the best programs cost relatively little, if even one-fifth of those short-term effects carry over into reductions in chronic dependent use of heroin, cocaine, methamphetamine, or alcohol, that would make prevention highly cost-effective as a means of reducing substance abuse and, presumably, crime as well. In other words, prevention programs may be cost-effective not because they are highly effective but because they do not cost much (Caulkins et al. 1999).

Those top-tier programs are not the most widespread. The best-known and most prevalent drug abuse prevention program is Drug Abuse Resistance Education (DARE), which is attractive to schools because the materials are federally subsidized and the instructor hours provided by the police, and to the police as good community relations. DARE is also popular among the officers involved, among students and alumni, among their parents, and, therefore, among elected officials. Unfortunately, none of the published evaluations has shown DARE to be effective in reducing substance abuse initiation (Dukes, Ullman, and Stein 1996; Brown and Kreft 1998; West and O'Neal 2004).

Formal evaluations agree with anecdotal reports in finding that DARE tends to improve student attitudes toward police—and police attitudes toward children—especially in low-income and minority neighborhoods. This may be more than ample justification for its continued deployment (Birkeland et al. 2005). But that effect is not the same as substance-abuse prevention, nor a close substitute for it.

It is possible that continued research, development, and evaluation will eventually come up with substantially more effective substance abuse prevention programs, but there seems no strong basis for optimism. Perhaps a narrow focus on substance abuse works less well than would a broader focus on self-management, health maintenance, and the avoidance of risky behaviors and/or on classroom behavior (cf., Furr-Holden et al. 2004).

Other programs, such as Gang Resistance Education and Training (GREAT) aim to prevent crime rather than drug use (see, e.g., Aos et al. 2004). Part of the goal is the prevention of drug dealing as opposed to drug use (Kleiman 1997b). Again, the crime-control benefits of such prevention efforts, were they successful, could be immediate and substantial; even if the youth prevented from dealing were replaced by adult dealers, that might reduce the overall level of violence associated with the drug markets. The risks of dealing are much greater than the risks of initiating drug use, and may be underestimated by potential dealers, who may also grossly overestimate its rewards.

Drug Abuse Treatment

Successful drug treatment, like prevention, is an unequivocal winner in terms of crime control. The criminal activity of addicted offenders seems to rise and fall in step with their drug consumption and, importantly, the relationship holds whether reductions in drug use are unassisted or are the product of formalized treatment and whether participation in treatment is voluntary or coerced (Anglin and Speckart 1986; Nurco et al. 1988; Anglin and Hser 1990). Moreover, a treatment-induced reduction in demand does not bring with it the side effects of an enforcement-induced reduction (higher drug prices, depletion of criminal justice resources).

So the question of how effective treatment is at reducing drug-related crime reduces to the question of how effective treatment is at reducing drug use. There is a mammoth literature assessing the effectiveness of drug treatment; that literature generally concludes that "treatment works" and is a good investment (e.g., Belenko, 2005), and yet the magnitude of the beneficial effect remains unclear.

One fact that is not in dispute is that rates of offending are usually lower after treatment than before (Gossop et al. 2005). But if people are particularly likely to enter treatment around a peak in use and/or criminality, then mere reversion to long-run average behavior ("regression to the mean") might create spurious favorable results in before-and-after studies.

The usual solution to the inherent limitations on before-and-after comparisons is to run controlled trials. This has been done for heroin, and the evidence is clear: Opiate Substitution Therapies (OSTs)—methadone, buprenorphine, and LAAM—work (Amato et al. 2005). Trials have also been conducted showing that counseling interventions reduce cannabis use among those who are cannabis dependent (MTP Research Group, 2004).

The evidence base for the effect of treatment on drugs other than heroin is soft. True randomized control trials are rare. Despite the great variety of psychosocial interventions, reviews of the comparative effectiveness of different approaches generally find, at most, modest differences (Prendergast et al. 2002). A National Research Council panel (Manski et al. 2001) found no definitive evidence of long-term treatment efficacy, other than for opiate substitution.

However, from a crime-control perspective, treatment can be worthwhile even without producing any long-term change in behavior, as long as users greatly reduce their criminal activity while the treatment is going on. The Treatment Outcome Prospective Study (TOPS) (Hubbard et al. 1989) found that about 60 percent of residential-treatment clients and about one-third of outpatient methadone and outpatient drug-free clients reported criminal activity in the year prior to entering treatment. Yet fewer than 10 percent of the outpatient clients and only 3.1 percent of the residential clients reported committing predatory crimes during treatment. The benefits of such dramatic reductions easily cover the relatively modest costs of outpatient treatment.

The inadequate availability and poor quality of substance abuse treatment—created in part by the reluctance of public and private health insurance to finance treatment for substance abuse and dependency on the same terms as treatment for other disorders—constitutes a major missed opportunity for crime control. Advocates of drug treatment are understandably frustrated that, in a political atmosphere in which the punitive side of the crime-control effort enjoys widespread support, drug treatment, which demonstrably reduces crime, remains neglected and underfunded.

A special source of outrage is the under-provision and over-regulation of opiate maintenance therapy. In terms of crime-control efficacy and other measurable improvements in the behavior and well-being of its clients, methadone treatment is the most successful kind of drug treatment (Amato et al. 2005). Unlike most treatment modalities, it has little trouble attracting and retaining clients. Yet only about one-eighth of U.S. heroin addicts are currently enrolled in methadone programs.

Methadone is restricted by the Narcotic Addict Treatment Act to hard-to-site specialty clinics that must deliver the drug directly to the patient rather than providing a prescription to be filled at a pharmacy, and which are under pressure to minimize dosage (at some risk to efficacy) to prevent diversion. This creates great inconvenience for methadone patients, especially those who live far from the clinics, which are limited in number by neighborhood resistance.

Because it does not aim at abstinence, maintenance therapy remains bitterly controversial. The controversy stems in part from the way methadone was oversold as a way to "wean" heroin addicts away from opiate use, rather than as a frank substitution of a less dangerous addictive drug under less dangerous conditions for the purchase and use of illicit heroin on the street. The reluctance of some ("low-threshold") methadone providers to insist that their clients desist from continuing to buy and use illicit heroin and cocaine adds to the controversy.

Yet the research is conclusive: methadone clients forced out of substitution treatment face substantial risks of relapse to active heroin addiction, a condition with annual mortality of about 2 percent. Nevertheless, most drug-diversion programs and drug courts insist on referring opiate-using clients to "drug-free" therapies, which are notably unsuccessful. In California; only 13 percent of heroin users in the Proposition 36 diversion program are sent to maintenance programs; they commit substantially fewer crimes than the 87 percent who are sent to "drug-free" therapies. (Urada et al. 2008)

The introduction of a second maintenance agent, buprenorphine, which can be prescribed rather than dispensed and which requires no special clinic, has substantially brightened the picture, but the failure to deliver maintenance therapy to criminally active opiate users remains a glaring policy failure and the source of completely preventable non-drug crimes.

While shortages of treatment capacity—especially for such difficult-to-treat clients as women with young children and persons suffering from serious mental illness as well as substance abuse disorders—remain significant, as reflected in long waiting lists for some treatment programs, adding more resources by itself would not make treatment a panacea. Not all substance abusers want to stop their drug-taking, though many would prefer to have better control over their use patterns. Even in those who do want to stop, that desire may be transient. Almost all treatment programs have dropout rates near or above the 50 percent level. Attempts to develop a comparable therapy for those dependent on cocaine and methamphetamine have so far come up dry, perhaps for fundamental reasons related to the differences between opiates and stimulants. (If the taste for opiates is satiating, so that each dose during a use session reduces the desire for the next, while the taste for stimulants is kindling, then the search for stimulant maintenance therapy is doomed to futility; as one researcher quipped, "You can't maintain a disturbance.")

Treatment in Lieu of Prison: Diversion Programs and Drug Courts

From the perspective of crime control, it is especially important to increase treatment use among those substance abusers who also commit non-drug crimes. While many drug-involved offenders will not seek out treatment voluntarily, perhaps they could be induced to enter and remain in treatment if the alternative were prison. As a means of partial incapacitation, drug treatment can be far more cost-effective than incarceration, reducing the rate of criminal activity among participants during the treatment period by more than half at perhaps a seventh of the cost of a prison cell.

Such is the thinking behind two sets of programs: the long-established "diversion" programs and the more recent drug treatment courts. Both rely on the threat of prison as a lever to secure treatment entry, retention, and compliance. Some such programs are limited to those charged with drug offenses, but others—sensibly, in terms of crime control—engage drug-involved offenders arrested for other offenses as well. The notion that drug addicts need treatment rather than prison is highly popular, as illustrated by the passage of Proposition 200 in Arizona in 1996 and Proposition 36 in California in 2000, both of which mandate treatment rather than incarceration for minor drug offenders.

While there is great variety among diversion programs, most take place under the administrative authority of probation departments. Offenders who fail to live up to their side of the bargain risk being found in violation of the terms of probation and incarcerated. Many probation departments contract with nonprofit organizations (frequently under the rubric TASC, Treatment Alternatives to Street Crime) to provide placement and monitoring services for diversion clients.

Since most probation agencies are underfunded, understaffed, short on technology and authority, and therefore demoralized (Kleiman 1998; Reinventing Probation Council 1999), diversion programs that rely on probation face major challenges. Not only are probation departments overwhelmed, with caseloads often in the hundreds, but they lack the capacity to impose sanctions without going to court, at significant cost in work effort, delay, and uncertainty about outcomes. This discourages aggressive supervision. Even when noncompliance comes formally to the attention of probation departments, sanctions are rare; often, the reaction is merely to record the failure, which will count against the offender if he or she is arrested again for a fresh crime.

Consequently, the "mandate" to treatment under many diversion programs remains merely nominal, with a quarter or more of diversion clients never even entering treatment, let alone remaining in it or complying with the advice of the treatment providers (Prendergast, Anglin, and Wellisch 1995; Anglin, Longshore, and Turner 1999). In the single largest state-level diversion program, California's Substance Abuse and Crime Prevention Act (formally SACPA, informally Proposition 36), only about three-quarters of offenders who accept SACPA treatment ever enter treatment; of those, only one-third complete treatment, for a net completion rate of 25 percent (Urada 2008). Sanctions are rare, with low sanctions rates and high violation rates being mutually supporting.

Drug courts attempt to use the power of the judge—over both offenders and other agencies inside and outside the criminal justice system—to make the treatment mandate real. Drug-court participants, like diversion-program participants, have their behavior periodically reviewed by the judge, with the prospect of praise or rebuke in open court and, to an extent varying considerably from court to court, sanctions for departure from the judge's rules. While outcome evaluations have been distinctly mixed, there seems little doubt that some drug courts are performing quite well, at modest cost, and that the judges involved tend to be passionate advocates of their program (Office of Justice Programs 1998; Roman 2008).

After more than 20 years of growth and despite widespread political support, drug courts have a total client count of fewer than 70,000 nationwide (Roman 2009), while the number of seriously drug-involved offenders is about 30 times as large. With the typical drug-court judge supervising 50–75 offenders—as that judge's full-time assignment—the sheer number of judges and courtrooms needed to serve hundreds of thousands rather than tens of thousands of drug-court clients is simply not available; managing 750,000 drug-court clients with judicial caseloads of 75 would require 10,000 judges, or about half of the total judicial workforce, even including traffic-court judges and magistrates (BLS 2009). Moreover, the drug court's capacity to commandeer resources from elsewhere, in particular probation officers and drug treatment slots, would run into capacity constraints were the number of drug-court clients to grow substantially.

Thus the inefficacy of diversion programs and the scale limits on drug courts mean that neither of them seems capable of making a major dent in the problem of drug-involved offenders.

Treatment in Prison

Providing treatment to people in prison avoids the problem of attracting users to treatment and keeping them in treatment. The incremental costs of providing treatment, once the subject is already confined, are modest. Programs on the therapeutic community (TC) model, for example, tend to have high success rates (among the minority of entrants who complete them), but since they provide room and board their costs are several times those of even intensive outpatient treatment: about $20,000 per participant per year. By contrast, the incremental cost of providing TC treatment in prison is only a few thousand dollars per year. Moreover, the recidivism rate among prisoners is so high (typically 40 to 60 percent, and higher among heroin and cocaine abusers) and the cost of imprisonment itself so great, that even expensive treatment would have its full costs recouped by even modest reductions in recidivism, which would likely follow from even modestly successful treatment programs.

On the other hand, prison-based treatment programs do not have the benefit of reducing criminal activity during treatment, because the users are already in prison; in order to prevent post-release crime, in-prison treatment must have lasting behavioral effects. Discouragingly, most prison-based drug treatment programs have not been shown to reduce recidivism rates (Gerstein and Harwood 1990). This may be due to the poor quality of the programs themselves. But it may also reflect a deeper problem. The prison environment is so different from the outside world that behavior patterns learned in prison are likely to carry over very imperfectly once prisoners have left. If the goal is for an offender to learn how not to use drugs in the community, much of that learning probably may have to take place in the community.

Accordingly, the small number of demonstrably successful in-prison treatment programs all have strong links to follow-up treatment in the community after the subject leaves prison (Lipton 1994). The gains from such programs easily cover their costs, even if we consider only reductions in future imprisonment and the gains to the offender, his or her family, and potential future victims.

Do Treatment and Enforcement Compete?

Other than legalization, the favorite policy prescription of the critics of enforcement-oriented drug policies is to shift from the current heavy reliance on enforcement and incarceration (which together account for approximately 80 percent of total U.S. drug control spending) toward a more nearly even division between enforcement and treatment. (Prevention is, and will remain, a low-budget item.)

The claim that treatment is generically more cost-effective than enforcement cannot be taken at face value; at minimum, it depends on details about what kind of enforcement is to be cut back, and what kind of treatment (in terms of quality, program type, and client base) is to expand. A complete analysis would also require facts not in evidence about the likely benefits of the marginal, as opposed to the average, treatment episode and the quantitative relationship between enforcement pressure and treatment entry.

Still, it seems reasonable to think that the crime-minimizing allocation of drug-control resources, if constrained to the current total budget, would provide somewhat more treatment and somewhat less enforcement than now occurs; drug treatment is unambiguously crime-reducing, while the effects of drug law enforcement on non-drug crime are far less clear. Moreover, given the current budget situation, a small (say, 10 percemt) reduction in enforcement would fund a doubling of publicly paid drug treatment.

However, all of this implicitly assumes that there is a budget for drug abuse control that some decision-maker then allocates among its component parts. While as a matter of calculation such a budget can be assembled, that calculation is rather remote from political and managerial reality. In practice, at the federal, state, and local levels, budgets are made separately for law enforcement agencies, health care agencies, and social service agencies, then allocated to various purposes within those agencies. Thus, moving money from drug enforcement to drug treatment is not within the power of any one decision maker. If enforcement budgets were cut, there is no assurance that drug enforcement would bear the brunt of those cuts. Similarly, if money were moved into health care and social services, drug treatment might not be the primary beneficiary.

LAW ENFORCEMENT

Drug law enforcement can both increase and decrease non-drug crime.

- The incarceration of drug offenders prevents whatever crimes they would have committed had they been free instead.
- Those offenders use up scarce prison and jail capacity; confining them thus in effect causes the crimes committed by people who would have been behind bars had they not been displaced by drug offenders.
- That displacement effect also reduces deterrence against non-drug crime.
- If drug enforcement increases the total number of people who serve time in prison, and if going to prison tends to increase the future non-drug criminal activity of former inmates by changing their attitudes and opportunities in ways less favorable to licit work, then drug-related incarceration has an additional crime-increasing effect.
- Drug enforcement tends to increase drug prices (Reuter and Kleiman 1986). Higher drug prices can reduce crime by reducing the volume of drugs consumed, but they can also increase crime by increasing the amount of money spent on drugs and increase the financial rewards for successful dealing; paradoxically, drug-law enforcers and the managers of drug cartels share the goal of restricting supplies and increasing prices (Schelling 1971).
- Drug enforcement can also make it harder for users to find drugs, or discourage them from seeking drugs for fear of arrest; that will reduce consumption without raising prices, unambiguously reducing non-drug crime through decreased expenditure and decreased intoxication and addiction (Moore 1973; Rochleau and Kleiman 1993).
- Enforcement can change the incentives facing drug dealers, leading either to more violence (e.g., if the presence of enforcement encourages violence to intimidate witnesses) or less violence (e.g., if enforcement and sentencing strategies create effective disincentives to violence).
- Enforcement can shape distribution patterns either toward more criminogenic "flagrant" forms, such as street markets and drug houses, or toward less criminogenic forms, such as home delivery (Caulkins 1992; Caulkins and Reuter 2009).

Drug-dealing is a transactional crime, in which buyers and sellers seek one another out, in contrast to predatory crimes, whose victims seek to avoid their victimizers.[1] When the perpetrator of a predatory crime is imprisoned, both deterrence and incapacitation effects lead us to believe that the result will be a lower incidence of that crime, if we hold constant the precautions taken by potential victims (Cook 1986). Crucially, there is nothing about deterring or incapacitating one predatory victimizer that encourages another such to take his place.

But when incapacitation or deterrence puts a purveyor of a forbidden commodity out of business, the result is to create a market niche for a new supplier or for the expansion of effort (e.g., hours of work) by an existing supplier (Kleiman 1997a; see Reuter, MacCoun, and Murphy 1990 on the prevalence of part-time dealing).

The same thing applies when it is drugs, rather than their dealers, that are seized. As long as there are retail dealers ready to sell and customers ready to buy, the drugs themselves can be replaced, at a price. Thus, while imprisoning a burglar directly prevents burglary, taking drugs and drug dealers off the streets does not directly prevent drug selling in anything like the same fashion.

It now appears that increased drug prices tend not to increase the total amount of money spent on drugs (Hyatt and Rhodes 1992; Grossman, 2005). Thus successful enforcement efforts to increase prices should not increase systemic or economic-compulsive crime and might decrease pharmacological crime (Caulkins et al. 1997). Unfortunately, the experience of the past 30 years suggests that even massive enforcement is not likely to increase the prices of mass-market drugs; both heroin and cocaine prices are trading at small fractions of their 1980 prices, despite more than a tenfold increase in drug-related incarceration in the meantime (Caulkins and Chandler 2006; Fries et al. 2008; Caulkins 2009). Thus the attempt to reduce crime by increasing the prices of illicit drugs may be doomed to failure. By contrast, increasing the difficulty of retail purchase remains a plausible strategy for controlling non-drug crime.

However, drug law enforcement can also influence illicit-industry "conduct"—how business is carried on—in ways that change the impact of the illicit drug trade on non-drug crime. It can do so by selectively winnowing out those dealers whose conduct, beyond delivering illicit drugs, creates the most noxious social side effects and by influencing the incentives facing the remaining market participants, in particular the risks they face from enforcement itself: arrest, conviction, prison time, and asset seizure. Since these risks are the most important costs of selling illicit drugs, there is every reason to hope that making them vary systematically with the behavior of dealers and dealing organizations could significantly change that behavior (Caulkins 2002; Caulkins and Reuter 2009). The UK Serious Organised Crime Agency (SOCA) is a leader in efforts to prioritize enforcement based on the overall harm generated, including collateral effects, not just the dealing itself (SOCA 2009).

The basic idea can be thought of as market jujitsu. The competitive pressures that frustrate efforts to suppress drug markets altogether can be exploited to good effect by cracking down on the most noxious types of dealing and the most noxious dealers. If those are replaced by techniques and organizations of only average noxiousness, some progress will have been made at ameliorating the damage caused by drug markets. What collateral effects of dealing are deemed most noxious will vary by drug, time, and place. Indeed, an argument can be made for bottom-up prioritization schemes that reflect community-based concern (Caulkins and Heymann 2001).

Drug dealers and drug-dealing organizations vary in their capacity and willingness to employ violence, though there is little systematic knowledge about the patterns or extent of that variation. If enforcement were focused, and known to be focused, on the most violent organizations, a dealer would have to weigh the benefits of violence in reducing enforcement vulnerability to its costs in moving his group up the target list. Moreover, those organizations and individuals "naturally" most prone to violence would be taken out of the trade by enforcement action at a higher rate than their less violent rivals. Insofar as the acquisition and use of capacities for violence by rival organizations have some of the characteristics of an arms race, there might also be indirectly beneficial effects: the reduction in the average level of violence through selective deterrence and incapacitation might lead to a reduction in the optimal level of violence for any given organization, even setting aside enforcement risks.

Dealing organizations, and the markets they create, also differ in flagrancy. At one extreme is highly discreet selling embedded within social networks or door-to-door delivery, pizza-style, arranged by cell phone. At the other is dealing openly in public spaces, or in dedicated drug locations such as crack houses. Flagrancy is of concern in part because it increases the availability of drugs to those not (yet) deeply knowledgeable about how to acquire them or strongly committed to their acquisition, but primarily because flagrant dealing may be linked to non-drug crime: the vulnerability of flagrant dealers to robbery gives them an incentive to become armed; flagrant dealing creates the sort of disorderly conditions that not only directly diminish neighborhood quality of life but have also been hypothesized to attract serious criminal behavior to the area by creating the (partially self-fulfilling) impression that the risks of arrest and punishment for offenses committed there are low (Wilson and Kelling 1982); and flagrant dealing can undermine public confidence in the criminal justice system and thus the capacity of law enforcement to secure citizen cooperation.

Thus enforcement agencies could try to reduce non-drug crime by focusing drug enforcement on those forms of flagrant dealing that create the most criminogenic disorder. Conversely, police and prosecutors might also consider carefully how tough they want to be on the more discreet dealing styles facilitated by new communications technology.

Given limited prison capacity, it makes sense to give priority to housing the most active and violent offenders. Current federal policy is perhaps the most prominent example of the wrong approach. Under the law, relatively minor participants in drug trafficking, some with no prior arrests, frequently face long mandatory prison terms. According to a Department of Justice analysis in the early 1990s (when drug offenders accounted for a smaller share of the federal prison population than today), 21 percent of all federal prisoners were "low-level drug law violators" with no record of violence or incarceration. Of these, 42 percent were drug couriers (or "mules"), rather than dealers or principals in trafficking organizations (Heymann 1994). Since those cells could instead be holding more dangerous offenders, the result of long mandatory sentences for minor drug offenders is to increase crime. Even if long sentences were given to offenders worth locking up, deterrence theory suggests that this would not be the best way to employ limited cell capacity to deter drug dealing: certainty (maximized by handing out many shorter sentences) is more important than severity (Cook 1981).

INNOVATIONS: HIGH POINT AND HOPE

This rather discouraging background highlights the importance of two innovations that hold out the promise of radical changes in the contribution of drugs and drug policy both to non-drug crime and to incarceration (which has shifted from one, albeit costly, contributor to crime control to being a massive social problem in its own right). Those two innovations are the low-arrest crackdowns on flagrant retail drug dealing (known, after the place of its first implementation, as the "High Point" strategy), and drug-testing and sanctions for drug-involved offenders on probation, parole, and pretrial release (known as HOPE, the name under which it has succeeded in Hawaii).

Low-arrest Crackdowns on Flagrant Drug Dealing

Large areas of flagrant drug dealing—either in the open or in dedicated locations such as crack houses—constitute serious problems for the neighborhoods where they exist. Violence and theft by and against both users and dealers can make flagrant market areas into hot spots for non-drug crime. Even when no actual non-drug crime is being committed, the presence of crowds of people, many of them armed and all of them engaged in illicit activity, instills fear into residents and drives non-residents, other than drug buyers and sellers, away. One reason that urban police continue to pursue the Sisyphean task of locking up drug dealers one by one, only to have them replaced by others, is that the neighbors demand it. The same community leadership that criticizes the police for overly aggressive and impolite enforcement activity often also complains about the failure of the police to stop a set of illegal activities that stand out in plain view. The presence of open dealing in minority neighborhoods can occasion accusations both of racism ("You wouldn't let this stuff go on in a white neighborhood") and of corruption ("The dealers couldn't operate like that if they hadn't paid off the cops").

It has been known since the early 1980s that intensive and sustained enforcement efforts ("crackdowns") can, under some circumstances, disrupt areas of flagrant drug dealing to the point at which open activity virtually disappears, and remains dormant even after enforcement levels return to normal (Kleiman 1988; Caulkins et al. 1993). At first blush, this is surprising; one might expect that buyers and sellers would quickly reassemble once the coast was clear, as in fact happens when a crackdown is short-lived. But the effect is different when a crackdown lasts long enough to change the expectations of market participants.

Drug dealing tends to be concentrated rather than dispersed because buyers tend to come to where they expect sellers to cluster, and sellers to come to where they expect buyers to cluster. Doing so increases the probability of quickly finding a transaction partner and reduces the risk of arrest, which tends to be lower for any illicit activity where the frequency of that activity is higher: any given level of enforcement attention is spread over a larger number of possible targets.

A drug market is thus a "focal point": once it has reached some critical level of activity, it becomes self-sustaining. But if a crackdown can push the level of activity below that critical level and keep it there long enough that buyers stop expecting sellers to be present and vice versa, the market may not reconstitute itself. By the same token, the belief that a new market area will automatically develop to replace the previous one is unsupported by either theory or evidence.

The problem with a crackdown such as Operation Pressure Point in New York is the heavy demand it puts on the scarce capacities within the criminal justice system: not so much the number of officers who need to be assigned to the task as the resulting burden on the court system. Pressure Point resulted in some 17,000 felony arrests, but there were no more felony convictions in New York County (Manhattan) courts than there had been the year before. In effect, any convictions that resulted from Pressure Point arrests squeezed out convictions for other offenses, presumably through dismissal and misdemeanor plea bargains. In the long run, Pressure Point saved enforcement resources by substantially eliminating the Alphabet City market that had been a steady source of arrests and prosecutions. But in the short run it imposed system burdens that could not be sustained (Kleiman 1988).

Therefore the Pressure Point success was followed, not by more Pressure Point operations in other drug-market areas, but by the much less resource-intensive, and much less successful, Tactical Narcotics Teams (Sviridoff 1992). That raised the question of whether the same results could be achieved at lower cost. If the goal was understood as "locking up drug dealers," the answer was pretty clearly "no." But if the goal was understood as "breaking up the market to return control of the neighbor-hood to law-abiding residents," the answer might be "yes." The problem was to shorten the number of days of crackdown effort and the number of arrests required to convince a critical mass of dealers that the effort was not merely a transitory "street-sweep" and that the target area was no longer an hospitable place for their businesses.

The key observation is that being the only dealer, or one of a few dealers, in a flagrant market is dangerous; the risk of arrest for each remaining seller goes up as the number of other dealers goes down. If it were possible to rapidly shift the expectations of dealers about one another's behavior, it might be possible to make the market collapse quickly.

That led David Kennedy (then at Harvard, now at John Jay College) to ask a question: "What if we put up posters?" If the police announced a crackdown in advance, promising that anyone dealing in a given area after some specified date would be arrested, and if sufficient number of dealers believed that threat, then a limited number of police would be able to deliver on that threat for the skeptical remainder. Again, if the goal is to break up the market rather than to make many arrests, there is actually a community of interest between the police, for whom arrests are a cost, and the dealers, who don't want to be arrested.

After several years, Kennedy managed to persuade one police depart-ment, in High Point, North Carolina, to try the new strategy. Instead of merely putting up posters, though, the police actually prepared felony cases against all of the dealers in the market, and then warned them at a meeting that anyone who continued dealing would be headed straight for prison. As a result, that market disappeared literally overnight, with only a handful of actual arrests, and has not reappeared in the intervening six years. Crack dealing was not eliminated, but flagrant crack dealing was eliminated, to the great benefit of the neighborhood, including lasting crime reductions (Kennedy 2008, 2009). That success has been replicated in East Hempstead, Long Island, and is being attempted in other jurisdic-tions. If it proves capable of dealing with the largest big-city drug markets, it holds out the prospect of substantially reducing the contribution of drug dealing to non-drug crime and disorder, while also reducing the flow of dealers in and out of prisons and jails.

Drug-Testing-and-Sanctions Programs for Offenders under Community Supervision

As argued above, neither voluntary nor coerced drug treatment has any prospect of greatly shrinking drug-related crime. If it were the case that all users of expensive illicit drugs were sufferers from clinically diagnosable substance abuse or dependency disorder, and that sufferers from such dis-orders have no volitional control over their drug-taking, and that such disorders are invariably chronic and go into remission only with professional intervention, then the limits on treatment would also be the limits on the capacity of the criminal justice system to influence the drug-taking of those under its jurisdiction.

Happily, however, all of those propositions are false. Many users, even frequent users, of cocaine, heroin, and methamphetamine do not meet clinical criteria for substance abuse or dependency. ("Drug abuse" as a legal matter merely means using a prohibited drug, or using a prescription drug for nonmedical reasons or without a valid prescription; "substance abuse" as a medical matter is defined by criteria such as escalation of dosage and frequency, narrowing of the behavioral repertoire, loss of control over use, and continued use despite adverse consequences.) Even for those who do meet clinical criteria, actual consumption depends in part on availability and on the consequences, especially the more-or-less immediate consequences. Incentives influence drug use, even within the treatment context; monitoring drug use by urine-testing enhances outcomes (Hser, Longshore, and Anglin 1994), as does the provision of even very small rewards for compliance (Higgins et al. 1994; Higgins 1997). Moreover, while the minority of substance-abusing or substance-dependent individuals suffering from chronic forms of those disorders makes up a large proportion of the population in treatment, the most common pattern of substance abuse is a single period of active disease followed by "spontaneous" (i.e., not treatment-generated) remission (Heyman 2001, 2009).

That being the case, persuading or forcing drug-using offenders into treatment is not the only way to reduce their drug consumption. An alternative to mandating treatment is to mandate desistance for persons on probation or parole. This mandate can be enforced by frequent drug tests, with predictable and nearly immediate sanctions for each missed test or incident of detected drug use. While in the long term drug-involved offenders who remain drug-involved are highly likely to be rearrested and eventually incarcerated, those long-term and probabilistic threats, even if the penalties involved are severe, may be less effective than short-term and virtually certain threats of much less drastic sanctions.

For those offenders whose drug use is subject to their volitional control, testing-and-sanctions programs can sharply reduce the frequency of that use. Those unable to control themselves, even under threat, will be quickly identified, and in a way that is likely to break through the denial that often characterizes substance abuse disorders. That will help direct treatment resources to those most in need of them and will help create a "therapeutic alliance" between providers and clients by giving clients strong incentives to succeed, as opposed to merely wanting the therapists off their backs.

Since probationers and parolees account for a large fraction—approximately one-half—of all the cocaine and heroin sold in the United States, and therefore for most of the revenues of the illicit markets, an effective testing-and-sanctions program would have a larger impact on the volume of the illicit trade—and presumably on the side effects it generates, including the need for drug law enforcement and related imprisonment—than any other initiative that could be undertaken: by one estimate, a national program of this type could reasonably be expected to shrink total hard-drug volumes by 40 percent, while also reducing the fraction of the lives of today's criminally active illicit drug users that will be spent behind bars.

Such a program requires money and facilities for drug testing, either judges willing to sanction predictably or authority for administrative sanctioning by the probation department, police officers (or probation officers with arrest authority) to seek out absconders, capacity for carrying out sanctions (such as supervisors for "community service" labor and confinement capacity appropriate for one- and two-day stays), and treatment capacity for those who proved unable to quit without professional help. If it were possible to provide rewards for compliance, as well as punishments for non-compliance, that should improve success rates and reduce overall costs. The key to success is the immediacy and certainty of the sanctions. This in turn depends on keeping the population assigned to the program small compared to the resources available, until the program has had a chance to establish the credibility that in turn will minimize violation rates and thus the need for the actual imposition of sanctions.

While the logic of that approach had seemed clear to some analysts for many years (DuPont and Green 1971; DuPont and Wish 1992; Kaplan 1983; Kleiman 1997, 1999, 2001), it had until recently failed to take hold as part of standard practice in any large jurisdiction; Maryland's well-publicized venture in this direction, under the rubric "Breaking the Cycle," seems to have suffered from a lack of sanctions credibility, which resulted from a combination of lack of administrative follow-through and judicial reluctance to punish detected drug use.

That pattern started to change in 2004, when Judge Steven Alm in Honolulu decided—unprompted, it should be noted, by any academic speculation—to impose randomized testing and formulaic sanctions on a group of 35 persistently non-compliant felony probationers. The offenders were mostly methamphetamine users on probation for property and violent crimes. The process—called Hawaii's Opportunity Probation with Enforcement, or HOPE—started with a "warning hearing," at which the probationers were given notice that each future violation of the rules would draw immediate jail time and were instructed to call in daily to learn whether they were required to come in that day for a drug test. Simplifying the process by which probationer officers report violations to the court made the program compatible with normal probation caseloads of 150–180; creating an abbreviated "probation modification" hearing in place of the more elaborate "probation revocation" hearing greatly economized on court time.

The results were dramatic: although participants were chosen precisely for their previous high violation rates (a combined "dirty" and "no-show" rate of about 30 percent, for drug tests scheduled well in advance), fewer than half ever earned an actual sanction under HOPE; for the rest, the threat alone was sufficient (Hawken and Kleiman 2007; Kleiman and Hawken 2008a, b; Kleiman 2009a [chap. 3], 2009b).

The annualized per-participant cost of the program comes to approximately $1,400, over and above the roughly $1,000-per-probationer cost of routine probation supervision. HOPE has now been expanded to cover 1,500 of the 8,000 felony probationers on the island of Oahu, and further expansion to cover 3,000 of them has been proposed. Judge Alm estimates that a single judge, freed of most trial work, could handle all 3,000 cases; the contrast with drug-court caseloads of 50–75 is stark. When other judges adopted the program, their probationers had results that matched those of Judge Alm's probationers.

HOPE provides direct fiscal savings to public agencies (chiefly prisons) of about $6,000 per participant per year, because HOPE probationers (as measured in a randomized controlled trial) reduce their days behind bars by about two-thirds compared to comparable offenders on routine probation; they have half as many arrests and only one-third as many probation revocations.

Most of the additional cost of HOPE, compared to routine probation, covers residential drug treatment for the roughly 8 percent of participants who repeatedly test "dirty" and are given the choice between residential treatment (lasting typically 3–6 months) and prison. Those are the only HOPE participants who are mandated to treatment; others have access to treatment but are not required to participate. Thus the program embodies what economist Angela Hawken (2009) calls "behavioral triage," as opposed to the current standard of "assess and treat." Instead of using clinical assessment tools to decide which criminal-justice clients need treatment and what kind of treatment they need, HOPE allows those who cannot quit on their own under the threat of sanctions to, in effect, identify themselves as in need of formal treatment. More than 80 percent of HOPE probationers—including some with very high scores on the Addiction Severity Index—were able to become stably abstinent in the community without undergoing residential treatment. Strikingly, the program is highly popular among the probationers themselves, even those interviewed while in jail serving a sanction. One probationer called the program "strict but fair," adding "You know where you stand."

Several other jurisdictions are in the process of starting HOPE-like programs for probationers, and one jurisdiction is contemplating its use with parolees. The Hawaii results seem to refute the claim that the nature of drug abuse makes desistance without treatment impossible. How well it will work in other jurisdictions remains to be seen, but there seems to be more reason to worry about whether the institutions of the criminal justice system in other places can work together well enough to deliver the promised swift and certain sanctions than about whether drug-using offenders will respond to those sanctions if they are actually put into practice.

The need for cooperation among multiple agencies—some state, some county, some municipal, some judicial, some administrative, some nongovernmental—greatly increases the difficulty of a successful implementation. Automatic sanctioning requires either limiting judicial discretion, getting the judges out of the process entirely, or persuading judges to put their actions on autopilot; the first two are unpopular with judges, who remain quite influential in making policy, and the third is extremely problematic (Harrell, Hirst, Mitchell 2000): as Adele Harrell remarked after evaluating such a program, "Changing addict behavior is easy; changing judge behavior is hard."

A comparable success in a very different context has been achieved by South Dakota's 24/7 Sobriety Project (http://www.state.sd.us/attorney/ DUI247/index.htm). The program began with twice-a-day pretrial testing of repeat DUI offenders for alcohol use, with the consequence for a positive test or "no-show" being an automatic and immediate 24-hour period in jail. The program web site reports that of 2.09 million tests given to almost 12,000 people in the program, 99.6 percent were clean (http://www.state.sd.us/attorney/DUI247/247stats.htm). On a per-person basis, of 1,021 participants, 680 (67 percent) never had a dirty or missed test, and another 277 (27 percent) had no more than two failed tests. Just 6 percent of those enrolled were not substantially compliant with the requirement to refrain from alcohol use pending trial. Strikingly, the testing and sanctions program was accompanied by a falling, not rising, jail census, as a result of lower rates of criminal recidivism (Long 2009).

The program was expanded over time to include electronic home monitoring for people for whom twice-a-day in person testing was not practical (e.g., in rural areas where driving times would be prohibitive) and testing for illegal drugs by urinalysis or drug patch. Compliance rates remained high, but tellingly, technologies that generated a longer gap between use and detection had higher rates of non-compliance.

The HOPE approach offers a plausible prospect for greatly reducing the extent of drug abuse, drug-related crime, and imprisonment. No other operationally feasible idea yet put forward for dealing with drug-involved offenders can make the same claim. Combined with the High Point approach to breaking up flagrant drug markets, HOPE could substantially sever the link between drug abuse and non-drug crime.

References

Amato, L., M. Davoli, C. A. Perucci, M. Ferri, F. Faggiano, and R. P. Mattick. 2005. "An Overview of Systematic Reviews of the Effectiveness of Opiate Maintenance Therapies: Available Evidence to Inform Clinical Practice and Research."*Journal of Substance Abuse Treatment* 28: 321–330.

Anderson, Elijah. 1994. The Code of the Streets. *The Atlantic Monthly* 273: 80–94.

Anderson, Elijah. 1999. *Code of the Street: Decency, Violence, and the Moral Life of the Inner City*. New York: W. W. Norton.

Anglin, Douglas M., and Yih-Ing Hser. 1990. "Treatment of Drug Abuse." In *Drugs and Crime*, eds. Michael H. Tonry and James Q. Wilson, 393–460. Vol. 13 of *Crime and Justice: A Review of Research*. Chicago: University of Chicago Press.

Anglin, Douglas M., D. Longshore, and S. Turner. 1999. Treatment Alternatives to Street Crime. *Criminal Justice and Behavior* 26 (2): 168–95.

Anglin, M. Douglas, and George Speckart. 1986. "Narcotics Use, Property Crime, and Dealing: Structural Dynamics across the Addiction Career." *Journal of Quantitative Criminology* 2: 355–75.

Anglin, M. Douglas, and George Speckart. 1988. "Narcotics Use and Crime: A Multisample, Multimethod Analysis." *Criminology* 26: 197–233.

Aos, S., R. Lieb, J. Mayfield, M. Miller, A. Pennucci. 2004. "Benefits and Costs of Prevention and Early Intervention Programs for Youth." Olympia: Washington State Institute for Public Policy. Available at <http://www.wsipp.wa.gov/rptfiles/04-07-3901.pdf>.

Arseneault, Louise, Cannon Mary, Witten John, Murray Robin M. 2004. "Causal Association Between Cannabis And Psychosis: Examination of the Evidence." *British Journal of Psychiatry* 184: 110–117.

Ball, John C. 1986. "The Hyper-criminal Opiate Addict." In *Crime Rates and Drug Abusing Offenders*, eds. Bruce D. Johnson and Eric Wish. New York: Narcotic and Drug Research.

Ball, John C., Lawrence Rosen, John A. Flueck, and David N. Nurco. 1981. "The Criminality of Heroin Addicts: When Addicted and When Off Opiates." In *The Drugs-Crime Connection*, ed. James A. Inciardi, 39–65. Beverly Hills: Sage.

Ball, John C., Lawrence Rosen, John A. Flueck, and David N. Nurco. 1982. "Lifetime Criminality of Heroin Addicts in the United States." *Journal of Drug Issues* 12: 225–239.

Ball, John C., John W. Shaffer, and David N. Nurco. 1983. "The Day-to-Day Criminality of Heroin Addicts in Baltimore: A Study in the Continuity of Offense Rates." *Drug and Alcohol Dependence* 12: 119–142.

Beaver, K. M., M. G. Vaughn, M. Delisi. J. P. Wright. 2008."Anabolic-Androgenic Steroid Use and Involvement in Violent Behavior in a Nationally Representative Sample of Young Adult Males in the United States " *American Journal of Public Health* 98 (12): 2185–2187. Available at doi:10.2105/AJPH.2008.137018 PMID 18923108 [DU1]

Becker, Gary S., Michael Grossman, and Kevin Murphy. 1991. "Rational Addiction and the Effect of Price on Consumption." *American Economic Review* 81 (2): 237–241.

Becker, G. S., M. Grossman, and K. M. Murphy. 1994. "An Empirical Analysis of Cigarette Addiction." *The American Economic Review* 84: 397–418.

Behrens, Doris A., Jonathan P. Caulkins, Gernot Tragler, and Gustav Feichtinger. 2000. "Optimal Control of Drug Epidemics: Prevent and Treat—But Not at the Same Time." *Management Science* 46 (3): 333–347.

Bejerot, Nils. 1970. "A Comparison of the Effects of Cocaine and Synthetic Central Stimulants." *British Journal of Addiction* 65: 35–37.

Belenko, Steven, Nicholas Patapsis, and Michael T. French, eds. 2005. *Economic Benefits of Drug Treatment: A Critical Review of the Evidence for Policy Makers.* Available at http://www.nsula.edu/laattc/documents/EconomicBenefits_2005Feb.pdf.

Birkeland, Sarah, Erin Murphy-Graham, and Carol Weiss. 2005. "Good Reasons for Ignoring Good Evaluation: The Case of the Drug Abuse Resistance Education (D.A.R.E.) Program." *Evaluation and Program Planning* 28 (3): 247–256.

Blackstone, William. [1778]1890. *Commentaries on the Laws of England.* Reprint of 8th ed. San Francisco: Bancroft-Whitney.

Block, Carolyn Rebecca, and Richard Block. 1993. *Street Gang Crime in Chicago*. National Institute of Justice, Research in Brief. Washington, DC: U.S. Department of Justice, December.

Blumstein, Alfred. 1993. "Making Rationality Relevant: The American Society of Criminology 1992 Presidential Address." *Criminology* 31 (1): 1–16.

Blumstein, A., and D. Cork. 1996. "Linking Gun Availability to Youth Gun Violence." *Law and Contemporary Problems* 59 (1): 5–24.

BOTEC Analysis Corporation. 1990. *Program Evaluation: Santa Cruz Street Drug Reduction Program*. Cambridge, MA: BOTEC Analysis.

Boyum, David. 1992. *Reflections on Economic Theory and Drug Enforcement*. Ph.D. diss., Harvard University.

Boyum, David. 1998. "The Distributive Politics of Drug Policy." *Drug Policy Analysis Bulletin* no. 4.

Brown, George F., and Lester P. Silverman. 1974. "The Retail Price of Heroin: Estimation and Applications." *Journal of the American Statistical Association* 69: 595–606.

Brown, Joel H., and Ita G. G. Kreft. 1998. "Zero Effects of Drug Prevention Programs: Issues and Solutions." *Evaluation Review* 22 (1): 1–14.

Brownsberger, William N. 2000. "Race Matters: Disproportionality of Incarceration for Drug Dealing in Massachusetts." *Journal of Drug Issues* 30 (2): 345–374.

Brownsberger, William N. 2001. "Limits on the Role of Testing and Sanctions: A Comment on Coerced Abstinence." In *Drug Addiction and Drug Policy*, eds. Philip B. Heymann and William N. Brownsberger. Cambridge, MA: Harvard University Press.

Brownsberger, William N., and Anne M. Piehl. 1997. "Profile of Anti-Drug Law Enforcement in Urban Poverty Areas in Massachusetts." Cambridge, MA: Harvard Medical School, Division on Addictions.

Bureau of Labor Statistics, U.S. Department of Labor, *Occupational OutlookHandbook, 2008–09 Edition*, Judges, Magistrates, and Other Judicial Workers. Available at http://www.bls.gov/oco/ocos272.htm.Accessed September 14, 2009.

Cameron, L., Williams J. 2001. "Substitutes or Complements? Alcohol, Cannabis and Tobacco." *Economic Record* 77: 19–34.

Caulkins, Jonathan P. 1992. "Thinking about Displacement in Drug Markets: Why Observing Change of Venue Isn't Enough." *The Journal of Drug Issues* 22 (1): 17–30.

Caulkins, Jonathan P. 1996. "Estimating the Elasticities and Cross Elasticities of Demand for Cocaine and Heroin." Pittsburgh: Carnegie Mellon University, Heinz School Working Paper 95–13.

Caulkins, Jonathan P. 2000. "Do Drug Prohibition and Enforcement Work?" White paper published in the What Works? series. Arlington, VA: Lexington Institute.

Caulkins, Jonathan P. 2002. "Law Enforcement's Role in a Harm Reduction Regime." *Crime and Justice Bulletin* Number 64. Crime and Justice Bulletin Number 64. (Sydney: New South Wales Bureau of Crime and Justice Research. Translated into Russian and Polish for distribution by the International Debate Education Association and reprinted in *War on Drugs, HIV/AIDS and Human Rights*.

Caulkins, Jonathan P. 2005. "Models Pertaining to How Drug Policy Should Vary over the Course of an Epidemic Cycle." In *Substance Use: Individual Behavior,*

Social Interactions, Markets, and Politics, eds. Bjorn Lindgren and Michael Grossman, *Advances in Health Economics and Health Services Research* 16: 407–439. New York: Elsevier.

Caulkins, Jonathan P. 2009. "Cost-Benefit Analyses of Investments to Control Illicit Substance Abuse and Addiction." In *Investing in the Disadvantaged: What Do (and Could) We Know about the Efficiency of Social Policies*, eds. David L. Weimer and Aidan R. Vining, Chapter 6. Georgetown University Press.

Caulkins, Jonathan P., and Sara Chandler. 2006. "Long-Run Trends in Incarceration of Drug Offenders in the US." *Crime and Delinquency* 52 (4): 619–641.

Caulkins, Jonathan P., and Philip Heymann. 2001. "How Should Low-Level Drug Dealers Be Punished?" In *Drug Addiction and Drug Policy: The Struggle to Control Dependence*, eds. Philip B. Heymann and William N. Brownsberger, 206–238. Cambridge. MA: Harvard University Press.

Caulkins, Jonathan P., and Mark A. R. Kleiman. 2008. "Drugs and Drug Policies in the United States." In *Understanding America: The Institutions and Policies that Shape America and the World*, eds. Peter H. Schuck and James Q. Wilson, 563–593. New York: Public Affairs Publishing.

Caulkins, Jonathan P., and Peter Reuter. 2009. "Toward a Harm Reduction Approach to Enforcement." *Safer Communities* 8 (1): 9–23.

Caulkins, Jonathan, Peter Rydell, Susan Everingham, James Chiesa, and Shawn Bushway. 1999. *An Ounce of Prevention, a Pound of Uncertainty*. Santa Monica, CA: RAND.

Caulkins, J. P., C. P. Rydell, W. L. Schwabe, and J. Chiesa. 1997. *Mandatory Minimum Drug Sentences: Throwing Away the Key or the Taxpayers' Money?* MR-827-DPRC. Santa Monica, CA: RAND.

Cavanagh, David P., and Mark A. R. Kleiman. 1990. *A Cost-Benefit Analysis of Prison Cell Construction and Alternative Sanctions*. Cambridge, MA: BOTEC Analysis.

Chaiken, Jan M., and Marcia R. Chaiken. 1990. "Drugs and Predatory Crime." In *Drugs and Crime*, vol. 13 of *Crime and Justice: A Review of Research*, eds. Michael H. Tonry and James Q. Wilson, 203–239. Chicago: University of Chicago Press.

Chaloupka, Frank J., and Adit Laixuthai. 1997. "Do Youths Substitute Alcohol And Marijuana? Some Econometric Evidence." *Eastern Economic Journal* 23 (3): 253–276.

Clayton, Richard R., and Harwin L. Voss. 1981. *Young Men and Drugs in Manhattan: A Causal Analysis*. NIDA Research Monograph No. 39. Rockville, MD: Alcohol, Drug Abuse, and Mental Health Administration.

Cleary, Paul D., Jan L. Hitchcock, Norbert Semmer, Laura J. Flinchbaugh, and John M. Pinney. 1988. "Adolescent Smoking: Research and Health Policy." *The Milbank Quarterly* 66 (1): 137–171.

Cohen, Jacqueline, and Daniel S. Nagin. 1993. "Criminal Careers of Drug Offenders: A Comparison." Paper presented at the annual meeting of the American Society of Criminology, Phoenix, October 29.

Collins, James J., Robert L. Hubbard, and J. Valley Rachal. 1985. "Expensive Drug Use and Illegal Income: A Test of Explanatory Hypotheses." *Criminology* 23: 743–764.

Compton, W. M., and N. D. Volkow. 2006. "Major Increases in Opioid Analgesic Abuse in the United States: Concerns and Strategies." *Drug and Alcohol Dependence* 81(2): 103–107.

Cook, Philip J. 1981. "Research in Criminal Deterrence: Laying the Groundwork for the Second Decade." In *Crime and Justice: A Review of Research*, vol. 2, eds. Michael H. Tonry and Norval Morris, 211–268. Chicago: University of Chicago Press.

Cook, Philip J. 1986. "The Demand and Supply of Criminal Opportunities." In *Crime and Justice: A Review of Research*, vol. 7, eds. Michael H. Tonry and Norval Morris, 1–27. Chicago: University of Chicago Press.

Cook, Philip J. 2007. *Paying the Tab: The Costs and Benefits of Alcohol Control.* Princeton, NJ: Princeton University Press.

Cook, Philip J., Mark H. Moore, and Anthony A. Braga. 2002. "Gun Control." In *Crime*, 2nd ed., eds. James Q. Wilson and Joan Petersilia, 291–330.

Cook, Philip J., and George Tauchen. 1982. "The Effect of Liquor Taxes on Heavy Drinking." *Bell Journal of Economics* 13 (2): 379–390.

Cork, Daniel. 1999. "Examining Space-Time Interaction in City-Level Homicide Data: Crack Markets and the Diffusion of Guns among Youth." *Journal of Quantitative Criminology* 15: 379–406.

Corman, Hope, and Naci Mocan. 2000. "A Time-Series Analysis of Crime, Deterrence and Drug Abuse in New York City." *The American Economic Review* 90 (3): 584–604.

Day, Carolyn, Louisa Degenhardt, and Wayne Hall. 2006. "Changes in the Initiation of Heroin Use after a Reduction in Heroin Supply." *Drug and Alcohol Review* 25: 307–313.

Degenhardt, Louisa, Peter Reuter, Linette Collins, and Wayne Hall. 2005a. "Evaluating Explanations of the Australian Heroin Drought." *Addiction* 100: 459–469.

Degenhardt, Louisa, Elizabeth Conroy, Stuart Gilmour, and Linette Collins. 2005b. "The Effect of a Reduction in Heroin Supply in Australia upon Drug Distribution and Acquisitive Crime." *British Journal of Criminology* 45 (1): 2–24.

Dewey, W. L. 1986. "Cannabinoid Pharmacology." *Pharmacology Review* 38: 151–178.

DiNardo, John. 1991. *Are Marijuana and Alcohol Substitutes? The Effect of State Drinking Age Laws on the Marijuana Consumption of High School Seniors.* Santa Monica, CA: RAND.

DiNardo, John. 1993. "Law Enforcement, the Price of Cocaine, and Cocaine Use." *Mathematical and Computer Modeling* 17 (2): 53–64.

Dukes, R. L., J. B. Ullman, and J. A. Stein. 1996. "Three-Year Follow-up of Drug Abuse Resistance Education (D.A.R.E.)." *Evaluation Review* 20 (1): 49–66.

DuPont, Robert L., and Mark H. Greene. 1973. "The Dynamics of a Heroin Addiction Epidemic." *Science* 181: 716–722.

DuPont, Robert L., and Eric D. Wish. 1992. "Operation Tripwire Revisited." *Annals of the American Academy of Political and Social Science* 521: 91–111.

Fagan, Jeffrey. 1990. "Intoxication and Aggression." In *Drugs and Crime*, vol. 13 of *Crime and Justice: A Review of Research*, eds. Michael Tonry and James Q. Wilson, 241–320. Chicago: University of Chicago Press.

Fagan, Jeffrey. 1992. "Drug Selling and Licit Income in Distressed Neighborhoods: The Economic Lives of Street-Level Drug Users and Dealers." In *Drugs, Crime, and Social Isolation*, eds. Adele V. Harrell and George E. Peterson, 99–146. Washington, DC: Urban Institute Press.

Faggiano, F., F. D. Vigna-Taglianti, E. Versino, A. Zambon, A. Borraccino, and P. Lemma. 2005. "School-Based Prevention for Illicit Drugs' Use." *The*

Cochrane Database of Systematic Reviews 2: 385–396. Art. no. CD003020. DOI: 10.1002/14651858.CD003020.pub2.

Farabee D., V. Joshi, and M. D. Anglin. 2001. "Addiction Careers and Criminal Specialization." *Crime and Delinquency* 47 (2): 196–220.

Farrelly, M. C., J. W. Bray, G. A. Zarkin, B. W. Wendling, and R.L. Pacula. 1999. "The Effects of Prices and Policies on the Demand for Marijuana: Evidence from the National Household Surveys on Drug Abuse." National Bureau of Economic Research Working Paper number 6940.

Ferguson, Ronald. 1993. Personal communication with the authors. December 14.

Fries, Arthur, Robert W. Anthony, Andrew Cseko, Jr., Carl C. Gaither, and Eric Schulman. 2008. "Technical Report for the Price and Purity of Illicit Drugs: 1981–2007." Office of National Drug Control Policy. Alexandria, VA: Institute for Defense Analyses.

Furr-Holden, C. Debra, Nicholas S. Ialongo, James C. Anthony, Hanno Petra, and G. Kellam Sheppard. 2004. "Developmentally Inspired Drug Prevention: Middle School Outcomes in a School-Based Randomized Prevention Trial." *Drug and Alcohol Dependence* 73: 149–158.

Gallegher, J. J. 1996. *Project Sentry Final Program Report*. Lansing, MI: Project Sentry.

Gallegher, J. J. 1997. *Project Sentry Quarterly Program Report*. Lansing, MI: Project Sentry.

Gates, S., J. McCambridge, L. A. Smith and D. R. Foxcroft. 2006. "Interventions for Prevention of Drug Use by Young People Delivered in Non-School Settings." *Cochrane Database of Systematic Reviews* Issue 1. Art. no.: CD005030. DOI: 10.1002/14651858.CD005030.pub2.

Gersh, Debra. 1988. "Some Newspapers Refuse to Run Anti-drug Ad, Object to Photo of a Man with a Gun Pointed Up His Nose." *Editor and Publisher* 23 January: 17.

Gerstein, Dean R., and Henrick J. Harwood. 1990. *Treating Drug Problems*, Vol. 1. Washington, DC: National Academy Press.

Gerstein, D. R., R. A. Johnson, H. J. Harwood, K. Fountain, N. Suter, and K. Malloy. 1994. *Evaluating Recovery Services: The California Drug and Alcohol Treatment Assessment (CALDATA) General Report*. Sacramento: California Department of Alcohol and Drug Programs.

Goldman, Fred. 1976. "Drug Markets and Addict Consumption Behavior." In *Drug Use and Crime: Report of the Panel on Drug Use and Criminal Behavior*, ed. Robert Shellow, 273–296. Washington, DC: National Technical Information Service.

Goldman, Fred. 1977. "Narcotics Users, Narcotics Prices, and Criminal Activity: An Economic Analysis." In *The Epidemiology of Heroin and Other Narcotics*, ed. J. Rittenhouse, 30–36. NIDA Research Monograph Series, No. 16. Rockville, MD: National Institute on Drug Abuse.

Goldman, Fred. 1981. "Drug Abuse, Crime and Economics: The Dismal Limits of Social Choice." In *The Drugs-Crime Connection*, ed. James A. Inciardi, 155–182. Beverly Hills: Sage.

Goldstein, Paul J. 1985. "The Drugs/Violence Nexus: A Tripartite Conceptual Framework." *Journal of Drug Issues* 15 (4): 493–506.

Goldstein, Paul J., and Henry H. Brownstein. 1987. *Drug Related Crime Analysis: Homicide*. Report to the National Institute of Justice Drugs, Alcohol, and Crime Program. Washington, DC: United States Department of Justice, July.

Goldstein, Paul J., Henry H. Brownstein, Patrick J. Ryan, and Patricia A. Bellucci. 1990. "Crack and Homicide in New York City, 1988: A Conceptually Based Event Analysis." *Contemporary Drug Problems* 16 (4): 651–687.

Golub, A., and B. D. Johnson. 1996. "The Crack Epidemic: Empirical Findings Support a Hypothesized Diffusion of Innovation Process." *Socio-Economic Planning Sciences* 30 (3): 221–231.

Golub, Andrew Lang, and Bruce D. Johnson. 1997. "Crack's Decline: Some Surprises across U.S. Cities." *Research in Brief*. Washington, DC: National Institute of Justice.

Gossop, M., K. Trakada, D. Stewart, and J. Witton. 2005. "Reductions in Criminal Convictions after Addiction Treatment: 5-Year Follow-up." *Drug and Alcohol Dependence* 79: 295–302.

Grinspoon, Lester, and James B. Bakalar. 1985. *Cocaine: A Drug and Its Social Evolution*, rev. ed. New York: Basic Books.

Grossman, M. 2005. "Individual Behaviors and Substance Use: The Role of Price." In *Substance Use: Individual Behaviors, Social Interactions, Markets and Politics*, eds. B. Lindgren and M. Grossman. Vol. 16 of *Advances in Health Economics and Health Services Resesarch*. Amsterdam: Elsevier.

Grossman, Michael, Frank J. Chaloupka, and Charles C. Brown. 1996. "The Demand for Cocaine by Young Adults: A Rational Addiction Approach." NBER Working Paper 5713. Cambridge, MA: National Bureau of Economic Research.

Haaga, John, and Peter Reuter. 1995. "Prevention: The (Lauded) Orphan of Drug Policy." In *Handbook on Drug Abuse Prevention*, eds. Robert Coombs and Douglas Ziedonis, 3–17. Englewood Cliffs, NJ: Allyn and Bacon.

Hamid, Ansley. 1990. "The Political Economy of Crack-Related Violence." *Contemporary Drug Problems* 17 (Spring): 31–78.

Harrell, A., S. Cavanagh, and J. Roman. 1999. *Findings from the Evaluation of the D.C. Superior Court Drug Intervention Program*. Washington, DC: The Urban Institute.

Harrell, A., A. Hirst, and O. Mitchell. 2000. *Implementing System-wide Interventions for Drug-Involved Offenders in Birmingham, Alabama: Evaluation of the Breaking the Cycle Demonstration*. Report submitted to the National Institute of Justice, Washington, DC: The Urban Institute.

Hawken, Angela. 2010. "Behavioral Triage: A New Model for Identifying and Treating Substance-Abusing Offenders." *Journal of Drug Policy Analysis* 3(1),

Hawken, Angela, and Mark A.R. Kleiman, 2007. "H.O.P.E. for Reform: What a Novel Probation Program in Hawaii Might Teach Other States." *American Prospect Online*, April 10.

Heyman, Eugene. 2001. "Is Substance Abuse a Chronic, Relapsing Condition?" In *Drug Addiction and Drug Policy*, eds. Philip B. Heymann and William N. Brownsberger. Cambridge, MA: Harvard University Press.

Heyman, Eugene. 2009. *Addiction: A Disorder of Choice*. Cambridge, MA: Harvard University Press.

Heymann, Philip. 1994. Personal communication with Mark Kleiman.

Higgins, Stephen. 1997. "Applying Behavioral Economics to the Challenge of Reducing Cocaine Abuse." In *The Economic Analysis of Substance Use and Abuse: An Integration of Econometric and Behavioral Economic Research*, eds. Frank J. Chaloupka, Warren K. Bickel, Michael Grossman, and Henry Saffer. Cambridge, MA: National Bureau of Economic Research.

Higgins, S. T., A. J. Budney, W. K. Bickel, F. E. Foerg, R. Donham, and G. J. Badger. 1994. "Incentives Improve Outcome in Outpatient Behavioral Treatment of Cocaine Dependence." *Archives of General Psychiatry* 51: 568–576.

Horgan, John. 1990. "An Antidrug Message Gets Its Facts Wrong." *Scientific American* 262 (5): 36.

Hser, Yih-Ing, Douglas Longshore, and M. Douglas Anglin. 1994. "Prevalence of Drug Use among Criminal Offender Populations: Implications for Control, Treatment, and Policy." In *Drugs and Crime: Evaluating Public Policy Initiatives*, eds. Doris Layton McKenzie and Craig D. Uchida, 18–41. Thousand Oaks, CA: Sage.

Hubbard, Robert L., Mary Ellen Marsden, J. Valley Rachal, Hendrick J. Harwood, Elizabeth R. Cavanaugh, and Harold M. Ginzburg. 1989. *Drug Abuse Treatment: A National Study of Effectiveness*. Chapel Hill: University of North Carolina Press.

Hyatt, Raymond, and William Rhodes. 1992. *Price and Purity of Cocaine: The Relationship to Emergency Room Visits and Deaths, and to Drug Use among Arrestees*. Report prepared for the Office of National Drug Control Policy, Washington, DC

Inciardi, James A. 1979. "Heroin Use and Street Crime." *Crime and Delinquency* 25: 335–346.

Inciardi, James A. 1980. "Youth, Drugs, and Street Crime." In *Drugs and the Youth Culture*, eds. Frank R. Scarpitti and Susan K. Datesman, 175–203. Beverly Hills: Sage.

Inciardi, James A., Ruth Horowitz, and Anne E. Pottieger. 1993. *Street Kids, Street Drugs, Street Crime: An Examination of Drug Use and Serious Delinquency in Miami*. Belmont, CA: Wadsworth.

Inciardi, James A., and Anne E. Pottieger. 1991. "Kids, Crack, and Crime." *Journal of Drug Issues* 21: 257–270.

Johnson, Bruce D., Kevin Anderson, and Eric D. Wish. 1988. "A Day in the Life of 105 Drug Addicts and Abusers: Crimes Committed and How the Money Was Spent." *Sociology and Social Research* 72 (3): 185–191.

Johnson, Bruce D., Paul J. Goldstein, Edward Preble, James Schmeidler, Douglas S. Lipton, Barry Spunt, and Thomas Miller. 1985. *Taking Care of Business: The Economics of Crime by Heroin Users*. Lexington, MA: Lexington Books.

Kakko, J., et al. 2003. "One-Year Retention and Social Function after Buprenorphine-Assisted Relapse Prevention Treatment for Heroin Dependence in Sweden: A Randomized, Placebo-Controlled Trial." *Lancet* 361: 662–668.

Kaplan, J. 1983. *The Hardest Drug: Heroin and Public Policy*. Chicago: Univ. of Chicago Press.

Kennedy, David M. 1993. "Closing the Market: Controlling the Drug Trade in Tampa, Florida." National Institute of Justice Program Focus, NCJ 139963. Washington, DC: U.S. Department of Justice, April.

Kennedy, David M. 1994. "Can We Keep Guns Away From Kids?" *The American Prospect* 5: 74–80.

Kennedy, David M. 1997. "Pulling Levers: Chronic Offenders, High-Crime Settings, and a Theory of Prevention." *Valparaiso University Law Review* 31 (2): 449–480.

Kennedy, David M. 2008. *Deterrence and Crime Prevention Reconsidering the Prospect of Sanction*. Toronto: Routledge.

Kennedy, David M. 2009. "Drugs, Race and Common Ground: Reflections on the High Point Intervention." *NIJ Journal* 262 (NCJ 225760).

Kleiman, Mark. 1988. "Crackdowns: The Effects of Intensive Enforcement on Retail Heroin Dealing." In *Street-Level Drug Enforcement: Examining the Issues*. Washington, DC National Institute of Justice Issues and Practices. (NCJ Number: 173155)

Kleiman, Mark A. R. 1992a. *Against Excess: Drug Policy for Results*. New York: Basic Books.

Kleiman, Mark A. R. 1992b. "Neither Prohibition nor Legalization: Grudging Toleration in Drug Control Policy." *Dædalus* 12 (3): 53–83.

Kleiman, Mark A. R. 1993. "Enforcement Swamping: A Positive-Feedback Mechanism in Rates of Illicit Activity." *Mathematical and Computer Modeling* 17 (2): 65–75.

Kleiman, Mark A. R. 1997a. "The Problem of Replacement and the Logic of Drug Law Enforcement." *Drug Policy Analysis Bulletin* no. 3.

Kleiman, Mark A. R. 1997b. "Reducing the Prevalence of Cocaine and Heroin Dealing among Adolescents." *Valparaiso University Law Review* 31 (2): 551–564.

Kleiman, Mark A. R. 1997c. "Coerced Abstinence: A Neo-Paternalistic Drug Policy Initiative." In *The New Paternalism*, ed. Lawrence A. Mead, 182–219. Washington, DC: Brookings Institution.

Kleiman, Mark A. R. 1999a. "Getting Deterrence Right: Applying Tipping Models and Behavioral Economics to the Problems of Crime Control." In *Perspectives on Crime and Justice: 1998–1999*. Washington, DC: National Institute of Justice.

Kleiman, Mark A. R. 1999b. "Community Corrections as the Front Line in Crime Control." *UCLA Law Review* 46 (6).

Kleiman, Mark A. R. 2001. "Controlling Drug Use and Crime among Drug-Involved Offenders: Testing, Sanctions, and Treatment." In *Drug Addiction and Drug Policy*, eds. Philip B. Heymann and William N. Brownsberger. Cambridge, MA: Harvard University Press.

Kleiman, Mark A. R. 2009a. *When Brute Force Fails: How to Have Less Crime and Less Punishment*. Princeton, NJ: Princeton University Press.

Kleiman, Mark A. R. 2009b. "Jail Break." *Washington Monthly* (July–August): 56–60.

Kleiman, Mark A. R., and Angela Hawken. 2008a. "Fixing the Parole System" *Issues in Science and Technology* (Summer): 45–52.

Kleiman, Mark A. R., and Angela Hawken. 2008b. "Research Brief: Evaluation of HOPE Probation " Washington, DC: Pew Center on the States. Available at http://www.pewcenteronthestates.org/uploadedFiles/HOPE_Research_Brief.pdf

Kleiman, Mark A.R., and Beau Kilmer. 2009. "The Dynamics of Deterrence." *Proceedings of the National Academy of Sciences* 106 (34): 14230–14235, August 25.

Kleiman, Mark A. R., Christopher E. Putala, Rebecca M. Young, and David P. Cavanagh. 1988. "Heroin Crackdowns in Two Massachusetts Cities." Report prepared for the Office of the District Attorney for the Eastern District, Commonwealth of Massachusetts, Hon. Kevin M. Burke, under National Institute of Justice Grant No. 85-JJ-CX-0027.

Kushner, Jeffrey. 1993. "Salient and Consistent Sanctions: Oregon's Key to Reducing Drug Use." *Treatment Improvement Exchange Communiqué*. Washington, DC: Center for Substance Abuse Treatment, Spring.

Lipton, D. S. 1994. "The Correctional Opportunity: Pathways to Drug Treatment for Offenders." *Journal of Drug Issues* 24 (1–2): 331–348.

Liu, Jin-Long, Jin-Tan Liu, James K. Hammitt, and Shin-Yi Chou. 1999. "The Price Elasticity of Opium in Taiwan, 1914–1942." *Journal of Health Economics* 18: 795–810.

Long, Larry. 2009. Address given at the Cosmos Club, Washington DC, June 30th, 2009, upon receipt of the John P. McGovern Award for Drug Abuse Prevention.

MacCoun, Robert, and Peter Reuter. 2001. *Drug War Heresies: Learning from Other Vices, Times and Places.* Cambridge: Cambridge University Press.

Macdonald, S., P. Erickson, S. Wells, A. Hathaway, and B. Pakula. 2008. "Predicting Violence among Cocaine, Cannabis, and Alcohol Treatment Clients." *Addictive Behaviors* 33 (1): 201–205.

MacIntyre, Alasdair. 1981. *After Virtue.* Notre Dame, IN: University of Notre Dame Press.

Manning, Willard G., Emmet B. Keeler, Joseph P. Newhouse, Elizabeth M. Sloss, and Jeffrey M. Wasserman. 1989. "The Taxes of Sin: Do Smokers and Drinkers Pay Their Way?" *Journal of the American Medical Association* 261: 1604–1609.

Manski, Charles F., and John Pepper. 2001. *What We Don't Know Keeps Hurting Us.* Washington, DC: National Academies Press.

Marijuana Treatment Project Research Group. 2004. "Brief Treatments for Cannabis Dependence: Findings from a Randomized Multisite Trial." *Journal of Consulting and Clinical Psychology* 72: 455–466.

Martin, W. R. 1983. "Pharmacology of Opioids." *Pharmacology Review* 35: 283–323.

McBride, Duane C., and Clyde B. McCoy. 1982. "Crime and Drugs: The Issues and the Literature." *Journal of Drug Issues* 12: 137–152.

Mill, John Stuart. [1859]1989. *On Liberty.* Reprint, Cambridge: Cambridge University Press.

Miron, Jeffrey A. 2003. "The Effect of Drug Prohibition on Drug Prices: Evidence from the Markets for Cocaine and Heroin." *The Review of Economics and Statistics* 85 (3): 522–530.

Model, Karyn. 1991. "The Effect of Marijuana Decriminalization on Hospital Emergency Room Drug Episodes: 1975–1987." Department of Economics, Harvard University. Unpublished paper.

Model, Karyn. 1994. Personal communication with Mark Kleiman.

Moore, Mark H. 1973. "Policies to Achieve Discrimination on the Effective Price of Heroin." *American Economic Review* 63: 270–277.

Moore, Mark H. 1979. "Limiting Supplies of Drugs to Illicit Markets." *Journal of Drug Issues* 9: 291–308.

Moore, Mark H. 1990. *An Analytic View of Drug Control Policies.* Program on Criminal Justice Policy and Management, John F. Kennedy School of Government, working paper no. 90–01–19. Cambridge, MA: Harvard University.

Moore, Mark H. 1991. "Drugs, the Criminal Law, and the Administration of Justice." *The Milbank Quarterly* 69 (4): 529–560.

Mumola, Christopher J., and Jennifer C. Karberg. 2006. *Drug Use and Dependence, State and Federal Prisoners, 2004.* U.S. Bureau of Justice Statistics, NCJ 215530. Available at http://www.ojp.usdoj.gov/bjs/pub/pdf/dudsfp04.pdf. Accessed on July 27, 2009.

Murray, Regan L, Stephen T Chermack, Maureen A Walton, Jamie Winters, Brenda M. Booth, Frederic C. Blow. 2008. "Psychological Aggression, Physical Aggression, and Injury in Nonpartner Relationships Among Men and

Women in Treatment for Substance-Use Disorders." *Journal of Studies on Alcohol and Drugs* 69 (6): 896–905.

Nadelman, Ethan A. 1988. "The Case for Legalization." *The Public Interest* 92 (Summer): 3–31.

National Institute of Justice. 2000. *1999 Annual Report on Drug Use among Adult and Juvenile Arrestees*. Washington, DC: U.S. Department of Justice.

Nisbet, C., and F. Vakil. 1972. "Some Estimates of Price and Expenditure Elasticities of Demand for Marijuana among UCLA Students." *Review of Economics and Statistics* 54: 473–475.

Nurco, David N., John C. Ball, John W. Shaffer, and Thomas F. Hanlon. 1985. "The Criminality of Narcotics Addicts." *Journal of Nervous and Mental Disease* 173: 94–102.

Nurco, David N., Thomas E. Hanlon, Timothy W. Kinlock, and Karen R. Duszynski. 1988. "Differential Criminal Patterns of Narcotic Addicts over an Addiction Career." *Criminology* 26: 407–423.

Nurco, David N., Timothy Kinlock, and Mitchell B. Balter. 1993. "The Severity of Preaddiction Criminal Behavior among Urban, Male Narcotic Addicts and Two Nonaddicted Control Groups." *Journal of Research in Crime and Delinquency* 30 (3): 293–316.

Office of Justice Programs, U.S. Department of Justice. 1998. "Looking at a Decade of Drug Courts." Prepared by the Drug Court Clearinghouse and Technical Assistance Project. Washington, DC: American University.

Office of National Drug Control Policy (ONDCP). 2009. *National Drug Control Strategy: Data Supplement 2009*. Washington, DC: The White House.

Office of National Drug Control Policy (ONDCP). 1994. *National Drug Control Strategy*. Washington, DC: The White House.

Office of National Drug Control Policy (ONDCP). 2001. *What America's Users Spend on Illegal Drugs*. Washington, DC: The White House.

Pacula, Rosalie L. 1998. "Does Increasing the Beer Tax Reduce Marijuana Consumption?" *Journal of Health Economics* 17 (5): 557–586.

Pacula, R. L., and F. J. Chaloupka. 2001. "The Effects of Macro-level Interventions on Addictive Behavior." *Journal of Substance Use and Misuse* 36(13): 1901–1922.

Pacula, L. R. 2001. "Marijuana and Youth." In *Risky Behavior Among Youths: An Economic Analysis*, ed. J. Gruber. National Bureau of Economic Research. Chicago: University of Chicago Press.

Pastrana, Andres, Andres Solimano, Caroline Moser, et al. 2000. *Colombia: Essays on Conflict, Peace, and Development*, ed. Andres Solimano. Washington DC: World Bank.

Piehl, Anne Morrison, and John J. DiIulio, Jr. 1995. "'Does Prison Pay?' Revisited." *Brookings Review* 13 (Winter): 20–25.

Pindyck, Robert S. 1979. *The Structure of World Energy Demand*. Cambridge, MA: MIT Press.

Post, Robert M. 1975. "Cocaine Psychoses: A Continuum Model." *American Journal of Psychiatry* 132: 225–231.

Prendergast, M., D. M. Anglin, and J. Wellisch. 1995. "Treatment for Drug-abusing Offenders under Community Supervision." *Federal Probation* 59: 66–75.

Prendergast, M. L., D. Podus, E. Chang, and D. Urada. 2002. "The Effectiveness of Drug Abuse Treatment: A Meta-Analysis of Comparison Group Studies." *Drug and Alcohol Dependence* 67: 53–73.

Rasmussen, D. W., and B. L. Benson. 1994. *The Economic Anatomy of a Drug War*. Lanham, MD: Rowman and Littlefield.

Rawson, Richard A. 1999. "Treatment for Stimulant Use Disorders." Treatment Improvement Protocol (TIP) Series 33, Substance Abuse and Mental Health Services Administration, Rockville, MD, DHHS Publication no. (SMA) 99–3296.

Reinventing Probation Council. 1999. *Broken Windows Probation: The Next Step in Fighting Crime*. New York: The Manhattan Institute.

Reiss, Albert J., Jr., and Jeffrey A. Roth, eds. 1993. *Understanding and Preventing Violence*. Washington, DC: National Academy Press.

Reuter, Peter, and Mark A. R. Kleiman. 1986. "Risks and Prices." In *Crime and Justice: A Review of Research*, vol. 7, eds. Michael Tonry and Norval Morris, 289–340. Chicago: University of Chicago Press.

Reuter, Peter, Robert MacCoun, and Patrick Murphy. 1990. *Money from Crime: A Study of the Economics of Drug Dealing*. Santa Monica, CA: RAND.

Rhodes, William, Paul Scheiman, and Kenneth Carlson. 1993. *What America's Users Spend on Illegal Drugs, 1988–1991*. Washington, DC: Office of National Drug Control Policy.

Riley, Kevin Jack. 1997. *Crack, Powder Cocaine, and Heroin: Drug Purchase and Use Patterns in Six U.S. Cities*. Washington, DC: National Institute of Justice.

Rocheleau, Ann Marie. 1994. Personal communication with David Boyum, March 7.

Rocheleau, Ann Marie, and Mark A. R. Kleiman. 1993. *Measuring Heroin Availability: A Demonstration*. Washington, DC: Office of National Drug Control Policy.

Roman, John K., Aaron Chalfin, Jay Reid, and Shannon Reid. 2008. *Impact and Cost-Benefit Analysis of the Anchorage Wellness Court*. Rockville, MD: NCJRS Photocopy Services.

Roth, Jeffrey A. 1994. *Psychoactive Substances and Violence*. National Institute of Justice, Research in Brief. Washington, DC: U.S. Department of Justice, February.

Rydell, C. Peter, and Susan M. Sohler Everingham. 1994. *Controlling Cocaine: Supply versus Demand Programs*. Santa Monica, CA: RAND.

Saffer, Henry, and Frank Chaloupka. 1995. "The Demand for Illicit Drugs." NBER Working Paper No. 5238. Cambridge, MA: National Bureau of Economic Research.

Saffer, Henry, and Frank Chaloupka. 1999a. "Demographic Differentials in the Demand for Alcohol and Illicit Drugs." In *The Economic Analysis of Substance Use and Abuse: An Integration of Econometric and Behavioral Economic Research*, eds. F. J. Chaloupka, M. Grossman, W. K. Bickel, and H. Saffer, 187–211. Chicago: University of Chicago Press for the National Bureau of Economic Research.

Saffer, Henry, and Frank Chaloupka. 1999b. "The Demand for Illicit Drugs." *Economic Inquiry* 37 (3): 401–411.

Sarrica, Fabrizio. 2008. "Drug Prices and Systemic Violence: An Empirical Study." *European Journal on Criminal Policy and Research* 14: 391–415.

Schelling, T. C. 1971. "What Is the Business of Organized Crime?" *Journal of Public Law* 20 (1): 71–84.

Serious Organized Crime Agency (SOCA). 2009. *Serious Organized Crime Agency Annual Plan, 2009/10*. The Home Office. Available at http://www.soca.gov.

uk/assessPublications/downloads/SOCA_Annual_Plan_2009_10.pdf.
Accessed on July 30, 2009.

Sharps, Phyllis, Jacquelyn C. Campbell, Doris Campbell, Faye Gary, and Daniel Webster. 2003. "Risky Mix: Drinking, Drug Use, and Homicide." *NIJ* (250). Available at http://www.ncjrs.gov/pdffiles1/jr000250d.pdf. Accessed on July 28, 2009.

Sheley, Joseph F., and James D. Wright. 1993. *Gun Acquisition and Possession in Selected Juvenile Samples*. National Institute of Justice, Office of Juvenile Justice and Delinquency Prevention, Research in Brief. Washington, DC: U.S. Department of Justice, December.

Silverman, Lester P., and Nancy L. Spruill. 1977. "Urban Crime and the Price of Heroin " *Journal of Urban Economics* 4: 80–103.

Spunt, Barry J., Henry Brownstein, Paul Goldstein, Michael Fendrich, and Hillary James Liberty. 1995. "Drug Use by Homicide Offenders." *Journal of Psychoactive Drugs* 27 (2): 125–134.

Stephens, Richard C., and Duane C. McBride. 1976. "Becoming a Street Addict." *Human Organization* 35: 87–93.

Stretesky, Paul B. 2009. "National Case-Control Study of Homicide Offending and Methamphetamine Use." *Journal of Interpersonal Violence* 24 (6): 911–924.

Sviridoff, M., Susan Sadd, Richard Curtis, Randolph M. Grinc, Michael E. Smith. 1992. *The Neighborhood Effects of Street-Level Drug Enforcement: Tactical Narcotics Teams in New York*. New York: Vera Institute of Justice.

Thies, C. F., and C. A. Register, Decriminalization of Marijuana and the Demand for Alcohol, Marijuana and Cocaine." *The Social Science Journal* 30: 385–399.

Tragler, Gernot, Jonathan P. Caulkins, and Gustav Feichtinger. 2001. "Optimal Dynamic Allocation of Treatment and Enforcement in Illicit Drug Control." *Operations Research* 49 (3): 352–362.

Trebach, Arnold S., and James A. Inciardi. 1993. *Legalize It? Debating American Drug Policy*. Washington, DC: American University Press.

Turner, David. 1991. "Pragmatic Incoherence: The Changing Face of British Drug Policy." In *Searching for Alternatives: Drug-Control Policy in the United States*, eds. Melvyn B. Krauss and Edward P. Lazear, 175–190. Stanford, CA: Hoover Institution Press.

Urada, D., Andrea Hawken, Bradley Conner, Elizabeth Evans, et al. 2008. *Evaluation of Proposition 36: The Substance Abuse and Crime Prevention Act of 2000*. 2008 Report. Los Angeles, CA: UCLA.

U.S. Department of Justice. 1992. *Drugs, Crime, and the Justice System*. Bureau of Justice Statistics. Washington, DC: U.S. Department of Justice.

U.S. Department of Justice. 1999. *Substance Abuse and Treatment, State and Federal Prisoners*. Bureau of Justice Statistics. NCJ-172871. Washington, DC: U.S. Department of Justice, January.

U.S. Department of Justice. 2000. *Correctional Populations in the United States, 1997*. Bureau of Justice Statistics. NCJ-177613. Washington, DC: U.S. Department of Justice.

U.S. Department of Justice. 2008. *Crime in the United States, 2007*. Available at http://www.fbi.gov/ucr/07cius.htm. Accessed July 27, 2009.

Van Ours, Jan C. 1995. "The Price Elasticity of Hard Drugs: The Case of Opium in the Dutch East Indies, 1923–1938." *Journal of Political Economy* 103 (2): 261–279.

Wasserman, Robert. 1993. Personal communication with the authors. December 14.

Watters, John K., Craig Reinarman, and Jeffrey Fagan. 1985. "Causality, Context, and Contingency: Relationship Between Drug Abuse and Delinquency." *Contemporary Drug Problems* 12 (3): 351–373.

Weisman, J. C., S. W. Marr, and P. L. Katsampes. 1976. "Addiction and Criminal Behavior: A Continuing Examination of Criminal Addicts." *Journal of Drug Issues* 6: 153–165.

Weiss, Roger D., and Steven M. Mirin. 1987. *Cocaine: The Human Danger, the Social Costs, the Treatment Alternatives*. New York: Ballantine Books.

West, Steven L. and Keri K. O'Neal. 2004. "Project D.A.R.E. Outcome Effectiveness Revisited." *American Journal of Public Health* 94: 1027–1029.

Wilkinson, Tracy. 2008. "Death Toll in Mexico's Drug War Surges." *Los Angeles Times*, December 9.

Williams, Jenny, Rosalie Liccardo Pacula, Frank J. Chaloupka, and Henry Wechsler. 2004. "Alcohol and Marijuana Use among College Students: Economic Complements or Substitutes?" *Health Economics* 13: 825–843.

Wilson, James Q. 1985. *Thinking About Crime*, rev. ed. New York: Vintage Books.

Wilson, James Q., and Richard J. Herrnstein. 1985. *Crime and Human Nature*. New York: Touchstone.

Wilson, James Q., and George Kelling. 1982. "Broken Windows: The Police and Neighborhood Safety," *The Atlantic Monthly* 249 (3): 29–38.

Notes

1. The distinction is an operational one, not a moral one, since a transactional crime need not be either victimless or morally innocuous: bribery and the "midnight dumping" of toxic waste are both transactional crimes.

Chapter 14

General Deterrence: A Review of Recent Evidence

Robert Apel, Daniel S. Nagin

The criminal justice system (CJS) dispenses justice by apprehending, prosecuting, and punishing individuals who break the law. These activities may also prevent crime by three distinct mechanisms—incapacitation, specific deterrence, and general deterrence. Convicted offenders are often punished with imprisonment. Incapacitation refers to the crimes averted by their physical isolation during the period of their incarceration. Specific deterrence and general deterrence involve possible behavioral responses. Specific deterrence refers to the reduction in reoffending that is presumed to follow from the *experience* of actually being punished. We note, however, that there are many sound reasons for suspecting that the experience of punishment might instead increase reoffending. The *threat* of punishment might also discourage potential and actual criminals in the general public from committing crime. This effect is known as general deterrence and is the subject of this chapter. For a review of the evidence on the effect of the experience of punishment on reoffending see Nagin, Cullen, and Jonson (2009), and for a review of the evidence on incapacitation effects see Spelman (1994) or Zimring and Hawkins (1995).

Going back at least to the Enlightenment-era legal philosophers Bentham and Beccaria, scholars have speculated on the general deterrent effect of official sanctions, but sustained efforts to empirically verify their effects did not begin until the 1960s. This review is not intended to be encyclopedic. Rather, its objective is to highlight key findings and conclusions. Because evidence through the late 1990s has been well summarized elsewhere (Zimring and Hawkins 1973; Andenaes 1974; Gibbs 1975; Blumstein, Cohen, and Nagin 1978; Cook 1980; Nagin 1998), our focus is primarily on research in the past decade, though important findings from the older literature will also be discussed.

KEY CONCEPTS OF DETERRENCE

Deterrence is a theory of choice in which would-be offenders balance the benefits and costs of crime. Benefits may be pecuniary in the case of property crime but may also involve intangibles such as defending one's honor, expressing outrage, demonstrating dominance, cementing a reputation, or seeking a thrill. The potential costs of crime are comparably varied. Crime can entail personal risk if the victim resists (Cook 1986). It may also invoke pangs of conscience or shame (Braithwaite 1989). In this review we are mainly concerned with offender responses to the costs that attend the imposition of official sanctions for crime, such as arrest, imprisonment, execution, fines, and other restrictions on freedom and liberty (e.g., mandated drug testing, electronic monitoring).

An example of a deterrence-based sanction policy is the "three strikes and you're out" law, which mandates a lengthy minimum sentence upon the third conviction for a "strike" offense (e.g., 25 years in California). Another example is the widespread requirement for a mandatory sentence enhancement if a firearm is used in the commission of another felony such as robbery or rape. More generally, any sanction policy that increases sentence length or mandates the imposition of a more onerous sanction (e.g., imprisonment rather than probation) is an example of a policy that may have a deterrence-based rationale.

The theory of deterrence is predicated on the idea that if state-imposed sanction costs are sufficiently severe, criminal activity will be discouraged, at least for some. Thus, one of the key concepts of deterrence is the severity of punishment. Our review of severity effects focuses on research findings concerning the penultimate and ultimate sanctions—imprisonment and capital punishment, respectively.

Severity alone, however, cannot deter. There must also be some possibility that the sanction will be incurred if the crime is committed. For that to happen, the offender must be apprehended, usually by the police. He must next be charged and successfully prosecuted, and finally sentenced by the judiciary. None of these successive stages in processing through the criminal justice system is certain. Thus, another key concept in deterrence theory is the certainty of punishment. In this regard the most important set of actors are the police—absent detection and apprehension, there is no possibility of conviction or punishment. For this reason we discuss separately what is known about the deterrent effect of police.

One of the key conclusions that emerged from the 1960s- and 1970s-era deterrence literature was that the certainty of punishment was a more powerful deterrent than the severity of punishment. The analyses of this era generally used cross-sectional data on states and involved testing the effects on the statewide crime rate of the certainty and severity of punishment, along with other demographic and socioeconomic control variables. (The statistical method is called regression analysis.) The certainty of punishment was measured by the ratio of prison admissions to the number of reported crimes, while the severity of punishment was measured by median time served of recent prison releases. The basis for the "certainty not severity" deterrence conclusion was that punishment certainty was consistently found to have a negative and significant association with the crime rate, whereas punishment severity generally had no significant association.

This conclusion at the time was probably based on faulty statistical inference. Two primary criticisms were leveled. The first was that the negative association between the certainty measure and crime rate was an artifact of the number of crimes appearing in the denominator of the certainty measure and the numerator of the crime rate. It can be mathematically demonstrated that errors in the measurement of number of crimes, of which there are many, will force a negative, deterrent-like association between the crime rate and certainty even if, in fact, the certainty of punishment had no deterrent effect on crime. The second involved the use of theoretically indefensible statistical methods for parsing out the cause-effect relationship between sanction levels and the crime rate. After all, sanctions may deter crime, but crime may also affect sanction levels (Nagin 1978). For example, perhaps overcrowded prisons might reduce the chances of newly caught offenders going to prison. However, subsequent findings from the so-called perceptual deterrence literature and economic studies of the effects of contact with the criminal justice system on access to legal labor markets provide a far firmer empirical and theoretical basis for the "certainty" contention. The perceptual deterrence literature examines the relationships of perceived sanction risks to either self-reported offending or intentions to do so, and was spawned by researchers interested in probing the perceptual underpinnings of the deterrence process. We review the contributions of research on perceptual deterrence as well.

THE DETERRENT EFFECT OF IMPRISONMENT

Imprisonment and Crime

There have been two distinct waves of studies of the deterrent effect of imprisonment. As already noted, studies in the 1960s and 1970s examined the relationship of the crime rate to the certainty of punishment, measured by the ratio of prison admissions to reported crimes, and the severity of punishment as measured by median time served. These studies suffered from a number of serious statistical flaws that are detailed in Blumstein, Cohen, and Nagin (1978). In response to these deficiencies, a second generation of studies emerged in the 1990s. Unlike the first-generation studies, which primarily involved cross-sectional analyses of states, second-generation studies had a longitudinal component in which data were analyzed not only across states but also over time. Another important difference is that the second-generation studies did not attempt to estimate certainty and severity effects separately. Instead they examined the relationship between the crime rate and rate of imprisonment as measured by prisoners per capita.

A review by Donohue (2007) identifies six such studies. All find statistically significant negative associations between imprisonment rates and crimes rates, implying a crime-prevention effect of imprisonment. However, the magnitude of the estimate varied widely—from nil in a study that allowed for the possibility of diminishing returns (Liedka et al. 2006), to an elasticity of –0.4 (Spelman 2000). (By an elasticity of –0.4, we mean that 10 percent growth in the imprisonment rate reduced the crime rate by 4 percent.) It is important to note that these studies are actually measuring a combination of deterrent and incapacitation effects. Thus, it is impossible to decipher the degree to which crime prevention is occurring because of a behavioral response by the population at large or because of the physical isolation of crime-prone people.

Donohue (2007) goes on to show that the small elasticity estimates imply that the current imprisonment rate is too large, while the high-end estimates imply the rate is too small. He lists a variety of technical shortcomings of these studies that, in our view, make it impossible to distinguish among the widely varying effect size estimates. The most important is the degree to which the studies were successful in separating cause from effect. While imprisonment prevents crime through a combination of deterrence and incapacitation, crime also generates the prison population. This is an example of what is called the "simultaneity problem," whereby we want to ascertain the effect of one variable (the imprisonment rate) on another variable (the crime rate) in a circumstance where we know or suspect that reverse causation is also present, namely that the crime rate simultaneously affects the imprisonment rate. Thus, statistical isolation of the crime prevention effect requires properly accounting for the effect of crime on imprisonment. The Levitt (1996) study is arguably the most successful in this regard. It uses court-ordered prison releases as an instrument for untangling the cause-and-effect relationship. However, even the Levitt analysis suffers from many of the technical limitations detailed by Donohue.

More fundamentally, this literature suffers from more than just technical shortcomings that future research might strive to correct. It also suffers from important conceptual flaws that limit its usefulness in devising crime-control policy. Prison population is not a policy variable; rather, it is an outcome of sanction policies dictating who goes to prison and for how long, namely the certainty and severity of punishment. In all incentive-based theories of criminal behavior, the deterrence response to sanction threats is posed in terms of the certainty and severity of punishment, not in terms of the imprisonment rate. Therefore, to predict how changes in certainty and severity might affect the crime rate requires knowledge of the relationship of the crime rate to certainty and severity as separate entities, which is not provided by the literature that analyzes the relationship of the crime rate to the imprisonment rate. The studies are also conducted at too global a level. There are good reasons for predicting differences in the crime reduction effects of different types of sanctions (e.g., mandatory minimums for repeat offenders versus prison diversion programs for first-time offenders). Obvious sources of heterogeneity in offender response include factors such as prior contact with the criminal justice system, demographic characteristics, and the mechanism by which sanction threats are communicated to their intended audience.

Three studies nicely illustrate heterogeneity in the deterrence response to the threat of imprisonment: the Weisburd, Einat, and Kowalski (2008) study on the use of imprisonment to enforce fine payment finds a substantial deterrent effect; the Helland and Tabarrok (2007) analysis of the deterrent effect of California's third strike provision finds only a modest deterrent effect; and the Lee and McCrary (2009) examination of the heightened threat of imprisonment that attends coming under the jurisdiction of the adult courts at the age of majority finds no deterrent effect.

Weisburd, Einat, and Kowalski (2008) report on a randomized field trial of alternative strategies for incentivizing the payment of court-ordered fines. The most salient finding involves the "miracle of the cells," namely, that the imminent threat of incarceration is a powerful incentive for paying delinquent fines. The miracle of the cells, we believe, provides a valuable vantage point for considering the oft-repeated conclusion from the deterrence literature that the certainty rather the severity of punishment is the more powerful deterrent. Consistent with the "certainty principle," the common feature of treatment conditions involving incarceration was a high certainty of imprisonment for failure to pay the fine. However, the fact that Weisburd and colleagues label the response the "miracle of the cells" and not the "miracle of certainty" is telling. Their choice of label is a reminder that certainty must result in a distasteful consequence, namely incarceration in this experiment, in order for it to be a deterrent. The consequences need not be draconian, just sufficiently costly to deter proscribed behavior.

Helland and Tabarrok (2007) examine whether California's "Three Strikes and You're Out" law deters offending among individuals previously convicted of strike-eligible offenses. The future offending of individuals convicted of two previous "strike" offenses was compared with that of individuals who had been convicted of only one "strike" offense but who, in addition, had been tried for a second "strike" offense but were ultimately convicted of a "non-strike" offense. The study demonstrates that these two groups of individuals were comparable on many characteristics such as age, race, and time in prison. Even so, it finds that arrest rates were about 20 percent lower for the group with convictions for two "strike" offenses. The authors attribute this reduction to the greatly enhanced sentence that would have accompanied conviction for a third "strike" offense.

For most crimes, the certainty and severity of punishment increases discontinuously upon reaching the age of majority, when jurisdiction for criminal wrongdoing shifts from the juvenile to the adult court. In an extraordinarily careful analysis of individual-level crime histories from Florida, Lee and McCrary (2009) attempt to identify a discontinuous decline in the hazard of offending at age 18, the age of majority in Florida. Their point estimate of the discontinuous change is negative as predicted, but minute in magnitude and not even remotely close to achieving statistical significance.

In combination, these three studies nicely illustrate that the deterrent effect of the threat of punishment is context-specific and that debates about whether deterrence works or not are ill posed. Instead, the discussion should be in terms of whether the specific sanction deters or not and if it does, whether the benefits of crime reduction are sufficient to justify the costs of imposing the sanction. To illustrate, while Helland and Tabarrok (2007) conclude that the third-strike effect in California is a deterrent, they also conclude, based on a cost-benefit analysis, that the crime-saving benefits are likely far smaller than the increased costs of incarceration. The Helland and Taborrok study is an exemplar of the approach that should be taken in evaluating different sanctioning regimes.

The Deterrent Effect of Capital Punishment

Like research on the deterrent effect of imprisonment, research on the deterrent effect of capital punishment has come in waves. The latest wave of research on capital punishment and deterrence is based on the data that have become available following the reintroduction of the death penalty in different states beginning in 1976, after a four-year moratorium on death sentences and executions resulting from the U.S. Supreme Court decision in *Furman v. Georgia* (408 U.S. 238 [1972]). Not all states reintroduced capital punishment at the same time when the decision in *Gregg v. Georgia* (428 U.S. 153 [1976]) lifted the Constitutional barrier; they acted at different times to restore capital punishment and used it at widely varying rates. The resulting natural variation in execution rates across states and over time forms the empirical basis for the new wave of studies.

This new body of work has failed to produce a consensus on whether deterrent effects are present. Dezhbakhsh, Rubin, and Shepherd (2003), Dezhbakhsh and Shepherd (2006), and Mocan and Gittings (2003) find strong deterrent effects from the death penalty. Yet their claims have been challenged by Donohue and Wolfers (2005), Berk (2005), Fagan (2006), and Cohen-Cole and colleagues (2009), who argue that the evidence that has been adduced in favor of strong deterrent effects is fragile, in that they may be reversed by small changes in model specification. Other studies have argued that more substantive differences in the formulation of the deterrence mechanism lead to different results. Katz, Levitt, and Shustorovich (2003), focusing on the fact that executions are relatively infrequent, argue that prison mortality rates represent a deterrent to serious crime, whereas capital punishment does not. Other studies find that deterrent effects are heterogeneous, so that important properties are masked by imposing a single measure on the statistical analysis. Shepherd (2005) draws mixed conclusions, suggesting that capital punishment will raise murder rates when the number of executions is small, producing what she calls a "brutalization effect." However, the brutalization effect is overcome by the deterrent effect when the number of executions exceeds some empirically identified threshold. Hjalmarsson (2008a) explores whether executions have short-run local deterrent effects by studying city-level, high-frequency (daily) data. Focusing on Texas, she finds little evidence of deterrence.

THE DETERRENT EFFECT OF POLICE

The police may prevent crime through many possible mechanisms. Apprehension of active offenders is a necessary first step for their conviction and punishment. If the sanction involves imprisonment, crime may be prevented by the incapacitation of the apprehended offender. The apprehension of active offenders may also deter would-be criminals by increasing their perception of the risk of apprehension and thereby the certainty of punishment. Many police tactics such as rapid response to calls for service at crime scenes or post-crime investigation are intended not only to capture the offender but to deter others by projecting a tangible threat of apprehension. Police may, however, deter without actually apprehending criminals because their very presence projects a threat of apprehension if a crime were to be committed. Indeed, some of the most compelling evidence of deterrence involve instances where there is complete or near complete collapse of police presence. In September 1944, German soldiers occupying Denmark arrested the entire Danish police force. According to an account by Andeneas (1974), crime rates rose immediately but not uniformly. The frequency of street crimes like robbery, whose control depends heavily upon visible police presence, rose sharply. By contrast, crimes like fraud were less affected. See Sherman and Eck (2002) for other examples of crime increases following a collapse of police presence.

The Andenaes anecdote illustrates two important points. First, sanction threats (or the absence thereof) may not uniformly affect all types of crime and more generally all types of people. Second, it draws attention to the difference between absolute and marginal deterrence. Absolute deterrence refers to the difference in the crime rate between the status quo level of sanction threat and a complete (or near) absence of sanction threat. The Andenaes anecdote is a compelling demonstration that the absolute deterrent effect is large. However, from a policy perspective, the important question is whether, on the margin, crime deterrence can be affected by incrementally manipulating sanction threats.

Research on the marginal deterrent effect of police has evolved in two distinct literatures. One has focused on the deterrent effect of the aggregate police presence measured, for example, by the relationship between police per capita and crime rates. The other has focused on the crime prevention effectiveness of different strategies for deploying police. We review these two literatures separately.

Aggregate Police Presence and Crime

Studies of police hiring and crime rates have been plagued by a number of impediments to causal inference. Among these are cross-jurisdictional differences in the recording of crime, feedback effects from crime rates to police hiring, the confounding of deterrence with incapacitation, and aggregation of police manpower effects across heterogeneous units, among others (see Nagin 1978, 1998). Yet the challenge that has received the most attention in empirical applications is the *simultaneity problem*, or the feedback from crime rates to police hiring. Simultaneity describes a situation in which two variables mutually influence one another in such a way that it is impossible, in the absence of exogenous variation or restrictive assumptions, to untangle the unique influence of one variable on the other.

The two studies of police manpower by Marvell and Moody (1996) and Levitt (1997) are notable for their different identification strategies as well as for the consistency of their findings. The Marvell and Moody (1996) study is based on an analysis of two panel data sets, one composed of 49 states for the years 1968–1993 and the other of 56 large cities for the years 1971–1992. To untangle the simultaneous causation problem, they regress the current crime rate on lags of the crime rate as well as lags of police manpower. If the lagged police measures are jointly significant, they are said to "Granger cause" crime. The strongest evidence for an impact of police hiring on total crime rates comes from the city-level analysis, with an estimated elasticity of –0.3, meaning that 10 percent growth in police manpower produces a 3-percent decline in the crime rate the following year. In the spirit of Marvell and Moody's multiple time series analysis, Corman and Mocan (2000) conduct tests of Granger causality using a single, high-frequency (monthly) time series of crime in New York City (January 1970 to December 1996). They find that the number of police officers is negatively correlated with some crimes (robbery, burglary) but not with others. In addition, the number of felony arrests is a robust predictor of several kinds of crime (murder, robbery, burglary, vehicle theft). They conclude that policymakers can deter serious crimes by adding more police officers, but also by allocating existing police resources to aggressive felony enforcement (see also Corman and Mocan 2005).

Levitt (1997) performs an instrumental variables (IV) analysis from a panel of 59 large cities for the years 1970–1992. Reasoning that political incumbents have incentives to devote resources to increasing the size of the police force in anticipation of upcoming elections, he uses election cycles to help untangle the cause-effect relationship between crime rates and police manpower. Levitt's model produces elasticities of about –1.0 for the violent crime rate and –0.3 for the property crime rate (but see McCrary 2002 for correction of a technical problem in Levitt's analysis, as well as a reply and new analysis by Levitt 2002). Following Levitt's use of the electoral cycle as an instrument for the number of sworn police officers, other studies have employed the number of firefighters and civil service workers (Levitt 2002), as well as federal subsidies disbursed through the Office of Community Oriented Policing Services for the hiring of new police officers (Evans and Owens 2007). These studies reach conclusions that are very similar to Levitt's study; for example, the elasticities estimated by Evans and Owens (2007) are –0.99 for violent crime and –0.26 for property crime.

In recent years, a number of more targeted tests of the police-crime relationship have appeared. These studies investigate the impact on the crime rate of reductions in police presence and productivity as a result of massive budget cuts or lawsuits following racial profiling scandals. Such studies have examined the Cincinnati Police Department (Shi 2007), the New Jersey State Police (Heaton forthcoming), and the Oregon State Police (DeAngelo and Hansen 2008). Each of these studies concludes that increases (decreases) in police presence and activity substantially decrease (increase) crime. By way of example, Shi (2007) studies the fallout from an incident in Cincinnati in which a white police officer shot and killed an unarmed African American suspect. The incident was followed by three days of rioting, heavy media attention, the filing of a class action lawsuit, a federal civil rights investigation, and the indictment of the officer in question. These events created an unofficial incentive for officers from the Cincinnati Police Department to curtail their use of arrest for misdemeanor crimes, especially in communities with higher proportional representation of African Americans out of concern for allegations of racial profiling. Shi demonstrates measurable declines in police productivity in the aftermath of the riot and also documents a substantial increase in criminal activity. The estimated elasticities of crime to policing based on her approach were –0.5 for violent crime and –0.3 for property crime.

The ongoing threat of terrorism has also provided a number of unique opportunities to study the impact of police resource allocation in cities around the world, including the District of Columbia (Klick and Tabarrok 2005), Buenos Aires (Di Tella and Schargrodsky 2004), Stockholm (Poutvaara and Priks 2006), and London (Draca, Machin, and Witt 2008). The Klick and Tabarrok (2005) study examines the effect on crime of the color-coded alert system devised by the U.S. Department of Homeland Security (in the aftermath of the September 11, 2001, terrorist attack) to denote the terrorism threat level. Its purpose was to signal federal, state, and local law enforcement agencies to occasions when it might be prudent to divert resources to sensitive locations. Klick and Tabarrok (2005) use daily police reports of crime (collected by the District's Metropolitan Police Department) for the period March 2002 to July 2003, during which time the terrorism alert level rose from "elevated" (yellow) to "high" (orange) and back down to "elevated" on four occasions. During high alerts, anecdotal evidence suggested that police presence increased by 50 percent. Their estimate of the elasticity of total crime to changes in police presence as the alert level rose and fell was –0.3.

To summarize, aggregate studies of police presence conducted since the mid-1990s consistently find that putting more police officers on the street—either by hiring new officers or by allocating existing officers in ways that put them on the street in larger numbers or for longer periods of time—has a substantial deterrent effect on serious crime. There is also consistency with respect to the size of the effect. Most estimates reveal that a 10 percent increase in police presence yields a reduction in total crime in the neighborhood of 3 percent, although studies that consider violent crime tend to find reductions ranging from 5 to 10 percent. Yet these police manpower studies speak only to the number and allocation of police officers and not to what police officers actually do on the street beyond making arrests. The next section proceeds from here by reviewing recent evaluations of deployment strategies used by police departments in order to control crime.

Police Deployment and Crime

Much research has examined the crime prevention effectiveness of alternative strategies for deploying police resources. This research has largely been conducted by criminologists and sociologists. Among this group of researchers, the preferred research designs are quasi-experiments involving before-and-after studies of the effect of targeted interventions as well as true randomized experiments. The discussion that follows draws heavily upon two excellent reviews of this research by Weisburd and Eck (2004) and Braga (2008). As a preface to this summary, we draw the theoretical link between police deployment and the certainty and severity of punishment. For the most part, deployment strategies affect the certainty of punishment through its impact on the probability of apprehension. There are, however, notable examples where severity may also be affected.

One way to increase apprehension risk is to mobilize police in a fashion that increases the probability that an offender is arrested after committing a crime. Strong evidence of a deterrent as opposed to an incapacitation effect resulting from the apprehension of criminals is limited. Studies of the effect of rapid response to calls for service (Kansas City Police Department 1977; Spelman and Brown 1981) find no evidence of a crime prevention effect, but this may be because most calls for service occur well after the crime event, with the result that the perpetrator has fled the scene. Thus, it is doubtful that rapid response materially affects apprehension risk. Similarly, because most arrests result from the presence of witnesses or physical evidence, improved investigations are not likely to yield material deterrent effects because, again, apprehension risk is not likely to be affected. A series of randomized experiments were conducted to test the deterrent effect of mandatory arrest for domestic violence. The initial experiment conducted in Minneapolis by Sherman and Berk (1984) found that mandatory arrest was effective in reducing domestic violence reoffending. Findings from follow-up replication studies (as part of the so-called Spouse Assault Replication Program, or SARP) were inconsistent. Experiments in two cities found a deterrent effect, but no such effect was found in three other cities (Maxwell, Garner, and Fagan 2002).

The second source of deterrence from police activities involves averting crime in the first place. In this circumstance, there is no apprehension because there was no offense. In our view this is the primary source of deterrence from the presence of police. If an occupied police car is parked outside a liquor store, a would-be robber of the store will likely be deterred because apprehension is all but certain. Thus, measures of apprehension risk based only on enforcement actions and crimes that actually occur, such as arrest per reported crime, are seriously incomplete because such measures do not capture the apprehension risk that attends criminal opportunities that were not acted upon by potential offenders because the risk was deemed too high (Cook 1979).

Two examples of police deployment strategies that have been shown to be effective in averting crime in the first place are "hot spots" policing and problem-oriented policing. Weisburd and Eck (2004) propose a two-dimensional taxonomy of policing strategies. One dimension is "level of focus" and the other is "diversity of approaches." Level of focus represents the degree to which police activities are targeted. Targeting can occur in a variety of ways, but Weisburd and Eck give special attention to policing strategies that target police resources in small geographic areas (e.g., blocks or specific addresses) that have very high levels of criminal activity, so-called crime "hot spots."

The idea of "hot spots" policing stems from a striking empirical regularity uncovered by Sherman, Weisburd, and others. Sherman and colleagues (1989) found that only 3 percent of addresses and intersections ("places," as they were called) in Minneapolis produced 50 percent of all calls to the police. Weisburd and Green (1995) found that 20 percent of all disorder crime and 14 percent of crimes against persons in Jersey City, New Jersey, arose from 56 drug crime hot spots. In a later study in Seattle, Washington, Weisburd et al. (2004) report that between 4 and 5 percent of street segments in the city accounted for 50 percent of crime incidents for each year over a fourteen-year period. Other more recent studies finding comparable crime concentrations include Brantingham and Brantingham (1999), Eck et al. (2000), and Roncek (2000). Just like in the liquor store example, the rationale for concentrating police in crime hot spots is to create a prohibitively high risk of apprehension and thereby to deter crime at the hot spot in the first place.

Braga's (2008) informative review of hot spots policing summarizes the findings from nine experimental or quasi-experimental evaluations. The studies were conducted in five large U.S. cities and one suburb of Australia. Crime-incident reports and citizen calls for service were used to evaluate impacts in and around the geographic area of the crime hot spot. The targets of the police actions varied. Some hot spots were generally high-crime locations, whereas others were characterized by specific crime problems like drug trafficking. All but two of the studies found evidence of significant reductions in crime. Further, no evidence was found of material crime displacement to immediately surrounding locations. On the contrary, some studies found evidence of crime reductions, not increases, in the surrounding locations—a "diffusion of crime-control benefits" to non-targeted locales.

The second dimension of the Weisburd and Eck taxonomy is diversity of approaches. This dimension concerns the variety of approaches that police use to impact public safety. Low diversity is associated with reliance on time-honored law enforcement strategies for affecting the threat of apprehension, for example, by dramatically increasing police presence. High diversity involves expanding beyond conventional practice to prevent crime. One example of a high-diversity approach is problem-oriented policing. Problem-oriented policy comes in so many different forms that it is regrettably hard to define.

One of the most visible examples of problem-oriented policing is Boston's Operation Cease Fire (Kennedy et al. 2001). The objective of the collaborative operation was to prevent inter-gang gun violence using two deterrence-based strategies. One was to target enforcement against weapons traffickers who were supplying weapons to Boston's violent youth gangs. The second involved a more innovative use of deterrence. The youth gangs themselves were assembled (and reassembled) to send the message that the response to any instance of serious violence would be "pulling every lever" legally available to punish gang members collectively. This included a salient severity-related dimension—vigorous prosecution for unrelated, non-violent crime such as drug dealing. Thus, the aim of Operation Cease Fire was to deter violent crime by increasing the certainty and severity of punishment but only in targeted circumstances, namely if the gang members were perpetrators of a violent crime. While there have been challenges to whether the decline in violence that accompanied Operation Cease Fire was attributable to the program, we concur with the judgment of Cook and Ludwig (2006) that Cease Fire seemed to play a role in the decline. Just as important, Operation Cease Fire illustrates the potential for combining elements of both certainty and severity enhancement to generate a targeted deterrent effect. Further evaluations of the efficacy of this strategy should be a high priority.

SANCTION RISK PERCEPTIONS

Deterrence is, fundamentally, a process of information transmission intended to discourage law violation (Geerken and Gove 1975). It entails communicating to a collection of individuals the sanctions that will potentially ensue when they fail to conform to proscribed behavior. Discourse about deterrence theory therefore acknowledges that risk perceptions are an important intermediate link between sanctions and behavior (Waldo and Chiricos 1972). But in order for a sanction policy to actually influence behavior, individual perceptions of the certainty and severity of sanctions must have some grounding in reality. Indeed, Nagin (1998, 18) observes that "behavior is immune to policy manipulation" to the degree that there is no link between policy and perceptions.

There are three distinct research traditions that examine correlations between criminal sanctions, risk perceptions, and criminal behavior, which we refer to as studies of the *contextual effect of sanctions*, studies of the *deterrent effect of risk perceptions*, and studies of the *experiential effect of behavior*.

The Contextual Effect of Sanctions on Risk Perceptions

One major research tradition in the study of perceptual deterrence entails estimating the degree of correspondence between area-level measures (usually the county) of criminal punishment and individual perceptions of sanction risk. This interest follows from studies that have identified a modest, inverse correlation between aggregate sanctions and individual delinquent and criminal behavior (Vicusi 1986; Mocan and Rees 2005). If these correlations reflect perceptual deterrence, at least in part, there should be a positive correlation between aggregate sanctions and individual perceptions of sanction risk—a contextual effect of sanctions on risk perceptions.

Recent studies of the contextual effects of sanctions on risk perceptions have revealed a generally weak and oftentimes negligible correlation. For example, Kleck and colleagues (2005) conduct a telephone survey of adults residing in 54 large urban counties, inquiring about estimates of the certainty, severity, and celerity of punishment pertaining to a variety of criminal offenses (homicide, robbery, burglary, aggravated assault). Their measures of actual and perceived punishments were generally uncorrelated. Lochner (2007) reports, in a nationally representative sample of youth, a positive and significant correlation between the county arrest clearance rate for auto theft and young males' estimates of the likelihood that they would be arrested if they stole a car. However, the correlation did not withstand inclusion of basic demographic (age, race/ethnicity) and spatial (metropolitan area residence) control variables. MacCoun et al. (2009) use data from a nationally representative sample of adults to study the relationship between prevailing state punishments and individual perceptions of the maximum penalty for first-time marijuana possession. Residents of states that decriminalized marijuana possession, compared to states in which marijuana possession was still criminalized, did indeed report more lenient sanctions for violation, but the actual differences were surprisingly modest in substantive terms. Moreover, almost one-third of the sample reported not knowing the maximum penalty for marijuana possession.

The recent research on perception formation that considers the contextual effects of sanctions has therefore yielded only modest correlations, at best, between area-level punishments and individual risk perceptions. On their face, these results are discouraging for perceptual deterrence. If people are only vaguely aware of the criminal punishments in their state or county, then the deterrence rationale of punishment is seriously undermined. However, there are a number of important limitations in this research relating to measurement, sampling, and contingencies.

First, articulations of risk perceptions in survey instruments are likely subject to a large degree of measurement error that will attenuate the strength of the correlation between perceptions and actual punishment risk. Measurement error may be large if people form punishment judgments in a fairly abstract way. Rather than forming crime-specific estimates of the certainty, severity, and celerity of punishment, the average individual (but not necessarily the average offender) might instead rely on an omnibus assessment or some generalized conception of punishment risk. Furthermore, individual risk perceptions are subject to well-known distortions and biases (for a review and discussion of research on crime decision-making, see Pogarsky forthcoming). Considered as a whole, these observations imply that researchers should place a premium on the refinement and validation of measures of sanction risk perceptions.

Second, a sizable proportion of the population is not "in the market" for law-violating behavior—they are committed law abiders. For committed law abiders, there is no reason to invest effort in forming accurate assessments of sanction risk because criminal activity is not an option that they consider. By the same token, another portion of the population is probably not "in the market" for law-abiding behavior—they are committed law violators. It might only be individuals in the middle of the criminal propensity continuum that are truly "deterrable" (Pogarsky 2002). It is these individuals who have an incentive to invest in forming accurate sanction risk perceptions. Population-based studies are likely to be composed largely of committed law abiders, especially when serious crimes are under consideration. Consequently the relationship between sanctions and perceptions will be modest at best.

Third, there are likely contingencies for perception formation whereby contextual factors moderate the strength of the correlation between sanctions and perceptions. A study by Apel, Pogarsky, and Bates (2009) considers this possibility in the school context. Using a nationally representative school-based survey, they find that the correlation between the prevailing sanctions in a school and student perceptions of rule strictness is strongest in schools that are the smallest and the least disordered. In the largest and most disordered schools, on the other hand, student perceptions are largely unrelated to changes in school sanctions. They conclude that large school size and disorder are contextual contingencies that impede the flow of information from school authorities to students and therefore dilute deterrence messages. Their findings might help to explain the weak correlation between sanctions measured at a highly aggregated level, such as the county or state, and individual-level risk perceptions.

The Deterrent Effect of Risk Perceptions on Behavior

Research on the deterrent effects of perceptions on behavior has proceeded along three distinctive methodological lines: cross-sectional surveys, panel studies, and vignette research. Cross-sectional surveys inquire about individuals' current perceptions of sanction risks (certainty, severity) and either their behavior within some reference period prior to the interview or their *behavioral intentions* to commit crime in the future. Cross-sectional surveys consistently show that risk perceptions are inversely correlated with both measures of offending behavior (see Paternoster 1987). Panel studies are designed to untangle temporal priority for the perceptions-behavior link that vexes cross-sectional research by relating perceptions in period t to actual behavior in period t + 1 (as opposed to intended future behavior in period t). Findings from panel studies tend to show that the actual perceptions-behavior correlation is smaller than that estimated from cross-sectional surveys and often diminishes to non-significance with the inclusion of control variables (see Paternoster 1987). But there are notable exceptions. A recent example of this approach is provided by Wright and colleagues (2004), who find long-term perceptual deterrent effects on behavior in a cohort of New Zealand youth. They find that the perceived risk of getting caught for criminal behavior in late adolescence is inversely and significantly correlated with criminal behavior at age 26.

Vignette research provides respondents with a detailed, hypothetical crime scenario and then asks them about their perceptions of the certainty and severity of punishment for the crime, as well as their own behavior if they found themselves in the same situation. A unique feature of this design is that situational characteristics can be experimentally manipulated in order to study how subjects respond to a variety of incentives, disincentives, and opportunity structures. A growing number of vignette designs in perceptual deterrence research have been employed in recent years (Nagin and Pogarsky 2001; Piquero and Pogarsky 2002; Pogarsky 2002, 2004; Pogarsky and Piquero 2003). To consider one example in detail, Nagin and Pogarsky (2001) issued to university students a scenario describing an incident of drunk driving in which they experimentally manipulated the severity and celerity of punishment. Respondents given a scenario with a longer length of license suspension upon conviction for drunk driving (higher severity) reported a significantly lower likelihood of driving drunk, although this effect appeared to be diminished among individuals who were more present-oriented or impulsive (i.e., those with a higher "discount rate"). On the other hand, a shorter delay between conviction and the suspension period (higher celerity) was unrelated to drunk driving intentions. When the authors inquired about subjects' own estimated likelihood of being apprehended and convicted for drunk driving (a measure of certainty) under the conditions described in the scenario, they found that it was a robust predictor of intentions to drive drunk.

Research on the perceptual deterrent effects of punishment has produced two other sets of findings that are important to understanding the sources of deterrence. The first concerns the comparative deterrent effects of the certainty and severity of punishment. Like the literature on the preventive effects of police and imprisonment, the perceptual deterrence literature finds more consistent evidence of the certainty of punishment as a crime deterrent relative to the severity of punishment. The second concerns the role of informal sanctions in the deterrence process. Zimring and Hawkins observe that formal punishment may best deter when it sets off informal sanctions: "Official actions can set off societal reactions that may provide potential offenders with more reason to avoid conviction than the officially imposed unpleasantness of punishment" (1973, 174). Andenaes (1974) makes the same argument. Much perceptual deterrence confirms this linkage. This research has consistently found that individuals who report higher stakes in conventionality are more strongly deterred by their perceived risk of punishment for law breaking.

A salient example of research supporting the "certainty principle" as well as untangling the link between formal and informal sanctions concerns tax evasion. In the United States, civil enforcement actions by tax authorities are a private matter unless the taxpayer appeals the action. Because tax authorities are scrupulous about maintaining the confidentially of tax return information, for civil enforcement actions non-compliers are gambling only with their money and not their personal reputations. In Klepper and Nagin (1989), a sample of generally middle-class adults was posed a series of tax non-compliance scenarios. The scenarios laid out the essential features of a tax report—income from different sources, number of exemptions, and various deductions. They then experimentally varied the amount and type of non-compliance (e.g., overstating charitable deductions or understating business income) across tax return line items and found that a majority of respondents reported a non-zero probability of taking advantage of the non-compliance opportunity described in the scenario. Plainly, the respondents were generally willing to consider tax non-compliance when only their money was at risk. They also seemed to be calculating: the attractiveness of the tax noncompliance gamble was inversely related to the perceived risk of civil enforcement.

The one exception to the rule of confidentially of enforcement interventions is criminal prosecution. As with all criminal cases, criminal prosecutions for tax evasion are a matter of public record. Here Klepper and Nagin found evidence of a different decision calculus—seemingly all that was necessary to deter evasion was the perception of a non-zero chance of criminal prosecution. Stated differently, if the evasion gamble also involved putting reputation and community standing at risk, the middle-class respondents were seemingly unwilling to consider taking the non-compliance gamble.

This finding helps explain why the certainty of punishment may be a greater deterrent than severity. If the social and economic costs of punishment are strictly proportional to the punishment received, for example, if the cost to the individual of a two-year prison term is twice that of a one-year sentence, certainty and severity will equally affect expected cost. This is because expected cost is simply the product of certainty, P, and severity, S. The value of the product, $P*S$, is equally affected by proportional changes in P or S. For example, the impact on expected cost of a 50 percent increase in P is the same as a 50 percent increase in S. However, the Klepper and Nagin study suggests that people do not perceive that costs are proportional to potential punishment. Instead it seems that they perceive there is fixed cost associated with merely being convicted or even apprehended if it is public record.

While Klepper and Nagin (1989) did not pin down the specific sources of these costs, other research on the impact of a criminal record on access to the legal labor market suggests a very real basis for the fear of stigmatization. For example, Freeman (1995) estimates that a prison record depresses the probability of employment by 15–30 percent and Waldfogel (1994) estimates that conviction for fraud reduces income by as much as 40 percent. More recent studies reinforce these earlier findings. Western (2002) estimates the wage reduction effect of incarceration to be about 16 percent. He also finds that incarceration deflects individuals onto a flatter wage trajectory in which wage growth is slowed by 31 percent relative to comparably high-risk men who were not incarcerated. Pager (2003) reports that employers advertising entry-level job openings were less than half as likely to call back applicants who reported a criminal history (a felony cocaine trafficking conviction with 18 months prison time). She concludes that "criminal records close doors in employment situations" (p. 956).

The Experiential Effect of Behavior on Risk Perceptions

An early conclusion of perceptual deterrence researchers was that people's own experiences with crime and punishment were more salient determinants of their risk perceptions than external sources of information about sanction risk (Parker and Grasmick 1979). Perceptual deterrence research also found that individuals who have experience as criminal offenders tended to have substantially lower risk perceptions and *more accurate risk perceptions* compared to individuals who lack such experience (Scheider 2001; Lochner 2007; MacCoun et al. 2009).

This raises the question of whether offenders' lower risk perceptions might be a consequence of their criminal behavior as well as a cause. Panel studies of the deterrent effect of perceptions are well positioned to speak to this question. The first wave of such studies indicated that there is a pronounced experiential effect of delinquent or criminal behavior on risk perceptions (e.g., Paternoster et al. 1982; Saltzman et al. 1982). Furthermore, among active offenders, the experience of being sanctioned (and sanctioned more severely) itself contributes to an increase in risk perceptions (Apospori and Alpert 1993). There are also compelling reasons to believe that individuals change their risk perceptions, in part, on the basis of the crime and punishment experiences of their friends and family members. Stafford and Warr (1993) refer to such effects as indirect or *vicarious* experiences (see also Paternoster and Piquero 1995).

Yet an equally important determinant of risk perceptions in addition to personal and vicarious *punishment experience*, according to Stafford and Warr (1993), is personal and vicarious *punishment avoidance*. There is evidence from a number of studies that, other things being equal, a higher level of unsanctioned offending lowers one's perceptions of formal sanction risk (e.g., Bridges and Stone 1986; Piliavin et al. 1986; Horney and Marshall 1992; Paternoster and Piquero 1995; Piquero and Paternoster 1998). For example, in the study by Horney and Marshall (1992), offenders with higher "arrest ratios" (i.e., more reported arrests per reported offenses) had higher perceptions of the risk of detection. Stated differently, offenders with more unsanctioned offenses—that is, more successful criminal careers, with success defined as avoidance of arrest—had lower risk perceptions.

These findings on the experiential effects of punishment and behavior on risk perceptions have led to an emerging, second-generation literature concerned with the development and testing of formal models of within-individual change in risk perceptions as a consequence of personal and vicarious experiences with, and avoidances of, arrest and punishment (Pogarsky and Piquero 2003; Pogarsky et al. 2004, 2005; Matsueda et al. 2006; Lochner 2007; Hjalmarsson 2008; Anwar and Loughran 2009). Many of these studies appeal to a Bayesian model of learning. A Bayesian model of risk perceptions and criminal behavior begins with an individual's initial assessment of the likelihood of apprehension for criminal conduct. This is known as the *prior probability* of the risk of arrest (among other sanctions). The perceptual deterrence literature strongly suggests that the prior probability estimates of individuals without offending experience systematically and often substantially overstate the true risk of apprehension. Over time, the individual will accumulate personal and/ or vicarious experiences as a successful or unsuccessful criminal offender. Note the parallel with Stafford and Warr's (1993) conceptualization of personal and vicarious punishment experience and punishment avoidance. The expectation is that the individual will then *update* his or her assessment of the risk of apprehension based on these experiences. The resulting *posterior probability* of the risk of arrest is a weighted sum of the individual's prior probability and the new information.

As an example of the Bayesian empirical approach, Hjalmarsson (2008b) takes advantage of cross-state variation in the age of criminal majority and finds that individual perceptions of the risk of jail following an arrest (for auto theft) increase discontinuously when youth become adults in the eyes of the law. Lochner (2007) also finds evidence for updating of risk perceptions in the same data set but with a different analytical focus. His results indicate that risk perceptions increase in response to arrest in the previous year, decrease in response to criminal behavior in the previous year, and decrease in response to sibling criminal behavior in the previous year as reported by siblings themselves, although the latter result is somewhat fragile.

Anwar and Loughran (2009) have significantly advanced empirical testing of the Bayesian updating model by looking for more fine-grained predictions of it. First, they observe that the effect of arrest within a reference window should depend on the number of crimes committed during that period. For example, being arrested once should matter more for an offender who committed only one crime as opposed to an offender who committed ten crimes. In the case of the former, the "experienced arrest certainty" (a term employed by Matsueda et al. 2006) is 100 percent, while in the case of the latter it is only 10 percent. Second, Anwar and Loughran observe that the effect of arrest should diminish as individuals gain more offending experience. In other words, since posterior risk perceptions are a function of prior risk perceptions and new information in the form of their arrest ratio (what they refer to as a "signal"), experienced offenders should place more weight on their prior risk perceptions in the sense that they should "update less" in response to new information simply because they have more experience upon which to draw. Inexperienced offenders, on the other hand, should "update more" to bring their risk perceptions closer in line with their actual punishment risk. Third, Anwar and Loughran observe that the effect of arrest should be crime specific, or at least specific within a class of criminal behaviors. That is, an arrest for a violent crime should influence risk perceptions of violent crime only, and not risk perceptions of property crime. All three of these predictions were tested and supported from a sample of serious juvenile offenders.

CONCLUSIONS

This chapter has reviewed the evidence on the general deterrent effect of sanctions. Evidence of a substantial effect is overwhelming. Just as important is the evidence that the effect is not uniform across different sanctions, jurisdictions, and individuals. Both conclusions are important to devising crime-control policies that make effective use of sanctions to prevent crime. The first conclusion implies that a well-balanced portfolio of strategies and programs to prevent crime must necessarily include deterrence-based policies. However, the second conclusion implies that not all deterrence policies will be effective in reducing crime or, if effective, that the crime-reduction benefits may fall short of the social and economic costs of the sanction. In this regard, our conclusions echo issues raised in two other recent reviews of the deterrence literature by Doob and Webster (2003) and Tonry (2008).

Future research on sanction effects will be most useful for policy evaluation if it moves closer to a medical model. Medical research is not organized around the theme of whether medical care cures diseases, the analog to the question of whether sanctions prevent crime. Instead, medical researchers address far more specific questions. Is a specific drug or procedure effective in treating a specific disease? Does the drug or procedure have adverse side effects for certain types of people? Furthermore, most such research is comparative—is the specific drug or procedure more effective than the status quo alternative? The analogous questions for deterrence research are whether and in what circumstances are sanction threats effective, and which threats are more effective and in what circumstances. There are many examples of "medical-model" type research in the policing literature on the effectiveness of alternative strategies for deploying police resources. Other examples outside the policing literature include the Helland and Tabarrok (2007) study of the California's "Three Strikes and You're Out" statute and the Lee and McCrary (2009) study of the deterrent effect of aging out of the jurisdiction of the juvenile court and into the jurisdiction of the adult court.

Devising sensible deterrence-based crime policies also requires much better knowledge of the determinants of sanction risk perceptions. In recent years, greater attention has been devoted to analyzing the linkage of sanction risk perceptions to policy and to personal and vicarious experiences with the criminal justice enforcement apparatus. The Bayesian learning model provides a valuable theoretical structure for organizing and building on this research. Continued testing and extension of this model should be given a high priority in deterrence research. Just as important is testing the Bayesian updating model with data from crime-prone populations.

References

Andenaes, Johannes. 1974. *Punishment and Deterrence*. Ann Arbor: University of Michigan Press.

Anwar, Shamena, and Thomas A. Loughran. 2009. "Testing a Bayesian Learning Theory of Deterrence among Serious Juvenile Offenders." Unpublished manuscript. Pittsburgh: Carnegie Mellon University.

Apel, Robert, Greg Pogarsky, and Leigh Bates. 2009. "The Sanctions-Perceptions Link in a Model of School-Based Deterrence." *Journal of Quantitative Criminology* 25: 201–226.

Apospori, Eleni, and Geoffrey Alpert. 1993. "Research Note: The Role of Differential Experience with the Criminal Justice System in Changes in Perceptions of Severity of Legal Sanctions over Time." *Journal of Research in Crime and Delinquency* 39: 184–194.

Bentham, Jeremy. [1871]1988. *The Principles of Morals and Legislation*. Amherst, NY: Prometheus Books.

Berk, Richard. 2005. "New Claims about Executions and General Deterrence: Déjá Vu All Over Again?" *Journal of Empirical Legal Studies* 2: 303–330.

Blumstein, Alfred, Jacqueline Cohen, and Daniel Nagin. 1977. *Deterrence and Incapacitation: Estimating the Effects of Criminal Sanctions on Crime Rates*. Washington, DC: National Academies Press.

Braga, Anthony A. 2008. "Police Enforcement Strategies to Prevent Crime in Hot Spot Areas." Washington, DC: Office of Community Oriented Policing Services, U.S. Department of Justice.

Braithwaite, John. 1989. *Crime, Shame, and Reintegration*. New York: Cambridge University Press.

Brantingham, Patricia L., and Paul J. Brantingham. 1999. "Theoretical Model of Crime Hot Spot Generation." *Studies on Crime and Crime Prevention* 8: 7–26.

Bridges, George S., and James A. Stone. 1986. "Effects of Criminal Punishment on Perceived Threat of Punishment: Toward an Understanding of Specific Deterrence." *Journal of Research in Crime and Delinquency* 23: 207–239.

Cohen-Cole, Ethan, Steven Durlauf, Jeffrey Fagan, and Daniel Nagin. 2009. "Model Uncertainty and the Deterrent Effect of Capital Punishment." *American Law and Economics Review* 11: 335–369.

Cook, Philip J. 1979. "The Clearance Rate as a Measure of Criminal Justice System Effectiveness." *Journal of Public Economics* 11: 135–142.

Cook, Philip J. 1980. "Research in Criminal Deterrence: Laying the Groundwork for the Second Decade." In *Crime and Justice: An Annual Review of Research, vol. 2*, eds. Norval Morris and Michael Tonry. Chicago: University of Chicago Press.

Cook, Philip J. 1986. "The Relationship between Victim Resistance and Injury in Noncommercial Robbery." *Journal of Legal Studies* 15: 405–416.

Cook Philip J. and Jens Ludwig. 2006. "Aiming for Evidenced-Based Gun Policy." *Journal of Policy Analysis and Management* 25: 691–735.

Corman, Hope, and H. Naci Mocan. 2000. "A Time-Series Analysis of Crime, Deterrence, and Drug Abuse in New York City." *American Economic Review* 90: 584–604.

Corman, Hope, and Naci Mocan. 2005. "Carrots, Sticks, and Broken Windows." *Journal of Law and Economics* 48: 235–266.

Crow, W., and J. Bull. 1975. *Robbery Deterrence: An Applied Behavioral Science Demonstration—Final Report*. La Jolla, CA: Western Behavioral Science Institute.

DeAngelo, Greg, and Benjamin Hansen. 2008. "Life and Death in the Fast Lane: Police Enforcement and Roadway Safety." Unpublished manuscript. University of California, Santa Barbara.

Dezhbakhsh, Hashem, Paul H. Rubin, and Joanna M. Shepherd. 2003. "Does Capital Punishment Have a Deterrent Effect? New Evidence from Postmoratorium Panel Data." *American Law and Economics Review* 5: 344–376.

Dezhbakhsh, Hashem, and Joanna Shepherd. 2006. "The Deterrent Effect of Capital Punishment: Evidence from a 'Judicial Experiment'." *Economic Inquiry* 44: 512.

Di Tella, Rafael, and Ernesto Schargrodsky. 2004. "Do Police Reduce Crime? Estimates Using the Allocation of Police Forces after a Terrorist Attack." *American Economic Review* 94: 115–133.

Donohue, John J., and Justin Wolfers. 2005. "Uses and Abuses of Empirical Evidence in the Death Penalty Debate." *Stanford Law Review* 58: 791–846.

Donohue, John J. 2007. "Assessing the Relative Benefits of Incarceration: The Overall Change over the Previous Decades and the Benefits on the Margin." Working paper. New Haven, CT: Yale Law School.

Doob, Anthony, and Cheryl Webster. 2003. "Sentence Severity and Crime: Accepting the Null Hypothesis." In *Crime and Justice: A Review of Research, vol. 30*, ed. Michael Tonry. Chicago: University of Chicago Press.

Draca, Mirko, Stephen Machin, and Robert Witt. 2008. "Panic on the Streets of London: Police, Crime and the July 2005 Terror Attacks." IZA Discussion Paper no. 3410. Bonn, Germany: Institute for the Study of Labor.

Eck, John E., Jeffrey S. Gersh, and Charlene Taylor. 2000. "Finding Crime Hot Spots Through Repeat Address Mapping." Pp. 49-64 in *Analyzing Crime Patterns: Frontiers of Practice*, edited by Victor Goldsmith, Philip G. McGuire, John H. Mollenkopf, and Timothy A. Ross. Thousand Oaks, CA: Sage Publications.

Evans, William N., and Emily G. Owens. 2007. "COPS and Crime." *Journal of Public Economics* 91: 181–201.

Fagan, Jeffrey. 2006. "Death and Deterrence Redux: Science, Law and Causal Reasoning on Capital Punishment." *Ohio State Journal of Criminal Law* 4: 255–319.

Freeman, Richard B. 1995. "Why Do So Many Young American Men Commit Crimes and What Might We Do About It?" *Journal of Economic Perspectives* 10: 25–42.

Geerken, Michael R., and Walter R. Gove. 1975. "Deterrence: Some Theoretical Considerations." *Law and Society Review* 9: 497–513.

Gibbs, Jack P. 1975. *Crime, Punishment, and Deterrence*. New York: Elsevier.

Heaton, Paul. Forthcoming. "Understanding the Effects of Anti-Profiling Policies." *Journal of Law and Economics*.

Helland, Eric, and Alexander Tabarrok. 2007. "Does Three Strikes Deter? A Nonparametric Estimation." *Journal of Human Resources* 42: 309–330.

Hjalmarsson, Randi. 2008a. "Does Capital Punishment Have a 'Local' Deterrent Effect on Homicides?" *American Law and Economics Review* 11: 310–334.

Hjalmarsson, Randi. 2008b. "Crime and Expected Punishment: Changes in Perceptions at the Age of Criminal Majority." *American Law and Economics Review* 11: 209–248.

Horney, Julie, and Ineke Haen Marshall. 1992. "Risk Perceptions among Serious Offenders: The Role of Crime and Punishment." *Criminology* 30: 575–593.

Kansas City Police Department. 1977. *Response Time Analysis*. Kansas City, MO: Kansas City Police Department.

Katz, Lawrence, Steven D. Levitt, and Ellen Shustorovich. 2003. "Prison Conditions, Capital Punishment, and Deterrence." *American Law and Economics Review* 5: 318–343.

Kennedy, David M., Anthony A. Braga, Anne Morrison Piehl, and Elin J. Waring. 2001. *Reducing Gun Violence: The Boston Gun Project's Operation Ceasefire*. Washington, DC: U.S. National Institute of Justice.

Kleck, Gary, Brion Sever, Spencer Li, and Marc Gertz. 2005. "The Missing Link in General Deterrence Research." *Criminology* 43: 623–659.

Klepper, Steven, and Daniel Nagin. 1989. "The Deterrent Effect of Perceived Certainty and Severity Revisited." *Criminology* 27: 721–746.

Klick, Jonathan, and Alexander Tabarrok. 2005. "Using Terror Alert Levels to Estimate the Effect of Police on Crime." *Journal of Law and Economics* 48: 267–279.

Lee, David S., and Justin McCrary. 2009. "The Deterrent Effect of Prison: Dynamic Theory and Evidence." Unpublished manuscript. Princeton, NJ: Princeton University.

Levitt, Steven D. 1996. "The Effect of Prison Population Size on Crime Rates: Evidence from Prison Overcrowding Legislation." *Quarterly Journal of Economics* 111: 319–352.

Levitt, Steven D. 1997. "Using Electoral Cycles in Police Hiring to Estimate the Effect of Police on Crime." *American Economic Review* 87: 270–290.

Levitt, Steven D. 2002. "Using Electoral Cycles in Police Hiring to Estimate the Effect of Police on Crime: Reply." *American Economic Review* 92: 1244–1250.

Liedka, Raymond V., Anne Morrison Piehl, and Bert Useem. 2006. "The Crime-Control Effect of Incarceration: Does Scale Matter?" *Criminology and Public Policy* 5: 245–276.

Lochner, Lance. 2007. "Individual Perceptions of the Criminal Justice System." *American Economic Review* 97: 444–460.

MacCoun, Robert, Rosalie Liccardo Pacula, Jamie Chriqui, Katherine Harris, and Peter Reuter. 2009. "Do Citizens Know Whether Their State Has Decriminalized Marijuana? Assessing the Perceptual Component of Deterrence Theory." *Review of Law and Economics* 5: 347–371.

Marvell, Thomas, and Carlisle Moody. 1996. "Specification Problems, Police Levels, and Crime Rates." *Criminology* 34: 609–646.

Matsueda, Ross L., Derek A. Kreager, and David Huizinga. 2006. "Deterring Delinquents: A Rational Choice Model of Theft and Violence." *American Sociological Review* 71: 95–122.

Maxwell, Christopher D., Joel H. Garner, and Jeffrey A. Fagan. 2002. "The Preventive Effects of Arrest on Intimate Partner Violence: Research, Policy and Theory." *Criminology and Public Policy* 2: 51–80.

McCrary, Justin. 2002. "Using Electoral Cycles in Police Hiring to Estimate the Effect of Police on Crime: Comment." *American Economic Review* 92: 1236–1243.

Mocan, H. Naci, and R. Kaj Gittings. 2003. "Getting Off Death Row: Commuted Sentences and the Deterrent Effect of Capital Punishment." *Journal of Law and Economics* 46: 453–478.

Mocan, H. Naci, and Daniel I. Rees. 2005. "Economic Conditions, Deterrence and Juvenile Crime: Evidence from Micro Data." *American Law and Economics Review* 7: 319–349.

Nagin, Daniel. 1978. "General Deterrence: A Review of the Empirical Evidence." In *Deterrence and Incapacitation: Estimating the Effects of Criminal Sanctions on Crime Rates*, eds. Alfred Blumstein, Jacqueline Cohen, and Daniel Nagin. Washington, DC: National Academies Press.

Nagin, Daniel S. 1998. "Criminal Deterrence Research at the Outset of the Twenty-First Century." In *Crime and Justice: A Review of Research, vol. 23*, ed. Michael Tonry. Chicago: University of Chicago Press.

Nagin, Daniel S., Francis T. Cullen, and Cheryl Lero Jonson. 2009. "Imprisonment and Re-Offending." In *Crime and Justice: A Review of Research, vol. 38*, ed. Michael Tonry. Chicago: University of Chicago Press.

Nagin, Daniel S., and Raymond Paternoster. 1993. "Enduring Individual Differences and Rational Choice Theories of Crime." *Law and Society Review* 27: 467–496.

Nagin, Daniel S., and Greg Pogarsky. 2001. "Integrating Celerity, Impulsivity, and Extralegal Sanction Threats into a Model of General Deterrence: Theory and Evidence." *Criminology* 39: 865–891.

Nagin, Daniel S., and Greg Pogarsky. 2003. "An Experimental Investigation of Deterrence: Cheating, Self-Serving Bias, and Impulsivity." *Criminology* 41: 167–193.

Pager, Devah. 2003. "The Mark of a Criminal Record." *American Journal of Sociology* 108: 937–975.

Parker, Jerry, and Harold G. Grasmick. 1979. "Linking Actual and Perceived Certainty of Punishment: An Exploratory Study of an Untested Proposition in Deterrence Theory." *Criminology* 17: 366–379.

Paternoster, Raymond. 1987. "The Deterrent Effect of the Perceived Certainty and Severity of Punishment: A Review of the Evidence and Issues." *Justice Quarterly* 4: 173–217.

Paternoster, Raymond, and Alex Piquero. 1995. "Reconceptualizing Deterrence: An Empirical Test of Personal and Vicarious Experiences." *Journal of Research in Crime and Delinquency* 32: 251–286.

Paternoster, Raymond, Linda E. Saltzman, Theodore G. Chiricos, and Gordon P. Waldo. 1982. "Perceived Risk and Deterrence: Methodological Artifacts in Perceptual Deterrence Research." *Journal of Criminal Law and Criminology* 73: 1238–1258.

Pierce, Glenn, S. Spaar, and L. R. Briggs. 1986. "The Character of Police Work: Strategic and Tactical Implications." Center for Applied Social Research. Boston, MA: Northeastern University.

Piliavin, Irving, Craig Thornton, Rosemary Gartner, and Ross L. Matsueda. 1986. "Crime, Deterrence, and Rational Choice." *American Sociological Review* 51: 101–119.

Piquero, Alex, and Raymond Paternoster. 1998. "An Application of Stafford and Warr's Reconceptualization of Deterrence to Drinking and Driving." *Journal of Research in Crime and Delinquency* 35: 3–39.

Piquero, Alex R., and Greg Pogarsky. 2002. "Beyond Stafford and Warr's Reconceptualization of Deterrence: Personal and Vicarious Experiences, Impulsivity, and Offending Behavior." *Journal of Research in Crime and Delinquency* 39: 153–186.

Pogarsky, Greg. 2002. "Identifying 'Deterrable' Offenders: Implications for Research on Deterrence." *Justice Quarterly* 19: 431–452.

Pogarsky, Greg. 2004. "Projected Offending and Contemporaneous Rule-Violation: Implications for Heterotypic Continuity." *Criminology* 42: 111–135.

Pogarsky, Greg. Forthcoming. "Deterrence and Decision-Making: Research Questions and Theoretical Refinements." In *Handbook on Crime and Deviance*, edited by Marvin D. Krohn, Alan J. Lizotte, and Gina P. Hall. New York: Springer.

Pogarsky, Greg, KiDeuk Kim, and Ray Paternoster. 2005. "Perceptual Change in the National Youth Survey: Lessons for Deterrence Theory and Offender Decision-Making." *Justice Quarterly* 22: 1–29.

Pogarsky, Greg, and Alex R. Piquero. 2003. "Can Punishment Encourage Offending? Investigating the 'Resetting' Effect." *Journal of Research in Crime and Delinquency* 40: 95–120.

Pogarsky, Greg, Alex R. Piquero, and Ray Paternoster. 2004. "Modeling Change in Perceptions about Sanction Threats: The Neglected Linkage in Deterrence Theory." *Journal of Quantitative Criminology* 20: 343–369.

Poutvaara, Panu, and Mikael Priks. 2006. "Hooliganism in the Shadow of a Terrorist Attack and the Tsunami: Do Police Reduce Group Violence?" Unpublished manuscript. Finland: University of Helsinki.

Roncek, Dennis W. 2000. "Schools and Crime." In *Analyzing Crime Patterns: Frontiers of Practice*, eds. Victor Goldsmith, Philip G. McGuire, John H. Mollenkopf, and Timothy A. Ross. Thousand Oaks, CA: Sage Publications.

Saltzman, Linda E., Raymond Paternoster, Gordon P. Waldo, and Theodore G. Chiricos. 1982. "Deterrent and Experiential Effects: The Problem of Causal Order in Perceptual Deterrence Research." *Journal of Research in Crime and Delinquency* 19: 172–189.

Scheider, Matthew C. 2001. "Deterrence and the Base Rate Fallacy: An Examination of Perceived Certainty." *Justice Quarterly* 18: 63–86.

Shepherd, Joanna M. 2005. "Deterrence Versus Brutalization: Capital Punishment's Differing Impacts among States." *Michigan Law Review* 104: 203–255.

Sherman, Lawrence W., and Richard A. Berk. 1984. "The Specific Deterrent Effects of Arrest for Domestic Assault." *American Sociological Review* 49: 261–272.

Sherman, Lawrence W., and John E. Eck. 2002. Policing for Prevention. In *Evidence Based Crime Prevention*, eds. Lawrence W. Sherman, David Farrington, and Brandon Welsh. New York: Routledge.

Sherman, Lawrence W., Patrick Gartin, and Michael E. Buerger. 1989. "Hot Spots of Predatory Crime: Routine Activities and the Criminology of Place." *Criminology* 27: 27–55.

Shi, Lan. 2009. "The Limits of Oversight in Policing: Evidence from the 2001 Cincinnati Riot." *Journal of Public Economics* 93: 99–113.

Spelman, William. 1994. *Criminal Incapacitation*. New York: Plenum Press.

Spelman, William. 2000. "What Recent Studies Do (and Don't) Tell Us about Imprisonment and Crime." In *Crime and Justice: A Review of Research, vol. 27*, ed. Michael Tonry Chicago: University of Chicago Press.

Spelman, William, and Dale K. Brown. 1981. *Calling the Police: A Replication of the Citizen Reporting Component of the Kansas City Response Time Analysis*. Washington, DC: Police Executive Research Forum.

Stafford, Mark C., and Mark Warr. 1993. "A Reconceptualization of General and Specific Deterrence." *Journal of Research in Crime and Delinquency* 30: 123–135.

Tonry, Michael. 2008. "Learning from the Limitations of Deterrence Research." In *Crime and Justice: A Review of Research, vol. 37*, ed. Michael Tonry. Chicago: University of Chicago Press.

Vicusi, W. Kip. 1986. "The Risks and Rewards of Criminal Activity: A Comprehensive Test of Criminal Deterrence." *Journal of Labor Economics* 4: 317–340.

Waldfogel, Joel. 1994. "The Effect of Criminal Conviction on Income and the Trust 'Reposed in the Workmen.'" *Journal of Human Resources* 29: 62–81.

Waldo, Gordon P., and Theodore G. Chiricos. 1972. "Perceived Penal Sanction and Self-Reported Criminality: A Neglected Approach to Deterrence Research." *Social Problems* 19: 522–540.

Weisburd, David, and John Eck. 2004. "What Can Police Do to Reduce Crime, Disorder, and Fear?" *Annals of the American Academy of Political and Social Science* 593: 42–65.

Weisburd, David, Tomar Einat, and Matt Kowalski. 2008. "The Miracle of the Cells: An Experimental Study of Interventions to Increase Payment of Court-Ordered Financial Obligations." *Criminology and Public Policy* 7: 9–36.

Weisburd, David, Shawn Bushway, Cynthia Lum, and Su-Ming Yang. 2004. "Trajectories of Crime at Places: A Longitudinal Study of Street Segments in the City of Seattle." *Criminology* 42: 283–320.

Weisburd, David and Lorraine Green. 1995. "Policing Drug Hot Spots: The Jersey City Drug Market Analysis Experiment." *Justice Quarterly* 12: 711–735.

Western, Bruce. 2002. "The Impact of Incarceration on Wage Mobility and Inequality." *American Sociological Review* 67: 526–546.

Wright, Bradley R. E., Avshalom Caspi, Terrie E. Moffitt, and Ray Paternoster. 2004. "Does the Perceived Risk of Punishment Deter Criminally Prone Individuals? Rational Choice, Self-Control, and Crime." *Journal of Research in Crime and Delinquency* 41: 180–213.

Zimring, Franklin E., and Gordon Hawkins. 1995. *Incapacitation: Penal Confinement and the Restraint of Crime*. New York: Oxford University Press.

Chapter 15

Prosecution

Brian Forst

One of the most memorable moments of the 2009 confirmation hearings of Supreme Court Justice Sonya Sotomayor was Minnesota senator Al Franken's quizzing of Sotomayor about their mutual interest in a classic TV show of the 1950s and 1960s: "What was the one case in 'Perry Mason' that [prosecutor] Burger won?" This was a joke with multiple punch lines,[1] perhaps least funny of which was the correct answer: Burger won not in one, but in three of the 271 episodes of the series.[2]

The real joke about prosecution is quite cruel: the public is entertained by media portrayals of the district attorney, but it has little way of knowing much about how prosecutors actually perform. Of all the actors in the criminal justice system, prosecutors are by many accounts the most powerful and least understood. Their power resides in the authority that they have to accept or reject arrests brought by the police and to determine how to charge each case accepted; how much time and effort to give to each, driven largely by the decision whether to prepare for trial or settle with a plea; and for those convicted, what sentence to recommend to judge or jury. As elected officials in most jurisdictions, prosecutors are publicly accountable for these decisions, but available evidence provides very little systematic basis for knowing how well the prosecutor in any community fares in exercising all this authority.

It seems in order to ask some fundamental questions about what prosecutors do and how they do it, beginning with what they do with people arrested for violating the law. Despite years of increases in prison populations, many still believe that our crime problem is largely the product of a system that is too soft on criminals. How tough are prosecutors *really*? Do they achieve a proper balance between the rights of the accused and the rights of victims? Is the main problem that offenders too often slip through the system on legal technicalities? Or is it that prosecutors have discretion that is unchecked and exercised arbitrarily, often against the poor and minorities? Should prosecutors be responsible for preventing crimes? How? What *are* the core problems of prosecution? What can be done about them?

These questions can be addressed by starting with basics. Most agree that case processing should be just, effective, and speedy, but authorities disagree broadly and often bitterly over the specifics. For prosecutors, central questions involve how to allocate scarce resources and how best to proceed for each type of a wide variety of cases involving street crime, domestic violence, drug violations, child abuse, white collar crimes, and repeat offenders in violation of court orders and warrants. For each arrest, the decision about whether and how to charge the suspect must take into account the often conflicting goals of crime prevention, fairness, reform of the offender and reintegration into the community, and resource conservation.

This chapter can be summarized as follows:

- Of all the actors in the criminal justice system, prosecutors are by many accounts the most powerful and least understood. Their power resides in the authority that they have to accept or reject arrests brought by the police and to determine how to charge each case accepted; how much time and effort to give to each, driven largely by the decision whether to prepare for trial or settle with a plea; and for those convicted, what sentence to recommend to judge or jury. As elected officials in most jurisdictions, prosecutors are publicly accountable for these decisions, but available evidence provides very little systematic basis for knowing how well the prosecutor in any community fares in exercising all this authority.
- One measure of the importance of the prosecutor is this: for every adult felony case that a judge presides over in trial, the prosecutor decides the fate of about 15 brought by the police. The cases that go to trial tend to be the most serious; while they consume a disproportionate share of resources, they represent a tiny share of the felony caseload of a typical prosecutor's office. Over an extraordinary 20-year period, 1988 to 2007, when the number of reported index crimes declined from 13.9 million to 11.3 million, the number of persons in prison or jail more than doubled, from 951,000 to 2,293,000. It is worth asking how the prosecutor contributed to this problem.
- It is widely believed that many, if not most, felony cases presented to prosecutors are dropped due to legal "technicalities" related to Fourth Amendment exclusionary rule violations. In fact, fewer than one percent of all felony arrests are dropped on such grounds; most of those are drug cases involving questionable drug searches. The vast majority of all felony cases dropped by the prosecutor are rejected due to insufficiency of evidence: the police fail to produce adequate physical evidence from crime scenes or testimonial evidence from victims or eye witnesses.
- Conventional wisdom holds that plea-to-trial ratios are driven by caseload pressures, but jurisdictions with huge caseloads often have

low ratios of pleas to trials, while those with much smaller caseloads often have high ratios. Prosecution policy—whether to aim for *quality* convictions by being more selective at the screening stage and then putting more effort into bringing cases to trial, or to aim for *more* convictions by accepting more marginal cases and putting greater effort into negotiating guilty pleas in return for charge reductions—appears to be no less important a determinant of the ratio of pleas-to-trials than the press of large caseloads.

- Since information about cases dropped by the prosecutor and all other case outcomes is not generally made available to the public, a prosecutor's legitimate crime control efforts, or lack thereof, will go unnoticed. The prosecutor, in short, is insulated by the virtual absence of a system of measured public accountability in most states. And the media, capable of enlightening the public on the folly of weak accountability for the vast majority of felony cases, have opted instead to feed the public's appetite for information about sensational cases.

- The incentives of prosecutors, in short, leave substantial opportunity for disparity and inefficiency in the exercise of discretion. The goals of prosecution have not been made sufficiently clear, and detailed information about the decisions made by prosecutors is not sufficiently accessible to allow anyone to know whether prosecutors tend to make decisions about individual cases that correspond closely or consistently to any particular standard of justice or efficiency.

- As elected officials, district attorneys aim to avoid embarrassment. This is usually accomplished by keeping their work below the horizon, staying away from risky cases and departures from conventional modes of operation and from collaborations with researchers on the assessment of policies, procedures, or performance, assessments that could become tomorrow's embarrassing headline. This problem is worsened by a reduction in publicly available information about prosecution in recent years. In a time of greater transparency throughout the public and private sectors, it is really remarkable that we have *less* useful information now about the routine prosecution of felony cases than we did 30 years ago.

- Community prosecution programs bring the prosecutor closer to the public, but they do not make the important decisions of the prosecutor more transparent. Nor do they restore the victims of crime. These programs leave intact the principle that the prosecutor represents the state, not the victim, in all criminal matters. One prospect for a revolutionary advance in prosecution might be to challenge that fundamental principle. Some have suggested that a shift to a process resembling our tort system might effectively work to remedy the serious deficiencies of our existing state-versus-defendant system. Genuine opportunities for victims to be restored could well increase their incentives to report crimes to the police, thus reducing recidivism rates and crime costs, stimulating general deterrent effects, and raising the both the perception and reality of legitimacy.

FROM VICTIMIZATION TO INCARCERATION

Given the goals stated above, what happens to the approximately 3 million arrests made each year in the United States for index crimes (homicide, forcible rape, robbery, burglary, aggravated assault, larceny, and arson)? We can begin to address this question by placing it in the larger context of what happens from victimization to incarceration, displayed in figure 15.1.

Before discussing the numbers, it must be noted that earlier versions of this essay showed the outcomes of 100 typical felony arrests. The data needed to support the level of detail presented in those displays are no longer available, following the discontinuance of the series by the U.S. Department of Justice. This is a serious problem. We will say more about it later.

Of the approximately 20 million felony victimizations that occur each year, about half are reported to the police, and about 20 percent of those wind up as arrests brought to the prosecutor.[3] Nearly half of the adult arrests do not end in conviction (Boland, Mahanna, and Sones, 1992). Arrestees who are convicted are considerably more likely to be incarcer-

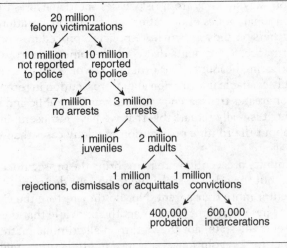

Figure 15.1. Approximate Outcomes of 20,000,000 Felony Victimizations in the United States, 2007

ated today, and for longer periods, than just 20 years ago, due to heightened public concern about crime. Over an extraordinary 20-year period, 1988 to 2007, when the number of reported index crimes declined from 13.9 million to 11.3 million—despite a 23 percent increase in the U.S. population—the number of persons in prison or jail more than doubled, from 951,000 to 2,293,000.[4]

How does the prosecutor contribute to the incarceration of one percent of the adult population?[5] To begin with, roughly 20 to 25 percent of the cases involving adults arrested for felony crimes are either rejected outright at the initial screening stage or dropped by the prosecutor or dismissed by a judge afterward, usually due to evidence insufficiency, procedural difficulty (e.g., the prosecutor is not prepared), or offense triviality. Others are dropped because the defendant fails to appear in court after having been released on money bond, personal recognizance, or third-party custody. Of those convicted, over 90 percent are by plea, typically to obtain a lighter sentence than if found guilty in trial. Of those who do go to trial, most are found guilty. About two-thirds of those convicted are incarcerated, the more serious receiving prison terms of at least one year and the others jail terms of up to a year. These numbers can vary substantially from one jurisdiction to the next.

One measure of the importance of the prosecutor is this: for every adult felony case that a judge presides over in trial, the prosecutor decides the fate of about 15 brought by the police. The cases that go to trial tend to be the most serious; while they consume a disproportionate share of resources, they represent a tiny share of the felony caseload of a typical prosecutor's office.

WHAT FACTORS PREDICT CONVICTION AND INCARCERATION?

So much for aggregate outcomes. What can be said about the factors that determine *which* cases are selected for prosecution and harsher sanctions in any jurisdiction? We can begin to address this question by focusing on the cases dropped and the reasons given by prosecutors for rejecting them.

The vast majority of all felony cases dropped by the prosecutor are rejected due to insufficiency of evidence—the police fail to produce adequate physical evidence (e.g., stolen property, implements of the crime) or testimonial evidence from victims or eye witnesses (Boland, Mahanna, and Sones, 1992). The next major reason given by prosecutors, although far less common than evidentiary insufficiency, is triviality of the offense (often reported as "declined in the interest of justice"). The defendants in these cases are generally not viewed as serious threats to the community. Most are dropped outright, while others are "diverted," often with the stipulation that the defendant must complete a program of counseling or instruction aimed at rehabilitation.

Many of the cases dropped or diverted are not trivial. Cases of assault and rape, in particular—often cases involving serious injury—are frequently dropped by prosecutors because they arise between people who knew each other prior to the offense, typically in domestic settings. Studies of felony arrest processing in several jurisdictions have shown that in the majority of violent offense cases, the assailant is known to the victim, and many involve members of the same family.[6] Prosecutors usually regard such cases as unattractive: the victims, after having called the police to arrest the offender, are frequently uncooperative.[7] Because of uncooperative witnesses, prosecutors reject arrests for crimes of assault within families at a rate of over 40 percent—nearly three times the rate for assault cases involving strangers.[8] Males who make a habit of assaulting their female partners may commit serious crimes in the home as frequently as other offenders with more serious criminal records do on the street.[9] Although considerable progress has been made on this front since 1980, prosecutors still are often reluctant to give the attention to such cases that is warranted by basic standards of justice.

Largely because of the importance of the relationship between offender and victim, conviction rates vary substantially from one index crime to another. Conviction rates for murder tend to be much higher than for larceny, and conviction rates for aggravated assault tend to be much lower (Solari 1992).

It is widely believed that many, if not most, felony cases presented to prosecutors are dropped for another reason—legal "technicalities" related to Fourth Amendment exclusionary rule violations. In fact, fewer than one percent of all felony arrests are dropped on such grounds; most of those are drug cases involving questionable procedures for searching for drugs (Forst, Lucianovic, and Cox 1977; Brosi 1979; Boland, Mahanna, and Sones 1992). While the exclusionary rule may retard the ability of the police to arrest offenders and bring them to the prosecutor, it does not appear to play a major role in the prosecutor's decision to reject or dismiss cases.[10]

Of course, the reasons for case rejections officially recorded by public agents are not necessarily to be believed. On this question, however, independent empirical evidence exists to validate the official reasons. Convictions are systematically more likely to follow arrest when police produce and document physical evidence than when such evidence is not produced. Likewise, when police produce information about two or more witnesses (including victims), convictions are more likely to follow. And when police make the arrest soon after an offense occurs, physical evidence is more likely to be found and conviction is more likely to follow than when more time elapses between the offense and the arrest (Forst, Lucianovic, and Cox 1977; Forst, et al. 1981).

It should not be surprising that arrests with the strongest tangible and testimonial evidence are most likely to produce convictions. The evidence needed to convict in court must be sufficient to prove guilt beyond a reasonable doubt. More important is the fact that the *police* are responsible for obtaining physical evidence and information about witnesses, as well as for providing information to witnesses that induces them to support the prosecutor in convicting offenders. While the police have little control over the amount and quality of relevant evidence available, some police officers show up consistently with arrests that end in conviction at a rate that substantially surpasses random chance.[11] Interviews have revealed that those officers tend to be more persistent about finding witnesses and more conscientious about follow-up investigation than officers with low rates of conviction (Forst et al. 1981).[12]

In short, whether an arrest ends in conviction depends in the first place on factors over which the prosecutor has no direct control: the strength of the evidence available to the police officer, the effectiveness of the officer in bringing the best available evidence (both tangible and testimonial) to the prosecutor, and the seriousness of the offense. Nonetheless, prosecution resources and practices—and the exercise of discretion—do play significant roles in determining whether arrests lead to conviction.

THE PROSECUTOR'S IMPACT ON SENTENCE SEVERITY AND DISPARITY

The prosecutor also influences sentencing outcomes, both in deciding which charges to pursue for conviction and in recommending sentences to the judge or jury. Sentencing outcomes became more predictable in the 1980s and 1990s, thanks largely to the replacement of "indeterminate sentencing" systems, in which the terms of incarceration were decided largely by parole boards, with sentencing guidelines and mandatory sentencing legislation (see chapter 16 in this volume by Kevin Reitz).

Reliance on more structured approaches to sentencing reduced discretion by judges and eliminated that of most parole officials, but the new rules did not restrict the discretion of prosecutors. Does this mean that sentencing discretion shifted from judges to prosecutors? Only if the process is viewed as a zero-sum game. What some see as a shift in discretionary authority from judge to prosecutor may be viewed alternatively as a net reduction in unwarranted disparity under sentencing guidelines, with no absolute increase in prosecutorial discretion. Judges have had less discretionary authority under the guidelines, but there is no evidence that prosecutors have had more, either in filing charges or reducing them, than they did before guidelines (Engen 2008). Prior to laws that structured sentencing practices, individual judges reported to no one in shaping sentences. If an imbalance of power between judge and prosecutor is regarded as the primary problem of structured sentencing policy, it becomes tempting to find solutions that return discretionary authority to judges and result in greater disparity in sentencing, with no less prosecutorial discretion—a cure that could be worse than the disease. This prospect has become more palpable following three landmark Supreme Court decisions from 2000 to 2005 that encourage a return to wider exercise of judicial discretion in sentencing: *Apprendi v. New Jersey*, 530 U.S. 466 (2000);[13] *Blakely v. Washington*, 542 U.S. 296 (2004);[14] *United States v. Booker*, 543 U.S. 220 (2005).[15]

Regardless of how much discretion judges have in sentencing, prosecutors will continue to influence sentences. Prosecution policy should be mindful of the effects of that influence on the offender and the community. Incarceration may be the most appropriate sanction for some offenders, but other sanctions may be more productive in reducing crime and may do so at a considerable saving to the public (See chapters by Petersilia and Reitz in this volume). An affluent nation may be able and willing to put a larger proportion of its population behind bars than any other in the world—about 2.3 million, as noted earlier (see also chapter 2 by Lynch and Pridemore in this volume)—but we will do well to consider alternatives to prison and jail for offenders who can be safely and effectively punished in other ways: fines, restitution, forfeiture, and community-based sanctions that encourage community reintegration without substantial risks. These sanctions are less expensive to administer, and they tend to produce less stigma than prison, enhancing the offender's prospects for community reintegration. Moreover, some alternatives to incarceration can provide compensation to the victim and society (Reitz).

The tough questions for prosecutors in making case-processing decisions that influence the sanction are these:

1. Will the resulting sanction best serve the collective interests of the community, taking into account the future behavior of the offender and victim(s) in the current case, and that of other prospective offenders and victims?
2. Will it be administered effectively and fairly, so as to make it transparent that the sanction is not out of line with that received by offenders with similar criminal histories and in similarly serious cases?
3. How much say should the victim and offender have in these matters?

Prosecutors in different jurisdictions will inevitably arrive at different answers to these questions. Whatever the answers, basic notions of justice warrant that they be uniformly applied to the offenders prosecuted in that jurisdiction.

VARIATION IN SCREENING AND PLEA BARGAINING PRACTICES

The practices and outcomes that follow arrest are anything but uniform across jurisdictions—prosecutors are free to operate in quite different ways from one jurisdiction to another, and even among offices within the same jurisdiction. The Constitution says nothing explicitly about prosecutorial rules and standards.[16] As a result, prosecutors in some offices are much more inclined to obtain convictions by plea rather than take cases to trial. Conventional wisdom holds that these differences are due to variations in the workloads per prosecutor from office to office, but pleas have been found not to be driven primarily by caseload pressure (Heumann 1978; Forst and Boland 1984). Jurisdictions with huge caseloads often have low ratios of pleas to trials, while those with much smaller caseloads often have high ratios.[17]

Prosecution *policy*—whether to aim for *quality convictions* by being more selective at the screening stage and then putting more effort into bringing cases to trial, or to aim for *more convictions* by accepting more marginal cases and putting greater effort into negotiating guilty pleas in return for charge reductions—appears to be no less important a determinant of the ratio of pleas-to-trials than the press of large caseloads. In screening arrests for prosecution, offices that aim for more convictions tend to be more inclined to apply the arrest standard of "probable cause," while those that aim for quality convictions tend to use a higher standard of "trial-worthiness." Offices with less-selective screening policies tend to have higher plea-to-trial ratios and higher conviction rates but lower rates of imprisonment than those that are more selective.[18] In jurisdictions where the police tend to bring weaker cases, or when crime waves or other shocks cause the quality of evidence in arrests to decline, a more selective screening policy appears to be more clearly warranted (Forst 2008).

How can a prosecution strategy that leans toward quantity and pleas rather than quality and trials be justified? Many have argued that plea bargaining is simply wrong and should be abolished—it deprives defendants of their day in court and deprives victims of the security of long terms of incarceration for offenders. But the abolition of or constraints on plea bargaining practices by legislation or voter referendum has proven to be at best ineffective and often counterproductive.[19] Many—perhaps most—pleas involve cases in which an offender has no defense and simply wishes to expedite the process, often in exchange for minor concessions by the prosecutor. A prosecution policy that tilts toward more convictions rather than more trials might obtain more crime reduction benefits through deterrence and incapacitation than one that allows culpable offenders to go free so that a few offenders get tougher sanctions.

Other pleas involve leniency in exchange for information from the defendant against other suspects. Such pleas can be indispensable for bringing offenders to justice, but they may tend to produce more miscarriages of justice, especially when the ones offering the information are a greater menace to the community than those about whom the information is given. Street offenders have been found, in any case, to be less inclined to assist prosecutors by providing such information than other offenders; many have been known to impose sanctions against collaborators who breach a bond of trust that are considerably harsher than those imposed by the criminal justice system (Forst and Lucianovic 1977).

UNBRIDLED PROSECUTORIAL DISCRETION?

District attorneys normally exercise considerable latitude in choosing which felony arrests to prosecute, what charges to file, and how aggressively to prosecute each case and charge. The typical urban prosecutor's office, presented with as many as 100 or more felony cases per attorney each year, obviously cannot give celebrity-status attention to every case. According to criminologist Albert Reiss (1974), the district attorney exercises "the greatest discretion in the formally organized criminal justice network" (See also Jackson 1940; Kress 1976; Worrall 2008).

For many, if not most, cases, the decision whether or not to prosecute is virtually automatic—cases in which the evidence is either extremely strong or weak and cases involving either very serious or trivial offenses. Numerous studies agree that prosecutors' case-screening and handling decisions are influenced primarily by the strength of the evidence and the seriousness of the offense (Landes 1971; Forst and Brosi 1977; U.S. Department of Justice 1977; Jacoby 1981; Feeney, Dill, and Weir 1983). In the late 1970s and early 1980s many prosecutors, induced largely by federal support, instituted programs to target resources as well on cases involving repeat offenders (Chelimsky and Dahmann 1981). Prosecutors' decisions have been anything but random.

Within those boundaries, however, substantial discretion is exercised. In deciding whether to accept cases, in selecting charges to file with the court, in negotiating pleas with defense counsel, in preparing cases more or less extensively for trial, and in recommending sentences to judges, prosecutors have considerable room to maneuver. Written policies used in even the most rule-bound offices do not provide unambiguous instructions about how to handle each and every type of case. Because of this discretion, even the best statistical models of prosecutors' decision-making cannot predict screening, charging, or plea bargaining decisions in particular cases with a significant degree of accuracy.

Ask a typical prosecutor to explain the rationale behind the decisions and you're likely to get an answer along the following lines: Case-handling decisions, like medical decisions, involve both science and craft, and experienced prosecutors know how to blend the technical requirements of the law with the wisdom that comes from years of practice. Unfortunately, this tells us nothing about the underlying goals that influence their actions. Nor do we know whether prosecutors consciously make case selection and handling decisions with such goals in mind. Most prosecutors argue that while justice, crime control, and speedy case processing are all worthy goals, each case is unique. Whether to accept a case, what charges to file, how much time to spend preparing it for a court proceeding, what charge or charges to allow the defendant to plead to in return for dropping other charges (or what sentence to recommend to the judge if the defendant pleads guilty to a particular charge) in any given case cannot be determined by contemplating abstract goals or resorting to a formula derived from such goals. Until a strong argument can be made for instituting a more explicit set of rules or guidelines for making case-processing decisions based on well-established factual links between the rules and such tangible goals as crime control and reduced case-processing time, decisions about individual cases are likely to continue to be made in a subjective and largely unpredictable manner.

At some point, however, prosecutors risk pushing the political, if not the Constitutional limits of their discretion. Authorities from both ends of the political spectrum have long voiced strong objection to the politicization of prosecution policies and practices. Here are three conspicuous prosecution events from the recent era involving excesses in the exercise of prosecutorial discretion in high-profile cases: independent prosecutor Kenneth Starr's freewheeling $52 million impeachment investigation of President Bill Clinton from 1994 to 1997 (Adams 2000; Will 1994); Durham District Attorney Mike Nifong's fraudulent 2006 prosecution of players from the Duke lacrosse team for rape (Taylor and Johnson 2008); and the 2009 dismissal of the conviction of Alaska Senator Ted Stevens's conviction for corruption because the prosecutors mishandled evidence and witnesses and failed to share exculpatory evidence with the defense and judge (Wilber 2009).

The central concern raised in these cases is not new. In 1940 former U.S. Attorney General and Supreme Court Justice Robert H. Jackson observed, "The prosecutor has more control over life, liberty, and reputation than any other person in America" (18). Jackson's remark had more resonance 70 years ago than today—a public with a low level of tolerance for crime might well accept extremes in the prosecutor's use of authority. For all the lip service paid to crime, prosecutors often have other interests that shape their operations.

Much less has been written about abuses of discretion in cases involving low-level street offenders, but the lack of any systematic review of prosecutors' decisions about which cases to file in court and how much attention to give to each should lead one to wonder about even-handedness in those cases as well.

Prosecutors may be less than clear about the proper goals of prosecution, or about the best way to achieve any particular goal. They are likely to find, however, that the development of guidelines for screening and case-processing decisions can at least produce greater consistency and coherence, if not critical and constructive thinking about the role of the prosecutor in society.

INCENTIVES OF PROSECUTORS

Given the substantial obstacles confronting prosecutors—large case loads, limited resources, and broadly conflicting views about what the system ought to be accomplishing—it seems reasonable to ask how they are motivated to solve these problems. District attorneys are typically publicly elected officials, so they are inclined to conduct themselves in a way that appeals to the general public (Worden 1989). But can we be sure that public appeal has much to do with the attainment of justice? Suppose a district attorney is especially conscientious about taking on cases involving highly active offenders, even when those cases require the commitment of additional resources (e.g., giving extra attention to the needs of reluctant witnesses). If, as a result, the crime rate were reduced by 10 percent, our inability to prove cause and effect would prevent even the district attorney from knowing for certain whether his or her conscientiousness paid off. Another district attorney may routinely drop cases involving repeat offenders unless they happen to be easy cases, taking on only those that do not require much attention, and may then boast of winning a few high-profile cases, or perhaps allude to a conviction rate over 90 percent for the narrow subset of cases that either go to trial or result in guilty pleas. Since information about cases dropped by the prosecutor is not generally made available to the public, a prosecutor's legitimate crime control efforts, or lack thereof, will go unnoticed.

The prosecutor is insulated by the virtual absence of a system of measured public accountability in most states. This derives in part from the origins of American prosecution, rooted in the English common law tradition of private prosecution. In the eighteenth century, the American colonies developed a system of elected public prosecutors, which evolved eventually into a system of federalism that puts the prosecutor outside the chain of command of the U.S. president (Shikita 1996; Worrall 2008). In other systems throughout the world, prosecutors are almost always appointed through a hierarchy, with the head of state at the top.

This evolution led to a system in which the success of prosecutors is assessed principally by the public's perception of the prosecutor's ability to convict offenders. These perceptions are shaped largely by a few prominent cases in the news and by occasional public pronouncements by a district attorney or attorney general asserting toughness against any and all who would dare to violate the law. Unlike police chiefs, who are appointed by and accountable to mayors, most prosecutors in the U.S. are elected district attorneys. They do not report to a higher political authority who might demand a comprehensive system of accountability. Political opponents have not been able to distract the voters from their preoccupation with celebrity cases and their obliviousness to the importance of systematic measures of performance. And the media, capable of enlightening the public on the folly of weak accountability for the vast majority of felony cases, have opted to feed the public's appetite for information about sensational cases.

Nor do prosecutors in most jurisdictions report information about the numbers and types of arrests received from the police and the dispositions of each type. To put this problem in perspective, imagine a police chief deciding not to provide comprehensive information about reported offenses, arrests, and clearances to anyone outside the office. Imagine him (or her) justifying such a decision on grounds that such information is too easily misinterpreted to be useful. Asked how, then, the public should hold the chief and the department accountable, suppose the chief responded that his frequent contacts with the public and attention from the local media make him more than sufficiently accountable. Such a stance would be regarded as arrogant and irresponsible. Yet this is essentially the position of most prosecutors in the United States.

Of course, most chief prosecutors are directly accountable to the voters. But they are politicians who have it in their best interest not to subject themselves to systems of accountability that opponents could use against them. Unlike the police chief, who may benefit from falling crime rates but must also suffer the inevitable upward swings in crime, the prosecutor is rarely called to task by the local press for a drop in the conviction rate. Conviction rates are not routinely reported to a national agency in the same way that crimes reported to the police and arrests made by the police are documented annually by the FBI. The federally operated National Judicial Reporting Program (NJRP) reports felony convictions and arrests for about 300 of the nation's 3,195 counties, but the data are aggregates rather than based on individually tracked felony cases (Solari 1992). Many of the convictions reported for any given year relate to arrests made in earlier years, which creates distortions, especially when the aggregates change from year to year. Moreover, the NJRP gives no information about cases rejected or dropped by prosecutors. More than a few people might like to know *why* over 80 percent of all arrests for motor vehicle theft fail to end in conviction, and why about 60 percent of all arrests for robbery and burglary fail as well.

Prosecutors in most jurisdictions are not required even to provide systematic information about case outcomes to other criminal justice agencies that deal with and rely on the prosecutor, most notably the police and victim-witness organizations. Some prosecutors do provide feedback, but it is usually voluntary and episodic.

Some prosecutors select cases and handle them in a way that gives more than the usual degree of political visibility, but this too tends to be opportunistic rather than systematic. It is tempting for big-city prosecutors to pursue high-profile cases aggressively, tilt strongly toward pleas in other cases, and eventually run for higher public office (Worden 1989). A prosecutor's career path can be driven, for better or worse, by the outcome of a single case that attains local or national prominence. (Criminologist Samuel Walker (1985) has alluded to these as "celebrity cases".)

The district attorney can gain public visibility also by projecting a tough image in press conferences and public appearances on a variety of crime issues. Many a prosecutor has gained visibility by announcing crackdowns on organized crime or drug-dealing. U.S. Attorney Rudolph Giuliani gained fame in his high-profile targeting of white-collar offenders in the Southern District of New York in the late 1980s and became mayor of New York City in 1995 and a leading presidential candidate in the election of 2008. If a prosecutor says he is tough on criminals and appears to put up a good fight in the exceptional cases that make the news, any failures in managing his office efficiently or in dealing effectively with the larger pool of cases involving predictably dangerous offenders—cases that rarely make the news—will not jeopardize his prospects for reelection or advancement to higher political office.

"Career criminal" prosecution programs, created in 1975, illustrate the tension that can arise between the somewhat abstract goals of justice and crime prevention, on the one hand, and the more immediate incentives facing prosecutors on the other. The programs were initiated by the Justice Department to deal with the problem posed by a relatively few offenders who, as researchers found repeatedly, account for a disproportionate share of cases involving serious crimes.[20] It had been perceived generally that prosecutors did not give special attention to cases involving those more criminally active offenders—cases that were often otherwise unattractive. This perception had been validated empirically (Forst and Brosi 1977). To provide an incentive for prosecutors to target more attorney time on such cases, the Justice Department offered additional resources to local prosecutors for the creation of career criminal programs. Many prosecutors, interested in the additional resources, applied for and obtained them, creating sections of the office in which attorneys worked on fewer cases and processed them through all the stages of prosecution ("vertically") rather than in the production-line process ("horizontally," from attorney to attorney) that characterizes municipal prosecution.

Evaluations of those programs, however, revealed that the criteria used by the prosecutors to identify career offenders were of limited value. Rather than pinpointing the most criminally active suspects, most jurisdictions developed criteria designed to be easily administered and to produce interesting cases. Career criminal units typically targeted offenders with at least one prior felony conviction and current charges involving a serious crime—often homicide, rape, or assault. Such criteria may be better than none, but prosecutors would do better still to base case selection on criteria that correspond more closely to the actual characteristics of dangerous, high-crime-rate offenders: prior arrests for serious crimes, a juvenile record, youthfulness, drug use, and known involvement in robbery or burglary. Those characteristics had been shown to be the strongest predictors of predatory crime in research at the University of Pennsylvania, the Rand Corporation, and elsewhere (Wolfgang, Figlio, and Sellin 1972; Williams, 1979; Forst, Rhodes, et al. 1982; Greenwood 1982; Chaiken and Chaiken 1982), yet they rarely turned up as career criminal targeting criteria. The public has been deeply concerned about crime and generally supportive of career criminal programs, but in practice, career criminal units have tended to employ criteria that focus largely on criminals in the twilight of their careers, often bypassing the offenders likely to inflict the most harm on society.

The incentives of prosecutors, in short, leave substantial opportunity for disparity and inefficiency in the exercise of discretion. The goals of prosecution have not been made sufficiently clear, and detailed information about the decisions made by prosecutors is not sufficiently accessible to allow anyone to know whether prosecutors tend to make decisions about individual cases that correspond closely or consistently to any particular standard of justice or efficiency.

RESISTANCE TO REFORM

These incentive systems have not placed prosecutors at the vanguard of criminal justice reform. The new millennium finds sea changes in every other sector of the criminal justice system. Policing has gone through the community policing revolution and transformations in systems of accountability (see chapter 20 in this volume by Sherman) and an explosion in privatization (Forst and Manning 1999). Companion chapters in this volume document equally remarkable changes in the spheres of sentencing and corrections: the conversion from extensive judicial discretion in sentencing to mandatory terms and legislatively imposed sentencing guideline systems, and now a shift back toward judicial discretion; large-scale shifts from a black-and-white world of either incarceration or probation to one with a myriad of intermediate sanction options, ranging from intensive supervision and electronically monitored home detention to more widespread use of community-based sanctions; and the expansion of private alternatives throughout the corrections sector.

Changes in prosecution have been modest by comparison. The typical prosecutor's office has a more modern appearance than it did in the mid-twentieth century, with laptop computers supporting operations and access to vastly greater sources of information and forensic technologies than ever before. Women and minorities play larger roles as prosecutors than in earlier times, paralleling their gains in virtually every other profession. And in the 1990s, prosecutors started developing community outreach programs that echoed community policing.

The fundamentals of prosecution, however, remain as they have for decades. The basic nature and goals of prosecution, the role of the citizen as victim or witness in a matter between the state and the defendant, the essential steps in processing cases through the courts, and the limited availability of transparent systems of public accountability all remain essentially as they were in 1970.

Prosecutors are not more inherently resistant to change than others. They are well-educated, they understand fine points of the law, and they must be able to decipher diverse and intricate case details quickly and interpret complex human behaviors accurately. Their work demands intelligence and ingenuity, resourcefulness and hard work. They have taken an oath to serve the public. And many have experienced that innovations can produce welcome political capital.

Still, as elected officials, district attorneys aim largely to avoid embarrassment. This is usually accomplished by keeping the bulk of their work below the horizon, staying away from risky ventures and drastic departures from conventional modes of office management and from collaborations with researchers on the assessment of policies, procedures, or performance—assessments that could become tomorrow's embarrassing headline.

A 1998 survey of over 500 scientific evaluations of crime prevention programs, sponsored by the National Institute of Justice and conducted by Lawrence Sherman and his former colleagues at the University of Maryland, found just one evaluation of an innovative prosecution program, an experiment run by David Ford that tested three alternative domestic violence interventions in Indianapolis. Innovation was found mostly in other parts of the justice system—programs initiated by the police, social service agencies, schools, drug treatment specialists, housing and correctional authorities.

The prosecutor's insulation derives in part from legal training. Prosecutors are trained in an adversarial system of law, not in principles of service delivery or systems of management. To the extent that they receive administrative training in law school, it pertains to the management of private law practice rather than the administration of a prosecutor's office.

A first rule of prosecution derives from the legal-adversarial culture: don't divulge the particulars of your case to anyone who is not in a position to help you win it. Prosecutors become accustomed to keeping their options open by revealing little about their objectives and about the information they have and do not have. They typically see little to gain and much to lose in divulging any information that is not required by law. Internal office policy manuals indicating the prosecutor's guidelines for screening cases and negotiating pleas are typically unavailable to the defense bar and the general public.

This culture stands in contrast to innovative efforts by other criminal justice agents, who sometimes find themselves attempting unsuccessfully to obtain needed support from the prosecutor. Sally Hillsman (1982) reported finding prosecutors converting an innovative attempt at rehabilitation in New York into a vehicle for controlling offenders who would otherwise have had their cases dismissed following diversion and the completion of job training. Sherman and colleaguges (1998) similarly documented pretrial diversion programs that "tend to get co-opted by prosecutors for purposes other than the intended purpose of rehabilitating offenders."

DIRECTIONS FOR REFORM

Structuring the Exercise of Prosecutorial Discretion

Aware of room for improvement, a few prosecutors, as well as state and federal legislators and criminal justice system reformers, have set out to introduce procedures designed to produce greater uniformity and efficiency in the decisions and practices that follow arrest. In the 1970s, prosecutors began to rely on computers to track individual cases and caseloads of individual attorneys, print subpoenas, produce periodic reports showing various aggregate dimensions of office performance, and provide data so that office policy could be analyzed in depth. Before that, prosecutors had neither the means nor much interest in monitoring office performance and assessing the effectiveness of alternative practices and policies.

Prosecutors have tended to focus traditionally on individual cases and litigation related to them rather than on jurisdiction-wide, or even office-wide constructs of performance (Szanton, 1972). Thoughtfully crafted guidelines and computerized decision-support systems have helped prosecutors to make screening and case-processing decisions more uniform and effective, and computerized information systems have helped district attorneys shift their thinking from the single-case litigation perspective instilled by conventional legal training to an orientation that considers aggregate information in the context of goals of prosecution and sentencing. Thus a basic aspect of reform in prosecution has been underway for some time now.

The Effective Use of Information

Despite the availability of these systems, most prosecutors continue to operate in a limited statistical environment, uncharacteristic of other major components of the criminal justice system and inconsistent with contemporary standards of management and public accountability (Nugent-Borakove 2008). Critical to the effective use of data to support criminal justice decisions is that the data be *reliable*. Prosecutors are usually quick to express concern, as they should, about the need for prompt, accurate information about evidence from investigators, forensic laboratories, and lineups. A crime-control-oriented prosecutor should be concerned as well with the quality of data indicative of defendant dangerousness, including arrest history ("rap sheet") information, juvenile record, and urinalysis test results to indicate whether the defendant was on drugs at the time of arrest. Prosecutors have not been conditioned to seek out such information to support prosecution decisions, despite widespread concern about "false positives"—people selected for targeting who in fact would not commit another crime if released. The availability and use of reliable rap sheets, juvenile records, and urinalysis test results, when combined with case information, would provide demonstrably more accurate assessments of defendant dangerousness than current information alone is capable of providing, and more accurate assessment means *fewer* false positives.[21]

Data used by prosecutors and courts, properly processed, could also help to improve performance in other areas of the criminal justice system. For example, district attorneys could induce the police to bring better arrests by periodically providing information to police supervisors about the outcomes of the arrests brought to prosecution, itemized by department, precinct, and officer. This information could include data about the frequencies of each major type of outcome and the reasons for case rejections and dismissals. Information about case outcomes could also be given routinely to the victims and witnesses in those cases. The systematic dissemination of information can also nurture cooperation between prosecutors and police, victims, and witnesses. Public support of the criminal justice system is not enhanced by the routine failure of prosecutors to provide feedback to victims and witnesses, and police incentives to produce better evidence are weakened when prosecutors fail to provide regular information about arrest outcomes to police officers and their supervisors.[22]

The federal government routinely gathered and reported case-tracking information on the prosecution of felony arrests from a large cross section of prosecution offices during the 1970s and 1980s, but this data series was discontinued in the 1990s. In a time of greater transparency throughout the public and private sectors, it is more than remarkable that we have *less* useful information today about the routine prosecution of felony cases than we did 30 years ago.

Community Prosecution

In the 1990s a few chief prosecutors attempted to improve the operations of their offices and improve relations with the public in the process by introducing community prosecution programs. Patterned after community policing programs that aim to improve police performance by building bridges to the community, these programs assign individual attorneys to cases involving crimes in specific neighborhoods. The basic idea is that prosecutors can be more effective when they become less insular and get to know the neighborhood better (Forst 1993; Coles and Kelling 1999; Coles 2008). Additional economies are likely to derive from working with the same few police officers who are responsible for particular neighborhoods. These programs are consistent with a central idea of success in a service economy: generating value by getting to know the customer better.

District attorneys in jurisdictions throughout the country have launched such programs of community outreach, assigning cases to assistant district attorneys by neighborhood, and encouraging these assistants to spend more time in the community. A common theme is to redirect service outside the court, with more sensitivity to the cultures and special needs of those served. Specific aspects of the programs include: working more closely with people who understand the unique characteristics of particular neighborhoods, assigning assistant district attorneys to work out of police precincts or storefronts, supporting community crime prevention programs, and converting from a production line approach that moves cases along impersonally to a system ("vertical prosecution") that reduces the need for traumatized victims to repeat harrowing experiences to a sequence of strangers.

A focus group commissioned by the Bureau of Justice Assistance developed this definition of community prosecution: "a long term, proactive strategy involving a partnership among the prosecutor's office, law enforcement, the community and public and private organizations whereby the authority of the prosecutor's office is used to solve problems and improve public safety and the quality of life in an identified community" (Stevens 1994, 13). Catherine Coles (2008) suggests a more nuanced definition revolving around increased collaboration with the police and other criminal justice agencies toward the solution of community problems, with seven basic defining elements: mission, base of authority, demand, organization, tactics, environment, and outcomes.

These ideas mirror ones initiated about 10 years earlier in policing. Municipal police departments throughout the country have worked to build bridges to the community and improve public relations by moving officers from squad cars to foot and bicycle patrols, working more closely with community leaders, and focusing more on prostitution, vandalism, and other crimes of disorder. Anecdotal evidence in support of these activities is compelling, but their effects on serious crime remains unclear. Reviews of the experimental research in several cities has found that these efforts have done more to reduce fear and increase public satisfaction with police service than to reduce crime rates, at least in the short term.[23]

In the late 1990s, federal funding became available to district attorneys to sweeten the community prosecution pot. Byrne Grant program funds, administered by the Bureau of Justice Assistance and authorized for amounts up to $16 million (for 2009), provide support to prosecutors to establish and participate in community prosecution programs generally and community justice centers and multi-jurisdictional task forces in particular.

Many prosecutors have responded by climbing aboard the community bandwagon. They have done so in much the same way as did police chiefs: first a few brave souls, then others, when the political benefits become more apparent and federal support available. Columnist Robert Samuelson has highlighted community-oriented justice programs that confer benefits on politicians rather than special interest groups as "the new pork barrel . . . propaganda disguised as a government program" (2000, A25). Prosecutors may be adopting these programs with noble intentions. There is, in any case, merit in bringing prosecutors down from the ivory tower, to induce greater sensitivity to the lives of the people whose fates are often at the mercy of the prosecutor's decisions. Still, it may be no coincidence that such programs are unheard of in other countries, where prosecutors are appointed rather than elected. Ten years ago it was common to hear police officers complain about learning of their department's conversion to "community policing" on the evening news. Assistant district attorneys today tell similar stories.

As appealing as community prosecution seems, it is really not clear that the prevailing bundle of interventions that have become associated with the community prosecution movement—more decentralized operations, lecturing to school children, police ride-alongs, and so on—are really the most effective ones for giving prosecutors their needed training on sensitivity toward community residents and problems. There is no guarantee that these experiences ensure that the prosecutors, thus enlightened, will exercise discretion more wisely from the case screening stage through final adjudication, or that the programs will make communities safer.

A basic premise of these programs warrants questioning: How much time *should* prosecutors spend supporting community crime prevention programs? Surely crime prevention is a worthy goal, but it is not clear that prosecutors are better situated to engage effectively in these efforts and in community reform than are the police and other public servants (Levine 2007). In any case, we have no clue as to the respective contributions to crime control of any given level of resources allocated to the pursuit of a conviction in a typical case in court and the same level allocated to the pursuit of any particular crime prevention activity.

The post-arrest options associated with community prosecution are another matter: focusing on dispute resolution, mediation, community service, restitution, and other community-based approaches to resolve minor crimes and problems at early stages before they blossom into serious felonies (Karp and Clear 2000). These programs fit the prosecution mandate more closely than many other crime prevention programs. In the meantime, prosecutors who win convictions in the ocean of run-of-the-mill cases that do not make the evening news are likely to produce more than an ounce of crime prevention.

Converting from a production-line approach to vertical prosecution may make sense in rape and homicide cases and cases involving victims who are very young or otherwise especially vulnerable. For a variety of less serious crimes, however, large municipal prosecution offices could be wasting resources and losing cases if they were to rely on systems of prosecution better suited to rural settings.

Assessments of community prosecution programs across the country have produced mixed results. Community prosecution offices do not appear to employ fundamentally different approaches or produce systematically different outcomes from those of conventional prosecution operations (Nugent-Borakove and Fanflik 2008).

One set of programs is noteworthy. Evidence from Boston in the late 1990s is consistent with the idea that interventions associated with community prosecution may reduce crime, especially cooperation between prosecutors and others in positions to prevent and solve crime. A constellation of projects has been credited with reducing gun homicides in

Boston, especially among juveniles. The number of homicides dropped from about 100 annually in the late 1980s, before the projects were launched, to 35 by 1998 and not a single juvenile homicide in that year. The number of shootings also plummeted. Ralph Martin II, the district attorney for Suffolk County (comprising Boston and immediately surrounding communities), played a pivotal leadership role in these projects.

A centerpiece of the Boston crime reduction efforts was the Safe Neighborhood Initiatives (SNI), which coordinated law enforcement activities, supported neighborhood revitalization efforts, and complemented conventional response activities with a focus on prevention. SNI prosecutors spoke at all the local schools and attended community organization meetings (Coles and Kelling 1999). They also participated in the Boston Youth Violence Strike Force, which coordinated Martin's SNI with the Massachusetts attorney general and local U.S. Attorney, as well as with 45 full-time Boston Police Department officers, 15 officers from nearby police departments, and federal agents, together with probation, parole, and other correctional agents (Department of Justice 1996). A third element of collaboration was the Boston Gun Project, which included the close support of agents from the Bureau of Alcohol, Tobacco and Firearms (Kennedy 1999).

In all three projects, coordination among prosecutors provided an array of creative options in determining which charges to file in which court or courts. Cross-deputization of prosecutors provided opportunities to file cases that fell under multiple jurisdiction authority in Suffolk County juvenile court, adult court, or federal court. Coordination with law enforcement officials appears to have been especially important, to support their program of "focused deterrence" on gang crimes and to ensure that the elements needed to satisfy various charging requirements were met (see chapter 9 by David Kennedy in this volume).

A broader set of prosecution strategies emerged from this coordination than had been traditionally applied. The Suffolk County district attorney aggressively filed charges against crimes of disorder—graffiti, truancy, noise, public drinking, and so on—to improve the quality of life, especially in areas of Boston that had suffered from chronic private abuse and public neglect. Federal, state, and local statutes were creatively applied to remove guns from the streets under laws against gun use, possession, and trafficking. The Massachusetts Commonwealth's criminal and civil forfeiture laws were exploited to take over drug dens and to permit their renovation into suitable low-income housing. Civil sanctions were also more aggressively applied to target chronic public blemishes, such as mechanics doing major vehicle repairs on the street and commercial establishments improperly disposing of waste.

A variety of interventions thus appears to have reduced crime in Boston, but this is by no means a clear victory for community prosecution. It may be a victory for aggressive programs to remove guns from juveniles and dangerous juveniles from the streets. It may be a victory for prosecutors effective at inducing support from others in positions to control crime, or for a unique way of targeting drugs. Several interventions were used, some having little to do with community prosecution, and we have no way of knowing which ones were the most effective; one or two may have even been counterproductive.

A key ingredient missing from the Boston experience was that the interventions were not individually tested by experimentation. Prosecutors in Boston and elsewhere are spending scarce resources on a loosely defined set of interventions having to do with "community outreach" and "cooperation" without the benefit of systematic evidence validating that some are really more effective than others, or indeed that *any* of those usually associated with community prosecution are useful for achieving the goals of prosecution. The primary problem with community prosecution programs as currently constituted is that even the best of the programs lack systematic bottom-line public accountability.

The Boston interventions make sense, but time and again criminal justice interventions based on common sense and theory (from random police patrols and rapid police response to boot camps and DARE programs) have been found to be ineffective when subjected to properly designed and executed experimental research. In some cases, such as mandatory arrests of unemployed spouse assaulters and "three strikes and you're out" for old offenders, the intervention has been shown to be worse than neutral (Sherman et al. 1998). Over the past several decades, a few courageous police chiefs—Clarence Kelley, Lee Brown, Darrel Stephens, and Gil Kerlikowsky are notable examples—have distinguished themselves and advanced their calling by allowing researchers to alter normal operations for the sake of learning what works, and there is no good reason why this should not happen in prosecution.

As they are currently conceived, community prosecution programs do little either to make prosecutors more systematically accountable to citizens for their workaday, behind-the-scene performance in *all* felony cases or to promote a deep, transformational sense of justice. While these programs may offer immediate political advantages for prosecutors, and may even produce marginal gains in crime abatement, they represent no "paradigm shift." They may, in fact, divert attention from reforms that could really serve members of the community most in need of relief from crime. We might do well to consider, instead of or in addition to community prosecution, a truly radical departure from current arrangements—not just for political gains, but primarily for the sake of victims and for the well-being of the community.

PROSPECTS FOR FUNDAMENTAL REFORM

While the operations of most other institutions are much more open to scrutiny today than when Justice Jackson made his observation about the prosecutor's power, systematic accounting of the prosecutor's day-to-day operations has diminished. Much of the work of the prosecutor is subject to abuses of discretion, despite posturing to the contrary. Contemporary standards of accountability warrant the casting of a brighter light on the work of prosecutors, to move beyond rhetoric and strengthen legitimacy by making their operations more transparent and subject to systematic evaluation.

If prosecutors really wish to serve the community, they will subject their workaday operations to more systematic reporting and their programs to more rigorous assessment. They could make data available to the public on the number of arrests in each neighborhood, by offense category, and the disposition of those arrests at each stage of prosecution from screening until the case leaves the court. They could routinely communicate information about the status and outcome of each case to the police, victims, and witnesses. They could work more diligently to nurture, maintain, and monitor the cooperation of witnesses and victims.

The potential for truly fundamental change in prosecution goes beyond even the critical matter of accountability. Change that could significantly advance the public's interests in justice and order would require a shift from our current system, which treats the victim primarily as a resource for promoting the interest of the state, to one that recasts justice as a matter of balancing the right of the defendant to a fair and full hearing under the presumption of innocence with the fundamental right of the victim to be restored. Under current arrangements, victims are not adequately compensated for costs imposed by the criminal justice system: lost income, time spent with police and court officials, out-of-pocket costs for transportation, child care, and related costs. Victims are not generally included in any meaningful way in case-processing decisions following arrest. Most significantly, they are rarely compensated for losses associated with the crime. Victims commonly end up feeling used, like little more than items of evidence, deprived even of basic rights corresponding to those extended to offenders. Even when the offenders are convicted, victims rarely benefit in any tangible way from conventional sentences of incarceration and probation. Nor are intermediate sanctions typically of much help to victims: community service programs do little for the community and less for the victim; fines are rarely collected; when they are, the proceeds typically do not go to the victim. In the exceptional case in which the judge orders restitution, the court rarely follows up to ensure that the terms of restitution are fully met. Victims are too often left with little incentive to cooperate in subsequent episodes (Rosen 1999).

When victims are asked how they have been treated by various components of the criminal justice system, prosecutors fare less well than police, despite the fact that the chief prosecutor is usually an elected official and the police chief is not.[24] Community prosecution programs aim principally to connect the prosecutor more closely to the community, not to restore the victim. These programs leave intact the principle that the prosecutor represents the state, not the victim, in all criminal matters.

One prospect for a revolutionary advance in prosecution might be to challenge that fundamental principle. Some have suggested that a shift to a process resembling our tort system might effectively work to remedy the serious deficiencies of our existing state-versus-defendant system (e.g., Benson 1998). Genuine opportunities for victims to be restored could well increase their incentives to report crimes to the police, thus reducing recidivism rates and crime costs, stimulating general deterrent effects, and raising the perception of system legitimacy (Bazemore 1998; Braithwaite 2002; Van Ness and Strong 1997).

Whether or not such basic transformation happens, prosecutors should be induced to take a larger, more systemic view of their operations. The one-case-in-a-vacuum perspective of case screening, plea bargaining, and sentencing—and the disparity that that approach engenders—has made cynics of many of the citizens upon whom prosecutors rely the most, those who have been victims or witnesses of serious crime.

How we use prosecutors to deal with offenders, crime, and the community will be assessed inevitably on grounds of justice and efficiency. But more is at stake. In the end, how we deal with offenders and victims of crime reflects what kind of people we are.

References

Adams, Lorraine. 2000. "$52 Million Starr Probe Costliest Ever." *Washington Post* (April 1), A2.

Bazemore, Gorgon. 1998. "Restorative Justice and Earned Redemption: Communities, Victims, and Offender Reintegration." *The American Behavioral Scientist* 41 (1998): 768–813.

Benson, Bruce L. 1998. *To Serve and Protect: Privatization and Community in Criminal Justice*. New York: New York University.

Boland, Barbara, and Brian Forst. 1985. "Prosecutors Don't Always Aim to Pleas." *Federal Probation* 49 (June), 10–15.

Boland, Barbara, Paul Mahanna, and Ronald Sones. 1992. *The Prosecution of Felony Arrests, 1988*. Washington, DC: Bureau of Justice Statistics.

Braithwaite, John. 2002. *Restorative Justice and Responsive Regulation*. New York: Oxford University Press.

Brown, Jodi M., Patrick A. Langan, and David J. Levin. 1999. *Felony Sentences in State Courts, 1996*—Report NCJ 173939. Washington, DC: Bureau of Justice Statistics.

Bureau of Justice Statistics. 1992. *Prosecutors in State Courts, 1990*. Washington, DC: U.S. Department of Justice.

Bureau of Justice Statistics. 2009a. *Jail Inmates at Midyear 2008—Statistical Tables*, Report NCJ-225709. Washington, DC: U.S. Department of Justice.

Bureau of Justice Statistics. 2009b. *Prison Inmates at Midyear 2008—Statistical Tables*, Report NCJ-225619. Washington, DC: U.S. Department of Justice.

Cannavale, Frank J., Jr., and William D. Falcon. 1976. *Witness Cooperation*. Lexington, MA: D. C. Heath.

Chaiken, Jan M., and Marcia R. Chaiken. 1982. *Varieties of Criminal Behavior*. Santa Monica, CA: Rand.

Coles, Catherine M. 2008. "Evolving Strategies in 20th-Century American Prosecution." In *The Changing Role of the American Prosecutor*, eds. John L. Worrall and M. Elaine Nugent-Borakove. Albany: State University of New York Press.

Coles, Catherine M., and George L. Kelling. 1999. "Prevention Through Community Prosecution." *The Public Interest* 136 (Summer): 69–84.

Department of Justice. 1996. *Youth Violence: A Community-Based Response—One City's Success Story*. Washington, DC: U.S. Department of Justice. Available at www.ncjrs.org/txtfiles/boston.txt.

Engen, Rodney L. 2008. "Have Sentencing Reforms Displaced Discretion over Sentencing from Judges to Prosecutors?" In *The Changing Role of the American Prosecutor*, eds. John L. Worrall and M. Elaine Nugent-Borakove. Albany: State University of New York Press.

Epstein, Julian. 2000. "A Prosecution Too Far, Again." *Wall Street Journal* (July 14), A14.

Federal Bureau of Investigation. *Uniform Crime Reports*. Washington, DC.

Feeney, Floyd, Forrest Dill, and Adrianne Weir. 1983. *Arrests Without Conviction: How Often They Occur and Why*. Washington, DC: National Institute of Justice.

Forst, Brian. 1993. "The Prosecutor and the Public." In *The Socio-Economics of Crime and Justice*, 291–302. Armonk, NY: M. E. Sharpe,.

Forst, Brian. 1995. "Prosecution and Sentencing." Chapter 16 of *Crime*, eds. James Q. Wilson and Joan Petersilia. San Francisco: ICS Press.

Forst, Brian. 2008. "Prosecution Policy and Errors of Justice." In *The Changing Role of the American Prosecutor*, eds. John L. Worrall and M. Elaine Nugent-Borakove. Albany: State University of New York Press.

Forst, Brian, and Barbara Boland. 1984. "The Prevalence of Guilty Pleas." *Bureau of Justice Statistics Special Report* (December).

Forst, Brian, and Kathleen Brosi. 1977. "A Theoretical and Empirical Analysis of the Prosecutor." *Journal of Legal Studies* 6., 177–191.

Forst, Brian, Frank Leahy, Jean Shirhall, Herbert Tyson, Eric Wish, and John Bartolomeo. 1981. *Arrest Convictability as a Measure of Police Performance*. Washington, DC: Institute for Law and Social Research.

Forst, Brian, and Judith Lucianovic. 1977. "The Prisoner's Dilemma: Theory and Reality." *Journal of Criminal Justice* 5 (Spring), 55–64. Forst, Brian, Judith Lucianovic, and Sarah Cox. 1977. *What Happens after Arrest?* Washington, DC: Institute for Law and Social Research.

Forst, Brian, and Peter K. Manning. 1999. *The Privatization of Policing: Two Views*. Washington, DC: Georgetown University Press.

Forst, Brian, William Rhodes, James Dimm, Arthur Gelman, and Barbara Mullin. 1982. *Targeting Federal Resources on Recidivists*. Washington, DC: INSLAW.

Greenwood, Peter W. 1982. *Selective Incapacitation*. Santa Monica, CA: RAND.

Greenwood, Peter, Sorrel Wildhorn, E. Poggio, M. Strumsasser, and P. Deleon. 1976. *Prosecution of Adult Felony Defendants in Lost Angeles County*. Santa Monica, CA: RAND.

Heumann, Milton. 1978. *Plea Bargaining: The Experiences of Prosecutors, Judges, and Defense Attorneys*. Chicago: University of Chicago Press.

Hillsman, Sally. 1982. "Pretrial Diversion of Youthful Adults: A Decade of Reform and Research." *Justice System Journal* 7: 361–387.

Hotaling, Gerald T., and Murray A. Straus. 1989. "Intrafamily Violence, and Crime and Violence Outside the Family." In *Family Violence*, eds. Lloyd Ohlin and Michael Tonry, 315–375. Chicago: University of Chicago Press.

Jackson, Robert H. 1940. "The Federal Prosecutor." *Journal of the American Judicial Society* 24.

Jacoby, Joan E. 1981. *Prosecutorial Decisionmaking: A National Study*. Washington, DC: Bureau of Social Science Research.

Karp, David R., and Todd R. Clear. 2000. "Community Justice: A Conceptual Framework." In *Criminal Justice 2000: Boundary Changes in Criminal Justice Organizations*, Vol. 2, 323–368. Washington, DC: U.S. Department of Justice.

Kennedy, David M. 1999. "Boston Proves Something Can Be Done." *Washington Post Outlook* (May 23), B3.

Kress, Jack M. 1976. "Progress and Prosecution." *Annals of the American Academy of Political and Social Science* 423: 99–116.

Landes, William M. 1971. "An Economic Analysis of the Courts." *Journal of Law and Economics* 14: 61–107.

Langan, Patrick A., and Richard Solari. 1992. *National Judicial Reporting Program, 1988*. Washington, DC: Bureau of Justice Statistics.

Levine, Kay. 2007. "Can Prosecutors Be Social Workers?" *Studies in Law, Politics and Society* 40: 125–151.

Loftin, Colin, Milton Heumann, and David McDowall. 1983. "Mandatory Sentencing and Firearm Violence." *Law and Society Review* 17.

McCoy, Candace. 1993. *Politics and Plea Bargaining: Victims' Rights in California*. Philadelphia: University of Pennsylvania Press.

Meehl, Paul E. 1954. *Clinical vs. Statistical Prediction*. Minneapolis: University of Minnesota Press.

Monahan, John. 1981. *Predicting Violent Behavior: An Assessment of Clinical Techniques*. Beverly Hills, CA: Sage.

Nugent-Borakove, M. Elaine. 2008. "Performance Measures and Accountability." In *The Changing Role of the American Prosecutor*, eds. John L. Worrall and M. Elaine Nugent-Borakove. Albany: State University of New York Press.

Nugent-Borakove, M. Elaine, and Patricia L. Fanflik. 2008. "Community Prosecution: Rhetoric or Reality?" In *The Changing Role of the American Prosecutor*, eds. John L. Worrall and M. Elaine Nugent-Borakove. Albany: State University of New York Press.

Petersilia, Joan, Allan Abrahamse, and James Q. Wilson. 1990a. *Police Performance and Case Attrition*. Santa Monica: RAND.

Petersilia, Joan, Allan Abrahamse, and James Q. Wilson. 1990b. "The Relationship Between Police Practice, Community Characteristics, and Case Attrition." *Policing and Society* 1: 23–38.

Reiss, Albert J., Jr. 1974. "Discretionary Justice in the United States." *International Journal of Criminology and Penology* 2.

Rosen, Marie Simonetti. 1999. "LEN Interview with Susan Herman." *Law Enforcement News* 25 (522) (November 30): 8–11.

Rubinstein, Michael L., and Teresa J. White. 1979. "Alaska's Ban on Plea Bargaining." *Law and Society Review* 13.

Samuelson, Robert J. 2000. "The New Pork Barrel." *Washington Post* (June 28), A25.

Sherman, Lawrence W., Denise C. Gottfredson, Doris L. MacKenzie, John Eck, Peter Reuter, and Shawn D. Bushway. 1998. *Preventing Crime: What Works,*

What Doesn't, What's Promising. Washington, DC: National Institute of Justice.

Shikita, Minoru. 1996. "The Role of the Public Prosecutor in a Changing World." Paper in *Proceedings of the Ninth United Nations Congress on the Prevention of Crime and Treatment of Offenders*. Cairo, Egypt.

Skogan, Welsey G., and Susan M. Hartnett. 1997. *Community Policing: Chicago Style*. New York: Oxford University Press.

Solari, Richard. 1992. *National Judicial Reporting Program, 1988*. Washington, DC: Bureau of Justice Statistics.

Steadman, Henry J., and Joseph Cocozza. 1978. "Psychiatry, Dangerousness and the Repetitively Violent Offender." *Journal of Criminal Law and Criminology* 69: 226–231.

Stevens, Norma Mancini. 1994. "Defining Community Prosecution." *The Prosecutor* 28 (March–April): 13–14.

Szanton, Peter L. 1972. *Public Policy, Public Good, and the Law*. Washington, DC: RAND.

Taylor, Stuart, Jr., and K. C. Johnson. 2008. *Until Proven Innocent: Political Correctness and the Shameful Injustices of the Duke Lacrosse Rape Case*. New York: St. Martin's Griffin.

U.S. Department of Justice. 1977. *Justice Litigation Management*. Washington, DC: U.S. Government Printing Office.

Van Ness, Daniel W., and Karen H. Strong. 1997. *Restoring Justice*. Cincinnati, OH: Anderson.

Vera Institute of Justice. 1977. *Felony Arrests: Their Prosecution and Disposition in New York City's Courts*. New York: Vera Institute of Justice.

Walker, Samuel. 1985. *Sense and Nonsense about Crime: A Policy Guide*. Monterey, CA: Brooks-Cole.

Wilber, Del Quentin. 2009. "Judge Tosses out Stevens Conviction." *Washington Post* (April 7).

Will, George F. 1994. "Fangs of the Independent Counsel." *The Washington Post* (January 7), A19.

Williams, Kristen M. *The Scope and Prediction of Recidivism*. Washington, DC: Institute for Law and Social Research, 1979.

Wolfgang, Marvin E., Robert M. Figlio, and Thorstein Sellin. 1972. *Delinquency in a Birth Cohort*. Chicago: University of Chicago Press.

Worden, Alissa Pollitz. 1989. "Policymaking by Prosecutors: The Uses of Discretion in Regulating Plea Bargaining." *Judicature* 73: 335–340.

Worrall, John L. 2008. "Prosecution in America: A Historical and Comparative Account." In *The Changing Role of the American Prosecutor*, eds. John L. Worrall and M. Elaine Nugent-Borakove. Albany: State University of New York Press.

Notes

I wish to thank Tom Brady, Jim Lynch, Kevin Reitz, John Worrall, and the editors for their helpful comments on drafts of this chapter. I alone am responsible any errors contained here.

1. Franken followed up Sotomayor's apology that she did not know the answer with this gem: "Didn't the White House prepare you for that?" He had previously commented: ". . . it amazes me that you wanted to become a prosecutor based on that show because, in *Perry Mason*, the prosecutor, Berger, lost every week, with

one exception. . . . " The joke was funny especially because Franken had spent the previous year trying to persuade the public that he was more serious statesman than Saturday Night Live comedian, the role that had made him famous.

2. "The Case of the Witless Witness," "The Case of the Deadly Verdict," and "The Case of the Terrified Typist" (*Perry Mason TV Show Book*, available at www. wendytech.com/moviesa-p.htm).

3. Several difficulties must be noted in tracking victimization outcomes. First, victimizations, reported crimes, and arrests are all fundamentally different units of observation. A single victimization may involve multiple offenders and court cases, and a single offender may attack multiple victims. In addition, about a third of all felony arrests are for drug crimes, which do not show up in the victimization statistics. About 30 percent involve juvenile offenders (many of whom are also drug offenders) who are not processed through criminal court. Of offenders not arrested for the reported crime, many are subsequently arrested for other crimes.

4. The decline in crime is likely due in part to an incapacitative effect of the additional incarcerations, as noted by Richard Rosenfeld in chapter 19 of this volume. The increase in incarcerations is almost surely not due to an increase in the average severity of crimes: the sharpest decline in crime over the 20-year span was in the most serious category—homicides—which fell by about half from 1988 to 2007. The explosion in prison and jail populations was fed in roughly equal measures by increases in the number of persons convicted, in the rate at which convicted people were incarcerated, and in the average terms of incarceration, with drug convictions contributing more than any other offense. Crime statistics are from the Federal Bureau of Investigation, *Uniform Crime Reports*, and the prison and jail population statistics are from the Bureau of Justice Statistics correctional surveys conducted under the National Prisoner Statistics Program and the Annual Survey of Jails (Bureau of Justice Statistics, 2009a and 2009b). Data were also used from selected BJS reports on state and federal sentences.

5. Statistics about the outcomes of the juvenile cases are not readily available, largely because of a widespread reluctance to maintain juvenile records and because the terms *conviction*, *ail*, and *prison* do not apply to juveniles. For adults, the results reported here are from the National Judicial Reporting Program (NJRP), which reports felony arrests and convictions for over 300 of the nation's 3,195 counties (Brown, Langan, and Levin 1999; Langan and Solari 1992; and Boland, Mahanna, and Sones 1992).

6. Such findings were reported for Washington, DC, by Forst, Lucianovic, and Cox (1977); similar findings were reported for New York by the Vera Institute (1977); for New Orleans, by Forst et al. (1981).

7. For an in-depth analysis of the prosecutor's view of the witness problem, see Cannavale and Falcon (1976).

8. Forst, Lucianovic, and Cox (1977, 28). Similar findings were found for New York by the Vera Institute (1977) and for New Orleans by Forst et al. (1981).

9. Some researchers have found that violent offenders in the family are also more likely to assault nonfamily members (Hotaling and Straus 1989).

10. This is not to suggest that the practice of aborting or retarding prosecution is an appropriate response to questionable police procedures of obtaining evidence. The 25,000 or so felony cases that are rejected annually in the United States due to such violations of rights to due process may be 25,000 too many from the public's point of view; these episodes erode police legitimacy. We wish

only to point out here that the problem is small from another perspective: for each case rejected due to an exclusionary rule violation, about 20 are rejected because the police failed to produce sufficient tangible or testimonial evidence.

11. This was found in Washington, DC, by Forst, Lucianovic, and Cox (1977), and in seven jurisdictions by Forst et al. (1981). In the latter study, arrests made by about 10,000 police officers during 1977–1978 were examined; half of the convictions that followed those arrests were the product of just 12 percent of the officers. Nearly twice as many officers (22 percent) made arrests that failed to yield a single conviction. This pattern held up after the researchers accounted for the officer's assignment, the number of arrests made by the officer, the normal conviction rate associated with each officer's offense mix (e.g., the conviction rate for robbery is considerably higher than for assault), and randomness associated with the small number of arrests made by most of the officers. Similar differences in conviction rates were found in a study of arrests for robbery and burglary by 25 different police departments operating in Los Angeles County in the 1980s— some departments produced arrests that resulted in conviction at twice the rate of others (Petersilia, Abrahamse, and Wilson 1990b).

12. Community policing may have raised the inclination of most police officers to work closely with members of the community to solve crimes and support prosecution, but variation across officers is likely to have persisted in policing, as in other occupations.

13. The *Apprendi* decision prohibited judges from enhancing criminal sentences beyond statutory maximums based on facts other than those decided by the jury beyond a reasonable doubt, such as information contained in a presentence investigation.

14. The *Blakely* decision applied the logic of *Apprendi* to cases involving mandatory sentencing guidelines under state law.

15. The *Booker* decision required a jury in a federal criminal case to decide, beyond a reasonable doubt, any fact that increased the sentence of the defendant above the maximum specified in the Federal Sentencing Guidelines.

16. Differences within Los Angeles County have been reported by Petersilia, Abrahamse, and Wilson (1990a), and earlier by Greenwood et al. (1976). Differences between United States Attorney offices in adjacent federal districts were reported by Boland and Forst (1985, 11).

17. Nationwide, the ratio of felony pleas to trials is roughly 10 to one. In the 1980s, plea-to-trial ratios ranged from lows of 4 or 5 to one for New Orleans, Portland, and Washington, DC, to ratios as high as 37 to one for Geneva, Illinois, and 19 to one for Littleton, Colorado (Forst and Boland, 1984, 2). Plea-to-trial ratios tend to be higher in urban areas than in rural ones.

18. Boland and Forst (1985, 11–13). In Manhattan, where the plea-to-trial ratio is 24 to one, only 3 percent of all felony arrests are rejected; the local crime unit in the U.S. Attorney's Washington, DC, office, with a plea-to-trial ratio of 5 to one, rejects 15 percent (Boland, Mahanna, and Sones 1992).

19. Legislative attempts to ban plea bargaining have been studied extensively, with conclusions that, while varied, are consistent in their generally negative assessments. When such attempts fail to enlist the full support of the prosecutor, charge bargaining has been found to be replaced with sentence bargaining and increases in the rate at which cases are dropped by the prosecutor (Blumstein et al. 1983; McCoy 1993). For analyses of the effects of attempts to ban plea bargaining under the 1973 New York drug law see Joint Committee (1979). Rubinstein and

White reported the findings of their study of the effects of a sweeping 1975 ban on plea bargaining in 1979. A 1977 plea bargaining ban in Michigan firearm cases was analyzed by Loftin, Heumann, and McDowall (1983, 287). The 1982 attempt to better serve victims with California's Proposition 8 referendum substantially accelerated the plea negotiation process in that state, but appears to have done so in a manner that undermines both the due process of defendants and the concerns of victims to have their views aired in court and receive appropriate levels of attention (McCoy 1993).

20. In 1972, Marvin Wolfgang and his associates at the University of Pennsylvania reported that 18 percent of all boys born in Philadelphia in 1945 accounted for 52 percent of all the offenses committed by the group (Wolfgang et al. 1972). A few years afterward Kristen Williams, analyzing PROMIS data from the District of Columbia for 1971–1975, reported that 7 percent of the 46,000 different defendants arrested accounted for 24 percent of the 73,000 felony and serious misdemeanor cases handled by the prosecutor for that jurisdiction (Williams 1979).

21. It is frequently argued that statistical prediction should not be used as a basis for criminal justice decision-making because of the false positives problem. In fact, nonstatistical assessment of dangerousness—the method preferred in most jurisdictions—has been found repeatedly to produce false positives at a *higher* rate than statistical assessments. See Monahan (1981); Steadman and Cocozza (1978); Meehl (1954).

The legitimacy of prediction as a basis for criminal justice decisions has been generally well established. Judges routinely base bail decisions on the perceived risk of defendant misbehavior prior to trial. The exercise of discretion by prosecutors in filing charges and in targeting cases involving dangerous offenders for special prosecution, and by judges in making bail and sentencing decisions, is rarely subjected to challenge and reversal.

22. Interviews with 180 police officers who made arrests in New York City and Washington, DC, revealed that none of the officers (or their immediate supervisors) routinely received information about the court outcomes of their arrests (Forst, Leahy, et al. 1981).

Fortunately, there are signs of improvement on this front. A 1992 survey of prosecutors revealed that the rate at which prosecutors notify police and victims of the outcomes of their cases more than doubled from 1974 to 1990.(Bureau of Justice Statistics 1992).

23. See, for example, Skogan (1990). Skogan and Hartnett (1997) later reported evidence of crime reduction effects of community policing in Chicago.

24. See Rosen's interview with Susan Herman, director of the National Center for Victims of Crime, at p. 9.

Chapter 16

Sentencing

Kevin R. Reitz

Sentencing is a legally constructed process for determination of the criminal sanctions applied to offenders as a consequence of their criminal convictions. A *sentence*, best understood from the viewpoint of the offender, is the sum total of criminal sanctions experienced because of a conviction.

The sentencing process typically unfolds through the cumulative decisions of many official actors and, in serious cases, can extend over many years. The ability to affect sentencing outcomes through the exercise of official authority is a good working definition of the elusive term *sentencing discretion*. There are many decision-makers with such discretion, although the particulars vary across jurisdictions and types of cases. Legislatures, sentencing commissions, prosecutors, probation officers, police officers, juries, trial judges, appellate judges, prison authorities, parole boards, and parole supervision agencies all make choices that contribute to sentencing outcomes in thousands upon thousands of cases per year (Zimring 1976; Knapp 1993; Reitz 1998). Sentencing discretion, as understood here, comes into being prior to conviction, and does not expire until a particular sentence has been fully executed.

The ability to influence sentencing outcomes is by no means limited to government officials. Certain private actors possess a *de facto* power akin to sentencing discretion when the legal system responds to their inputs. Crime victims, victims' families and friends, community representatives, and offenders themselves can all exert great influence over sentences. For instance, a negotiated plea is a bilateral agreement, not dictated solely by the prosecutor. A defendant's ability to insist on a particular penalty, or a cap on sentence, depends on the parties' relative bargaining strengths and the defendant's willingness to hold out, threatening to go to trial (Scott and Stuntz 2002). As a second example, if crime victims' views are routinely weighed by prosecutors in deciding what charges to file or whether to accept a plea agreement, or by probation officers when preparing pre-sentence reports, or by judges at sentencing hearings, then decisions by victims may affect the nature and severity of ultimate sentences (Cassell 2009). A victim who chooses to speak in favor of mercy can change the dynamics of the process, in contrast to a victim who asks for the full measure of authorized punishment. We lack terminology for talking and thinking about *private* sentencing discretion, or shared public-private discretion, but it is important to recognize that these things exist. Otherwise we are missing the true complexity of what goes on, and we may underestimate the difficulty of managing the process toward beneficial social ends.

This chapter will examine issues of sentencing law and policy primarily from wide-angle and systemic perspectives. Because criminal justice systems have so many moving parts, and yet are so powerful in their uncoordinated forward momentum, it is essential—regularly—to step back and examine the large patterns in what they are doing. The sections that follow will:

- Examine long-term trends in American crime and punishment
- Discuss the uneasy coexistence of retributive and utilitarian purposes of sentencing
- Tour the major variants of sentencing system types in operation across the United States today
- Offer criteria for evaluating the successes and failures of different system types
- Address the politics of sentencing reform
- Distinguish the case of fiscal emergency from long-term reform.

MACRO PERSPECTIVES ON CRIME AND PUNISHMENT

The explosion in aggregate sentencing severity over the past 40 years has been one of the most dramatic transformations in American history. Few exercises of governmental domestic power—anywhere in the world, in any time period—have affected so many so greatly. Any consideration of contemporary U.S. sentencing policy, writ large, must begin with an awareness that we live in extraordinary times. Although the causes of large sociocultural phenomena are never simple, and it is wise to avoid reductionist analyses, it is illuminating to survey changes over the past several decades in the most basic of indicators: crime rates and overall correctional populations.

From the late 1950s through the mid-1970s, rates of serious crimes in the United States increased considerably. Homicide rates more than doubled, with similar or greater upsurges in serious assaults, rapes, and robberies. From the mid-1970s until the early 1990s, American crime rates for the most serious offenses remained at distressing levels, compared with recent history and with other developed nations (Ruth and Reitz 2003, 16–17). During this 20-year "high crime plateau," for example, homicide death rates, while oscillating somewhat from year to year, remained at levels between 2 and 3 times those of the early 1960s. In 1993, the U.S. homicide rate stood at more than 4 times the rates in Canada and Australia, 9 times the rates in Spain, France, and Germany, and 15 to 20 times the rates in England and Japan (Zimring and Hawkins 1997, 8). After two decades of red-line violence, however, things began to change. Starting in 1992 and 1993, U.S. crime rates fell steadily for about 10 years, with an apparent flattening-out in the early 2000s—although one cannot know where the future trend line is going.

During the high crime plateau from (roughly) 1974 to 1993, all 50 states and the federal system experienced immense growth in their prison and jail systems—and in numbers of offenders on probation and parole. The period of punitive expansionism continued through the 1990s and the first decade of the 2000s, extending several years after crime began to drop. The pace of incarceration growth slackened appreciably, however, once crime rates returned to relatively low levels not seen since the 1960s (Ruth and Reitz 2003, 22–25, 73–80). While the link between crime rates and aggregate punishment policy is hotly contested among academics (Useem and Piehl 2008; Beckett 1997), today one does not hear the same calls to increase prison populations that were extant well into the 1990s (Bennett et al. 1996; Murray 1997).

The explosion in use of prisons and jails was unprecedented in American history, and among other developed democracies. The expansionist period left the United States with the largest per capita confinement population in the world—a phenomenon often called "mass incarceration" (e.g., Clear 2007; Useem and Piehl 2008). By 2007, there were an estimated 2.3 million inmates in the nation's prisons and jails, up from only 357,292 in 1970. Correcting for population growth, the incarceration rate had quintupled over this span. The U.S. rate in 2007—counting prisons and jails—was 762 inmates per 100,000 general population, compared with an average rate of 95 per 100,000 in western and southern European nations, 153 in England and Wales, 116 in Canada, and 129 in Australia. Russia was the United States' nearest competitor with a rate of 629 (Bureau of Justice Statistics 2008; Walmsey 2009).

The stunning scale of the use of confinement is one of the most salient features of the nation's criminal justice complex. It is often cited as proof in itself that U.S. sentencing policy is indefensible and in need of drastic change (e.g., Tonry 2004; Whitman 2003; Rubin 2003; Mauer 1999).

Concern over mass confinement is also inextricably bound up in questions of distributive justice. Racial and ethnic disparities in U.S. incarcerated populations are severe. In 2008, an estimated 60 percent of all inmates in America's prisons and jails were either African American or Hispanic. Compared with a white male incarceration rate of 727 per 100,000 nationwide, the black male rate was 4,777 and the Hispanic male rate was 1,760 (Bureau of Justice Statistics 2009). This translates into a "disparity ratio" for black and white males of 6.5 to one, and a ratio of 2.4 to one for Hispanic and white males.

Compared to Canada, England, and Australia, U.S. disparity ratios by race and ethnicity are not unusually large (Tonry 1994). However, because incarceration rates *overall* are so high, the absolute impact of confinement on minority communities in the United States is breathtaking. The powerful growth trend in prisons and jails over the past 35 years has had small impact on the likelihood of being incarcerated for the majority white population, but a concentrated and pronounced impact for defined subsegments of the population (Raphael and Stoll 2009, 4). Nearly 5 percent of all black men in the United States were in prison and jail on any one day in 2008 (Bureau of Justice Statistics 2009). For certain subgroups, the numbers are higher. Using 2000 Census data, Raphael and Stoll (2009, 6–9) estimated that, among black male high-school dropouts aged 26 to 35, roughly one-third were incarcerated on any given day. Raphael (2005) estimated that, by the close of the 1990s, over 90 percent of black male high-school dropouts in California had previously served prison time.

The raw facts of racial and ethnic disparities in U.S. incarceration are another source of criticism of—and outrage toward—American criminal justice policy (e.g., Tonry and Melewski 2008; Wacquant 2001; Beckett 1997; Mauer 1994). The subject is as complex as it is painful, however. To a substantial degree, disparities in punishment reflect differences in rates of offending by race (we know less about ethnicity and crime), which are in turn associated with conditions of poverty and disadvantage (Frase 2009; Tonry and Melewski 2008). Because crime victims tend to resemble offenders demographically, victimization rates in minority communities have been shockingly high (Ruth and Reitz 2003; Zimring and Hawkins 1997; DiIulio 1994). To the extent that the incarceration boom has reduced crime rates (see Piehl and Useem, Chapter 18, and Rosefeld, Chapter 19, in this volume), African Americans have been important beneficiaries. For 20 years, from 1973 to 1994, the serious violent victimization rate for African Americans—including homicide, rape, robbery, and aggravated assault—hovered around 30 to 40 per 1,000, then fell steadily over 1995 to 2007 to 10.3 per 1,000 (Bureau of Justice Statistics 2008b). The black homicide victimization rate fell from 39.3 per 100,000 in 1991 to 18.2 in 2008 (Bureau of Justice Statistics 2007; Federal Bureau of Investigation 2009; U.S. Census Bureau 2009).

Whatever one's attitude toward punitive expansionism and racial and ethnic disparities in incarceration, both are issues of overriding importance that cannot be ignored by policymakers going forward. America's vast investment in prisons and jails was neither planned nor anticipated (Zimring and Hawkins 1991), and it unfolded in a period of sorely inadequate information about the costs and benefits of imprisonment. The prisons also exploded during an era when searching analysis into questions of race, crime, and punishment was taboo, although this seems to be changing for the better (Tonry 1995; Kennedy 1998). As later sections will suggest, it is not naïve to think that we are developing better tools for the management of sentencing systems, including their aggregate punishment outcomes, and to hope that an improving knowledge base may help ameliorate even the most painful and intractable problems of the past.

SENTENCING PURPOSES

Other contributors to this volume have surveyed the empirical literatures relevant to crime-reductive goals such as rehabilitation, deterrence, and incapacitation (See chapters in this volume by Cullen and Jonson (11), Petersilia (17), Piehl and Useem (18), Rosenfeld (19)). An understanding of sentencing policy cannot end with utilitarianism, however. Many people believe that sentences should be influenced or determined by a moral calculus, and should reflect *justice* or *desert* or *proportionality* in punishment. These are called *deontological* or *retributive* ideas about sentencing. They are relevant to a discussion of crime control because moral preferences, in one form or another, can supplant, limit, or reinforce utilitarian objectives.

For present purposes, I will focus on the moral axiom that a criminal sentence should not be *disproportionate* to the seriousness of the offense committed and the blameworthiness of the offender (American Law Institute 2007, 1). Stated this way, it is hard to find anyone who would disagree. However, there is much room for dispute over the meaning of "proportionality." Retributive theories, and ideas for their implementation, come in many different sizes, shapes, and colorations (Moore 1987; Robinson 2008). A small sample will be discussed below.

In *just deserts* theory, penalties must be closely fitted to crime seriousness and a tightly defined view of offender culpability, restricted to the offender's state of mind when the offense was committed (von Hirsch and Ashworth 2005; von Hirsch 1993). I call this an example of *defining* desert theory, because the moral reference points for punishment tell us all we need to know when fixing sentence. There is no room for utilitarian goals to influence penalty severity.[1] The background of the criminal does not matter much, either, including circumstances of poverty or hardship (von Hirsch 1993; Ashworth 2005). Just deserts theorists have an exceedingly difficult time explaining why a defendant's prior convictions should be allowed to influence the severity of a current sentence (Fletcher 1978; Dressler 2001). Public opinion about appropriate punishments is not to be consulted in carrying out the just deserts scheme. Moral valuations of proportionality must be carefully reasoned from first principles (von Hirsch and Ashworth 2005).

The theory of *empirical desert*, in contrast, treats public opinion as the touchstone of proportionality. To derive a penalty scale, proponents have crafted sophisticated survey instruments to record people's collective moral judgments when responding to various scenarios of offenses and offenders (Robinson and Darley 1995; Roberts 2008). Like just deserts theory, empirical desert is defining of punishment; utilitarian objectives may not drive sentence severity. The sentencing system strives for moral legitimacy or, more precisely, widespread acceptability in light of people's intuitions about just punishments. The foundation of empirical desert—or, at least, its most prominent school—is thought to be biological: human beings have evolved over thousands of centuries to react in certain ways to behaviors that seriously violate group norms. Moving from "is" to "ought," the theory posits that these adaptive responses are sound starting points for development of sentencing policy. Legal systems are said to act at their peril if they stray too far from the hardwiring of human belief structures (Robinson, Kurzban, and Jones 2007; Hoffman and Goldsmith 2004).

Limiting retributivism is an example of a *non-defining* moral theory of sentencing; instead, as its name foretells, it is a *limiting* theory. Here, proportionality in punishment is understood as an imprecise concept with a margin of error, not reducible to a specific sanction for each case. The "moral calipers" available to human beings are set wide, the theory asserts, producing a substantial range of justifiable sentences for most cases. At some upper boundary, we begin to feel that a penalty is clearly disproportionate in severity and, at a lower point, we intuit that it is clearly too lenient (Morris 1974; Frase 2002). Imagining a generous spread between the two, limiting retributivism would permit utilitarian purposes to determine sentences within the morally permissible range (Morris and Miller 1985; American Law Institute 2007). One difficulty for limiting retributivism is that it has no ideas of its own about how the morally-informed limits on punishment should be located (Ristroph 2009). Its proponents have tended to borrow from just deserts theory and the snapshot reference points of offense and offender culpability during the offense (American Law Institute 2007; Frase 2002).

Beyond the contested terrain of proportionality, moral judgments pervade sentencing policy formation at every turn. For example, I have come to believe that many people feel society has an ethical duty to try to rehabilitate offenders, even when the evidence of success is mixed or disappointing (cf. Rubin 2002; Wilson 1975). This moral impulse seems most visibly at work in the history of the juvenile courts (Zimring 2005). Strong moral views likewise buffet the debate of selective incapacitation policy. Some find it indefensible to imprison people for "crimes they have yet to commit," or to force offenders to bear the risk that the system has incorrectly identified them as future serious offenders (Tonry 1999). Others assign greater moral value to the claims of prospective crime victims who, after all, have not been convicted of a serious offense, and whose injuries can be avoided through incapacitative policies (Walker 1991).

Policymakers must be cognizant of the ideological realities that can deflect or scramble the pursuit of crime-control objectives. We would not want to remove the moral content from sentencing systems, of course, but it is necessary to recognize that conceptions of desert and proportionality are every bit as complex—and in need of examination—as the utilitarian theories with which they interact.

SENTENCING SYSTEMS

Across America, the legal and institutional architectures of sentencing systems are remarkably varied—and many states have changed their configurations in recent years or are in the process of contemplating major reforms (American Law Institute 2003). In one sense, Justice Brandeis's vision of the states as laboratories is vindicated by all of this diversity, innovation, and flux (Brandeis 1932). On the other hand, policymakers have difficulty making good use of the information, much of which has not been distilled into accessible, published sources. Most criminal justice professionals are familiar with the sentencing framework in their own state and in the federal system. It requires a large time investment to investigate the workings of multiple other systems, and still more to evaluate their comparative merits. Most responsible officials and opinion leaders, quite understandably, do not make such efforts. All too often, debates of sentencing system policy are rooted in local experience and unreliable conventional wisdom about how things are working out elsewhere. To improve on this picture, we require a language, and a metric, to make better use of the raw information that has been piling up from Brandeis's laboratories (Weisberg 2007).

This section will describe a number of the essential building blocks, or design features, of contemporary sentencing systems. It will focus most heavily on sentencing guidelines structures, which have been endorsed by national law reform organizations as the most successful among existing system types (American Bar Association 1994; American Law Institute 2007) and have been called the "consensus" model for reform among academics and policymakers (Weisberg 2007). It will also posit a number of evaluative criteria for sorting successes and failures in system design.

In the early 1970s, all jurisdictions in the United States used fundamentally similar *indeterminate sentencing systems*, invented by the Progressives near the turn of the twentieth century (Frankel 1973; Rothman 1980). From the mid-1970s forward, a host of new system types has emerged, but roughly half of the states still follow the traditional indeterminate approach for the bulk of criminal cases (American Law Institute 2003). The indeterminate structure is characterized by expansive judicial sentencing discretion, unguided and unreviewable so long as the judge stays within the ceiling of statutory maximum penalties, followed in prison cases by an even greater discretionary power—also unguided and unreviewable—held by the parole board to decide what actual confinement terms will be. For example, for a reasonably serious felony, the judge might impose a sentence of "three to ten years." Once the offender has served a minimum term of three years, perhaps reduced by credits for good behavior, it is left to the parole board to decide whether the offender will be released after three years, three years and one day, four years—or any length of stay up to the maximum available 10 years, which again might be lowered somewhat by a good-time allowance (id.).

In the 1970s, indeterminate sentencing came under strong attack. Critics claimed that judicial sentences were arbitrary and parole board decisions inexplicable—even to the boards themselves (Frankel 1973). At root, indeterminate systems became vulnerable because they were designed on the assumptions that nearly all offenders could be rehabilitated, that judges were wise enough to tailor sentences to the goal of reform, and that parole boards were capable of watching prison inmates over a period of years and discerning when the process of rehabilitation had taken hold (Rothman 1980).

When faith in rehabilitation theory suffered its greatest blow in the 1970s (see chapter 11 of this volume by Cullen and Jonson), all of the unstructured, individualized, and unreviewable discretion within the indeterminate structure began to look like an evil. Lacking a clear rehabilitative sense of direction, sentencing policy was being made atomistically, one judge at a time, with vast differences from one courtroom to another. At best, the critics maintained, criminal punishment was too much determined by the luck of the draw—which judge a defendant happened to get, and what that judge had eaten for breakfast; at worst, it was a vehicle for racial and other biases (American Friends Services Committee 1971). In some views, indeterminate sentences were not only unprincipled, but tended toward undue severity; for others, indeterminacy appeared the source of sloppy, unjustified lenity. Criminal justice conservatives and liberals, for different reasons, found themselves in agreement that the system had failed (Tonry 1996; Stith and Cabranes 1998).

Since the 1970s, sentencing system "reform" in the United States has largely taken the shape of efforts to improve upon the traditional indeterminate structure. Indeterminacy, in other words, is regarded as the "before picture" by sentencing reformers. Currently, more than half the states and the federal government have made ambitious systemic changes away from the traditional plan. There is no single "after picture," but a patchwork of different approaches. Some classification among the experiments is therefore in order.

Determinate sentencing systems are those that have extinguished the parole board's control over prison-release dates (although post-release supervision still takes place). Sixteen states and the federal system have taken this step (Petersilia 2003). In determinate systems, provisions for good time typically remain in place to encourage rule compliance among inmates and participation in prison programs (Jacobs 1982). Thus, for example, in a jurisdiction offering good time credits of 15 percent, a judicially pronounced sentence of five years will result in actual time served of somewhere between four years three months and five years. The determinate scheme thus tightens the "fit" between judicial ruling and sentencing consequence. In rough terms, the sentencing discretion over prison durations formerly held by the parole board is transferred to the sentencing court. This is often described as a shift in discretion from the "back end" to the "front end" of the sentencing process. Proponents maintain that determinacy fosters "truth in sentencing," on the theory that tough-sounding maximum terms in indeterminate schemes have lost their public credibility (Knapp 1993).

There is no such thing as a *pure* determinate system. Virtually all determinate jurisdictions allow for the shortening of prison terms through good time or earned time allowances, mechanisms for compassionate release (as for the terminally ill), and executive clemency (National Conference of State Legislatures 2009; Reitz 2009). Formulas for good time and earned time are particularly important because large numbers of inmates are affected. These vary a great deal, from 0 to 50 percent depending on the offense and the jurisdiction (American Law Institute 2009). Generally the allowances are administered by departments of corrections. Where this form of release discretion is especially robust, the dividing line between determinacy and indeterminacy becomes blurred, as substantial portions of the back-end authority formerly exercised by parole boards is relocated in corrections agencies.

Sentencing guidelines systems differ from the traditional indeterminate plan in that they seek to provide guidance at the moment of judicial sentencing, through rules or recommendations addressed to sentencing judges. About 20 states and the federal system now employ sentencing guidelines of one kind or another, but the systems are distinct and must themselves be sub-classified according to a number of important features (Frase 2005; American Law Institute 2007). One widespread misconception is that *state* sentencing guidelines systems bear resemblance to the much-criticized *federal* guidelines system. In fact, most state systems have chosen to be as different as possible from their federal counterpart (American Law Institute 2003; Weisberg 2007).

Table 16.1, created by Richard Frase (2005), identifies a number of key variables and shows how they have been incorporated into sentencing system designs across the United States. The "Frase Table," by itself, is a major contribution for its distillation of comparative information about American sentencing systems. The next several subsections of this article will concentrate on the "major structural features" identified in four columns of the Frase Table.

1. Is There a Permanent Sentencing Commission?[5]

Both the American Bar Association (1994) and the American Law Institute (2007) have recommended that every jurisdiction should charter a permanent sentencing commission. Commissions are made up of state leaders from the judiciary, prosecutors' offices, defense bar, corrections

Table 16.1. American Sentencing Guidelines Systems as of Fall 2004 † [from: Richard S. Frase, *State Sentencing Guidelines:* ..., 105 COLUM. L. REV. 1190 (2005)] †= major changes since Fall 2004 ✓ = feature is present to a substantial degree

Jurisdiction	Initial effective date	Major Structural Features					ALSO regulates/covers:		
		Permanent Sentencing Commission	Resource-Impact Assessments	Enforced by appeals or otherwise	Parole Release Abolished	Intermediate Sanctions	Misdemeanor Offenses	revocation of probation	revocation of SR/parole
Utah	Jan. 1979	(1983)	(1993)	(reasons)		(some)	(some)		(some)
Alaska	1-1-80	✓	✓	✓	(mostly)			(some)	
Minnesota	5-1-80	✓	(some)	(some)	✓	(1994)	✓		
Pennsylvania	7-22-82	(1996)	(1996)	(reasons)			✓		
Maryland	7-1-83	(until 1998)	(1988–98)	(some)	✓	(some)			
Florida	10-1-83	(1995–2002)	(1995–97)	(some, 1999)	✓	(some)			
Michigan	1-17-84	✓	✓	(reasons)	(1990)	(some)		(some)	
Washington	7-1-84	✓	✓	(reasons)	✓	✓		(some)	✓
Delaware	10-10-87	✓	(some)	(until 2005)	✓	(some)	(some)		
FEDERAL †	11-1-87	✓		(some until 2005)	✓	✓			(some)
Oregon	11-1-89	(some)			(some)	✓	✓		
Tennessee †	11-1-89	(until 1995)	(until 1995)	(some until 2005)	✓	✓			
Virginia	1-1-91	(1995)	(1995)	(reasons)	(1995)	(some)		(2004)	(2004)
ABA Stds (3rd edit., 1993)		✓	✓	✓	✓	✓	✓	(some)	(some)
Kansas	7-1-93	✓	✓	(reasons)	(some)	✓			(some)
Arkansas	1-1-94	✓	✓	(some)	✓	✓	✓		(some)

North Carolina					
Ohio †	7-1-96	✓	(until 2006)	✓	(some)
Missouri	March 97	✓			(some)
Wisconsin	1985–95	✓			
† 2-1-03 [11 crimes]	(until 2007)	(some until 2007)		✓	(some)
Wash. D.C.	6-14-04 [pilot]	✓	(some)	✓	(some)
Alabama †	10-1-06	✓	(some)	✓ (Oct 1, 2009?)	(some)

departments, public at large, and sometimes the legislature. Because commissions represent constituencies across the criminal justice system, they can strive for a reputation of nonpartisanship. The better-funded commissions have their own administrative and research staffs, although some commissions are forced to borrow research capacity from other state agencies.

The first order of business of a new commission is usually to consider the wisdom of adopting sentencing guidelines, and to draft proposed guidelines. By state law, the commission's proposed guidelines sometimes take effect unless the legislature acts to block them, but in some jurisdictions guidelines must be affirmatively enacted by the legislature. Most commissions then have continuing duties to collect information, monitor the operation of the system, publish reports, project the use of correctional resources, amend the guidelines as needed, and respond to legislative requests for information and policy recommendations (American Law Institute 2007).

By recent count, there were 17 permanent sentencing commissions in the United States charged with oversight of sentencing guidelines systems (American Law Institute 2007, 54). A handful of states, including Florida and Tennessee, disbanded their sentencing commissions after guidelines were put into effect.[2]

2. How Enforceable Are Sentencing Guidelines?

Potentially, sentencing guidelines can be enormously restrictive of judicial sentencing discretion, but they may also be fashioned as loose prescriptions or mere recommendations. The degree of enforceability is a fundamental policy choice that individual jurisdictions can fine-tune as they like, along a continuum from *mandatory* to *advisory* guidelines (Reitz 2005a; Frase 2005).

To flesh out the range of possibility, an illustration is helpful. Say that a state's criminal code assigns aggravated robbery authorized penalties of anything from probation to 20 years in prison. Typically, sentencing guidelines will designate a much narrower sentencing range, somewhere within the statutory range.

In most guidelines systems, the guidelines sentence is a function of the offense of conviction and the defendant's prior convictions. Figure 16.1, taken from Minnesota, is an example of a sentencing grid built on these two axes. The guidelines range for a first offender convicted of aggravated robbery (Offense Severity Level VIII, Criminal History Column 0) is 41–57 months—a far more specific prescription than the full statutory penalty range. The sentences within the grid cells ratchet upward in severity for repeat offenders, depending on how extensive their criminal histories (moving from left to right in the Severity Level VIII row), but all of the guidelines ranges are nested within statutory limits.

Italicized numbers within the grid denote the range within which a judge may sentence without the sentence being deemed a departure. Offenders with non-imprisonment felony sentences are subject to jail the time according to law.

SEVERITY LEVEL OF CONVICTION OFFENSE (Common offenses listed in italics)		CRIMINAL HISTORY SCORE						
		0	1	2	3	4	5	6 or more
Murder, 2nd Degree (intentional murder; drive-by-shootings)	XI	306 261-367	326 278-391	346 295-415	366 312-439	386 329-463	406 346-480[2]	426 363-480[2]
Murder, 3rd Degree Murder, 2nd Degree (unintentional murder)	X	150 128-180	165 141-198	180 153-216	195 166-234	210 179-252	225 192-270	240 204-288
Assault, 1st Degree Controlled Substance Crime, 1st Degree	IX	86 74-103	98 84-117	110 94-132	122 104-146	134 114-160	146 125-175	158 135-189
Aggravated Robbery, 1st Degree Controlled Substance Crime, 2nd Degree	VIII	48 41-57	58 50-69	68 58-81	78 67-93	88 75-105	98 84-117	108 92-129
Felony DWI	VII	36	42	48	54 46-64	60 51-72	66 57-79	72 62-84[2]
Controlled Substance Crime, 3rd Degree	VI	21	27	33	39 34-46	45 39-54	51 44-61	57 49-68
Residential Burglary Simple Robbery	V	18	23	28	33 29-39	38 33-45	43 37-51	48 41-57
Nonresidential Burglary	IV	12[1]	15	18	21	24 21-28	27 23-32	30 26-36
Theft Crimes (Over $5,000)	III	12[1]	13	15	17	19 17-22	21 18-25	23 20-27
Theft Crimes ($5,000 or less) Check Forgery ($251-$2,500)	II	12[1]	12[1]	13	15	17	19	21 18-25
Sale of Simulated Controlled Substance	I	12[1]	12[1]	12[1]	13	15	17	19 17-22

☐ Presumptive commitment to state imprisonment. First-degree murder has a mandatory life sentence and is excluded from the guidelines by law. See Guidelines Section II.E. mandatory Sentences, for policy regarding those sentences controlled by law

■ Presumptive stayed sentence; at the discretion of the judge, up to a year in jail and/or other non-jail sanctions can be imposed as conditions of probation. However, certain offenses in this section of the grid always carry a presumptive commitment to state prison. See, Guidelines Sections II.C. Presumptive Sentence and II.E. Mandatory Sentences.

[1] One year and one day

[2] M.S. § 244.09 requires the Sentencing Guidelines to provide a range for sentences which are presumptive commitment to state imprisonment of 15% lower and 20% higher than the fixed duration displayed, provided that the minimum sentence is not less than one year and one day and the maximum sentence is not more than the statutory maximum. See, Guidelines Sections II, H. Presumptive Sentence Durations that Exceed the Statutory Maximum Sentence and II.I. Sentence Ranges for Presumptive Commitment Offenses in Shaded Areas of Grids.

Effective August 1, 2009

Figure 16.1. Sentencing Guidelines Grid Presumptive Sentence Lengths in Months

The restrictive or nonrestrictive character of guidelines is partly a function of their breadth. Some states use guidelines with much wider ranges than Minnesota. The federal guidelines are a bit more pinpointed. But far more critical is the formulation of the legal standards that govern trial courts' ability to *depart* from the guidelines range in individual cases. The substantive content of the *departure standard*—often no more than a short phrase buried somewhere in state law—is a cornerstone that affects everything else in the system.

Roughly half of American guidelines systems use *presumptive* guidelines, which are binding on the sentencing court unless the court can give adequate reasons on the record for imposing a non-guidelines penalty. In Minnesota, Washington, Oregon, and Kansas, the judge must cite "substantial and compelling reasons" in support of a departure sentence. The American Law Institute (2007) recommends the looser requirement of "substantial reasons." Whatever the standard, it has bite only if trial courts' departure sentences are reviewable. In a presumptive system, this is generally the case. Ultimately it is up to the state's appellate courts to pass on the adequacy of reasons for departure given by sentencing courts in particular cases. The intensity of appellate review is controlled in large part by the state's departure standard, but appellate courts in guidelines states have usually granted sentencing courts the additional insulation of a deferential standard of review. All told, reversals of guidelines departures by state appellate courts have been rare, though not unheard of. True outlier sentences are the most likely to prompt appellate rebuke, or those resting on a legally impermissible rationale (Reitz 1997). This stands in contrast to most of the history of the federal system—until it was converted into an advisory system in 2005—where the departure standard was forbidding, and appellate reversals of trial-court sentences were far more frequent than in the states (id.).[3]

In sum, legally enforceable guidelines can be designed to be modestly binding, as in states like Minnesota—yet not so weakly reinforced that they can be casually disregarded. Or, as in the federal system from 1987 to 2005, guidelines may be rigorously enforced—to the point that federal judges used to refer to them, not as presumptive, but "mandatory" (Stith and Cabranes 1998). Adjustments along the enforceability scale have large effects on the allocation of discretion within the system. In a Minnesota-style system, sentencing courts retain significant discretion in individual cases. If a judge feels at all strongly that the guidelines sentence is inappropriate, the judge may move up or down with little fear of reversal. In contrast, in the high-enforcement model of the former federal system, the sentencing commission's authority eclipses that of trial courts.

At the opposite end of the system-design continuum, about half the states that have adopted sentencing guidelines make no provision for their enforcement at all. These are called *voluntary* or *advisory* systems. Among these states, there is usually a legal requirement that sentencing courts give reasons when departing—but there is no appellate review of the sufficiency of those reasons (Wool and Stemen 2004). Here, trial courts' discretion is much the same as in traditional indeterminate schemes. Any sentence within statutory boundaries, unless a rare constitutional error has occurred, cannot be reassessed for its substance. The sentencing commission in such a regime is a weakened discretionary player. It must try to persuade judges to hew closely to the guidelines, or to respect them at all, but the commission has no formal power in the matter.

Experience shows that, in some advisory systems, the guidelines are influential with trial judges. In other states this is not so, and advisory guidelines are all but nullities (American Law Institute 2007). One recent study found that advisory systems overall have been roughly one-half as successful as presumptive systems in their efforts to control prison population growth and reduce racial disparities in sentencing (Pfaff 2006).[4] Much depends on local circumstances, such as the size of the court system and the degree to which the guidelines were created with judges' involvement, and were designed to capture preexisting judicial preferences (Hunt and Connelly 2007).

3. Is the System Determinate or Indeterminate?

About one-third of American jurisdictions that have adopted sentencing guidelines still empower parole boards to make the final decisions about lengths of prison stays in most cases. The other two-thirds have abrogated this back-end release authority, usually in conjunction with the creation of guidelines. The discretionary implications of this design choice are straightforward. The greater the parole board's discretion over prison terms, the lesser the discretion held by judges. Because sentencing guidelines do not regulate parole boards—and probably could not, in any legally binding way—a healthy measure of parole-board release discretion also tends to diminish the commission's importance in the system (Reitz 1998).

From a policy standpoint, the choices of whether to cabin judicial discretion through guidelines and whether to have (or not have) parole release discretion are closely interactive, and together have profound effects on the system as a whole. In a modestly presumptive guidelines system with no parole release, for example, it is fair to say that judges are the most powerful decision-makers—and hold significantly more authority than judges in traditional indeterminate structures (Knapp 1993; American Law Institute 2003). In an advisory guidelines system with no parole release, trial courts reign supreme.

These are especially important observations because most uninformed observers believe that judges automatically lose a great deal of their sentencing discretion when a guidelines scheme is adopted. The actual state of affairs is much different. In most American guidelines systems implemented to date, judges have been net winners in the discretionary sweepstakes, not losers.

4. Does the System Take Correctional Resources into Account?

If there is one dominant reason for states' decisions to create sentencing commissions and guidelines, or for the preservation of such systems once in place, it is money. Starting with Minnesota in 1980, sentencing-commission states have demonstrated that, under guidelines, it is possible to generate better forecasts of prison growth than in non-guidelines systems (American Law Institute 2003, 72–85; Zimring and Hawkins 1991). The improved accuracy is possible because guidelines generate predictable bell curves of judicial sentencing practices. With retrospective data, even departure patterns can be anticipated with reasonable confidence (Hunt 1998). Computer projections, in the form of *fiscal impact statements*, are routinely attached to any proposal to create or amend guidelines, or to change other laws affecting criminal punishment. More importantly, in states where commissions have established track records of accurate projections, legislators are more likely to consider the information credible, and to weigh it heavily in their deliberations (Frase 2005; Wright 2002).

For example, in North Carolina, the state sentencing commission's initial set of proposed guidelines was forecast to cause significant prison population growth. By statute, however, the commission had been instructed to provide the legislature with an alternative set of guidelines that were projected to be "resource neutral"—that is, to fit sentences within existing prison resources. When faced with this choice, the legislature set aside the commission's formal proposal, and enacted the zero-growth guidelines instead (Wright 2002). From the inception of North Carolina's guidelines system in 1995 through the present, the state has experienced an overall reduction in prison rates— a noteworthy change in light of national prison-growth trends over the same period (Weisberg 2007; American Law Institute 2009). Most other guidelines states have seen increases in their incarceration rates. In general, however, states with sentencing commissions charged with taking correctional resources into account when formulating guidelines have experienced less prison growth than other states (Marvell 1995; Weisberg 2007). Overwhelmingly, states that have adopted sentencing guidelines while abolishing the parole board's release discretion have seen less prison growth than other states (Reitz 2006; Stemen and Rengifo 2005).

Not all guidelines systems have been designed with resource management in mind, however, and not all jurisdictions have used correctional impact tools to the same effect. For example, in the federal system, total corrections expenditures are a tiny part of the total U.S. budget and, as opposed to state legislatures, Congress does not operate under a balanced budget requirement. Thus, money pressure has never been an important brake on federal sentencing policy. The first iteration of the U.S. Sentencing Guidelines took effect in 1987 (under federal law, when Congress failed to block them), despite forecasts of rapid prison growth (Tonry 1996). Since then, the U.S. Sentencing Commission has not been charged with regular production of correctional impact statements. Over the last two decades, the federal prison system has been one of the fastest growing in the nation, outpacing most states even during the highest prison-growth period of the 1990s (Bureau of Justice Statistics 1988, 2009).

Because the federal sentencing system is one of the most visible in the country, many people who are uninformed about state guidelines systems assume that guidelines have everywhere fueled prison growth comparable to federal experience. Some academics even cite the advent of American sentencing commissions as one of the causes of mass incarceration (e.g., Berman 2009). The actual history—at least, to date—is that most states have tried to employ guidelines as inhibitors on prison growth, and most have succeeded (Reitz 2006).

Other Design Features

The regulatory scope of sentencing guidelines is not everywhere the same, as indicated in the last four columns of Table 16.1. Some guidelines speak only to prison sentences, while others, including those in Washington, Pennsylvania, Delaware, and North Carolina, comprehend the full menu of community sanctions. Guidelines with the broader coverage can bring their resource management capacity to bear on intermediate sanctions as well as prison spaces. Thus, for example, in North Carolina, a major proposal to divert property and drug offenders out of the prisons was accompanied by an impact projection showing the additional funding that would be needed to supply new treatment and community corrections slots for the diverted populations. The legislature was persuaded to make an adequate appropriation (much of which had to be passed down to local governments) to make ready for the projected upsurge in demand for non-prison programming (Wright 2002). This episode stands in contrast to another major prison-diversion effort: the passage of Proposition 36 in California, which contemplated the movement of many prison-bound drug offenders into drug treatment. Among the problems with Prop 36, the funding needed for new needed treatment slots was badly under-estimated. California has spent years trying to catch up (see chapter 13 in this volume by Boyum, Caulkins, and Kleiman).

In addition, existing guidelines systems vary in whether they reach misdemeanor offenses and questions of sentence revocations. If misde-meanors are not covered, then many jail sentences are, literally, off the grid. Also, because of the range of authorized penalties in most states, it is possible for some of the more serious misdemeanors to be sentenced more severely than crimes at the low end of the felony scale. For these reasons, Frase has argued that it is best practice for guidelines to extend to both felonies and misdemeanors (2003, 2005; see also American Bar Association 1994; American Law Institute 2007).

The extension of sentencing guidelines to sentence revocations is still in an early, experimental stage. In theory, however, this is an important subject to explore. Nationwide, parole revocations make up more than one-third of all prison admissions, and in some states the number is much higher (Bureau of Justice Statistics 2002, table 5.10a). An overly parochial view, that "sentencing" occurs only in courtrooms, may be responsible for the failure of most sentencing commissions, until recently, to study possible avenues for the regulation of revocations, and sanctions for sentence violations short of revocation.

Mandatory Penalties

Statutes imposing mandatory penalties do not add up to "systems" in and of themselves, but all American jurisdictions have mandatory penalty provisions—in varying shapes and sizes, and with very different effects. Some mandatory penalty laws have had large impacts on states' overall sentencing practices. They tend to work as pockets of extreme determinacy, regardless of the type of system otherwise in place. For example, California's three-strikes law has had a big effect on prison growth in the state, even though California judges in most other cases have discretion over imprisonment decisions and the selection of an ordinary, mitigated, or aggravated prison term for those offenders they decide to incarcerate (Vitiello 2004; Zimring, Hawkins and Kamin 2001). In New York, a state still working with a traditional indeterminate system, the Rockefeller Drug Laws, with tiers of mandatory penalties for drug offenses, have been important contributors to prison growth in some years (Weiman and Weiss 2009).

Both in California and New York, recent history supports the view that prosecutorial discretion is a primary determinant of how mandatory sentencing laws are applied. In California, the three-strikes law is invoked heavily in some counties and infrequently in others. In New York, the Rockefeller Laws lay mostly dormant through the 1970s, when prosecutors—especially in New York City—viewed them as too harsh, but the same laws became a major driver of prison use in the 1980s, when local officials decided to enforce them with greater vigor (Weiman and Weiss 2009). The U.S. Sentencing Commission, in a major study of mandatory penalties in federal law, likewise found that prosecutorial discretion in charging and plea bargaining resulted in serious disuniformities in how the laws were applied (U.S. Sentencing Commission 1991; see also Tonry 2009).

EVALUATING SENTENCING SYSTEMS

This section will suggest a number of systemic goals that might be pursued by a sentencing system, and will venture assessments of how well different system types have performed in meeting those objectives. Concededly the discussion is subjective, but it does draw on current themes of policy debate in the United States (Weisberg 2009; Frase 2005; American Law Institute 2003, 2007). For purposes of analysis, let us suppose that we have agreement on the desirability of the following systemic goals.

A sentencing system should:

- Allow policymakers deliberately to manage the changing sizes of correctional populations, and set priorities for how correctional resources should best be used
- Allow policymakers to better understand the causes of racial and ethnic disparities in sentenced populations, and take effective steps toward the elimination of unwarranted disparities
- Generate and consume information about the system's workings and potential improvements, and have the capacity for continuous change in light of that information
- Achieve fairness, consistency, and rationality in the pursuit of identified sentencing goals in individual cases
- Preserve substantial judicial sentencing discretion, particularly in relation to prosecutors.

As shorthands, these goals might be called: resource management, racial and ethnic disparity reduction, reflexivity, goal-driven consistency, and preservation of judicial sentencing discretion.

Resource Management

Through most of U.S. history, sentencing systems were not designed to produce aggregate outcomes tailored to a state's existing or planned correctional resources. Sentencing laws and case decisions were made one at a time, and everyone assumed that future governments would pay the bill for the accumulated results (Zimring and Hawkins 1991). In my experience, this is still the operative assumption in most Western democracies outside the United States.

This funding strategy works tolerably well when per capita prison and jail counts are low, but is less viable in a high-punishment, high-cost milieu. Since the beginning of the expansionist period in American corrections, overcrowding in prison and jails has been a commonplace problem, often reaching crisis proportions. And in emergency circumstances, "solutions" rarely represent good sentencing policy; too often they have taken the form of court orders or consent decrees (Feeley and Rubin 1998). It is perhaps no accident that resource-sensitive sentencing systems were pioneered in the United States during the extraordinary prison boom years of the 1980s and 1990s, and still exist nowhere else in the world. Necessity breeds invention.

It is illuminating to review the prison-growth history of states with different types of sentencing systems over the past 30 years. Regardless of one's policy preferences, there is much in the historical record that challenges conventional wisdom.

As we saw in an earlier section, most sentencing guidelines systems have been designed to inhibit prison growth, and they have generally succeeded. This has been especially true of guidelines systems in which parole board release discretion has been abolished. In a recent study (American Law Institute 2009), all nine of the American guidelines systems of this description, with at least five years of operation, had experienced lower per capita prison growth than the national average. Figure 16.2 gives the particulars, comparing incremental growth in prison rates among parole-abolition-guidelines states with national growth among all states, focusing on the specific time periods of operation for each guidelines system.

In the absence of sentencing guidelines, determinate sentencing states have a mixed record of prison expansion: half (California, Indiana, and Mississippi) have been high-growth states—Mississippi spectacularly so—and half have been low-growth (Maine, Illinois, and Arizona) when compared to the nation as a whole (American Law Institute 2009, 23).

In contrast, traditional indeterminate sentencing systems—especially those with no sentencing guidelines—have been the primary engines of incarceration growth in the United States. In 2006, eight of the ten states with the highest prison rates were jurisdictions that retained parole-release discretion (Bureau of Justice Statistics 2007b).[6] Eight of the ten states with the highest rate of prison population growth from 1980 to 2006 were likewise parole-release jurisdictions (id.; Bureau of Justice Statistics 1991).[7] The five states with the largest per capita prison rates in 2006 included Louisiana, Texas, Oklahoma, and Georgia—all indeterminate jurisdictions.

The historical facts just recited, of course, are at war with common perceptions. Most people equate indeterminate sentencing and the possibility of "early release" through parole with leniency in punishment. This is an unfortunate instance of romanticism trumping reality. For those concerned about issues of the aggregate scale of incarceration in America, it is better not to work from a backwards understanding of the factual record.

Racial and Ethnic Disparity Reduction

No sentencing system can claim major progress on this front. In part this is because numerical disproportionalities in correctional populations by race (we know less about ethnicity) are linked to real differences in rates of crime commission (Frase 2009; Tonry and Melewski 2008). However, there is evidence that determinate sentencing structures (Klein, Petersilia, and Turner 1990) and sentencing guidelines systems (Pfaff 2006; Tonry 1996) have made marginal inroads in reducing disparities unexplained by differential crime rates or criminal records.

The future may be brighter. In 2007, inspired by the American Law Institute's recommendation in its revised Model Penal Code (2007), Minnesota became the first state to attach racial and ethnic impact projections to proposed changes in sentencing laws, similar to the fiscal impact projections. In 2008, Iowa passed legislation requiring the preparation of racial impact statements, as well (Mauer 2009). It is much too early to tell if this innovation will spread to other states, nor do we have

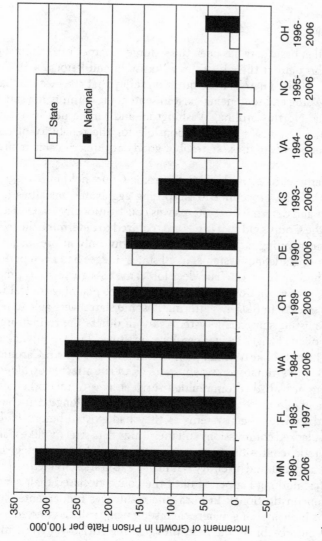

Figure 16.2. Growth in Prison Rates in Parole Release Abolition States with Sentencing Guidelines Through Year-end 2006

much experience with how it works in practice. In Minnesota, since the racial and ethnic impact statements have been in use, budgetary pressures have foreclosed *any* measure projected to increase prison populations. The true test of the demographic impact statement as a policy tool will come when an otherwise viable sentencing bill is projected to exacerbate racial disparities in punishment (Reitz 2009).

Reflexivity

A shortfall in basic data has been the scourge of American criminal justice systems throughout their histories (Blumstein and Petersilia 1995; Ruth and Reitz 2003). There is little question today that the best databases on case processing and sentencing exist in sentencing commission states such as Virginia, North Carolina, Washington, and Minnesota. Investment in information systems is partly responsible for the reliability of resource impact statements in these states, but good data are critical in many other contexts.

For example, in 2004 the U.S. Supreme Court held in *Blakely v. Washington* that the procedure for imposing aggravated penalties in many guidelines and determinate systems was constitutionally inadequate. Specifically, the Court held that juries are required to determine the existence of some aggravating factors at sentencing—but only in presumptive and not advisory guidelines systems. In all states, judges had been performing this fact-finding function. The decision came as a surprise to practically everyone; no jurisdiction had done any advance planning to deal with its potential effects. In *Blakely*'s aftermath, some states were able to preserve their preexisting sentencing systems, but in others the ruling forced unwanted policy changes (American Law Institute 2007). Sentencing commissions in states like Washington, Minnesota, and North Carolina were able quickly to estimate how many cases would be affected by *Blakely*, and in a few months had recommended surgical fixes to meet the new legal requirements. In these jurisdictions, there were no long-term changes in the foundations of their systems as they had existed before *Blakely*. In states that lacked commissions and their thick data streams, like California and Colorado, confusion reigned. No one knew what percentage of cases would be affected, and no entity was in place to craft a targeted response. In both states, nothing happened until the courts declared their sentencing systems unconstitutional. In both, the result was fundamental systemic change via judicial ruling; where their sentencing rules addressed to judges had been enforceable in the past, they became advisory. (These might be called "involuntary voluntary" systems.)

Goal-Driven Consistency

In the early days of reform initiatives to address the perceived arbitrariness of indeterminate sentences, many suggested that "uniformity" in sentencing should be a primary goal (American Friends Services Committee 1971). Observers, including Federal Judge Marvin Frankel (1973), charged that each judge in indeterminate systems brought an idiosyncratic set of values to sentencing hearings, so that sentences depended as much upon which judge happened to be assigned as upon the facts of the case.

In the intervening decades, uniformity in sentencing has proven an elusive goal and, when (arguably) achieved, a mixed blessing. The underlying difficulty is that uniformity, as an intellectual tool, has no meaning except with reference to external criteria. If uniformity means that everyone convicted of crime x should receive sentence y, it is not a difficult policy to understand or to implement. But very few people would sponsor such a program. If uniformity means that there should be precise weights and measures that judges must apply mechanically at sentencing, then such a system did exist for many years under the federal sentencing guidelines—but it was unrelentingly criticized as inflexible, perverse, and dehumanizing (Freed 1992; Schulhofer 1992; American Bar Association 1994; Stith and Cabranes 1998; American Law Institute 2003). Practically every guidelines system ever invented has made the defensible claim that, based on compliance data—tracking how often judges comply with the guidelines—the goal of uniformity in sentencing has largely been achieved in their jurisdiction (Tonry 1996). What this tells us, I think, is that the goal of uniformity is so plastic that it is not worth very much. It may be that *consistency of thought process*, in light of designated sentencing purposes favored by policymakers in a jurisdiction, is a more salutary goal than uniformity of outcomes.

In Virginia, for example, the sentencing guidelines were created to incorporate criminological knowledge about criminal careers and the recidivism risks presented by individual offenders (Kern 1995; Ostrom et al. 2002). Actuarial risk assessments, based on the sentencing commission's ongoing recidivism studies of ex-prisoners in the state, are used most frequently to divert low-risk offenders from prison. True diversion is achieved by targeting drug and property offenders who would otherwise be given a prison sentence under the guidelines. In other instances, however, most pronouncedly for sex offenders, projections of high risk of recidivism are an authorized basis for long, incapacitative sentences (Virginia Criminal Sentencing Commission 2001). Some find this whole approach reprehensible, partly because offenders who commit like offenses frequently receive unlike punishments, and partly because the guidelines differentiate penalty recommendations based on age and gender (Tonry 1999). Putting this controversy to one side, however, the system has succeeded in providing a jurisdiction-wide policy template for sentencing decisions. Every trial court in Virginia works in a system in which selective incapacitation—or selective diversion from prison, as the case may be—is understood as an overarching goal.

Preservation of Judicial Sentencing Discretion

One of the most long-standing indictments of sentencing guidelines systems is the assertion that they leach sentencing discretion away from the courts and transfer it to prosecutors (Alschuler 1978). The theory is that inflexible guidelines force judges to impose lock-step penalties based on the charges of conviction and other predetermined guidelines factors. Therefore, the argument goes, prosecutors may control sentences through their charging decisions and by insisting that defendants plead guilty to certain counts, and perhaps also by pressuring defendants to stipulate to aggravating factors relevant to guidelines calculations. Once the plea is entered, there is nothing remaining for the judge to do but assign the preordained penalty.

This account is plausible when penalty prescriptions are truly mandatory, giving sentencing courts no room to maneuver after a conviction is in place (Tonry 1996). It is also plausible for a near-mandatory regime, such as the federal sentencing guidelines as they existed in 1987–2005. During this period, many observers protested loudly that federal prosecutors had become the real sentencers, and judges mere functionaries (Alschuler 1993; Tonry 1996; Stith and Cabranes 1998). But strong complaints of this sort have not been heard in *state* guidelines systems over the last 30 years. Why should that be?

The explanation, I believe, has two parts. First, most sentencing guidelines systems, with the sole exception of the former federal system, have given judges flexibility in the sentences they impose. As argued earlier, judges often have more effective sentencing discretion in a guidelines framework than in indeterminate structures. When judges' hands are not tied, the charge of conviction negotiated by the prosecutor is no guarantee of what the sentence will be. No prosecutor can force a sentence without the ratification of the sentencing judge, who may depart from the guidelines with relative freedom.

Second, prosecutorial power is affected by the severity of the punishments that are built into a particular system. To the extent that a prosecutor can threaten fearsome penalties, defendants are in a weakened bargaining position. Most American guidelines systems, however, have not been designed to ratchet up penalties overall. Once again, the federal system is an exception. The combination of unusual inflexibility and severity goes a long way toward explaining the perception that federal prosecutors circa 1987–2005 held undue power under the federal sentencing law. This diagnosis, however, should not be carelessly generalized to other guidelines systems.

THE POLITICS OF SENTENCING REFORM

In current parlance, *sentencing reform* means wholesale change in a jurisdiction's sentencing system away from the traditional model of indeterminacy. Hopefully this can result in better institutional arrangements, better legal structures for sentencing decisions, better process, better information, and better policy implementation. The substantive use to which a new sentencing system will be put, however, is very much a separate question. "Reformed" sentencing guidelines systems in America have been used to further policies of greater severity in punishment—in some places at some times—as well as policies of increased lenity (Tonry 1996; American Law Institute 2007). In this sense, sentencing reform is ideologically neutral.

Even so, the pathways toward achieving systemic reform are highly political. Large institutional changes affect the professional lives of many stakeholders in the criminal justice system, and the perceived interests of important constituencies vary from place to place. For example, notwithstanding the wide belief that prosecutors' powers are multiplied in a sentencing guidelines system, prosecutors' organizations have been formidable opponents of guidelines reform in many states, including Colorado, Texas, Massachusetts, and California. In other states, like Washington and Oregon, prosecutors have led the call for reform. Judges, too, have staked out different positions across jurisdictions: Judicial leadership was key to the adoption of guidelines systems in Minnesota, Delaware, North Carolina, Missouri, and the District of Columbia (and ongoing attempted reforms in Massachusetts). In other places, judges have been unsupportive or hostile to reform efforts, such as Colorado, New York, Georgia, and the federal system.

The criminal justice needs and political realities of each jurisdiction are distinctive. Chronic problems of prison crowding and corrections costs, in states that have felt them most, are associated with the adoption of guidelines reforms (Barkow and O'Neill 2006). Successful reform may also be easier to engineer in relatively small jurisdictions, where criminal justice communities are manageable in size, and individual leadership can play out within smaller networks. In larger jurisdictions like New York, Texas, and California, efforts at reform have foundered or, in the federal system, have led to an unstable framework weakened by continuous barrages of criticism (Freed 1992; Schulhofer 1992; Tonry 1996; Stith and Cabranes 1998; American Law Institute 2003).

SENTENCING SYSTEMS AND ACUTE BUDGETARY STRESS

Periods of budgetary crisis recur for all state governments. When immediate belt-tightening is needed, as in the early and late 2000s, corrections is one major area of state spending that must be examined. For fiscal year 2008, total spending on corrections for all states was estimated to exceed $52 billion. Corrections, on average, consumed 6.9 of state general fund expenditures (Pew Center for the States 2009).

In the early 2000s, and again late in that decade, states took a number of steps to realize short-time reductions in correctional costs. Some cut operating budgets for the prisons, targeting food costs, health care, and programming, or have cut funding for community-based sanctions. Others pared back the reach of mandatory sentencing laws, particularly for nonviolent offenses. A number of states changed their formulas for good-time or earned-time credits, or have otherwise accelerated prison release dates for designated inmates. Elsewhere, parole boards have been encouraged to expedite their normal processes, and some states have enlarged their compassionate release provisions for inmates who are elderly or seriously ill. A number of jurisdictions have acted to cut the number of offenders on probation or parole—all of whom are potential subjects of sentence revocation and new admission to prison—and some have encouraged the greater use of sanctions short of confinement for technical sentence violators (Wool and Stemen 2004b; Scott-Hayward 2009; National Conference of State Legislatures 2009).

Emergency cost-cutting measures do not necessarily comport with the best longer-term sentencing policy. While policymakers sometimes view crisis as opportunity, it is useful to draw distinctions between quick fixes—perhaps regrettable—and true reforms that allow the system to better manage costs, set priorities, and respond to evidence.

CONCLUSION

We live in an era of great changes in the theories and empirical understanding of what criminal sentences can do, the legal and institutional structures for sentencing decisions, and the sizes and compositions of sentenced populations. At the same time, we have paid too little attention as a society to the implications of these developments—and some of them have been vast indeed. By hypothesis, there is much that is positive to be learned from the dramatic upheavals in sentencing law and policy over the past 30 to 40 years, and much to be regretted. Given the great complexity of the subject, however, and to counteract the human tendency to be self-confident even in our ignorance, we must always be looking for better tools to examine the big picture outcomes of sentencing policies, the operations of sentencing systems as a whole, and the comparative merits of different systems.

References

Alschuler, Albert W. 1978. "Sentencing Reform and Prosecutorial Power: A Critique of Recent Proposals for 'Fixed' and 'Presumptive' Sentencing." *University of Pennsylvania Law Review* 126: 550–577.

Alschuler, Albert W. 1993. "The Failure of Sentencing Guidelines: A Plea for Less Aggregation." *University of Chicago Law Review* 58: 901–951.

American Bar Association. 1994. *Standards for Criminal Justice, Sentencing*, 3rd ed. Washington, DC: American Bar Association.

American Friends Service Committee. 1971. *Struggle for Justice: A Report on Crime and Punishment in America*. New York: Hill and Wang.

American Law Institute. 2003. *Model Penal Code: Sentencing, Report*. Philadelphia: American Law Institute.

American Law Institute. 2007. *Model Penal Code: Sentencing, Tentative Draft No. 1* (approved May 16, 2007). Philadelphia: American Law Institute.

American Law Institute. 2009. *Model Penal Code: Sentencing, Discussion Draft No. 2*. Philadelphia: American Law Institute.

Ashworth, Andrew A. 2005. *Sentencing and Criminal Justice*, 4th ed. Cambridge: Cambridge University Press.

Barkow, Rachel, and Kathleen M. O'Neill. 2006. "Delegating Punitive Power: The Political Economy of Sentencing Commission and Guideline Formation." *Texas Law Review* 84: 1973–2022.

Beckett, Katherine. 1997. *Making Crime Pay: Law and Order in Contemporary American Politics*. New York: Oxford University Press.

Bennett, William J., John J. DiIulio, Jr., and John P. Walters. 1996. *Body Count: Moral Poverty and How to Win America's War Against Crime and Drugs*. New York: Simon and Schuster.

Berman, Douglas A. 2009. "The Enduring (and Again Timely) Wisdom of the Original MPC Sentencing Provisions." *Florida Law Review* 61: 709–725.

Blakely v. Washington. 2004. 542 U.S. 296.

Blumstein, Alfred, and Joan Petersilia. 1995. "Investing in Criminal Justice Research." In *Crime*, eds. James Q. Wilson and Joan Petersilia. San Francisco: ICS Press.

Brandeis, Louis D. 1932. In *New State Ice Co. v. Liebmann*, 285 U.S. 262.

Bureau of Justice Statistics. 1986. *Historical Corrections Statistics in the United States: 1850 to 1984*. Washington, DC: U.S. Department of Justice, Bureau of Justice Statistics.

Bureau of Justice Statistics. 1988. *Prisoners in 1987*. Washington, DC: U.S. Department of Justice, Bureau of Justice Statistics.

Bureau of Justice Statistics. 1991. *Sourcebook of Criminal Justice Statistics—1990*. Washington, DC: U.S. Department of Justice, Bureau of Justice Statistics.

Bureau of Justice Statistics. 2002. *Correctional Populations in the United States 1998—Statistical Tables*. Washington, DC: U.S. Department of Justice, Bureau of Justice Statistics. Online. Available at http://www.ojp.usdoj.gov/bjs/pub/pdf/cpus9805.pdf.

Bureau of Justice Statistics. 2006. *Prison and Jail Inmates at Midyear 2005*. Washington, DC: U.S. Department of Justice, Bureau of Justice Statistics.

Bureau of Justice Statistics. 2007. *Homicide Trends in the U.S.: Trends by Race*. Washington, DC: U.S. Department of Justice, Bureau of Justice Statistics. Online. Available: http://www.ojp.usdoj.gov/bjs/homicide/tables/vracetab.htm.

Bureau of Justice Statistics. 2007b. *Prison and Jail Inmates at Midyear 2006*. Washington, DC: U.S. Department of Justice, Bureau of Justice Statistics.

Bureau of Justice Statistics. 2008a. *Prison Inmates at Midyear 2007*. Washington, DC: U.S. Department of Justice, Bureau of Justice Statistics.

Bureau of Justice Statistics. 2008b. *Serious Violent Victimization Rates by Race, 1973–2005*. Washington, DC: U.S. Department of Justice, Bureau of Justice Statistics. Online. Available at www.ojp.usdoj.gov/bjs/glance/tables/racetab.htm.

Bureau of Justice Statistics. 2009. *Prison Inmates at Midyear 2008—Statistical Tables.* Washington, DC: U.S. Department of Justice, Bureau of Justice Statistics.

Cassell, Paul. 2009. "In Defense of Victim Impact Statements." *Ohio State Journal of Criminal Law* 6: 611–648.

Clear, Todd R. 2007. *Imprisoning Communities: How Mass Incarceration Makes Communities Worse.* New York: Oxford University Press.

DiIulio, John J., Jr. 1994. "The Question of Black Crime." *The Public Interest* 117: 3–32.

Donohue, John J., III. 2009. "Assessing the Relative Benefits of Incarceration: Overall Changes and the Benefits on the Margin." In *Do Prisons Make Us Safer?: The Benefits and Costs of the Prison Boom,* eds. Steven Raphael and Michael A. Stoll, 269–341. New York: Russell Sage Foundation.

Dressler, Joshua. 2001. *Understanding Criminal Law,* 3rd ed. New York: Lexis Publishing.

Federal Bureau of Investigation. 2009. *Crime in the United States 2008.* Washington, DC: U.S. Department of Justice.

Feeley, Malcolm M., and Edward L. Rubin. 1998. *Judicial Policy Making and the Modern State: How the Courts Reformed America's Prisons.* Cambridge: Cambridge University Press.

Fletcher, George. 1978. *Rethinking Criminal Law.* Boston: Little, Brown.

Frase, Richard S. 2002. "Limiting Retributivism." In *The Future of Imprisonment,* ed. Michael Tonry, 83–119. New York: Oxford University Press.

Frase, Richard S. 2005. "State Sentencing Guidelines: Diversity, Consensus, and Unresolved Policy Issues." *Columbia Law Review* 105: 1190–1232.

Frase, Richard S. 2009. "What Factors Explain Persistent Racial Disproportionality in Minnesota's Prison and Jail Populations?" In *Crime and Justice: A Review of Research,* ed. Michael Tonry, 38: 201–80. Chicago: University of Chicago Press.

Frankel, Marvin E. 1973. *Criminal Sentences: Law Without Order.* New York: Hill and Wang.

Freed, Daniel J. 1992. "Federal Sentencing in the Wake of Guidelines: Unacceptable Limits on the Discretion of Sentencers." *Yale Law Journal* 101: 1681–1754.

Gall v. U.S. 2007. 552 U.S. 38.

Hoffman, Morris G., and Timothy H. Goldsmith. 2004. "The Biological Roots of Punishment." *Ohio State Journal of Criminal Law* 1: 627–641.

Hunt, Kim S. 1998. "Sentencing Commissions as Centers for Policy Analysis and Research: Illustrations from the Budget Process." *Law and Policy:* 20: 465–489.

Hunt, Kim S., and Michael Connelly. 2005. "Advisory Guidelines in the Post-*Blakely* Era." *Federal Sentencing Reporter* 17: 233.

Jacobs, James B. 1982. "Sentencing by Prison Personnel: Good Time." *U.C.L.A. Law Review* 30: 217–270.

Kennedy, Randall. 1998. *Race, Crime, and the Law.* New York: Pantheon Books.

Kern, Richard. 1995. "Sentencing Reform in Virginia." *Federal Sentencing Reporter* 8: 84–88.

Kimbrough v. U.S. 2007. 552 U.S. 85.

Klein, Susan, Joan Petersilia, and Susan Turner 1990. "Race and Imprisonment Decisions in California." *Science* 847: 212–216.

Knapp, Kay A. 1993. "Allocation of Discretion and Accountability Within Sentencing Structures." *University of Colorado Law Review* 64: 679–705.

Marvell, Thomas B. 1995. "Sentencing Guidelines and Prison Population Growth." *Journal of Criminal Law and Criminology* 85: 696–709.

Mauer, Marc. 1994. *Race to Incarcerate*. New York: The New Press.

Mauer, Marc. 2009. "Racial Impact Statements." *Criminal Justice* (Winter): 16–20.

Moore, Michael S. "The Moral Worth of Retribution." In *Responsibility, Character, and the Emotions: New Essays in Moral Psychology*, ed. Ferdinand Schoeman, 179–219. New York: Cambridge University Press.

Morris, Norval. 1974. *The Future of Imprisonment*. Chicago: University of Chicago Press.

Morris, Norval, and Marc Miller. 1985. "Predictions of Dangerousness." In *Crime and Justice: An Annual Review of Research*, eds. Michael Tonry and Norval Morris, Vol. 6, 1–50. Chicago: University of Chicago Press.

Murray, Charles. 1997. *Does Prison Work?* London: Institute of Economic Affairs.

National Conference of State Legislatures. 2009. *Cutting Corrections Costs: Earned Time Policies for State Prisoners*. Denver: National Conference of State Legislatures.

Ostrom, Brian J., Matthew Kleiman, Fred Cheesman II, Randall M. Hansen, and Neil B. Kauder. 2002. *Offender Risk Assessment in Virginia: A Three-Stage Evaluation*. Williamsburg: National Center for State Courts.

Petersilia, Joan. 2003. *When Prisoners Come Home: Parole and Prisoner Reentry*. New York: Oxford University Press.

Pew Center for the States. 2009. *One in 31: The Long Reach of American Corrections*. Washington, DC: The Pew Charitable Trusts.

Pfaff, John F. 2006. "The Continued Vitality of Structured Sentencing Following *Blakely*: The Effectiveness of Voluntary Guidelines." *U.C.L.A. Law Review* 54: 235–306.

Raphael, Steven. 2005. "The Socioeconomic Status of Black Males: The Increasing Importance of Incarceration." In *Poverty, the Distribution of Income, and Public Policy*, eds. Allen Auerbach, David Card and John Quigley, 319–358. New York: Russell Sage Foundation.

Raphael, Steven, and Michael A. Stoll. 2009. "Introduction." In *Do Prisons Make Us Safer?: The Benefits and Costs of the Prison Boom*, eds. Steven Raphael and Michael A. Stoll, 1–24. New York: Russell Sage Foundation.

Reitz, Kevin R. 1997. "Sentencing Guidelines Systems and Sentence Appeals: A Comparison of Federal and State Experiences." *Northwestern Law Review* 91: 1441–1506.

Reitz, Kevin R. 1998. "Modeling Discretion in American Sentencing Systems." *Law and Policy* 20: 389–428.

Reitz, Kevin R. 2005. "The Enforceability of Sentencing Guidelines." *Stanford Law Review* 58: 155–73.

Reitz, Kevin R. 2006. "Don't Blame Determinacy: U.S. Incarceration Growth Has Been Driven by Other Forces." *Texas Law Review* 84: 1787–1802.

Reitz, Kevin R. 2009. "Demographic Impact Statements, O'Connor's Warning, and the Mysteries of Prison Release: Topics from a Sentencing Reform Agenda." *Florida Law Review* 61: 683–707.

Ristroph, Alice. 2009. "How (Not) to Think Like a Punisher." *Florida Law Review* 61: 727–749.

Roberts, Julian V. 2008. *Punishing Persistent Offenders: Exploring Community and Offender Perspectives*. New York: Oxford University Press.

Robinson, Paul H. 2006. "Competing Conceptions of Modern Desert: Vengeful, Deontological, and Empirical. *Cambridge Law Journal* 67: 145–75.

Robinson, Paul H., and John M. Darley. 1995. *Justice, Liability, and Blame: Community Views and the Criminal Law*. Boulder, CO: Westview Press.

Robinson, Paul H., Robert Kurzban, and Owen D. Jones. 2007. "The Origins of Shared Intuitions of Justice." *Vanderbilt Law Review* 60: 1633–1688.

Rothman, David J. 1980. *Conscience and Convenience: The Asylum and Its Alternatives in Progressive America*. Boston: Little, Brown and Co.

Rubin, Edward. 2002. "The Inevitability of Rehabilitation." *Law and Inequality* 19: 343–377.

Rubin, Edward. 2003. "Just Say No to Retribution." *Buffalo Criminal Law Review* 7: 17–83.

Ruth, Henry, and Kevin R. Reitz. 2003. *The Challenge of Crime: Rethinking Our Response*. Cambridge: Harvard University Press.

Scott, Robert E., and William J. Stuntz. 1992. "Plea Bargaining as Contract." *Yale Law Journal* 101: 1909–1968.

Scott-Hayward. 2009. *The Fiscal Crisis in Corrections: Rethinking Policies and Practices*. New York: Vera Institute of Justice.

Schulhofer, Stephen J. 1992. "Assessing the Federal Sentencing Process: The Problem is Uniformity, Not Disparity." *American Criminal Law Review* 29: 833–873.

Spears v. U.S. 2009. 129 S. Ct. 840.

Stemen, Don, and Andres Rengifo, with James Wilson. 2005. *Of Fragmentation and Ferment: The Impact of State Sentencing Policies on Incarceration Rates, 1972–2002*. New York: Vera Institute of Justice.

Stith, Kate and José A. Cabranes. 1998. *Fear of Judging: Sentencing Guidelines in the Federal Courts*. Chicago: University of Chicago Press.

Tonry, Michael. 1994. Racial Disproportion in U. S. Prisons. *British Journal of Criminology* 34: 97–115.

Tonry, Michael. 1995. *Malign Neglect: Race, Crime, and Punishment in America*. New York: Oxford University Press.

Tonry, Michael. 1996. *Sentencing Matters*. New York: Oxford University Press.

Tonry, Michael. 1999. "Rethinking Unthinkable Punishment Policies in America." *U.C.L.A. Law Review* 46: 1751–1791.

Tonry, Michael. 2004. *Thinking About Crime: Sense and Sensibility in American Penal Culture*. New York: Oxford University Press.

Tonry, Michael, and Matthew Melewski. 2008. "The Malign Effects of Drug and Crime Control Policies on Black Americans." *Crime and Justice: A Review of Research* 37: 1–44. Chicago: University of Chicago Press.

U.S. Census Bureau. 2009. *Annual Estimates of the Resident Population by Sex, Race, and Hispanic Origin for the United States: April 1, 2000 to July 1, 2008*. Washington, DC: U.S. Census Bureau. Online. Available at http://www.census.gov/popest/national/asrh/NC-EST2008-srh.html.

U.S. Sentencing Commission. 1991. *Special Report to Congress: Mandatory Minimum Penalties in the Federal Criminal Justice System*. Washington, DC: U.S. Sentencing Commission.

U.S. v. Booker. 2005. 543 U.S. 220.

Useem, Bert, and Anne Morrison Piehl. 2008. *Prison State: The Challenge of Mass Incarceration*. New York: Cambridge University Press.

Violence Policy Center. 2009. *Black Homicide Victimization in the United States: An Analysis of 2006 Homicide Data*. Washington, DC: Violence Policy Center.

Virginia Criminal Sentencing Commission. 2001. *Assessing Risk Among Sex Offenders in Virginia*. Richmond: Virginia Criminal Sentencing Commission.

Vitiello, Michael. 2004. "Reforming Three Strikes' Excesses." *Washington University Law Quarterly* 82: 1–42.

von Hirsch, Andrew. 1985. *Past and Future Crimes: Deservedness and Dangerousness in the Sentencing of Criminals*. New Brunswick, NJ: Rutgers University Press.

von Hirsch, Andrew. 1993. *Censure and Sanctions*. Oxford: Clarendon Press.

von Hirsch, Andrew, and Andrew Ashworth. 2005. *Proportionate Sentencing*. London: Hart Publishing.

von Hirsch, Andrew, Anthony E. Bottoms, Elizabeth Burney, and P.O. Wikstrom. 1999. *Criminal Deterrence and Sentence Severity: An Analysis of Recent Research*. London: Hart Publishing.

Wacquant, Loïc. 2001. "Deadly Symbiosis: When Ghetto and Prison Meet and Mesh." *Punishment and Society* 3: 95–133.

Walker, Nigel. 1991. *Why Punish? Theories of Punishment Reassessed*. New York: Oxford University Press.

Walmsey, Roy. 2009. *International Centre for Prison Studies, World Prison Population List*, 8th ed. London. Online. Available at http://www.kcl.ac.uk/depsta/law/research/icps/downloads.php?searchtitle=world+prison&type=0&month=0&year=0&lang=0&author=&search=Search.

Weiman, David F. and Christopher Weiss. 2009. "The Origins of Mass Incarceration in New York State: The Rockefeller Drug Laws and the Local War on Drugs." In *Do Prisons Make Us Safer?: The Benefits and Costs of the Prison Boom*, eds. Steven Raphael and Michael A. Stoll, 73-116. New York: Russell Sage Foundation.

Weisberg, Robert. 2007. "How Sentencing Commissions Turned Out to Be a Good Idea." *Berkeley Journal of Criminal Law* 12: 179–230.

Weisberg, Robert. 2009. "Tragedy, Skepticism, and the MPCS." *Florida Law Review* 61: 797–826.

Whitman, James Q. 2003. "A Plea Against Retributivism." *Buffalo Criminal Law Review* 7: 85–107.

Wilson, James Q. 1975. *Thinking About Crime*. New York: Basic Books.

Wool, Jon, and Don Stemen. 2004. *Aggravated Sentencing*: Blakely v. Washington: *Practical Implications for State Sentencing Systems*. New York: Vera Institute of Justice.

Wool, Jon, and Don Stemen. 2004b. *Changing Fortunes or Changing Attitudes? Sentencing and Corrections Reforms in 2003*. New York: Vera Institute of Justice.

Wright, Ronald F. 2002. "Counting the Cost of Sentencing in North Carolina, 1980–2000." *Crime and Justice: A Review of Research* 29: 39–112. Chicago: University of Chicago Press.

Zimring, Franklin E. 1976. "A Consumer's Guide to Sentencing Reform: Making the Punishment Fit the Crime." *Hastings Center Report* 6: 13–17.

Zimring, Franklin E. 2005. *American Juvenile Justice*. New York: Oxford University Press.

Zimring, Franklin E., and Gordon Hawkins. 1991. *The Scale of Imprisonment*. Chicago: University of Chicago Press.

Zimring, Franklin E., and Gordon Hawkins. 1997. *Crime Is Not the Problem: Lethal Violence in America*. New York: Oxford University Press.

Notes

1. The leading proponents of just deserts theory believe that general deterrence might be a happy by-product of their scheme. In addition, utilitarian goals may be consulted to choose among various sanctions options of equivalent severity (von Hirsch and Ashworth 2005).

2. A number of states have created temporary sentencing commissions that decided not to recommend or promulgate sentencing guidelines. These include Georgia, New York, and Texas.

3. The federal departure standard under 18 U.S.C. 3553(b) requires the sentencing court to find "an aggravating or mitigating circumstance of a kind, or to a degree, *not adequately taken into consideration by the Sentencing Commission in formulating the guidelines* that should result in a sentence different from that described" in the guidelines (my emphasis). Because the federal sentencing guidelines are so detailed and compendious—far more so than any state's guidelines—the federal appellate courts rarely agreed that a trial judge's reasons for departure had not been considered and rejected by the commission (Reitz 1997). The Supreme Court reworked the federal guidelines system by constitutional decision in 2005, transforming it into an advisory system. This has in theory loosened the guidelines' grip, although the Supreme Court continues to hear federal cases in which trial courts' discretion has been unduly constricted on appeal (U.S. v. Booker 2005; Gall v. U.S. 2007; Kimbrough v. U.S. 2007; Spears v. U.S. 2009).

4. This study mistakenly classified Pennsylvania as a presumptive system, however. Correcting for this error, the presumptive systems would probably have looked even more effective in relation to advisory systems.

5. The only exception among state systems to my knowledge is Pennsylvania, where sentencing guidelines originally were promulgated with the express purpose of increasing the state's use of imprisonment. In 1982, when the guidelines took effect, Pennsylvania was far below the national average in its per capita prison rate, and out of step with neighboring states. Under guidelines, the prison rate shot up dramatically for many years, although the state's policy has since shifted to a low-growth model.

6. These states were, from highest prison rate, Louisiana (835), Texas (687), Mississippi (661), Oklahoma (658), Alabama (587), Georgia (560), Arizona (529), South Carolina (527), Missouri (524), and Michigan (502). Of the top 10, only Arizona and Mississippi employed determinate systems.

7. The top 10 prison-growth states from 1980 to 2006 were Louisiana, Mississippi, Oklahoma, Texas, Alabama, Connecticut, Missouri, Idaho, California, and Colorado. Of these, only Mississippi and California have determinate sentencing systems.

Chapter 17

Community Corrections: Probation, Parole, and Prisoner Reentry

Joan Petersilia

A fundamental fact about punishment in the United States is that the vast majority of those under correctional supervision are *not* behind bars, but living in the community. At year-end 2007, 7.3 million adults were under some form of correctional supervision—incarcerated in jails and prisons, or supervised on probation or parole. Just 2.2 million of them were physically in custody. The remaining 5.1 million persons (*or 70 percent of all adult criminals under sentence*) were on probation or parole (Glaze and Bonczar 2008). In 2007, 19 percent of all adults on probation or parole had been convicted of violent crimes (about one in five), and 29 percent had been convicted of drug crimes (nearly one in three) (Glaze and Bonczar 2008). In addition, 560,000 juveniles were placed on probation in 2005—nearly half of all cases that received a juvenile court sanction (Puzzanchera and Sickmund 2008). These non-prison programs are known as community corrections, because they permit an offender to reside in the community while serving a criminal sentence. In fact, despite the addition of 1.1 million prison beds in the past decade and the quadrupling of the prison population, the proportion of offenders behind bars versus in the community has changed very little over the past 25 years. Today, as has always been the case, the U.S. criminal justice system is primarily a system of community-based sanctioning.

Despite the fact that most convicted offenders remain in the community, community corrections has always been undervalued and undersupported. It suffers from a soft on crime image, and as a result, does not get much financial or community support. A national survey recently reported that the average annual cost of housing a prisoner in the United States was nearly $29,000, compared to $1,250 for supervising a probationer, and $2,750 for supervising a parolee (Scott-Hayward 2009). Prison understandably costs more, but the price gap is staggering. While three out of four offenders are on probation or parole rather than behind bars, almost nine of every ten dollars of corrections funding goes to fund prisons.

In many ways, the underfunding of community corrections fuels the ever-expanding funding for prisons: probation and parole failures eventually end up occupying prison beds. About two-thirds of all prison admissions each year consist of persons who have had their probation or parole revoked, many for technical violations such as testing positive for drugs (Petersilia 2003). Nearly everyone who goes to prison eventually comes home, and the never-ending churning cycle begins again. In essence, the entire correctional system feeds on itself, as increases in probation and parole populations create more violations and new crimes, which in turn creates pressure to expand the prison system. Second only to Medicaid, corrections has become the fastest growing general fund expenditure in the United States, and the United States now spends about $52 billion a year on its corrections system, a 20-year jump of over 300 percent (Scott-Hayward 2009).

It is not just the high and growing costs of prisons that cause concern. Scholars have demonstrated the negative impact of incarceration on racial minorities, labor markets, political participation, community well-being, and family formation. Researchers have also studied the long-term psychological impacts on those incarcerated, and how these and other aspects of imprisonment negatively impact the prospects of successful reentry when offenders are released (for examples, see Haney 2006; Petersilia 2003; Travis 2005).

Within this context, community corrections looms large. Policymakers at all levels of government are asking the same question: Can probation and parole be strengthened and improved, thereby increasing public safety, decreasing system costs, and fostering offender reintegration? The question is not new. In fact, it is the exact question that was asked in the mid-1980s when the "intermediate sanctions" movement took hold. The issues were identical: cash-strapped states were looking for alternatives to incarceration, and state legislatures responded by funding a variety of punishment options that did not require a prison cell. Between 1985 and 1995, hundreds of intermediate sanction programs (ISPs) were implemented, many funded by the federal government (Petersilia 1998). Virtually every large probation and parole agency developed programs of intensive supervision, electronic monitoring, house arrest, drug testing, and, to a lesser extent, day reporting centers. The *Washington Post* and the *New York Times* ran major stories touting early program successes in Georgia, and called such programs the "future of American corrections."

But the enthusiasm was short-lived, squelched by dismal evaluations showing that the intermediate sanctions did not achieve their core objectives of relieving prison crowding, saving money, or rehabilitating offenders (Petersilia and Turner 1993; Tonry and Hamilton 1995). In fact, they often did just the opposite: offenders in intermediate sanction programs were watched more closely—as evidenced by a greater number of contacts—but the programs did not reduce new arrests. Close surveillance uncovered more technical violations, and ISP managers took punitive action—often revocation to prison—to maintain the program's credibility in the eyes of the judiciary and the community. Programs that were started primarily to save money and avoid prison costs ended up costing more in the long run as violators were increasingly returned to prison and jail.

These disappointing results led to the closure of many intermediate sanction programs. A few programs were redesigned to increase treatment services, but on the whole, the ISP experiment was characterized as yet another failed justice experiment, and state after state—now facing rising crime rates as well—moved away from endorsing community sanctions and became more punitive, convinced that community sanctions had been tried and did not work.

This leads to the current conundrum: overcrowded prisons, a community corrections system starved for funding, and a bloated prison system that is unsustainable as the nation's economic woes become widely felt. States are again looking for ways to trim corrections costs while maintaining public safety. One attractive option is to reduce prison populations by making better use of community corrections. But the $64,000 question is, *"If not prison, what?"* That is, can we reduce the growth of prisons while keeping communities safe? The short answer is yes—but only if we have realistic expectations, an understanding of community correction history and current operations, and knowledge of the scientific "what works" in corrections rehabilitation literature. This chapter provides an overview of these issues.

Section I defines probation, parole, and prisoner reentry. Section II provides a brief history of probation and parole development in the United States. Section III describes the growth, funding, and characteristics of community corrections populations. Section IV discusses issues related to supervision (e.g., caseload size), and the civil disabilities governing a probationer or parolee's life (e.g., voting restrictions). Section V presents data on recidivism, revocations to prison, and the public safety consequences of lax community supervision. Section VI, the final section, provides recommendations for creating a more effective community corrections system.

The main conclusions of this chapter are as follows:

- Probation and parole have been part of America's criminal justice system for more than one hundred years, and despite the fact that prisons dominate our thinking on punishment, about two-thirds of all adults under correctional supervision in the United States are on probation or parole. Just 10 percent of all corrections spending in the United States goes to community correctional agencies.
- Community corrections has never had much public support and suffers from a "soft on crime" image, despite having moved in recent years from a "casework" to "surveillance" approach to supervision. Agencies struggle for resources and credibility, and officers often

handle 100-plus caseloads, where few rehabilitation services can be provided.

- Community corrections is not very effective, and most felons fail to successfully complete their probation or parole terms. Offenders most often fail due to committing a technical or rule violation rather than committing a new crime. Probation and parole failures are major contributors to recent increases in U.S. prison populations.

- Several promising programs have improved traditional probation and parole by intensifying supervision for violent offenders and providing specialized treatment programs tailored to moderate offenders' criminogenic needs. These programs appear to reduce both recidivism and system costs.

- The current fiscal crisis may well provide a window of opportunity to rigorously test and replicate these promising programs, paving the way for reductions in historically high prison populations.

I. DEFINING KEY TERMS

Probation and parole are the core of community corrections. While the terms are often used interchangeably, probation is a dispositional *alternative* to prison, whereas parole implies that the offender has already served a portion of his or her sentence incarcerated. There are two other important differences: probation is a sentencing option available to local judges, who determine the form that probation will take. Parole results from an administrative decision made by a legally-designated paroling authority. Under parole, the power to determine when an offender may be released, and to fix supervision conditions, passes from the hands of the court to an agency within the executive branch of the state. Probation can be a state or local activity, administered by one of more than 2,000 separate agencies in the United States. Parole is always a state function, administered by a single state agency.

In other major respects, probation and parole are similar. In both, information about an offender is gathered and presented to a decision-making authority, and that authority has the power to release the offender under specific conditions, which are articulated in a contract signed by the offender. The principal responsibility of the probation or parole officer is to monitor this court-imposed contract and conditions. If offenders fail to live up to their conditions, they can be revoked and returned to jail or prison to serve out the remainder of the original sentence or to serve a new sentence. Probation and parole can be revoked for two reasons: (1) the commission of a new crime, or (2) the violation of the conditions of parole (a technical violation). Technical violations pertain to behavior that is not criminal, such as the failure to refrain from alcohol use or remain employed. In either event, the violation process is rather straightforward. Given that probationers and parolees are technically still in the legal custody of the court or prison authorities, their constitutional rights are severely limited. Offenders do have some rights in revocation proceedings. Two U.S. Supreme Court cases, *Morrissey v. Brewer* (1972) and *Gagnon v. Scarpelli* (1973), established minimum due process standards for the revocation of probation and parole. Offenders must be given written notice of the nature of the violation and the evidence obtained, and they have a right to confront and cross-examine their accusers (del Carmen, Barnhill, and Bonham 2000).

The goals of probation and parole supervision are identical: to protect the community and help rehabilitate offenders. These dual functions are referred to as the law enforcement function, which emphasizes surveillance of the offender and close control of behavior, and the social work function, which attempts to provide supportive services to meet offenders' needs. Both have always been part of community corrections, and debating which should be of higher priority has always caused strain. Currently, the social work function has given way to the law enforcement function, and probation and parole officers are less interested today in treating clients than in controlling their behavior.

Another term—*prisoner reentry*—began affecting community corrections in early 2000. Unlike probation and parole, prisoner reentry is not a legal status or program, but a new conceptual framework for thinking about the processing of criminal offenders, from sentencing to parole discharge. Prisoner reentry is defined as the process of leaving incarceration and returning to society, and includes all activities and programming conducted to prepare ex-convicts to return safely to the community and to live as law-abiding citizens (Petersilia 2003). Reentry is also virtually universal. As Jeremy Travis (2005, xxi) reminds us, "reentry is not a form of supervision, like parole. Reentry is not a goal, like rehabilitation or reintegration. Reentry is not an option. Reentry reflects the iron law of imprisonment: they all come back." Reentry is simply the inevitable consequence of incarceration.

Refocusing the justice system around a reentry perspective represents a fundamental paradigm shift that impacts decisions about the timing of release, the procedures for making the release decision, the preparation of the prisoner for release, supervision after release, and the linkages between in-prison and post-release activities.

As U.S. incarceration increased, interest in reentry grew, and today it is often referred to as a full-fledged movement (Travis 2007). Current parole discussions now often focus on parole as a sanction as well as a method of transitioning offenders to the community. And as states struggle with gaping budget shortfalls, there is a window of opportunity for community corrections to demonstrate they can effectively carry out their mission. But there is also the possibility that community corrections will be asked to deliver the impossible—greater public safety and more rehabilitation with stagnant or declining funding. Understanding probation and parole's historical roots puts the current policy discussions in useful context.

II. A BRIEF HISTORY OF PROBATION AND PAROLE

The history of probation and parole can best be understood in relationship to prisons and jails, as they both developed as reactions to the harshness and conditions of incarceration. Probation developed as a result of the perceived harshness of jails, and parole developed as a prison-crowding management tool and a means to induce prisoners to participate in rehabilitation programs (Friedman 1993; Morris and Rothman 1995). Today, this history repeats itself as renewed attention to community corrections is being driven primarily by the high costs of prisons, both for offenders and the community, rather than a fundamental commitment to community corrections.

The Origins and Evolution of Probation

Probation in the United States began in 1841 with the innovative work of John Augustus, a Boston bootmaker who was the first to post bail for a man charged with being a common drunk under the authority of the Boston Police Court. Mr. Augustus was a religious man of financial means, and had some experience working with alcoholics. When the man appeared before the judge for sentencing, Mr. Augustus asked the judge to defer sentencing for three weeks and release the man into Augustus's custody. At the end of this brief probationary period, the offender convinced the judge of his reform and therefore received a nominal fine. The concept of probation had been born.

From the beginning, the "helping" role of Augustus met with the scorn of law enforcement officials who wanted offenders punished not helped. But Augustus persisted, and the court gradually accepted the notion that not all offenders need to be incarcerated. During the next fifteen years (from 1841 until his death in 1859), Augustus bailed out over 1,800 persons in the Boston courts, making himself liable to the extent of $243,234 and preventing these individuals from being held in jail to await trial. Augustus is reported to have selected his candidates carefully, offering assistance "mainly to those who were indicted for their first offense, and whose hearts were not wholly depraved, but gave promise of better things" (Augustus 1852). He provided his charges with aid in obtaining employment, an education, or a place to live, and also made an impartial report to the court.

Augustus reported great success with his charges, nearly all of whom were accused or convicted of violating Boston's vice or temperance laws. Of the first 1,100 offenders he discussed in his autobiography, he claimed only one had forfeited bond, and asserted that, with help, most of them eventually led upright lives.

Buoyed by Augustus's example, Massachusetts quickly moved into the forefront of probation development. In 1878, Massachusetts was the first state to formally adopt a probation law for juveniles. Interestingly, it was also the concern for mitigating the harshness of penalties for children that led to the international development of probation.

Public support for adult probation was much more difficult to come by. It was not until 1901 that New York passed the first statute authorizing probation for adult offenders—over 20 years after Massachusetts passed its law for juvenile probationers. By 1956, all states had adopted adult and juvenile probation laws (Petersilia 1997).

John Augustus's early work provided the model for probation as we know it today. He originally conceived virtually every basic practice of probation. He was the first person to use the term *probation*—which derives from the Latin term *probatio*, meaning a "period of proving or trial." He developed the ideas of the pre-sentence investigation, supervision conditions, social casework, reports to the court, and revocation of probation.It is unfortunate that such a visionary died destitute.

Initially, probation officers were volunteers who, according to Augustus, just needed to just have a good heart. Early probation volunteer officers were often drawn from Catholic, Protestant, and Jewish church groups. In addition, police were reassigned to function as probation officers while continuing to draw their pay as municipal employees. But as the concept spread and the number of persons arrested increased, the need for pre-sentence investigations increased, and the volunteer probation officer was converted into a paid position (Dressler 1974). The new officers hired were drawn largely from the law enforcement community—retired sheriffs and policemen—and worked directly for the judge.

Gradually the role of court support and probation officer became synonymous, and probation officers became "the eyes and ears of the local court." As Rothman (1980) observed some years later, probation developed in the United States very haphazardly, and with no real thought. Missions were unclear and often contradictory, and from the start there was tension between the law enforcement and rehabilitation purposes of probation. But most importantly, tasks were continually added to probation's responsibilities, while funding remained constant or declined. A survey by Fitzharris (1979) found that probation departments were responsible for more than 50 different activities, including court-related civil functions (for example, step-parent adoption investigations, minority-age marriage investigations).

Between the 1950s and 1970s, U.S. probation evolved in relative obscurity. But a number of reports issued in the 1970s brought national attention to the inadequacy of probation services and their organization. The National Advisory Commission on Criminal Justice Standards and Goals (1973, 112) stated that probation was the "brightest hope for corrections," but was "failing to provide services and supervision." In 1974, Martinson's widely publicized review of rehabilitation programs purportedly showed probation's ineffectiveness, and two years later the Comptroller General's Office released a report concluding that probation as currently practiced was a failure, and that the U.S. probation systems were "in crisis." They urged that, "Since most offenders are sentenced to probation, probation systems must receive adequate resources. But something more fundamental is needed. The priority given to probation in the criminal justice system must be reevaluated (Comptroller General of the United States 1976, 74).

In recent years, probation agencies have struggled—with continued meager resources—to upgrade services and supervision. But there is no doubt that probation plays a critical role in justice system case processing. Anyone who is convicted, and many of those arrested, come into contact with the probation department; probation officials, operating with a great deal of discretionary authority, dramatically affect most subsequent justice-processing decisions. Their input affects not only the subsequent liberties that offenders will enjoy, but their decisions influence public safety, since they recommend (within certain legal restraints) which offenders will be released back to their communities, and judges follow their sentence recommendations 70 to 90 percent of the time (Clear, Cole, and Reisig 2009).

When the court grants probation, probation staff have great discretion about which court-ordered conditions to enforce and monitor. For persons who violate probation conditions, probation officers are responsible for deciding which violations will be brought to the court's attention and what subsequent sanctions to recommend. And even when an offender goes to prison, the offender's initial security classification (and eligibility for parole) will be based on information contained in the probation officer's presentence investigation. Finally, when the offender is released from jail or prison, probation staff often provide his or her community supervision. In fact, it is safe to say that no other justice agency is involved with the offender and his case as comprehensively as the probation department.

Parole's Historical Roots and Modern Development

Parole comes from the French word *parole*, referring to "word," as in giving one's word of honor or promise. It has come to mean an inmate's promise to conduct him or herself in a law-abiding manner and according to certain rules in exchange for release from prison. In penal philosophy, parole is part of the general nineteenth-century trend in criminology from punishment to reformation. Chief credit for developing the early parole system is usually given to Alexander Maconochie, who was in charge of the English penal colony at Norfolk Island, 1,000 miles off the coast of Australia, and to Sir Walter Crofton, who directed Ireland's prisons (Morris 2002).

Maconochie criticized definite prison terms and developed a system of rewards for good conduct, labor, and study. Through a classification procedure he called the mark system, prisoners could progress through stages of increasing responsibility and ultimately gain freedom. In 1840, he was given an opportunity to apply these principles as superintendent of the Norfolk Island penal settlement in the South Pacific. Under his direction, task accomplishment, not time served, was the criterion for release. Marks of commendation were given to prisoners who performed their tasks well, and they were released from the penal colony as they demonstrated willingness to accept society's rules. Returning to England in 1844 to campaign for penal reform, Maconochie tried to implement his reforms when he was appointed governor of the new Birmingham Prison in 1849. However, he was unable to institute his reforms there because he was dismissed from his position in 1851 on the grounds that his methods were too lenient.

Walter Crofton attempted to implement Maconochie's mark system when he became the administrator of the Irish prison system in 1854. Crofton felt that prison programs should be directed more toward reformation, and that "tickets-of-leave" should be awarded to prisoners who had shown definite achievement and positive attitude change. After a period of strict imprisonment, Crofton began transferring offenders to "intermediate prisons" where they could accumulate marks based on work performance, behavior, and educational improvement. Eventually they would be given tickets-of-leave and released on parole supervision. Parolees were required to submit monthly reports to the police, and a police inspector helped them find jobs and generally oversaw their activities. The concepts of intermediate prisons, assistance, and supervision after release were Crofton's contributions to the modern system of parole (Clear, Cole, and Reisig 2009).

By 1865, American penal reformers were well aware of the reforms achieved in the European prison systems, particularly in the Irish system. At the Cincinnati meeting of the National Prison Association in 1870, a paper by Crofton was read, and specific references to the Irish system were incorporated into the Declaration of Principles, along with other such reforms as indeterminate sentencing and classification for release based on a mark system. Because of Crofton's experiment, many Americans referred to parole as the Irish system.

Zebulon Brockway, a Michigan penologist, is given credit for implementing parole in the United States. He proposed a two-pronged strategy for managing prison populations and preparing inmates for release: indeterminate sentencing coupled with parole supervision. He put his proposal into practice in 1876 when he was appointed superintendent at a new youth reformatory, the Elmira Reformatory in New York. He instituted a system of indeterminacy and parole release, and is commonly credited as the father of both in the United States. His ideas reflected the tenor of the times—a belief that criminals could be reformed, and that every prisoner's treatment should be individualized.

On being admitted to Elmira, each inmate (males between the ages of 16 and 30) was placed in the second grade of classification. Six months of good conduct meant promotion to the first grade but misbehavior could result in being placed in the third grade. The inmate would have to work his way back up from third to second or first. Continued good behavior in the first grade resulted in release. Paroled inmates remained under the jurisdiction of authorities for an additional six months, during which the parolee was required to report on the first day of every month to his appointed volunteer guardian (from which parole officers evolved) and provide an account of his situation and conduct (Abadinsky 2008). Written reports became required and were submitted to the court after being signed by the parolee's employer and guardian.

Indeterminate sentencing and parole spread rapidly through the United States. In 1907, New York became the first state to formally adopt all the components of a parole system: indeterminate sentences, a system for granting release, post-release supervision, and specific criteria for parole violation. By 1927, only three states (Florida, Mississippi and Virginia) were without a parole system, and by 1942, all states and the federal government had such systems (Petersilia 1999).

Recent years have seen a major decline in the percentage of prisoners released through the discretionary actions of parole boards. The percentage of U.S. prisoners released on discretionary parole rose from 44 percent in 1940 to a high of 72 percent in 1977, after which some states began to question the very foundations of parole, and the number of prisoners released in this fashion began to decline. By 2006, mandatory parole has surpassed discretionary parole release (48 percent versus 33 percent) (Glaze and Bonczar 2007). Mandatory parole is basically a matter of bookkeeping: one calculates the amount of time served plus good time and subtracts it from the prison sentence imposed. When the required number of months has been served, prisoners are automatically released, conditionally, to parole supervision for the rest of their sentence. Parole supervision generally lasts from one to three years, with the average parole supervision lasting 26 months (Austin et al. 2007). Mandatory parole release is now used by federal jurisdictions and the 16 states with determinate sentencing. The implications of these modern changes in the way that inmates are released from prison are profound and have gone rather unnoticed and undebated by the American public.

III. THE GROWTH, FUNDING, AND CHARACTERISTICS OF COMMUNITY CORRECTIONS POPULATIONS

The disproportionate number of criminals serving sentences in the community is not new. There have always been more people convicted of crimes in the United States than there are prison cells to hold them. In fact, despite mandatory minimum sentences, "three strikes and you're out" legislation, and other tough-on-crime policies of the past decade, the absolute numbers of offenders serving sentences in the community is larger than ever before in our history (probation up 284 percent since 1980), and the percentage of the total correctional population under community supervision (versus incarceration) has declined only slightly in that period—from 72 percent in 1982 to 69 percent in 2007 (Pew Center on the States 2009).

The Growth of Community Corrections Populations

As the U.S. population has grown, more citizens are being arrested and convicted, and *all* corrections populations (prisons, jails, probation, and parole) have grown simultaneously (see table 17.1). The number of offenders in prison and jail reached 2.3 million and, for the first time, one in 100 adults was in prison or jail. With far less notice, however, the number of people on probation or parole has also skyrocketed to more than 5 million, up from 1.6 million just 25 years ago. This means that a stunning 1 in every 31 adults, or 3.2 percent, is under some form of correctional control in the United States (Pew Center on the States 2009).

It is important to note that the national picture of correctional populations is disproportionally influenced, or skewed, by relatively few states. Four states from four different regions in the United States dominate corrections: California, Texas, New York, and Florida. They account for about two-fifths of all offenders under correctional control.

Funding for Community Corrections

Despite wide usage and its essential role in supervising serious offenders, community corrections has often been the subject of intense criticism. It is often depicted as permissive, uncaring about crime victims, and committed to a rehabilitative ideal that ignores the reality of violent, predatory criminals. Americans have very low confidence in and little knowledge of probation and parole. A national survey conducted by Longmire and Sims (1995) found that roughly 60 percent of those surveyed reacted favorably to the performance of the police, while only 25 percent expressed confidence in probation. In a 1996 national poll, 53 percent of the sample agreed that "community corrections programs are evidence of leniency in the criminal justice system" (Cullen, Fisher, and Applegate 2000). Citizen surveys repeatedly show that the public thinks that prisons and jails make people worse, but it does *not* believe that probation and parole make them better, hold offenders accountable, or protect the public (Reinventing Probation Council 2000).

However, a recent national public opinion poll by Zogby International found that Americans strongly support alternatives to prison for nonviolent, nonserious crimes (those where the loss of property was less than $400) (Hartney and Marchionna 2009). Nearly 80 percent of respondents felt that the most appropriate sentence for a nonserious offender is supervised probation, with no prison or jail unless these alternatives fail. But, 60 percent of those polled felt that incarceration was necessary if violations of probation or parole were detected, even if no new crime was committed. It appears that the public favors community corrections for

Table 17.1. Adult Correctional Populations, 1980–2007

	1980	1988	2007	% Change 1980 to 2007
Prisons	319,598	607,766	1,512,576	+373%
Probation	1,118,097	2,356,483	4,293,163	+284%
Parole	220,438	407,977	824,365	+274%
Jails	182,288	341,893	780,581	+328%
Total	1,840,400	3,714,100	7,410,685	+303%
U.S. Population	227 million	245 million	306 million	+35%
Reported Index Crimes	13.4 million	13.9 million	11.3 million	−16%
Index Arrest Rate Per 100,000	1,056	1,124	744	−30%

Sources: Bureau of Justice Statistics, *Correctional Populations in the United States,* Annual, *Prisoners in 2007* and *Probation and Parole in the United States, 2007.* Available at http://ojp. usdoj.gov/bjs/glance/corr2.htm. Population and crime data taken from Austin (2007).

certain offenders but wants it to be a more credible sanction, where violations are detected and consistently punished.

Unfortunately, the current economic woes have left probation and parole agencies woefully underfunded, undermining their potential effectiveness. However, in the aggregate, community-based supervision has never been shown to decrease recidivism, contributing to their weak position to argue for increased funding. Despite the fact that community corrections populations have grown at a rate similar to that of prisons and jails, funding for prisons and jails has increased significantly while spending for probation and parole remains unchanged from what it was in 1977. Jacobson (2005, 137) wrote that, with few resources and growing caseloads, parole agents "experience constant pressure, including anxieties about whether someone on their caseload will be the next murderer of a Polly Klass. Indeed, a combination of high caseloads, few internal resources, and frequent political condemnation makes their job one of the most difficult and stressful in the criminal justice system."

The Demographic and Crime Profiles of Probationers and Parolees

Probationers, as a population, are less seriously criminal than parolees. As shown table 17.2, 47 percent of the probationers were convicted of felonies (as opposed to misdemeanors), as were 100 percent of the parolees. We have much less information on the probation population (and almost no information on misdemeanant probationers), but the available evidence suggests that adult probationers are younger, more often female and non-minority, and have less serious criminal histories than parolees. Of course, this makes sense since probation is imposed earlier in the criminal career in the hopes of effectively preventing future crime. When probation fails, the criminal career continues and many are eventually sent to prison and parole—hence as a population, parolees are older and have more serious criminal records.

Probation and parole populations have not only grown in numbers, but the characteristics of persons under supervision have become more serious, which of course makes the decline of funding more problematic. Most probation and parole officials believe their current caseloads (the number of offenders an officer is responsible for supervising) are becoming more difficult to manage because more of their populations are drug users or sexual offenders, are mentally ill, have gang affiliations, and have few marketable skills.

Beck (2000) reported that 74 percent of released prisoners are drug or alcohol involved, 15 percent are mentally ill, and 11 percent have co-occurring disorders (substance abuse plus mental illness). He also reports that just 22 percent of the alcohol or drug abusers will have participated in treatment while in prison, while 60 percent of those having a mental illness will have received treatment. As the prison population boomed and inmate needs became more acute, money to support rehabilitation programs did not keep pace. Analysis by Lynch and Sabol (2001) shows that the rate of prison program participation has declined for state inmates since the early 1990s. As a result, large numbers of prisoners are released to parole without their treatment needs met.

IV. SUPERVISION CONDITIONS, CASELOAD SIZE, ACCESS TO SERVICES, AND CIVIL DISABILITIES

Every probationer and parolee is required to sign a contract stating that they agree to abide by certain conditions. Conditions generally can be grouped into standard conditions applicable to all offenders, and special conditions that are tailored to particular offenders. Standard conditions are similar throughout most jurisdictions, and include payment of supervision fees, finding employment, not carrying weapons, reporting changes of address and employment, not committing crimes, and submitting to search by the police and parole officers. Special conditions are tailored to the offenders' particular circumstances, such as periodic drug testing for substance abusers and law enforcement registration for sex offenders.

Ironically, while caseloads have grown and funding has declined, the proportion of offenders subject to special conditions—particularly drug testing—has increased. The public's more punitive mood, combined with inexpensive drug testing (now about $5 per test) and a greater number of

Table 17.2. Characteristics of Adult Probationers and State Parolees

	Percentage of Total	
	Probationers	State Parolees
Gender		
Male	77	88
Female	23	12
Race/Hispanic origin		
White	55	42
Black	29	37
Hispanic or Latino	13	19
Other	2	2
Mean age	NA	34 yrs
Convicted of Felony	47	100
Most Serious Offense or Current Conviction Crime		
Violent	17	26
Property	24	24
Drug	27	37
Public-Order	18	7
Other	13	6
Status of Supervision		
Abscond	9	7
No Prior Adult Sentences to Probation or Incarceration	50	22
Has High School Diploma or GED	40	42

offenders with substance abuse problems, contributes to the increased number of conditions imposed. The Bureau of Justice Statistics (BJS) reports that nearly half of all probationers had five or more conditions to their sentence required by the court or probation agency (Bonczar 1997). A monetary requirement was the most common condition (84 percent), and more than 2 of every 5 probationers were required to enroll in some form of substance abuse treatment. Nearly a third of all probationers were subject to mandatory drug testing—43 percent of felons and 17 percent of misdemeanants.

Parole requirements are more stringent. Rhine et al. (1991) found that 80 percent of parolees were required to have "gainful employment," 61 percent "no association with persons of criminal records," 53 percent "pay all fines and restitution," and 47 percent "support family and all dependents." It was estimated that more than a third of all U.S. probationers and parolees have court-ordered drug testing conditions in 1998 (Camp and Camp 1999). Surely the number is higher today, but there are no more recent statistics on the issue.

The problem, however, is that while many probationers and parolees have dozens of supervision conditions, the enforcement of those conditions is usually quite lax. Caseloads have risen and funding has remained stagnant or decreased, so that most conditions remain unenforced. Mark Kleiman studied drug testing orders for probationers in California and concluded that, "infrequent testing and lax sanctioning make offenders confident that they can continue using drugs with impunity" (Kleiman et al. 2003, 32).

The problem Kleiman discovered was that existing resources were spread so thinly across so many probationers that the drug testing had lost credibility both with offenders and the courts. He recommended concentrating resources on fewer offenders, drug testing more frequently, reducing the turnaround time for test results, and imposing brief jail terms for every failure to appear or instance of drug use. Kleiman's demand-reduction idea is now being tested in Hawaii's Opportunity Probation with Enforcement (or HOPE). Under it, probation officers refer to the judge offenders who have failed a (frequent) drug test. A prosecutor and public defender are available to hear these cases quickly. After a warning, each violator is given a short jail sentence. Early results show that drug offenses among these probationers quickly declined (see chapter 13 in this volume).

Many in the field agree that the "piling up" of supervision conditions has created unrealistic expectations and has hurt the credibility of community corrections. Carl Wicklund, executive director of the American Probation and Parole Association, advocates the "three R's" of supervision conditions: they should be realistic—few in number and attainable; relevant—tailored to individual risks and needs; and research-based—supported by evidence that they will change behavior and result in improved public safety and reintegration outcomes (Wicklund 2004).

Sex Offenders under Community Supervision

While the average probationer or parolee usually receives little supervision, convicted sex offenders are sometimes an exception. In recent years, a number of laws have been passed that have significantly altered the conditions for sex offenders on probation or parole. Megan's Law is the informal name given for laws requiring community notification when a person convicted of certain crimes is released on probation or parole. The first Megan's Law was passed in New Jersey in 1994, where seven-year-old Megan Kanka was kidnapped and murdered by a man who had two prior sex crime convictions. Federal legislation was passed the following year requiring that every state develop a procedure for notifying the public—and the offender's victim—when convicted sex offenders reside in their neighborhood.

The public's concern over sex offenders in the community continued to produce tighter restrictions with the passage of Jessica's Laws. In 2005, John Couey—a repeat sex offender—abducted nine-year-old Jessica Lundsford from her bedroom in Florida, and raped and murdered her. Public outrage over this case spurred Florida officials to pass Jessica's Law in 2005 and Congress to create the Jessica Lundsford Act. Versions of Jessica's Law have now been passed in many states, including California, New York, and Texas. Key provisions of all these laws are mandatory minimum prison sentences, community notification of the whereabouts of certain offenders, lifetime parole registration at release, and residency restrictions (see chapter 12 by Beauregard and Lieb in this volume).

California's law is the most stringent and impacts the greatest number of parolees. Voters there approved Jessica's Law in 2006 (known as Proposition 83), which requires all high-risk sex offenders to wear satellite tracking devices or global positioning system (GPS) tracking devices *for life* and forbids them from living within 2,000 feet of schools and parks. GPS tracking technology also allows users to create "geofences" to mark forbidden hot zones, giving victims a sense of safety. By January 2009, California had placed all 6,622 sex offender parolees on GPS (California Department of Corrections and Rehabilitation 2009). Florida, with the second most GPS units in use in the country, currently monitors about 1,800 adult parolees on GPS.

The average cost of GPS in California is $9 per day, compared to $90 per day for a California prison cell. California acknowledges that sex offenders on parole are just 11 percent of all registered sex offenders in the state but believes the extra investment is worth the public safety benefits. While some hoped that GPS would reduce the workload of parole officers, it appears to do the opposite. An evaluation of the GPS program in San Diego, California, showed that officers had to reduce their caseloads from 30 to 1 to 20 to 1 to keep up with the additional paperwork generated by the GPS technology. The early evaluation also showed that while GPS monitoring did not reduce recidivism, it did increase information-sharing between law enforcement and parole agencies (Turner and Jannetta 2008). Law enforcement agencies were able to compare crime data with the GPS information to determine whether a GPS-monitored parolee was in the vicinity of a reported crime.

Residency laws, which dictate where sex offenders can live, have also grown in recent years and have greatly impacted community supervision. Twenty-two states currently have some form of residency laws that restrict where sex offenders can life. States often prohibit sex offenders from living within 1,000 to 2,500 feet of schools, bus stops, day-care centers, or public parks. Parole and probation officers spend a great deal of time trying to locate suitable housing and monitor that the location does not violate residency restrictions. The expense might be worthwhile if there were evidence that it were reducing sex crimes, yet research has found no connection between where a sex offender lives and the likelihood that he will offend again (Walker 2007). Since California passed its residency restrictions in 2006, there has been a 12-fold increase in the number of homeless sex offenders, and some believe that a lack of stable housing may increase recidivism. As California's Sex Offender Management Board (2008, 3) recently wrote, "Residency restrictions that preclude or eliminate appropriate offender housing can threaten public safety instead of enhancing it." States such as Washington and Colorado have employed innovative housing methods such as shared living arrangements, secure community transition facilities, and mobile trailers as transitional housing. Of these housing methods, only the shared living arrangement has been studied to determine its effects on violations by paroled sex offenders. Colorado found that high-risk sex offenders living in a shared living arrangement had significantly fewer violations than those in other living arrangements (living alone or with family or friends) (California Sex Offender Management Board 2008).

This is not the place to discuss the pros and cons of these various restrictions. But it is important to acknowledge that probation and parole supervision in the twenty-first century is increasingly focused on sex offenders, which are less than 10 percent of overall community supervision caseloads (Langan, Schmitt, and Durose 2003). As a result, other offenders are being deprioritized, resulting in little supervision and few services.

Caseload Size

Monitoring offender behavior and delivering services is managed through caseloads (the number of parolees assigned to a single agent), and community corrections has always struggled with what the ideal caseload size should be. Higher-risk offenders are placed on smaller caseloads, where more intensive services and surveillance can be provided. In larger agencies, caseload assignment is usually based on a structured assessment of the offender's risk, and an assessment of the needs or problem areas that have contributed to the criminality. By scoring personal information relative to the risk of recidivism, and the particular needs of the offender (i.e., a risk/need instrument), a total score is derived, which dictates the particular level of supervision (for example, intensive, medium, regular, administrative). The Association of Paroling Authorities International (APAI) recently reported that two-thirds of all U.S. parole boards use a formal risk assessment instrument to assign caseload type and supervision conditions, with the most common instrument used being the Level of Service—Revised (LSI-R) (Kinnevy and Caplan 2008). Each jurisdiction then establishes its own policies dictating the contact levels (times the officer will meet with the offender) within each caseload type. Officers may also have "collateral contacts" with family members or employers to inquire about the offender's progress.

But what is the ideal caseload size? To some, this might seem to be a rather straightforward question, but in practice it is quite complex. As Burrell (2007) notes, not all offenders or court orders are alike, and the political and policy environments of jurisdictions provide services that vary greatly. The American Probation and Parole Association (APPA) urges agencies to adopt a "workload" rather than "caseload" approach, where time factors weigh into the case. For example, a case with a high priority would require 4 hours per month equaling 30 as a total caseload (if an officer has 120 hours per month to supervise offenders). But the APPA has also published "not to exceed" caseload standards (see table 17.3).

Unfortunately, a large body of research now exists showing that smaller caseloads and stricter reporting requirements do not necessarily reduce recidivism. Petersilia and Turner (1993) found that offenders on smaller (25 to 30 cases per officer versus 50 to 75 per officer) were no less likely to have new arrests but were more likely to have their parole and probation revoked because of technical violations (due to closer surveillance). But Petersilia and Turner did find one positive finding from the evaluation: offenders who were on smaller caseloads *and* completed counseling, were employed, and paid restitution had lower rearrest rates. This suggests that interventions that focus on diminishing behaviors associated with crimi-

Table 17.3. American Probation and Parole Association's Caseload Standards for Probation and Parole Supervision

Case Type	Cases to Staff Ratio	
	Juvenile	Adult
Intensive	15:1	20:1
Moderate to High Risk	30:1	50:1
Low Risk	100:1	200:1
Administrative	Not recommended	No limit? 1,000?

Source: Burrell (2007)

nality are more important to reducing recidivism than simply increasing contacts between officer and offender.

The Bureau of Justice Statistics (BJS) recently reported that the average adult parole caseload was 38 active parolees for each officer, but the average does not really describe the experiences of most parolees (Bonczar 2008). Two-thirds of adult offenders on parole are required to have face-to-face contact with their parole officer at least once a month, including 14 percent who are required to have weekly face-to-face contact. An additional 17 percent of paroled offenders are required to meet with their parole officers less than once a month or to maintain contact by mail, telephone, or other means. An additional 13 percent of paroled offenders are no longer required to report on a regular basis. In sum, this means that about 30 percent of all U.S. parolees are basically being supervised "on paper" with few services or active surveillance. This type of paper-parole is becoming more popular because, even though the parolee has no formal reporting requirements, they are still considered in the custody of corrections agencies and their legal rights are severely limited. Parolees can be visited in their homes and on the street and searched without a warrant by law enforcement or parole agents. If they are found to be in violation of parole conditions, they can be returned to prison as a parole violator without a criminal court proceeding. Parole board officials use the more lenient legal standard of "preponderance of the evidence," as opposed to the "beyond a reasonable doubt" standard that is required in criminal court convictions. This most lenient standard is deemed appropriate because a parolee is still in the legal custody of the state's prison system.

Many serious offenders are left unsupervised, and this undoubtedly contributes to high recidivism rates. Langan and Cunniff (1992) found that nearly half of all probationers do not comply with the terms of their sentence, and only a fifth of those who violate their sentences ever go to jail for their noncompliance. It is also true that thousands of probationers and parolees abscond (that is, whereabouts unknown) from supervision. The BJS estimates that in 1990 just 1 percent of all adult probationers and parolees had absconded from supervision, but by 2007, 9 percent of adult probationers were on abscond status (Glaze and Bonczar 2008), and 7 percent of parolees were on absconder status (Glaze and Bonczar 2007). In California the figure is even higher. On any given day, 20 percent of all parolees had absconded supervision (Petersilia 2008). While a majority of jurisdictions issue warrants for such violators, funding shortages mean that little is done systematically to locate absconders. It is also worth noting that probation and parole officers play a vital role to crime victims, providing them information about the offender's whereabouts, conditions of supervision, and other issues affecting victim safety. When offenders abscond, the victim's peace of mind and safety are threatened.

The justice system simply cannot afford to do much monitoring for the majority of offenders under supervision. Agencies are trying to deploy more staff and rehabilitative resources to higher-classified offenders and—because budgets are limited—spend correspondingly fewer dollars on lower-classified offenders. The New York City Department of Probation, for example, uses automated check-in kiosks for the city's low-risk probation population, a strategy that could be applied to low-risk parolees as well. The limited use of kiosks began in the 1990s, and by 2003 about 70 percent of all New York adult probationers were on kiosk supervision. After being trained on how to use the system, probationers assigned to kiosk supervision report to the kiosk and answer questions about their conditions (e.g., residence, updated contact information, employment, and new arrests). The kiosk system uses a biometric hand scanner that generates a receipt when used. A recent assessment of the city's kiosk system found that it helps improve compliance with reporting conditions without sacrificing public safety. Moreover, kiosks allow the department to allocate more resources to those who pose the greatest risk to public safety—probationers who are identified as high-risk for recidivism. Arrest rates for both low- risk and high-risk probationers are down (Wilson, Naro, and Austin 2007).

Civil Disabilities for Probationers and Parolees

In addition to the formal probation and parole conditions that the offend-er must follow while under supervision, a number of statutory restrictions or civil disabilities also apply to many convicted offenders. These restrictions differ by state, apply more often to parolees than probationers, and are statutory, stemming from a common-law traditional that people who are incarcerated are "civilly dead" and have lost all civil rights (Travis 2005). Offenders' criminal records may preclude them from voting, eliminate their parental rights, be grounds for divorce, and bar them from serving on a jury, holding public office, and owning firearms. In 13 states, current and former prisoners, parolees, and felony probationers cannot vote (Manza and Uggen 2006).

Employers are also increasingly forbidden from hiring probationers and parolees for certain jobs and are mandated to perform background checks for many others. The most common types of jobs with legal prohibitions against convicted offenders are in the fields of childcare, education, security, nursing, and home health care—exactly the types of jobs that are expanding. Since the mid-1980s, the number of barred occupations has increased dramatically. And, even if an offender is not legally barred from a particular job, research shows that ex-offenders face bleak prospects in the labor market, with the mark of a criminal record representing an important barrier to finding work (Pager 2003). Indeed, more than 60 percent of employers claim that they would not knowingly hire an applicant with a criminal background (Holzer, Raphael, and Stoll 2002). Overcoming the barriers that ex-offenders face in finding a job is critical to successful reintegration, since employment helps ex-prisoners take care of their families, develop valuable life skills, and strengthen their self-esteem and social connectedness. Research has also empirically established a positive link between job stability and reduced juvenile offending. Lipsey's (1995) meta-analysis of nearly 400 studies found that the single most effective factor in reducing reoffending rates was employment.

V. RECIDIVISM, REVOCATIONS TO PRISON, AND PUBLIC SAFETY

Most probationers and parolees do not succeed. For the probation population as a whole, we do not know the percentage who are re-arrested while on probation because 48 percent of all adult probationers have been convicted of misdemeanors and are not tracked in recidivism research. For *felony* probationers, the best recidivism data come from the Bureau of Justice Statistics (BJS) study by Langan and Cunniff (1992). They found that within three years of sentencing, while still on probation, 43 percent of felons were re-arrested for a crime within the state. Half of the arrests were for a violent crime or a drug offense.

Parolees fare no better. The BJS tracked a national sample of parolees released from prison in 1994. They found that within three years, 67 percent of them had been rearrested for a felony or serious misdemeanor, and 52 percent were back in prison, serving time for a new prison sentence or for a technical violation of their release (Langan and Levin 2002).

Opponents of parole also assert that there is no evidence that placing offenders on parole supervision helps reduce their recidivism rates. In fact, a controversial study by the Urban Institute entitled "Does Parole Supervision Work?" found no difference in the rearrest rates of offenders released from prison with and without parole supervision. After statistically controlling for the offenders' demographic characteristics and criminal histories, the researchers found that 61 percent of mandatory parolees (those without supervision) were rearrested, as compared to 57 percent of discretionary (with supervision) parole releasees. Solomon, Kachnowski, and Bhati (2005, 37) concluded that "Parole has not contributed substantially to reduced recidivism and increased public safety." This is not to say that parole supervision *couldn't* reduce recidivism, only that at the aggregate level in which it was studied, there was no evidence that it reduced rearrests.

For both probationers and parolees, the risk of recidivism is highest in the first year after sentencing or release on parole. Rosenfeld and his colleagues (2005) recently reported that the probability of arrest during the first month out of prison is roughly double that during the 15th month. These results have led to calls to front-load parole services and surveillance so as to reduce these and other negative outcomes during the first six months after release (National Research Council 2008; Petersilia 2003; Travis 2005).

But while recidivism rates are high nationally, just like other aspects of community corrections, they vary greatly among states. Levin and Levin

(2002) report that the three-year reincarceration rate in California is over 60 percent but for Texas it is about 30 percent. Why are these states' rates so different? Analysis completed by Ryan Fischer (2005) revealed that when one defines recidivism equivalently across states, using the same follow-up time period and comparing similarly serious offenders, California's technical violation rates are higher than other states, but its rates of new arrest and new criminal convictions are not always higher. Unfortunately, it is nearly impossible to compare recidivism rates across states, as state differences can be attributed to longer lengths of stay and the associated aging of prisoner release cohorts. It could also be due to widely divergent approaches to measuring recidivism, better employment conditions for parolees, or mere changes in revocation practices as prison systems become crowded.

Offender recidivism rates are one way to measure the effectiveness of probation and parole. But another way is to look at arrest and conviction statistics and see the proportion that are attributable to persons under community supervision. Rosenfeld and colleagues (2005) reanalyzed the BJS recidivism data and estimated that parolees accounted for 15 to 28 percent of all arrests for violent crimes and 10 to 18 percent of all arrests for property crimes. If former prisoners are accounting for nearly one-fifth of all the nation's arrests, then investing in prisoner reentry is unquestionably a matter of public safety. Such evidence has encouraged law enforcement organizations such as the International Association of Chiefs of Police (IACP) and the National District Attorneys Association to develop policies, training, and other tools that support effective prisoner reentry (La Vigne et al. 2006; National District Attorneys Association 2005).

In a recent study of the impact of returning parolees on neighborhood crime rates in California, Hipp and Yates (2009) found that, in most cases, reports of aggravated assault, robbery, and burglary go up when parolees return to their neighborhoods, and that if parolees have violent backgrounds, murder rates increase. But Hipp and Yates (2009) also found that crime rates decrease when parolees move back to neighborhoods characterized by residential stability, and they increase at a lower rate in areas with nonprofit groups offering economic resources and youth intervention programs. These findings suggest that social factors and the availability of treatment can play a role in how communities can counter the influx of parolees.

Probation and Parole Violators Returned to Prison

When parolees or probationers commit new crimes or fail to comply with supervision conditions, they may be revoked and returned to prison; most of them will eventually be re-released, and the revolving door process continually repeats itself. The constant churning of probationers and parolees in and out of incarceration is one of the major factors linked to the growing U.S. prison population. As a percentage of all admissions to state prisons, parole violators more than doubled from 17 percent in 1980 to nearly 35 percent in 2006 (Sabol and Couture 2008). California had both the largest absolute number and the largest percentage increase of admissions for parole violations. In 2006, 65 percent of *all* prison admissions in California—more than 70,000 persons—were for parole violations, not the result of new convictions (Grattet, Petersilia, and Lin 2008). Excluding California, parole violations represented slightly more than a quarter of all state prison admissions in 2006 (Sabol and Couture 2008).

Community supervision failures certainly impact the costs and effectiveness of the prison system, but their consequences are more widespread. The research literature now details how failed prisoner reentry impacts communities, racial justice, families and children, civic and workforce participation, and public health (for reviews, see Bushway, Stoll, and Weiman 2007; Clear 2007; Jacobson 2005; Pattillo, Weiman, and Western 2004; Thompson 2008; Travis and Waul 2003). The overarching problem is that failed probation and parole supervision ends up creating pressures on prisons, which in turn reduces rehabilitation and work programs, which in turn increases recidivism. It is a vicious cycle. But that begs the all-important question of whether we can implement probation and parole programs to increase the odds of success, the subject we now turn to.

VI. WHAT NEEDS TO BE DONE? STRATEGIES FOR AN EFFECTIVE COMMUNITY CORRECTIONS SYSTEM

Ever since probation and parole agencies were established in America, they have struggled for legitimacy, public support, and resources. There have been dozens of reports published over the last several decades detailing how to "reform," "reinvent," and "restructure" community corrections (see, for example, Burke and Tonry 2006; National Research Council 2008; Solomon et al. 2008). A reading of these reports shows a great deal of consensus about what needs to be done. It involves a number of steps, the most important of which are detailed below.

Use a Validated Risk Assessment Instrument to Sort Offenders by Risk to Public Safety

Reforming community corrections must start with the use of a validated risk assessment tool. Empirically based risk assessments have repeatedly demonstrated their ability to sort the offender population into sub-groups that have different probabilities of recidivism (Washington State Institute for Public Policy 2003). It is now possible to identify a group of high-risk offenders who are four to five times more likely to recidivate than low-risk offenders. This knowledge should be used to allocate resources to offenders who present the greatest risk to public safety. Parole and probation officers can then focus on the highest-risk offenders by seeing them more frequently (e.g., once a week) or placing them on GPS, electronic monitoring, or frequent drug testing. Lower risk offenders can be seen less frequently.

Risk prediction instruments should also be used to prioritize treatment services, since focusing on high- and moderate-risk offenders produces the greatest returns in terms of the benefits of treatment programming. Research has shown that when rehabilitation treatment programs are delivered appropriately to higher-risk offenders, recidivism can be reduced. But when the same rehabilitation programs are provided to low-risk offenders, a very minimal reduction or even an increase in recidivism results (Lowenkamp, Latessa, and Smith 2006). Risk assessments, used in conjunction with needs assessment, can be used to "match" offenders to the type of programs and services most appropriate for them. Risk assessments can also be used in decisions about the duration of supervision. Low risk offenders might not be assigned active parole supervision at all, moderate risk offenders who adjust well to supervision might be discharged early.

Implement Intermediate Sanctions That Incorporate Both Surveillance and Treatment for Moderate Risk Offenders

Well-implemented intermediate sanctions restore credibility to the justice system and provide a much-needed spectrum of punishments to match the spectrum of risk posed by criminals. Policymakers, judges, corrections practitioners, and the public strongly support intermediate sanctions for nonviolent offenders. Offenders judge certain ISP programs as more punitive than short incarceration terms. This is particularly true in ISPs that include mandatory work and drug testing requirements. Intermediate sanctions may offer promise as a way to get and keep offenders in drug and other treatment programs. With drug treatment programs at least, there is evidence that coerced treatment programs can reduce both later drug use and later crimes, and there is evidence in the ISP and boot camp literatures that these programs can increase treatment participation.

The most important finding from the intermediate sanctions literature is that programs must deliver high "doses" of *both* treatment and surveillance to assure public safety and reduce recidivism. "Treatment" alone is not enough, nor is "surveillance" by itself adequate. Programs that can increase offender-to-officer contacts *and* provide treatment have reduced recidivism. Programs such as Hawaii's HOPE (described earlier and in chapter 13 in this volume) combine drug testing with predictable sanctions, thus reducing recidivism.

Identify the Most Dangerous And Violent Offenders, for Whom Surveillance Through Human And Technological Means Is a Top Priority

We have no evidence that intensive human services with the highest risk, extremely egocentric offenders will reduce reoffending. We must harness technology for these offenders, including electronic monitoring, GPS technology, and random drug testing. The overall record of electronic monitoring in reducing recidivism is mixed, but GPS tracking devices and other electronic sensors can be useful in monitoring offenders' whereabouts and making victims feel safer. There is also emerging evidence that GPS systems increase communication between law enforcement and community corrections, and may help solve some crimes committed by probationers and parolees.

Deliver Treatment Programs That Are Evidence-Based

There is now a body of evidence that well-designed rehabilitation programs that target the right offenders and are implemented effectively can reduce recidivism rates. The Washington Institute for Public Policy provides a comprehensive overview of well-designed studies that provide evidence that programs for criminal offenders do reduce recidivism (AOS et al. 2006). The Institute also provides a comprehensive overview of what works for drug, alcohol, and mental health treatment. The National Institute of Drug Abuse (2009) provides principles of what works in treating substance abusers. Data on the success of drug courts is growing and positive (Carey et al. 2008). Recent research on the national "Ready 4 Work" program also indicates reduction in recidivism (Farley and McClanahan 2007).

Several reviews of education and vocational programs have also shown that these programs can reduce recidivism by 5 to 30 percent (for a recent review, see National Research Council 2008). Effective programs have the following features:

- They were intensive and behavioral. Intensity was measured by both the absorption of the offenders' daily schedule and the duration of the program over time. Appropriate services in this respect will occupy 40–70 percent of the offender's time and last an average of six months.
- They targeted high-risk offenders and criminogenic needs. Treatment modalities and counselor must be matched with individual offender types, by, for example, matching the learning style and personality of the offender. Linking the style of the therapist with the personality of the offender (for example, anxious offenders should be matched with especially sensitive counselors) also is critical.
- They provide pro-social contexts and activities and emphasize advocacy and brokerage. Effective programs will replace the normal offender networks with new circles of peers and contacts who are involved in law-abiding lifestyles.

Research has also consistently shown that cognitive behavior treatments are more effective than any other form of correctional intervention because these treatment types address criminal thinking and behaviors in offenders. The therapeutic community treatment model, which uses cognitive-based treatment strategies, is the most effective documented method for treating alcohol and other drug dependencies. In the case of treatment effectiveness, the devil is in the details.

A systematic review of over 800 studies of faith-based programs seem to suggest that such programs are associated with somewhat higher rates of success in reducing prisoner recidivism, and in achieving other positive social outcomes (reducing drug abuse, for example) than otherwise comparable secular programs or no programs at all (Johnson 2002). But the research designs and methods are so problematic that at this stage of research it is really impossible to know the impacts of faith-based programs, even though the results appear promising.

Implement Behavioral Contracting and "Earned Discharge" Probation and Parole Terms to Enhance Success

Having a good assessment and evidence-based programs are a necessary but insufficient condition to bring about offender change. Those tools must be used to motivate and engage offenders in efforts at self-change. Probation and parole agents are in an ideal position to create incentives to engage offenders in efforts at self-change. Today, probationers and parolees are successfully discharged from parole if they adhere to their parole conditions (mostly remain crime-free) for the length of a pre-assigned time period. Offenders have little opportunity to reduce the length of their imposed term once it has been imposed. By providing the opportunity for an accelerated release date as an incentive, agents can motivate probationers and parolees to participate in targeted interventions and behavior that will increase their chances of success.

Low-level, nonviolent probationers and parolees who are least likely to commit new crimes should be eligible to earn discharge from parole or probation after six months if they meet strict guidelines. By allowing low-risk offenders to earn discharge from supervision by completing rehabilitation, education, and job training programs, we create an incentive for inmates to participate in rehabilitation programs, which in turn reduces recidivism. Removing low-risk offenders demonstrating good behavior from the overburdened caseloads of agents will free them to keep a closer eye on the more serious threats to commit new crimes in our communities. The earned discharge strategy is an evidence-based practice that has been shown in numerous studies to reduce recidivism and the commission of new crimes by offenders (Petersilia 2007).

Recidivism studies have consistently shown that inmates who are going to return to crime do so quickly. Reallocating scarce parole resources away from those who have demonstrated they do not need the services and the surveillance will allow agents to focus on those who pose a higher risk. By rewarding participation in work, education, and substance abuse programs we will motivate parolees to complete rehabilitation programs as an incentive to earn their way off supervision. Parolees and probationers self-select into low-risk-of-recidivism groups, so the public safety implications of an earned discharge are minimal, and the cost efficiencies will increase because offenders who do not need supervision will be removed from crowded caseloads.

Implement a Structured Parole and Probation Violations Matrix

States continue to struggle with how they might respond to violations of probation and parole—particularly technical violations that do not involve, of themselves, new criminal behavior. Many believe that for probation and parole to work, sanctions must be in place for violations. Even the smallest violations must be met with a meaningful response from probation and parole officers. But responding with a prison cell may be both unnecessary and expensive. Several states are now restructuring the court's responses to technical violations.

Many agencies are adopting policy-driven approaches to violations, using a decision-making matrix and graduated community-based sanctions. Such tools allow officials to respond consistently to parole and probation violations, using a well-developed range of intermediate sanctions. The response usually reflects the original risk level of the offender, coupled with a proportionate response to the seriousness of the violation. These guidelines or matrixes assure that the system's response to low-risk offenders who violate parole is very different from its response to high-risk violators. Parole and probation violation matrixes also assure that responses to violations are more consistent across locations and agents. Consistent decisions made for similar situations also increase parolee compliance, while dramatically different responses undermine trust and legitimacy for the system. Of course, in order for the guidelines to work, they must be accompanied by an expanded and credible array of intermediate sanctions programs.

Commit to a Community-Centered Approach to Offender Supervision and Management, Which Means Getting Officers Out of Their Offices and Having Them Work Interactively with Victims, Law Enforcement, Offenders, and Families

Crime and criminality are complex, multifaceted problems; real long-term solutions must come *from* the community and must include active participation *by* the community and those that surround the offender. This model of community engagement is the foundation of community policing, and its tenets are now spreading to community corrections.

At the philosophy's core is the notion that for probation and parole supervision to be effective, they must take place where offenders live and recreate. Proponents of this model argue that community corrections has suffered from a fortress or bunker mentality, where supervision takes place in offices far removed from neighborhoods and the factors that contribute to crime and disorder. Moreover, firsthand knowledge of where the offender lives, his family, and his immediate and extended environment are critical elements of meaningful supervision. Meaningful supervision also means that it is conducted at times not confined to the traditional 8:00 A.M. to 5:00 P.M., Monday through Friday. To be effective, it must be delivered at nights, on weekends, and on holidays.

This new probation and parole model is referred to as "neighborhood parole," or "broken windows" probation (Reinventing Probation Council 2000). Regardless of the name, the key components are the same. They involve strengthening community corrections linkages with law enforcement and the community; brokering treatment and work resources; and attempting to change the offenders' lives through personal, family, and neighborhood interventions. At the core, these models move away from managing offenders on conventional caseloads and toward a more "activist supervision," in which agents are responsible for close supervision as well as procuring jobs, social support, and needed treatment. Effective supervision then is attentive to the social ecology of community life.

The "broken windows" model of community supervision is attracting a lot of attention from professionals in the field. Boston, Phoenix, Los Angeles, and numerous districts throughout Iowa, Maryland, and elsewhere have adopted many of its elements (Reinventing Probation Council 2000). The Washington State Department of Corrections has also developed a program called Neighborhood Based Supervision (NBS). NBS corrections officers share office space with local police officers and other shareholders, along with neighborhood volunteers housed at Community Oriented Policing Substations (COPS). Being located in the neighborhoods' COPS shop has enabled the community corrections officers (CCOs) to work cooperatively with police officers and community members while supervising offenders on their caseloads who live in their neighborhoods. The program reports a 35 percent reduction in burglaries since the beginning of the program in 1993 (Lehman 2000).

Unfortunately, few of these efforts have been rigorously evaluated using a control group. An exception is Boston's Reentry Initiative (BRI), which is an interagency initiative to help transition violent adult offenders released from the local jail back to their Boston neighborhoods through mentoring, social service, active supervision, and vocational development. The authors found that BRI was associated with significant reductions—on the order of 30 percent—in the overall and violent arrest failure rates (Braga, Piehl, and Hureau 2009).

As noted in the National Research Council's (2007) report on parole and criminal desistance, true criminal desistance must include informal social support and community involvement. In fact, these are the *only* factors consistently related to desistance outcomes. Community partnerships increase such support and involvement for a variety of community supervision activities, as well as for services provided inside institutions by nonprofit agencies, faith-based organizations, and volunteers. Ultimately, the long-term sustainability of probation and parole initiatives may well rest with these emerging community partnerships.

CONCLUSION

The current fiscal crisis has provided an opening to discuss the appropriate role for a strong community corrections system in the United States. Most Americans agree that chronic and violent offenders belong behind bars for a long time, and they are willing to pay for it. But for hundreds of thousands of nonviolent, nonserious offenders, a strong system of community-based penalties may provide greater crime reduction benefits in the long run. This approach is not being soft on crime, as it is often portrayed, but rather smart on crime.

Criminologists have spent the last 20 years improving risk assessments and evidence-based program data to reliably separate those offenders who belong in prison from those who can be kept in the community. It would be a shame if the current prison-crowding crisis served to simply dump offenders into overloaded probation and parole agencies without commensurate financial support. If that happens, history will again repeat itself: offenders will recidivate, community corrections will be blamed for their high failure rates, the public will be again convinced that "nothing works," and increases in prison commitments will follow. On the other hand, if we use this crisis as an opportunity to implement evidence-based community correctional programs, we might finally demonstrate the critical role that community corrections agencies can play in the promotion of community safety, successful reintegration, and individual accountability.

References

Abadinsky, Howard. 2008. *Probation and Parole: Theory and Practice.* Upper Saddle River, NJ: Prentice Hall.

Augustus, John. 1852. "A Report of the Labors of John Augustus." Boston: Wright and Hasty Printers.

Austin, James. 2007. "Reducing America's Correctional Populations: A Strategic Plan." Washington, DC: JFA Associates.

Austin, James, Todd Clear, Troy Duster, David Greenberg, John Irwin, Candace McCoy, Alan Mobley, Barbara Owen, and Joshua Page. 2007. "Unlocking America: Why and How to Reduce America's Prison Population." Washington, DC: JFA Associates.

Beck, Allen J. 2000. "State and Federal Prisoners Returning to the Community: Findings from the Bureau of Justice Statistics." Bureau of Justice Statistics, Washington DC.

Bonczar, Thomas. 1997. "Characteristics of Adults on Probation, 1995." Washington, DC: Bureau of Justice Statistics.

Bonczar, Thomas P. 2008. "Characteristics of State Parole Supervising Agencies, 2006." Washington, DC: Bureau of Justice Statistics.

Braga, Anthony, Anne Piehl, and David Hureau. 2009. "Controling Violent Offenders Released to the Community: An Evaluation of the Boston Reentry Initiative." *Journal of Research in Crime and Delinquency*, Vol. 46, No. 4, 411–436.

Burke, Peggy, and Michael Tonry. 2006. *Successful Transition and Reentry for Safer Communities: A Call to Action for Parole*. Silver Spring, MD: Center for Effective Public Policy.

Burrell, William D. 2007. "Caseload Standards for Probation and Parole." American Probation and Parole Association. Lexington, KY.

Bushway, Shawn, Michael Stoll, and David Weiman. 2007. "Barriers to Reentry? The Labor Market for Released Prisoners in Post-Industrial America." New York: Russell Sage Foundation.

California Department of Corrections and Rehabilitation. 2009. "CDCR Places Entire Sex Offender Parolee Population on GPS Monitoring." Sacramento, CA. State of California.

California Sex Offender Management Board. 2008. "Homelessness Among Registered Sex Offenders in California: The Numbers, The Risks and the Response." Sacramento, CA.

Camp, Camille, and George Camp. 1999. *The Corrections Yearbook 1998*. Middletown, CT: Criminal Justice Institute.

Carey, Shannon, Kimberly Pukstas, Mark S. Waller, Richard Mackin, and Michael Finigan. 2008. "Drug Courts and State Mandates Drug Treatment Programs: Outcomes, Costs and Consequences." Portland, OR: NPC Research.

Clear, Todd R. 2007. *Imprisoning Communities: How Mass Incarceration Makes Disadvantaged Neighborhoods Worse*. New York: Oxford University Press.

Clear, Todd, George Cole, and Michael Reisig. 2009. *American Corrections*. Belmont, CA: Thomson Wadsworth.

Comptroller General of the United States. 1976. "State and County Probation: Systems in Crisis, Report to the Congress of the United States." Washington, DC: U.S. Department of Justice.

Cullen, Francis, Bonnie Fisher, and Brandon Applegate. 2000. "Public Opinion About Punishment and Corrections." In *Crime and Justice: A Review of Research*, vol. 27, ed. M. Tonry, 1–79. Chicago: University of Chicago Press.

del Carmen, Rolando, Maldine Barnhill, and Gene Bonham. 2000. "Civil Liabilities and Other Legal Issues for Probation and Parole Officers and Supervisors." Washington, DC: National Institute of Corrections.

Dressler, David. 1974. *Practice and Theory of Probation and Parole.*: New York: Columbia University Press.

Farley, Chelsea, and Wendy S. McClanahan. 2007. "Ready4Work in Brief: Update on Outomes." Philadelphia: Public Private Ventures.

Fischer, Ryan. 2005. "Are California's Recidivism Rates Really the Highest in the Nation?" Vol. 1. Irvine, CA: UCI Center for Evidence-Based Corrections.

Fitzharris, Timothy. 1979. "Probation in an Era of Diminishing Resources." Sacramento, CA: The Foundation for Continuing Education in California.

Friedman, Lawrence. 1993. *Crime and Punishment in American History*. New York: Basic Books.

Glaze, Lauren E., and Thomas P. Bonczar. 2007. "Probation and Parole in the United States, 2006." Washington, DC. Bureau of Justice Statistics.

Glaze, Lauren E., and Thomas P. Bonczar. 2008. "Probation and Parole in the United States, 2007—Statistical Tables," ed. Bureau of Justice Statistics. Washington, DC: U.S. Department of Justice.

Grattet, Ryken, Joan Petersilia, and Jeffrey Lin. 2008. "Parole Violations and Revocations in California." Washington, DC: National Institute of Justice.

Haney, Craig. 2006. *Reforming Punishment: Psychological Limits to the Pains of Imprisonment*. Washington, DC: American Psychological Association.

Hartney, Christopher, and Susan Marchionna. 2009. "Attitudes of US Voters Toward Nonserious Offenders and Alternatives to Incarceration." San Francisco: National Council on Crime and Delinquency.

Hipp, John R., and Daniel K. Yates. 2009. "Do Returning Parolees Affect Neighborhood Crime? A Case Study of Sacamento." *Criminology* 47: 619–656.

Holzer, Harry, Steven Raphael, and Michael Stoll. 2002. "Can Employers Play a More Positive Role in Prisoner Reentry?" Washington, DC: Urban Institute.

Jacobson, Michael. 2005. *Downsizing Prisons: How to Reduce Crime and End Mass Incarceration*. New York: New York University.

Johnson, Bryon. 2002. "Objective Hope: Assessing the Effectiveness of Faith-Based Organizations, A Review of the Literature." Philadelphia: Center for Research on Religion and Urban Civil Society.

Kinnevy, Susan, and Joel Caplan. 2008. "Findings from the APAI International Survey of Releasing Authorities." Philadelphia: University of Pennsylvania. Published by the Association of Paroling Authorities International, San Houston State University.

Kleiman, Mark, Thomas Tran, Paul Fishbein, Maria-Teresa Magula, Warren Allen, and Gareth Lacy. 2003. "Opportunities and Barriers in Probation Reform: A Case Study of Drug Testing and Sanctions." Sacramento: California Policy Research Seminar.

La Vigne, Nancy G., Amy Solomon, Karen Beckman, and Kelly Dedel. 2006. "Prisoner Reentry and Community Policing: Strategies for Enhancing Public Safety." Washington, DC: Urban Institute.

Langan, Patrick, and Mark Cunniff. 1992. "Recidivism of Felons on Probation 1986–1989." Washington, DC: Bureau of Justice Statistics.

Langan, Patrick, and David Levin. 2002. "Recidivism of Prisoners Released in 1994." Washington, DC: Bureau of Justice Statistics.

Langan, Patrick, Erica Schmitt, and Matthew Durose. 2003. "Recidivism of Sex Offenders Released from Prison in 1994." Washington, DC: Bureau of Justice Statistics.

Lehman, Joseph. 2000. "Neighborhood Based Supervision." In *Correctional Best Practices: Directors Perspectives*, ed. R. Wilkinson. Middletown, CT: Association of State Correctional Administrators.

Lipsey, Mark W. 1995. "What Do We Learn from 400 Research Studies on the Effectiveness of Treatment with Juvenile Delinquency?" In *What Works: Reducing Reoffending*, ed. J. McQuire, 63–78. West Sussex, UK: John Wiley.

Longmire, Dennis, and Barbara Sims. 1995. "The 1995 crime poll: Texas and the nation." Huntsville, TX: Sam Houston State University.

Lowenkamp, Christopher T., Edward J. Latessa, and Paula Smith. 2006. "Does Correctional Program Quality Really Matter? The Impact of Adhering to the Principles of Effective Intervention." *Criminology and Public Policy* 5: 575–594.

Lynch, James P., and William J. Sabol. 2001. "Prisoner Reentry in Perspective." Washington, DC: Urban Institute.

Manza, Jeff, and Christopher Uggen. 2006. *Locked Out: Felon Disenfranchisement and American Democracy*. New York: Oxford University Press.

Martinson, Robert. 1974. "What Works? Questions and Answers About Prison Reform." *Public Interest* 35: 22–35.

Morris, Norval. 2002. *Maconochie's Gentlemen: The Story of Norfolk Island, the Roots of Modern Prison Reform*. New York: Oxford University Press.

Morris, Norval, and David J. Rothman. 1995. "The Oxford History of the Prison: The Practice of Punishment in Western Society." New York: Oxford University Press.

National Advisory Commission on Criminal Justice Standards and Goals. 1973. "Corrections." Washington, DC: U.S. Department of Justice.

National District Attorneys Association. 2005. "Policy Positions on Prisoner Reentry Issues." Alexandria, VA.

National Institute of Drug Abuse. 2009. "Principles of Drug Addiction Treatment: A Research-Based Guide." Washington, DC. National Institute of Drug Abuse.

National Research Council. 2008. "Parole, Desistance from Crime, and Community Integration." Washington, DC: National Academy of Sciences.

Pager, Devah. 2003. "The Mark of a Criminal Record." *American Journal of Sociology* 108: 937–975.

Pattillo, Mary, David Weiman, and Bruce Western. 2004. "Imprisoning America: The Social Effects of Mass Incarceration." New York: Russell Sage Foundation.

Petersilia, Joan. 1997. "Probation in the United States." In *Crime and Justice*, vol. 22, ed. M. Tonry, 149–200. Chicago: University of Chicago Press.

Petersilia, Joan. 1998. "A Decade of Experimenting with Intermediate Sanctions: What Have We Learned?" *Federal Probation* 62: 3–9.

Petersilia, Joan. 1999. "Parole and Prisoner Reentry in the United States." In *Prisons*, vol. 26, *Crime and Justice: A Review of Research*, eds. M. Tonry and J. Petersilia, 479–530. Chicago: University of Chicago Press.

Petersilia, Joan. 2003. *When Prisoners Come Home: Parole and Prisoner Reentry*. New York: Oxford University Press.

Petersilia, Joan. 2007. "Employ Behavioral Contracting for 'Earned Discharge' Parole." *Criminology and Public Policy* 6: 807–814.

Petersilia, Joan. 2008. "California's Correctional Paradox of Excess and Deprivation." In *Crime and Justice: A Review of Research*, vol. 37, ed. M. H. Tonry. Chicago: University of Chicago Press.

Petersilia, Joan, and Susan Turner. 1993. "Intensive Probation and Parole." In *Crime and Justice: An Annual Review of Research*, vol. 17, ed. M. Tonry, 281–335. Chicago: University of Chicago Press.

Pew Center on the States. 2009. "One in 31: The Long Reach of American Corrections." Washington, DC: The Pew Charitable Trusts.

Puzzanchera, Charles, and Melissa Sickmund. 2008. "Juvenile Court Statistics 2005." Pittsburgh: National Center for Juvenile Justice.

Reinventing Probation Council. 2000. "Transforming Probation Through Leadership: The "Broken Windows" Model." New York: Manhattan Institute for Policy Research.

Rhine, Edward, William Smith, Ronald Jackson, Peggy Burke, and Roger LaBelle. 1991. "Paroling Authorities: Recent History and Current Practice." Laurel, MD: American Correctional Association.

Rosenfeld, Richard, Joel Wallman, and Robert Fornango. 2005. "The Contribution of Ex-Prisoners to Crime Rates." In *Prisoner Reentry and Crime in America*, eds. J. Travis and C. A. Visher. New York: Cambridge University Press.

Rothman, David. 1980. *Conscience and Convenience: The Asylum and Its Alternatives in Progressive America.* Boston: Little, Brown.

Sabol, William J., and Heather Couture. 2008. "Prison Inmates at Midyear 2007." Washington, DC: Bureau of Justice Statistics.

Scott-Hayward, Christine. 2009. "The Fiscal Crisis in Corrections: Rethinking Policies and Practices." New York: Vera Institute of Justice.

Solomon, Amy L., Vera Kachnowski, and Avinash Bhati. 2005. "Does Parole Work? Analyzing the Impact of Postprison Supervision on Rearrest Outcomes." Washington, DC: Urban Institute.

Solomon, Amy, Jenny Osborne, Laura Winterfield, and Brian Elderbroom. 2008. "Putting Public Safety First: 13 Parole Supervision Strategies to Enhance Reentry Outcomes." Washington, DC: Urban Institute.

Thompson, Anthony C. 2008. *Releasing Prisoners, Redeeming Communities: Reentry, Race, and Politics.* New York: New York University Press.

Tonry, Michael H., and Kate Hamilton. 1995. *Intermediate Sanctions in Overcrowded Times.* Boston: Northeastern University Press.

Travis, Jeremy. 2005. *But They All Come Back: Facing the Challenges of Prisoner Reentry.* Washington, DC: Urban Institute.

Travis, Jeremy. 2007. "Reflections on the Reentry Movement." *Federal Sentencing Reporter* 20, 2: 84–87.

Travis, Jeremy, and Michelle Waul. 2003. "Prisoners Once Removed: The Impact of Incarceration and Reentry on Children, Families, and Communities." Washington, DC: Urban Institute.

Turner, Susan, and Jesse Jannetta. 2008. "Implementation and Early Outcomes for the San Diego HIgh Risk Sex Offender GPS Pilot Program." Irvine, CA: Center for Evidence-Based Corrections.

Walker, Jeffrey. 2007. "Eliminate Residency Restrictions for Sex Offenders." *Criminology and Public Policy* 6: 863–870.

Washington State Institute for Public Policy. 2003. "An Analysis of the Department of Corrections' Risk Assessment." Olympia, WA.

Wicklund, Carl. 2004. "Assessment, Treatment, and Compliance: Recommendation to the Community Correcdtions Field." Alexandria, VA: Institute for Law and Justice.

Wilson, James A., Wendy Naro, and James Austin. 2007. "Innovations in Probation: Assessing New York City's Automated Reporting System." Washington, DC: JFA Associates.

Chapter 18

Prisons

Anne Morrison Piehl, Bert Useem

A prison term is a punishment imposed by a duly constituted public authority for a serious transgression against an officially recognized norm for behavior. If the transgression is less serious (in most states, a misdemeanor rather than a felony), the offender may serve time in a jail or in a community-based punishment. Prisons have long been the subject of scholarly study. Until recently, however, prisoners have been a tiny fraction of the U.S. population. To study prisoners was to investigate a fascinating, but not a critically significant, population. With the U.S. prison buildup, a quintupling of the number of prisoners in just three decades, prisons have become far more central to the operation of American society. Prisons writ large—the system of punishing serious criminal offending in the United States—can be expected to have a non-trivial impact on the crime rate, the labor market, the fiscal purse, race relations, and the futures of the large number of people serving time behind bars. This essay describes the current state of incarceration in the United States, the prison buildup, and the direction and magnitude, where possible, of these impacts.

RATES OF INCARCERATION

There are 1.6 million inmates in U.S. prisons, and another half-million employees whose job it is to keep them there and provide for their needs. If congregated in one location, this "city" of 2.1 million people would surpass Phoenix as the fifth largest U.S. city and would be more populous than 13 states. A majority of the inmates, 1.4 million, are in state prisons; the other 200,000 are in federal prisons. In general, offenders convicted of breaking federal laws are sent to federal prisons; those convicted of breaking state laws are incarcerated in state prisons.[1] In addition to these adults, there are 93,000 juvenile offenders held in residential placement facilities (Office of Juvenile Justice and Delinquency Prevention 2009).

This large a prison population is relatively new (see Figure 18.1). In 1930, there were 130,000 state and federal inmates, or a rate of 162 inmates per 100,000 residents 18 years and older.[2] Over the next four and a half decades, the prison population experienced little sustained growth or contraction. An uptick occurred in 1939, up to 199 per 100,000, but this was followed by a downtick in 1945 to 136 per 100,000. The 1975 rate of 161 prisoners per 100,000 adult population was almost identical to the 1930 rate.

In the second half of the 1970s, the prison population embarked on a large scale, long-term buildup. By century's end, 1.3 million offenders were confined to state and federal prisons, a rate of 629 per 100,000. The pace of growth slowed somewhat after this. Still, the numbers added were non-trivial: 280,000 more people by year-end 2008–greater than the *entire* prison population of 1975. By year-end 2008, one in every 143 adult residents in the United States was in prison.

Variation across States

U.S. federalism permits states to punish crime as heavily or as lightly as they choose (within Constitutional limits). Figure 18.21 shows each state's prison population denominated by the number of residents 18 years and older in that state. Variation among states is the rule. The most "punitive" state, Louisiana, has a ratio (1,162 per 100,000) six times greater than the least punitive Massachusetts (193 per 100,000).

Perhaps states imprison at different prisoner-to-population ratios simply because some states have more crime than others. For example, Louisiana may be six times more "punitive" than Massachusetts only because it has six times as much imprisonable crime. Figure 18.3 shows the number of prisoners in each state divided by the number of violent crimes in that state.[3] Large inter-state variation persists. Calculated this way (prisoners per violent crime), Massachusetts remains at the low end of punishment scale, but another New England state, Vermont anchors the other end. The difference between the top and the bottom remains large (278 versus 41).

Variation across Countries

Worldwide, there are about 10 million people in prison or jail (Walmsley 2008). (No breakout of prisoners from jail inmates is available at the cross national level. Here jail inmates include both convicted offenders and pre-trial detainees.) While the United States has 4.5 percent of the world's population, it holds almost a quarter (23.4 percent) of the world's penal population. The U.S. rate of prison and jail incarceration, 756 inmates per 100,000 population, exceeds the rate of Russia (629), and far exceeds those of the western European industrial counterparts: Germany (89), Denmark (63), Belgium (93), France (96), and Spain (160).

Why is the U.S. imprisonment rate so high? A nation's prison rate is a function of four factors: the scope of the criminal law (e.g., what behavior

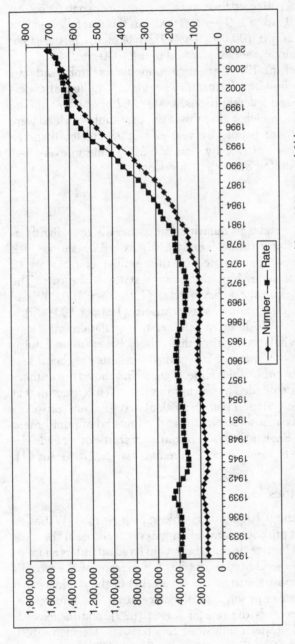

Figure 18.1. Number and Rate of State and Federal Inmates per 100,000 Residents 18 Years and Older

Sources: Sourcebook of Criminal Justice Statistics Online http://www.albany.edu/sourcebook/ [September 3, 2009].

Sourcebook of Criminal Justice Statistics, Online, 2009, Table 6.13.2008. Available: http://www.albany.edu/sourcebook/ [September 3, 2009].

Historical Statistics of the United States, Millennial Edition, Online, edited by Susan B. Carter, Scott Sigmund Gartner, Michael R. Haines, Alan L. Olmstead, Richard Sutch, and Gavin Wright. (New York: Cambridge University Press, 2006). Available: http://hsus.cambridge.org/HSUSWeb/ HSUSEntryServlet [September 1, 2009].

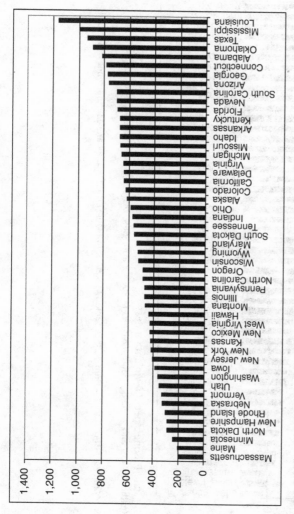

Figure 18.2. State Prisoners per 100,000 Adult Population (18 Years and Older)
Sources: Heather C. West and William J. Sabol, *Prisoners in 2007* (Washington, DC: Bureau of Justice Statistics, 2008 [revised 5/12/2009]).

Statistical Abstract of the United States.Available http://www.census.gov/compendia/statab/tables/09s0016.xls [September 3, 2009].

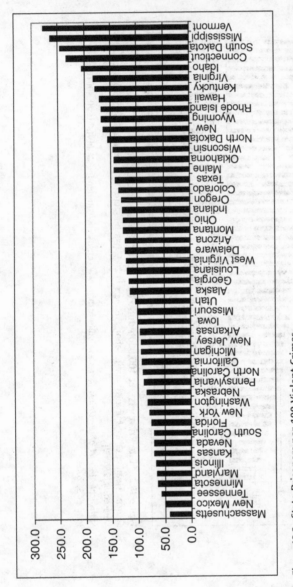

Figure 18.3. State Prisoners per 100 Violent Crimes

Sources: Heather C. West and William J. Sabol, *Prisoners in 2007* (Washington, DC: Bureau of Justice Statistics, 2008 [revised 5/12/2009]).

Sourcebook of Criminal Justice Statistics, Online, 2009, Table 3.106.2007. Available http://www.albany.edu/sourcebook/ [September 3, 2009].

is considered criminal); the crime rate for offenses that can lead to a prison sentence (e.g., murder, but not shoplifting); the proportion of such crimes that result in an arrest and conviction; and, among those convicted, the length of time they serve in prison. All four of these factors contribute to the high rate of imprisonment in the United States. (For a discussion of this issue see the Chapter 2 by James Lynch and William Pridemore in this volume).

Demographics—Which Groups Go to US Prisons?

Young male adults dominate the federal and state prison populations—93 percent are males (West and Sabol 2008, 3). Figure 18.4 shows the age distribution of male inmates (again as the rate per 100,000 population). Incarceration rates peak in the late 20's and early 30s.

Prisoners have lower levels of educational attainment than the general population (see table 18.1). In 2004, 12 percent of the state and 11 percent of federal prisoners had not gone beyond the 8th grade, compared to 6 percent of the general population.[4] Twelve percent of state prisoners and 20 percent of federal prisoners had started college, compared to 52 percent of the general population.

At 2007 yearend, whites accounted for 34.0 percent of the federal and state prison populations, blacks made up 38.2 percent of the prison population, and Hispanics were 20.8 percent (West and Sabol 2008, 3). (The remaining 6 percent included American Indians, Alaska Natives, Native Hawaiians, other Pacific Islanders, and inmates identifying two or more races.) White males were imprisoned at a rate of 481 per 100,000 residents, black males at 3,318 per 100,000 residents; and Hispanics males at 1,259 per 100,000 inmates (West and Sabol 2008, 4). In 2007,

Table 18.1. Education Completed for State and Federal Inmates and the General Population in 2004

Education completed	State prison inmates	Federal prison inmates	General population 18 years and over
8th grade or less	12.3%	10.8%	5.8%
Some high school	24.3	16.0	9.9
GED	29.9	28.8	–
High school graduate	21.6	24.1	31.7
Some college or more	11.8	20.2	52.4

Sources: Lauren Glaze and Laura M. Maruschak, *Parents and Their Minor Children* (Washington, DC: Bureau of Justice Statistics, 2008) (underlying data, Survey of State and Federal Inmates, 2004).
U.S. Census Bureau, Current Population Survey, Internet release. Available:http://www.census.gov/population/socdemo/education/cps2004/tab01-01.pdf [August 28, 2009].

one in 31 black men was a prisoner, in contrast to one in 79 Hispanic men and one in 208 white men. Ten percent of all black men between the ages of 20 and 39 are in prison.

The high rate of incarceration of African Americans has been one of the most studied, but least understood, aspects of the U.S. correctional system. Early work by Alfred Blumstein (1982) and Patrick Langan (1985) found that much of the racial disparity could be accounted for by differential crime rates. Using 1979 data, Blumstein showed that while over one half (52.3 percent) of the inmates imprisoned for murder were black, this corresponds closely to the proportion of blacks arrested for murder (51.6 percent). Overall, black arrest rates accounted for 80 percent of the racial disproportionality among prisoners, leaving 20 percent unexplained. Langan took the analysis one step further back in the criminal justice process, asking if black offenders were arrested in disproportionate numbers relative to white offenders. To establish the race of offenders, Langan used reports by the victims of crime on the race of their assailants (murder had to be excluded). Blacks were arrested at about the same rates as victims reported that they committed crimes. Langan concluded that even if police act with racial bias, it could only explain a small portion of the overrepresentation of blacks in prison.

More recent work has raised new questions. Michael Tonry and Matthew Melewski (2008) replicated Blumstein's analysis using 2004 data. The results using the newer data differed: the black/white arrest patterns could explain a smaller portion of the racial disparities in imprisonment. For example, Blumstein found that black-white differences in arrests for homicide could explain all but 2.8 percent of the differences in white/black rates for imprisonment in homicide. By 2004, the percentage unexplained increased to 11.6 percent. Across all crimes, the percentage of racial variation unexplained by crime increased from 20 percent to 39 percent.

What has changed to reduce the share of racial disproportionally in imprisonment explained by differential crime? Tonry and Melewski suggest several explanations, giving the greatest weight to the war on drugs. They argue that blacks are "much easier to arrest" because more of the drug dealing occurs on the streets in open-air drug markets (Tonry and Melewski 2008, 27). Another source of disparity arises from the fact that blacks are more likely to reside in high-density neighborhoods (as in central cities) and, as a result, are more likely to spend time within the "drug free" zones around schools (and other public places). These zones provide for enhanced criminal penalties for drug crimes within the zones, regardless of whether children are involved or whether school is in session when the offense occurs (Brownsberger and Aromaa 2001; New Jersey Commission to Review Sentencing 2007). A long literature details the ways in which differences between blacks and whites—in types of drugs preferred, length of criminal history, residential geography, and so on—are associated with differential outcomes in criminal justice. Each of these subjects requires scrutiny before one can judge a disparity as justified by the crime context or not, so a full assessment is not possible within this essay. But it is worth noting that the general view of criminal justice scholars is increasingly emphasizing structural reasons in addition to differential crime rates. This view is succinctly stated by Tonry and Melewski (2008, 29), "[M]any more blacks than whites are in prison because police officials have adopted practices, and policy makers have enacted laws, that foreseeably treat black offenders much more harshly than white ones."

REASONS FOR THE BUILDUP

While the facts of the buildup of the prison population are both know-able and well known, just why and how it occurred is the subject of great debate. Prison populations are the outcome of a large number of decisions by many different types of actors in society—the protective efforts of regular people, the predatory actions of offenders, policing and prosecution decisions, and the laws set by legislators, among many others. Any complete explanation for the prison buildup would have to account for the behavior of all of these actors. Several sets of scholars have analyzed the sources of change in prison populations, concluding that the major reasons for the increases since 1980 are changes in policy and practice that increased the likelihood that a person who committed a crime would go to prison *and* increased the length of prison terms for those who were sentenced to prison (Blumstein and Beck 1999, 2005; Raphael and Stoll, 2009).

To explain these changes, some authors take a broad perspective of social change. Frances Fukuyama (1999a) has called the period from mid-1960s through the early 1990s the "great disruption." The period saw deeply unsettling changes in the family structure; a decline of popular trust in institutions; and soaring crime rates, especially in the inner cities. With regard to the latter, Fukuyama (1999b, 55) states, "crime and social disorder began to rise, making inner city areas of the wealthiest societies on earth almost uninhabitable." In fact, with regard to crime, over a 30-year period, from 1961 to 1991, the rate of violent crime increased nearly five-fold, from 158 per 100,000 residents to 758 per 100,000. The property crime rate increased three-fold from 1,726 to 5,140 per 100,000 residents (*Sourcebook of Criminal Justice Statistics*, Online, 2009, table 3.106.2007). One explana-tion the prison buildup is that a social movement—people mobilized to favor social change—arose to help restore society to a more balanced order, at least on the streets, in order to reverse the great disruption. From this perspective, the social movement had a purpose.

Another position also links the prison buildup to broad social change, but here construes the buildup as an effort at social domination and exploitation. From this perspective, the U.S. prison buildup had no ratio-nal content. Behind the mass movement demanding more imprisonment were excited, but unaware, masses; politicians taking advantage of these lower sentiments; and large doses of collective irrationality.

In an essay highly critical of the prison buildup, economist Glenn Loury argues that the legacy of racism continues to keep us apart, and that racial animus carries over to how we treat criminal offenders. He states, "We have met the enemy, and the enemy is them" (2008, 25). Perhaps stronger identification with "them"—mainly, poor residents of high-crime cities— would lead to different criminal justice policies.

Our own analysis of these arguments and public opinion data about policy options suggests that the social movement grew out of a pragmatic effort to solve a pressing social problem.[5] Escalating crime was a real issue for supporters of prison buildup, not merely emblematic of hidden frustrations or diffuse anxieties nor a smoke screen for hegemonic domination. The movement's expressed rationale should be taken at face value. For example, we found that from the mid-1960s through the 1980s there was a broad shift in public opinion toward more conservative positions on crime and punishments, without a decline in support for the civil liberties of criminal defendants (Useem and Piehl 2008, 15–41). Moreover, in our multivariable statistical analyses, supporters for the more punitive policies, compared to supporters for more lenient policies, were hard to distinguish in terms of social losses or economic insecurity.

But reasoning people may have gotten it wrong. Even if the intent was to restore order, this does not necessarily imply that quintupling the prison population was the only—or best—way to achieve it. For pragmatists, how one feels about the appropriateness of high rates of incarceration in the United States would depend upon how central prison is to crime control. We turn to this issue next.

PRISON AND CRIME RATES

Prison has multiple purposes, as we have discussed. And how extensively it is used is the result of myriad policy choices and the decisions of many actors, from offender behavior to the crime prevention actions of ordinary citizens to police budgets, to sentencing decisions of judges and others. Yet in the midst of this complexity stands one central question: What is the "right" size of the prison sector? Justice is one part of the balance— sentences must in rough balance the criminal conduct. Pragmatism is another part of the balance. How well does the correctional population achieve society's broader goals? How much increased reliance on prisons reduces crime rates is central to this latter concern.

To the extent that higher rates of incarceration cause reductions in crime, expanding the use of prison has practical social value. (Of course, other approaches to controlling crime may have even greater social value.) The size of the impact is likely to depend on the scale of imprisonment. Expansions of prison populations will add to deterrence, but if deterrence is already high, then its impact on crime may be low. Similarly, prison expansion will increase incapacitation, but if these expansions involve less serious offenders, either by expanding the categories of crime or by the inclusion of less serious offenders within crime type, again the practical gains may be small. And some authors argue that expansions of prison will lead to increases in crime rates, as the community disruption impacts swamp the other mechanisms (Rose and Clear 1998). The crucial issue is not whether some negative effects occur in communities; they most certainly do (Lynch and Sabol 2004). Rather, the key question for the policy debate is whether those effects overwhelm the crime-reducing mechanisms of prison—deterrence and incapacitation—which also most certainly occur under present conditions.

The research literature generally models the statistical relationship between states' incarceration rates and crime rates as an "elasticity," the percentage reduction in the crime rate brought about by a percentage increase in the imprisonment rate. An unavoidable issue in regressions of crime rates on incarceration rates is that of simultaneity bias. While changes in incarceration rates cause changes in crime rates, the process also operates in the opposite direction—increases in crime rates lead to a growth in the incarceration rate. When simultaneity occurs, the regression estimate of the effect of incarceration on crime will be understated. (A metaphor: Imagine spraying a lawn to eliminate its crabgrass. If absent spraying, the crabgrass would spread like wildfire, the treatment would appear less effective than it really is if one simply compared the amount of crabgrass after the treatment to the amount before the treatment.) The research studies cited in this section have attempted to deal with simultaneity using a variety of statistical strategies. While none is entirely satisfactory, they provide our best estimates of how prison impacts crime.

A burst of regression analyses in the 1990's addressed the empirical question of the overall impact of expanding incarceration on crime in the United States, all relying on similar data, collected at county or state levels. Although they relied on somewhat different statistical models, the best of these studies yielded roughly similar estimates—that the elasticity of crime with regard to the prison rate is between −0.16 and −0.55 (Marvell and Moody 1994; Levitt 1996; Witt and Witte 2000). That is, a 10 percent increase in the prison rate will result in a 1.6 percent to 5.5 percent drop in the crime rate.[6] (For a full explanation of this issue, see Chapter 14 by Robert Apel and Daniel Nagin in this volume).

How big are these effects? Steven Levitt (2004) and William Spelman (2008) have assessed the size of these elasticities relative to the drop in violent crime over the 1990s, both concluding that about 25 percent of the violent crime drop can be attributed to the increased use of incarceration. It has become common for this finding to be cited in policy debates as an estimate of expected gains from further expansions, or expected increases in crime if prison populations are reduced.

The above studies, and the policy implications drawn from them, presume that the relationship between imprisonment and crime does not vary with the scale of imprisonment. But our recent work with Raymond Liedka (Liedka et al. 2006) shows that allowing for the elasticity to vary with the scale of imprisonment was critical for drawing inference about the relationship between prison populations and crime rates. When we estimated the key relationships between prison populations and crime using state-level data from 1972 to 2000 and using models similar to those of Marvell and Moody, Levitt, and Witt and Witte, the results were within the same ballpark. From this, we concluded that the addition of another decade's worth of data on prison growth has not drastically changed the conclusions drawn in the empirical literature of the mid-1990s.

However, when we estimated a model that allowed for the elasticity to vary, we found that the effect of incarceration did indeed depend on the scale of incarceration, rejecting the constant elasticity framework. We found negative elasticities at low rates of imprisonment, which become less negative as the incarceration rates rise, eventually reaching an inflection point at which the elasticity turns positive. It is harder to summarize the results of an elasticity that varies with the scale of the prison population precisely because the estimates vary. Here we provide just a few of the results (many more can be found in Liedka et al. 2006). At the median value of the state prison population, our preferred estimate indicates that a 10 percent increase in the incarceration rate would lower crime rates by 0.58 percent. However, at a lower level—the twenty-fifth percentile of the state prison population—that same 10 percent increase would reduce crime rates by 1.12 percent, and at the higher seventy-fifth percentile, the reduction would only be 0.08 percent. This pattern is robust to a wide range of alternative specifications of empirical models. These estimates come from models that separate out short-term from long-term impacts in order to address simultaneity bias. While we are cautious about interpreting their precise magnitudes, we are fully confident of the more general point that the effect of prison on crime at a point in time depends on how extensively prison is used.

These estimates demonstrate diminishing proportional returns to the use of incarceration. Note that these results go beyond the more typical claim of declining marginal returns. Rather, they document accelerating declining marginal returns, that is, a percent reduction in crime that gets smaller with ever-larger prison populations. The findings imply several conclusions about the usual, constant-elasticity, statistical analyses of incarceration's effect on crime: (1) at low levels of incarceration, these analyses underestimate the negative relationship between incarceration and crime; (2) at higher levels of incarceration, the analyses overstates the negative effect; and (3) analyses from one time period cannot be extrapolated to other points in time with vastly different incarceration experience.

The elasticity underlying the assessment that a quarter of the violent crime drop in the 1990s is accounted for by increasing incarceration is based on the Levitt (1996) paper, which in turn relied on data running through 1993 and that was identified using statistical variation primarily from the 1980s. The Liedka-study findings indicate the problem with extrapolating such findings to today's debates, with today's much higher rate of incarceration. Our estimated elasticities are much lower than Levitt's. Another way to form an estimate of the current relationship from incarceration rates to crime rates is to adjust the Levitt elasticity for today's incarceration rates. Our findings indicate that shifting from 1993 levels of incarceration to 2006, cuts the elasticity to one-seventh. Then, taking one-seventh of Levitt's elasticity as the estimate of today's elasticity, indicates a crime-reducing impact of increasing incarceration, but a small one on the order of 1 percent decline for a 10 percent increase in incarceration. Whether one relies on our estimates or adjusts Levitt's, the marginal impact of further expansions of incarceration is minimal (a 10 percent increase in incarceration leading to a 0.1 percent drop in crime, from Liedka et al. 2006) or small (the same increase leading to a 1 percent drop in crime rates from adjusting Levitt 1996). This is the magnitude that should be at center of society's deliberations about how well the correctional population achieves society's broader goals.

The research literature leads us to draw two broad conclusions. First, the prison buildup has achieved crime reduction. Even the sternest critics of the buildup do not demand to return to pre-buildup level of imprisonment. Using data from the United States over 30 years, researchers have found quite consistent results using a range of research methodologies that there is a negative relationship between prison size and the crime rate. In a phrase, more prison, less crime. Second, the prison buildup has not been equally effective across the buildup period. The regression results showed not just declining marginal returns but *acceleration* in the declining marginal return to scale. These findings provide an important caution for many jurisdictions. Using old estimates of the effect of prison on crime to predict future impacts will greatly overstate the crime reductions.

PRISON MANAGEMENT

The challenge of correctional management arises, in the first instance, from the fact that prisoners are forced to be there. No one chooses prison. The quality of life is low, at least when compared to life on the "outside." Nearly everything that would make an inmate's life a little more pleasant— a radio, a snack, a pair of shoes, a breath of fresh air—is not his or hers for the taking or purchase, but must be requested from a correctional employee. Inmates have only what they are given. Cell phones and the Internet are disallowed. Sexual relations are prohibited (though not always effectively). Visits with loved ones are limited in duration and awkward in setting. Food typically lacks variety and flavor. The coercive nature of prison may be met by inmate resistance, through unfettered criticism, rule breaking, violent attacks against staff and other inmates, formation of gangs, riots, and attempts to escape.

The first task of correctional management is to ensure that acts of resistance are exceptions rather than rule. Even though prisons are coercive institutions, they require the cooperation of inmates. In its absence, ordinary activity and day-to-day operations cannot go on. With some exceptions, inmates leave their general confinement cells for much of the day, to participate in work assignments, recreate on the yard, go to the mess hall, attend religious services, use the law library, receive counseling, and participate in educational programs. Moreover, the overall trend is toward more, rather than less, inmate movement. In New York, for example, "violent offenders are now let out of their maximum-security general confinement cells to interact for some 16 hours each day, compared to the 6-8 hours of daily out-of-cell time allowed during the era of the proverbial 'Big House'" (Goord 2006, 1). In lower security dormitory-style units, inmates freely interact the entire day. Exceptions are those inmates who are housed in protective custody units, punitive units, or "supermax facilities" for very high security inmates, the latter discussed further below. If acts of inmate resistance become the rule rather than the exception, prison authorities may have little choice but to "lock down" a facility. Inmates are confined to their cells. Daily life—rehabilitative programs, work, visitation, out-of-cell feeding, religious services—come to a grinding halt. The costs are for all parties are great.

During the course of the prison buildup and even toward its end, many criminologists predicted that the buildup would be extremely difficult to implement. They expected a crisis of order exemplified by high rates of violence and escapes. Criminologist John Hagan, for example, warned that "increased imprisonment will lead to more disruptions and riots in prisons" (1995, 524). With the very unfair advantage of hindsight, we now know that these predictions were false.

In fact, prison riots went from frequent, long, and costly to infrequent, relatively short, and resolved with little loss of life or damage (Useem and Piehl 2006). The most notorious riots—Attica in 1971 (41 dead, 4 days in duration) and New Mexico (3 days in length, 33 dead)—have almost no contemporary parallels. Correctional agencies developed specialized units to respond quickly to disturbances to prevent their spread and lower the costs of resolution to all parties. And, in doing this, they discouraged their occurrence, under the Latin dictum, "Si vis pacem, para bellum"—if you want peace, prepare for war. The riots that have occurred more recently appear to lack the fury of their earlier counterparts; they were not deadly, destructive affairs. For example, in a recent riot in an Indiana prison, inmates transferred there from California's overcrowded prison system demanded to be returned to their home state of California, closer to family and friends. Inmates took no hostages and destroyed little property.

Other measures of order/disorder have tracked in the same direction. The trends include lower rates of escapes, of staff assaulted and murdered, and of inmate violations of prison rules (Useem and Piehl 2008, 93–99). To illustrate, crime researchers, when they are especially concerned about the validity of their data, typically turn to homicide as the best measured crime. Figure 18.5 shows a 94 percent decline in the rate of inmate homicides over three decades among state inmates. In 1973, there were 63 homicides per 100,000 state inmates. In 1990, there were 8, and in 2003 the homicide rate dropped further to 4. During the 2003, the homicide rate in prison (4 per 100,000) was lower than the rate for the U.S. resident population (6 per 100,000). As a further check on these trends, prison suicide rates dropped sharply. Figure 4 shows that in 1980, there were 34 inmate suicides per 100,000 inmates. This rate decreased to 16 suicides per 100,000 in 1990 and has remained stable since then. The suicide rate in prison is higher than in the general population. (In 2006, the overall rate was about 11 suicide deaths per 100,000 people. National Institute of Health 2009).

Improvements in security equipment appear to have had a substantial impact on order, although we know of no systematic evidence to support this. For example, many jurisdictions are beginning to use the BOSS Chair (Body Orifice Scanning System)—a device that can detect metal hidden on an inmate, including in the rectum and hair, even when fully clothed. In some prisons, observation cameras cover almost all areas in which inmates move. While the precise contribution of these technical improvements to order has not been measured, neither can they be doubted.

How much has the proliferation of supermaxes prisons in the late 1980s and 1990s responsible for decreasing rate of disorder? To define the term: Supermaxes are extremely high security facilities, in effect,

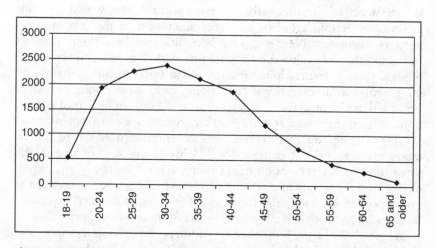

Figure 18.4. Prisoners in State and Federal Prison (per 100,000 Population) by Age
Source: Heather C. West and William J. Sabol, *Prisoners in 2007* (Washington, DC: Bureau of Justice Statistics, 2008 [revised 5/12/2009]),19.

prisons within prisons. Inmates typically spend 23 hours a day locked in their cells and have little or no contact with other inmates. Services to inmates, such as food and medical care, are provided to inmates in their cells. When inmates are taken out of their cells, they are usually hand-cuffed, shackled, and escorted by a four-person team. Inmates most often are allowed to exercise in a small fenced-in yard.[7]

To date, Chad Briggs, Jody Sundt, and Thomas Castellano (2003) have conducted the only test of the effect of supermaxes on order in correctional systems. They selected four correctional systems to study, based in part on the availability of reliable data on violence over time. Three of the systems (Arizona, Illinois, and Minnesota) had opened a supermax in the time period covered. A fourth system (Utah) had not, providing a comparison system. They asked whether inmate-against-inmate and inmate-against-staff violence declined, system-wide, after a supermax facility opened. A formal data analysis found little effect. Specifically, the opening of a supermax did not reduce the level of inmate-against-inmate assaults. Inmates were no safer after the opening of a supermax than before. The opening of supermaxes had mixed effects on inmate-against-staff violence. The opening of a supermax institution left unaffected inmate-against-staff assaults in one prison system, decreased it in another, and increased it in a third. This study, based on a small number of states, cannot definitely answer the question of whether supermaxes have a negative effect on prison violence. Still, if supermaxes were a major causal force in the broader trend toward order, some trace of that effect is likely to have shown up in the study.

A central lesson to be drawn from the experience of the prison buildup is the capability of correctional agencies to be agile: adaptable, flexible, and constructive.[8] Traditionally, observers of corrections would view this pairing (corrections/agile) to be a contradiction in terms. Yet in many agencies, correctional leadership has been able transform their organization into effective, value-driven, enterprises. But, as with all aspects of prisons, there is tremendous variation across states in this domain. The improvements in correctional functioning came over a long period of time, and as the product of many influences. Professionalism of correctional officers improved as it did in other areas of law enforcement, most notably policing. And many correctional systems improved due to judicial intervention to protect constitutional rights of inmates, or due to the threat that such intervention might occur. As one metric of the extent of this intervention, Schlanger (2006) reports that 30–40 percent of the prison population during the 1980s and 1990s was housed in correctional facilities under court orders governing one or more areas of prison life.

What will the future bring to order within prisons? While a prophecy of gloom and doom should be avoided (as unrealistic), so too should unrealistic optimism. The problems of managing the care, custody, and treatment of 1.6 million people (for whom life is unpleasant) are daunting. Prison riots—the ultimate breakdown in authority, however temporary—

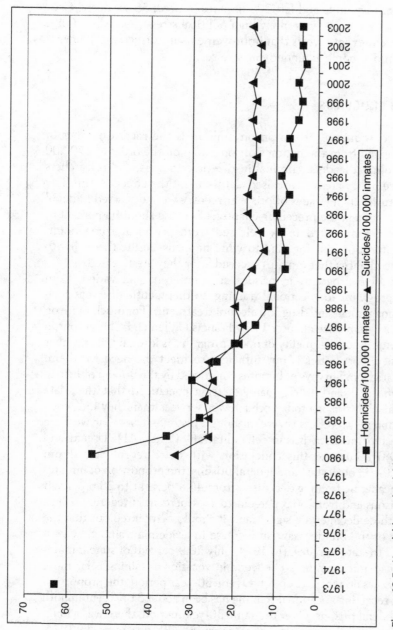

Figure 18.5. Homicide and Suicide Rates in State Prisons

Sources: Bureau of Justice Statistics, "Suicide and Homicide Rates in State Prisons and Jails." Available: http://www.ojp.usdoj.gov/bjs/glance/tables/shipjtab.htm [August 28, 2009].

The 1973 Figure: Sawyer F. Sylvester, John H. Reed, and David O. Nelson. *Prison Homicide* (Jamaica, NY: Spectrum Publications, 1977).

Legend: ■ Homicides/100,000 inmates ▲ Suicides/100,000 inmates can still be expected. As an example, in August 2009, black and Hispanic inmates attacked one another in a four-hour long brawl at the California Institution for Men in Chino, a medium-security facility. They destroyed several dormitory units and left 200 inmates injured, 55 seriously. California prisons are under extremely high political stress (Petersilia 2008). And this recent event reveals that improvements in correctional management cannot overcome all underlying stresses.

IN-PRISON PROGRAMS

A natural consequence of the prison buildup is the record number of inmates released from the nation's prisons, now on the order of 670,000 per year. Political leaders, criminal justice practitioners, and researchers from diverse policy areas have raised alarms about the effects of this flow on communities. (The issues of prisoner reentry were discussed in detail by Joan Petersilia in the preceding chapter.) Because about 95 percent of all inmates are expected to be released from prison at some point, increasing attention is being paid to what happens "inside the walls" to improve the chances that inmates succeed after they are released.

Rehabilitative programs in prisons are numerous and varied, from education programs to vocational training, to therapeutic offerings such as anger management and drug and alcohol treatment. (For much more on particular programs, see chapter 11 by Francis Cullen and Cheryl Jonson in this volume.) But the quality of many programs is low, and the number of program opportunities is not sufficient to meet the need for them. Based on data from Surveys of Inmates conducted by the Bureau of Justice Statistics in 1991 and 1997, Joan Petersilia concluded that the "data suggest that U.S. prisons today offer fewer services than they did when inmate problems were less severe, although history shows that we have never invested much in prison rehabilitation" (2005, 41). Useem and Piehl (2008) reinforced this conclusion with more recent data. From 1991 to 2004, in both state and federal prisons, the proportion of inmates receiving academic training decreased from 46.4 percent to 28.6 percent in state prisons and from 56.3 percent to 35.4 percent in federal prisons. Although these declines are significant, it should be pointed out that the early years of the buildup saw an increase in academic training, at least with regard to state inmates. (In 1974, only 20.9 percent of state inmates received academic training.) The trend in vocational training is far more even and shows no recent drop off. Over a 30-year period, the proportion of inmates receiving vocational training has been about 31 percent in both state and federal prisons. Over the same 30-year period, there was a long-term decline in the proportion of inmates in work programs. In 1974, 72.1 percent of state prison inmates had work assignments. In 2004, only 60.1 percent of the inmates had such assignments. In federal prisons, the proportions, in the 3 years for which we have surveys, are higher and more stable. The extremely tough fiscal conditions of state governments is likely to result in increased pressure on the already underprovided in-prison programming opportunities.

Whether or not any given program is effective depends on its design and its implementation. While we cannot assess the vast array of programs here, we can provide some general conclusions from the research literature. LoBuglio (2007, 6) identifies four principles of effective treatment programming: "first, the programs need to target high risk offenders; second, they need to focus on factors that lead to recidivism; third, they need to incorporate a curriculum that is responsive to this population; and fourth, the programs need to be well-designed, implemented, and enjoy institutional support (i.e. the programs need to demonstrate 'fidelity' to these goals)."

The Washington State Institute for Public Policy (WSIPP) undertook an ambitious effort to summarize evaluations of in-prison programs. They reviewed over 500 studies that met their criteria for rigorous research design. (Results are summarized in Drake et al. [2009a]; full details are in Aos et al. [2006]). The latter is an extremely useful reference document.) The WSIPP review identified certain treatment programs as more effective than others. For instance, general education programs in prison can reduce recidivism by 8 percent, vocational education programs by 10 percent, drug treatment and cognitive behavioral programming by 6–7 percent. Other programs, such as boot camps and domestic violence education, were found to be ineffective at reducing recidivism (Drake et al. 2009a).[9]

The numbers above come from carefully implemented research studies of well-implemented programs. So they show what is possible for programs to achieve. But in practice, program quality varies greatly from one prison to the next, and from one program provider to the next. For example, Ann Chih Lin (2002) studied rehabilitation programming, including educational programs, in five medium-security prisons. All five prisons had mandatory GED classes for inmates without a high school education. Real education took place in three of the prisons, but in the two others, classes amounted to little more than required attendance and busywork. An assessment by Barnoski (2004) found that the recidivism results of therapeutic programs also varied tremendously, with therapists who closely followed the relevant treatment program having much greater recidivism reductions for their clients compared with therapists who deviated from treatment protocols.

The low rates of participation in programs in prison reflect, in part, the fact that prison administrators face enormous challenges in developing and implementing reentry and other treatment programs. Classification is the institutional process that determines where inmates reside within an institution and which programs they receive. Ideally, the process determines institutional placement by balancing the risks and needs of the inmates. Inmates who are suicidal, who have "enemies" within the institution, who are disruptive, and who fall within a number of categories, are generally placed in specialized living units. Most inmates, though, are placed in general population living units and receive an institutional service plan that requires them to participate in a variety of education, treatment programming, and work assignments. The plan is often a wish list of activities because the institution does not offer enough programs to engage fully the whole inmate population at any point in time. The classification status of inmates is reviewed periodically and they are rewarded for following their plans by placement in living units of lower security with greater privileges (e.g., more recreation time, greater access to visits, better institutional jobs, opportunities to earn time off their sentences). In this way, the institution provides incentives for good behavior and steps inmates down from higher- to lower-custody living areas.

State laws and regulations, and correctional department policies and procedures, can override the classification process—and have done so. Many state legislatures passed laws (mostly in the 1980s and 1990s) prohibiting inmates with particular offenses from participating fully in probation, parole, furlough, work release, and earned "good time" for particular offenses. At the same time, departmental policies also frequently become more restrictive. These constraints can be surprisingly far reaching, and can constrain even the well-intentioned efforts of correctional administrators to prepare inmates for release.

Gresham Sykes (1958), in *The Society of Captives* (along with other scholars since then), argued that prison's task to rehabilitate inmates is undone by the need to maintain security. But John DiIulio conducted in-depth case-studies in several prison systems and found just the opposite. In *Governing Prisons*, DiIulio (1987) reported that prisons with high levels of service and amenities provide more effective programming. This is because (1) order, amenities, and service share a common cause in effective management; (2) prisons with high levels of order can provide more effective programs; and (3) programming facilitates order by providing an opportunity for inmate—staff communication.

Changes in the law and practice since DiIulio's pathbreaking work have in general increased the constraints on corrections, both leading to and reflecting the increased emphasis on security and punishment. For example, the opportunity for discretionary release has declined dramatically. This led to declines in both the prison culture valuing rehabilitation and the associated pressure to participate in programs. In spite of this, some jail and prison systems have embraced the ethos that effective correctional management furthers the goals of rehabilitation by developing systems of "inmate accountability." In these correctional institutions, all of the practices are designed to modify inmate behavior by setting and communicating expectations, providing incentives (sanction and reward) for good conduct and for effort in rehabilitation or work programs, and holding inmates accountable for meeting expectations. These systems allow gradual expansion of liberty for inmates whose conduct merits a reduction in the intensity of supervision. In this way, then, the entire period of incarceration is used to improve the chances of success following release (Lyman et al. 2001).

SUMMARY: THE PRISON BUILDUP

The theory behind the prison buildup was that higher rates of incarceration would strengthen the predisposition to obey law and incapacitate those for whom this predisposition is especially weak. The theory was right. Crime rates *did* fall, due in part to the expanded use of prison.

Critics of the buildup were certain that the country had embarked on a self-destructive course, arguing that the prison system would collapse under its own weight because of the flaws inherent to prisons. With the advantage of hindsight—buttressed by reasonably good data—we now know they were wrong. The prison buildup has been associated with a sharp decline in chaos behind bars. Prison riots have become rare, the homicide and suicide rates have declined dramatically, and a smaller proportion of inmates are held in segregation and protective custody. Escapes are less common. If Americans want to have mass-scale imprisonment, we can have it without out-of-control conditions behind bars.

What caused the trend toward greater, rather than less, order? The data are consistent with the position that the political and correctional leadership made the institution more effective. The negative social consequences of the buildup—its expense, the impact on communities that have large numbers of residents removed to prison and later returning from prison, and the impact on inmates and their families—need to be assessed in light of the gains of crime reduction and prison order.

What is new, different, and still crucially needed is the capacity of correctional leadership to see the broader mission of corrections in society, and how it has changed as a consequence of the buildup. Partly this entails recognizing the limits of further correctional expansion. We need to learn how to apply the brakes to correctional expansion, while still serving the ends of crime control and justice. Flat, even negative, growth may be indicated.

Another aspect is to take into full account the impact of prison on the futures of many people. They are mainly young men, who are disproportionately minority, with little education, and personal deficits making it difficult for them to participate in the labor market upon release. A significant portion of inmates suffer mild to severe mental illness. Precise numbers necessarily depend on how mental illness is defined and assessed; recent estimates are on the order of half of inmates (James and Glaze 2006).[10] In addition, prisons contain a substantial number of older inmates. In 2007, over 40,000 inmates were age 60 and older (West and Sabol 2008). Health problems of these older inmates and of the general prison population are leading to increasing cost and other pressures on prison systems. While prisoners have always been a troubled population, they are no longer a group of unimportant size.

WHAT LIES AHEAD FOR PRISONS? POLICY REFORM

Although there was opposition to the buildup before its effects were visible, few now advocate a return to the previously low levels of incarceration, at least in one fell swoop. The economic recession has led to very tight budgetary conditions at the state and local levels which in turn has caused most states to consider seriously whether there are more effective approaches for punishing criminal behavior (Scott-Hayward 2009). Senator Webb from Virginia has introduced legislation in Congress to establish a commission to review state and federal criminal justice laws and practices to recommend reforms to "responsibly reduce the overall incarceration rate; improve federal and local responses to international and domestic gang violence; restructure our approach to drug policy; improve the treatment of mental illness; improve prison administration; and establish a system for reintegrating ex-offenders" (Webb 2009).

But while policy reform is called for, even crucial, it is likely to be incremental. One increment is the effort to trim prison populations where reductions can be done without threatening public safety, or at least where the tradeoffs appear to be reasonably good bets. As an example, 31 states now permit low-risk inmates to reduce their minimum sentence through "earned time" (Lawrence 2009). In contrast to "good time," which allows inmates to reduce their sentence for following prison rules, earned time accelerates the date of release from confinement in return for active participation in education, work, substance-abuse or other sorts of rehabilitative programming. States vary in the precise programs that count toward earned time, the formulas for calculating it, who is eligible, and the cost saving achieved.

Whether the early releases are "safe" enough is a matter of judgment. But a recent study from Washington State suggests that they are, at least under some conditions. An evaluation of 2003 law that increased the availability of earned release for adult prison inmates showed that recidivism rates were lower under the expanded program. Therefore, the state benefited from both shorter prison stays and the lower recidivism, yielding a substantial saving from the law (Drake et al. 2009b).

The room for incremental reforms such as earned good time is sometimes narrowly circumscribed by state sentencing laws, including ones that specify mandatory minimum terms and detail the terms under which inmates are released from custody. As a result, the policy reforms that would have the greatest impact on prison populations are outside the realm of prison per se. For example, consider the populations of convicted offenders serving sentences under community supervision. At the end of 2007, there were over 4 million people on probation and over 800,000 on parole in the United States (U.S. Department of Justice 2009). That makes the parole population slightly larger than the 750,000 admitted to prison each year (West and Sabol 2008). The probation population is five times as large. Therefore, even modest changes to parole or probation practice (such as how readily violations of the conditions of supervision are sanctioned by periods in prison) can have huge impacts on state prisons (Piehl and LoBuglio 2005). While states are reassessing their sentencing laws and practices that govern how many go to prison, and for how long, whether they will turn out to lead to reductions in prison populations remains to be seen.

WHAT LIES AHEAD FOR PRISONS? CORRECTIONAL LEADERSHIP

Regardless of the path that sentencing and other reforms take, pressures on correctional agencies will remain high for the foreseeable future. Where is corrections headed, and where should it be headed? Its immediate problems are evident. They include dealing with budgetary shortfalls in the state capitals; over-crowding in some agencies; and managing the ever-present dangers of prison violence. Dealing with these immediate problems are formidable tasks.

We believe, however, that corrections can increasingly move toward a more deeply value-driven agenda. By this we mean that correctional agencies assess and reassess their missions, and build programmatic responses around those missions. Mission statements should be taken seriously and, in fact, sometimes (although not always) will be implemented in new forms of practices. For example, the mission statement of the New York State Department of Correctional Services includes, under its goals, "create and maintain an atmosphere where both inmates and staff feel secure;" "develop and implement positive individualized treatment plans for each inmate;" "teach inmates the need for discipline and respect, and the importance of a mature understanding of the work ethic." These goals are then to be translated into policies, such as "offer opportunities for inmates to improve their skills, and to receive individual treatment services, based on their ability and willingness to participate; establish a structure environment that fosters respect through discipline learning" and "enhance positive relationships by providing opportunities for interaction between inmates and their families." Many other correctional agencies have also broadened their mission statements over the past decade, in some cases in recognition of the agency's role in prisoner reentry.

While one should be cautious about over-interpreting mission statements, they do provide a basis for defining agency's purposes. One then has to look at actual implementation and, most importantly, results. To follow up on the New York example, even the agency's most difficult population—those inmates being confined in a "special housing unit" (SHU, pronounced "shoe") for serious infraction of prison rules, such as striking an officer or another inmate—are provided educational and rehabilitative programs. They can earn privileges or reduce the length of their SHU confinement through cooperative behavior. The agency's mission is not lost, even, indeed especially, for this group of inmates.

Speaking generally, we are confident that the range of possibilities—new sorts of programs, new ways of doing things, new fixes to old problems—are large. Not everything tried will come to fruition. Those that do can become embedded as standard practices more widely.

The overall point of this essay is that prisons, when properly governed and right-sized, are useful social arrangements for reeling in crime and serving justice. To be well-governed, prisons must have leadership that defines missions suitably and inspires fellow-employees to make good choices. To be right-sized, prisons must not exceed a sensible limit in numbers of inmates and must hold the right sorts of offenders. Prisons are limited in what they can achieve. Prisons may deter; they certainly incapacitate; they can educate; they can provide drug and alcohol counseling. They are not, however, especially good at instilling personal virtue and individual restraint. More broadly, prisons' limitations are reflected in E. V. Walter's (1959, 642) comment, "Sanctions, penalties, and the fear of punishment are merely braces and not foundations." Finally, prisons are costly to all parties involved—but so is crime.

References

Aos, Steve, Marna Miller, and Elizabeth Drake. 2006. *Evidence-Based Public Policy Options to Reduce Future Prison Construction, Criminal Justice Costs, and Crime Rates.* Olympia: Washington State Institute for Public Policy.

Barnoski, Robert. 2004. *Outcome Evaluation of Washington State's Research-Based Programs for Juvenile Offenders* (document No. 04–01–1201). Olympia: Washington State Institute for Public Policy.

Blumstein, Alfred. 1982. "On Racial Disproportionality of the United States' Prison Populations." *Journal of Criminal Law and Criminology* 73 (3): 1259–1281.

Blumstein, Alfred, and Allen J. Beck. 1999. "Population Growth in U.S. Prisons, 1980–1996." In *Prisons*, eds. Michael Tonry and Joan Petersilia, 17–61. Chicago: University of Chicago Press.

Blumstein, Alfred, and Allen J. Beck. 2005. "Reentry as a Transient State Between Liberty and Recommitment." In *Prisoner Reentry and Crime in America*, eds. Jeremy Travis and Christy Visher, 50–79. New York: Cambridge University Press.

Briggs, Chadd S., Jody L. Sundt, and Thomas C. Castellano. 2003. "The Effect of Supermaximum Security Prisons on Aggregate Levels of Institutional Violence." *Criminology* 41(4): 1341–1376.

Brownsberger, William N., and Susan Aromaa. 2001. *An Empirical Study of the School Zone Law in Three Cities in Massachusetts.* Boston: Join Together. Available at http://www.jointogether.org/resources/pdf/school_zone.pdf. Accessed September 1, 2009.

DiIulio, John J., Jr. 1987. *Governing Prisons: A Comparative Study of Correctional Management.* New York: The Free Press.

Drake, Elizabeth, Steve Aos, and Marna Miller. 2009a. *"Evidence-Based Public Policy Options to Reduce Crime and Criminal Justice Costs: Implications in Washington State".* Victims and Offenders 4: 179–196. Olympia: Washington State Institute for Public Policy.

Drake, Elizabeth K., Robert Barnoski, and Steve Aos. 2009b. *Increased Earned Release from Prison: Impacts of a 2003 Law on Recidivism and Crime Costs, Revised.* Document No. 09–04–1201. Olympia: Washington State Institute for Public Policy.

Fisher, William, Jeffery L. Geller, and John A. Pandiani. 2009. "The Changing Role of the State Psychiatric Hospital." *Health Affairs* 28(3): 676–684.

Fukuyama, Francis. 1999a. "Human Nature and the Reconstruction of Social Order." *Atlantic Monthly* 283 (5): 55–80.

Fukuyama, Francis. 1999b. *The Great Disruption: Human Nature and the Reconstitution of Social Order.* New York: The Free Press.

Gamson, William A. 1990 [1975]. *The Strategy of Social Protest,* 2nd ed. Belmont, CA: Wadsworth.

Glaze, Lauren E., and Laura M. Maruschak. 2008. *Parents and Their Minor Children.* Washington, DC: Bureau of Justice Statistics.

Goord, Glenn. S. 2006. *Prison Safety in New York.* Albany: NYDOCS. Available online at http://www.docs.state.ny.us/PressRel/06CommissionerRpt/06Prison-Safety Rpt.pdf.

Hagan, John. 1995. "The Imprisoned Society: Time Turns a Classic on Its Head." *Sociological Forum* 10: 520–24.

Historical Statistics of the United States, Millennial Edition. 2006. Online, edited by Susan B. Carter, Scott Sigmund Gartner, Michael R. Haines, Alan L. Olmstead, Richard Sutch, and Gavin Wright. New York: Cambridge University Press.

James, Doris J. and Lauren E. Glaze. 2006. *Mental Health Problems of Prison and Jail Inmates.* Washington, D.C.: Bureau of Justice Statistics.

Kanter, Rosabeth Moss. 2008. "Transforming Giants." *Harvard Business Review* 86: 43–52.

Krueger, Alan B. 2007. *What Makes a Terrorist: Economics and the Roots of Terrorism.* Princeton, NJ: Princeton University Press.

Langan, Patrick. 1985. "Racism on Trial: New Evidence to Explain the Racial Composition of Prisons in the United States." *Journal of Criminal Law and Criminology* 76: 666–683.

Lawrence, Alison. 2009. *Cutting Corrections Costs: Earned Time Policies for State Prisoners.* Washington, DC: National Conference of State Legislatures.

Levitt, Steven D. 1996. "The Effect of Prison Population Size on Crime Rates: Evidence from Prison Overcrowding Litigation." *Quarterly Journal of Economics* 111: 319–352.

Levitt, Steven D. 2004. "Understanding Why Crime Fell in the 1990s: Four Factors That Explain the Decline and Six That Do Not." *Journal of Economic Perspectives* 18: 163–190.

Liedka, Raymond, Anne Morrison Piehl, and Bert Useem. 2006. "The Crime-Control Effect of Incarceration: Does Scale Matter?" *Criminology and Public Policy* 5: 245–275.

Lin, Ann Chih. 2002. *Reform in the Making: The Implementation of Social Policy in Prison*. Princeton, NJ: Princeton University Press.

LoBuglio, Stefan F. 2007. *Gauging the Effectiveness of Jail Reentry Programs: Evidence from the Hampden County, Massachusetts Sheriff's Department Transitional Program*. Ph.D. dissertation, Harvard University.

Loury, Glenn. 2008. *Race, Incarceration, and American Values*. Cambridge: MIT Press.

Lyman, Martha A., David A. Morehouse, and M. A. Perkins. 2001. "Maximizing Accountability Through Programming: Targeting Criminogenic Factors for Successful Offender Reintegration." Ludlow, MA: Hampden County Sheriff's Department.

Lynch, James P., and William Sabol. 2004. "Assessing the Effects of Mass Incarceration on Informal Social Control in Communities." *Criminology and Public Policy* 3: 267–294.

Marvell, Thomas B., and Carlisle E. Moody. 1994. "Prison Population and Crime Reduction." *Journal of Quantitative Criminology* 10: 109–139.

National Institute of Health, National Institute of Mental Health. 2009. Suicide in the U.S.: Statistics and Prevention: A fact sheet of statistics on suicide with information on treatments and suicide prevention. http://www.nimh.nih.gov/health/publications/suicide-in-the-us-statistics-and-prevention/index.shtml.

New Jersey Commission to Review Criminal Sentencing. 2007. *Supplemental Report on New Jersey's Drug Free Zone Crimes and Proposal for Reform*. April. Available at http://www.sentencing.nj.gov/downloads/supplemental%20schoolzonereport.pdf. Accessed September 2, 2009.

Office of Juvenile Justice and Delinquency Prevention (OJJDP). 2009. OJJDP *Statistical Briefing Book*. Online. Available online at: http://ojjdp.ncjrs.gov/ojstatbb/corrections/qa08201.asp/qaDate=2006. Accessed September 23, 2009.

Petersilia, Joan. 2005. "From Cell to Society: Who Is Returning Home?" In *Prisoner Reentry and Crime in America*, eds. Jeremy Travis and Christy Visher, 15–49. New York: Cambridge University Press.

Petersilia, Joan. 2008. "California's Correctional Paradox of Excess and Deprivation." In *Crime and Justice: A Review of Research*, ed. Michael Tonry, 207–278. Chicago: University of Chicago Press.

Piehl, Anne Morrison and Stefan F. LoBuglio. 2005. "Does Supervision Matter? Pp. 105–138 in *Prisoner Reentry and Crime in America*," eds. Jeremy Travis and Christy Visher, New York: Cambridge University Press.

Randall, Michael. 2009. Tamms closed maximum security unit: Overview and ten-point plan. Submitted to Governor Pat Quinn. (September 3). Available online: http://www.idoc.state.il.us/subsections/reports/other/Tamms%20CMAX%20Overview%20and%20Ten%20Point%20Plan.pdf

Raphael, Steven, and Michael A. Stoll. 2009. "Why Are So Many Americans in Prison?" In *Do Prisons Make Us Safer? The Benefits and Costs of the Prison Boom*, eds. Steven Raphael and Michael A. Stoll, 27–72. New York: Russell Sage Foundation.

Rose, Dina R., and Todd R. Clear. 1998. "Incarceration, Social Capital, and Crime: Examining the Unintended Consequences of Incarceration." *Criminology* 36: 441–479.

Schlanger, Margo. 2006. "Civil Rights Injunctions Over Time: A Case Study of Jail and Prison Court Orders," *New York University Law Review*, 81: 550–630.

Scott-Hayward, Christine S. 2009. *The Fiscal Crisis in Corrections: Rethinking Policies and Practices.* New York: Vera Institute of Justice.

Sourcebook of Criminal Justice Statistics, Online, 2009. Available http://www. albany.edu/sourcebook [accessed September 3, 2009].

Spelman, William. 2008. "Specifying the Relationship Between Crime and Prisons." *Journal of Quantitative Criminology* 24: 149–178.

Sykes, Gresham M. 1958. *The Society of Captives: A Study of a Maximum Security Prison.* Princeton, NJ: Princeton University Press.

Tonry, Michael, and Matthew Melewski. 2008. "The Malign Effect of Drug and Crime Control Policies on Black Americans." In *Crime and Justice: A Review of Research,* ed. Michael Tonry. 1–44. Chicago: University of Chicago Press.

U.S. Department of Justice. 2009. *Probation and Parole Statistics.* Available at http://www.ojp.usdoj.gov/bjs/pandp.htm. Accessed September 8, 2009.

Useem, Bert and Anne Morrison Piehl. 2006. "Prison Buildup and Disorder." *Punishment and Society,* 8(1): 87–115.

Useem, Bert and Anne Morrison Piehl. 2008. *Prison State: The Challenge of Mass Incarceration.* New York: Oxford University Press.

Walmsley, Roy. 2008. *World Prison Population,* 8th ed. London: King's College.

Walter, E. V. 1959. "Power, Civilization, and the Psychology of Conscience." *American Political Science Review* 53(3): 641–661.

Webb, James. 2009. *Sen. Webb's National Criminal Justice Commission Act of 2009.* Fact sheet. Available at http://webb.senate.gov/email/incardocs/ FactSheeti.pdf. Accessed September 8, 2009.

West, Heather C., and William J. Sabol. 2008 (revised May 12, 2009). *Prisoners in 2007.* Washington, DC: Bureau of Justice Statistics.

Witt, Robert, and Anne Witte. 2000. "Crime, Prison, and Female Labor Supply." *Journal of Quantitative Criminology* 16 (1): 69–85.

Wright, Richard F. 2006. "Federal or State? Sorting as a Sentencing Choice." *Criminal Justice Magazine* (Summer). Available at http://www.abanet.org/ crimjust/cjmag/21-2/federalorstate.pdf.

Notes

1. Precisely the same conduct can violate both state and federal laws. In these instances, there is no single model for sorting the cases into federal or state prosecution. In some circumstances, state and federal prosecutors will decide the cases each will pursue. In others, law enforcement investigating agents may make the call. Sometimes the outcome is determined by a well-structured meeting, other times through informal phone calls. Not a great deal is known about this sorting process (Wright 2006).

2. More typically, this ratio is expressed as the number of prisoners per 100,000 resident population. Since persons below the age of 18 are not generally admitted to state or federal prisons (except in some states, where the age cutoff is 17), the dominator used here is the adult resident population 18 years and older. Prisons hold a small number of residents below the age of 18, in more recent years about 3,600 in state prison (*Sourcebook of Criminal Justice Statistic, Online,* Table 6.39.2008) This biases the prisoners/residents upward from its true value, but only slightly.

3. We are unable to distinguish violent crimes committed by adults from violent crimes committed by juveniles. In the present context, this is problematic only if in some states more juveniles commit crimes relative to adult crime.

4. The data on educational attainment collected by the CPS are not fully comparable to the Survey of Inmates data. The CPS asks a single question, "What is the highest grade of school...has completed, or the highest degree...has received?" Only years attending "regular" schools are recorded. U.S. Census Bureau, "Current Population Survey—Definitions and Explanations, Available at http://www.census.gov/population/www./cps/cpsdef.html. [September 2, 2009] The Survey of Inmates asks five questions about educational attainment, and records GED.

5. Students of social movements will not be surprised at this finding, as it is consistent with their work on popular support for a broad range of social movements—both Left and Right, from peaceful protest to terrorism. See, for example, Gamson (1990) and Krueger (2007).

6. William Spelman's (2008) recent work includes a detailed discussion of how specific modeling assumptions affect the estimates.

7. The protocol for "supermaxes" is actually less rigid than this implies, and may evolve over time. For example, in September, 2009, the director of the Illinois Department of Corrections submitted to the governor a plan for changing its sole supermax prison, Tamms CMAX, substantially away from this model (Randall 2009). New York corrections made this move several years ago.

8. For a useful discussion of the transformation of large-scale organizations, see Kanter (2008).

9. Different evaluation criteria, however, can produce different results. In New York, for example, shock incarceration (boot camp) for non-violent offenders has allowed program graduates to be released on average one year prior to the completing of their court-determined minimum period of incarceration. The costs savings for the state have been large.

10. It is common to observe that large numbers of individuals with mental illness are cycling though the prison system, in part because of effort to reduce the use of state hospitals ("deinstitutionalization"). Yet, in 2006, there remained 228 state hospitals with 49,000 beds. The reverse process also holds: state mental hospitals are increasingly used to handle individuals with serious criminal justice histories (Fisher, Geller, and Pandiani 2009).

Chapter 19

Changing Crime Rates

Richard Rosenfeld

The study of change is central to social science and ideally underlies policy interventions intended to alter the course of significant social outcomes, from educational attainment, to employment, to rates of illness and disease. In principal, crime is no different. In practice, however, research on changing crime rates remains limited in comparison with studies of individual criminal propensities and differences between the crime rates of groups or communities at a single point in time. The reasons for this imbalance are unclear, but the consequences should concern criminologists and policymakers alike.

The relative inattention to change in the study of crime fosters the impression that crime trends elude criminological theory, research methods, data, and by extension, the policies they might inform. A *New York Times* article on crime trends during the 2008–2009 recession thus concludes that crime "is a mystery with a direction all its own, one that may be beyond the reach of public policy" (Dewan 2009). I believe this is a mistaken view of crime, of the current state of knowledge regarding the factors that underlie changes in crime rates over time, and of the influence of public policy on crime rates. But it is a misimpression that should be corrected, lest the public and policymakers conclude that crime control policy informed by research evidence is no better than that based on ideology, advocacy, or the latest headlines.

Although research on crime trends remains relatively limited, it has grown in recent years and has begun to disclose, in general terms, some of the factors underlying changes in crime rates over time. In this chapter, I discuss the primary data sources and measurement issues related to the study of crime trends, present some illustrative trends in crime over the past 30–50 years, review the promising recent research, recommend steps to better explain past changes in crime rates, including those resulting from policy initiatives, and forecast future crime rates. The chapter's major conclusions are as follows:

- Major swings in U.S. crime rates have occurred over the past several decades, notably a marked increase in crime during the 1960s and

1970s and a major decline during the 1990s, but crime trends differ by type of crime and demographic subgroup.

- The 1990s crime drop was a wake-up call for criminologists to take the study of crime trends more seriously and devote greater attention to systematic crime forecasting.
- Recent research offers three guiding principles for the study of crime trends: disaggregate the trends by population subgroup, select the unit of analysis and time period according to the purposes of the research, and investigate the multiple causes of variation in crime rates.
- Current research emphasizes five explanatory factors underlying recent crime trends: demographic shifts, especially changes in the age composition of the population; the changing dynamics of illegal drug markets; growth in imprisonment; variation in the size and strategies of police forces; and changes in economic conditions.
- Future research should comprehensively assess the multiple factors underlying crime rate changes and evaluate policy impacts in multivariate, comparative frameworks using common outcome measures.
- Criminal justice planning and policy should be based on reliable projections of crime rates that combine the individual estimates from multiple forecast models.

MEASURING CRIME TRENDS

Careful and reliable measurement is essential for scientific explanation. The measurement of crime trends historically has been plagued by crude counting methods, unreliable and sometimes conflicting data sources, uneven data quality across different units of analysis, and variations in population coverage, crime definitions, and classification procedures across data sources and over time. Nonetheless, it is possible to make broad generalizations regarding the movement of crime over time, especially during the past several decades. The following discussion focuses on temporal changes in homicide rates, non-lethal violent crime rates, and property crime rates in the United States. Throughout the discussion, the implications of changing crime rates within and across the different offense categories for explanations of crime trends are considered.

Homicide Trends

Despite crude measures and differing units of analysis, several studies using historical data from multiple sources have documented very substantial homicide declines in Europe over the past several centuries (see the review in Eisner 2001). The long-term homicide drop is consistent with Norbert Elias's theory of the "civilizing process," which explains the reduction of interpersonal violence as resulting from the emergence of the modern centralized state, the diffusion of self-control in European populations, and the rise of modern individualism (Eisner 2001; Elias 1994; Gurr 1989). The absence of reliable data makes it difficult to assess homicide trends in the United States until well into the twentieth century, with the incorporation of death certificates in a national system of vital statistics and, beginning in 1931, the publication of the FBI's *Uniform Crime Reports*. Homicide rates evidently increased somewhat from 1900 to the early 1930s, peaking at a rate of 9.6 per 100,000 population in 1933, although the early-twentieth-century rise was much less steep than assumed in anecdotes about the "lawless" 1920s and uncritical inspection of the limited vital statistics available prior to the 1930s (Archer and Gartner 1984; Eckberg 1995; Lane 1997, 239–242). Homicide rates fell during the remainder of the 1930s, rose slightly at the end of World War II, and fell again at mid-century, where we begin our assessment of recent trends.

Figure 19.1 presents homicide rates from 1950 to 2007. The homicide data are from the FBI's *Uniform Crime Reports* (UCR), which compiles crime records from local police departments. Therefore, crimes that are not reported to the police are not captured in the UCR data; criminal homicide is by far the best-measured crime in the UCR because, at least in recent decades, very few homicides escape the attention of the police. A brief glance at figure 19.1 indicates that the United States has experienced two primary shifts in homicide over the past half century: a major increase beginning in the mid-1960s and a major decline during the 1990s. Any credible explanation of homicide trends should account for, or at least not contradict, these highly important changes.

But a closer look at the figure reveals other changes worthy of note as well, beginning with the fall in homicide during first half of the 1950s and the rise in homicide during the second half of the decade. The homicide rate increased by 28 percent between 1957 and 1960, resulting in over 1,000 more victims in 1960 than in 1957. Sizable shifts also occurred during the 1970s and 1980s. Such changes are clearly important, and they cannot be easily explained by measurement error in the UCR. As noted earlier, an independent monitoring system, the National Vital Statistics System (NVSS), also compiles U.S. homicide data, derived from death certificates (http://www.cdc.gov/nchs/deaths.htm). Homicide time series from the NVSS and the UCR correspond very closely (Riedel 1999). The best explanations of homicide changes over time should be able to accommodate these notable swings.

Thus far we have been concerned with change in the total homicide rate, that is, the number of homicide victims per 100,000 U.S. population, irrespective of the victim's sex, age, or race. But we cannot assume for purposes of measurement or explanation that homicide trends are similar across population groups. Group-specific homicide rates often diverge substantially from one another. A good example is the homicide

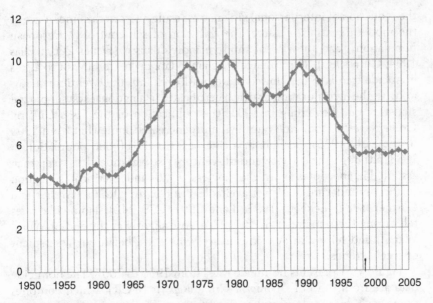

Figure 19.1. U.S. Homicides per 100,000 Population, 1950–2007
Source: Bureau of Justice Statistics (http://www.ojp.usdoj.gov/bjs/homicide/hmrt.htm) and Uniform Crime Reports (http://www.fbi.gov/ucr/cius2007/data/table_01.html). Accessed August 7, 2009.

rise that occurred during the 1980s and early 1990s in the United States. As shown in figure 19.1, the total homicide rate increased about 25 percent, from roughly 8 to 10 per 100,000 population, between 1984 and 1991. It turns out that increasing rates of youth homicide accounted for nearly all of the increase in the total homicide rate during that period (Blumstein and Rosenfeld 1998; Cook and Laub 1998). Adult homicide rates were basically flat by comparison (Rosenfeld 2006a). Moreover, the spike in homicide was concentrated among minority youth, African American males in particular (Blumstein 2006). We will take a closer look at these age and race differences later in the chapter. The important point for now is that an adequate explanation of recent homicide trends must account for, or not contradict, these group-specific patterns.

The NVSS provides homicide data by the victim's sex, age, race, and ethnicity (Hispanic, non-Hispanic). The FBI's *Supplementary Homicide Reports* (SHR) also furnish homicide data, extending back to 1976, disaggregated by victim characteristics. In addition, the SHR data contain demographic characteristics of the homicide offender, for incidents in which the offender has been identified, as well as the relationship between the victim and offender (e.g., friend, acquaintance, stranger), and the circumstance of the killing (e.g., felony, argument, drug-related).[1] Researchers have used the SHR data to investigate trends in both youth and adult homicide, and have devoted special attention to one category of adult

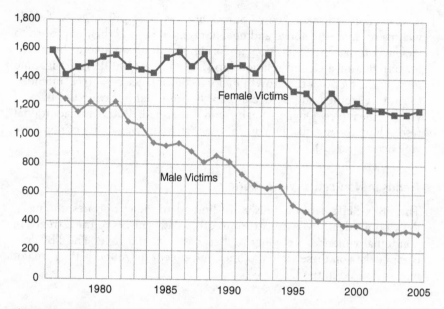

Figure 19.2. Intimate Partner Homicides, 1976–2005
Source: Supplementary Homicide Reports data from the Bureau of Justice Statistics (http://www.ojp.usdoj.gov/bjs/intimate/ipv.htm). Accessed August 11, 2009.

homicide in particular: killings involving intimate partners (Browne and Williams 1989, 1993; Dugan, Nagin, and Rosenfeld 1999; Rosenfeld 2006a).

Intimate partner homicides (killings involving spouses, ex-spouses, boyfriends, girlfriends) have declined over the past 30 years in the United States. The decrease in male victims has been particularly pronounced, as shown in figure 19.2. The number of men killed by their intimate partners declined by 75 percent between 1976 and 2005. In contrast, the number of women killed by their partners fell by 26% over the same period, and all of this decrease occurred since the early 1990s. Because intimate partner homicides are defined by the relationship between the victim and offender, part of the drop in these killings reflects changes in the relationships between men and women over the past several decades, specifically, declining marriage rates (Dugan et al. 1999; Rosenfeld 1997, 2006a).

But the decline in intimate partner killings is not restricted to married (or separated or divorced) partners (Catalano 2007). Research has linked the overall drop in intimate partner homicide to the increasing availability of resources, such as hotlines, shelters, protection orders, and legal advocacy for victims of domestic violence (Browne and Williams 1989; Dugan et al. 1999). These results help to explain the sex difference in the decline. Female-perpetrated intimate partner killings are much more likely than those perpetrated by males to be "victim-precipitated," that is, committed in response to past or present violence by male partners (Rosenfeld 1997).

Because domestic violence resources are available primarily to female victims of domestic abuse and enable them to reduce their exposure to violent intimate partners, they are a nonviolent alternative to homicide for terminating a violent relationship (Dugan et al. 1999). There is some irony in the fact that the growth in domestic violence resources, intended to protect women and their children, has resulted in saving the lives of violent men (see Dugan, Nagin, and Rosenfeld, 2003, for additional research on the unequal benefits of the increasing availability of domestic violence resources).

Trends in Non-Lethal Violent Crime

The FBI's SHR data obviously are limited to violent crimes ending in the victim's death. We must turn to other data sources to track trends in non-lethal violence, including robbery, assault, and rape. The FBI does compile data on these violent crimes but, except for robbery, they are not well measured in the UCR.

Rape

Recall that the UCR data are limited to crimes known to the police. Only 38 percent of rapes and other sexual assaults were reported to the police in 2005 (Catalano 2006). An alternative source of rape data is the National Crime Victimization Survey (NCVS), administered by the Bureau of Justice Statistics and U. S. Census Bureau. Since 1973, the NCVS has collected information on non-fatal criminal victimization from representative samples of the U.S. population age 12 and older. The NCVS data include crimes that the victim (or others) did not report to the police.[2] The NCVS has documented major declines in crime rates during the past several decades, perhaps none more dramatic than the 86 percent decrease in rape rates between the peak rate of 2.8 rapes per 1,000 population age 12 and older registered in 1979 and the trough of 0.4 in 2004 (see figure 19.3). A reduction in serious violence of this magnitude and duration demands explanation, yet it is hardly mentioned in recent reports on the U. S. crime drop (Blumstein and Wallman 2006; Rosenfeld 2004; Zimring 2006).

Aggravated Assault

Trends in non-sexual assaults also are portrayed more accurately in data from victim surveys than data reported to and filtered by police departments. When a victim reports an incident to the police, it does not become a crime and part of the UCR crime statistics until it has been "founded" as such by the police. The police first make a determination that a crime was actually committed. Then they must classify it as a crime of a particular type. There is much to recommend this filtering process for

Figure 19.3. Rape Victimizations per 1,000 Population Age 12 and Older, 1973–2005
Source: National Crime Victimization Survey data from the Bureau of Justice Statistics (http://www.
ojp.usdoj.gov/bjs/glance/rape.htm). Accessed August 12, 2009. The data shown exclude other
sexual assaults and include both male and female victims.

ensuring the validity and accuracy of crime statistics, but there is no
reason to believe that the criteria, standards, and judgments used in
founding and classifying crimes are constant across police agencies or
over time. Consider the curious case of the conflicting trends in aggravated assault derived from victim surveys and police records.

Figure 19.4 compares NCVS and UCR aggravated assault trends between 1973 and 2005. The dark lines represent the best-fitting trends
calculated for each series. The trends in the two series clearly differ. The
UCR aggravated assault rates rose through the early 1990s and fell thereafter, while the NCVS rates fell through the early 1980s, rose for a few
years, and then dropped again through 2005. Little of this difference is
explained by changes in the rate at which victims reported crimes to the
police or by the minimal differences in the way the UCR and NCVS
nominally define aggravated assaults (Rosenfeld 2007).

Although some of the divergence in the two trends may reflect the
omission of victims under the age of 12 from the NCVS data, for the most
part it appears to result from change over the period in police crime-
recording practices. Aggravated assaults are defined in both the UCR and
NCVS as assaults involving a firearm or other weapon, or those resulting
in serious injury to the victim. Absent these "aggravating" factors, assaults
are defined as simple assaults in both the NCVS and UCR. The NCVS
assault definition and classification criteria have not changed over time,
and there is little reason to suspect that police departments altered the

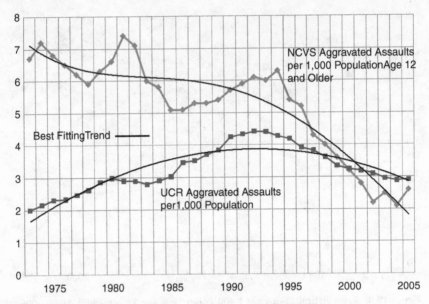

Figure 19.4. UCR and NCVS Aggravated Assault Rates, 1973–2005
Source: National Crime Victimization Survey and Uniform Crime Reports data from the Bureau of Justice Statistics (http://bjsdata.ojp.usdoj.gov/dataonline/Search/Crime/Crime.cfm and http://www.ojp.usdoj.gov/bjs/glance/tables/viortrdtab.htm). Accessed August 12, 2009. The UCR data have been converted to rates per 1,000 population. The NCVS rates are limited to victims age 12 and older.

classification of the most serious assaults, those committed with a firearm, which unambiguously qualifies an assault as aggravated. Any classification changes that occurred, therefore, should have been limited primarily to how the police categorize non-firearm assaults. If this interpretation is correct, we should expect the time trends in NCVS and UCR firearm assaults to correspond very closely and the contrasting trends in the two series to be limited to non-firearm assaults. That is precisely what prior research on the NCVS and UCR assault trends shows (Rosenfeld 2007).

What happened over the past 30 years that might explain why police departments altered the classification of assaults that do not involve a firearm? Although we must conjecture, it is reasonable to assume that the advent of 911 crime reporting and the computerization of crime records have increased the number of assaults recorded by the police. Further, police departments have come under increasing pressure by victim advocates, especially those concerned with domestic violence, to treat assault victims seriously. Again, these changes should have had the greatest effect on the way the police handle non-firearm assaults. If they responded by recording more of such incidents as aggravated assaults, that would help to explain the increase in UCR aggravated assaults over time shown in figure 19.4.

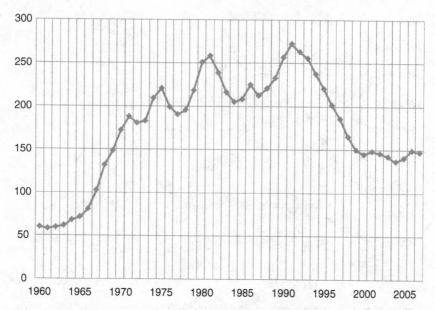

Figure 19.5. UCR Robberies per 100,000 Population, 1960–2007
Source: Uniform Crime Reports data from the Bureau of Justice Statistics (http://bjsdata.ojp.usdoj.gov/dataonline/). Accessed August 12, 2009.

Robbery

Robbery is defined in both the UCR and NCVS as theft accompanied by force or the threat of force. Unlike rape, most robberies are reported to the police (Catalano 2006). Unlike aggravated assault, changes over time in NCVS and UCR robbery rates correspond rather closely (Blumstein, Cohen, and Rosenfeld 1991). UCR robbery rates between 1960 and 2007 are displayed in figure 19.5.

Figure 19.5 prompts an immediate observation: we have seen it before. It looks a lot like the homicide trend shown in figure 19.1. Robbery and homicide rates both rose during the 1960s and 1970s, fell in the early 1980s, increased again in the late 1980s, and declined from the early 1990s through the end of the twentieth century. A very strong correlation exists between the two trends ($r = .90$), which suggests that many of the same factors underlying changes in robbery rates also may affect homicide rates. Both aggravated assault and robbery have been characterized as homicide "siblings" because most homicides result from the application or threat of force to resolve a dispute or to secure the victim's compliance with the offender's objectives (Block and Block 1991; Felson 1993). Robbery is a hybrid offense, in that it applies the forceful means of violent crime to the acquisitive ends of property crime. As a result, we should expect explanations of robbery trends to encompass factors that account for changes in property crime as well as violent crime.

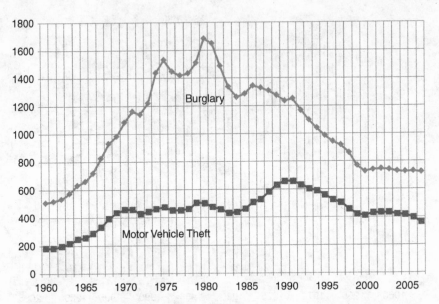

Figure 19.6. UCR Burglaries and Motor Vehicle Thefts per 100,000 Population, 1960–2007

Source: Uniform Crime Reports data from the Bureau of Justice Statistics (http://bjsdata.ojp.usdoj. gov/dataonline/). Accessed August 13, 2009.

Property Crime Trends

The three major types of property crime are burglary, larceny, and motor vehicle theft. Larceny, theft that does not involve breaking and entering or force, is an extremely heterogeneous offense category and is not well measured in the UCR. Only 32 percent of larcenies are reported to the police, compared with 56% of residential burglaries and 83% of motor vehicle thefts (Catalano 2006). Figure 19.6 displays UCR burglary and motor vehicle theft trends from 1960 to 2007.

Although a modest correspondence exists between the two series $(r = .64)$, burglary and motor vehicle theft rates clearly have not moved in unison over the past several decades. Rates of both crimes increased during the 1960s, but afterward vehicle theft rates were essentially flat through the mid-1980s and then rose again, while burglary rates peaked in 1980 and began a long decline, briefly interrupted in the mid-1980s, through the end of the century. After increasing by more than 50% during the late 1980s, vehicle theft rates also fell through the following decade. Explanations intended to explain trends in property crime should account for the differences as well as commonalities between the trends in burglary and vehicle theft. Indeed, the best explanations should account for temporal changes in both violent and property crimes. We have a long way to go to meet this admittedly exacting standard, as indicated by the following discussion of current explanations of changing crime rates.

EXPLAINING CRIME TRENDS

It is fair to say that recent changes in crime trends have caught social scientists and policymakers off guard. Criminologists did not anticipate the dramatic reduction in crime that took place during the 1990s; in fact, several prominent observers were warning of an impending crime increase well after the historic crime drop had begun (Zimring 2006). In part, this lack of foresight can be attributed to delays in the dissemination of crime data in the United States. The complete UCR and NCVS data are typically released nine months to a year after the collection period.[3] But time delays in the release of crime data are not the whole story. Criminologists lack the forecasting capabilities to anticipate changes in crime rates and the cumulative knowledge base needed to explain those changes once they occur. Even with such resources, we may not have been able to predict the coming of the 1990s crime drop, which in many respects was truly unprecedented (Zimring 2006). The important point, however, is that criminologists did not have any systematic basis to anticipate changes in crime rates, regardless of their direction or magnitude. The crime drop may have been a surprise, but not because it undermined rigorous analyses or well-developed theories of crime trends. When crime rates abruptly reversed course and began their historic plunge, the field was left speechless.

The crime drop may have served as a wake-up call to begin taking crime trends more seriously. Two editions of an edited volume on the crime drop have appeared in recent years (Blumstein and Wallman 2000, 2006), along with a thoughtful assessment of the crime drop by a leading criminologist (Zimring 2006). Several recent papers have analyzed the role of economic and other factors in the crime drop and the crime increases of preceding decades (e.g., Arvanites and Defina 2006; Gould, Weinberg, and Mustard 2002; Raphael and Winter-Ebmer 2001; Rosenfeld and Fornango 2007). Finally, the National Research Council held a workshop in 2007 resulting in a volume entitled *Understanding Crime Trends* (Goldberger and Rosenfeld 2008) that recommends greater scientific attention to changing crime rates. These are promising indications of growing interest in the study of crime trends, and they offer some basis for informed speculation about the factors underlying recent changes in crime (see Blumstein and Rosenfeld 2008). Recent research also provides several object lessons for establishing the adequacy of any explanation of crime trends. Those lessons can be summarized as follows: *disaggregation, trend duration*, and *multiple causation*.[4]

Disaggregation

Disaggregation might be termed the first principle of explaining crime trends. For any given offense category, the aggregate crime rate represents the average of the rates of separate population subgroups (defined by sex, age, race, geographic location, or other characteristics), weighted by population size. Different subgroups may exhibit quite distinct patterns or rates of temporal change in crime, as we have already seen in the comparison of male and female intimate partner homicide trends shown in figure 19.2. Blumstein (2006) emphasizes the importance of disaggregating violence trends by age and race for identifying factors responsible for the rise and fall of violence rates in the United States over the past 25 years (see, also, Cook and Laub 1998, 2002). The point is illustrated by figures 19.7a and 19.7b, which display homicide victimization rates by race and age between 1976 and 2005.

Comparing the two figures, we first notice the large race difference in homicide levels, with the black rates 10 times higher than the white rates. However, the general age-specific patterns of change in homicide appear roughly similar for blacks and whites. Among adolescents (age 14–17) and young adults (age 18–24) in both race groups, we observe a sizable homicide increase during the 1980s, followed by a decline in the 1990s, and a flattening of the rates since 2000. We also see that the homicide rates among adults in both groups generally declined over the entire 30-year period. Blumstein (1995, 2006) highlights these age differences in homicide trends to support his argument that the youth homicide rise resulted from the expansion of the crack markets beginning in the mid-1980s, as young sellers were recruited into the markets to replace older drug dealers, who faced a heightened risk of incarceration during the nation's war on drugs. As they acquired firearms for protection against rival sellers and street robbers, youth homicide rates rose during the crack era. This interpretation is consistent with evidence that youth firearm homicides account for nearly all of the homicide increase in the late 1980s (Blumstein 1995, 2006; Blumstein and Rosenfeld 1998).

Blumstein went further, however, by emphasizing the race differences in the timing and magnitude of the youth homicide epidemic. As shown in figures 19.7a and 19.7b, the homicide increase among black youth began a few years earlier and was considerably greater than among young whites. For example, the homicide rate among 18–24 year-old black males increased by 173 percent between 1984 and the peak rate in 1993, while the rate among 18–24 year-old white males rose by 53% between 1984 and the series peak in 1991. These differences, according to Blumstein (2006), reflect the greater involvement of black than white youth in the urban crack markets.

Subsequent studies by other researchers lend support to Blumstein's hypothesis linking recent trends in youth homicide to the dynamics of urban drug markets and, by extension, they underscore the importance of demographic disaggregation for explaining crime trends (e.g., Baumer, Lauritsen, Rosenfeld, and Wright 1998; Cork 1999; Messner, Deane, Anselin, and Pearson-Nelson 2005; Ousey and Lee 2002). But this research is also notable for its demographic omissions, specifically, sex and ethnicity. After a brief flurry of research during the 1980s directed at

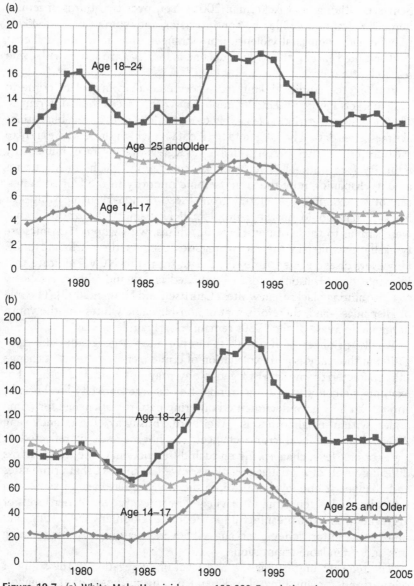

Figure 19.7. (a) White Male Homicides per 100,000 Population, by Age, 1976–2005.
(b) Black Male Homicides per 100,000 Population, by Age, 1976–2005
Source: Supplementary Homicide Reports data from the Bureau of Justice Statistics (http://www.
ojp.usdoj.gov/bjs/homicide/tables/varstab.htm). Accessed August 14, 2009.

claims that women's liberation was resulting in a rise in female violent
crime (e.g., Adler 1975; Austin 1982; Simon 1975; Steffensmeier and
Cobb 1981), studies of sex-specific violence trends have been largely
restricted to intimate partner violence (for recent exceptions, see Heimer
and Lauritsen 2009; Lauritsen, Heimer, and Lynch 2009; Steffensmeier,

Schwartz, Zhong, and Ackerman 2005). Yet, over two-thirds of female homicide victims are killed by non-intimates, and women are more likely to experience non-fatal violence from strangers than intimate partners.[5] And, as noted earlier, the striking decline in rape has attracted virtually no research attention.

Further, the studies linking race-specific changes in violent crime to drug markets ignore potentially important within-race ethnic differences. That omission is attributable largely to limitations in the available national time-series data. The UCR and SHR data on which these studies rely to measure crime rates permit reliable disaggregation by race, but not by ethnicity (see note 1). The result is that nationwide homicide trends among Hispanics, now the largest ethnic minority in the United States, cannot be examined separately from those of non-Hispanic whites or blacks. That would not be a problem if Hispanic victimization trends were similar to those of non-Hispanic whites, with whom Hispanics are typically classified in the race categories used in the UCR and SHR. However, disaggregated time-series data from the NCVS indicate that Hispanic victimization trends in aggravated assault and robbery are closer to those among blacks than whites (Lauritsen and Heimer 2009). The role of Hispanics—and, therefore, that of non-Hispanic whites—in the youth homicide increase of the 1980s remains poorly understood.[6]

Finally, prior research reveals the importance of geographic disaggregation in the analysis and explanation of crime trends. Patterns of change that characterize one level of geography may not hold at another. For example, neighborhood crime trends often diverge from city-level trends, and researchers have documented differing patterns of change for crime nodes within neighborhoods (Weisburd, Bushway, Lum, and Yang 2004). National-level crime changes are not necessarily reflected in state- or city-level changes. Given such differences in crime trends across differing levels of spatial aggregation, as well as the fact that crime rates and changes at one level are simply the weighted average of those at a lower level, it is tempting to privilege lower levels over higher levels of aggregation as more meaningful for theory development and testing, and more suitable for policy intervention. Several reasons exist for resisting this understandable temptation.

The relevant unit of analysis and level of aggregation in the study of crime trends or anything else depend on the purposes of the analyst. Researchers interested in the influence of biological or psychological factors on criminal propensities necessarily study variation in such factors within and between individuals (see chapter 3 by Moffit, Ross, and Raine in this volume). Those concerned with how parents or peers affect delinquency will be drawn to the study of families, schools, gangs, neighborhoods, or other micro environments (see chapters 5, 6, and 8 in this volume). Policy interests also help to determine the appropriate unit of analysis. For example, because corrections policy is set primarily by state legislatures, it makes sense to study U.S. imprisonment or parole trends at the state level. Because economic policy is generally promulgated at the national level, nation states are pertinent units of analysis for investigating the effects of economic conditions on crime rates.

Yet, studies of social aggregates such as states or nations are sometimes criticized on the grounds that such extremely heterogeneous social units cannot be meaningfully compared with one another. A related criticism is that units of analysis should have natural or socially meaningful boundaries, which often do not coincide with political divisions such as states, counties, or census tracts. Such criticisms apply in principle to research conducted at any level of aggregation, beyond the individual level, that contains within it even lower levels of aggregation and smaller units of analysis that are presumed to be more homogeneous and more proximate to individuals and their decisions to engage in or refrain from criminal behavior.

These criticisms are not without substantive merit, but they also reflect the persistence of methodological individualism in the study of crime, the belief that social phenomena reflect nothing more than the aggregation of individual actions. In addition, they betray a strong tradition of localism in American law enforcement and crime control (see Rosenfeld 2006b). From this perspective, each community has its own crime problems, which may or may not resemble those of others, and is responsible for finding its own solutions. An alternative view, one much closer to the study of economic or health problems, is that local crime patterns represent more or less predictable variations on a common theme. For example, epidemiologists direct attention to national trends in diabetes, even though the death rate from diabetes is twice as high in Oklahoma as in Massachusetts (http://www.statehealthfacts.org/index.jsp). Economists proceed similarly when explaining differences across communities in income and job growth. The same approach—viewing empirical variations at one level of geographic aggregation as manifestations of common explanatory factors operative at a higher level of aggregation—holds promise in the study of crime trends. Thus a recent study shows that crime trends in U. S. cities tend to follow a national-level pattern and, by implication, share common causes (McDowall and Loftin 2009).

In sum, disaggregating crime trends by sex, age, race, ethnicity, and spatial unit is important for purposes of identifying points of commonality and difference across levels of aggregation. But one level is not necessarily superior to another for informing explanations of changing crime rates, and the same explanatory factors may operate at different levels. In particular, a myopic emphasis on the local community, while understandable in the context of American political institutions, is more likely to impede than facilitate the scientific explanation of crime.

Trend Duration

Thus far we have considered crime changes that occur over greatly different time spans, from centuries, to decades, to a few years. The duration of

the trend has important implications for the plausibility of the explanations that are applied to it. Crime changes occurring over centuries, such
as the decline in European homicide rates discussed earlier, are appropriately explained with reference to social changes, such as the spread of
formal education or growth of centralized states, that unfold over long
time spans. On the other hand, such long-term changes cannot plausibly
account for year-to-year fluctuations in crime, which are better explained
by factors that also exhibit short-run temporal variation, such as cyclical
economic conditions or abrupt changes in crime control policy. The same
factor may have differing, even opposing, effects on crime trends, depending on the length of the period under examination. A good example is the
relationship between property crime and economic growth. As will be
discussed below, year-to-year increases in growth rates are associated with
decreases in property crime in the United States and other developed
nations. Even so, the long-term growth in consumption accompanying
industrialization and urbanization resulted in major increases in property
crime rates in both capitalist and socialist nations (Shelley 1981).

Explanations that account for long swings in crime are not necessarily
superior to those that apply to short-term changes. As with the appropriate level of spatial aggregation, the temporal scope of the explanation
should coincide with the theoretical or practical purposes of the analyst.
Historians generally prefer explanations that encompass time spans
measured in centuries or decades, whereas police chiefs will be more
concerned with crime changes that take place over years, months, or
weeks. Unfortunately, many studies do not delineate the time period
that is relevant to the explanatory purposes at hand, leading to indeterminacy or ambiguity in the conclusions that can be drawn. As a rule,
investigators should specify the conditions under which a given explanation is expected to hold. The relevant time period for evaluating the
explanation then becomes the period during which those conditions are
present. This kind of contextual analysis is rare in studies of crime trends
(for an exception, see Batton and Jensen 2002).

Finally, a common analytical error in quantitative crime studies is to
draw causal inferences regarding crime trends from cross-sectional research. It is an elementary methodological principle, but one that bears
repeating: Snapshot cross sections are useful for identifying associations
between crime and other conditions at a single point in time, but they
cannot be used to support claims that changes in crime are brought about
by—or are even related to—changes in putative causal factors. For well-
known philosophical and methodological reasons, causal claims of any
sort are notoriously difficult to substantiate in non-experimental research.
In the study of an inherently dynamic phenomenon such as crime, findings from cross-sectional research often cannot be replicated in longitudinal studies involving the same factors. A good example is the relationship
between crime and unemployment, which is quite robust in cross-
sectional studies but less consistent in analyses of change over time

(Pratt and Cullen 2005). Conflicting findings from cross-sectional and longitudinal research often reflect the weakness of cross-sectional designs in detecting spurious associations, but whatever their source, they are an important reminder that the study of change—in crime or anything else—requires observations that vary over time.

Multiple Causation

The press and policymakers often ask social scientists to explain "the cause" of major social changes, such as the 1990s crime drop, as if a single, overriding cause existed. It is not a silly question. The search for unitary explanations of important or dramatic social transformations is quite understandable, even laudable, on scientific grounds. Science craves both generality and simplicity of explanation: The best theories explain the most facts with the fewest propositions (Black 1995). We are a long way from such theorizing about crime trends. The most thoughtful appraisals of the 1990s crime decline, for example, identify several factors underlying the crime drop (Blumstein and Wallman 2006; Levitt 2004; Zimring 2006). And none of these factors or accompanying explanations amounts to a "theory" of the crime drop, although such theories have been developed to explain other crime trends (e.g., Cohen and Felson 1979; Eisner 2001; LaFree 1998). In this discussion, I direct attention to five factors that prior research has linked to crime rate changes in the United States over the past several decades: demographic change, specifically the changing age composition of the population; the expansion and contraction of the urban crack markets; growth in imprisonment; changes in police size and strategies; and changing economic conditions. These factors do not exhaust the explanations, some widely publicized,[7] of recent crime changes, but they have received the greatest attention in the research literature.

Demographic Change

The crime increase of the 1960s and 1970s and the decrease during the early 1980s have been attributed, in part, to alterations in the age structure of the population (Blumstein and Rosenfeld 2008; Fox 2006; Steffensmeier and Harer 1991). As the baby-boom cohorts born in the late 1940s and 1950s reached adolescence beginning in the mid-1960s, crime rates rose for more than a decade, peaked around 1980, and then declined over the next several years, as the baby-boom cohorts were entering adulthood. (The largest baby-boom cohort was born in 1957.) This pattern corresponds with the well-known "age-crime curve" in criminology, which depicts increasing involvement in crime as children move into adolescence and decreasing involvement as they move out (Hirschi and Gottfredson 1983). A related explanation attributes the crime rise *within* the youthful age cohorts during the 1960s and 1970s to increases in the relative size of those cohorts as crowded classrooms and labor markets weakened social controls, diminished economic opportunities, and stimulated the emergence of an autonomous "youth culture" among adolescents and young adults (Easterlin 1987). Finally, a widely publicized account attributes the 1990s decline in youth violence to selective attrition in birth cohorts reaching adolescence and young adulthood in the early 1990s, resulting from abortion policy changes in the 1970s (Donahue and Levitt 2001; see Foote and Goetz 2008, Joyce 2009, and Zimring 2006 for thoughtful appraisals).

Drug Markets

Although growth in the youthful segment of the population undoubtedly contributed to the crime rise of the 1960s and 1970s, it cannot explain the marked increase in youth violence during the late 1980s, when the relative size of the adolescent and young adult cohorts was not growing. As noted earlier, the leading explanation of the rise in youth violence is Blumstein's hypothesis linking the urban crack markets to increases in firearm violence during that period, especially among young minority males. As the crack markets waned during the early 1990s (e.g., Golub and Johnson 1997), violent crime rates began their historic plunge.

Imprisonment

Changing crime rates also have been linked to the dramatic growth in imprisonment in the United States over the past several decades. Prison populations nearly quadrupled in size between 1980 and 2007. The evidence for the crime-reduction effects of imprisonment growth is quite strong (e.g., Levitt 1996, 2002, 2004; Marvell and Moody 1994; Spelman 2006). But the effects of imprisonment on crime are complex. Recent research indicates that the crime-reductions associated with imprisonment diminish as the scale of imprisonment increases (Liedka, Piehl, and Useem 2006; chapter 18 by Piehl and Useem in this volume), vary substantially across states (DeFina and Arvanites 2002), and differ by crime type (Rosenfeld 2009; Rosenfeld and Fornango 2007).

Estimates of the effect of imprisonment growth on the 1990s crime drop also vary across studies. Spelman (2006) concludes that imprisonment growth accounted for about one-quarter of the crime drop. Rosenfeld and Fornango (2007) find similar prison impacts for robbery, burglary, and motor vehicle theft, but no impact on the decline in larceny rates during the 1990s. On the other hand, Western (2006) maintains that growth in imprisonment accounted for no more than 10 percent of the crime drop. Resolving these discrepancies between studies regarding the contribution of imprisonment to the crime drop is an important task for future research. But taken together, the research evidence indicates that imprisonment growth in the United States has resulted in nontrivial crime reductions, albeit not everywhere or for all types of crime.

Policing

Evidence on the effects of policing on recent crime trends is less consistent across studies than the evidence pertaining to imprisonment. The research should be divided between two types of studies: those that estimate the effects of police *size* on crime rates and those that estimate the effects on crime of police *activity*. The first type of investigation asks whether adding officers to a police agency lowers the crime rate. The second asks whether changes in deployment practice and strategy affect the crime rate. Early studies found little impact of marginal increases in police strength on crime rates, but methodological weaknesses in this research prevent strong conclusions. More recent research that addresses the problem of reverse causation in the police-crime relationship has found that adding police officers does reduce crime (Levitt 1997); however, this research has been criticized for failing to account for the confounding effects on crime of police size and police activity (Skogan and Frydl 2004).

So-called "hot spots" policing—focused patrols in geographic areas with high or rising crime rates—has been shown to be effective in reducing crime and disorder, with minimal displacement to other areas (see chapter 20 by Sherman in this volume; Skogan and Frydl 2004). The impact of hot spots and other promising enforcement strategies on general crime trends, however, remains unknown (Eck and Maguire 2006).

A somewhat different enforcement strategy, aggressive order maintenance or "broken windows" policing, has been evaluated for its impact on New York City's dramatic crime drop during the 1990s. New York City implemented the order-maintenance strategy in the early 1990s as part of a package of policing reforms initiated by then Police Commissioner William Bratton. Order-maintenance policing, which entails vigorous enforcement of minor crimes and disorder to avert more serious crime, is typically measured by arrest rates for misdemeanors, although one study combines misdemeanor arrests with those for city ordinance violations (Rosenfeld, Fornango, and Rengifo 2007). The results of precinct-level research that investigates the effects of order-maintenance policing on New York's crime drop are decidedly mixed. One study finds that all of the crime drop is attributable to increases in misdemeanor arrests during the 1990s (Kelling and Sousa 2001). Another finds that changes in misdemeanor arrests had no effect on crime rates (Harcourt and Ludwig 2006). Two additional studies find a statistically significant but modest impact of order maintenance policing on reductions in violent crimes; both conclude that New York would have experienced a sizable crime decline without the change in enforcement strategy (Messner et al. 2007; Rosenfeld, Fornango, and Rengifo 2007).

Clearly, additional research is needed to determine the impact of order-maintenance policing on New York City's crime drop, as well as the effectiveness of similar strategies in other cities (for an excellent review of prior research, see Weisburd and Eck 2004). That research should seek to untangle the effects of police size and police activity on crime trends. A point of departure is a finding from the Rosenfeld and Fornango (2007) study, indicating that changes in the number of police per capita in New York City precincts had an indirect effect on both homicide and robbery rates through misdemeanor and ordinance violation arrests. That is, increases in police size produced more order-maintenance arrests which, in turn, reduced homicide and robbery rates. Future research on the relationship between policing and crime should incorporate measures of both police size and activity.

Economic Change

Popular opinion has long held that crime rates increase as economic conditions worsen. The logic of the popular view is straightforward: As unemployment rises and incomes fall, people will be more likely to pursue illegitimate means to obtain economic goals, and property crime rates will increase. Related views attribute increases in violent crime to adverse economic conditions that heighten goal frustration, disrupt families and communities, and weaken stakes in conformity. These popular accounts have been distilled in economic and sociological theories that link crime to economic cost-benefit calculations (Becker 1968; Ehrlich 1973), the cultural emphasis on economic success (Merton 1938; Messner and Rosenfeld 2007), and social disorganization in disadvantaged communities (Shaw and McKay 1969; Wilson 1987).

Popular opinion and its more refined social science counterpart have not fared well in the research literature on crime trends—but that may be changing. Studies of the impact of economic conditions, typically measured by the unemployment rate, on crime trends have produced mixed results, with some research showing the expected positive relationship between increases in unemployment and crime, other investigations showing just the opposite, and many studies finding no relationship (see chapter 7 by Bushway in this volume). One reason for the disparate results of prior research is the use of the unemployment rate to measure economic effects on crime rates. The unemployment rate is a narrow measure of economic conditions (e.g., labor force dropouts are excluded) and a lagging indicator of economic change. Recent research that employs broader measures, such as per capita growth rates, and leading economic indicators, such as consumer sentiment, tells a more consistent story about the influence of the economy on crime trends: Crime rates tend to rise during economic downturns and fall during recoveries (Arvanites and Defina 2006; Rosenfeld and Fornango 2007). In addition, recent studies indicate that the economic expansion during the 1990s explains a sizable fraction of the drop in property crime, in both the United States and Europe (Rosenfeld and Messner 2009) and in violent crime, although the effect on violent crime appears to be largely indirect through property crime (Rosenfeld 2009).

While promising, the recent research on the economy and crime remains sparse and requires replication using demographically disaggregated measures of crime, additional covariates, including indicators of changing drug markets, and larger and more diverse samples of cities and nations. It is too early to tell whether the relationship between crime and economic change is robust or whether the research literature will revert to form and conclude that the connection is illusive.

THE FUTURE

Even though social scientists have long been intrigued by temporal change in crime rates, systematic research on crime trends remains in its infancy. Significant progress on two fronts is necessary to strengthen the science base of research on crime trends and its relevance to policymakers and criminal justice practitioners: (1) enhancing explanatory research and policy evaluation; and (2) improving forecasting methods and models. Both will require substantial and ongoing investments from agencies charged with supporting criminal justice research.

Research and Evaluation

Future research on the factors underlying changes in crime over time should comprehensively assess the multiple explanations of changing crime rates, particularly those that have sought to account for marked reversals or "turning points" in crime trends, such as the dramatic crime drop of the 1990s (see Blumstein and Rosenfeld 2008). A model for such research is Baumer's (2008) longitudinal study of city crime rates in the United States. Baumer's study is by far the most comprehensive assessment to date of local change in crime rates, with estimates of the effects of 24 explanatory variables on burglary, motor vehicle theft, robbery, and homicide rates, the latter disaggregated by firearm use and victim age. He reports separate estimates of the relative impact of the explanatory variables for the period 1984–1992, when crime rates were generally rising, and 1993–2000, the period of the crime drop. His results indicate that changes in drug markets, imprisonment, and the relative size of the 15–24-year-old age cohort had sizable effects on crime rates between the mid-1980s and early 1990s, although the effects vary somewhat across different types of crime. He also found notable effects for demographic variables rarely examined in crime trends research, specifically, the proportion of adolescents born to teen mothers and the proportion of households occupied by unmarried cohabiting couples.

Importantly, Baumer's (2008) analysis suggests that the factors under-lying the 1990s crime drop differ somewhat from those accounting for the preceding crime increase (see, also, Cook and Laub 2002). For example, while drug market changes contributed to increasing crime rates, particu-larly firearm and youth homicide, during the earlier period, they had little impact on the crime drop within cities. In contrast, improving economic conditions, measured by unemployment and wage rates, helped to drive down crime rates during the 1990s, but played only a modest role at best in the crime rise of the previous decade. Changes in the relative size of youth cohorts were of little importance in the crime drop, but growth in adult cohorts contributed significantly to falling crime rates in the 1990s. The lagged measure of teen births and the imprisonment rate had impor-tant effects on crime rates during both the crime drop and the preceding increase.

Baumer's study also provides an analytical framework for assessing the impact of crime control policies and strategies across a large sample of jurisdictions. The effectiveness of criminal justice policies is usually eval-uated in single-case research designs, often using ad hoc or special purpose outcome measures, which greatly limits the generalizability of results (Rosenfeld 2006b; Rosenfeld, Fornango, and Baumer 2005). In principle, Baumer's multivariate panel framework allows for assessments of policy effects on the same outcome indicators across local contexts that vary in size, socioeconomic characteristics, and (prior) levels of crime. He illus-trates the utility of the framework for evaluating enforcement policy in an analysis of the effects of order maintenance policing, measured by arrest rates for minor offending, on rates of serious crime. The results reveal little to no relationship between arrests for minor crime and city-level trends in serious crime.

Baumer is careful to point to the limitations of his analysis. His analysis is confined to crime trends within cities; whether the results hold at other levels of aggregation (e.g., neighborhoods or states) is uncertain. He did not adjust his data for possible nonstationarity in the city crime trends or predictors, and he conducted no formal assessments of endogeneity in his models.[8] Perhaps most importantly, his forecasts of future crime rates, in his words, "do not appear to be very good—one could do better in predicting the direction of changes in these crimes by flipping a coin" (Baumer 2008, 168). He recommends greater attention to the methodo-logical challenges associated with explaining past crime rates and forecasting future changes. A particularly important task is to improve forecasting methods and models.

Forecasting

If the central objective of science is prediction, criminology remains in a pre-scientific state. Reliable forecasting of the future values of a time series is essential for program planning and policy evaluation in economics (e.g., to gauge future consumer spending, unemployment, industrial output) and health care (e.g., to assess the need for hospital beds, emergency care, inoculations). By comparison, reliable forecasts of crime rates—the demand component of the criminal justice system—are rarely used to guide criminal justice planning.

The key word is *reliable* forecasting, not to be confused with forecast *accuracy*. A reliable forecast has known properties, is repeatable, and most importantly, is subject to systematic modification. The ultimate goal of any forecasting effort is accurate prediction of future conditions, ideally with a high degree of precision.[9] Reliability is a means to that end. Between the two, forecast reliability is more important than forecast accuracy. A good guess is accurate but conveys little information about the relationship between past and future conditions. A reliable forecast may be inaccurate or imprecise but, in principle, leads to modifications of the underlying forecast model and improves subsequent forecasts.

From this perspective, the problem with the predictions of an impending wave of youth violence just as the historic crime drop began in the early 1990s was not their inaccuracy but their unreliability. The errors in prediction could not be used to revise the forecast model because there was no forecast model, or none whose features were systematically knowable, repeatable, and hence modifiable (cf. Blumstein and Rosenfeld 2008; Zimring 2006, 21–24). As noted earlier, the 1990s crime drop may have served as a wake-up call to criminologists to take the study of crime trends more seriously. It should also stimulate interest in the reliable forecasting of future crime rates.

Criminologists can take advantage of recent developments in economic forecasting for developing more reliable crime forecasts.[10] The principles of *model uncertainty* and *model instability* guide current econometric thinking about forecasting in realistic environments. The uncertainty principle reflects the difficulties in identifying, from among the multiple causal influences on crime rates, the variables that are most useful for forecasting and specifying a single, parsimonious model that incorporates all of the relevant variables. Model instability reflects the fact that model specification will change over time or across investigators. Given that any single model is likely to be uncertain or unstable, it makes sense to estimate multiple models and combine the resulting forecast estimates. This also helps to avoid the problem of "over-fitting" forecasts to the data generating the model, which may produce poor out-of-sample projections. Combinations of individual forecasts have been shown to be more accurate than the individual forecasts themselves (Bates and Granger 1969) and recent research demonstrates that combination forecasts improve forecasts of macroeconomic variables (Rapach and Strauss 2008).

As an example, consider the various factors discussed above that researchers have shown to be associated with recent crime rate changes. Suppose we want to forecast future crime rates based on these factors.

The principle of model uncertainty suggests that we should estimate many different models containing differing (but plausible) measurements and combinations of variables. The principle of model instability implies that we base our forecast models on data that cover time periods of varying length (e.g., 10 years, 20 years, 50 years). To avoid over-fitting, we should forecast crime rates for time periods not included in the data used to generate the models. Finally, we should combine the individual forecasts obtained from the multiple models, on the assumption that these combination forecasts will minimize the errors associated with any single forecast taken alone.

Crime rate forecasting also can be improved by recognizing the practical needs of criminal justice planners and policymakers. Practitioners rarely need to know next year's or quarter's exact crime rate. More often, they plan and allocate resources on the basis of the expected change in crime. Consequently, *density forecasts* are likely to be more useful for most crime forecast users than *point forecasts*. Density forecasts provide estimates of the range of projected outcomes and their associated probabilities of occurrence. Given the primitive state of crime forecasting, just outperforming Baumer's (2008) coin-toss test for predicting crime increases or decreases may represent a significant improvement over current practice. Here, too, recent developments in the econometrics literature on combination density forecasting (i.e., combining several different density forecasts; Hall and Mitchell 2007) should be of interest to researchers concerned with enhancing the reliability and utility of crime rate forecasts.

If the explanation of past crime trends remains limited and crime forecasting capabilities are primitive, what are the grounds for optimism about the future of research on changing crime rates? It may be more difficult to accurately forecast trends in criminology than trends in crime. But there are some hopeful signs of progress. Accumulating research evidence has begun to disclose some of the factors underlying recent crime trends. Advances in econometric forecasting methods hold promise for improving the reliability of crime forecasts. Recent National Research Council reports contain specific recommendations for strengthening the science base and policy relevance of data and research on crime rates (Goldberger and Rosenfeld 2008; Groves and Cork 2009). The continuing challenge is to nurture and capitalize on these developments by increasing the nation's investment in research on changing crime rates.

References

Adler, Freda. 1975. *Sisters in Crime*. New York: McGraw-Hill.

Archer, Dane, and Rosemary Gartner. 1984. *Violence and Crime in Cross-National Perspective*. New Haven, CT: Yale University Press.

Arvanites, Thomas M., and Robert H. Defina. 2006. "Business Cycles and Street Crime." *Criminology* 44: 139–164.

Austin, Roy L. 1982. "Women's Liberation and Increases in Minor, Major, and Occupational Offenses." *Criminology* 20: 407–430.

Bates, J. M., and C. W. J. Granger. 1969. "The Combination of Forecasts." *Operational Research Quarterly* 20: 451–468.

Batton, Candice, and Gary F. Jensen. 2002. "Decommodification and Homicide Rates in the Twentieth Century United States." *Homicide Studies* 6: 6–38.

Baumer, Eric P. 2008. "An Empirical Assessment of the Contemporary Crime Trends Puzzle: A Modest Step Toward a More Comprehensive Research Agenda." In *Understanding Crime Trends*, eds. Arthur S. Goldberger and Richard Rosenfeld. Washington, DC: National Academies Press.

Baumer, Eric P., Janet L. Lauritsen, Richard Rosenfeld, and Richard Wright. 1998. "The Influence of Crack Cocaine on Robbery, Burglary, and Homicide Rates: A Cross-City, Longitudinal Analysis." *Journal of Research in Crime and Delinquency* 35: 316–340.

Becker, Gary. 1968. "Crime and Punishment: An Economic Approach." *Journal of Political Economy* 73: 169–217.

Black, Donald. 1995. "The Epistemology of Pure Sociology." *Law and Society Review* 21: 563–584.

Block, Carolyn Rebecca, and Richard Block. 1991. "Beginning with Wolfgang: An Agenda for Homicide Research." *Journal of Crime and Justice* 14: 31–70.

Blumstein, Alfred. 2006. "Disaggregating the Violence Trends." In *The Crime Drop in America*, rev. ed., eds. Alfred Blumstein and Joel Wallman. New York: Cambridge University Press.

Blumstein, Alfred, Jacqueline Cohen, and Richard Rosenfeld. 1991. "Trend and Deviation in Crime Rates: A Comparison of UCR and NCS Data for Robbery and Burglary." *Criminology* 29: 237–263.

Blumstein, Alfred, and Richard Rosenfeld. 1998. "Explaining Recent Trends in US Homicide Rates." *Journal of Criminal Law and Criminology* 88: 1175–1216.

Blumstein, Alfred, and Richard Rosenfeld. 2008. "Factors Contributing to U. S. Crime Trends." In *Understanding Crime Trends*, eds. Arthur S. Goldberger and Richard Rosenfeld. Washington, DC: National Academies Press.

Blumstein, Alfred, and Joel Wallman, eds. 2000. *The Crime Drop in America*. New York: Cambridge University Press. [Yes, OK—RR]Blumstein, Alfred, and Joel Wallman, eds. 2006. *The Crime Drop in America*, rev. ed. New York: Cambridge University Press.

Browne, Angela, and Kirk R. Williams. 1989. "Exploring the Effect of Resource Availability and the Likelihood of Female-Perpetrated Homicides." *Law and Society Review* 23: 75- [75-94—RR].

Browne, Angela, and Kirk R. Williams. "Gender, Intimacy, and Lethal Violence: Trends from 1976 through 1987." *Gender and Society* 7: 78–98.

Catalano, Shannan M. 2006. *Criminal Victimization in the United States, 2005*. Washington, DC: U.S. Department of Justice.

Catalano, Shannan M. 2007. *Intimate Partner Violence in the United States*. Washington, DC: US Department of Justice. Available at http://www.ojp.usdoj.gov/bjs/intimate/ipv.htm. Accessed August 12, 2009.

Cohen, Lawrence E., and Marcus Felson. 1979. "Social Change and Crime Rate Trends: A Routine Activities Approach." *American Sociological Review* 44: 588–608.

Cook, Philip J., and John H. Laub. 1998. "The Unprecedented Epidemic in Youth Violence." *Crime and Justice* 24: 27–64.

Cook, Philip J., and John H. Laub. 2002. "After the Epidemic: Recent Trends in Youth Violence in the United States." *Crime and Justice* 29: 1–37.

Cork, Daniel. 1999. "Examining Space-Time Interaction in City-Level Homicide Data: Crack Markets and the Diffusion of Guns among Youth." *Journal of Quantitative Criminology* 15: 379–406.

DeFina, Robert H., and Thomas M. Arvanites. 2002. "The Weak Effect of Imprisonment on Crime: 1971–1992." *Social Science Quarterly* 83: 635–653.

Dewan, Shaila. 2009. "The Real Murder Mystery? It's the Low Crime Rate." *New York Times* (August 2): Week in Review, 4.

Donohue, John J., III, and Steven D. Levitt. 2001. "The Impact of Legalized Abortion on Crime." *Quarterly Journal of Economics* 116: 379–420. [OK—RR]

Dugan, Laura, Daniel Nagin, and Richard Rosenfeld. 1999. "Explaining the Decline in Intimate Partner Homicide: The Effects of Changing Domesticity, Women's Status, and Domestic Violence Resources." *Homicide Studies* 3: 187–214.

Dugan, Laura, Daniel Nagin, and Richard Rosenfeld. 2003. "Exposure Reduction or Retaliation? The Effects of Domestic Violence Resources on Intimate Partner Homicide." *Law and Society Review* 37: 169–198.

Easterlin, Richard A. 1987. *Birth and Fortune*. Chicago: University of Chicago Press.

Eck, John E., and Edward R. Maguire. 2006. "Have Changes in Policing Reduced Violent Crime? An Assessment of the Evidence." In *The Crime Drop in America*, rev. ed., eds. Alfred Blumstein and Joel Wallman. New York: Cambridge University Press.

Eckberg, Douglas Lee. 1995. "Estimates of Early Twentieth-Century U. S. Homicide Rates: An Econometric Forecasting Approach." *Demography* 32: 1–16.

Ehrlich, Isaac. 1973. "Participation in Illegitimate Activities: A Theoretical and Empirical Investigation." *Journal of Political Economy* 81: 521–565.

Eisner, Manuel. 2001. "Modernization, Self-Control, and Lethal Violence: The Long-Term Dynamics of European Homicide Rates in Theoretical Perspective." *British Journal of Criminology* 41: 618–638.

Elias, Norbert. 1994. *The Civilizing Process*. New York: Blackwell.

Felson, Richard B. 1993. "Predatory and Dispute-Related Violence: A Social Interactionist Approach." In *Routine Activity and Rational Choice: Advances in Criminological Theory*, eds. Ronald V. Clarke and Marcus Felson, Vol. 5. New Brunswick, NJ: Transaction.

Foote, Christopher L., and Christopher F. Goetz. 2008. "The Impact of Legalized Abortion on Crime: Comment." *Quarterly Journal of Economics* 123: 407–423.

Fox, James Alan. 2006. "Demographics and U.S. Homicide." In *The Crime Drop in America*, rev. ed., eds. Alfred Blumstein and Joel Wallman New York: Cambridge University Press.

Goldberger, Arthur S., and Richard Rosenfeld, eds. 2008. *Understanding Crime Trends*. Washington, DC: National Academies Press.

Gollub, Andrew, and Bruce D. Johnson. 1997. *Crack's Decline: Some Surprises across U.S. Cities*. Washington, DC: National Institute of Justice.

Gould, Eric D., Bruce A. Weinberg, and David B. Mustard. 2002. "Crime Rates and Local Labor Market Opportunities in the United States: 1979–1997." *Review of Economics and Statistics* 84: 45–61.

Groves, Robert M., and Daniel L. Cork. 2009. *Ensuring the Quality, Credibility, and Relevance of U.S. Justice Statistics*. Washington, DC: National Academies Press.

Gurr, Ted Robert. 1989. "Historical Trends in Violent Crime: Europe and the United States." In *Violence in America*, Vol. 1: *The History of Crime*, ed. Ted Robert Gurr. Newbury Park, CA: Sage.

Hall, S. G., and J. Mitchell. 2007. "Combining Density Forecasts." *International Journal of Forecasting* 23: 1–13.

Harcourt, Bernard E., and Jens Ludwig. 2006. "Broken Windows: New Evidence from New York City and a Five-City Social Experiment." *University of Chicago Law Review* 73: 271–320.

Heimer, Karen, and Janet L. Lauritsen. 2009. "Gender and Violence in the United States: Trends in Offending and Victimization." In *Understanding Crime Trends*, eds. Arthur S. Goldberger and Richard Rosenfeld. Washington, DC: National Academies Press.

Hirschi, Travis, and Michael Gottfredson. 1983. "Age and the Explanation of Crime." *American Journal of Sociology* 89: 552–584.

Joyce, Ted. 2009. "A Simple Test of Abortion and Crime." *Review of Economics and Statistics* 91: 112–123.

Kelling, George, and William H. Sousa, Jr. 2001. *Do Police Matter? An Analysis of the Impact of New York City's Police Reforms*. Manhattan Institute Civic Report. Available at http://www.manhattan-institute.org/cr_22.pdf.

LaFree, Gary. 1998. *Losing Legitimacy: Street Crime and the Decline of Social Institutions in America*. Boulder, CO: Westview.

Lane, Roger. 1997. *Murder in America: A History*. Columbus: Ohio State University Press.

Lauritsen, Janet L., and Karen Heimer. 2009. "Long-term Trends in Exposure to Serious Violent Crime by Race, Ethnicity, and Gender." Paper presented at the annual meetings of the American Association for the Advancement of Science, Chicago, IL (February).

Lauritsen, Janet L., Karen Heimer, and James P. Lynch. 2009. "Trends in the Gender Gap in Violent Offending: New Evidence from the National Crime Victimization Survey." *Criminology* 47: 361–399.

Levitt, Steven D. 1996. "The Effect of Prison Population Size on Crime Rates: Evidence from Prison Overcrowding Litigation." *Quarterly Journal of Economics* 111: 319–352.

Levitt, Steven D. 1997. "Using Electoral Cycles in Police Hiring to Estimate the Effect of Police on Crime." *American Economic Review* 87: 270–290.

Levitt, Steven D. 1999. "The Limited Role of Changing Age Structure in Explaining Aggregate Crime Rates." *Criminology* 37: 581–598.

Levitt, Steven D. 2002. "Deterrence." In *Crime: Public Policies for Crime Control*, eds. James Q. Wilson and Joan Petersilia. Oakland, CA.: ICS Press.

Levitt, Steven D. 2004. "Understanding Why Crime Fell in the 1990s: Four Factors That Explain the Decline and Six That Do Not." *Journal of Economic Perspectives* 18: 163–190.

Liedka, Raymond V., Anne Morrison Piehl, and Bert Useem. 2006. "The Crime-Control Effect of Incarceration: Does Scale Matter?" *Criminology and Public Policy* 5: 245–276.

Marvell, Thomas B., and Carlisle E. Moody. 1994. "Prison Population and Crime Reduction." *Journal of Quantitative Criminology* 10: 109–139.

McDowall, David, and Colin Loftin. 2009. "Do US City Crime Rates Follow a National Trend? The Influence of Nationwide Conditions on Local Crime Patterns." *Journal of Quantitative Criminology* 25: 307–324.

Merton, Robert K. 1938. "Social Structure and Anomie." *American Sociological Review* 3: 672–682.

Messner, Steven F., and Richard Rosenfeld. 2007. *Crime and the American Dream*. 4th ed. Belmont, CA: Wadsworth.

Messner, Steven F., Glenn D. Deane, Luc Anselin, and Benjamin Pearson-Nelson. 2005. "Locating the Vanguard in Rising and Falling Homicide Rates across U. S. cities." *Criminology*: 661–696.

Messner, Steven F., Sandro Galea, Kenneth J. Tardiff, Melissa Tracy, Angela Bucciarelli, Tinka Markham Piper, Victoria Frye, and David Vlahov. 2007. "Policing, Drugs, and the Homicide Decline in New York City in the 1990s." *Criminology* 45: 385–413.

Nevin, R. 2000. "How Lead Exposure Relates to Temporal Changes in IQ, Violent Crime, and Unwed Pregnancy." *Environmental Research* 83: 1–22.

Ousey, Graham C., and Matthew R. Lee. 2002. "Examing the Conditional Nature of the Illicit Drug Market-Homicide Relationship: A Partial Test of the Theory of Contingent Causation." *Criminology* 40: 73–102.

Pratt, Travis C., and Francis T. Cullen. 2005. "Assessing Macro-Level Predictors and Theories of Crime: A Meta-Analysis." *Crime and Justice* 32: 373–450.

Rapach, D. E., and J. K. Strauss. 2008. "Forecasting U.S. Employment Growth Using Forecast Combining Methods." *Journal of Forecasting* 27: 75–93.

Raphael, Steven, and Rudolf Winter-Ebmer. 2001. "Identifying The Effect of Unemployment on Crime." *Journal of Law and Economics* 44: 259–283.

Reyes, Jessica Wolpaw. 2007. *Environmental Policy as Social Policy? The Impact of Childhood Lead Exposure on Crime*. NBER Working Paper 13097. Available at http://www.nber.org/papers/w13097.

Riedel, Marc. 1999. "Sources of Homicide Data: A Review and Comparison." In *Homicide: A Sourcebook of Social Research*, M. Dwayne Smith and Margaret A. Zahn. Thousand Oaks, CA: Sage.

Rosenfeld, Richard. 1997. "Changing Relationships Between Men And Women: A Note on the Decline in Intimate Partner Homicide." *Homicide Studies* 1: 72–83.

Rosenfeld, Richard. 2004. "The Case of the Unsolved Crime Decline." *Scientific American* (February): 82–89.

Rosenfeld, Richard. 2006a. "Patterns in Adult Homicide: 1980–1995." In *The Crime Drop in America*, rev. ed., eds. Alfred Blumstein and Joel Wallman. New York: Cambridge University Press.

Rosenfeld, Richard. 2006b. "Connecting the Dots: Crime Rates and Criminal Justice Evaluation Research." *Journal of Experimental Criminology* 2: 309–319.

Rosenfeld, Richard. 2007. "Explaining the Divergence Between UCR and NCVS Aggravated Assault Trends." In *Understanding Crime Statistics: Revisiting the Divergence of the NCVS and the UCR*, eds. James P. Lynch and Lynn A. Addington. New York: Cambridge University Press.

Rosenfeld, Richard. 2009. "Crime is the Problem: Homicide, Acquisitive Crime, and Economic Conditions." *Journal of Quantitative Criminology* 25: 287–306.

Rosenfeld, Richard, and Robert Fornango. 2007. "The Impact of Economic Conditions on Robbery and Property Crime: The Role of Consumer Sentiment." *Criminology* 45: 735–769.

Rosenfeld, Richard, Robert Fornango, and Andres Rengifo. 2007. "The Impact of Order-Maintenance Policing on New York City Robbery and Homicide Rates: 1988–2001." *Criminology* 45: 355–383.

Rosenfeld, Richard, Robert Fornango, and Eric Baumer. 2005. "Did *Ceasefire, Compstat,* and *Exile* Reduce Homicide?" *Criminology and Public Policy* 4: 419–450.

Rosenfeld, Richard, and Arthur S. Goldberger. 2008. "Introduction." In *Understanding Crime Trends,* eds. Arthur S. Goldberger and Richard Rosenfeld. Washington, DC: National Academies Press.

Rosenfeld, Richard, and Steven F. Messner. 2009. "The Crime Drop in Comparative Perspective: The Impact of the Economy and Imprisonment on American and European Burglary Rates." *British Journal of Sociology* 60: 445–471.

Shaw, Clifford R., and Henry D. McKay. 1969. *Juvenile Delinquency in Urban Areas,* rev. ed. Chicago: University of Chicago Press.

Shelley, Louise I. 1981. *Crime and Modernization: The Impact of Industrialization and Urbanization on Crime.* Carbondale, IL: Southern Illinois University Press.

Simon, Rita James. 1975. *Women and Crime.* Lexington, MA: Lexington Books.

Skogan, Wesley, and Kathleen Frydl, eds. 2004. *Fairness and Effectiveness in Policing: The Evidence.* Washington, DC: National Academies Press.

Spelman, William. 2006. "The Limited Importance of Prison Expansion." In *The Crime Drop in America,* rev. ed., eds. Alfred Blumstein and Joel Wallman. New York: Cambridge University Press.

Steffensmeier, Darrell, and Michael J. Cobb. 1981. "Sex Differences in Urban Arrest Patterns, 1934–79." *Social Problems* 29: 37–50.

Steffensmeier, Darrell, and Miles D. Harer. 1991. "Did Crime Rise or Fall during the Reagan Presidency? The Effects of an "Aging" U.S. Population on the Nation's Crime Rate." *Journal of Research in Crime and Delinquency* 28: 330–359.

Steffensmeier, Darrell, Jennifer Schwartz, Hua Zhong, Jeff Ackerman. 2005. "An Assessment of Recent Trends in Girls' Violence using Diverse Longitudinal Sources. Is the Gender Gap Closing?" *Criminology* 43: 355–405.

Weisburd, David, and John E. Eck. 2004. "What Can Police Do to Reduce Crime, Disorder, and Fear?" *The Annals* 593: 42–65.

Weisburd, David, Shawn Bushway, Cynthia Lum, and Sue-Ming Yang. 2004. "Trajectories of Crime at Places: A Longitudinal Study of Street Segments in the City of Seattle." *Criminology* 42: 283–322.

Western, Bruce. 2006. *Punishment and Inequality in America.* New York: Russell Sage Foundation.

Wilson, William Julius. 1987. *The Truly Disadvantaged: The Inner City, the Underclass, and Public Policy.* Chicago: University of Chicago Press.

Zimring, Franklin E. 2006. *The Great American Crime Decline.* New York: Oxford University Press.

Notes

1. Like the NVSS, the SHR codes the ethnicity (Hispanic, non-Hispanic) of the victim and offender, but the ethnicity data are missing in well over half of the reported homicide incidents, which makes them unusable for research purposes. See the Bureau of Justice Statistics web site (http://www.ojp.usdoj.gov/bjs/homicide/homtrnd.htm) for a description of the SHR and illustrative data. NVSS data on homicide and nonfatal assaults can be accessed through the CDC's Web-based Injury Statistics Query and Reporting System (http://www.cdc.gov/injury/ wisqars/index. html).

2. See Lynch and Addington (2007) for a discussion of the measurement properties of the UCR and NCVS. In 1992 the NCVS underwent a significant redesign, resulting in part from concerns that the surveys undercounted sexual assaults and domestic violence. New screening items and interview protocols increased the number of sexual and other assaults reported by female respondents. The trend data reported below are adjusted to reflect these changes.

3. As of mid-August, 2009, the most recent available UCR crime figures consisted of incomplete preliminary data for 2008 (http://www.fbi.gov/ucr/08aprelim/index.html). The most recent NCVS data were for 2007 (http://ojp.usdoj.gov/bjs/abstract/cv07.htm). Accessed August 13, 2009.

4. The following discussion elaborates on arguments originally presented in Rosenfeld and Goldberger (2008).

5. According to the NCVS, in 2005 about 22 percent of non-fatal violence against women age 12 and older was committed by intimate partners and 33 percent was committed by strangers (see Catalano 2006).

6. As discussed above, Hispanic homicide victimization rates are recorded separately from those of non-Hispanic whites and blacks in the NVSS, but the available ethnic-specific homicide trends extend back only to 1990 (see http://webappa.cdc.gov/sasweb/ncipc/mortrate.html). Cook and Laub (2002) use these data to discuss Hispanic homicide trends during the early 1990s.

7. For example, recent research has identified reductions in childhood exposure to lead in the environment during the 1970s as an important contributor to the youth violent crime decline of the 1990s (Nevin 2000; Reyes 2007). This work has yet to be widely replicated. An important limitation of prior research is that the lead-exposure effects are restricted to change in violent crime rates (Reyes 2007), even though the effects of impulsivity, cognitive deficits, and other long-term neurological consequences of exposure to lead would be expected to influence rates of property crime as well.

8. A time series is "stationary" if its basic properties, such as the mean and variance, do not change over time. "Endogeneity" in this context means that crime can affect the conditions that are thought to cause changes in crime rates. A good example is the relationship between crime and the size of police forces discussed above.

9. A crime forecast is accurate if it correctly predicts the direction and size of future crime rates. A forecast is precise if the difference between the predicted crime rate and actual crime rate is small. Precise forecasts are always accurate, but an accurate forecast is not necessarily precise. For example, if this year's homicide rate is five homicides per 100,000 population and we predict that next year's homicide rate will be somewhere between one and 20 homicides per 100,000, our forecast would probably be accurate but it would not be very precise.

10. This section draws from work in progress with David Rapach and Eric Baumer.

Chapter 20

Democratic Policing on the Evidence

Lawrence W. Sherman

Democracy and policing have a troubled relationship. Democracy requires widespread participation in public decisions, no matter how much time it takes to reach a conclusion. Policing requires quick and independent decisions by a non-political agent of the law when something must be done immediately (Bittner 1970). It is little wonder that the mother of all Parliaments, the British House of Commons, took almost a century to decide whether or not to create an organization of salaried police officers in England. While democracies around the world have all made similar decisions since England created the Metropolitan Police of London in 1829, they have also continued to struggle with the desire to have their cake and eat it too: to have an effective means to prevent or intervene quickly in crime and disorder, while maintaining the fairness of lengthy democratic deliberation over how policing should be accomplished.

This chapter describes those twin demands as the *democratic policing dilemma*. It describes two solutions to the dilemma that democracies have used for centuries: reshuffling the *external oversight* of police agencies, and enhancing the internal *technical knowledge* of police practices. It then suggests that the latter strategy, in its most recent form called *evidence-based policing*, offers the most promise to minimize, but never eliminate, the democratic policing dilemma. In summary, the chapter describes how:

- Democracy will always debate the moral choices in policing, but
- Technical knowledge in policing is less subject to debate
- Police know, for example, that they can prevent more crime if they focus resources on high-crime places, people, and victims, and that
- Arrest and prosecution often causes more crime than informal action
- Adopting "evidence-based policing" may be initially controversial, but in the long run should increase both liberty and public safety.

The classic solution to the democratic dilemma is an endless restructuring of external oversight, transparency, accountability, and control of policing. England, for example, began the twenty-first century by debating whether police agencies should be led by elected commissioners, much like an American district attorney's office—even though no judges, prosecutors, police chiefs, or other criminal justice officials have ever been elected in England. In the United States, in the last decades of the twentieth century, police authority was restructured in Los Angeles, Milwaukee, and Baltimore, even though police in most U.S. large cities were directly accountable to an elected mayor (also unheard of in Britain, until 2008).

There is little evidence, however, that the *structures* of external police governance make much difference in how police do their job, how much controversy they generate, or how well they secure public safety and human rights. The constant rearranging of police oversight powers may "work" for democracy, which must be seen to be responsive to their continuing dilemma of deploying force quickly against their own voters, in order to protect other voters. The fact that the dilemma itself persists suggests the general failure of the structural solutions.

The classic competition to this solution is the idea of promoting *technical expertise* within the police profession—especially the profession of police leaders. Even before the Progressive Era of the early twentieth century, the idea of governing democracies by science rather than politics has waxed and waned in its public appeal. The idea has had the most appeal at the local level, with such functions as highways, water and sewage, education and policing. Thousands of cities—but not one state—have translated this scientific principle into the professional post of a "city manager" (or "chief executive" in Britain), who is an expert in the technical aspects of government but is structurally accountable to part-time, lower-paid, untrained elected officials. When extended to policing, this idea suggests that the police dilemma can be resolved by policing "smarter," but not necessarily "tougher," in order to reflect a democratic consensus under the rule of law. This consensus especially values police using "just enough" force—but not too much—to foster public safety without infringing on civil liberties.

This chapter examines present-day uses of the structural and technical approach to addressing the dilemma of policing democracies. It begins by introducing key concepts in both policing and democracy. Second, the chapter applies these concepts to a bedrock issue in policing, one that forces technical limitations to confront democratic debate: the power to kill. Third, the chapter traces the parallel development of structural and technical solutions over two centuries, showing how neither approach has ever resolved the dilemma for long. Finally, it describes a new and promising version of the technical approach, one that may help reduce the gap between democratic deliberation and decisive deployment of legitimate force: "evidence-based policing." Modeled on the new field of evidence-based medicine, this recent approach seeks to develop and test ever-more-effective responses to recurring challenges, using controlled experiments to choose among competing choices of action. While it is unlikely that evidence-based policing will ever resolve the dilemma of democratic policing, it may at least reduce the level of tension associated with that dilemma.

KEY CONCEPTS IN DEMOCRACY AND POLICING

Policing

The modern meaning of the word *policing* is only some two centuries old. The ancient Greek origin of the word referred to all matters of governance in a city-state. Adam Smith's 1763 lectures (as cited in Barrie 2008, 12) even defined "police" to include cleanliness (public sanitation) and food supply. Not until after the creation of the Bow Street Runners in the 1750s as the first publicly paid investigators in England (Fielding 1755) did the word *police* acquire its current association with crime prevention and investigation. That development occurred first in the 1786 legislation for the policing of Dublin, Ireland, the first law to define police as "a body of men" (Barrie 2008, 13). At the same time, the French Revolution saw the development of the word "police" to mean agents of the national government, distinct from the army, in its role of both catching criminals and spying on private citizens to suppress statements and actions opposing the government. That conception of police was at the heart of decades of English opposition to creating a police force in London (Hurd 2007). When the London Metropolitan Police were finally created, they were described as "citizens" (not soldiers or agents of the government in power) under the rule of law, with special responsibilities to keep the peace, preventing crime and disorder.

Even today, the tension between defining police with a specific focus on "crime control" or by the more general functions of "peacekeeping" stirs the emotions of police scholars, who battle each other over what policing is "really" about. What we know about how police can help reduce crime is sometimes even portrayed as dangerous knowledge that threatens the many other functions that police must perform, from traffic safety to public health (Skogan 2009). Yet there is broad scholarly agreement on Bittner's (1990, 131) definition of the role of the police as " . . . a mechanism for the distribution of non-negotiably coercive force employed in accordance with the dictates of an intuitive grasp of situational exigencies," and specifically situations in which there is " . . . something-that ought-not-be-to-happening-and-about-which- someone-had better-do- something-NOW" (1990, 249).

Legitimacy

The most important distinction between democratic and non-democratic policing is "policing by consent." Democratic ideals require that "non-negotiably coercive force" should be broadly accepted by the public as morally right, or "legitimate." The idea of legitimacy is defined by a leading police scholar as "a property of an authority or institution that leads people to feel that that authority or institution is entitled to be deferred to and obeyed" (Tyler 1990, 25). It represents an "acceptance by people of the need to bring their behavior into line with the dictates of an external authority" (Sunshine and Tyler 2003, 514). Non-democratic policing can use the same (or greater) force than police in democracies, but without a political culture in which that force must be morally justified.

Prediction

"Predictive policing" has rapidly gained prominence in the early twenty-first century. Prediction of where, when, how, and by whom crime will be committed plays a growing role in police strategy. These predictions were once limited to subjective or clinical assessments of crime patterns and criminals. Today, they are more likely to be derived from statistical analyses of large data bases. These data bases are now generating more accurate forecasts about crime and criminals than were ever possible before a new generation of super-computers, as well as advanced statistical techniques for "mining" the data (Berk et al. 2009).

Hot Spots

This term is widely used to describe locations with a highly elevated risk of crime, by which 3 percent or so of the street addresses (or address clusters) in any city generate some 50 percent of all police calls for service (Sherman et al. 1989). Even greater concentrations are reported for violent crimes. While some police agencies define hot spots over far broader areas, such as 10 or 20 square blocks, the most extensive empirical evidence (Weisburd et al. 2004) presents data showing long-term crime concentrations at the level that Sherman and colleagues (1989) described: address-specific or address-cluster micro-areas that can be taken in by the human eye turning in a complete circle.

Risk Factors

A risk factor is a characteristic of a person, situation, area, or community that predicts an elevated probability that something bad will occur, such as crimes or accidents. They include simple counts of previous events in the past year or more (Sherman et al. 1989). They also include elaborate computer models of 15 or more factors in combination that can predict who is likely to commit a homicide (Berk et al. 2009). The concept is inherently statistical, even though it may be used in an intuitive way—such as police suspicion at seeing a white man walking at night in an area that is predominantly African American (Shaw 1995). Risk factors are the basic tools of prediction, and are increasingly used to allocate police resources for proactive strategies (Reiss 1971).

Prevention versus Punishment

The most profound division within police ranks, as well as among citizens, is whether police should give priority to preventing crime or punishing it. This dilemma arises every time police go into a station for hours to process an arrest. Every minute they spend away from patrol duties, they reduce the documented preventive effects of police patrol on crime (Apel and Nagin, chapter 14 of this volume; see also below). At the same time, it is not clear that the arrest itself has any crime prevention value, and may even prompt more crime (see below). Yet under a utilitarian view of policing, the greatest good for the greatest number may entail reducing the investment in punishment in order to increase the investment in prevention. That, in turn, collides with a widespread moral sense that crimes should be punished in some way, even if the modern justice system makes such punishment very costly in policing diverted from prevention.

Evidence: Cases versus Consequences

The concepts presented above all suggest the importance of what scholars call "evidence" in policing. They do not mean fingerprints or DNA, but rather facts in support of a hypothesis, prediction, or description. In its broadest sense, "evidence" includes any observations that help to answer an empirical question about the real world. But in the growing knowledge about police behavior, the term *evidence* is used in a more restricted way: to describe the likely (but not certain) consequences of taking any particular course of action. This evidence is about *cause and effect*: the impact of police action, for example, on the likelihood of a future crime.

Unbiased Evidence

Researchers from medicine to agriculture to criminology are concerned about the potential for "bias" in evidence about cause and effect. By that they do not mean racial or ethnic prejudice. They mean that certain kinds of research designs may create bias in favor of a particular conclusion about causation, even if that conclusion is wrong. This usually happens when there is some bias toward certain kinds of cases getting one treatment rather than another—cases that would have done better regardless of which treatment they received. The result makes it look like the treatment "worked" better, when all it did was to get chosen by better cases. The best way to avoid bias is to have an otherwise-identical comparison group. Fair comparisons are best achieved by using random assignment of different practices to similar cases—then comparing the results (Sherman, 2011). When it is not possible to randomly assign different police methods over a large number of units, the next best option is a "quasi-experimental" design comparing a few similar units (such as police precincts) getting different practices.

Evidence-Based Policing

Basing police practices on what unbiased research evidence shows to be the most cost-effective option (Sherman 1998) is the core idea of evidence-based policing (EBP). The kind of evidence needed is best produced by a synthesis—or "meta-analysis"—of the results of seven or more randomized controlled experiments. That is the usual practice in the emerging field of "evidence-based medicine" (www.cochrane.org), which is the model for evidence-based policing. Where the unbiased evidence is replicated in multiple studies across different kinds of police agencies and communities, there is more confidence that the results are likely to apply in any policing setting—not just in one or two places where the research was done. Using such evidence in practice is still rare in policing (Lum 2009). But the prospects for attaining more widespread use of EBP have recently improved.

What may help EBP to thrive in the coming decades is a better understanding of two limitations. One is the fact that many dilemmas in police work are not curable by better evidence. The power to kill is a prime example, as discussed below. The other limitation is that political oversight alone is also unable to resolve key dilemmas in policing. The possibility of developing more knowledge appears greater than the possibility of developing better political oversight of police. Both facts point in the direction of improved commitments to knowledge as a pathway to cultural change within democratic police agencies, as a contribution to democracy itself.

TECHNICAL SOLUTIONS VERSUS EXTERNAL OVERSIGHT

The modern police institution was a technical solution to a democratic problem. The problem was how to reduce crime and disorder, including (in the case of Ireland) terrorism, without restricting civil liberties. The technical solution, at least in the English-speaking nations, was to create an organized agency of well-paid peacekeepers, who would apply the new theory of deterrence to potential and actual lawbreakers. The key to this solution was, in effect, "socialized prosecution," by which crime victims no longer had to pay private lawyers to prosecute criminals for crimes (Radzinowicz 1956). Instead, the police would prosecute criminal defendants at the expense of the monarch.

Wherever this technical solution was adopted, it was accompanied by a system of democratic oversight. Yet the systems of oversight varied widely. The technical solution apparently first appeared in late-eighteenth-century Scotland, where unpaid "police commissioners" were elected by voters in each city for the sole purpose of supervising the police (Barrie 2008). When the technical solution spread to Ireland (Hurd 2007), police were put under control of special magistrates, who were appointed by the British prime minister's representative in Dublin. The first modern urban police agency in England was also controlled for almost two centuries by magistrates (confusingly, also called "commissioners") appointed by the (elected) national government, and not by voters in the metropolis being policed (London). The United States saw a wide array of external control systems, including direct election of police executives in Philadelphia (Sprogle 1887) and even of precinct commanders in New York (Richardson 1970), while most cities eventually settled on a police executive serving at the pleasure of the mayor.

That summary of external oversight systems is, admittedly, a vast oversimplification. Wherever democracies created police organizations, they also created heroic struggles for control over police resources: jobs, bribes, and capacity to influence elections. These struggles sometimes resulted in competing police agencies created by two different levels of government. Two New York City police agencies, one appointed by the state and one by the city, once fought a battle on the steps of New York City Hall (Richardson 1970), only to be broken up by the U.S. Army. More often, scandals provoked new legislation reorganizing control of police. Kansas City and St. Louis lost local control of their police agencies in scandals over their political machines, with the state governor given powers to appoint a police commission in each of the state's two biggest cities. Maryland gave its governor the power to directly appoint Baltimore's police commissioner.

The history of police control in democracies has often moved away from local democracy, in favor of a more "disinterested" approach to police administration. This was the basis for the 1964 Police Act in England and Wales, which merged over 150 police agencies into 43 larger units. The theory of the merger was, in part, to keep police leaders from having too close (or corrupting) a relationship with the people they policed. But size alone has not guaranteed impartiality. One example is the Indian Police Service, a national senior officer corps (selected by merit under an 1861 colonial law) that is assigned to lead state-hired police in vast populations. Serving very populous states of about 50 million people each—larger than most nations—has been no guarantee against political pressures and challenges of police preference for powerful people.

In the United States and the United Kingdom, recent years have seen demands for more democracy in policing. These demands often take the form of making it easier for locally elected officials to fire a police executive. The Los Angeles police chief's position was stripped of its civil service life tenure, as was the Milwaukee police chief's. In both cases, the job was converted to a fixed-term contract that could be bought out at any time. In London, the national government voluntarily devolved its exclusive control of the Metropolitan Police in favor of a local police authority, placed under control of the new position of an elected mayor. On the same day in 2008 that the mayor became chair of the Metropolitan Police Authority, his first act was to remove the professional police commissioner (Blair 2009).

From 2007 through 2009, the British Conservative Party campaigned for local election of a single, non-professional police commissioner for all 43 police forces in England and Wales. This plan would replace, in each agency, a large board called a "Police Authority," which already consisted of locally elected officials. It would also greatly constrain the 43 professional chief constables in England and Wales, also (as in India) selected by a national system of certifying professional and technical competence. The association of chief constables announced its strong opposition to the plan, which the Conservatives said was borrowed directly from the United States. Not one big city in the United States, however, has a directly elected official whose sole job is to oversee the police.

What the United States does have is two decades of experience with local community consultations, often called "community policing." These consultations have been the subject of extensive research (e.g., Skogan and Hartnett 1997; Skogan and Frydl 2004). The evidence suggests that regular police consultations with community leadership helps neighborhoods and improves police relationships with those communities. It does not show, however, that engaging self-selected local citizens in the setting of priorities for police action reduces serious crime. As yet another form of external participation in the conduct of police agencies, the community policing movement can be seen as far more political than technical, about democracy more than police work. The fact that it disappeared so quickly from U.S. police discourse in the twenty-first century further suggests that it had little effect on how police work was done. Yet it was strongly supported by a wide range of political leaders, in both the United States and the United Kingdom.

What feeds this intermittent stream of demands for reform of police oversight? In general, it is dissatisfaction with police conduct in critical incidents (Wilson 1968). Riots, shootings, political demonstrations, "preventable" murders, and torture or corruption scandals: these are the fuel of police reform (Sherman 1978). These incidents, in turn, may stem from a technical failure of police leaders to obtain compliance within their agencies. It is remarkable how few police executives have been held personally culpable for condoning police misconduct, even when the agency itself is stained by clear misconduct. The most common "culprit" is a failure of internal regulation, by which police must follow agency rules and leaders are able to know when they do not.

These critical incidents are windows of opportunity for change. When that change takes the form of more democracy, non-professionals gain more power over the police. They may bring more passion to police reform. But without technical knowledge, it is not clear that they can change police conduct. The better police conduct gets, the harder it is to improve by good intentions alone. By many indications, police conduct is far better today than it has been in recent memory. In both the United

Kingdom and the United States, most observers cite far less brutality, corruption, racism, sleeping and drinking on the job in 2009 than in 1969. Yet these improvements will not prevent critical incidents over terrorism, or failures to prevent domestic homicide or other critical incidents that cause distrust in democracies.

Over two centuries of rearranging external police oversight, democracies have occasionally embraced new technical reforms. August Vollmer (1936), the police chief who founded the American Society of Criminology, was the leading exponent of this approach. He saw the hope of police progress in the new ideas and knowledge produced by scientific discoveries. Long a friend of many leading scholars at Berkeley, he went on to become a professor at the University of Chicago before returning to California as a Berkeley professor. He also made profound changes in the technical content of police work, including radio-dispatched police cars. Yet his vision was far broader, embracing the potential of almost all of science.

Vollmer notwithstanding, the techniques of policing have actually changed very little in 200 years. Police still patrol the streets to prevent crime, and prosecute defendants they believe have committed crime. Put that simply, police today use the same techniques as they did in London in 1829, in New York in 1845, and in Sydney and Bombay in 1861. Elaborations in police bureaucracy—red tape—may have constrained police freedom. Far more training is done today, and police are universally literate in most democracies. Those changes are not minor. But they are merely changes to infrastructure. They do not address the core of police work. They are like air conditioning in an operating room where doctors still perform surgery with eighteenth-century tools and techniques. Until police tools and techniques change, modern officers cannot be expected to get much better results than their predecessors did. No amount of external control, moreover, is likely to do any better.

Yet doctors, as well as farmers, get far better results today than they did two centuries ago. What pulled them ahead of the police in those years was public investment in technical knowledge. An influx of public resources has made a large difference—perhaps even more in farming than in medicine. In 1900, food consumed 40 percent of US household income, and took half the labor force to produce it. Today, on even less land, food consumes only 8 percent of household income and 2 percent of the labor force (Gawande 2009). Those improvements come *not* from public investment in operations (like putting "more cops on the street"), but rather from research and development: testing techniques in the field to compare results. From a rapid start in 1914, the U.S. Department of Agriculture Cooperative Extension Service had established over 750,000 field testing farms by 1930, with over 7,000 knowledge brokers called "extension service agents" employed to tell the farmers what techniques could help them to produce more and better food.

That same approach could arguably improve the outcomes of policing. A substantial body of research has now accumulated that could be put into practice in police agencies. Even more could be generated by creating the equivalent of field testing stations or research and teaching hospitals for policing. Such a movement is already developing in the United Kingdom with some of the largest police agencies, led by the Greater Manchester Police (see www.crim.cam.ac.uk/experiments). Rather than waiting for central government investment, these agencies are using their own resources to discover how to yield better results.

What is needed to make knowledge work in policing, as in other fields, is a combination of good *evidence* and persuasive *communication* methods. Even farmers have been reluctant, for example, to manage the rotation schedule of grazing animals from field to field with as much precision as the research results suggest is optimal (Gawande 2009). Their failure costs them substantial losses in income, but they may not notice it. Similarly, doctors have been reluctant to wash their hands as they go from patient to patient in their hospital rounds. Their reluctance may kill thousands of people a year by spreading infections. No one questions the research on these points. But no one has yet found a technique to make most doctors wash their hands between touching patients, most of the time.

The challenge of evidence-based policing is thus twofold. First, it must generate and synthesize research at a rapidly growing rate. Second, it must also test the techniques of communicating research results to police officers and leaders, so that they will want to use the most effective methods available. It is not clear which of these two tasks is more beneficial to accomplish first. In light of the substantial number of field tests already completed in policing, it may well be time to start testing how to convey the results of those tests.

What follows is a summary of those results. As a medium for communication and persuasion, this summary is definitely not recommended; an extension agent, for example, would rather present technical knowledge to farmers in one-on-one conversations. As a place for readers to evaluate whether research knows enough about policing for evidence-based policy, the next section provides an overview of more detailed road maps to the key research evidence (Sherman 1997; Sherman and Eck 2005; Skogan and Frydl 2004).

EVIDENCE-BASED POLICING

In 1989, a young police officer parked her police car in a high crime "hot spot" in Minneapolis. After 5 minutes, she drove away. For the next 15 minutes after her police car had departed, the likelihood of a crime occurring was lower than it had been before the officer had parked there for 5 minutes. This persisting benefit of a short police presence is called *residual deterrence* (Sherman 1990): a free bonus effect of deterrence even when police are not visible. That fact may not have surprised the officer as she patrolled that day. But her police chief was surprised to learn what a National Institute of Justice (NIJ) study later revealed: had the officer parked in the hot spot for 10 minutes, the residual deterrent period would have been about twice as long as after only 5 minutes (Sherman 1995).

The conclusions about the optimal amount of time to patrol a hot spot are derived from the "Koper Curve" of residual deterrence: an analysis of over 7,000 police arrivals and departures from high-crime street corners during the Minneapolis hot spots patrol experiment (Sherman and Weisburd 1995). The Koper Curve is a prime example of the benefits of evidence-based policing (EBP), by which the same number of police officers can deter much more crime with such knowledge than without it. The Curve shows that for every minute a police car or uniformed officer remains in a hot spot, the length of time *without crime* after police leave goes up—until the presence lasts 15 minutes. After 15 minutes, the time without crime starts to decline, in a pattern of diminishing returns. It suggests that the optimal time for a uniformed police officer to remain at a high crime location is just around 15 minutes—and not much more or less.

The discovery of the Koper Curve answers the most fundamental questions about moving forward with the current body of research. What evidence do we have about the comparative effectiveness of police practices? What can we tell police officers and leaders, based on unbiased test results, about how best to spend their time, in different kinds of communities with different kinds of crime problems? Research evidence can offer only partial answers to those questions. But the part they answer is important: how a police decision today can affect a community tomorrow, how a decision this minute can affect what happens 10 minutes later.

Evidence-based policing is often contrasted with the "craft" of policing based on experience. Experience alone, however, does not produce reliable guidance to complex decisions. Farming is some 5,000 years old, but its results did not improve substantially until systematic testing began a mere 100 years ago. Police patrol is centuries old, but no one had tested the dose-response curve from patrol presence until the Police Foundation conducted the first controlled experiment in police patrol dosage in the early 1970s (Kelling et al. 1974). That experiment ignited a blaze of police research that has spread around the world, greatly multiplying the amount of systematic evidence about the comparative effectiveness of police practices. While the pace of growth in new knowledge is never as fast as many would hope, it is far faster today than ever before.

The pace of police research may increase when more research is put into practice, which in turn may create demands for more research. Before concluding the chapter with the challenges of applying research to policing, this section shows how much knowledge we already have to apply. The goal of this section is to show not only what we know, but how we know it. The key areas of our knowledge so far match the most expensive areas of police practices and the crime problems they address: patrol, problem-solving, investigations, repeat stranger offenders, domestic and gun violence, youth crime, and public drug dealing. We also have extensive knowledge from a long-term effort to invent and test entirely different approach to policing called restorative justice. While the gaps in our knowledge remain substantial, we at least know how we can fill them in.

Patrol

For at least 800 years (Lee 1901), the core "technology" of police work has been patrolling of public areas to deter and interrupt crime. Like most human services, it has been performed with great variation in quality and quantity. The night watch portrayed by William Shakespeare in his play *Much Ado about Nothing* is a drunken, oafish collection of poorly paid and unarmed men of low intelligence, reflecting the state of patrol in six-teenth-century London. Other world capitals chose to rely on armed soldiers to provide patrol, with the risk that they would use too much force against the populace. The "citizen police" idea developed in the British Isles from the late eighteenth century chose a third route: a well-paid, tightly supervised group of unarmed but highly reliable people of excellent character who would comply with the rule of law. A later innovation put them into uniforms, in order to increase their visibility in public places.

Armed or unarmed, the citizen police had many choices about how to conduct patrols. They could, for example, arrest everyone they saw break-ing the law. Or they could just make minor lawbreakers stop what they were doing and send them on their way. Patrol work has always required police to balance staying on the streets to keep order against taking them off the streets to seek justice. Police could also patrol alone, in pairs, or in larger groups. They could patrol primarily in highly dense areas of com-merce, or in quiet side streets as well. For varying parts of the past century, they could choose between patrols on foot, bicycle, motorcycle, automo-bile, two-wheeled Segway personal transporters, or three-wheeled electric chariots. All of these variations may, or may not, matter in causing police to be more or less effective. The potential knowledge about all these choices could be as complex as knowledge about brain surgery.

What we have learned most about to date is the *dosage* of police patrol in relation to the *crime density* of patrol locations. What we have learned is that more patrol can substantially reduce crime in locations with high density of crime per square foot ("hot spots" of crime). How we learned that is a story of increasingly refined experiments that systematically varied patrol dosage in different kinds of locations. These experiments are not yet refined enough, however, to allow us to distinguish between different means of patrol *mobility*, such as walking versus driving.

The first systematic testing of patrol dosage began in the 1950s in New York City. The research was done with a crude before-and-after comparison of crime in a precinct that was given a large increase in the number of police on patrol. The conclusion was that crime went down when patrol dosage went up, but with some evidence of "displacement" from increases in crime in the areas surrounding the precinct where police patrolling was increased. The issue of displacement plagues all patrol research, and has since acquired a growing evidence base of its own.

This kind of research design is now called a "Level 2" on the Maryland Scientific Methods Scale (Sherman 1997), a scale of 1 to 5 with 5 as the best. This scale ranks crime prevention evaluation designs on the strength of their internal validity, or the extent to which the conclusions can be considered *unbiased* in relation to such issues as self-selection of treatments. A "Level 1" design is merely a correlation of two characteristics at one point in time, such as evidence that murder rates are higher in poorer areas than in wealthier ones. A Level 2 design is a before-and-after comparison of crime rates in the same area, with and without a new program designed to reduce the crime rates. The reason a Level 2 design is better than Level 1 is that the Level 2 difference is more clearly linked to the new program than a (Level 1) correlation across areas at a single point in time. While Level 1 could be explained by a wide range of characteristics of areas with lower crime rates, Level 2 findings with a sharp drop in crime just after a new program would not have to compete with other factors that remained unchanged.

The problem with Level 2 designs is that they still cannot rule out many other competing explanations. At the same time that patrol increased, for example, there could have been sharp changes in the weather. Or a band of very active criminals could have been locked up. Or a new prosecutor could have been elected. Or a new traffic pattern could have made fleeing the police more difficult. Any of these "plausible rival hypotheses" could have fit the facts just as well as a change in patrol. The classical fallacy of *post hoc, ergo propter hoc?* (after this, therefore because of this?) is just what limits conclusions based on Level 2 research designs.

The Kansas City Patrol Experiment

The first study to reach (but not grasp) above Level 2 was the Police Foundation's Kansas City Preventive Patrol Experiment (Kelling et al. 1974). This study tried to reach not only to Level 3, but also to Level 4. It compared the before-and-after crime data where patrol had been increased to an area where it had not been. That comparison alone would have pushed it up to Level 3: a design with a measure of what might have happened in the target area even if patrol had not changed. If crime in the comparison area remained unchanged while crime dropped where patrol increased, that finding would have ruled out many competing explanations (Campbell and Stanley 1966). Any changes that could have occurred in both the target and comparison areas, such as the weather or a change in the county prosecutor, would be ruled out as a threat to the theory that more patrol caused less crime. The difference of trends between the two areas, and not just a before-after trend within one area, provides a stronger case for inferring causation—or lack of it—from any correlation with higher patrol. Thus many people were convinced by the experiment's finding that crime was not affected by higher or lower doses of police patrol.

Even better for good evidence, the Kansas City experiment reached beyond Level 3 to Level 4. Rather than just comparing two areas, the experiment compared five areas with a patrol increase to five areas without an increase. With a larger number of comparisons, the study helped to rule out another rival theory: mere coincidence. A difference between two areas is more likely to occur by chance than a consistent difference between five areas with and five areas without more patrol. To make the test even more powerful, the experiment added a third group of five areas, in which routine patrol was eliminated altogether. This design is a kind of Super Level 4, in which the logic of the theory is checked in two ways at once.

The Kansas City experiment reached for Levels 3 and 4 with even more enhancements to the research design. It was the first patrol study to use victimization surveys to supplement official crime records. It was the first to claim to use random assignment in deciding which area would get each of the three dosage levels of patrol. It was the first study to ask large samples of citizens in each area if they had noticed any change in the visibility of patrol—either increases or decreases. It was also the first study to use interviews with known offenders to ask if they had noticed any difference in patrol.

Unfortunately, the Kansas City study did not quite grasp Level 3 or Level 4. According to various calculations by independent analysts (reviewed in Sherman 1986), there was probably no difference in the amount of patrol presence actually provided in the three groups of areas. The reason that patrol presence was equal despite a clear difference in policy is that responses to calls for service were left unchanged. These responses generate such a high proportion of police visibility that it did not matter what the policy was on non-response patrol in each area. Even the areas banned from routine patrol received as much patrol as the areas with standard patrol levels, simply by driving into the areas to answer calls and driving out again when each call was finished. The requirement to leave the area may have led to more driving than if they had been allowed to stay in the area and had patrolled more slowly with less distance covered.

If there was no difference in patrol visibility between the three intended patrol levels, then there was no test conducted. The actual research design was not a Level 4, but no level at all. Even if there had been a difference in dosage, other calculations suggested that the volume of crime in the 15 beats was so low that only a huge impact of patrol dosage variance on crime would have been found to be "statistically significant"—or not due to chance. Significance, to statisticians, depends greatly on how much "power" a statistical test has to discern what is true as not just a chance coincidence. An underpowered study is particularly bad for a conclusion of "no difference," since that conclusion could always be due to the weak power of the test. On two counts, then, the test is not considered a fair assessment of the impact of patrol dosage on crime. This interpretation of the evidence is essential for understanding the basis of the study's conclusion: that the level of patrol dosage has no effect on crime. This conclusion was widely cited and accepted by public officials, some of whom laid off thousands of police in the mid-1970s in the aftermath of the study being reported on the front page of the *New York Times*. While the layoffs were driven by an economic recession, the Kansas City experiment was cited as a justification. Yet by a fairly clear consensus of reviewers, that justification was incorrect.

Newark Foot Patrol Experiment

Similar issues beset the Police Foundation's (1981) second major patrol experiment, a test of foot patrol in Newark. This experiment was arguably stronger than the Kansas City test, if only because foot patrol is a more distinctive strategy than automobile patrol. Officers on foot patrol, by the late 1970s, had to be assigned to do it; few officers did it voluntarily. At the time this Level 4 experiment began, there had been consistent foot patrol in 8 beats in Newark. The experiment discontinued foot patrol in 4 of the 8 beats, and added it to 4 new beats, for a total of 12 beats in which public surveys of crime victimization and official crime reports were analyzed. The report found no differences in crime, but clear differences in public perceptions of disorder. In beats that retained or added foot patrol, the public perceived less disorder than in the 4 beats in which it had been discontinued. This result led to an influential article by Wilson and Kelling (1982), which has been widely cited as "broken windows theory" (see below).

The most widely accepted conclusion from the Newark evidence is that foot patrol does not reduce crime. This conclusion, like the Kansas City finding, was based on comparisons of relatively large beat areas. While such areas have traditionally been the basis for organizing patrol activity, it is not clear that large beats are the optimal approach for preventing crime. If they are too large for police to communicate a credible threat of intervention in crime, then they may simply dilute policing too much. Organizing police patrols around very small spaces with very high densities of crime, however, could well provide a different result from spreading the same resources too thinly across larger areas. That was only one of the many ideas that emerged from almost two decades of discussion about the two path-breaking patrol experiments conducted by the Police Foundation. Those discussions show that the initial report of a study may not, in the long run, be as important as a broader discussion of the evidence by a community of scholars and police professionals.

Evidence-based policing thus requires a careful review of the evidence, not just by the authors of each study but also by knowledgeable reviewers. As in evidence-based medicine, the ownership of evidence is public and collective. It is not up to a journalist to decide what is scientifically valid. It is, instead, the job of a scientific and professional community to determine, for each question, what the evidence really shows. The medical community has done that world-wide with the Cochrane Collaboration, a group that commissions and regulates systematic reviews of the evidence on specific medical treatments and prevention programs. Fortunately, the Cochrane Collaboration helped to initiate a similar group for human services programs, including crime and justice. With funding from the Norwegian government, the human services review group called the Campbell Collaboration is now 10 years old. Its web site (www.campbellcollaboration.org) now posts several systematic reviews of evidence on the effectiveness of police practices, including patrols in hot spots (Braga 2007). That review, in turn, reflects the second generation of patrol studies, organized around small, high-crime places rather than traditional patrol beats.

Minneapolis Hot Spots Experiment

The first Level 5, randomized controlled trial of patrol dosage was also the first patrol experiment to use hot spots, rather than beats, as the unit of analysis. In 1988–1989, the Minneapolis Police Department assigned uniformed officers in patrol cars to perform extra patrols in 55 hot spots that were selected at random from a list of 110, with no change to the other 55 (Sherman and Weisburd 1995). The NIJ-funded test counted both patrols and crimes from 7 P.M. to 3 A.M. (the times of day in which crimes were most heavily concentrated), seven days a week.

This one-year experiment was also the first to use systematic observation to measure the number of minutes that police were present in both control and experimental hot spots. A team of trained independent observers, stop watches in hand, counted each arrival and departure of a police car at a high-crime street corner, including those that simply drove right by, for a total sample of 7,542 hours. The observations were assigned to sample each of the hot spots equally, showing that on average the experimental group had twice as much police patrol as the control group. While the ratio varied substantially across the four seasons, the difference in public calls to police about crime in the hot spots overall was around two-thirds less crime in hot spots receiving extra patrol. These results were confirmed by the independent observers, who counted about half as many events of "disorder" (from drug dealing and using to prostitution transactions) at the experimental street corners as at the controls.

These findings appear to have been applied in a number of police agencies, including New York City during the rapid drop in crime in the 1990s. The application of the findings was aided by the spread of computerized crime statistics updated weekly, combined with crime mapping software—neither of which had been available at the time the Minneapolis experiment was conducted. The COMPSTAT method of regular reviews of crime concentrations in each police district also encouraged police to focus more on hot spots than on "random" patrols. Without a controlled test of this method across police agencies, it is impossible to conclude whether it helped reduce crime nationally. Yet it is at least one of several plausible hypotheses. It has also led several British police agencies to plan replications of the Minneapolis experiment, with new technologies for tracking police officers' whereabouts by satellite transponders in their personal radios.

Jersey City

While the exact Minneapolis design has never been replicated, a growing number of tests using patrols in crime hot spots have been reported (see the review by Braga 2007). These results show consistent benefits of adding uniformed patrol time in crime hot spots, either in crime prevention or in disorder reduction. The closest replication of the Minneapolis design was the Jersey City Drug Market Analysis Experiment in 1988–1989 (Weisburd and Green 1995). This 15-month experiment had fewer locations, and employed additional forms of policing besides uniformed patrol. Like many experiments, it had an uneven implementation of the treatment across the 28 experimental hot spots, and it lacked systematic measures of the dosage of uniformed patrol presence in the experimental and control spots. The sample size was also smaller than is conventionally required to create equivalence between experimental and control groups. These factors limited its evidence about the effects of uniformed patrol on violent and property crime, which showed no significant difference. Nonetheless, the results showed substantially fewer calls for service about disorder in the hot spots receiving extra patrols.

Displacement

The most important finding of the Jersey City experiment is that there was no displacement of disorder calls to the catchment areas surrounding the target areas. This was the first experiment to systematically test for such effects by comparing control and experimental locations. The results actually showed that the catchment areas around the locations with increased patrols also had reductions in calls for service. This "diffusion of benefit" (Clarke and Weisburd 1994) from increased police dosage has since been reported elsewhere (Weisburd et al. 2006), and has done much to deflect a widespread criticism of location-focused crime prevention: the idea that it "just moves crime around the corner." This hypothesis has been repeatedly tested by Weisburd and his colleagues, as well as by independent assessors of displacement effects. The most comprehensive review of a wide range of strategies, including police patrol, found that in a total of 574 tests, displacement to surrounding buffer zones was no more likely to happen than that crime or disorder would go down in those areas—each occurring in about 1 in 4 cases, with half of all cases showing no change in surrounding areas (Guerette and Bowers, 2009). But a further concern beyond local displacement is whether repeat offenders in targeted hot spots will move to other parts of the city. That hypothesis has yet to be tested, but is also part of the protocol the Greater Manchester Police have developed for their own hot spots experiment (see the Registry of police experimental protocols at www.crim.cam.ac.uk/experiments).

Other Costs

Place-focused policing has also been criticized with evidence that the increased arrests it may generate cause a range of problems in the criminal justice system, and create more fugitives from justice (Goldkamp and Vilcica 2008). This critique, however, can only apply to increases of enforcement, and not to all increases in patrol. Because enforcement takes officers off the streets, there is a clear trade-off between arrest and patrol. The evidence cited above shows that increased patrol makes a difference; it does not provide clear evidence that increasing arrests in places causes either crime reductions or increases.

Broken Windows Theory

One of the most widely debated policy issues in police patrol has been what is loosely called "broken windows theory," sometimes equated with "zero tolerance" or massive increases in misdemeanor arrests. This debate does not reflect an accurate reading of the science on which it is purportedly based. There are, for example, at least two broken windows theories, neither of which claims that massive increases in misdemeanor arrests will reduce crime. The first is a theory of crime *causation*, which hypothesizes that minor disorder is infectious, and may lead to more serious crime if left unchecked (Wilson and Kelling 1982). The evidence for this theory include's Zimbardo's (1970) field tests with abandoned cars, and more robustly, the series of field experiments by Keizer and his colleagues (2008) in the Netherlands. It also includes Sampson and Raudenbush's (1999) extensive analysis of videotapes of street behavior over time, which found that social disorder in small locations was a moderately strong predictor of robbery, but not as strong a predictor as the area's "collective efficacy"—a measure from public surveys showing whether local residents think they can make a difference in the quality of life in their neighborhoods.

The other broken windows hypothesis is a theory of crime *prevention*, which holds that if police regulate disorder more effectively, serious crime will go down or be prevented. The most direct evidence on this prediction is the randomized experiment by Braga and Bond (2008) with a "policing disorder" strategy across 17 pairs of hot spots in Lowell, Massachusetts. That experiment found that disorder reduction strategies reduced: (1) observations of social disorder in the target hot spots relative to the controls, and (2) calls for service about assault, robbery, burglary, and disorder. The police strategies included alterations in physical and social environmental characteristics (labeled "situational crime prevention") as well as increases in misdemeanor arrests. The authors attribute more of the crime reduction to the environmental strategies than to the misdemeanor arrests. The effect of misdemeanor arrests on serious crime was tested with non-experimental evidence by Corman and Mocan (2005), controlling for economic conditions and felony arrests. They found that misdemeanor arrest increases were followed by statistically significant but small declines in robbery, auto theft, and grand larcenies. Many other non-experimental tests of the prevention theory have been published, but experimental tests have focused more broadly on a wide range of "problem-solving" techniques.

Problem-Solving

The advent of problem-oriented policing (Goldstein 1979, 1990; Eck and Spelman 1987), or POP, created a major new police technique that rivals uniform patrol. That technique requires police to systematically identify crime patterns, and the potential causes of those patterns. Like public health physicians, police are then required to intervene in the causes of the ongoing harm in order to reduce it. If they think that public prostitution markets are supported by hotels that rent rooms by the hour, then they can regulate the hotels to prevent short rentals. If police think that a violent tavern is serving drinks to intoxicated people, they can try to revoke the tavern's liquor license. While such efforts are far rarer than uniformed police patrol, they have been subjected to roughly as many controlled tests.

The results of a Campbell Collaboration systematic review of 10 controlled tests of this strategy found a statistically significant average effect in reducing calls about crime and disorder, crime reports, or other measures (Weisburd et al. 2008). The review included four "Level 5" randomized controlled trials, which also showed a significant pattern of crime or disorder prevention. The size of the average effect was smaller than in the overlapping Campbell review of hot spots policing (Braga 2007), but the overlap in the studies sampled makes such a direct comparison inappropriate. More useful will be the results of a direct comparison of problem-solving and pure patrolling in a randomized experiment currently being completed by the Police Executive Research Forum (PERF). By comparing the very different techniques of patrol and POP in the same kinds of hot spots in the same police department, the PERF experiment will provide the best evidence yet on the cost-effectiveness of the two approaches.

Investigations

A third major technique of policing is criminal investigation, generally (but not always) performed in plainclothes by people called detectives. The most crucial part of investigations may actually be done by the uniformed patrol officers who make the initial contact with a crime scene or victim, or by a forensic technician who has special skills in gathering physical evidence of the identity of offenders. The statistical evidence on the effectiveness of all aspects of investigations is thin, but like all police knowledge it has recently been growing.

The most notable advance is the 2008 publication of a multi-city, Level 5 NIJ experiment on the analysis of DNA evidence from crime scenes in Phoenix, Denver, Topeka, Los Angeles, and Orange County (CA) (Roman et al. 2008). The experiment tested the hypothesis that in cases where DNA evidence has been collected, analyzing it will increase the likelihood that police will identify suspects, make arrests, and have cases referred for prosecution. The experiment did not examine the effect of DNA analysis on conviction rates or future recidivism of suspects. It did show, however, that for an average cost of around $4,000, the analysis of DNA evidence had the following effects in comparison to control cases in which randomly assigned cases had DNA evidence that was not analyzed:

- Property crime cases where DNA evidence is processed have more than twice as many suspects identified, twice as many suspects arrested, and more than twice as many cases accepted for prosecution compared with traditional investigation;
- DNA is at least five times as likely to result in a suspect identification compared with fingerprints;
- Suspects identified by DNA had at least twice as many prior felony arrests and convictions as those identified by traditional investigation;
- Biological material collected by forensic technicians is no more likely to result in a suspect being identified than biological material collected by patrol officers. (Roman et al. 2008, 3)

This experiment must be seen the context of earlier evidence on criminal investigations, which addressed the chronic inability of police to make arrests for most reported crimes. The first generation of research on investigations was focused on developing a better "triage" system for setting priorities among criminal cases. Identifying 25 information elements that predicted at the start of an investigation whether a suspect could be identified, the Stanford Research Institute found that six of them were statistically significant predictors of an arrest. Eck (1979) then tested the model in over 12,000 investigations by 26 police agencies. He found that the model's predictions were accurate in 86 percent of the cases, and were more accurate than predictions based on qualitative case analysis by experienced investigators.

The political problem in applying the research on case "solvability factors" is that writing off cases entirely creates an appearance of callous indifference to crime victims. It is not clear how widely these findings are used, but an announced triage policy based on the factors could evoke emotional concerns that would swamp the technical rationality of the model—just as medical triage sometimes does.

Repeat Stranger Offenders

Investigations done in the reverse direction—from suspect to crime rather than crime to suspect—may be even more rational. In 1983 the Police Foundation conducted a controlled experiment of the Washington, DC, Repeat Offender Project (ROP), using quasi-random assignment to subject half of a sample of over 200 highly active stranger offenders to 24-hour covert surveillance (Martin and Sherman 1986). The targeted group of robbers, burglars and others was arrested at a rate over four times higher than the control group not put under surveillance, with most arrests of the target group made by the covert ROP investigators. Because the evidence from such arrests was provided by testimony of police who had witnessed the offender start to commit a crime, the conviction and incarceration rate was also much higher in the experimental group.

Similarly, the Phoenix Police worked with the RAND Corporation to conduct a randomized test of intensive post-arrest investigations of a list of repeat offenders (Abrahamse et al. 1991). This experiment also found an effect of policing on incapacitation: significantly higher rates of imprisonment, and longer average prison sentences. While longer incapacitation does not necessarily mean a net reduction in crime (depending on its effect on offending after release from prison), it is a common goal for policing that has now been subject to two controlled experiments.

Domestic Violence

The evidence on reducing repeat domestic violence is stronger, but less encouraging, than the evidence on stranger criminals. It is this topic that provided the first controlled field testing of arrest by random assignment, on a topic about which the wisdom of arrest was once hotly debated. Such arrests for misdemeanors not witnessed by police were not even legally possible in Minnesota until the late 1970s. With the unanimous support of the Minneapolis City Council, Sherman and Berk (1984) reported that randomly assigned arrest produced less than half as much official recidivism in six months as two non-arrest alternatives (mediation, and separation for the night). This experiment received substantial publicity, and was followed by over half of the states making such arrests mandatory (against the authors' recommendations). But it was also followed by the first program of experimental replications in the history of police experiments.

With NIJ support, five more experiments were independently conducted and reported: in Omaha, Milwaukee, Charlotte, Dade County (FL), and Colorado Springs (see Sherman 1992). The results of the experiments were not consistent across the five new tests, but they generally failed to replicate the Minneapolis result. Meanwhile, Gartin (1992) found that the Minneapolis results varied according to which data analysis strategy was employed. His most important finding was that because Sherman had given the officers their numbered random assignment sequence (of arrest, separation, and mediation responses) in advance (a method that Sherman has since advised strongly against!), some officers were omitting cases from the study when the random assignment called for an arrest. They apparently waited for a suspect they did not like to resume the sequence and impose an arrest. This meant they were non-randomly assigning arrests to suspects with longer criminal histories than were found for non-arrest cases, thus biasing the results against arrest having lower recidivism rates. (This problem was solved in the replications by having random assignment disclosed only after officers declared the case eligible.) The fact that the result went in the other direction suggests that, if anything, the original analysis may have underestimated the deterrent effect. Yet the failure to confirm that effect in other cities means that mandatory arrest for domestic violence cannot be considered evidence-based policing.

What can be considered evidence-based policing of domestic violence is politically impractical. In all four out of four domestic violence arrest experiments examined, the effects of arrest on recidivism vary according to the employment of the suspect (Sherman and Smith 1992; Pate and Hamilton 1992; Berk et al. 1992). Suspects who are reportedly employed at the time of random assignment were consistently deterred by arrests. Arrested suspects who were not employed were either not deterred, or were substantially more likely than unemployed controls (who were not arrested) to be arrested again for domestic violence. In some analyses, recidivism of unemployed suspects was twice as high after a randomly assigned arrest as after a non-arrest alternative.

These facts caused widespread consternation among practitioners, and brought further experiments on domestic violence to a virtual halt for almost two decades. Policymakers took refuge in retribution as a justification for arrest, while one criminologist published an essay saying that arrest was the right policy, even if it did cause more women to be assaulted in the future. Fortunately, the Staffordshire Police in England have resumed research on the question, after the assistant chief constable (Beale 2009) completed his master's thesis on his own agency's responses to domestic "common assaults." His experimental protocol compares randomly assigned mandatory arrest to a policy of police consulting with victims about their preference for handling the situation. Notably, it includes the use of arrest for offenders who have already fled the scene. Such cases may constitute half of all domestic assaults reported to police (Sherman 1992), and still have the only unrefuted experimental evidence that arrest (warrants) will produce deterrent effects on repeat violence (Dunford 1990).

Unless and until new experiments produce more politically palatable results, however, domestic violence will remain an issue with one of the best bodies of evidence, yet the least application of that evidence to standard police practice. This contrasts sharply with police responses to gun violence, where the evidence does not use strong research designs, but at least the research produces more consistent results.

Gun Violence

The crucial issue of gun violence has a highly plausible theory for police practice: gunfire can be reduced by deterring gun carrying in public places (Moore 1980; Wilson 1994). This theory does not require that police confiscate massive numbers of guns carried by young men on the streets. It only requires that young men in areas of high levels of gun crime leave their guns at home. The theory holds that patrolling for guns, especially with stop-and-frisk tactics under the 1968 *Terry v. Ohio* decision of the U. S. Supreme Court, will discourage gun owners (or borrowers, or even renters!) from risking the loss of the gun to the police.

This theory has consistently been supported by the evidence, including five Level 3 studies and two Level 2 tests (Koper and Mayo-Wilson 2006). The Level 3 comparisons (control versus experimental) in Indianapolis and Pittsburgh each used either homicide or gunshot wounds as one of their outcomes, replicating the results of the original field test of the theory in Kansas City (Sherman et al. 1995). The Level 2 comparisons, both in Colombia, also used homicide as the outcome measure. In every test, the gun injury data showed less harm where or when police intensified stop-search tactics to look for guns. While other kinds of outcome data (such as violent crime reports) are less consistent, they are also arguably less relevant to the theory.

There is also some evidence that police put these data to work in the 1990s, when weapons arrests spiked in relation to homicides, after which homicides started a sharp and then steady decline nationwide (Sherman 2000). While this technique is not without controversy, several recent mayoral campaigns in U.S. cities have featured promises to institute more intensive use of gun patrols in gun crime hot spots.

Juvenile Crime

In sharp contrast to gun crime, juvenile crime would appear to benefit by a radically different approach to policing. While the advent of serious violence among very young people (e.g., 12-year-old robbers) is a strong predictor of homicide (Berk et al. 2009), most offenders under 18 come to police attention much later. When they do, they are most likely to desist from further official crime. But when they are prosecuted formally in court, as recent review of randomized experiments concludes, they will become more likely to go on being arrested than if they had not been prosecuted. That was the conclusion of the 1997 Maryland Report to the U.S. Congress (Sherman 1997). And with an even more comprehensive review, that is also the conclusion of the Campbell Collaboration's more recent analysis.

In the Campbell review, Petrosino and his colleagues (2009) found 29 eligible experiments conducted over a 35-year period, with a total of 7,304 juveniles. In each of the studies, cases were assigned either at random or by a quasi-random procedure (such as alternating cases in sequence). Level 4 or lower SMS studies using matched comparisons were excluded. The 29 studies examined were therefore all likely to have had unbiased, internally valid results. The main issue with summarizing them is that they had a wide variety of "experimental" conditions in comparison to prosecution, ranging from doing nothing to a diversion program. Yet that variety is also a strength of the analysis, making it generalizable to a broad range of alternatives to formal processing of suspects under age 18.

The meta-analysis of these 29 tests shows that, on average, formal processing of juvenile suspects in court causes statistically significant patterns of *increases* in the prevalence and incidence of future crime, as well as an increase in severity of crime that is near the borderline for statistical significance. The one exception is that in four tests of formal processing of offenders with no prior records, the processing caused a *decrease* in future offending. All other studies had samples with varying extensiveness of prior criminal records. It is also important that diversion to some combination of programmatic services generally did much better at reducing repeat crime than mere diversion to "doing nothing."

While these findings might be considered a matter for prosecution, there is actually a major policy implication for police. Fifty years ago, police handled a wide range of juvenile matters by informal resolution, rather than putting juveniles into the legal system. They are still legally entitled to do that under the case law of police discretion. Police agencies that decide not to bring these kinds of juvenile cases to court—especially if they could divert the offenders to some mandatory services—would not just be returning to traditional police practices. They would be practicing evidence-based policing.

Drug Dealing

A substantial body of evidence has been created on police responses to drug dealing, both in open-air markets and inside "drug houses." It generally shows better results from sustained pressure of regulatory tools (Green 1995; Mazerolle et al. 2000; Eck and Wartell 1998) than from the more dramatic tactics of raids (Sherman and Rogan 1995). Eck and Wartell, for example, randomly assigned 121 San Diego drug houses on rental property to three conditions: no action (42), police meetings with property owners to discuss eviction procedures (42), or letters to property owners offering such meetings (37). The meetings produced the largest number of evictions and the largest drop in crime on the properties. Letters did better than control (no action), but not as well as meetings. Mazerolle and colleagues (2000) randomly assigned civil code enforcement to half of a sample of 100 drug dealing locations in Oakland, with routine patrol responses as the control group. The code enforcement strategy reduced reported crime, but showed evidence of displacement when applied to commercial locations.

Restorative Justice

Since 1989, police in New Zealand and Australia have been involved to varying degrees in face-to-face meetings between crime victims, their offenders, and their respective families and friends. These meetings occur only after an offender has accepted responsibility for the crime and has agreed to discuss it with the victim. The twin goals of the process are for the offender to help repair the harm suffered by victims and loved ones, as well as to give the offender more reasons for not committing crime in the future. These meetings fall generally under the rubric of "restorative justice," much of which actually involves no face-to-face contact between victims and offenders. There is a substantial evidence base, however, on the variety called "Restorative Justice Conferencing" (RJC).

This strategy was first tested in four randomized trials in the Australian capital of Canberra (Strang et al. 1999). Those trials were followed by seven independently evaluated Level 5 tests in England, as well as one in Indianapolis. A total of 12 randomized trials with almost 3,000 offenders have been included in the systematic review of RJC effects for the Campbell Collaboration (Strang et al. 2009). Almost all of the tests compared police-led RJC to a variety of control conditions involving no RJC. Overall, these studies show a statistically significant pattern of RJC reducing the frequency of repeat convictions over the two years after random assignment. While the effect sizes are modest, the cost benefit gains are substantial. Shapland and her colleagues (2008) estimated that Sherman and Strang's 7 English RCTs, for example, produced an average return on investment of 9 to 1, the ratio of the estimated costs of crime prevented by RJC to the cost of delivering it by police in London and Northumbria, and by prison and probation staff in Thames Valley (Sherman 2009).

Knowledge Gaps

The evidence on policing may be substantial and growing, but there are enormous gaps in the evidence. Perhaps the highest priority is to generate more replications of previous experiments in other countries. The question of whether what works in policing can become knowledge without borders is crucial for interpreting all future police research. Given the lack of replication that can be found even within countries, it is even more important for each nation or region (such as Scandinavia) to conduct their own crucial tests. Simply relying on research done in other nations or cities will not provide a firm enough foundation for predicting the likely effects of police practices. The growing number of international research reviews, such as the juvenile prosecution and restorative justice examples, demonstrates that such cross-national replication is possible.

Another major knowledge gap concerns the use of alternatives to arrest. While police once relied heavily on informal social control, the age of legalism has pressed police to use criminal law more exclusively as a response to any situation. Yet the evidence on drug dealing suggests that civil remedies are more effective than criminal prosecution. The evidence on juvenile policing suggests that prosecution causes even more crime. The evidence on restorative justice shows that informal social control greatly augments formal controls, and can even do better at crime prevention. Rather than viewing alternatives to prosecution as "not" doing something, police could develop a new portfolio of evidence-based peacekeeping techniques that would stay away from the courtroom.

The key concept in all police innovation, of course, must be evidence. British police have been criticized for using informal diversion from prosecution in egregious cases. But no controlled test of police diversion to "fixed penalty notices" (like a traffic ticket) or "conditional cautioning" (like a pre-trial probation sentence) was ever conducted. The government simply created the legal tools, and told police to use them. That is perhaps as sound as telling doctors to prescribe new pharmaceuticals for their patients without testing the drugs for safety and effectiveness.

KNOWLEDGE, POWER AND POLICING

The fundamental issue in evidence-based policing is democracy. The question is whether police methods should be chosen by democratic votes, or by expert reviews of unbiased evidence. At the same time that police knowledge has been growing, elected officials have become more assertive in ordering police to do things that are at odds with the evidence. In both London and New York, there is a claim to be following evidence-based government. But on both sides of the Atlantic, there is much doubt about how elected officials interpret scientific evidence. They are not required, of course, to be experts on any technical questions. But as long as they may see electoral advantage in shaping police policy, there will be a continuing clash between doing what works for politics and what works for crime prevention.

There is unlikely to be any easy or early resolution of this tension. Democracy needs to be moderately distrustful of police if only as a matter of checks and balances. Yet if democracy is unwilling to trust in police knowledge—even when it is co-produced with scientists—then it may suffer higher levels of crime. It is not necessary to trust police blindly when the evidence on policing is transparent. Ultimately, police themselves can contribute to their own evidence-based independence by accepting this point. If police repeatedly base their expert authority on objective evidence, rather than on subjective opinions, they can challenge their critics to show how the objective evidence is wrong.

In the long sweep of history, both evidence and democracy have been growing. In recent years, the growth of research evidence has pulled ahead. There are so many missed opportunities for citizens to vote at present that some observers conclude that democracy has met its limits. In the discovery of new knowledge about democratic police practices, the possibilities are limitless.

References

Abrahamse, Allan F., Patricia A. Ebener, Peter W. Greenwood, Nora Fitzgerald, and Thomas E. Kosin. 1991. "An Experimental Evaluation of the Phoenix Repeat Offender Program." *Justice Quarterly* 8: 141–168.

Apel, Robert, and Daniel Nagin. 2010. *General Deterrence: A Review of Recent Evidence*. Chapter 14, this volume.

Barrie, David G. 2008. "Police in the Age of Improvement: Police Development and the Civic Tradition in Scotland, 1775–1865." Cullompton, UK: Willan.

Berk, Richard A., Alec Campbell, Ruth Klap, and Bruce Western. 1992. "The Deterrent Effect of Arrest in Incidents of Domestic Violence: A Bayesian Analysis of Four Field Experiments." *American Sociological Review* 57: 698–708.

Berk, Richard, Lawrence Sherman, Geoffrey Barnes, Ellen Kurtz, and Lindsay Ahlman. 2009. "Forecasting Murder within a Population of Probationers and Parolees: A High Stakes Application of Statistical Learning." *Journal of the Royal Statistical Society*. Series A. *Statistics in Society* 172: 191–211.

Bittner, Egon. 1990. *Aspects of Police Work*. Boston: Northeastern University Press.

Blair, Ian. 2009. Policing Controversy. London: Profile Books.

Braga, Anthony. 2007. "The Effects of Hot Spots Policing on Crime." A Campbell Collaboration Systematic Review. Available at http://www.campbellcollaboration.org/library.php.

Braga, Anthony, and Brenda J. Bond. 2008. "Policing Crime and Disorder in Hot Spots: A Randomized, Controlled Trial." *Criminology* 46: 577–607.

Campbell, Donald T., and Julian C. Stanley. 1966. *Experimental and Quasi-Experimental Designs for Research*. Chicago: Rand-McNally.

Corman, Hope, and Naci Mocan. 2005. "Carrots, Sticks and Broken Windows." *Journal of Law and Economics* 48: 235–266.

Dunford, Franklyn W. 1990. "System-Initiated Warrants for Suspects of Misdemeanor Domestic Assault: A Pilot Study." *Justice Quarterly* 7: 631–653.

Eck, John E. 1979. *Managing Case Assignments: The Burglary Investigation Decision Model Replication*. Washington, DC: Police Executive Research Forum.

Eck, John, and William Spelman. 1987. *Problem-Solving: Problem-Oriented Policing in Newport News*. Washington, DC: Police Executive Research Forum.

Eck, John, and Julia Wartell. 1998. "Improving the Management of Rental Properties with Drug Problems: A Randomized Experiment."*Crime Prevention Studies*, Vol. 9, 161–185. Monsey, NY: Criminal Justice Press.

Fielding, Henry. 1755. *Journal of a Voyage to Lisbon*. London. Available at http://ebooks.adelaide.edu.au/f/fielding/henry/lisbon&/introduction2.html.

Gawande, Atul. 2009. "Testing, Testing." *The New Yorker*, December 14, 34–41.

Goldkamp, John, and E. Riley Vilcica. 2008. "Targeted Enforcement and Adverse System Side Effects: The Generation of Fugitives in Philadelphia." *Criminology* 46: 371–409.

Goldstein, Herman. 1977. *Policing a Free Society*. Cambridge: Ballinger.

Goldstein, Herman. 1979. "Improving Policing: A Problem-Oriented Approach." *Crime and Delinquency* 25: 236–258.

Goldstein, Herman. 1990. *Problem-Oriented Policing*. New York: McGraw-Hill.

Guerette, Rob T., and Kate Bowers. 2009. "Assessing the Extent of Crime Displacement and Diffusion of Benefits: A Review of Situational Crime Prevention Evaluations." *Criminology* 47: 1331–1368.

Hurd, Douglas. 2007. *Robert Peel: A Biography*. London: Weidenfield and Nicolson.

Keizer, Kees, Siegwart Lindenberg, and Linda Steg. 2008. "The Spreading of Disorder." *Science* (December 12): 1681–1685.

Koper, Christopher. 1995. "Just Enough Police Presence: Reducing Crime and Disorderly Behavior by Optimizing Patrol Time in Crime Hot Spots." *Justice Quarterly* 12: 649–672.

Koper, Christopher, and Evan Mayo-Wilson. 2006. "Police Crackdowns on Illegal Gun Carrying: A Systematic Review of Their Impact on Gun Crime." *Journal of Experimental Criminology* 2: 227–261.

Lee, W. L. Melville. 1901 *A History of Police in England*. London: Methuen.

Lum, Cynthia. 2009. *Translating Police Research into Practice: Ideas in American Policing Series*. Washington, DC: Police Foundation.

Martin, Susan, and Lawrence Sherman. 1986. "Selective Apprehension: A Police Strategy for Repeat Offenders." *Criminology* 24: 55–72.

Mazerolle, Lorraine Green, James F. Price, and Jan Roehl. 2000. "Civil Remedies and Drug Control: A Randomized Field Trial in Oakland, California." *Evaluation Review* 24: 212–241.

Moore, Mark. 1980. "The Police and Weapons Offenses." *Annals of the American Academy of Political and Social Sciences* 452: 22–32.

Pate, Antony, and Edwin E. Hamilton. 1992. "Formal and Informal Deterrents to Domestic Violence: The Dade County Spouse Assault Experiment." *American Sociological Review* 57: 691–698.

Petrosino, Anthony, Carolyn Turpin-Petrosino, and Sarah Guckenberg. 2009. "Formal System Processing of Juveniles: Effects on Delinquency." Campbell Collaboration Review. Available at http://www.campbellcollaboration.org/library.php.

Radzinowicz, Leon. 1956. *A History of English Criminal Law and Its Administration from 1750*, Vol. 3: *Cross-Currents in the Movement for the Reform of the Police*. London: Stevens & Sons.

Reiss, Albert J., Jr. 1971. *The Police and the Public*. New Haven: Yale University Press.

Richardson, James F. 1970. *The New York Police: Colonial Times to 1900*. New York: Oxford University Press.

Roman, John K., Shannon Reid, Jay Reid, Aaron Chalfin, William Adams, and Carly Knight. 2008. *The DNA Field Experiment: Cost-Effectiveness Analysis of the Use of DNA in the Investigation of High-Volume Crimes*. Washington, DC: Urban Institute.

Sampson, Robert J., and Stephen W. Raudenbush. 1999. "Systematic Social Observation of Public Spaces: A New Look at Disorder in Urban Neighborhoods." *American Journal of Sociology* 105: 603–651.

Shapland, Joanna, Anne Atkinson, Helen Atkinson, James Dignan, Lucy Edwards, Jeremy Hibbert, Marie Howes, Jennifer Johnstone, Gwen Robinson, and Angela Sorsby. 2008. *Does Restorative Justice Affect Reconviction? The Fourth Report from the Evaluation of Three Schemes*. London: Ministry of Justice.

Shaw, James. 1995. "Community Policing Against Guns: Public Opinion of the Kansas City Gun Experiment." *Justice Quarterly* 12: 695–710.

Sherman, Lawrence W. 1980. "Execution Without Trial: Police Homicide and the Constitution." *Vanderbilt Law Review* 33 (1): 71–100.

Sherman, Lawrence W. 1983. "Reducing Police Gun Use: Critical Events, Administrative Policy and Organizational Change." In *Control in the Police Organization*, ed. Maurice Punch, 98–125. Cambridge, MA: MIT Press.

Sherman, Lawrence W. 1986. "Policing Communities: What Works?" In *Communities and Crime*, Vol. 8, *Crime and Justice*, eds. Albert J. Reiss, Jr. and Michael Tonry, 343–386. Chicago: University of Chicago Press.

Sherman, Lawrence. 1992. *Policing Domestic Violence: Experiments and Dilemmas*. New York: Free Press.

Sherman, Lawrence W. 1997. "Thinking about Crime Prevention." In *Preventing Crime: What Works, What Doesn't, What's Promising*, eds. Lawrence W. Sherman, Denise Gottfredson, Doris MacKenzie, John Eck, Peter Reuter, and Shawn D. Bushway, Washington, DC: U.S. Department of Justice. Available at http://www.ncjrs.gov/works/.

Sherman, Lawrence. 1998. *Evidence-Based Policing*. Washington, DC: Police Foundation.

Sherman, Lawrence. 2000. "Gun Carrying and Homicide Prevention." Editorial. *Journal of the American Medical Association* 283: 1193–1195.

Sherman, Lawrence. 2009. "Evidence and Liberty: The Promise of Experimental Criminology." *Criminology and Criminal Justice* 9: 5–28.

Sherman, Lawrence. 2011. *Experimental Criminology*. London: Sage.

Sherman, Lawrence, and Richard Berk. 1984. "The Specific Deterrent Effects of Arrest for Domestic Assault." *American Sociological Review* 49 (2): 261–271.

Sherman, Lawrence, Patrick Gartin, and Michael E. Buerger. 1989. "Hot Spots of Predatory Crime: Routine Activities and the Criminology of Place." *Criminology* 27 (1): 27–55.

Sherman, Lawrence, and Dennis P. Rogan. 1995. "Deterrent Effects of Police Raids on Crack Houses: A Randomized, Controlled Experiment." *Justice Quarterly* 12: 755–781.

Sherman, Lawrence, Dennis P. Rogan, and James Shaw. 1995. *The Kansas City Gun Experiment*. Washington, DC: National Institute of Justice, Research in Brief.

Sherman, Lawrence, and Douglas A. Smith. 1992. "Crime, Punishment and Stake in Conformity: Legal and Informal Control of Domestic Violence." *American Sociological Review* 57 (5): 680–690.

Sherman, Lawrence, and David Weisburd. 1995. "General Deterrent Effects of Police Patrol in Crime Hot Spots: A Randomized, Controlled Trial." *Justice Quarterly* 12 (4): 635–648.Yes

Skogan, Wesley. 2009. Personal Communication, Nov. 4.

Skogan, Wesley, and Kathleen Frydl, eds. 2004. *Fairness and Effectiveness in Policing: The Evidence*. Washington, DC: National Academies Press.

Skogan, Wesley, and Susan Hartnett. 1997. *Community Policing, Chicago Style*. New York: Oxford University Press.

Strang, Heather, Geoffrey C. Barnes, John Braithwaite, and Lawrence W. Sherman. 1999. *Experiments in Restorative Policing: A Progress Report on the Canberra Reintegrative Shaming Experiments (RISE)*. Canberra: Australian National University.

Strang, Heather, Lawrence Sherman, Daniel Woods, and Evan Mayo-Wilson. 2009. *Effects of Restorative Justice Conferencing on Victims and Offenders: A Systematic Review*. Draft Review for the Campbell Collaboration. Cambridge, UK: Cambridge University, Institute of Criminology, Jerry Lee Centre of Experimental Criminology.

Sunshine, J., and T. R. Tyler. 2003. "The Role of Procedural Justice and Legitimacy in Shaping Public Support for Policing." *Law and Society Review* 37 (3): 513–48.

Sunstein, Cass. 2009. "Some Effects of Moral Indignation on Law." *Vermont Law Review* 33: 405–433.

Tankebe, Justice. 2008. "Police Effectiveness and Police Trustworthiness in Ghana: An Empirical Appraisal." *Criminology and Criminal Justice* 8: 185–202.

Tyler, Tom. 1990. *Why People Obey the Law*. New Haven, CT: Yale University Press.

Vollmer, August. 1936. *The Police and Modern Society*. Berkeley: University of California Press.

Weisburd, David, Shawn Bushway, Cynthia Lum, and Sue-Ming Yang. 2004. "Trajectories of Crime at Places: A Longitudinal Study of Street Segments in the City of Seattle." *Criminology* 42: 283–322.

David Weisburd, Cody W. Telep, Joshua C. Hinkle, and John E. Eck. 2008. "The Effects of Problem-Oriented Policing on Crime and Disorder." A Campbell Collaboration Systematic Review. Available at http://www.campbellcollaboration.org/library.php.

Weisburd, David, Laura Wyckoff, Justin Ready, John E. Eck, Joshua C. Hinkle, and Frank Gajewski. 2006. "Does Crime Just Move Around the Corner?: A Controlled Study of Spatial Displacement and Diffusion of Crime Control Benefits." *Criminology* 44 (3): 549–591.

Westley, William A. 1970. *Violence and the Police A Sociological Study of Law, Custom, and Morality*. Cambridge, MA: MIT Press.

Wilson, James Q. 1968. *Varieties of Police Behavior: The Management of Law and Order in Eight Communities*. Cambridge, MA: Harvard University Press.

Wilson, James Q. 1994. "Just Take Away Their Guns: Forget Gun Control." *New York Times Magazine*, March 20, 46–47.

Wilson, James Q., and George L. Kelling. 1982. "Broken Windows: The Police and Neighborhood Safety." *Atlantic Monthly* (March): 29–38.

Zimbardo, P. G. 1970. "The Human Choice: Individuation, Reason, and Order Versus Deindividuation, Impulse, and Chaos." In *The 1969 Nebraska Symposium on Motivation*, eds. W. J. Arnold and D. Levine, 237–307. Lincoln: University of Nebraska Press.

Chapter 21

Crime and Public Policy

James Q. Wilson

There are two great questions about crime: Why do people differ in the rate at which they break the law, and why do crime rates in a society rise and fall? You might think that the answer to each question would be the same, but they are not. As Terrie Moffitt and her colleagues explain in chapter 3 of this volume, some people are biologically more likely to commit crimes than are others. But when our nation's crime rate rose sharply, as it did in the 1960s and 1970s, it was not because there was a sudden increase in our biological predisposition to crime. Other factors must have played a role. We also know that young men are much more likely to commit crimes than are young women, but most societies have the same proportion of men and women, even though their crime rates differ sharply.

The chapters in this book provide fascinating answers to both questions: we know much more than we used to about why people differ in how many crimes they commit, and we have learned a lot (though not yet enough) about what factors make the crime rate go up or down. In this chapter I will draw on these findings to provide my overview of what this knowledge means for public policy, but in doing so I am not providing an agreed-upon summary of what has been learned. The authors of the other chapters have not reviewed what I have written here; some may agree, some may not. If you are a student, do not read this chapter to find a condensed version of the whole book; instead, read the book.

CRIME RATES

Everyone knows that the United States has a high level of homicide, though one much reduced from what it was 20 years ago. But some people forget, as James Lynch and William Pridemore point out in chapter 2, that this country has a level of less-serious crime, including most property crimes, that is about the same as what we find in other democratic countries.

Explaining why we have so many murders and (relatively) so few burglaries is not an easy task. We have probably kept the burglary rate lower than what one finds in some European nations because we are more likely to imprison burglars. Lynch and Pridemore point out that this country is more likely to convict a person for burglary and robbery than are England, Scotland, and Switzerland and more likely to send convicted persons to prison than are Australia, England, Scotland, and Sweden, and to keep people in prison for longer periods than are England, the Netherlands, Scotland, Sweden, and Switzerland.

These differences suggest, but do not prove, that America's criminal justice system has helped keep the rates of burglary and robbery lower than what one finds in many comparable nations. To prove this argument, of course, would require us to take into account all of the many differences among the countries, an analysis that is very difficult to do. One personal anecdote may explain why I take this possibility seriously. When I visited England in the 1980s, that country sent a higher fraction of its robbers to prison than did California, and the English robbery rate was lower than California's. When I returned to England 20 years later, the situation had reversed itself: now the English sent a much smaller fraction of robbers to prison than did California, and its robbery rate had become higher than here. One is entitled to suppose that imprisonment affects national differences in crime rates (Wilson 1976, 1997).

But if that is so, it does not explain why this country has so high a homicide rate. We convict and imprison murderers at about the same rate as do European nations, but our homicide rate is more than five times higher than England's. The only answer we can give is that America is a more murderous country than is England or any other European nation. We have been that way for a long time. The late Eric Monkkonen has shown that the homicide rate in New York City has been 10 to 15 times higher than it has been in London for at least 200 years (Monkkonen 2001). That level of violence occurred long before televised violence, widespread drug use, and the advent of semiautomatic weapons.

Why is that so# Imagine that you are asked this question on an exam. Your answer could plausibly list all of the distinctive features of American history. We are a nation of immigrants; we never had a powerful aristocracy that could keep ordinary people in their place; our government has always been weaker and more decentralized than most governments abroad; we had to settle an open frontier inhabited by sometimes hostile Native Americans; we settled it before there was a government to manage it; we practiced racial slavery that used force to suppress black Americans and when they became free, especially during the Jim Crow period, we did not have the police enforce criminal laws if the offense took place among blacks. Prohibition created violent gangs that outlasted the dry years. The South has long had a culture of honor that placed a high value on maintaining status by means of dueling. And so on.

Some may suppose that the prevalence of guns in this country may explain our high homicide rate. No doubt it explains some of it; as Philip Cook and his colleagues point out in chapter 10, we do not have drive-by knifings, but we do have drive-by shootings. But guns cannot explain the whole difference. As Franklin Zimring and Gordon Hawkins have pointed out, in 1984 the rate at which we kill people *without* using guns (with knives, clubs, fists, and poison) is three times higher than the rate at which British kill each other without using guns (Zimring and Hawkins 1997). With the recent decline in homicide rates that connection may or may not still be true, but it remains the case that Americans are more violent with or without guns

THE RECENT DECLINE IN CRIME

Crime rates rose from the early 1960s until the early 1980s, then leveled off a bit, then increased sharply in the late 1980s and early 1990s, and then dropped again right into 2009. Part of this decline is the result, as Greenwood and Turner show, of a decline in the proportion of juveniles in the population. When there are fewer young people, there is less crime. But that is not the whole story; the late Marvin Wolfgang and his colleagues have shown us that young people in the 1970s were not only a bigger share of the population, they had also become, as individuals, more likely to commit serious crimes (Tracy, Wolfgang, and Figlio 1990).

Several authors suggest that the spike in violent crime in the late 1980s was the result of the emergence of street-level crack dealing, an enterprise that involved young people who, in order to protect themselves and harass other dealers, acquired guns. But as the crack trade either diminished or came under tighter control in the mid-1990s, the need for violence declined (Blumstein, Rivara, and Rosenfeld 2000).

In addition, we made heavier use of prison. The number of people in prison rose from about 320,000 in 1980 to 1.1 million in 1995. This country is often criticized for putting a lot of people in prison, but as Apel and Nagin point out in chapter 14, there are several important studies that show that increasing the risk of going to prison for a crime reduces the rate at which that crime is committed. Deterrence works, though the studies disagree about how large this deterrent effects is.

One reason for this uncertainty is that the effect of prison on crime rates changes with the amount of imprisonment. Piehl and Useem make this point in chapter 18. If a state imprisons very few people, adding more prisoners drives the crime rate down by a large amount. But if the state already imprisons a lot of offenders, adding more prisoners has only a modest effect on the crime rate.

If punishment reduces crime, why doesn't every nation punish more? There are several reasons. One is cost: it takes a lot of money to build and manage a prison. But an even more important reason is politics. In this country, the criminal justice system is under popular control: district attorneys and many judges are elected. When people worry about crime, prosecutors and judges worry also. But in most industrialized nations, prosecutors and judges are appointed by the national government, and these officials are sensitive, not to what the public wants, but to what their national superiors prefer. These superiors are upper-middle-class people who can afford to protect themselves against crime and who may be more concerned with other issues.

But there is much we still need to know. Gangs cause a lot of crime; in some cities, such as Los Angeles, they may cause most of the murders. It would be nice to know how gang activity changes and in response to what political or community activities. Maxson in chapter 6 shows that, in many cities, gangs have become less common in recent years, though in some large ones, such as Chicago and Los Angeles, they remain powerful and increase sharply the number of crime that their young members commit.

There are accounts by journalists suggesting that, in some large cities, gangs have reduced the conflict among them and may even have begun to cooperate in selling drugs and other criminal activities. If true, this suggests that we may have less violence but more illegal business transactions, a trade-off that, though worrisome, may make people safer from drive-by shootings.

People have also invested more heavily in self-defense. They have moved to the suburbs, hired security guards to watch over their big-city apartments, equipped their cars with alarms and special locks, and stayed away from dangerous neighborhoods. We do not know how big a difference this change has made, but we do know that much street crime is committed by people who live near their targets. Crime not only requires criminals, it also requires opportunities. When there are fewer opportunities, there is less crime because most offenders do not travel far to find new targets.

But when middle-class people move out of a crime-ridden neighborhood in order to be safer, they leave behind people who cannot or will not move out and who therefore become less safe. As Robert Sampson points out in chapter 8, crime is more common in unstable neighborhoods where it is hard to maintain an adequate sense of mutual trust and a shared willingness to act to reduce crime. What Sampson calls the "collective efficacy" of a neighborhood is reduced when people with a commitment to sustaining it move away.

Our culture changes also, with people at some times being somewhat tolerant of crime or at least resigned to its being commonplace and at other times being intolerant of it and determined to do something about it. Public policies aimed at solving other problems may also reduce crime rates. The spread of shelters for abused women has not only helped them but may well have reduced the rate at which women are killed by abusive males. There is evidence that in the 1960s and 1970s that crime rose not only in America but everywhere in Europe despite rising levels of economic progress, because people, especially young ones, felt that they had been freed from traditional restraints on their behavior (Wilson 1983). Today society seems less tolerant of "doing your own thing"; perhaps that has helped reduce crime rates.

Police tactics have also changed. Sherman points out in chapter 20 that some departments have become skillful at reducing crime rates by improving how they manage police patrols, respond to calls for help, and manage the ways in which officers spend their time. When the police focus on known offenders and the "hot spots" where crime is likely to occur, they can have a larger impact than when they merely drive around on patrol or wait for 911 calls. In several cities the police are directed, through management techniques like CompStat that was pioneered in New York City by William Bratton, to focus not on maximizing arrests but on reducing crime. This police management technique makes detailed analyses of crime rates in particular neighborhoods and holds the precinct or district commanders accountable for reducing those rates, sometimes by arrests but sometimes by relocating patrols or changing the physical environment.

Finally, changes in public health affect crime rates. Lead can cause reductions in intelligence and increases in crime. When government policies led to a reduction in the amount of leaded gasoline and paint, data suggests that this may have helped reduce crime levels (Reyes 2007).

CAN MORE BE DONE TO REDUCE CRIME?

When the crime rate in America began rising sharply in the early 1960s, scholars did not know much about how it might be controlled. Many denied that deterrence works; to them, crime was entirely the result of human factors (attitudes, peer connections, family difficulties, school problems, and the like) that made would-be offenders immune to the risk of punishment. It was customary then to say that crime could only be reduced by changing its "root causes."

No doubt reducing the causes of crime would help, but 40 years ago we did not have a very good idea of what those causes were. Many people thought that unemployment caused crime, but in the 1960s that was a curious view since the American economy was booming and unemployment rates were quite low.

The connection between crime and the economy is much more complicated than popular discussions recognize. As Bushway shows in chapter 7, the link between unemployment and crime is dependent on time. When people first become unemployed, they stay at home, draw on savings, or work on homely tasks. Crime rates stay low. But if unemployment persists it may well drive up crime rates. And more is at stake than unemployment. One is the share of people who participate in the labor market. When this is high, people feel connected to work even when they are unemployed. But when people have never joined the labor market or have left it because they have a prison record or are engaged in drug dealing, they become detached from the goal of finding legitimate work.

Moreover, it may be the condition of the economy as a whole (the gross domestic product, or GDP) rather than the unemployment rate that affects human behavior. A decline in GDP may push burglary rates up, but an *increase* in GDP may drive auto theft rates up. Economists continue to puzzle over these connections. One possibility is that imprisonment has affected so many offenders that they find the legal labor market either unappealing or inaccessible.

Others thought that family problems were the cause, but no one knew much about how the government could affect family life. Still others blamed gangs and bad companions and urged gang workers to reduce these bad influences. That was a good idea except that then—and to a considerable extent, still today—we do not know very much about reducing gang influences.

But the rising crime rate produced at least one good result: a sharp increase in intelligent research on crime. Today we know vastly more than we once did about individual differences in the tendency to break the law and about the effect (or in some cases, the non-effect) of policies aimed at reducing crime rates. The most important thing to do is to move toward evidence-based criminal justice policies. This book contains a summary of much of that evidence.

DETERRENCE

We know that punishment deters crime, but we also know that it is probably the swiftness and certainty of being imprisoned more than the severity of the penalty that has the largest effect. This raises the question of whether we keep some people in prison too long. Typical offenders commit most of their crimes when they are in their early twenties, and very few after they reach their forties. Perhaps we could cut prison costs and open up more prison space by shortening sentences.

But we can only do that if we think that the chief purpose of punishment is deterrence. If punishment also has a moral role by conveying society's view about the wrongness of some behavior, then there are important limits to how short sentences can be. You go to prison if you are convicted of murdering your spouse, but how long you stay there does not depend on whether, after your release, you will murder your next spouse; indeed, convicted wife murderers are not likely to marry again. You are kept in prison for a long time because society thinks murder is a terrible crime, not because we simply want to discourage more murders. Prison terms for some offenses can be safely reduced; for example, it may make little sense to keep an auto thief in prison for a long time since theft, though a serious crime, is not one that arouses powerful (and desirable) retributive instincts.

And it may make even less sense to keep a drug dealer in prison very long because when one dealer leaves, a rival takes his place on the street. Punishing people who deal in certain drugs is a good idea because we want to make it clear that using these substances is a big mistake, but long sentences for drug dealing are not likely to reduce that dealing.

A better way to shorten prison terms and thus create more space for new offenders is to rethink the practice, common in many states, of sending people who violate the terms of their parole back to prison. Some parolees do things that merit reimprisonment, but others commit only technical violations that could be handled more easily by toughening up community controls.

The creation of global positioning satellites makes it possible today to require people on probation or parole to wear a GPS monitor around their ankles, accompanied by a device that warns the police if they try to remove it. The GPS monitor can tell probation and parole officers exactly where their charges are and can be fitted with devices that set off an alarm if they go to forbidden places (for example, a school or a dangerous bar).

Another strategy is to give an incentive to persons to avoid crime. Project HOPE, described by Boyum, Caulkins, and Kleiman in chapter 13, is a major advancement in how to keep people on probation, most of whom have committed felonies, from committing more. It shows how overworked probation officers can be mobilized to write up short, simple violation notices and get judges quickly to warn and then punish with short jail terms people who fail to obey the terms of probation. The result of swift deterrence was a sharp drop in crime rates, even though no "root causes" were eliminated.

PREVENTING CRIME

Preventing people from becoming criminal is an ideal strategy: it spares us the later and high costs of more police, more judges, and more prison time. The problem is to discover and test programs that in fact prevent crime and to be sure that a program that works on a few people in one place when it is run by gifted researchers will work across the country for thousands of people when it is run by ordinary employees.

Happily, we have learned a lot about what works. There are several sources of such knowledge. One is the Center for the Study and Prevention of Violence at the University of Colorado, which has produced short, readable accounts of prevention programs that meet at least two tests. The first is that they have been evaluated by randomly assigning people to either the program or to the status quo. Random assignment is important because it eliminates the possibility that a program only appears to work owing to the fact that those in the program are predisposed to benefit and those not in it are inclined to resist change. Random assignment means that both participants and the control group are equal. The second requirement is to test the program in more than one place. This is important because it reduces the chance that some exceptional feature of one locale, or the people in that locale, explain the gains.

The University of Colorado survey lists about a dozen programs that have survived these two tests. Some of them seem obvious: for example, a program that teaches children to avoid drug use (Project STAR), another that makes foster homes work better (Treatment Foster Care), and yet another that helps improve family life (Functional Family Therapy). But some successes may strike you as puzzling. One is the Nurse Home Visitation Program, which sends trained nurses into the homes of poor young girls who have just become pregnant. The nurses explain how to care for newborn babies by feeding, clothing, and handling their health care needs. Why should any of this affect later criminality? But it does: in one study, done in Elmira, New York, the female children of these mothers 19 years later were one-fifth as likely to be arrested or convicted of a crime as those in the control group (Eckenrode, 2010). But there was no improvement for the male children. For the girls, early care made a difference.

There no doubt are other good programs, but because they have not been rigorously evaluated we do not know that they work. One may be the High/Scope Perry Preschool Project in Ypsilanti, Michigan. About one hundred three- or four-year-old children were randomly divided between being in and out of a new preschool project. They were followed for over 20 years, and those in the program were less likely than those not in it to have been arrested, to be unemployed, or to receive welfare (Schweinhart, Barnes, and Weikart 2005). But for reasons that I do not know, the program was only done in one city and so it did not meet the Colorado test.

As David Farrington shows in chapter 5, we have learned some things about reducing the extent to which bad families can cause crime among their children. These programs are not easily managed, as many involve dealing with family members in special clinics or as part of a program that involves children, their schoolteachers, and their parents.

Unfortunately, programs that work are not nearly as well-known as those that do not. Millions of people have heard of DARE (Drug Abuse Resistance Education), a program that sends police officers into fifth-grade classes to teach students to avoid drugs. The several studies that have been done show that it has not reduced later drug use. (It may still be a helpful program if it makes the police and young people get along better, but that was not what it was intended to achieve.) Everybody knows about DARE; hardly anybody knows about nurse home visitations.

GUNS AND CRIME

For many people, America's high homicide rate would go down sharply if we just got guns off the street. But public opinion polls and a recent Supreme Court decision make it clear that this will not happen. The Court held that the Second Amendment gives to individual citizens the right to own a gun, but it allows the states to impose reasonable restrictions on the kinds of guns and how they may be purchased (*District of Columbia v. Heller* 2008). However, if guns did disappear, we would still have a higher murder rate than does England because we kill people at a higher rate without using guns than does England.

Government restrictions may limit gun purchases to people who are not criminals but they may not ban (as has been tried in a few places) every citizen from owning any gun. And such bans would probably not make much difference; after they were enacted, violent crime rates in many of those places continued to rise. The reason is simple: there are hundred of millions of guns in private possession. A criminal can easily steal one or, in places where their sale is legal, get a person without a criminal record to buy one and pass it on to him.

But surely we can reduce the number of guns carried by people who are ready to use them for criminal purposes. Yes, but this tactic requires certain restrictions on civil rights and a great need for a better technology.

The civil rights problem is that the police must be able to justify a search of another person. That is easily done if the person is arrested or the police have a search warrant. But it is not so easily done if the police spot a suspicious person on the street and try to search him. It can be done under certain circumstances. The Supreme Court has ruled that the police may stop and frisk someone if an officer observes unusual conduct that leads him or her reasonably to conclude that the person may be armed or dangerous (*Terry v. Ohio* 1968). A "stop and frisk" means patting down a person's clothing and, if a gun is felt, seizing it. These street stops have become very important in some big cities, with thousands of guns being taken off the streets.

The police can also search for guns when they make traffic stops; Lawrence Sherman has reported that when this was done in a part of Kansas City, many guns were seized and in that neighborhood the crime rate fell.

The police in some cities have asked parents to allow their homes to be searched for guns that might be owned by their children on the understanding that, if a gun is found, no one will be arrested. And in every state, probation and parole officers have the authority to take guns from anyone under their supervision.

It is possible that technology might be devised that would allow the police to detect from a distance whether a person was carrying a concealed weapon on the street. Of course, some people carrying a concealed weapon may have a permit that allows this. But others who lack such permits could have their gun seized. This technology has been produced. It uses millimeter-band radar. But the device is too cumbersome for the police to carry. More research is needed to create a more useful apparatus.

Guns play a role in self-defense. Studies have been done to estimate how frequently a gun protects a person threatened with assault or robbery. The results vary; no one is sure what the correct number is, but it is much larger than zero. One study argues that places where people find it easy to get a permit to carry a concealed weapon have, other things being equal, a lower risk of being murdered (Lott 2000). Other studies have challenged this finding (Donohue and Ayres 2003; Black and Nagin 1998). A committee appointed by the National Academy of Sciences examined the issue and, with one dissent, agreed with the critics. I was the dissenter (Wellford, Pepper, and Petrie 2004).

REDUCING CRIME AMONG EX-CONVICTS

About two-thirds of the people released from prison commit new crimes. This high recidivism rate is a major source of our crime rate. If we could reduce this rate, it would make a big difference in how many new crimes are committed.

But this is a very hard task. Unlike crime prevention programs for children, treatment programs for adults must cope with people who, in most cases, are leading completely dysfunctional lives. Most are on drugs, many belong to gangs, few have much education or job skills, some are psychopaths who find it very hard to learn any rules, and a lot leave prison to go back to neighborhoods where circumstances had already pushed them into crime.

Joan Petersilia in chapter 17 writes about the importance of this group. Judging from how many are involved (there were 828,000 adults on parole in 2008), it may be impossible to deal effectively with many of them. That means, I imagine, dealing with those that are either amenable to change or who constitute the greatest risk.

I have written "dealing" with them, but frankly we do not yet know how best to deal with them. One possibility is to keep them under close supervision using a GPS anklet that cannot be removed without sending out a signal. We might then be able to keep close track of them and be able to intervene if they go to places (a dangerous barroom, a place where drugs are sold, a public school) that we wish them to avoid.

But today we know more than we used to. Forty years ago a committee from the National Academy of Science wrote that there was very little evidence that any program to rehabilitate criminals worked. But today, as Francis Cullen and Cheryl Jonson point out in chapter 11, we can say with some confidence that there are such programs that make a difference. By looking at all such efforts taken together (the process is called meta-analysis) we learn that they will, on average, reduce the recidivism rate by about 10 percent. A gain, but a small one, and we are not certain it is worth the cost.

But the same meta-analysis tells us that certain kinds of programs will reduce recidivism by much more, perhaps by 20 to 30 percent. These successful programs focus on what specialists call cognitive-behavioral or social learning approaches. In plain language, they involve helping criminals learn how to handle the environment they face. They do this in two ways. First, they alter what the offenders think about crime (for example, by learning that it is they, and not some outside force, that is to blame for what they do). A striking finding about criminals is they often think that "outside forces" explain their behavior. Second, offenders are taught how to manage themselves as they confront the environment (by, for example, controlling their anger and their impulsive urges).

We have also learned what does not work, such as boot camps and "scared straight" programs. And there is much about which we are uncertain, such as the effect on crime of many educational and job training programs. If there is any one area of criminal justice on which new research is most needed, handling ex-cons is it.

JUSTICE AND CRIME

Policies to deal with crime must not only be effective and worth the cost, they must be just. In chapter 9, Randall Kennedy describes the long and still incomplete struggle this country has had in trying to ensure that crime control policies are not racially biased.

But even when we try to be fair, we are still likely to think up policies to deal with crime on the basis of our ideological predispositions. If you are a liberal, you will tend to blame crime on poverty, too many guns, and unemployment and argue for more civil rights and more jobs—whatever the facts may be. If you are a conservative, you will be inclined to blame crime on personal irresponsibility and lenient courts that have hurt the police and argue in favor of capital punishment and longer prison terms—whatever the facts may be. Picking your way through this ideological swamp is difficult, and no one, including the authors in this book, is entirely successful at doing it.

Crime control in this country is essentially a local matter, but there is one thing that local authorities find it hard to, and that is to find out what works. A local police chief may be eager to learn what patrol strategy is best, but he faces two problems: he or she needs to find enough money to test different strategies (but money is scare at the local level), and he or she has to be willing to risk political embarrassment if a strategy fails. To help with these problems, it is important that the federal government give money to carefully test new ideas.

In the past, federal authorities, notably the National Institute of Justice, have done this, but only on occasion. Politically, it is much easier to send money to law enforcement agencies without asking them to find out what works. That episodic approach is a mistake. The nation needs a continuous and systematic commitment to the development of evidence-based law enforcement.

References

Black, D. A., and D. S. Nagin. 1998. "Do Right-to-Carry Laws Deter Violent Crime?" *Journal of Legal Studies* 27: 221.

Blumstein, A., F. P. Rivara, and R. Rosenfeld. 2000. "The Rise and Decline of Homicide—and Why." *Annual Review of Public Health* 21: 505–541.

Bureau of Justice Statistics, *Key Facts at A Glance*, Available at http://bjs.ojp.usdoj.gov/content/glance/tables/corr2tab.cfm.

District of Columbia v. Heller. 2008. 554 U.S. 128 S. Ct. 2783, 171 L. Ed 2d 637.

Donohue, J., and I. Ayres. 2003. "Shooting Down the "More Guns, Less Crime' Hypothesis." *Stanford Law Review* 51: 4.

Eckenrode, et al., 2010. "Long-Term Effects of Prenatal and Infancy Nurse Home Visitation on the Life Course of Youths: 19-Year Follow-Up of a Randomized Trial." Archives of Pediatric Adolescent Medicine 164: 9–15.

Lott, J. R. 2000. *More Guns, Less Crime: Understanding Crime and Gun Control Laws*, 2d ed. Chicago: University of Chicago Press.

Monkonnen, E. 2001. *Murder in New York City*. Berkeley: University of California Press.

Reyes, J. W. "Environmental Policy as Social Policy? The Impact of Childhood Lead Exposure on Crime," National Bureau of Economic Research, Working Paper 13097, 2007. Available at http://www.nber.org/papers/w13097.

Schweinhart, L. J., H. V. Barnes, and D. P. Weikart. 2005. *Significant Benefits: The High/Scope Perry Preschool Program Through Age 40*. Ypsilanti: High/Scope Press. Available at http://www.highscope.org/content.asp/contentid=219.

Terry v. Ohio. 1968. 392 U.S. 1.

Tracy, P. E., M. E. Wolfgang, and R. M. Figlio. 1990. *Delinquency Careers in Two Birth Cohorts*. New York: Plenum.

Wellford, C. F., J. V. Pepper, and C. V. Petrie, eds. *Firearms and Violence: A Critical Review*. Washington, DC: National Academy Press, 2004.

Wilson, J. Q. 1976. "Crime and Punishment in England." *The Public Interest* 43 (Spring): 3–25.

Wilson, J. Q. 1983. "Crime and American Culture." *The Public Interest* 70 (Winter): 22–48.

Wilson, J. Q. 1997. "Criminal Justice in England and America." *The Public Interest* 126 (Winter): 3–14.

Zimring, F. E., and G. Hawkins. 1997. *Crime Is Not the Problem: Lethal Violence in America*. New York: Oxford University Press.

Index

Note: Page numbers followed by *n* indicate numbered endnote. Page numbers followed by *t* denote tables.